Guerrillas in Power

By the same author

Visa for Poland
Khrushchev and the West
China: The Other Communism

Guerrillas in Power

The Course of the Cuban Revolution

K. S. KAROL

Translated from the French by ARNOLD POMERANS

Jonathan Cape Thirty Bedford Square London

FIRST PUBLISHED IN GREAT BRITAIN 1971
© 1970 BY K. S. KAROL
PUBLISHED IN FRENCH UNDER THE TITLE *Les Guérilleros au Pouvoir:
L'Itinéraire Politique de la Révolution Cubaine*

JONATHAN CAPE LTD, 30 BEDFORD SQUARE, LONDON WCI

ISBN 0 224 61959 4

PRINTED IN GREAT BRITAIN
BY LOWE & BRYDONE (PRINTERS) LTD, LONDON
ON PAPER MADE BY JOHN DICKINSON AND CO. LTD.
BOUND BY G. & J. KITCAT LTD, LONDON

Contents

Guerrillas in Power

Foreword

One does not have to be a Latin American expert to realize that the Cuban Revolution has changed course more than once during the eleven years of its colorful existence. Fidel Castro's international outlook was not the same on his adoption of socialism in 1961 as it had been after his victory in 1959; it changed again in 1965, when Ernesto Che Guevara left to put heart into the guerrilla movement in Latin America, and once more after Che's death in 1967. None of these vacillations can be attributed to an excess of pragmatism on the part of the Cuban leader and his team, or even to Cuba's dependence—however real—on foreign trade.

Lying at the very door of the United States, a mere ninety miles off the coast of Florida, Cuba is closely tied to the faraway Soviet bloc, itself in the throes of a grave internal crisis. Historically and geographically, Cuba is part of Latin America and, like all countries on that subcontinent, bears the marks of colonial and neocolonial exploitation. It was Cuba's wish to make a radical break with that past which exposed it to the gravest dangers and, incidentally, turned it into a living witness to the crises and contradictions currently shaking the West, as well as the East and the Third World. Cuba has been transformed into a kind of sound box, reacting to the smallest vibration, to the least drama in any part of the modern world. That is a political fact Cubans cannot afford to ignore if they are to forge ahead and to choose, at each stage of their progress, solutions that will least mortgage their future.

This task has been a difficult one, to say the least; yet the Castroists have tackled it with enthusiasm and with a great deal of originality. In so doing, they have highlighted many of the problems, of the present and of the near future. It was their destiny to reveal to the rest of the world the real nature of America's foreign policy and to pierce the veil of its liberal and anti-colonialist rhetoric. Later they laid bare the true nature of the Soviet bloc. True, the U.S.S.R. did not come to Cuba's aid in order to seize its sugar or tobacco—for the Soviet Union was still pretending to be a socialist and anti-imperialist country—but it was not by chance that it failed utterly to grasp the objectives, needs, and implications of Cuba's young revolutionary movement. Being a great power, the Soviet Union could only treat the island as a pawn on the international chessboard. It is against this background that the Cuban example reveals the difficulties facing any underdeveloped country determined to break with the past but unable to rely on fraternal aid from the industrialized powers, whatever their political color.

However, my purpose is not to produce a long list of Cuba's unresolved problems or to offer a theoretical analysis of them all; instead I shall try to retrace the course of the Cuban Revolution, relying chiefly on what direct experience I have gained during four visits to Cuba: two in 1961, one in 1967, and the last in 1968. All these visits coincided with major political turning points. In 1961, I was privileged to be present at the birth of the Socialist Republic; a few months later, I witnessed Cuba's first clash with its Eastern allies and with their local supporters. In 1967, I was in Cuba just when Castro's "heretical" attempt to define "the Cuban path toward socialism and Communism" was reaching its climax. Finally, in 1968, a few months after the death of Che Guevara, I was able to watch Castro's first faltering steps on his return to the Soviet road to "socialism."

The structure of this book reflects my desire to bear witness to the political climate and economic conditions I observed on the island during each of my visits. I have let the Cubans themselves speak of their problems and hopes, and have carefully refrained from updating my own reactions of the time. Thus, when reporting my interview with Che Guevara in 1961, I have set down my thoughts on leaving his office in the Ministry of Industry, rather than what I know today, ten years after the event. In 1967, I had a long series of meetings with Fidel Castro, in which he set forth his views on desirable social changes, and discussed his economic projects for the immediate future. His remarks constitute an important documentary in their own right, and I have not censored them in the light of subsequent developments.

In short, I have done my utmost not to run ahead of the events, and to let the reader follow the Castroist movement along the actual road it has pursued. I have, however, thought it best to include a fairly long historical digression, to emphasize the very special character of the first socialist revolution to have been made without the participation of the Communist Party, or any other offshoots, however heretical, of the Third International. Many other books on the same subject can be found in Havana, but all of these struck me as being too stamped by postrevolutionary developments to describe the birth of Castroism as an original revolutionary project. I have therefore compiled my own dossier on this subject, based on documents and eye-witness accounts collected during a long investigation in Havana in 1968.

My researches, whether of the past or the present, have been

A*

made in a spirit of solidarity with the Cuban Revolution; I have the utmost sympathy for a country to which fate has reserved an outstanding historical role. But I have been careful not to gloss over any of the flaws, not to deceive either the reader or myself. Some of the criticisms contained in these pages were bitterly challenged by the Cuban leaders and their foreign followers when the book was first published in France in the spring of 1970. Subsequently Fidel Castro himself was much more critical in his famous speech of July 26, 1970. What matters, however, is not my criticism as such but its purpose. After all, truth, as Gramsci put it, is always revolutionary.

August, 1970   **K. S. KAROL**

Part one

"If Fidel is a socialist

so are we"

No coexistence with Cuba

I did not discover Cuba until after Castro's Revolution, and
when I did it was thanks to the Americans. The dramatic event
on the island—General Batista's coup d'état of 1952 and the
subsequent struggle of the people against his dictatorship—
failed to arouse any great passions in Europe. For us, 1953 was
the year of Stalin's death and not of Fidel Castro's attack on
the Moncada Fortress. In 1956, when Fidel and his eighty-two
men disembarked from *Granma* to begin their guerrilla campaign in the Sierra Maestra, we were preoccupied with the Polish
"October," with the Hungarian tragedy, with the Algerian war,
and with the Suez adventure. Even after Batista's fall in January
1959, when the papers were full of the *barbudos'* triumphal
entry into Havana, we were not sure just what to make of this
revolution.

For us in the Old World, "revolution" has for more than a

3

century been more or less identical with "socialism"—we think of it in terms of profound social changes. The overthrow of a dictatorship like Batista's, joyful news though it was, struck us as just another step on the slow road to parliamentary democracy in Latin America, where military tyrants had ceased to be safe in their beds. Reports from Havana in no way suggested that the new Cuban Republic would be appreciably different from, say, Venezuela, where democrats of all persuasions had, a year before, put an end to the detestable regime of General Pérez Jiménez.

Then, in September 1959, I went to the United States to be present at the great reconciliation attempt between Russia and America. For two weeks, Nikita Khrushchev, the Soviet premier, toured the American continent, explaining to groups of business-men and other V.I.P.'s that the two atomic superpowers were not just condemned to share one world, but had a mutual interest in doing so. "One day our grandchildren will choose peacefully between the capitalist and Communist systems, and since the latter is the more efficient, that's the one they are bound to favor," he repeated time and again. This hint at a thaw, after so many years of Cold War, greatly perplexed U.S. public opinion, conditioned by years of anti-Communist propaganda, though the more enlightened were quick to grasp that a détente might greatly benefit their country. People began to listen to Khrushchev with growing interest, and at the end of his tour the ice seemed indeed to have been broken—no one was shocked by references to the personal charm of First Secretary Khrush-chev and his family. The most audacious even went so far as to admit that the Russian Communists might perhaps not be quite as evil as had been thought.

Yet amid all this coexistential euphoria, it was still in poor taste to talk of Fidel Castro; the mere mention of his name aroused Americans to frenzies of anti-Communist passion. No epithet seemed harsh enough to describe his "band of juvenile delinquents" who, having seized power in Havana, were now trying to transform a wonderful island—Christopher Columbus had called it "the fairest island human eyes have yet beheld"—

into a base of Communist subversion, right inside the Western hemisphere.

When I first heard such views expressed, I could hardly believe my ears. But then I was visiting America at a time when left-wing Europeans were cut off from the U.S. Establishment by a high wall of incomprehension. Most of the people I spoke to in Washington had apparently turned into Manicheans: for them the world was plainly divided into good and evil. Anyone wanting to change the status quo was either a willing tool or a dupe of the Communist totalitarians and hence a "bad guy"; all the "good guys" were ranged behind the star-spangled banner, determined to help the United States preserve and protect the democratic decencies—sacrosanct free enterprise chief among them. Hence it was enough simply to call Castro "some kind of Communist" to put him beyond the pale.

What had Castro done to merit this distinction? He had inaugurated "totalitarian" land reforms involving the virtual confiscation of foreign estates and investments; he had expelled the North American military mission from Havana; he had apparently unleashed a smear campaign against the United States, and he seemed to have every intention of violating democracy and private property even further. According to the "irrefutable" testimony of refugees, his camp was infested with "crypto-Communists" and even with fully paid-up Party members. "You see," continued my American informants, "Cuba is ninety miles from Florida. We have strong emotional ties with that island, especially as we liberated it from the Spanish yoke and think of it almost as another state of the Union."

All this was happening in September 1959, when the "crypto-Communist" of Havana was still making overtures to the United States. He had expressed his willingness to pay an indemnity to U.S. companies hit by the land reforms. He had offered to extend trade with the United States, and had undertaken to supply up to eight million tons of sugar on the best possible terms.[1] But

1. In his speech of June 4, 1959, Fidel Castro offered the United States delivery in 1961 of eight million tons of sugar at four cents per pound (see *Revolución*, June 5, 1959).

no one in Washington paid the slightest attention to these offers, and for a very good reason: it was not the policy of the United States to reach agreement with Castro but to overthrow him by fair means or foul, and in the briefest possible time.[2] At the time, the United States was still convinced that economic pressure would quickly persuade the Cubans of the error of their ways, and encourage them to get rid of "this bragging psychopath."

In these circumstances, it was not at all surprising that anti-Cuban sentiment in the United States should have turned into hysterical frenzy once it became clear that, far from achieving the desired objects, these "peaceful" measures had led to the complete nationalization of American estates in Cuba and to closer Cuban ties with the Soviet Union.

I returned to the United States exactly one year after my 1959 trip, once again in the traces of the indefatigable Nikita Khrushchev, who had decided to grace the Fifteenth General Assembly of the United Nations in New York with his presence. Most leaders from other Communist countries and the Third World had followed his example. Fidel Castro, accompanied by a large Cuban delegation,[3] was present as well, and his arrival on

2. On April 15, 1959, Fidel Castro went to the United States at the invitation of the American Society of Newspaper Editors. He was unable to meet President Eisenhower, since the latter had, most discourteously, absented himself from Washington to show his disapproval of the way the Cuban Revolution had gone. However, Castro had a long meeting with Vice-President Nixon who, according to his own testimony, concluded that this man had to be removed from office. He accordingly drafted a memo to all departments concerned, recommending the training of Cuban exile commandos that would help to overthrow the new regime. It is worth noting that the Castro-Nixon meeting took place two months *before* Cuba passed its land-reform laws, and that the only Cuban exiles at the time were former Batista men. (See Manuel Semides: *Les États Unis et la révolution cubaine,* Armand Colin, 1968, p. 53; and Richard Nixon: *Six Crises,* Doubleday, 1962, pp. 351–357.)

3. It included Raúl Roa, Minister of Foreign Affairs; Commander Juan Almeida, one of Castro's oldest comrades in arms; Carlos Franqui, editor of *Revolución;* Regino Botí, Cuba's leading economist, and a host of other associates and experts.

6

"If Fidel is a socialist so are we"

September 14, 1960, caused a great stir in the United States. When the management of the elegant hotel in which Cuban diplomats usually stayed asked for payment in advance, Fidel and his men packed their bags and moved to Harlem, at the same time issuing incendiary declarations against racial discrimination in the United States. It was in Harlem, at the Hotel Theresa, an old, blackened, and cheap-looking hotel on 125th Street, that I finally met the Cubans in the flesh.

The occasion was a meeting organized, on the eve of Castro's address to the United Nations, by the "Fair Play for Cuba Committee," a body comprising intellectuals from the "other America" and such European sympathizers as Jean-Paul Sartre and Kenneth Tynan. I shall always remember that evening, not least for its fraternal and free-and-easy atmosphere, which formed a glaring contrast to that of all the diplomatic receptions—including the "socialist" ones—I had attended on previous evenings in Manhattan. The proletarian staff of the hotel, the olive-green uniforms of the *guerrilleros,* the general lack of formality, all helped to emphasize the gaiety and the stimulating, if not revolutionary, character of the meeting. Fidel Castro arrived rather late, and was immediately surrounded by a group of Negroes, each as imposing in stature as Fidel himself. They flung themselves into his open arms. Everyone else then wanted to follow their example, and there were a few moments of pandemonium. In the midst of the general hubbub, a committee member presented Fidel with a small statue of Abraham Lincoln, and the ensuing applause drowned the voice of the Cuban leader; the absence of a microphone rendered his thanks completely inaudible. After a while, we found out that we were to sit around the small tables at the end of the hall, and that Fidel would come around to greet us all in turn.

My table was Franco-American: Claude Bourdet and Henri Cartier-Bresson shared it with I. F. Stone, as spritely as ever, and with Maria Winn, the young assistant of Rickey Leacock, the film director. We waited patiently, occasionally beckoning to men in olive-green who were not otherwise occupied and whose

7

names or rank we did not know. There seemed little hope that
Castro would ever get around to us. And then, there he was.
With a somber expression and in a confidential tone of voice, he
informed us that his speech to the United Nations next day
would be very hard to put across. "Cuba's case is almost identical
with that of the Congo and Algeria," he said. "We want our
independence and the North Americans reply by waging the
most perfidious war against us, trying to bring further ruin on a
country they have been systematically bleeding for more than
half a century." He was speaking in a low voice, as if his words
were meant for us alone, with obvious sincerity and great conviction. And by way of farewell he added: "But they won't get
away with it. Sooner or later, the American people will come to
realize what injustices they are inflicting on Cuba."

We carried on chatting with other Cubans for some time, and
I was struck forcibly by the extraordinary difference between
their tone and that of the anti-Castro leaders in the American
press. I won't say they were moderate, but they were certainly
calm and collected. Theirs was the typically neutralist attitude
of the Third World; they were not anti-American; they simply
believed that the U.S.S.R. and the Communist bloc would prove
more sympathetic. But they took this position regretfully, insisting that the United States, too, would "sooner or later" be
forced to revise her attitude toward them. Neither their language
nor their arguments were the least bit "Communistic." When
some of us insisted on a more precise definition of their political
attitude, they came out, rather reluctantly, with a phrase of
one who was already their chief ideologist, Ernesto Che Guevara.
"As an oversimplification, one could call our regime a 'left-wing
nationalist' one."[4]

Other stray encounters with the Cubans in the corridors of
the United Nations confirmed the impression I had formed in
the Hotel Theresa. Moreover, I was lucky enough to have a

4. "*Se podría esquematizar llamándole nacionalismo de la izquierda*"
(as reported in *Bohemia* on January 31, 1960).

8

friend in New York who was better placed than most to enlighten me on the subject of Cuba—it was this man I had in mind when I said that I discovered Cuba thanks to the Americans. He was C. Wright Mills, professor at Columbia University and a sociologist of world renown.[5]

In August 1960, Mills had gone to Havana, mainly to satisfy his own curiosity, and certainly without any precise scientific or political goals. He had not been to Cuba before, but his knowledge of Mexico and Brazil made him highly sensitive to the drama that was being played out in Latin America. One day, Fidel Castro had looked him up in his hotel, telling him straight out that his *Power Elite* had been the bedside book of most of the *guerrilleros* in the Sierra Maestra. Castro invited him to come on a tour—*una vuelta*—of the country. They spent three and a half days together, devoting an average of eighteen hours in every twenty-four to discussions. Then Mills went on to Oriente, where he spent an additional six days traveling with Major René C. Vallejo,[6] who was then the director of the provincial section of the INRA (*Instituto Nacional de Reforma Agraria*)[7] and was Castro's close friend and personal physician. During this tour, Mills was able to meet Cubans of all ages and social conditions and, making full use of his special experience, to record their opinions and comments in full.

When I called on him at his home in West Nyack, a suburb of New York, he was busily organizing the mine of information he had tapped in Cuba for his forthcoming *Listen, Yankee*,[8] a book in which he lets the Cubans themselves explain why and how they made their revolution and what they hoped to gain from it. Mills was a true radical, revolted by the smugness of his country, and suffocating in its conformist atmosphere. In

5. The best known of his writings are: *White Collar* (1951), *The Power Elite* (1956), *The Sociological Imagination* (1959).

6. Major Vallejo died in 1969.

7. The INRA was, in fact, much more than its title suggests—it was a state institute for planning and land management, and played a decisive role in the organization of the socialist sector of the Cuban economy.

8. C. Wright Mills: *Listen, Yankee* (New York, McGraw-Hill, 1960).

Havana he had breathed fresh air; he had met revolutionaries of a new type, imbued with all the best ideas of the Left. He had been profoundly moved. But Mills was also familiar with socialist countries in Europe,[9] and he knew better than most what difficulties blocked the path to a new society. Above all, he had nothing of the hidebound propagandist about him, was not given to letting his enthusiasm run away with him, to seeing everything through rose-tinted glasses. "I am for the Cuban Revolution. I do not worry about it, I worry for it and with it," he wrote at the end of his book. Eight years later, we can see how right his predictions were, and how shrewdly he discerned some of the obstacles on the Cuban road to socialism.

The greatest danger, according to him, was the total lack of understanding with which American public opinion treated the Cuban Revolution. Conditioned to anti-Communist reflexes, Americans allowed themselves to be manipulated by a "power elite," men who were prepared to fight an underhand battle with Cuba for private advantage. Not that Mills accused journalists or certain anti-Castroist university lecturers of being in the pay of the sugar companies or the administration; he simply argued that they were too caught up in their Manichean universe to grasp the profound meaning of a revolution sparkling with new ideas.

In particular he was worried about the failure of the American Left to step into the breach. He knew that the instinct of self-preservation would inexorably drive Cubans into the arms of the Soviet bloc, and that the latter would be quick to fill the ideological semi-void of Castroism with its own peculiar brand of Marxism. Mills was full of praise for the Cubans' openness of mind and intellectual curiosity. "In twenty years of teaching and writing, and of considerable travel, I have never before encountered such a sustained passion for learning and such an in-

9. In his book *The Causes of World War Three*, Mills had strongly attacked the social stratification that was rife in the East and also the formation of "socialist power elites" on the American pattern.

telligent awareness of the kind of things that must be studied,"
he wrote.[10] But he also realized that underdeveloped Cuba,
long a cultural appendage of the United States, would suffer
cruelly from a lack of qualified men, men of sufficient intellectual stature to ensure the rapid adoption and absorption of new
ideas demanded by the new situation. Hence he called upon his
fellow Americans to forget their blind aggression and join in
the building of a "critical university"—one in which left-wing
intellectuals from all parts of the world would help Cuba to
discover the manifold currents of revolutionary thought and
history. Thanks to this "laboratory of ideas," the Cuban Revolution would be able to preserve its libertarian character, and
eventually emerge as an entirely new type of society.

But who, in the United States, was ready to heed this appeal?
Today, after the bitter Vietnamese experience, many American
intellectuals have rediscovered the virtues of nonconformism and
freedom of criticism. But in 1960, C. Wright Mills was preaching
in a wilderness. His was one of those lone voices that evoked
no echo either in American society at large, or even in academic
circles—both still haunted by the specter of McCarthyism.[11] It
made one sad to see this Texan—and I have never met anyone
more typical of the free and independent American pioneer—
up against a solid wall of hostility and vilification.

Mills' personal drama was played out against a background of
national hysteria. "The red peril is upon us!" was the tone set
from above. After the UN meeting, I stayed on for the presidential election, and witnessed an incredible spectacle: the two
candidates, Kennedy and Nixon, were outbidding each other in

10. *Listen, Yankee,* p. 186.
11. C. Wright Mills was not, of course, the only American to defend
the Cuban Revolution. A few months before the appearance of his *Listen,
Yankee,* L. Huberman and P. Sweezy had published their excellent *Cuba:
Anatomy of a Revolution* (Routledge & Kegan Paul, 1960). They had even
been the first to demonstrate that Cuba was experiencing a socialist
revolution, one that for the first time in history had not been organized
by Communists. But at the time I was more familiar with Mills' ideas
on the subject.

11

martial pronouncements and in their failure to grasp the Cuban problem. They faced each other four separate times on television, before some seventy million viewers whom, each time, they treated to homilies on the best method of liquidating Castroism. Kennedy, the more enlightened of the two, was worse even than his blunt adversary: he called quite openly for the dispatch to Cuba of an expeditionary force, recruited from among the "democratic" refugees who, with the help and the blessing of the United States, would quickly put an end to that "Communist enclave." Nixon, who had been promoting this solution since 1959 and knew that it was about to be translated into practice, thought it best to appear more discreet, and even spoke of the international risks involved. But the average viewer wanted Castro's head at any price. I heard decent people, the peaceable fathers of families, many with college degrees, discussing whether it was best to shave Castro's beard before hanging him, or to execute him as he was.

In the spring of 1961 the United States was ready to pounce. I happened to be back in Washington to report on Kennedy's new Democratic administration. I had never been so well received. The political machine was not all that had changed: the outlook of the Kennedy team seemed radically different from that of the outgoing administration. The new President was surrounded by a brilliant galaxy of "eggheads," recruited from among the best colleges in his native Massachusetts, men whose intellectual outlook and knowledge by far surpassed those of the older Republican bureaucrats. Primitive Manicheanism was no longer in vogue. Far from thinking of European leftists as "pinkos" busily aiding the Communist devil, Kennedy's academics saw them as potential allies in their great struggle to reshape the world. The *New Statesman*, my London weekly, was read more at that time in the White House, and in the State Department, than in Whitehall. All doors were now open to me.

My hosts turned harshly on their predecessors and agreed that it was their folly that had caused America to play the unfortunate role of guardian of the world economic and social status

12

quo, at a time when her own interests and inclinations should have encouraged her to promote changes, however revolutionary. The old division between Communism and liberalism, they said, was largely gone. Russians and Americans had similar problems to resolve if they were to ensure economic growth in their complex industrial societies. Instead of competing with one another in the Third World, they ought both to be preparing the developing countries for rapid economic "take-off"; only industrialized societies could become true trading partners of the two great giants.

Clearly, the Kennedy administration was ready to go some way toward meeting the Russians, who, for their part, were anxious to wipe out the after-effects of the Cold War and to put an end to what had become a "vain ideological battle." I was told that the United States was going to do everything it could to rid the world of those stagnant regimes, both conservative and dictatorial, that impeded all progress in the Third World. Henceforth the United States would only give economic aid to governments capable of putting U.S. dollars to good use for the fundamental transformation of their countries. "Leftist regimes, far from frightening us, are likely to prove our best friends," my informants went on to assure me.

It was all very interesting. But why, I wondered, was this enlightened program being kept from the American public—particularly during the election campaign? My academic friends smiled and referred me to the history books: "Do you think Abraham Lincoln would have won elections by preaching abolitionism? Or Roosevelt by advocating the New Deal? In this country, you must seize the reins of power first; molding public opinion with the vast resources and prestige of the administration then becomes a simple matter." Kennedy was handicapped by the bare majority that had carried him into the White House, and he was highly sensitive to the fact that one American in two had voted for his conservative rival. One simply had to take him on trust: as he gathered strength, he would apply himself to the task of transforming the mood of the entire country.

13

At this stage one had either to ignore the bad smell under one's nose or to ask point-blank, "What about Cuba?" Suddenly the enlightened Democrats turned as uncompromising as the most narrow-minded Republicans. Their reasoning was, of course, more subtle. They did not defend the sanctity of private property, or the need to protect American investments abroad at any cost. Far from it—they declared that they accepted the social changes that had taken place in Cuba, that they were not opposed to the land reforms, and had no intention of restoring the old regime. The reason they could not accept Castro was simply that the people of Cuba did not accept him; he had betrayed his own revolution by aligning himself with the Communists and by turning his country into a Soviet base. The Cubans wanted no part of him or his crazy ideas.

On April 3, 1961, the State Department put out a White Paper on the need for "Castroism without Castro," for a revolution without Communism. It struck an unaccustomed intellectual note and was unashamedly highbrow: while not going so far as to quote Marx, it did make use of some phrases of I. F. Stone. The author, Professor Arthur Schlesinger, Jr., had no difficulty in rising to this plane. He was a well-known leftist member of the Establishment, a former president of Americans for Democratic Action, a biographer of Roosevelt, and a Pulitzer Prize winner. President Kennedy had brought him to the White House straight from his chair in Harvard.

It was in the White House, in his office on the ground floor of the presidential mansion, that we spoke at length one afternoon in early April. He found me "doctrinaire," and I thought he must be joking when he explained that 90 per cent of Cubans were against Castro, and that the United States "could not possibly defend this regime against its own people." He did not at the time believe a word he was saying—he disclosed this later in his book[12]—and one could sense it. But he did me a great

12. In his book, *A Thousand Days; John F. Kennedy in the White House* (1965), Professor Schlesinger explains that he was opposed from the very start to the Cuban invasion project which the Democratic administration had inherited from its predecessor and which it could not apparently

service on the professional level: through talking with him I realized the invasion of Cuba must be imminent. Until then my American colleagues had somewhat misled me, unwittingly perhaps, by swearing that "that idea has been dropped, or anyway shelved." Although Schlesinger told me nothing definite, by the time I left him I knew that the die was cast. That same evening I wrote an article saying just that for *L'Express* in Paris. It appeared on Friday, April 14, 1961; twenty-four hours afterward Cuban airfields were being bombarded by "deserters from Castro's air force," men who, needless to say, were never produced for the benefit of foreign correspondents. Two days later, at dawn on April 17, 1,500 anti-Castro volunteers disembarked on the Playa Girón, Bay of Pigs, southern Cuba.

I heard this news in New York and left at once for Miami, hoping to catch a plane for Havana—to no purpose, however, since the air links with Cuba had been cut. In the town, full of overexcited anti-Castroists and American journalists who had flocked there from all over the country, it was suggested that I should become accredited by the "democratic government" which was about to take over on liberated territory. To believe the local papers, the assault forces were sweeping all before them. One paper even claimed that Fidel Castro had taken to his heels, that his brother Raúl had been killed, that there had been an uprising on the Isle of Pines, etc. Plainly much of this was pure propaganda, but even the most skeptical among us feared that Cuba might witness an American repetition of the Spanish Civil War. Not wanting to have anything to do with the new "Francoists," I declined the offer to have myself accredited by

countermand. However, his opposition did not prevent him from producing the State Department White Paper which appeared on April 3, 1961. Hence Claude Julien had every reason to write in his *L'Empire américain* (Paris, Grasset, 1968, p. 347): "Unconsciously and no matter what his reservations on the subject of the CIA, a great liberal had come to accept the fundamental ideas of that organization. Worse still, he invested them with an elegant style, high motivations, an apparent inner consistency, a generous tone, and a deceptive breadth of outlook that were bound to influence many readers. He moreover stood moral surety for them with his reputation as a leading liberal intellectual."

15

them. Instead, three British colleagues and myself departed for Jamaica hoping to reach Cuba from there.

The logic of history

On the Playa Girón, the American mountain labored hard to produce a mouse. Seventy-two hours after disembarking, the expeditionary force was indeed on its way to Havana, but in prison trucks. The American attempt to overthrow Fidel had proved a "perfect failure," to use the very words of one of Castroism's chief detractors, Theodore Draper.[13] The world marveled. Despite chaste disclaimers from Washington, it was common knowledge that the notorious Central Intelligence Agency had been directly involved in the whole fiasco. Now, the CIA was considered to be an efficient organization, endowed both with daring and vast resources. It was even called "the invisible government" of the United States, and had, in fact, proved its mettle all over the world, in "solving" crisis after crisis by quick action behind the scenes. In these circumstances who would have thought that the powerful CIA would be stupid enough to throw to the Castroist lions a thousand "volunteers" whom nothing short of a miracle could save from a humiliating disaster?

In fact, the Americans had been taken in by their own propaganda, and had gravely underestimated their opponents. For this they were made to pay a heavy price. Those who win wars are able to rewrite history, and to allot the best parts to themselves. But in defeat blunders recoil upon their instigators. The Americans had not been too careful about their methods. In the psychological warfare they waged on Castro, anything went. Adlai Stevenson,[14] the U.S. representative at the UN, was allowed to exhibit fake photographs before the Security Council, "proving" that the Cuban airports had been bombed by Castroist de-

13. Theodore Draper: *Castroism: Theory and Practice* (London, Pall Mall Press, 1965).
14. Before his death in London in 1966, Adlai Stevenson made a clean breast of the whole matter to Eric Sevareid.

16

fectors. As for the American press, it excelled in churning out lies from the very start of the invasion. Internationally known agencies who flattered themselves on their objectivity sent out the most fantastic dispatches on the downfall of the Cuban regime. When the truth became known, the whole world began to wonder about the basic principles of a policy that required such massive recourse to duplicity.

The myth of Castro's unpopularity had been shattered, and there were other premises in the State Department's White Paper that stood up no better to the light of day. An examination of the list of prisoners was all that was needed to throw doubt on the much-vaunted American readiness to "preserve the social achievements of the revolution." The invading force contained no fewer than 194 of Batista's militia and police, including the unhappily notorious torturer Calvino. Most of the contingent was made up of exiled landowners or their children—the *niños bien*, as they used to be called in Havana—and their only concession to the wind of social change was the presence in their ranks of 112 vagrants and ex-convicts. Claude Julien, who had followed Cuban affairs since before the Revolution and knew them well, observed that for the invaders "the chief object was the recapture of 371,930 hectares of land, 9,666 estates, 70 factories, 10 sugar refineries, 3 banks, 5 mines, and 12 nightclubs."[15]

The Castroists were jubilant; the "great U.S. debate" on the Cuban debacle daily brought discreditable revelations. In particular, it became clear that the Cuban refugee organizations, which on March 22 had set up a sort of provisional government presided over by Miró Cardona,[16] had had no say over their own

15. In *L'Empire américain*, p. 364. See the same author's *La Révolution cubaine*, Paris, 1961. Even American writers whom no one could accuse of pro-Castroism, such as Tad Szulc and Karl E. Meyer, have deplored the influence of Batista supporters on the expeditionary corps (see their *Cuban Invasion*, New York, Ballantine, 1962).

16. Miró Cardona, president of the Havana Bar Association under Batista, was active in the civilian resistance movement against the dictator. He was prime minister from January 2 to February 17, 1959, when Fidel Castro took over his office. Cardona was made Cuban Ambassador to Spain and a year later asked for political asylum in the United States. On

"military forces." The invasion force had been recruited, trained, equipped, and controlled solely by U.S. intelligence, and had been a jealously guarded tool in its hands. Moreover, in an attempt to explain the failure of the expedition, the American press itself was forced to mention the heroism of the peasant militiamen who had alerted Castro's army and who had strenuously held out until its arrival on the battlefield. It was they who had spoiled the surprise effect and had prevented the invaders from establishing a bridgehead in that marshy and sparsely populated part of Cuba. All this gave Americans plenty to think about, and Cubans as much cause for rejoicing.

Unfortunately, humiliating defeat does not generally prompt a country to change its policies. The Americans were no exception to this rule—most public figures called upon the nation to close ranks at this difficult time, rather than question the political fitness of men who had meddled so ineffectually and so illegally in the affairs of another country. Even right-wing extremists agreed to defer their attacks on Kennedy, and particularly not to press their charge that he had been most remiss in not providing the "liberators" with the necessary air cover. As far as the President himself was concerned, he gallantly took full responsibility for the disaster, and to boost the morale of his people promised to pay Castro back in the near future. He announced that he would try to mobilize the entire hemisphere in the fight against Communist penetration, and even made special provisions lest his neighbors should prove unequal to this glorious task. "My government will not hesitate to do what is necessary for the safety of our nation. . . . We shall not allow men whose hands are covered with blood from the streets of Budapest to teach us a lesson in non-interference. Communism in this hemisphere is not negotiable."[17]

March 22, 1961 he became president of the Council of Cuban Refugees in Miami; a post from which he resigned in 1963 when it had become clear that, despite his exhortations, the United States was not prepared to launch a new invasion.

17. *The New York Times*, April 20, 1961.

"If Fidel is a socialist so are we"

And while waiting for the great crusade on the American continent to begin, President Kennedy decided to act more vigorously against Communists in other parts of the world—in Asia, for example. Immediately after the rout on the Playa Girón, he stepped up U.S. pressure against "Communist infiltration in Laos and South Vietnam." At the end of the eventful month of April 1961 the first contingents of American experts in anti-guerrilla warfare and in "pacification" techniques left for Saigon. Today some former associates of President Kennedy—Professor Arthur Schlesinger, Jr., for one[18]—denounce the futile horror of American aggression in Southeast Asia, and speak of the fatal chain reaction by which their country was dragged into this venture. They seem to forget that their own administration made a unique contribution to setting it in motion.

I was unable to follow the happenings of this historic week from either the Cuban side or the American because, infuriatingly, my three English companions and I were stuck in Jamaica;[19] all our ingenious attempts to reach Santiago de Cuba from Kingston had come to nothing. We had embarked in a small boat belonging to a Canadian, Captain Frank, who had promised for a large reward to ferry us across. During the night there was a terrible storm. At dawn on April 22, still sick from the crossing, we at last sighted dry land; it was, unfortunately, Jamaica once again, or more precisely Bowden Saint Thomas, a godforsaken hole.[20]

---

18. See Arthur Schlesinger: *Bitter Heritage* (London, Sphere, 1967).
19. My English associates were Eric de Mauny of the B.B.C., Roy Perrot of the *Observer,* and Eldon Griffiths, then working for *Newsweek* and now a Conservative Member of Parliament.
20. Our futile maritime adventures nevertheless taught me something about the unholy fear Cuban ideas inspired in the Caribbean. In order to leave Kingston legally for Santiago, we were forced to make a host of representations to the local authorities, the Cuban Consul, and, for good measure, the U.S. Consul General, so as to make sure that the U.S. Fleet would not intercept us. We divided the tasks, mine consisting chiefly of carrying on negotiations with Alfonso Herrera, a young man in charge of the Cuban Consulate. To be precise, Herrera was both captain and crew: he acted as his own secretary, advisor, and even accountant, fulfilling this last task with great ease as the Consulate budget was modest. He was

Guerrillas in Power

Back in Kingston again, we decided to make another try for Havana. This time it was our European logic that let us down. We were convinced that neutral countries such as Jamaica would restore air services to Havana long before the United States. We therefore began to lay siege to the KLM offices in Kingston while our respective newspapers exerted pressure in Amsterdam on the company's headquarters. But even as the timid Dutchmen wavered, Pan American in Miami quietly resumed its daily flight to Havana. One member of our quartet, Eldon Griffiths, felt too humiliated by the whole thing to continue, and the rest of us went back to the United States.

Finally, on April 27, we found places on a plane full of Cubans going home. They burst into frenzied applause when the hostess announced that we were about to land at Rancho Boyeros airport. Below, reunited families embraced each other,

---

living on the second floor of a dusty old house which he kept in order as best he could. Herrera was very keen to help but he had never had to deal with anything like us before. He agreed to phone the Cuban Embassy in London—at our expense—and having been given the go-ahead, to cable Santiago and Havana—again at our expense—to receive us as friends. He himself was most amicable and anxious that we should meet with success. He came to our hotel quite often, and even invited us to draft the cables with him. For all that, we had the clear impression that the times—and his lack of resources—were such that his influence in Jamaica was extremely small.

Eldon Griffiths, who had been put "in charge" of the American sector, took me to dinner with the U.S. Consul General on the eve of our departure. The Consulate was an impressive building in the center of town and employed as large a staff as Her Britannic Majesty's Governor. The Consul himself lived in a luxurious villa in the hills and his cool rooms were filled with Africana, mementos of his time as U.S. Consul in the Congo. His wife had previously told us that the Belgians had done a "magnificent job" there, which brought us to the situation in Jamaica. Our host seemed deeply concerned about social unrest on the island which, in his view, was assuming alarming proportions. What was the cause of these problems on the eve of independence? Were they perchance economic? Not at all. According to the Consul the blame was entirely Alfonso Herrera's; it was only since the arrival of "that revolutionary agitator" that the normally peaceful tenor of Jamaican life had become explosive. Even Eldon Griffiths, now a leading pro-American in the House of Commons, found it very difficult not to burst out laughing.

guitarists in national costume sang Afro-Cuban melodies, photographers took souvenir snapshots; all under the benevolent gaze of militiamen in blue shirts and soldiers in olive-green, armed to the teeth. Cuban flags framed two enormous placards on the front of the airport building: CUBA, PRIMERO TERRITORIO LIBRE DE AMÉRICA and VIVA NUESTRA REVOLUCIÓN SOCIALISTA.

Socialist? Since when? It was only in town, when we were settled in the Habana Riviera Hotel, that my colleague Juan Arcocha,[21] a writer on the staff of *Revolución*, who was to show me around Cuba, supplied me with some sort of explanation. On April 16, at the burial service for those killed during the bombing of Havana airport (which had preceded the invasion) Fidel had said that the Americans were waging war on Cuba "because they refuse to accept our socialist revolution." It was expected that he would go into greater details during his forthcoming May Day address.

Meanwhile, socialism did not apparently prevent the functioning of the hotel casino as before; it was even possible to win American dollars provided one bet in hard currency. The lively districts of the capital, celebrated throughout the world, were livelier than ever—Sloppy Joe's, the rendezvous of film stars, was chock-full every evening, and the Floridita, Hemingway's favorite restaurant, still mixed the best daiquiris in the world. The public, however, had changed—the Revolution had opened up what used to be places of privilege to the people at large. Admission charges had been lowered dramatically and, since the new social climate stimulated consumption, the circle of people with the means of enjoying themselves had been greatly widened. Even my room in the Habana Riviera, which in the old days had cost forty dollars a day, was now let to me for just twelve pesos.[22] Moreover, several floors were rented out

21. Juan Arcocha, author of *Candle in the Wind*, is now a translator with UNESCO in Paris. He is an outstanding linguist who can interpret in four or five languages with astonishing facility. Arcocha accompanied C. Wright Mills on his trip in the summer of 1960.

22. Before the Revolution, 1 peso equaled 1 dollar; this rate has been maintained ever since.

free to "provincial revolutionaries," with a strong contingent of children who played a happy game of up-and-down in the elevators, shouting "Yankee NO!" every time we had to interrupt them in order to reach our rooms. My British companions, Eric de Mauny and Roy Perrot, who in other circumstances would not have appreciated being treated in this manner, proved full of indulgence. Indeed, having looked around the capital for several days, one of them said: "If this is socialism, then I'm all for it."

After provincial Kingston, we were struck by Havana's metropolitan atmosphere, by its great vitality and infectious gaiety. The Cubans sang as they made their revolution, brimming over with joy and confidence. They were naturally proud of their victory at Playa Girón, but beyond that felt that they had just participated in an extraordinary social transformation, one that benefited all who had neither been exploiters nor been foolish enough to fall for the myth of "the American way of life." They liked to talk about their agrarian reforms,[23] which had

23. Pre-revolutionary Cuba was a country of large latifundia: fewer than 3,000 men owned more than 70 per cent of the land. "So high a concentration is rare even in Latin America," wrote Michel Gutelman in his *Agriculture socialisée à Cuba* (Paris, Maspero, 1967). Moreover, of the 125,619 smaller holdings of less than 70 acres, only 40,643 were farmed by their owners—the rest were sublet. It was these tenants who were the first to benefit from the land reform decree of May 17, 1959. They were given the titles to the land they farmed, had their holdings increased to a total of 190 acres, and were granted subsidies to work them efficiently. The Castroists refused to split up the lands of the large estates and did not set up "minifundia" which would have meant a considerable drop in productivity. Instead they entrusted INRA or the cooperatives with the running of the old latifundia. In 1961, the area administered by the state in one form or another represented 44 per cent of Cuba's arable land.

European agricultural experts such as Michel Gutelman or René Dumont (*Cuba, socialisme et développement*, Paris, Seuil, 1964) thought the first Cuban reform law rather tepid. Castroist courage manifested itself chiefly in the determination to put an end to U.S. domination of the Cuban sugar industry. At the same time, the Cuban definition of "medium-sized" properties remained highly elastic. The old proprietors were authorized to retain up to 30 *caballerías* (i.e., approximately 1,000 acres), and in cases of farms with a productivity greater by 50 per cent than the national average, as much as 3,500 acres. In Europe, farms of that size would easily qualify as latifundia.

22

given the land to those who worked it, thus repairing an age-old injustice against the poverty-stricken peasants. "As a result our harvest has been nearly doubled, and that's just the beginning. No revolution, anywhere, has achieved comparable results on the land," they declared. There were also "urban reforms,"[24] whose immediate effect was the cutting of rents by 50 per cent. Furthermore, a whole new district had gone up in East Havana, where most of the factories were located; previously building activity had been mainly restricted to the rich residential West. The price of electricity and telephone calls was cut by a third as soon as these services were nationalized and their erstwhile masters, the Americans, had left the country. The list of social achievements in the countryside was even longer. Some hundred million dollars had been allocated for the construction of houses, schools, hospitals, and roads. And this time the peasants got modern homes instead of improvised shanties. Under the aegis of INIT, the National Institute of the Tourist Industry, a great effort had been made to set up new rest centers and public facilities at the beaches. I wondered how so many apparently costly projects could be realized in so short a time. This was no mystery to the young intellectuals whom I asked about it. "All that was needed was to abolish all those disgraceful privileges and to put an end to the foreign exploitation of our island," they told me.

"The Revolution," these young Cubans continued, "has al-

In fact, the political background—and American resistance above all—quickly caused the liberal scope of the reforms to be overtaken by events. Thus systematic opposition on the part of farmers who, though entitled to hang on to their lands in the central and eastern parts of the island, preferred to obstruct the regime and to boycott its social policies, led, at the beginning of 1960, to the confiscation of some one and a half million acres of land. When sugar growers proved equally obstructive, INRA quickly took over their medium-sized farms as well. Conversely, most surviving small-peasant holdings owe their existence to the agrarian reforms of 1959.

24. The urban reforms consisted, by and large, of the municipalization of accommodation, followed by the resale of apartments to their tenants. The former owners were paid compensation of up to 600 pesos per month, while the tenants paid the state a fixed sum over a fixed number of years. From the start, that sum was considerably smaller than the old rent.

lowed an almost spontaneous redistribution of wealth in favor of the humble—the *humildes*. Anything was possible just as soon as imperialist overlordship was ended. Other South American countries still under the heel of the American business community have been quick to 'read the lesson. That is the real reason for their vicious hostility to Cuba. For the Americans, the Revolution represents not only the loss of some eight hundred million to a billion dollars in confiscated properties—they are rich enough to stand that—but it endangers all their investments in the rest of the South American subcontinent."

While visiting the capital, we happened to pass the Coca-Cola factory, and my guides exclaimed: "Have a good look, that used to be only one of the U.S. embassies here. And as one U.S. ambassador himself said, he was at least as important as the president of the Cuban Republic. He said so while giving evidence before a Senate subcommittee.[25] Yet he himself was answerable to the big American investors no less than to his superiors in the State Department. Representatives of Standard Oil and Texaco, of the telephone and electricity companies, the automobile distributors and tire manufacturers, all had a hand in shaping Cuban policy. Their slogan was: 'What's good for the American business community is good for Cuba.' Nothing could be allowed to upset the applecart; no matter what the color of the administration in Washington or what its policy statements, the main thing was to bleed our country white."

This said, they candidly agreed that the quality of the Coca-Cola had sadly deteriorated since nationalization and that the great beverage now resembled a rather nasty syrup. Luckily, the American embargo on trade with Cuba seemed to have few other untoward effects. Not only had it not led to the threatened paralysis of the country's economy, but one could buy almost anything in the shops including a number of goods "made in U.S.A." Visitors from the East, particularly from Russia, began

25. See the evidence of Ambassador Smith, quoted in R. Smith: *What Happened in Cuba* (New York, Twayne, 1963) , p. 273.

24

their stay—so I was told—by stocking up on American shirts, transistors, and every kind of gadget. It was plain that Cuban shopkeepers had shown great foresight in laying in supplies against a prolonged siege. But what would happen once the supplies were exhausted? Being very careful not to rub my guides the wrong way, I asked if Fidel might not have blundered in his dealings with the United States, and, in particular, if he could not have done more to avoid a rupture. Far from being annoyed, my Cuban friends said cheerfully: "Do you really think that a revolution which touches the vital interests of the United States can be made acceptable to Washington with beautiful and soothing speeches? Even if Fidel had never opened his mouth or had picked Donald Duck as the symbol of our revolution, we still wouldn't have escaped the fury of the Americans. No matter what we did, once we started our revolution, the American response was a foregone conclusion.

"As soon as we announced the agrarian reforms, the United States demanded full compensation. This was one way of warning us off—no Cuban government had enough cash to buy up the three million or so acres of land and the sixty-one sugar refineries, some of them the biggest in the country, which were owned by American companies. Sure, things could have been arranged if these companies had agreed to take the ten dollars per acre, which was what they'd paid in the first place. But they didn't even agree to the values they themselves had declared in their last tax returns, and they were shocked by our offer to repay them over twenty years at 4 per cent interest. So we were forced to go it alone, which was enough to earn us the full measure of their anti-Communist indignation. To begin with, they threatened to cut our sugar quota on the U.S. market; for the past thirty years that quota had enabled us to sell some three million tons of sugar per year at the preferential price fixed for American-grown sugar. This represented the bulk of our income from foreign trade. In January 1960, Congress authorized President Eisenhower to settle the whole matter at his discretion, which was one way of putting a gun to our heads. So to get in first, we approached the neutral countries, and then the Soviet Union, to make sure that, if the worst came to the worst, all our sugar wouldn't just pile up in the warehouses. The Russians straightaway bought a small amount and promised to take over any quota the Americans didn't want. In exchange they offered us some 300,000 tons of oil, at a preferential price, and also gave us credit to buy industrial equipment. You know what happened next: Standard Oil, Texaco, and Shell, who were the sole managers of the Cuban oil business, not content with refusing to refine 'red petroleum,' suspended supplies of their own fuel, and without oil our industries, our transport system, and our electricity works would have ground to a halt. We no longer had a choice. We had to take over the management of the refineries ourselves and ask the Russians to send us their oil as quickly as possible. Then the American electricity company refused to use 'red petroleum' or to lower its tariffs by the 30 per cent our government had demanded. So we had to confiscate that company as well, in spite of even more violent American threats about our sugar. Fidel then told them: 'If you cut our quota pound by pound, we will nationalize your factories one by one.' None of this did any good: on July 9, 1960, President Eisenhower stopped the purchase of 700,000 tons of sugar, the balance of our annual quota. A month later, on August 6, Fidel nationalized thirty-six American sugar refineries and all American-owned property in this key sector of the economy. Then in October the United States placed an embargo on the export of a host of commodities to Cuba, in the hope of whipping up the anger of all the large landowners and traders who had remained on the island. On October 13, 1960, our government responded to this act of aggression by nationalizing approximately four hundred banks and other concerns. From that date on we have been our own masters; our nickel has been our own and so has our sugar; we have gained control over our own finances—in other words, we have become an independent country."

My friends were all agreed on this version, and differences of opinion arose only when I tried to find out whether Fidel had known what would happen from the very start. Some argued that he had been afraid the Americans would retaliate even more quickly, and had accordingly fought for time to train new political and economic administrators. Hence he had at first entrusted important government posts—including the presidency of the republic—to men who would be likely to placate the Americans.[26] In addition, Fidel had paid a good-will visit to the United States himself. Thanks to these precautions, he was not caught unprepared when the inevitable trial of strength came in 1960. By that time he was able to pay the Americans back tit for tat with no harm at all to the economy of his country.

According to others, Fidel had not been playing for time at all but had been genuinely anxious to make the Cuban Revolution palatable to the Americans—he was determined to spare his country the horrors of economic and military aggression. When, for example, he first opened negotiations with the East, his aim was to let the Americans know that their threats and pressures would be of no use since Cuba could count on new markets at any time. And he remembered that in 1938, when President Cárdenas had nationalized oil in Mexico, the United States had also blustered, threatening to "drown Mexico in its own oil," but as soon as Cárdenas made it clear that he could sell his chief export in Europe, the U.S. government had quickly backed down. Fidel probably hoped to get the same result by signing trade agreements with the U.S.S.R. and China. But then in 1938, Roosevelt's administration had been quick to realize that Cárdenas would stand firm on the oil question and that it was better forgotten if profitable relations with Mexico were to be preserved. In 1959–60, unfortunately, the Eisenhower government was not nearly so subtle: determined not to give an

26. Manuel Urrutia, President of the Cuban Republic after the fall of Batista, was a liberal judge who, in 1957, had voted for the acquittal of the rebels captured after the *Granma* landing. Strongly anti-Communist and disturbed at the radical course of the Revolution, Urrutia clashed with the Castroists and was forced to tender his resignation (July 16, 1959).

inch, it lost a whole country. For all that, even Cubans who spoke of Ike's "cosmic stupidity" agreed that their longing for independence had been far too strong to allow of a Mexican type of compromise solution. Hence "historical inevitability" would have led to the same result, even had Eisenhower dis-played all the subtlety of a Franklin D. Roosevelt.

Our hosts' analysis of Cuban-American relations ended here, and at their suggestion we decided that immediately after Fidel's speech on May 1 we would set off for Pinar del Río province, to see Cuban socialism at work in the field.

The guerrilleros *turn administrators*

On the way to Pinar del Río we had to run a veritable obstacle race around anti-tank holes in the road. The Cubans had been prepared for an invasion, and not knowing where to expect it, had taken precautions everywhere. We were not the only ones to be inconvenienced: the peasant trucks returning from Havana after the big May Day celebrations also had great difficulty in weaving their way between these traps.

The country folk had swarmed to the capital to take part in a great *fiesta* and, most important, to hear Fidel's speech. Now they were returning, tired and a little sleepy, their heads full of what he had told them about the dawn of popular power, their power, which was now called socialism. Fidel had not elaborated on the precise meaning of that word, nor on the society he was planning to build; he had merely dealt with a controversy that had been at the center of Cuban political life for the past twenty years. The democratic constitution of 1940,[27] which the old

27. The 1940 Constitution had been voted under the impetus of radical opinion when Cuba had just emerged painfully from the long crisis of the 1930s. It contained a number of progressive social clauses limiting the privileges and rights of the rich and land ownership by foreigners. The United States was not prepared to accept even these limitations of its economic prerogatives on the island and the Cuban government lacked the means to impose them, particularly in view of the international situation caused by the outbreak of the Second World War. The social provisions

regime had never been able to apply, had now been superseded and a socialist constitution, adapted to the new social conditions, would be presented to the people in the near future. Fidel also reiterated the chief points of the "Havana Declaration,"[28] to which he added the extension of social justice and the right of the workers to enjoy to the full the fruits of their labor. Everybody had cheered wildly; dancing and singing in Revolution Square had continued until late in the night. Some people, however, had set to work plastering the walls of Havana with such slogans as: "If the Yanks can't live with a socialist revolution ninety miles from their shores, why don't they get out?"

We have said that many of the celebrants were simple peasants, and we wondered how the new ideas had so quickly managed to take root in the countryside. Juan Arcocha, who led our international team—Timur Gaidar of *Pravda* had meanwhile joined us—took us straight to the man with his finger on the pulse of the province. *Comandante* Escalona, young, slim, and with an impressive black beard, received us in a pretty villa, inherited from an exiled *latifundista,* and offered us a fine Cuban breakfast. I do not now recall if he was military commander of the province, or director of INRA (*Instituto nacional de Reforma Agraria*). However, I have put together a rough outline of his account, taken from my notes.

Cuban revolutionaries were not apparently aware of the full

---

in the Constitution thus remained so many dead letters, even though the Left never ceased clamoring for their implementation, and indeed made this the most important question of national life.

28. In reply to the declaration of the Organization of American States in San José de Costa Rica condemning Cuba's policy for the first time, Fidel Castro called a National Assembly of the People of Cuba on September 2, 1960, and before a million people read an eight-part document, the last section of which stipulated that the document would be known as the "Havana Declaration." Its content was anti-imperialist and denounced American misdeeds in the hemisphere. The "Second Havana Declaration" (February 4, 1962), which followed the exclusion of Cuba from the Organization of American States at their Conference in Punta del Este, was a much longer and more elaborate document, including a social and economic analysis of the problems of the Third World.

extent of peasant misery until they started their guerrilla war. In the Sierra Maestra, they came across some three hundred thousand human beings living on the fringes of society, as good as forgotten by the rest of the world, cultivating land that was rarely their own, pitilessly exploited by a series of profiteers ranging from landlord and moneylender to the shopkeeper on the corner. The vast majority of their children did not go to school, and although the mountain climate was cold, did not, as a rule, own a single pair of shoes. No one had ever seen a doctor, no one knew what a hospital was; electricity and roads had not yet reached the Sierra Maestra. The situation was no better in the Sierra Cristal where, in 1958, Raúl Castro had opened the second front in the anti-Batista guerrilla war. The revolutionaries had to take charge of the administration of more than a million people, bringing them both material aid and the rudiments of civilization.

The rebel army's officer corps, which took shape during that testing time, afterward provided the framework of INRA, the organization charged first of all with distributing *latifundista* lands among the tenant farmers and later with agrarian reform. The six Cuban provinces were divided into twenty-eight agricultural development zones in each of which the administrator helped the people to form cooperatives, especially in sugar cane plantations, or else organized *granjas del pueblo,* state farms under the direct administration of INRA. The small owners were invited to join ANAP—The National Association of Small Farmers—which proposed to coordinate the new agricultural policy. Others, particularly the sugar workers, formed associations that fell somewhere between private farms and cooperatives. The whole program was run on a purely voluntary basis, with no pressure of any sort and amid much popular enthusiasm. *Comandante* Escalona stressed this point "because foreigners often go away with the idea that the peasants have to be forced to join cooperatives."

Thus, in Pinar del Río province, more than 5,500 poor peasants had benefited from the reform by the spring of 1961, cultivating between them some 13,500 acres of land. Almost 60 per

cent of them belonged to ANAP. However, Escalona frankly
pointed out that those old owners who had hung on to their own
land had proved more reticent toward ANAP, which had only
been able to enroll 30 per cent of them.

As for INRA, it comprised 29 cooperatives whose 6,000 members worked 75,000 acres of land, and the same number of
granjas del pueblo with more than 20,000 workers and 750,000
acres of land. The *granjas* were more popular and bigger in size
simply because they opened up new land and, for the rest,
specialized in stock-farming and hence needed large areas for
grazing. In any case, the *comandante* and his assistants who gave
us these figures made no secret of the fact that at the time INRA
was running the cooperatives as well as the *granjas*.[29]

This was in itself a considerable undertaking, and INRA had
many other responsibilities besides: its industrial department
managed the repair shops and generally looked after machinery
and other essential agricultural equipment; its commercial department ran several thousand *tiendas del pueblo* (people's
shops) which sold almost everything and freed the peasants
from the clutches of crooked tradesmen. INRA also distributed
the products of the cooperatives and *granjas* in the towns. Here
the theoretical report ended. But how did things work out in
practice? What problems troubled the comrades in Pinar del Río
most? Our concern amazed the revolutionaries. Everything was
going extremely well; it had become clear that there was absolutely no need for *latifundistas* and professional administrators. Without them, and despite counterrevolutionary raids by
saboteurs from Miami, production of the principal commodities
—sugar and tobacco—had reached a record in 1961. For the
first time in the history of Cuba, the *zafra*—the sugar-cane har-

29. In fact, like the *granjas*, the cooperatives were chiefly composed of
former land workers who contributed no property except a few cattle.
I should think that the sponsors of INRA were simply trying to discover
which of the two would prove more effective. But since both were under the
direct control of INRA—the heads of all cooperatives were appointed by,
and answerable to, that organization—it was difficult to arrive at a
satisfactory conclusion. Later they opted for the *granjas* all the same and,
as we shall see, the cooperatives have tended to disappear.

vest—had been brought in, not by overexploited workers, but by the people themselves, and in particular by volunteers from the towns. In addition, their great effort had coincided both with the state of alert of December 1960[30] and with the Bay of Pigs invasion; that is, it had occurred during full-scale military mobilization. Despite the fact that harvesting had to be relegated to pauses in military training, the first returns showed that, in 1961, Cuba would have the largest *zafra* of the century.[31] Fidel had himself given the lead: one day in February he had cut 364 *arrobas* of cane at a time when the daily norm had been fixed at 100 *arrobas*.[32] One of our hosts even claimed that Fidel had cut 1,000 *arrobas* but we did not dwell on this minor difference of opinion.

Escalona told us before leaving for another appointment that Cuba did not, strictly speaking, have an agricultural problem— the development of its vast potential had been artificially held back by the *latifundistas* and the American sugar companies. Sugar production in Cuba in the '20s had not been much less than in the '50s, although the Cuban population had grown from three and a half to almost six and a half million. This was the result of deliberate policy with a double objective: to limit the production of sugar so as to stabilize world prices, and to prevent the growing of other crops in order to have an army of seasonal workers permanently on tap at ridiculous wages. The companies rented vast areas of arable land which they often left barren; occasionally they would plant "reserve cane" which did not have to be cut each year. They neither invested nor did

30. The Castroists, alarmed by American preparations, were afraid that President Eisenhower might decide to go out on a trail of glory and order the invasion of Cuba before departing the White House. In December, Cuba accordingly declared a state of general alert, i.e., the mobilization of the army and the entire civilian population. The emergency measures were only lifted on the inauguration of John F. Kennedy, on January 19, 1961.

31. In fact the *zafra* of 1961 (approximately 7 million tons) was the second largest in Cuban history. The record (7.2 million tons) was the *zafra* of 1952.

32. One *arroba* = 25 pounds.

anything to increase the yield, with the result that the Cubans became "the biggest sugar growers with the lowest productivity." "Every year we had to import agricultural products from the United States. That cost us hundreds of millions of dollars, almost half what our own sugar earned us, when we could easily have grown it all on good Cuban soil."

Given these conditions, the only real problem was the quickest possible eradication of the worst effects of cultural and technical underdevelopment. It was accordingly decided to make literacy the number one job of 1961. The *comandante* advised us to visit the teaching brigades attached to INRA; they were all made up of volunteers—young schoolteachers, students, and even school children—and did remarkable work. I asked Escalona if we could also meet political leaders of the July 26th Movement in his province, or leaders of other parties (the Communist Party, for example), but he was already moving away in his jeep. His slightly ironical smile seemed to say: "Don't waste your time, I am the July 26th Movement and no one can tell you any more than I have told you already."

Perhaps he was thinking nothing of the kind, but in the next few days we learned that he would have had every right to do so. We visited *granjas* and cooperatives, we admired the pretty wooden cottages in the new village of El Rosario, we slept in recreation centers built by INIT (The National Institute of the Tourist Industry), but nowhere did we meet local leaders or anybody capable of giving us an overall picture of the situation. INRA officials, no less than the managers of the *granjas,* discussed nothing except the diversification of agriculture, quoting repeatedly from a speech of Fidel's on this very subject.[33] Many of their own projects struck us as rather unsophisticated, but the

33. In his television address of December 9, 1960, Fidel for the first time called for the diversification of agriculture and insisted that this was far more important than the cultivation of virgin soil. Cuba, he explained, had no need to buy tens of thousands of bulldozers to open up new land, when all it needed was to cultivate existing fields in a more rational and efficient manner.

rank and file declared themselves content and spontaneously told us how much their condition had improved thanks to the Revolution. They were at last getting fixed wages, enough to eat, and could even afford meat, chicken, and other "luxury" foods. They were grateful to Fidel and had nothing but good to say of the men in olive-green, but they were far more concerned with day-to-day problems than with questions of state or the organization of their *granjas* and cooperatives.

When I went back to Havana, I learned that INRA was still far too "*guerrillero*"—to use Che Guevara's famous expression—i.e., neither coordinated enough nor properly planned. The Castroists themselves were the first to admit this and half amused, half shocked, they told entertaining stories about certain *granja* leaders who had come forward with all sorts of harebrained schemes. It was customary to laugh at them, rather than suppress them, because they always had the very best of intentions,[34] and because their mistakes were inevitable, given their lack of experience and the scope of the task they had taken on.[35]

34. Edward Boorstein, an American then working for the National Bank, tells a characteristic story on this subject in his *The Economic Transformation of Cuba* (London, *Monthly Review Press, 1968*). One day in the spring of 1960, Che Guevara's economic assistant and Boorstein were visited by an old *guerrillero*, in charge of a thousand *tiendas del pueblo*—nearly half of the total. He asked for a loan of 16 million pesos, because his shops were in financial difficulties. He brought along no papers, but simply explained that, if he was refused, he would have no stock within six or seven weeks. When asked how his shops were run, whether he gave a great deal of credit, whether his customers paid their debts, and how he fixed his prices, he replied most amiably that he did, indeed, give a great deal of credit and that many of his customers failed to pay up—but what could he possibly do about it? Before the Revolution, the poor countryfolk had been crushed by the traders who seized on their debts to grind their faces even further in the dust. Today the *tiendas del pueblo* were their own *tiendas* and there must be nothing to remind them of the old days. A great deal of time and patience was needed to settle the outstanding credit problems, and while this was being done, the peasants must, under no circumstances, be allowed to find empty shelves in their shops. And the two financial advisers decided to grant his request, although it was not at all in accordance with the normal tenets of good banking.

35. In his *Cuba, socialisme et développement*, René Dumont remarks on some of the errors committed by INRA. Above all he rightly objects

"If Fidel is a socialist so are we"

It was decided that the damage done was not too serious, and in any case the time for improvisation was rapidly coming to an end. Since February 1961 Havana had been planning the introduction of a complete and coherent planning system that would run like clockwork, ensure the rapid advancement of the economy, and, above all, provide for the industrialization of the island. "This year, our economy is still freewheeling a bit, but 1962 will really be the year for planning."

We made no comments ourselves on any of the obvious deficiencies of the guerrilla methods in Pinar del Río province, but in spite of our sympathy for the new administrators, we were rather perplexed by some of their efforts. For instance, in the cooperative (or was it a *granja?*) Los Pinos, we were shown a large crop of tomatoes and peppers grown on a specially prepared bed of pebbles, surrounded by water works so complex that it took more than an hour to explain how they worked. Our colleague from *Pravda* was fascinated and determined not to miss a single word. Juan Arcocha helped him by translating the instructions into English which I then retranslated into Russian. Being unfamiliar with the vocabulary of hydroponics, I had to make an extraordinary linguistic effort, and could think of nothing else. Hence I never found out what exactly were the advantages of growing tomatoes and peppers by this scientific method. I gained the clear impression, however, that all the energies of the workers in the place were thrown into this venture. What, I wondered, was the reason for all these complications when Cuba abounded in fertile soil and sun?

I never discovered the answer to this question because Gaidar rather monopolized the conversation. He came from Arkhan-

to the absence of rank-and-file autonomy and initiative. According to him, many errors could have been avoided, if the members of the peasant cooperatives and *granjas* had been allowed to have their say on the running of these enterprises. I do think, however, that Dumont is wrong to blame Captain Antonio Nuñez Jiménez, the first head of INRA, who had the thankless task of directing this body during the first, and most difficult, eighteen months of its existence. Captain Jiménez, a geographer, is now president of the Academy of Sciences.

gelsk, in the cold north, and was enchanted by his discovery of semitropical agriculture. The atmosphere in our group was one of perfect courtesy and he succeeded admirably in conveying both his good humor and the freshness of his reactions to all of us.[36] In addition most of the provincials, hearing Russian spoken, took us for Soviet citizens, which gave me a good idea of their feelings about the U.S.S.R. By and large, these views were of three kinds.

Those few who were aware of the importance of *Pravda* stood out clearly from the rest. They kept pumping Gaidar's hand while congratulating him on the power of the Soviet Union and her historic role in the anti-American struggle. This group, however, was exclusively made up of officials. Most of the people looked upon *los soviéticos* with a mixture of fearful astonishment and gratitude. Arcocha discreetly told me about remarks made "between Cubans" from which it emerged that the image of the Bolshevik with a knife between his teeth was still firmly rooted in the local mind. This did not stop comments like: "Even so, they're better than the Yankees"; "At least they're not trying to get rich at our expense"; and so on. It should be said that Gaidar, always smiling and perfectly peaceable, shooting no one except with his camera, was able to dispel their worst fears. On one occasion only did I hear frankly disagreeable remarks about the Russians, but they were made by some elegant Havana people who were passing the evening in a bar, taking advantage of the new recreational possibilities in Pinar del Río province. They left later in a Cadillac which had lost much of its original glitter.

All in all, the general Cuban attitude toward Russia showed how difficult it is to eradicate the consequences of long-term membership in the U.S. ideological empire. Even young men

36. In 1966 Timur Gaidar published a short book on his stay in Cuba. In it he gave a most faithful account of his strange experiences during the Playa Girón invasion: though he was admitted to Castro's staff he knew no Spanish and hence had very little idea of what was going on. His book ends, very prudently, with the end of the invasion.

and women who had not been politically active until after the Revolution were not free from some of the old prejudices. The nature of the resulting "ideological vacuum," with which my friend C. Wright Mills had been so preoccupied, was driven home to me while I was on a visit to the literacy brigade at El Rosario.

These young teachers had already become legendary in Cuba and had even produced their own martyrs. One of their number, a black youth called Conrado Benítez, had been hung by counterrevolutionaries in the Escambray mountains,[37] and this crime, carried out against a volunteer armed only with his spelling books, had shaken the country. It had not, however, dampened the enthusiasm of a large army of volunteer teachers, who tackled their task with redoubled determination. At that time two peasants out of five could neither read nor write[38] and no law could make them learn. The "brigaders," by slowly gaining their confidence, did, however, bring them around. They worked with their pupils in the fields, but had their own camps with their own canteens, so as not to be a burden on the needy peasants. They also ran libraries and there were other, more experienced, teachers to lead them, which meant that they, too, could study in their free time. Each literacy brigade headquarters thus formed a focus of intellectual and political life, from which the ideas of the Revolution radiated out far and wide.

Everything that our young hosts of El Rosario told us about

37. The Escambray mountains (Las Villas province) counted two distinct *guerrillero* centers during the anti-Batista struggle. The first was founded by student militants of the *Directorio Revolucionario;* the second was known as the Escambray Second Front, and most of its leaders subsequently turned against Castro. According to the current version, this group adopted a rapacious attitude toward the peasants, who came to hate the Revolution so much that in 1960 they formed a counterrevolutionary center subsidized by the CIA.

38. At the time of the Revolution 23 per cent of all Cubans were illiterate. Some of these lived in the poorer district of Havana, but the great majority was found in the countryside.

their work and the way they lived was extraordinary. These sixteen- and seventeen-year-olds appeared very much aware of the tragedy of the poverty-stricken peasants, and were deeply moved by the destitution of some of the villages. They had reacted with outrage, almost with shame, to the abject condition of their country. For the rest, they had a measure of patience not normally found in people of their age, and their devotion to Fidel knew no bounds.

The head of the brigade led me to the library. Fidel's *History Will Absolve Me*,[39] Che Guevara's book on guerrilla warfare, and popular editions of the works of José Martí y Pérez (1853–1895), the apostle of Cuban independence, were all given pride of place. International socialist literature was there, too, neatly stacked in the political section. And it was here that I made a most painful discovery. One could excuse the presence of Makarenko's *Pedagogical Poem*, and of Ostrovsky's *How the Steel Was Tempered*, but to what possible use could these young people, thirsty for knowledge, put the *Rudiments of Marxist Philosophy* by academician Konstantinov, the works of academician Mitin, or those of the unfortunately renowned academician Lysenko? What was the point of filling their heads with these typically Stalinist works which the Russians themselves, including Gaidar, looked upon with embarrassment?

My guide, uneasy as he saw me making notes of these titles, was quick to explain that his pupils enjoyed *Weekend in Guatemala* by Miguel Angel Asturias and Cuban or Latin American literature best of all. "They are shaping well politically because of it," he said.

For all that, they certainly knew very little about socialism and Communism. It even seemed to me that these two words, so long equated with hell by the mass media of the preceding regime, still filled them with a kind of terror. When I asked a young girl of seventeen, Julia L., if she would call herself a socialist, she turned red as a beet and then, after a moment's

39. Written after the Moncada attack on July 26, 1953.

hesitation, replied: "I am a revolutionary." Her friends, even more bashful than she was, gave a sigh of relief. However, I pressed her: "Don't you know that Fidel has said that your revolution is a socialist revolution?" Julia blushed again and her comrades maintained a thoughtful silence. "If Fidel said that our revolution is a socialist one, he knows better than I do. And if he is a socialist, then so am I." This time the girl's answer produced general applause, including that of the head of the brigade who had listened without interruption to our conversation.

"El Che" confronts the orthodox

"We will even arm the cats," Fidel Castro joked in 1959, "if only we can teach them how to handle a gun."[40] In fact the number of armed men and women two years later was impressive. The militia stood guard day and night in front of every kind of business, ministry, newspaper building, and even the most innocent-looking office. If one adds a large sprinkling of veterans and young recruits in olive-green, one can indeed say that Cuba was a nation under arms, conforming fully to the heroic picture of all revolutions. The columns of soldiers in ragged file, with their prewar guns in the May Day parade, together with the rhythmic choruses in Spanish, reminded me of the volunteer brigades during the battle of Madrid; for Europeans of my generation there could be nothing more moving than this victorious resurrection of the *grande armée* of socialism.

For the comparison to remain valid, however, these enthusiastic people would have had to talk about their "soviets" or about their "socialist plans." Now I had tried in vain, in the provinces as well as in Havana, to find signs of any great enthusiasm for either among the rank and file. There was an impressive amount of support for the Revolution, but the absence of any political initiative even among the militants and the

40. In a letter to *Bohemia* on June 14, 1959.

rather primitive level of their socialism were rather surprising. Moreover it was not easy to penetrate the mysteries of the administrative structure or the inner workings of their new society, a society in which a large sector of the economy had been nationalized. Everything seemed to be working smoothly, but very few people could tell you how. In general, they were content to explain that the new Cuba had released so much untapped energy and so many fresh resources that she could, for a time at least, allow herself the luxury of living without bothering about a complete social blueprint.

If one adds to this the presence in the libraries of those "famous" Soviet manuals, with their hidebound explanations of the irreplaceable role of the proletarian party—a party which did not even exist in Cuba—one must admit that it was not very easy to make sense of the situation. Carlos Franqui, editor of the Castroist daily *Revolución* and an *impenitente discutidor*,[41] talked to me nonstop, from midnight to dawn, of Fidel's genius, of their life together in the Sierra, and of the marvelous spirit

41. In a letter to Armando Hart, written from the Sierra Maestra in April 1958, Major Faustino Pérez, one of the members of the *Granma* expedition and later chief of the resistance movement in Havana, described Carlos Franqui as an "impenitent debater," but this was meant as a tribute to his vigilant critical spirit. Carlos Franqui, the self-taught son of a poor peasant from Las Villas province, was at first active in the PSP and worked as a proofreader on the Party journal *Hoy*. However, his tendency to discuss rather than obey earned him the censure of Aníbal Escalante, and led to his expulsion in 1947. This did not dampen Franqui's revolutionary ardor and in fact helped turn him into a leading member of the Cuban avant-garde in the '50s. From the beginning of the anti-Batista struggle he distinguished himself as organizer of the underground press in Havana. Later he continued the struggle from his Costa Rican exile, before joining the Sierra Maestra at the end of 1957. Once there he ran *Radio Rebelde* and, in fact, took charge of the entire Castroist propaganda machine. He also set up the forerunner of *Revolución*, the organ of the July 26th Movement. In January 1959, after the liberation of Havana, this paper became the chief daily of Cuba and remained such until 1964, when it fused with *Hoy* and changed its name to *Granma*. Carlos Franqui has also published one of the best eyewitness accounts of the Castroist resistance movement, the *Book of the Twelve*, a mine of information on the guerrilla movement and the life of Cuban revolutionaries.

of the people. However, for further information he advised me
to go to other leaders more qualified to pronounce on the practical and ideological implications of the new socialist program.
Fidel was unfortunately out of reach; he was traveling the
country from one end to the other. So Carlos arranged a series
of meetings at a somewhat lower level. It was at one of these
that I first met Ernesto Guevara, "El Che."

*El compañero ministro de industrias, el comandante doctor
Ernesto Guevara de la Serna* was not yet the legendary hero of
the Latin American revolution, but in Cuban eyes he was already "the other Fidel"—admittedly less important, but abounding in talent and exemplary worth. President Dorticós, Raúl
Castro, or even Armando Hart, had as high a status in the
Castroist hierarchy, but Che seemed to have a more independent persona, more clearly delineated and hence more obviously
charismatic. One fact alone singled him out—he was not a
Cuban.

Che Guevara was born in the Argentine, and had done his
medical studies, all the while "dreaming of the glory of the
scientist who puts his discoveries to the service of mankind."
But his restless nature urged him on to travel, and, faced with
the misery and destitution of Latin America, he quickly realized
the vanity of his medical ambitions. In 1954, in the Guatemala
of Jacobo Arbenz, he had already prepared his notes on "the
conduct of a revolutionary physician," when "the United Fruit
Company, the State Department, and John Foster Dulles—they
were, in fact, one and the same—unleashed their dogs of war."
Then it was, at the age of twenty-five, that Che discovered a
fundamental truth: "To become a revolutionary physician, one
must first of all make a revolution."[42]

That revolution would be made in Cuba. He met Fidel, in
exile, on "one of those cold Mexican nights"; and they remained friends for life. Fate was to separate them, however, on

42. The phrases in quotation marks are taken from a speech by Che
given in 1960, and quoted in *Cuba,* 67, November 1967.

the very eve of their armed departure for the Sierra. The Castroists had had trouble with the Mexican police, and Che was thrown into jail. He told the story himself: "I was a foreigner, living in Mexico illegally, and with a series of charges against me," but felt that "under no circumstances should the Revolution be held back for me." It would have been much simpler to "leave me behind"; and he laid claim to another assignment for later. Fidel replied brusquely: "I will not abandon you."[43]

An ordinary comrade on board the *Granma,* Che rapidly stood out from the rest. Fidel always entrusted him and Camilo Cienfuegos[44] with the most important tasks; it was they who led the "invasion brigades of the plain" and delivered the *coup de grâce* to the *Batistiano* army. But the Sierra had not been simply a military test for the Castroists; it was also a social experiment, and had a decisive effect on the future of the Revolution. In the political debates of the time—we shall examine them later—Che's advice counted for a great deal, indeed was often the determining factor. His turn of mind and his Latin American experiences made him better suited than anyone else to becoming the theorist of the guerrilla war, an expert on relations between the guerrillas and the peasantry and on the repercussions of the war on the nature of the Revolution.

It was natural in these circumstances that the "moderates" and opponents of the Revolution should have seen Che as "Fidel's evil Communist genius." This judgment was incorrect to a large extent, since it is impossible to divide Fidel's development into two distinct portions, one "democratic" and the other "socialist." However, it was universally recognized that Che played an important part in the political and intellectual maturation of the *guerrilleros.*

It is also a fact that Che's promotion in November 1959 to president of the National Bank marked a decisive turning point

43. Quoted from *Reminiscences of the Cuban Revolutionary War* (London, Pelican, 1968), p. 39.
44. Camilo Cienfuegos, liberator of Havana and a legendary figure in Castro's ranks, died in a plane accident in November 1959.

in the direction of the Revolution. From that moment on, socialist measures began to rain down with the force of a tropical
storm. Later, in 1960, Che took charge of the industrial department of INRA, which led, in fact, to his assuming the leadership of the nationalized sector of the economy. At the end of
the same year, it was Che again who went on a long tour of
the East and laid the foundations for systematic cooperation between Cuba and the socialist bloc. Last but not least, as Minister
of Industry he paved the way for the industrialization of the
island.

Some people close to Fidel feared a public outcry against the
promotion of a foreigner, and a leftist at that, to the nation's
key posts. But the revolutionary impetus very quickly swept
aside all xenophobic prejudices and all opposition to Guevara's
radicalism. Indeed, the ease with which the Cubans adopted Che
put an end to the old "theory" that all Latin American countries
are in the grip of nationalist frenzy, and suffer from the kind of
provincial mentality that inevitably causes them to rise up
against one another. In Cuba, Ernesto Che Guevara, despite his
Argentinian origins, had neither a greater nor a smaller number
of difficulties than the other leaders. Like the rest, he had his
enemies, and not all his ideas were adopted by the Castroist
movement.

Everybody in command knew that "socialism with the
pachanga," as Che called it, could not last forever. The economy
of the country was already running into problems that could not
be resolved by guerrilla methods. Many sprang directly from the
administrative vacuum and from the lack of organization during
the period when everything was running *por la libre*. Remedies
had to be found as quickly as possible, and since they did not
place great reliance in rank-and-file initiative, the leaders tried
to take charge themselves. They had already discussed the formation of a "revolutionary party" which would mobilize all forces
and introduce discipline into all sectors of public life. But how
could this party be established? And precisely what sort of discipline was needed? Would the inspiration have to come from

the textbooks sent by Soviet comrades, and would Cubans have to make amends for their crime of *lèse-orthodoxie:* the victory of a revolution that ran counter to the doctrine of the only "true Marxist-Leninist party"? The official guardian of that doctrine in Cuba, the *Partido Socialista Popular* (PSP), was one of eighty-one Communist parties which, in 1960, had just returned from a get-together in Moscow, and was not very keen on making common cause with the men of the Sierra; much better if the Castroists formed a nationalist movement with socialist aspirations, a sort of Cuban version of the "Revolutionary Kuomintang" of Maoist China. The Castroists themselves were cool toward the PSP; indeed many of them could not disguise their sour faces every time the name of that party or those of its leaders were mentioned.

In the last resort, it was up to Fidel to settle the question. Che, however, had very definite ideas on the subject, and his advice could not be ignored. According to him, time was pressing; it was important to act quickly, and since the only available model was the one described in the Soviet manuals, the best thing was to adapt it to the Cuban situation. His haste could no doubt be explained by the fact that he was in daily contact with the most complex economic problems and found it hard to put up with the "creative chaos" the guerrillas and their young helpers had caused so blithely to prevail. But it was also suggested that he had been seduced, even enraptured, by his tour of the East; in his own words, he had felt like Alice in Wonderland in the Soviet bloc.[45] He saw no disadvantage, therefore, in Cuba's drawing inspiration from these countries

45. Captain Nuñez Jiménez, then director of INRA, was the first to publish an extraordinary account of his trip to the U.S.S.R. in the autumn of 1960. The Cubans said that it read like Alice in Wonderland. Che Guevara, who visited nearly every country in the Eastern bloc, from Czechoslovakia and the U.S.S.R. to China and Korea, anticipated similarly skeptical remarks when, on his return, he said in a television address (December 31, 1960) that during his entire tour he had felt "like Alice in a continent of marvels." See Che's *Oeuvres*, Vol. 3, Paris, Maspero, 1968.

and had high hopes that by doing so she might obtain the most spectacular results.

Che had never been a Communist—"if I were a Communist, I would not hesitate to shout it from the rooftops"[46]—but he had an almost visceral reaction toward those manifestations of anti-Communism with which he had grown familiar since adolescence and which he attributed to the baleful influence of the Yankee ideology. While in the Sierra he had already criticized what he considered to be the excessive suspicions of many of his comrades with regard to the PSP. All this helped to make him intransigent, even uncompromising, when talking with his more cautious comrades. On top of this, if one adds that, according to Che himself, he had a somewhat quarrelsome nature which often made him blow up, it is easy to understand that he was a difficult character to live with.

Hence I must frankly confess that as I entered the Ministry of Industry on May 9, 1961, my great curiosity and my admiration for Che were tempered with apprehension. But the conversation got off to a good start, and what is more, in French—Che could handle that language with great facility, only inquiring from time to time, a little coyly, whether his vocabulary was not perhaps too Spanish. We talked at first about the United States and then of my Jamaican fiasco, which seemed to amuse him a great deal. He had a sense of humor and our conversation was extremely relaxed.

Continuing in this vein, I tried to repeat, as entertainingly as I could, my talks with ordinary Cubans about socialism. "Of course," he agreed wholeheartedly, "people here are learning by doing, and they have only just started. Quite recently, I happened to speak to some comrades, who said that they were not too pleased with 'all this socialist business.' So I asked them: 'Do you mean to say that you are against land reforms? Or against expropriation of Yankee holdings? Or against nationalization, social justice, and the right of everyone to enjoy the fruits of his

46. See Che's letter to *Bohemia*, June 14, 1959.

labor?' They indignantly denied this, and swore that they were so enamored of all these things that they were ready to lay down their lives for them. 'Well then,' I said to them, 'if you are for all that, then you are for socialism,' and they went away happy."

So far so good. But then I asked whether, given this rather elementary plane of political education, it might not be dangerous to throw into what C. Wright Mills had called this "ideological vacuum" a whole lot of Soviet literature of questionable value. At this question, he became furious. He spoke scathingly of "liberals" who wanted the Revolution to remain ideologically neutral, and to give everyone perfect freedom to choose between a host of social philosophies and doctrines. "We reject such 'freedom' precisely because our view is that the first duty and most urgent need of the Revolution is the political and ideological education of our people. In a country which has to face death every day, which has to tackle tasks without equal in the history of this continent, it would be nothing less than criminal to give the people the privilege of hesitating between true and false ideologies." He ended soberly, his face suddenly clouded.

I contented myself with giving him my own views on the works of academicians Konstantinov, Mitin, and Lysenko, which had adorned the shelves of the library at El Rosario. Che raised his arms up to heaven: "We want to turn our young people into socialists as quickly as we possibly can, and that means consulting textbooks from the Eastern bloc. Have you got any others you can recommend?"

"I certainly know of better ones than those. Besides, there are different currents in socialist thought; why pick on just one, and not the most marvelous either?"

This time he was more than a little irritated. But his smile quickly returned; on the whole his attitude revealed a kind of impatience at this idle polemical joust, rather than annoyance or real anger. "So you would like us to turn Cuba into a sort of seminar for intellectuals, a Parisian café where people can sit down and rave about the latest literary hits. But what kind of country do you think ours really is? Cuba is in the midst of a revolution, besieged by U.S. Marines; she must see to her defenses and build her future. It is not for fun that we have decided to rush our children from secondary schools to high schools and from high schools to universities. It is because we have to act quickly and because we have no choice in the matter."

While he spoke, his look seemed to say: "Please, try to forget all your preconceptions and put yourself in our shoes." He did not attempt to defend the Marxism of Konstantinov and Mitin any more than he approved my opinion of them. He let it be understood that he had never read these works and that the political education of Cuba did not depend on the sort of marginal aberration they might represent. I insisted: "I have seen the havoc caused by false ideas of how to build socialism; first they gave rise to conformism on an incredible scale, and next they led to apolitical feelings and finally to cynicism. I lived in the U.S.S.R. for seven years, I attended courses in Marxism-Leninism at one of the biggest universities, and I have met many Soviet citizens in recent years. Why on earth must young Cubans be launched on the same path, the path of intellectual Stalinism and mental semiparalysis, followed by a period of recantation with all the anguish that entails?"

"Listen to me," he replied slowly and deliberately. "Every revolution, like it or not, inevitably has its share of Stalinism, simply because every revolution faces capitalist encirclement. In very quick succession, we have been taught the meaning of economic blockade, subversion, sabotage, and psychological warfare. We have had to defend ourselves against the imperialist threat, and the invasion of April 17 reminded us that no measure, no sacrifice, is too great as far as this is concerned.

"In any case," he continued, "the situation in Cuba cannot be compared with that of the U.S.S.R. The Soviet Union not only had to protect herself against threats from outside but had also to create, by her own unaided efforts, the basic industries essential to her economic development and defense. Our situa-

47

tion is quite different. We get all we want from the other social-ist countries. For us, industrialization means immediate benefits for the whole population and the end of unemployment, a chronic scourge of Latin America. Moreover, we do not have an agricultural problem. In the U.S.S.R., peasant resistance to collectivization played a decisive role in the development of Stalinism. Here, land reform has kept step with the demands of the peasants and is one of our most popular measures. That is why conditions for Stalinist developments do not exist in Cuba; that phenomenon simply cannot be repeated here.[47]

"Moreover," Che continued, "I believe that in order to learn how to run a country, to plan its economy, and to construct socialism, our young people can do no better than consult books from those socialist countries that have preceded us along our path.

"The country closest to us, from the economic point of view, is Czechoslovakia. It has a surface area comparable to ours and it has developed a very efficient planning system that starts on the factory floor. We like that very much and we hope to do the same thing in our first four-year plan. But we still have a lack of trained people to put such a system into operation. So what do you want us to do? Let our young people struggle along for several years or invite the Czechs to help us and to train our economic experts? We don't even have to think about it: we invite the Czechs!"

The slight tension between us disappeared as soon as we changed the subject. Che replied freely to my questions about the island's economic situation and said he felt highly satisfied

47. Theodore Draper has seized upon this part of the interview, published in the *New Statesman* of May 19, 1961, to explain that Guevara's idea of "capitalist encirclement of the U.S.S.R." was a myth. According to this exponent of anti-Castroism, the Soviet Union ceased to be encircled the moment the United States established diplomatic relations with it (in 1932). Draper seems incapable of conceiving that any power other than the United States could ever have headed the anti-Bolshevik crusade. Has he never heard of the existence of Hitler or of the anti-Comintern pact? Is he quite unaware that certain Western powers, and not the least among them either, did their utmost to encourage Hitler's *Drang nach Osten?* See his *Castroism, Theory and Practice.*

"If Fidel is a socialist so are we"

with the results of the land reforms. One of his chief concerns, however, remained the continuance of unemployment, that plague handed on by the old regime. But Che was optimistic: "Within a year, industrialization will have eradicated unemployment throughout the country. Nothing comparable has ever been done in the history of Latin America!"

Many hopes were mingled with much indignation as he spoke of poverty on the continent. I thought he was taking a specifically Latin American view of the struggle and strongly counted on "Cuban contagion" south of the Río Grande. Perhaps this was because I remembered that he was an Argentinian, and that he had just published an article showing that the Cuban Revolution, far from being an exceptional case, had simply opened up a new path for all Latin American revolutionaries.[48] In any case, that article was merely the draft of a thesis on the possibility of the spread of guerrilla warfare, and not yet the enunciation of a complete strategy or a call to arms. The most urgent task was the transformation of revolutionary Cuba into a showcase. It would prove to Latin Americans at large not only that the old social order could be destroyed, but also that the new order was fully capable of satisfying the needs of the people, eradicating underdevelopment and its terrible consequences once and for all. Che's great continental design placed an exceptional stress on humanity, a stress that left no room for doctrinaire ideas or personal ambitions.

Meanwhile, a great deal depended on how much harm the United States could do to Cuba's future. In one of his last speeches, Che outlined the difficulties which had arisen in coal mining through a lack of American spare parts. And one had only to look at the cars in Havana, by far the greatest number of which had been "made in U.S.A.," to realize that Cuban transport would grind to a complete halt unless spare parts were quickly brought in.

Che did not, however, seem unduly worried about the nickel

48. See *Cuba, cas exceptionnel ou avant-garde?* in Che Guevara: *Oeuvres,* Vol. 13 (Paris, Maspero, 1968).

49

industry.[49] He had been assured of prompt Soviet aid which would even allow an increase in the production of this metal, so vital to the Cuban economy. As far as the rest of the economy was concerned, the Americans could indeed cause trouble but not nearly so much as they thought. They had no way of halting the island's economic progress, and their very impotence might possibly drive them into new military adventures. This threat was the reason for struggling with might and main for the speedy restoration of normal relations between Washington and Havana.

Knowing the political temper then of the United States, I was

---

49. Cuba has the world's largest nickel reserves (24 million tons). The United States consumes 40 per cent of the world output, producing a mere 3 per cent itself. Without Cuba, she has had to rely chiefly on nickel supplies from Canada, whose reserves at the time were 4 million tons. Now, United States firms had invested a great deal of money in Cuban mining, and contrary to normal practice, the U.S. government had made a direct contribution for the construction of an ultra-modern nickel refinery at Moa, in Oriente province. Another mechanized but nonautomated factory had been set up in nearby Nicaro. Americans looked upon Cuban nickel as part of their own "strategic pile" and, ever since the end of the Korean war, had cut down production in their factories in Oriente (13,200 tons in 1954). After the Revolution, Cuba was determined to increase its nickel output, but came up against technical difficulties: Moa and Nicaro did not manufacture the finished product. To obtain metallic nickel they would have had to send their output for final processing to American factories. This was no longer possible after nationalization and, moreover, most of the technicians who could have helped had meanwhile left for the United States. In his address of December 31, 1960, Che Guevara admitted freely that the Nicaro factory was half paralyzed and the Moa one completely so. But he reassured Cubans by telling them that the Soviet Union had not only promised to render technical aid, but had also undertaken to build new nickel factories so that the production of this precious export would quickly reach 70,000 tons per year. In reality Che was much too optimistic: the Soviet technicians were dumbfounded by the ultra-modern factories they found in Nicaro and Moa, and proved of little further use. The Cubans themselves had to set matters right, and of this they are legitimately proud. However, Cuban nickel production is far from the target set by Che in his speech of December 1960. For the implications on U.S.-Cuban relations see particularly C. Julien: *L'Empire Américain*, pp. 25–26. For Che's address of December 31, 1960, see Che Guevara, *Oeuvres*, Vol. 3.

highly skeptical about this possibility, but Che repeated his line of argument with great assurance: "After all, the United States has to coexist with the U.S.S.R. and the people's democracies, like it or not. The world has changed and the imperialists have been forced to swallow a great many things they would have scorned in the past. Tomorrow they will have to put up with even more. Cuba's European friends are wrong to appeal to America's better nature. They say to them, 'Don't invade Cuba because you would be perpetrating a grave injustice.' That's a very poor argument. With the Americans you have to talk business. You have to say: 'If you attack Cuba, you will lose the whole of Latin America, you will ruin your world position, and it's just possible that you will unleash an atomic war and see your own country devastated.' That's the only language they understand. Two things are clear to me: if the Americans attack us, we shall fight to the last man and lose everything in the process; but U.S. imperialism will not survive either. I am absolutely convinced of that. I don't know if the Americans realize the danger; let's just hope it can be brought home to them in time."

This was not the first time I had heard a Cuban leader alluding to the Soviet nuclear shield around their country. The Russian colleagues I met in Havana, carried away by the atmosphere, also kept brandishing intercontinental missiles during conversations. However, in their official pronouncements, the leaders of the U.S.S.R. did not seem to place any great reliance in the rapid spread of revolutions, let alone call for a showdown with the United States for the benefit of their foreign comrades. True, Khrushchev had made a great number of speeches of solidarity with Cuba and, since the abortive summit conference of May 1960 in Paris, he had even gone to unexpected lengths—we shall try to show why later on—in his support of the Castroist Revolution. But at the same time, he had made at least as many speeches in favor of coexistence between the U.S.S.R. and the United States. Such coexistence, he explained, was absolutely essential, because in a thermonuclear war there

51

would be neither victors nor vanquished, and all mankind would probably perish. And since the advent of the Kennedy administration, the Soviet leader seemed more than ever convinced that at long last there was someone in Washington who really wanted to put an end to the Cold War and to all conflict between the two superpowers. In the circumstances how could anyone possibly conclude that the U.S.S.R. would always and under all circumstances give priority to its "international and revolutionary commitments"?

But there was no time to put this question to Che. Our discussion had lasted more than two and a half hours and he was expecting a delegation of Soviet nickel experts. It was clearly not the right moment to embark on the subject of Russia's international policy. Che only had time to tell me that, in his opinion, it was based on socialist principles, and that that was enough to make it radically different from the policy practiced by any capitalist country, no matter how democratic and open-minded. As proof he quickly mentioned his experience of economic transactions with Eastern countries: "The Russians want to build steelworks here, capable of turning out 700,000 tons of steel in 1964 and 1,500,000 tons a few years after that. And we shall not have to start paying them back until one year after the factory is operational, which means that we shall be able to settle with them out of our profits. Moreover, the Russians are giving us credit to buy equipment over the next ten years, at 2½ per cent. As for the Chinese, they don't ask for any interest at all. Find me a capitalist country that would do the same!"

I would be lying if I pretended today that in May 1961 I was convinced by Che's arguments. His strong personality and intellectual charm made an instant impression, but I had the feeling that he had closed his eyes to certain facts about the socialist bloc, because it suited him to do so. No man of his intellect and sensitivity could help being troubled by the many defects and shortcomings of those socialist countries he had just discovered. Unlike the true believers, he did not keep repeating the oversimplified slogans of Soviet propaganda, and even his explanation of the Stalinist phenomenon was not nearly as oversimplified as that of the "de-Stalinizers" in Moscow. Thus he was not one of those sectarians who, wrapped up in their particular truth, are deaf to all arguments. Some of the uneasiness he felt seemed at times to break through his praises of the Soviet system.

In fact, Che demanded much of Cuba's socialist allies. He hoped in particular that by their behavior toward the Cuban Revolution they would demonstrate their moral superiority to the "champions of capitalist culture"; that they would match their actions to their words. As long as there was no proof to the contrary, not in the world at large, but in the specific context of Cuba, Che refused to attack or condemn them. The U.S.S.R. could be expected to make a definite contribution to the success of the first socialist country in the Americas, and she had to be given every chance to show that, in spite of past errors and setbacks, she was able to fulfill this historic task.

This said, it is only fair to add that Fidel, Che, and their comrades in olive-green were not the only ones to determine the course of Cuban politics. Even when they had made a pro-Soviet choice, the Sierra rebels retained their genuine revolutionary ardor and were clear about the objectives they pursued. But the revolutionary movement had meanwhile been joined by former members of the *Partido Socialista Popular*. This small but articulate part of the movement had always confused the priorities of the U.S.S.R. with those of the international proletariat, and bore the marks of its long tradition of unconditional support for the country of Lenin and Stalin. Recent events seemed to bear out the views of these orthodox converts to the movement. They may have failed to make the Revolution, but they knew better than anyone else how to take advantage of post-revolutionary developments. They used the authority of Marxist-Leninist dogma and their old ties with the Communist bloc to intervene forcefully in the ideological and political training of young Cubans. Since December 1960 this orthodox wing has held sway in the new Schools of Revolutionary Instruction and, adding yet another paradox, it was they who taught a large number of heroes and veterans of the Castroist struggle the "true history" of a revolution that had left them far behind.

But to grasp this strange situation and the personality of the future founders of Cuba's Unified Party of the Socialist Revolution, we must first take a brief look at the history of Cuba's Communist old guard and of the new revolutionary wave around Fidel Castro.

The Communists and
the Revolution

"The crisis of a whole people"

Whenever we visit a new country, its history is likely to trip us
up. We tend to argue by analogy, and believe that events abroad
must necessarily follow the same logic as they do at home and
that the same political labels must needs describe the same
goods. But appearances are deceptive. In Cuba, for example,
liberals were often more conservative than the conservatives,
and every self-respecting party called itself "revolutionary." To
find out if a statesman or intellectual is progressive or reactionary we must look not so much at his professions of faith as at
his attitude toward the United States. It served as a touchstone,
enabling us to distinguish authentic leftists from so-called revolutionaries.

I learned all this during my first day on the island, but I also
discovered that this knowledge is not enough to reconstruct the
historical picture. To do that, one must first fit together the

C

scattered pieces of a great jigsaw puzzle: names, speeches, and events, many of which seem completely out of place. I did not tackle this task seriously until 1967–1968, when a few days in the José Martí National Library in Havana drove it home to me that, in the Cuban puzzle, part of the basic design has been distorted to the point of erasure. Had the Castroists succumbed to the Stalinist disease of rewriting history? Had they carefully consigned all embarrassing documents to the bottom of a secret vault?

Nothing could be further from the truth; in Havana one quickly realizes that the only reason why there are no books on contemporary history is that such books have never been written. If you comment on this fact, express astonishment that the library should contain no cuttings from the underground press, or refer to other surprising gaps in the shelves, you are told: "Our eyes are fixed on the future," or else you are advised to consult the dramatis personae in the recent historic events.

"You are interested in the revolution of 1933? Then talk to Raúl Roa; the 'chancellor' knows more about it than anyone else." And an interview is arranged for you there and then. If you want to know more about the days in the Sierra, you must obviously talk to Fidel, to Celia Sánchez, or perhaps to Carlos Franqui. All these heroes are great storytellers who don't worry about diplomatic protocol. Not only will they apparently answer all your questions but they will also put you in contact with other eyewitnesses who can fill in some of the details. Still, there was one subject that did not seem to fill anyone with great enthusiasm, and that was the history of the PSP, the old Communist Party of Cuba. Here the edges of the jigsaw puzzle have become amazingly blurred.

"Ah, if only you knew!" my Havana guides sighed in 1961, when I asked about those "confessed Communists" who were causing the Americans so much heartache. And they quickly added that it was best to drop the whole matter lest the enemies of the Revolution receive fresh grist for their mills. Fidel himself had warned against anti-Communist recriminations or prej-

The Communists and the Revolution

udicial remarks about the PSP. But seven years later I still heard the same "Ah, if only you knew!" from those who had told me in 1961 that it was best to draw a curtain on past disagreements and misunderstandings between revolutionaries.

What, one begins to wonder, is so terrible about the history of the old Communist Party that no one can either tell you about it openly or forget it completely? Why are old Party members still scarred by their political origins? Why is the rift between them and the Castroists still as deep as ever? A Castroist prefers not to answer such questions; he will tell you nothing about the PSP that you, or anyone else in Havana, do not know already, namely that the PSP saw fit to collaborate with Batista on the eve of, and during, the Second World War, and that it opposed Fidel's armed struggle until his triumph was a foregone conclusion. For the rest, you are referred to ex-members of the PSP, and you can almost hear the tacit rider: "Let them get themselves out of their own mess if they can."

In 1961, the PSP was incorporated into a new party which in October 1965 adopted the name of Communist Party of Cuba, and under the leadership of Fidel now embraces Castroists, Communists, and former members of the *Directorio Revolucionario*. Before it lost its identity, the PSP never bothered to write a general version of its history, and the new party is unlikely to do so either, since it is most anxious to gloss over the old and sad quarrels of its three constituent parts. It has no intention of prying into the past of any of them, particularly the past of the one with the longest and most complex history, the one most closely implicated in the international tactics of the Soviet Union.

As for the publication of an unofficial history by any of the leading characters, Carlos Rafael Rodríguez, who of all the old "veterans" is certainly the one most fully at home in Castro's party, told me that it was still too early. "There are too many heart cases among them for us to do that," is how Fidel himself put it to me. Meanwhile the foreign student is advised to find out for himself.

57

Personal contact with the old Party members is not difficult. They are not much given to polemics these days, and experience has stripped them of the arrogance with which Communists habitually refer to their own party. They seem most eager to help you reach an objective understanding of their strange past, and some do not bother to hide their astonishment that anyone should be interested in them in the first place. And when they do begin to unburden themselves, you suddenly find yourself immersed in the history of a party caught in its own logic, in a world far removed from the complex framework of Cuban reality. For all that, this same party was able, not so long ago either, to infuse its members with a remarkable degree of self-abnegation and self-sacrifice. It had its heroes and martyrs, its own morality and its own rules of conduct. From joining Batista's government of national union during the war, the Communist Party gained none of the typical rewards commonly associated with Latin American political deals; a unique and greatly respected performance on its part. The PSP remained a party of the poor, highly disciplined, devoted, and often persecuted. And then someone else made the revolution in its place, and in so doing cast doubt on all its theories, tactics, and on its very *raison d'être*. A party born for revolution and convinced that it had a monopoly in this field was suddenly forced to stand by almost idly while socialism triumphed all around.

The resulting shock was in no way lessened by the fusion of the parties. True, Blas Roca, leader of the PSP, stood on the balcony of the presidential palace that day in October 1960 when Fidel announced his nationalization decrees, but he kept to the rear and stood well behind the revolutionaries in olive-green, some of whom had not the least idea who he was and wondered why Fidel had brought him there. All the old Communists realized only too well that they owed their presence in the revolutionary ranks to nothing but the benevolence of Fidel, Che, and some others, and that many Castroists would have greatly preferred to ostracize them.

The old stagers have since come to appreciate that their

The Communists and the Revolution

"savior," Fidel, was as critical as anybody of their political tactics. Fidel did not blame them for their conduct during the anti-Batista struggle, simply because he had reached the conclusion that, at that stage, the Communist Party was no longer capable of making a revolution. If it had given the order for an insurrection against Batista, no one would have listened. This was due not only to the anti-Communist atmosphere prevalent on the entire American continent during the '50s, but also to memories of the tortuous history of the PSP. Fidel thus blamed historical circumstances rather than the men. But his judgment nevertheless implied a crushing political indictment, because what stronger condemnation is there of a Communist Party than the claim that it was honest, morally irreproachable, but had ceased to be a force capable of guiding or even influencing the course of events?

After his victory Fidel did not propose to revive the Party as such; all he wanted was its members. This, as we shall see, proved rather difficult, but even if it had not, there is no reason to believe that Castro would have whitewashed the PSP in general or its history in particular. This blot remains and does not affect Cuba alone; it blights all discussions of revolutionary movements in Latin America. For no one can forget that the past of the Cuban PSP is the present of the Communist parties on that part of the continent.

In this book, I shall not treat the reader to a detailed analysis of the history of Cuban Communism. To do so I should have to write volumes. Instead, I shall simply try to answer the three main questions that still appear to bother the man in the street in Havana. Why did the PSP collaborate with Batista? Why did it keep aloof from Fidel until just before victory in the Sierra? Why did Fidel reinstate the "old guard" and admit it into his revolutionary movement?

Any attempt to answer these questions must place Cuban Communism in the context of the international workers' movement. The PSP, like all Communist parties, was a creature of the Comintern, and remained true to the Communist International until the latter's dissolution in 1943, when it transferred all its loyalty directly to the Soviet Union. Its links with the "socialist fatherland" have always been so close and strong that it is quite impossible to separate its own strategy from the theoretical and practical aims of the U.S.S.R.

Now the Communist Party, or rather the Cuban section of the Third International, was founded fairly late in the day, in August 1925, at a time when Stalin had gained control of his own party and the Comintern. The Cuban section therefore based its charter on a current in Communism that was opposed to all forms of internal discussion, was intolerant of minorities, and demanded blind submission to the dogma of socialism in one country—the U.S.S.R. In other words, Cuban Communism was Stalinist from the very outset. This did not at first prevent it from making spectacular advances, or from becoming the most important Communist Party in Latin America.

But then Cuba had for decades been the scene of wars, battles, and repeated crises. The Cubans started their struggle for national independence in 1868, long after the other Latin American colonies (with the exception of Puerto Rico) had shaken off the Spanish yoke. And it was perhaps because they were the last that Spain clung to them with such grim determination. The war lasted for thirty years, during which foreign troops ravaged the island as they had not ravaged any other part of America. And just when Cuba, exhausted and ruined, was about to snatch victory, her powerful northern neighbor, the United States, "volunteered" to finish the Spaniards off, and having done so refused to relinquish its hold over the island. True, America gave the Cubans their independence, but only after having forced them to inscribe the Platt Amendment[1]

1. The Platt Amendment has been the subject of scores of books in Cuba and the United States. In *Our Cuban Colony*, Leland H. Jenk gives a detailed account of the political and economic factors responsible for its adoption first by Congress and later by the Cuban Parliament. The Americans made its adoption a condition of withdrawing their troops

The Communists and the Revolution

into their 1901 constitution. This amendment entitled the United States to intervene in Cuba whenever its interests demanded it.

Cuba had made indescribable sacrifices, only to exchange the domination of a distant and declining power for that of a nearby and far more powerful one, a country in the process of rapid economic expansion. Paradoxically, it was at the point of acquiring her "independence" that Cuba began to develop, and develop fast, all the characteristics of a colonial dependency.

Creole landowners, lacking economic resources to prevent massive American penetration,[2] could not turn themselves into that class of entrepreneurs which presides over "normal" capitalist development and helps to run the kind of bourgeois republic described in the Cuban Constitution. Cuba was transformed into a paradise for *compradores,* speculators, and other agents in the service of the new masters. The enrichment of this "elite" necessarily led to the impoverishment of the people, and social contrasts became more glaring from year to year. The misery of the countryside, which contained 52 per cent of all Cubans before the Second World War, defies the imagination. Those who pulled up their roots in the hope of finding work in the cities found themselves in shantytowns, where they barely eked out a living on the fringe of society. Sugar, the country's chief crop, accounted for 80 per cent of the gross national income, but provided no more than 30,000 permanent jobs– the number of employees went up to 400,000 during each *zafra*

---

from the island. Despite U.S. pressure, the Cuban opposition, led by a remarkable black politician, Juan Gualberto Gómez, nearly succeeded in having the amendment rejected. In the end, it was adopted by a slender majority and even then not before June 12, 1901.

2. Purely by way of illustration, we quote the following figures on U.S. investments in Cuba:

1902–1906	$ 80,000,000	(excluding the public debt)
1909	$ 200,000,000	(including the public debt)
1922	$1,200,000,000	(with control of 75 per cent of the sugar industry)

See *Historia de Cuba* (Havana, Dirección Política de las FAR, 1967), p. 583.

or sugar harvest. However, the sugar companies, most of them American or under direct U.S. control, preferred to "import" large contingents of Jamaican or Haitian "semi-slaves," who proved even more tractable when it came to wages than did the Cuban seasonal workers. All in all, by the end of the '20s, the Cuban proletariat accounted for a mere 16.4 per cent of the working population, while the tertiary sector, hypertrophied as in all colonial countries, had already absorbed 35 per cent.[3]

Most Cubans found it difficult to resign themselves to the marriage of extreme corruption with extreme poverty. "Cuban society is about to disintegrate. Cuba is rapidly sinking into barbarism." So wrote Fernando Ortiz,[4] the great ethnologist and one of the most respected intellectuals of his country. "We live in an unprecedented crisis, not of a particular government or class, but of a whole people," Raimundo Cabrera, another respected Cuban, wrote at the same time.[5]

Memories of the patriotic war were still fresh in many minds, and a country that had made so many sacrifices and had had such high hopes was unlikely to resign itself to so much blatant dishonesty and moral decay. What was more, the apostle of Cuban independence, José Martí, had prophetically warned Cubans against Yankee imperialism ("I have lived in the entrails of the North American monster, I know of what crimes it is capable") and had taught them that "rights are not obtained by begging but must be seized by force." Hence it was not at all astonishing that young Cubans should have had a fondness for violence. "To get rid of gangsters you need dynamite," the young poet Rubén Martínez Villena proclaimed in 1923.

3. All these data are taken from Julio Alienes y Urosa: *Características fundamentales de la economía cubana* (Havana, Barco Nacional de Cuba, 1950).
4. In his classic *La Decadencia Cubana* (Havana, Imprenta La Universal, 1924).
5. Raimundo Cabrera (1852–1924) was chiefly a novelist and memorialist. He belonged to the patriotic generation of the civil war, and the remark we quote was made during the last year of his life.

The Communists and the Revolution

It was in this explosive atmosphere that the young Communist Party was founded. Everything seemed to favor it: as a branch of the Third International, it was anti-imperialist, and its anti-Yankee denunciations re-echoed José Martí's. It was anti-racist and so appealed to the numerically important colored sector, which after supplying more than 60 per cent of the soldiers in the anti-Spanish army, was now suffering rank economic and social discrimination. Last but far from least, its political rivals were groups split into numerous factions based on personal ambition and a great deal of ideological confusion. In short, the Communist Party was in an excellent position to establish what Antonio Gramsci has called its hegemony.

And at first, it did look as if it would do just that. "The Communist Party has scored such notable successes because its leaders are intelligent, dynamic, and honest men. It enjoys the support of the foremost Cuban intellectuals and of a growing number of teachers, writers, and white-collar workers among the young generation. Many of its members belong to that minority with a religious sense of duty which, capable of deep devotion to a cause, is prepared to sacrifice its entire time, even its life. . . . The profound influence of the Communist movement stems not only from the presence in its ranks of thousands of members accepting its rigid discipline, but also from the sympathy that hundreds of thousands of Cubans bear, in various degrees, toward the ideas and aims of Communism. These Cubans have welcomed Communism as a redemptive force capable of freeing them from the misery and poverty which Cuba now suffers."[6] Such were the conclusions of the twelve members of the commission of inquiry sent by the Foreign Policy Association of the United States, and no one could have called them sympathizers of the extreme Left. Another factor favoring the Communists was their rapid infiltration of workers' circles. They controlled the National Labor Confederation of Cuba and

6. See Foreign Policy Association: *Problemas de la Nueva Cuba* (Havana, Cultural S.A., 1935) , p. 219.

the Labor Federation of Havana, and they were on the point of forming a vast trade union of sugar plantation workers which, in view of the location of the sugar refineries far from the towns, would have been a truly remarkable success.

Moreover, in 1925, the year the Communist Party was founded, Cuba found herself with a new president, elected on the liberal ticket: General Gerardo Machado. He immediately declared that under his reign no strike would be allowed, even for fifteen minutes. Two years later, this liberal extended his stay in office for a further seven years by tampering with the Constitution. This caused a furor particularly at the University of Havana and drove into the welcoming arms of the opposition all those who still nurtured illusions about "republican legality." Cuba now entered a period of antidictatorial struggle, and this suited no one so well as the Communists.

For all its initial successes, the Communist Party suffered from what we may call a congenital fault: it tried to transfer into the neo-colonial situation of Cuba, an underdeveloped country, the precise revolutionary scheme its comrades had developed for the capitalist countries of Europe. The fact that in Cuba "the crisis of a whole people" was the result of subordination to American interests seemed to concern the Communist Party far less than the contrasts—admittedly glaring—between capital and labor. Hence it failed to appreciate the potential value of all those anti-Machado and anti-American forces which did not acknowledge the truths of Leninism or even of socialism. The Communists were fighting on only one battlefield: the labor front. In Cuba's particular situation this was by no means the most important area—here the American throttlehold was thwarting "normal" capitalist developments. The tensions created by this domination overrode the contradiction that, in less dependent countries, would have given rise to the typical social crystallizations. Failing to grasp this fact, the Communists were unable to use, let alone control, those "other forces" which they dismissed as "petty bourgeois anarchists."

This blindness to the facts—this dogmatism—marked the Communist Party from its very beginnings. People in Cuba will tell you today—and perhaps they have always said so—that the founder and first secretary of the Communist Party was Julio Antonio Mella, a brilliant young intellectual. But though Mella was a Communist throughout his short active life, he neither founded nor led the Party—in full accordance with the European tradition, Communist Party secretaries had to be of working-class origin. Julio Antonio Mella was only a student, founder in 1923 of the FEU (*Federación Estudiantil Universitaria*) and later of the José Martí Popular University (1924). He also did outstanding work in organizing Havana tobacco workers, and in Cuba may be said to have played much the same role as Rudi Dutschke did more recently in Germany, though, of course, under quite different conditions. He began as a leading critic of university life and ended as a critic of society at large. For him Communism was the normal result of his libertarian and fiercely anti-imperialist sentiments, of his utter devotion to the cause of social justice. And he applied his theories with the gusto of an intellectual deeply rooted in the moral climate of his country and tradition.

His passionate temperament appealed to the spirit of youth and has, in fact, become legendary. People still speak admiringly of his extraordinary exploits. When the Cuban government refused to let the Soviet ship *Vorovski* dock in Havana, Mella jumped into the sea, and ignoring the sharks, swam out to carry fraternal greetings to the Red sailors. When he was arrested on a charge of having carried a bomb into the Payret Theater, he refused to accept the right of Machado, that "tropical Mussolini," as he called him, to try anybody. He immediately went on a hunger strike which lasted for nineteen days, and there was such an outcry that Machado was forced to release him. However, he managed to drive Mella from Cuba, and in 1929 had him assassinated in Mexico. Mella was twenty-six years old when he died.

Martyrdom helped to turn Mella into an idol of his party; but only his martyrdom. For the rest, his militant tactics had been breaches of Party discipline, and were deplored as such by his comrades. Thus the Party opposed his hunger strike on the grounds that only intellectuals, who could eat as much as they liked, were able to appreciate this type of protest—the workers would consider the whole thing quite pointless. Mella went on fasting all the same, and for this he was severely taken to task after his release from prison—some even say that he was expelled from the Party. The Italian Communist Vittorio Vidali (Carlos), at the time Comintern delegate to the Cuban Communist Youth Movement, has denied this story. What he does admit is that Mella was the subject of long discussions, and that the young Cuban exile later had serious differences with the Mexican Party.

The Mella case highlighted a problem that was more than purely disciplinary. It revealed how difficult Communist Party organizations find it to absorb this kind of revolutionary, a young man typical of his age. Another famous intellectual, the poet Rubén Martínez Villena, suffered much the same fate. Like Mella he has passed into legend as a Communist hero, but in his lifetime he, too, never rose to the top of the Party hierarchy, even though he had greater responsibilities and took part in fewer quarrels than Julio Antonio. Like Mella, he became famous for his protests even before he joined the CP. As early as 1923, at the head of thirteen young men, he challenged the then president, Alfredo Zayas, in the middle of a solemn session of the Academy of Sciences. He participated in the conspiracy of the Association of Veterans and Patriots, and volunteered to pilot a plane and to bomb military objectives in Havana. This scheme came to nothing. He further headed the *minorista* movement, a group of avant-garde intellectuals, and participated in every conceivable debate. His far-flung intellectual and political activities overstretched his tubercular body and, despite the valiant struggle he fought against this dreadful disease, he succumbed to it in 1934, at the age of thirty-five.

The lives of these two Communist pioneers show clearly that the Party[7] started off with a whole galaxy of youthful talent, who

7. The first leader of the Cuban Communist Party was José Miguel Pérez. But since he was of foreign birth, Machado had him deported

might well have been able to forge ties with the "rebel intelligentsia" from which sprang Castro and some of his closest companions. Mella and Martínez Villena had come from the same background; they were profoundly rooted in the special reality of their country; they drew from it their intellectual training, their anti-imperialist and libertarian ideas, their individualism and taste for heroic deeds, and a style of life that would be resuscitated decades later—and not by chance either—by the young Castroists. For Mella and Martínez Villena the conversion to Communism was not a break with, but an extension and deepening of, their intellectual experience. They kept up their links with those of their comrades in arms at the university who had not followed their example, and who preferred to continue the struggle outside the Communist Party. As yet, no wall had risen up between these two forces, one might almost say two worlds, both determined to challenge the established order.

And when this wall did appear at the decisive moment in the anti-Machadoist struggle, it was to play havoc with the Cuban Left. The Communist Party, which was to be its chief victim, also bore the greatest responsibility for it, as we shall see when we look more closely at the 1930s.

For a country as dependent on the United States as Cuba, the great American slump of 1929 was a ghastly tragedy. Sugar exports, difficult enough to get rid of since 1926, went into a giddying decline, dropping from 200 million dollars' worth in 1929 to 129 million in 1930, 78 million in 1931, and 42 million in 1932.[8] This was ruin. Famine appeared in the countryside; unemployment and despair reigned in the towns. The American financiers who had underwritten Machado, the

---

to the Canaries. His successor, José Peña Vilaboa, led the Party until 1927, when he fell ill and was replaced by Joachim Valdés. All three were simple workers. During the crucial period in 1933, Jorge Vivo, an advocate, acted as party secretary, but four years later his comrades expelled him. From 1934 almost to the "integration" of 1961, the Party was led by Blas Roca.

8. See *Historia de Cuba,* cited above.

Chase National Bank chief among them, not only refused further aid but even called for settlement of the old debts.

The struggle against the dictator became transformed almost overnight: even the Right now joined the opposition. However the two dates which stand out as landmarks during the first year of the rebellion both belong to the calendar of the Left. On March 19, 1930, a general strike paralyzed Cuba and delivered a terrible blow to Machado's prestige. On September 30, 1930, students came out into the street in response to an indirect appeal by Enrique José Varona,[9] one of Cuba's leading intellectuals. The police blocked the students' way to the great philosopher's house, and one of the student leaders, Rafael Trejo, fell to their bullets. The dictator then decided to close the university, but in so doing helped only to strengthen the bond between the poverty-stricken staff and the rebellious students. The first shots in a civil war had been fired.

Who precisely were the contenders? The dictator evidently relied on the support of the army, on his "expert squad" (secret political police), and on the Patriotic League, the so-called *porros*. His enemies represented all shades of public opinion, ranging from Communists to the conservative Right led by Colonel Mendieta. However, two groups were particularly prominent, namely the *Directorio Estudiantil Universitario*, or Student Directorship and, to a lesser degree, the ABC Party.

The *Directorio*, as its name suggests, was a student body, but

9. Enrique José Varona, philosopher, sociologist, and friend of José Martí, later president of the Conservative Party and vice-president of the Republic (1912), was eighty-one years old in 1930. An intransigent opponent of the Machado regime, he declared in an interview on September 25, 1930, that he was astonished at the passivity of Cuban youth. It was by way of an answer that the *Directorio* decided to organize a massive anti-Machado demonstration and to march in procession to the philosopher's house. It should be added that, toward the end of his life, Enrique José Varona tended increasingly toward the Left, and this despite his repeated declarations that he was too old to change his philosophic opinions. He openly expressed his admiration of the Soviet Union and his support for the anti-imperialist struggle.

one with very wide ramifications. It could count on the support of a broad spectrum of young people, and on the good advice of such "professional conspirators" as José Rafael García Bárcena, editor of *Mundo Social*. The *Directorio* itself had no leader; it was run by a committee of some forty to fifty people representing the various faculties and colleges. Every member of the executive had a proxy who could step into his shoes the moment he was arrested. The list of those who at one time or another served on the committee includes nearly every great name in Cuban politics, from Eduardo Chibás (who, in 1947, founded the Ortodoxo Party in which Fidel Castro started his political career) to Raúl Roa, the present Minister of Foreign Affairs. To be fair, we must add that it also included the name of the "corrupt" future president Prío Socarrás, and of a great many other people who later became die-hard reactionaries.

Alma Mater, the clandestine paper of the *Directorio,* did not call for workers' emancipation from the capitalist yoke or for anti-imperialist struggle. Its political guidelines were much simpler: it supported justice against fraud, honor against corruption; it declared war on poverty, and spoke up for the dignity of man. Its denunciations of Machadoist crimes were hard-hitting, though not nearly critical enough to satisfy the more doctrinaire students. A Marxist group led by Aureliano Sánchez Arango[10] formed the "student left wing" and published its own journal, *Línea,* with brilliant contributions, particularly by Pablo de la Torriente Brau and Raúl Roa. This paper chose as its motto a line from the famous poem of Mayakovsky: "Enough speeches; over to you, Comrade Mauser!"[11]

But the *Directorio* did not simply leave it at propaganda;

10. Unlike Raúl Roa and Pablo de la Torriente Brau, Aureliano Sánchez Arango was a member of the Communist Party at that time. Later he left the Party to become minister of education in the Prío administration (1948). During the anti-Batista struggle, he led a right-wing resistance movement, the Triple-A. He is an anti-Castroist and now lives in the United States.

11. In Russian the poem is called *"Levyi marsh."*

it also ran a military branch which manufactured bombs and detonators, and a direct action group which distributed these products to good purpose. The president of the Machadoist senate, the founder of the *porros,* and the chief of the "expert squad"—all fell to attacks by these young champions of justice, and the dictator himself only just escaped death on several occasions. The *Directorio* never sang the praises of terrorism as such, but practiced it purely as "a matter of necessity." After the fall of Machado, none of its members boasted about his terrorist activities.[12] One of the co-founders of the *Directorio,* Antonio Guiteras Holmes, was as prominent as any in the field of direct action. Guiteras is extremely difficult to fit into a precise political current. He had to leave the university in 1929, for lack of funds, and became a pharmaceutical salesman. It was while traveling the length and breadth of the island with his wares that he recruited young men of like mind, men determined to save their country. But Guiteras did not at first start a party of his own,[13] or acknowledge a particular doctrine. What few articles he wrote show merely that he was closer to the Communists than he was to the anarchists. He may be called the embodiment of the impatience and activism of his entire generation. He was a leader of men and, as events were to show, an intelligent politician. But for the time being Guiteras was above all the great conspirator, a sort of pioneer in the art of guerrilla warfare; as early as April 29, 1933, he took the barracks of San Luis in Oriente province by storm.

As for the ABC Party—which became notorious for its plots and (unsuccessful) landing attempts—it was a very curious body. One of its members was Jorge Mañach, an important name in Cuban literature and the biographer of José Martí. For the

12. Ambassador Villaseca, the former head of the *Directorio* and now the Cuban representative in Rome, made this clear during a lecture on the 1933 Revolution, given on May 17, 1966, at the University of Havana.
13. He did not found the *Jóven Cuba* movement until after the 1933 Revolution.

The Communists and the Revolution

rest, however, the forty-one-point program the ABC published in 1931 revealed a very suspect liking for corporatist solutions, borrowed directly from the arsenal of Mussolini. Its demagogy only rivaled its confusion; the party called itself the spokesman of youth, but saw fit to take its cues from the old stagers of Cuban politics. It included a Gandhian wing that preached nonviolence, and another so-called radical wing that extolled violent action.

Despite these many rifts in his opponents' camp, the dictator was unable to divide and rule. "Machado is a donkey with claws," Rubén Martínez Villena said of him, and events were to confirm this diagnosis. Machado practiced a form of primitive counterterrorism, hitting out wildly at strikers no less than at the scions of the "great patriotic families." He suspended the Constitution, sat by while factories lay idle, allowed the treasury to remain deeply in the red, and closed the university for three years.

It was against this background that the newly elected President of the United States, Franklin Delano Roosevelt, sent to the pearl of the Caribbean one of his best diplomats, Mr. Sumner Welles, who, no doubt as part of America's good-neighbor policy, promised Machado U.S. assistance in calming the opposition, provided only that the dictator agreed to retire in 1934, at the end of his present term of office. And Sumner Welles did, in fact, contact Machado's opponents so as to discuss the best means of improving Cuban political life. Unfortunately for him, no opposition spokesmen of any importance—from the *Directorio* to the highly conservative General Méncal—wanted to meet him; those who were prepared to accept his mediation were men with little say on the island. Moreover, the dictator himself was only concerned with gaining time, and not at all with finding an honorable solution. By and large, the very presence of Sumner Welles in Havana merely encouraged the revolutionaries to press on, when he was trying to hold them back. For to all good Cubans, any politician subjected to pressure by, and relying on the help of, the United States is a man who

71

must be fought tooth and nail. Hence far from solving the crisis, the presence of the U.S. envoy merely precipitated an open confrontation. It started almost spontaneously, three months after his arrival in Havana. On August 2, 1933, a bus depot in the capital went on strike; two days later the entire transport system of Havana was paralyzed. On August 6, the strike spread to the whole country. On August 7, the rumor went around that the dictator had resigned, whereupon the overjoyed population came out into the streets and marched on the capitol. They were met and fired upon by the police; dozens lay dead, and hundreds were wounded.

The dictator was determined not to give in, and made ready for a fight to the bitter end. The next morning, however, after a dramatic reversal of policy, he held out an olive branch to those whom he had pilloried for the past eight years as the most deadly enemies of the fatherland: to the Communists of the Central Strike Committee. One day later came an even more dramatic development: the Strike Committee agreed to negotiate, provided only that all the claims of the transport workers were met. The dictator agreed to everything. After twenty-four hours of discussion and consultation, César Vilár, in the name of the Central Strike Committee and the Cuban Labor Confederation, gave orders for a resumption of work at noon on August 11.

But the workers themselves thought otherwise. At the appointed day and hour, not a bus, not a single tram, left the depot. The cornered dictator appealed to the army, but the officers turned a deaf ear to his appeals. There was nothing for it now: Machado fled the country and bequeathed his office to the Minister of Defense. The latter, in agreement with Sumner Welles, declined this honor in favor of the more acceptable Carlos Manuel de Céspedes, the son of the "great de Céspedes," hero of the War of Independence. The people came out into the streets once again, and this time there were no policemen to fire on them; instead the crowd rounded on the "expert squad"

The Communists and the Revolution

and settled old scores with the *porros* and other Machadoists.[14]
This was revolution.

To the magic sound of his name, de Céspedes could add none
of the skills needed to control an explosive situation. He
accordingly did nothing, said nothing, and promised nothing.
"He is not a tyrant; he is incapable," the Student Directorship
proclaimed. It called for his resignation, denounced his subservience to the United States, and demanded *inter alia* that all
corrupt and guilty officials be brought to justice and that all
mayors, governors, and judges appointed by Machado be dismissed. Sumner Welles informed Washington that Cuba was in
danger of sinking into utter chaos. On September 4, a group of
noncommissioned officers led by Sergeant Fulgencio Batista came
out in revolt: all they really wanted was an increase in pay,
and a revocation of the proposed cuts in the armed forces,
but their uprising proved the last straw for the de Céspedes
regime. Members of the *Directorio* rushed to the military camp
in Columbia, joined the sergeants in the formation of a
Revolutionary Reconstruction Group,[15] and put full power in

14. In fact, lynchings and attacks on policemen and politicians continued
for several days, and not in Havana alone. *"El espíritu de venganza y el
anhelo de sanción se manifesterón en saqueo, incendio y destrucciones"*
(The spirit of vengeance and the longing for retribution express themselves
in pillage, fire and destruction), wrote Ramiro Guerra in his *History of the
Cuban Nation*, Vol. 8, p. 80. Fidel Castro was extremely anxious to ensure
that the same spirit did not come to the fore after his own victory, and
to that end he immediately inaugurated legal procedures which, while brief
and to the point, prevented summary executions and provided suspects
with a number of safeguards. Thus while the American press immediately
accused him of the execution of countless *Batistianos*, Castro himself has
stressed that in 1959 no one fell victim to excesses of the kind seen in
1933, and this despite the fact that the struggle against Batista had been
no less bitter than the fight against Machado, and that Batista's police
had claimed far more victims, and with much more refined brutality,
than Machado's.
15. In fact, the Revolutionary Reconstruction Group was an ad hoc
organization, which lent greater respectability to the *Directorio*, the
only real force behind the new government. It is significant that the
manifesto informing Cuba of the birth of the revolutionary regime on
September 5, 1933, was signed by all the members of the *Directorio*.

the hands of a *pentarquía,* a junta of five, presided over by Ramón Grau San Martín,[16] professor of physiology in the University of Havana. Five days later, the junta decided to co-opt new members and to transform itself into a veritable government, once again with student support. Antonio Guiteras, who obtained the largest number of votes, took over the *Secretaria de Gobernación,* the Ministry in charge of home affairs, and so became the second in command. Fulgencio Batista was offered another portfolio, but he declined modestly on the grounds that it would be more "useful" to the revolution if he became the head of the army. He already knew where he was going.

Exasperated, Sumner Welles now alleged that the Communists had stage-managed the entire "mutiny," and declared that under no circumstances would the United States recognize the Grau-Guiteras government. He could not have been more mistaken: the Communists had had nothing to do with the course of events; indeed their relations with the other revolutionary groups were worse than ever before. Their strike committee's last-minute negotiations with the discredited Machado regime had played straight into the hands of those in the *Directorio* who were opposed to any form of collaboration with them, and had weakened the hand of all leftists anxious to form a common front. The Central Committee of the Communist Party met in

It is equally remarkable that of the 33 signatories, fifteen should be living in exile today; seven were killed in the successive battles or died for other reasons; ten remained in Cuba and have taken their place in the Revolution; one is in prison.

16. Professor Ramón Grau San Martín (1887–1969) owed his popularity among the students to the courageous stands he took in 1927 and 1930 during the two tests of strength between the dictator and the student movement. Professor Grau was considered one of the educators most engaged in the fight against Machado, although his action was limited, at first glance, to signing petitions in favor of the students and protests against the dictatorship. In the absence of any personal writings it is difficult to establish whether Professor Grau had at this time—as some people have maintained—very radical and anti-imperialist ideas. After the Revolution of 1959 Professor Grau refused either to emigrate or to collaborate with the Castro regime. He spent his last years in his retreat at Miramar.

The Communists and the Revolution

plenary session on August 26, in Havana, to see what lessons there were to be drawn from the unhappy Machado deal, and to determine what tactics were demanded by the new situation. It concluded that the Strike Committee had gravely under-estimated the militancy of the masses, and had been quite wrong to conclude that all the workers wanted was a wage increase. And since no Communist Party must ever lag behind the revolution-ary masses, the Party decided to atone for its sins by calling on the Cuban proletariat to form soviets, "organs of popular power in every locality preparatory to the seizure of power at the top."[17] The Party did not evidently bother to consult any other political groups, nor did it try to enlist outside support for its new tactics. It was convinced that the present popular upsurge would force all the rest to fall into line, would persuade them to accept Communist decisions and Communist leadership. The unexpected emergence of a government that was well to the left of de Céspedes, and which the United States refused to recognize, seemed to corroborate their view of the situation. To the Communists, Grau was just another Kerensky, and it was more urgent than ever to press for the formation of soviets, which alone could express the true will of the people. There could therefore be no question of Communist support for the new government, which, in its turn, was quick to denounce the "Red diversionists."

The revolution now developed on two almost parallel planes: that of the Grau-Guiteras government and that of the "soviets." The first promulgated decrees which, by Cuban standards, were highly revolutionary: an eight-hour working day, a minimum daily wage for cane cutters, restriction of the number of sea-sonal workers brought in from abroad, recognition of trade union rights, a 45 per cent cut in the electricity rate (the prelude to the nationalization of the U.S.-owned electricity company) ; a moratorium on all debts Machado had contracted with the Chase National Bank; a limitation on the purchase of

17. See *Historia de Cuba*, p. 637.

75

land by foreigners; sequestration of the estates of Machadoist collaborators; the promise of agrarian reforms; and the convocation, in the near future, of a constituent assembly charged with the repeal of the Platt Amendment, and with presenting a new "social" constitution.

The Communists, for their part, succeeded in establishing a few soviets in the provincial sugar centers, though in Havana even their own rank and file did not follow their lead. The Party fared best in the provinces of Oriente, Camaguey, and Las Villas. The Mabey soviet, in particular, became a sort of microcosm of the proletarian state, took over the management of the sugar refineries and the administration of the adjacent estates, organized supplies, and formed a workers' militia. Other soviets were established at Jaronu, Senado, Santa Lucía, and a host of other places.[18]

At first, the two revolutions proceeded apace while ignoring each other. But a clash between them was inevitable—the government simply could not tolerate islands of Communist dissent, particularly on the eve of the *zafra*. And so the army, now under the command of Batista, was sent out to attack them in force. Batista was no less ruthless in stifling the protests of a group of conservative officers which had gathered in the Hotel National, under the very nose of Sumner Welles.[19] On October 6, 1933, the government promulgated the historic Decree 2059,

18. Carlos Rafael Rodriguez has told me—rather ironically—about the soviets near his native village of Cienfuegos, which were apparently quite ineffectual. In the village itself, the leading militants had left their posts to help hoist the red flag on a little windmill. The whole thing ended in tragedy when the founders of this soviet were shot by the triumphant reaction.

19. Discontented officers had moved into the Hotel National, where Sumner Welles was staying and, on October 2, organized an armed demonstration that had little chance of success and, in fact, ended in massacre. In his "History Will Absolve Me," Castro accuses Batista of murdering some officers after they had surrendered. The same thing happened during yet another army protest, on November 6, 1935 at Fort Atarés where, as Castro himself has explained, "the besiegers' machine guns cut down a row of prisoners." (See Fidel Castro: *History Will Absolve Me* (Cape Editions No. 23, Jonathan Cape, London, 1968).

granting full autonomy to the university, and at the same time calling for calm and discipline. The appeal was heeded by the *Directorio* on the grounds that "for the past two months Cuba has been a free country at long last."[20] The *Directorio* called for a vote of confidence in the government and in the future constituent assembly. The Communists did nothing at all. Though the soviets in the sugar refineries were falling to the army in quick succession, on November 10 the Party still kept sounding its famous clarion call: "All power to the soviets!"

Harassed on the Left, sabotaged on the Right, threatened by the United States which had brought up its fleet, the Grau-Guiteras government was forced to resign on January 15, 1934. The chief of the army, Batista, acting in accord with the Americans, had struck it a final blow. Although he held no official post in the government, Batista quickly became the strong man of a new regime, directing his country with an iron fist for the next ten years.[21]

Even without Batista's intervention, the Grau-Guiteras government could not have survived much longer, given Cuba's economic dependence on the United States, and the balance of world power at that time. In fact, the Grau-Guiteras government was the first and only government on the American continent to denounce United States interventionism publicly—in December 1933, before an assembly of all the Latin American states. On that occasion it also called for the abrogation of the Platt Amendment. And though most of its social legislation was quickly repealed by the new president, Carlos Mendieta, the Grau-Guiteras government may be said to represent a turning

20. The *Directorio* was paraphrasing Mella's famous book *Cuba, the Country That Has Never Been Free.*
21. Fulgencio Batista did not have himself elected president of the Republic until 1940, but during the six preceding years, the three presidents—Cárlos Mendieta, Miguel Mariano Gómez, and Federico Laredo-Bru—were his puppets. In fact, their importance in Cuban public life was so insignificant that the whole world considers the period 1934–1944 as that of the reign of Fulgencio Batista.

point in Cuban history. No wonder, therefore, that it was able to capture the imagination of the whole nation.

But later, when he returned to power, Ramón Grau San Martín demonstrated that he had been a false messiah all along, "a prophet of disintegration."[22] And many of his revolutionary comrades of 1933 were able to make themselves comfortable in a society they had solemnly promised to transform. In spite of this, radical opinion in Cuba continued for a very long time to place its hopes in Grau and his party—the Authentic Cuban Revolutionary Party or *Auténticos* for short—in the belief that they would continue the good work begun by the ephemeral government of September 1933. This illusion contributed largely to the degeneration of Cuban political life. As we shall see, it also weighed heavily on the moral climate in which the new generation of rebels grew up—the generation of Fidel Castro.

Antonio Guiteras entered history and legend with a good record. He fought courageously against the new conservative regime, founded the *Jóven Cuba* movement, and came to adopt an increasingly anti-imperialist stand. He was assassinated in May 1935 by Batista's men, while about to leave Cuba with plans for an armed landing. His followers clung to the old methods of direct action which, now that the tide had turned against them and they lacked a leader, proved of little avail.

As for the Communists, they were completely cut off from the whole generation of "unengaged" revolutionaries, who never forgave them their "mistakes." They condemned the Party's political opportunism in general and its dealings with Machado in particular—by these acts it had demonstrated that it was neither sincerely revolutionary nor truly Cuban. Even in 1959, its right-wing enemies, Andrés Valdespino among them, were still harping on that affair, when calling upon the nation to ignore the Communists.[23] Others blamed the Communist Party

22. This is how Raúl Roa described him in a recent interview in *Cuba*, No. 78.

23. See *Bohemia*, April–June, 1959.

more particularly for its attitude to the Grau-Guiteras government, although they themselves would have found it difficult to justify that government's authorization of Batista's army to crush the soviets.[24] But pangs of conscience rarely diminish the bitterness of political polemics.

In 1934, the Communist Party changed leaders and went into a period of self-criticism. The new team under Blas Roca admitted that the Party had been guilty of left-wing deviationism and that the call for soviets had been mistaken. But Blas Roca's analysis did not really get to the bottom of things; in particular, it failed to explain why the Party had changed tactics during those dramatic days of August 1933 when, passing from one extreme to the other, it first entered into negotiations with Machado and then refused to have any dealings with the Grau-Guiteras government.[25] Why had it suddenly swung from

24. One of the darkest episodes in the ephemeral history of the Grau San Martín government occurred on September 29, 1933, during the interment in Havana of Julio Antonio Mella, whose ashes had been brought from Mexico with the special authorization of Antonio Guiteras. While a vast crowd accompanied the remains of the martyr of the Machado terror, an army detachment opened fire, wounding dozens. In the *Historia de Cuba* (*op. cit.* p. 602) this act is attributed to the men around Batista if not to Batista himself. Several former members of the *Directorio* have, however, told me that a most careful inquiry at the time failed to establish who was really responsible for this piece of anti-Communist aggression. According to them it was probably an unauthorized act on the part of an ultraconservative army group. Immediately after the event, many leftists in Cuba passed severe strictures on the Grau-Guiteras government and Raúl Roa, for example, even spoke of a "second death of Julio Antonio Mella." See Raúl Roa, *Retorno a la Alborada* (Las Villas University, 1964).

25. As an example of the quality of the "historical" explanations proffered by the PSP, we can do no better than to quote from J. Arnault's *Marxisme à Cuba* (*Nouvelle Critique*, August 1962): "During this decisive period in the fight against Machado, discussions took place in the Communist Party. . . . One section upheld the view that the fundamental problem was the economy. The most important thing was to obtain maximum satisfaction on the wage-claim front, even from Machado. This section carried the day. . . . But the movement was too strong; the masses were out in full force, and Machado was forced to take to his heels. And still the discussion continued: the Communist Party had constantly to face up to

mere wage claims to a call for insurrection? To answer this question honestly, Blas Roca would have had to admit that the Party had failed to appreciate how weak the Machado regime really was, and that later, when the Communist appeal to return to work had misfired, it made the opposite error of thinking that the workers had the situation under control and could prevent any attempt to restore the bourgeoisie to power. What the Communists failed to see was that Machado was not only opposed by the strikers and the working class, but by a much vaster social front, within which the proletariat ought to have pressed its own claims, but outside of which it did not represent a force strong enough to seize power.

Admittedly, their assessment of the situation was conditioned by the theory of the "struggle of class against class," which the Communist International had preached since 1928 and which it upheld until its Seventh Congress in 1935. Then, quite suddenly, the Comintern realized that the main enemy was fascism and that in order to destroy it, any alliances with other social and political forces were not only permissible but desirable. Up to that point, the Communist International had failed to see any difference between the various nonproletarian parties, on the grounds that one bourgeois government was as bad as the next.

As a result Cuban Communists had failed utterly to understand such forces as the *Directorio* and Guiteras, which were neither conservative nor socialist but represented an advanced form of revolutionary radicalism. And failing to understand them, the Communists refused to have any dealings with them. Before the fall of Machado, they opposed all calls for direct

---

economist tendencies within its ranks. The Party emerged all the greater from this struggle" (pp. 42–43).

What does all this mean? Why precisely did the Party "emerge all the greater"? What were the "economist tendencies"? Arnault does not bother his reader with an account of the Cuban soviets, later decried as examples of left-wing deviationism. All that apparently mattered to him was to reiterate that the Party grew bigger and better through whatever struggle it happened to be engaged in.

action and referred to the radical groups as adventurers or anarchists; after the fall of Machado they dismissed the same groups as petty bourgeois, and failed to perceive that the Grau-Guiteras government might have a positive role to play in Cuban politics. At either stage, they remained isolated and in the minority, quite incapable of grasping the real nature of Cuba's crisis or of affecting its development.

Here then is the background of an intriguing problem: why the Communist Party began in 1936 to make approaches to Batista, the man who had "drowned the general strike of 1935 in blood," and who by definition should have been the prime enemy of the Communists and of the entire Cuban Left.

A strange partner in the anti-fascist front

"There must be a *zafra* or there will be bloodshed," Colonel Batista had warned in January 1934, in the name of his Government of National Concentration. He kept his promise: within the next eighteen months the workers' resistance movement was crushed with unprecedented brutality. Here is the account of Blas Roca, the new leader of the Communist Party, to the Sixteenth Plenary Assembly of the Central Committee, in the autumn of 1935.[26]

"Batista, that national traitor in the pay of the imperialists, the faithful executioner of the orders of Caffery,[27] has drowned the March [general] strike in blood, has turned the university into a barracks, has smashed the workers' trade unions and burned down their headquarters, has destroyed the Medical Federation of Cuba, has filled the prisons with more than 3,000 men, women, and adolescent defenders of liberty and democracy,

26. The photocopy of his lecture, supplied by the José Martí National Library, is undated. However, since he was referring to the Seventh Congress of the Communist International, which was held in Moscow between July 25 and August 25, 1935, we may assume that the lecture was delivered in the autumn, and probably in October, of the same year.

27. Ambassador Caffery took over from Sumner Welles in December 1933.

has unleashed a barbarous terror campaign of street murder against his adversaries, has banned all anti-imperialist parties, and would now like to profit from his temporary victory by liquidating the revolution altogether."

Batista, Blas Roca went on to say, must be stopped at any price, and to that end all anti-fascists would have to build a popular front. He did not disguise the fact that this message had been inspired by the resolutions of the Seventh Congress of the Comintern in Moscow; there Comrade Dimitrov, "the giant of Leipzig"[28] and then general secretary of the Communist International, had used the occasion to "assign new and important tasks to the Communist movement." All Communist parties had been asked to do their utmost to halt the swing to the extreme right, and to make common cause with "whatever forces are capable of stemming the rising tide of fascist dictatorships."

Now, continued Blas Roca, in Cuba, fascism meant Batista and Batista alone. The criticisms leveled at certain leaders of the ABC Party "whom we previously accused of fascist tendencies have become pointless, because that party has changed leaders, and because it would be absurd, indeed ridiculous, to treat it as the fascist peril at a time when Batista and his 23,000 armed men have stepped into Machado's shoes and are spreading terror throughout the country." In the new circumstances, all attacks against the ABC Party had to cease, and Communists had to consider seriously the possibility of making common cause with them.

Blas Roca gave details of his contacts with the anti-imperialist and anti-fascist forces, and tried to win his comrades over to the new strategy. He pleaded eloquently for the "magnificent historical approach of the Communist International and its correct application to Cuba." To those who argued that the

28. Georgi Dimitrov, the Bulgarian Communist leader, was accused by Hitler of burning the Reichstag. At his trial in Leipzig, in 1934, Dimitrov was able to turn the tables on the prosecution.

The Communists and the Revolution

Party must "neither compact nor compromise" with its former rivals, Blas recalled the extreme gravity of the hour: "The traitor Batista and his formidable military machine pose a mortal threat to our country." In these circumstances, adherence to the old slogan of *solos contra todo y contra todos*[29] was tantamount to suicide.

Less than three years later, on July 18, 1938, the Party Central Committee held its Tenth Plenary Assembly in Havana. On that occasion Blas Roca delivered himself of yet another historical speech, although his central message had changed. Cuba now was said to be experiencing "semi-democratic conditions," and Batista to have "ceased to be the leading figure in the reactionary camp." And Blas Roca explained his strange about-turn as follows:

"We must remember Batista's social origins. Although he has grown rich, like all the new officers, and although he can now be described as a man of property, reactionary and aristocratic circles continue to treat him as a mere sergeant, a man in whom they cannot place their trust. Moreover, his links with the revolutionary movement are still very strong; he is still friendly with his old messmates—sergeants, corporals, and privates—all of whom remember his oath of loyalty to Cuba. I firmly believe that the force of the revolutionary tide which, in September 1933, drove this man to fight the then government, continues to exercise a pull on him and on all the other participants in these events."

But as Blas Roca knew perfectly well, Batista's social origins had not prevented him from happily mowing down revolutionaries. Hence he preferred to link up the "objective conditions" that had apparently helped to shape Batista's policies. "The situation in the United States has always influenced Cuban life. Now everyone knows the democratic intentions of the Roosevelt administration, and its attempts to inaugurate a good neighbor policy. Roosevelt is opposed to the warmongers and has

29. "Alone, against one and all."

83

asked that the fascist states be put outside the pale. He has gone to some lengths to ensure the restoration of democracy in our country. In particular, he has been anxious to increase the purchasing power of our people so that we can step up our consumption of his country's products. Unlike his predecessors, controlled by Wall Street, i.e., by exporters of capital who are interested in nothing but high yields from their investments and who have imposed starvation wages upon us, Roosevelt sympathizes with our desire for a higher standard of living and with our democratic aspirations."

Blas Roca also recalled that Cuba was once again going through a period of economic difficulties; the price of sugar on the world market had fallen by 18 per cent and the Americans had reduced by 200,000 tons the Cuban quota for 1938. The threat of crisis had split the Cuban Right into two distinct camps: the fascists, who relied on brute force, and *Batistianos*, who favored reforms and a popular dialogue. And that was precisely why Batista had agreed to convoke the Constituent Assembly, as the Left had demanded ever since 1933, and why he was under constant attack by such reactionary papers as the *Diario de la Marina*.

"In this situation," continued the general secretary of the Communist Party, "when asked if we would come to an agreement with Batista we reply quite openly, before the whole world, that it all depends on Batista's attitude to the basic problems of democracy: the Constituent Assembly, the improvement of social conditions, and independence. Batista is not a representative of a political party out of power; he is the actual head of the government. We cannot rely on his promises alone; we must judge him by his concrete actions."

While waiting for Batista to prove himself, Blas Roca announced that a leftist group led by "Pablo" and "Nieto" had been expelled from the Party, and recommended a merciless struggle against all Trotskyites and other "minor and impotent" groups who dared to oppose the march of the victorious people and sabotaged their unity and fruitful activities.

The Communists and the Revolution

Finally, the Communist leader explained his relations with "the revolutionary and fraternal party of Dr. Grau San Martín." Not very impressed by the new popular front policy, the latter had proposed the formation of a single revolutionary party. The Communist Party had no objections to this plan in principle, but it was skeptical of its chances of rapid success. And time was pressing: "The elections to the Constituent Assembly are about to usher in a new epoch in our history. This time we shall not simply be electing a president, or deputies with a restricted and temporary mandate, but we shall be choosing representatives of the people who will be able to give the country a fundamentally new constitution." The Communist Party thus left the door wide open both for an understanding with Batista and for an agreement with his "enemy-brothers" in the fight against Machado.

The third act of the drama was played out six months later, on January 11, 1939, at Santa Clara. On that day the Cuban Communist Party opened its Third National Congress. By having granted it legal recognition[30] for the first time in its history, Batista had given concrete proof of his good will and the Communists had not remained insensible to these overtures. As early as November 1938, when the dictator returned from the Armistice Day celebrations in Washington, the Communist Party had mobilized all its members to give him a tumultuous welcome home. Blas Roca had appeared on the balcony of the presidential palace side by side with the ex-sergeant, ex-fascist, "ex-assassin" of Antonio Guiteras, now the Communists' number one ally in the great "anti-fascist front." At the Congress of Santa Clara, Blas Roca himself justified the new Party line as follows:

"We must impress upon the people the need for a positive attitude toward Batista, and do our utmost to support his progressive endeavors. We are saying unequivocally at this moment

30. The Communist Party was given legal recognition on September 13, 1938. But in fact a para-Communist organization, led by Juan Marinello, had been legally operating in Havana since 1936.

that the first task of the revolutionary movement is to struggle for national unity based on a democratic program. Faced with the advance of Hitlerism and fascism, with the possibility of a German-Italian victory in Spain, the threat of the Rome-Berlin-Tokyo axis against America, Cuba must work in close collaboration with the democratic governments of the world, and in particular with that of the United States. Whenever we state these simple truths, some revolutionaries, influenced by the calumnies of such extreme right-wing journals as *Alerta* or *Diario de la Marina,* call us traitors, accuse us of abandoning the revolution, and so on. The Nazis who run the *Diario de la Marina* and the Trotskyites alike claim that we are sacrificing the interests of our people to the international aspirations of the Soviet Union. Their arguments are ridiculous. National unity, the defense of our country against a Nazi-fascist invasion, and collaboration with democratic countries, are all in the interests of our own people, correspond to their most urgent needs, and spring from the concrete conditions in which our country finds itself."

After these explanations, Blas Roca went on to examine the positive achievements of Batista: his cabinet had been reshuffled and three left-wing ministers had been co-opted; the heavy tax burden had been eased. During his trip to Washington, Batista had laid "the basis for effective collaboration between Cuba and the United States against the fascist menace." At the Seventh Pan-American Conference he had declared himself in favor of "the formation of a continental bloc against fascism" and had demanded "the outlawing of racial or religious persecution." Finally, Batista had promised to abolish Decree No. 3 of 1934, which prohibited trade unions' joining together in national federations.

"Batista would have gone much further still, had Congress not sabotaged his progressive projects. And the blindness of some revolutionaries who insist on seeing him as their principal enemy facilitates this type of reactionary sabotage and thus endangers the interests of the people." On that concise note the Communist

86

The Communists and the Revolution

leader ended his eulogy of the head of the army. Unfortunately he could not just leave it at that, simply ignoring what for the last fourteen years had been the chief bugbear of the Communist Party—the United States' grip on the island, exploitation by Yankee imperialists, and the semi-colonial or neo-colonial situation in which America was determined to maintain Cuba.

"We have never been anti-American but only anti-imperialist," the Communist leader insisted. "But in 1939 the most threatening form of imperialism is not that of the United States but that of the Nazi-fascists. In Cuba they have recently begun to spread their tentacles with extraordinary persistence. Their chief strongholds are the North German company Lloyd, and Bayer of Hamburg. The latter ostensibly deals in pharmaceutical products but is in fact one of the world's biggest manufacturers of chemical weapons; its Cuban subsidiary is run by one Reiman, who is appointed directly by the German government, and who spends several months of each year in Germany. As for Lloyd, whose headquarters are at 307 Obispo Street, they have a transmitting station and dubious connections with the Ministry of Communications.

"Despite this," Blas Roca continued, "and despite the intensification of Nazi propaganda, certain leftists pretend that Cuba is not really up against a fascist threat, and that we must devote ourselves entirely to the struggle against Yankee imperialism, even if this really means Roosevelt's democratic administration. This is precisely what the Nazi imperialists want, the very men who have just armed the Brazilian Integralists for a *golpe*[31]—which luckily has failed—who have shipped arms through Guatemala to the fascist enemies of Lázaro Cárdenas, the Mexican president, who have engineered a putsch in Chile, who occupy entire provinces in Costa Rica and now prepare the colonization of all America. There is no doubt that all of us are threatened by the criminal gravediggers of the Spanish Republic!" When speaking of Roosevelt, Blas Roca could not

31. Coup d'état.

87   D

help repeating the praises he had already accorded the President, though he also reminded his comrades of the words spoken in Havana, at a mass meeting held on November 12, 1938, by a leading Communist from the United States, James W. Ford: "President Roosevelt's speech [on the subject of Latin America] fully expresses the mood of the progressive movement which is rapidly sweeping across America. His good-neighbor policy does not require superhuman or impossible sacrifices from any nation. American imperialism was an unpopular policy because it served the interests of a small minority. The good-neighbor policy serves the interests of the masses of people in all parts of North and South America."

Finally, to put the last nail into the coffin of his *izquierdista*[32] critics, Blas Roca quoted an authority that no revolutionary could afford to ignore, namely Dolores Ibarruri, *la Pasionaria* of the Spanish Republic. Addressing the Central Committee of her party in Madrid on May 23, 1938, she had said: "There are some who claim that our thirteen-point program will win us the war but lose us the revolution. I cannot help smiling when I think of the revolution that they are dreaming of. . . . We declare in the face of their unjust attacks that here in Spain we are fighting neither for libertarian Communism nor for a socialist government nor for a dictatorship of the proletariat. We are fighting for a parliamentary democratic republic, with a profound concern for justice and social progress. Obviously, those who confuse the revolution with Messianism and fatalism, who forget the historical conditions and political conditions of our country, cannot understand us. . . . Lenin has taught that in order to educate the people we must sometimes swim against the tide. And we shall not weaken in our determination because we happen to be swimming against a particularly noisy tide, in this case the revolutionary *bambolla*, which, at root, has nothing constructive to offer, either for winning the war or for improving the lot of the masses." To which Blas Roca merely

32. "Leftist."

added that these words of *la Pasionaria* were admirably "Cuban."

The General Secretary of the Party did not say that he had already signed an electoral pact with Batista, but one could easily have deduced it from his speech. In fact, on November 15, 1939, when Cubans were given the chance to elect their long-awaited Constituent Assembly, two main groups competed for their votes: the Batista-led Socialist Democratic Coalition which included the Communist Party, and the Opposition Bloc, consisting of the *Auténticos*, the ABC Party, the Democratic Republican Party, and the Action Party. The Opposition Bloc, led by Dr. Grau San Martín and boasting strong ties with the revolution of 1933, won by a comfortable majority (45 seats out of 81), while the Communists obtained a mere 6 seats within the Batista coalition.[33]

The six Communist deputies played an important and praise-worthy part in the work of the Assembly. Good speakers, and intimately familiar with the island's social problems, they distinguished themselves by the high quality of their debates and other contributions. Thanks to them, the new constitution included a great many advanced clauses. It was passed on July 1, 1940, but did not become law until October 10, the anniversary of the outbreak of the 1868 war of independence. The new democratic electoral code was not to be applied until 1943. On July 25, 1940, Cubans were called to elect a new president, and thanks to the time-honored practice of indirect representation no less than the support of a number of prominent people, General (no longer Colonel) Fulgencio Batista succeeded in beating his inveterate enemy, Dr. Grau. Batista's tactics were not very elegant, but then he was in no position to put the issue honestly to the electorate. Aware of his continued unpopularity, he redoubled his efforts to pacify the opposition, and invited

33. Of 1,940,444 registered electors, only 1,105,709 (56.9 per cent) cast their vote. The bloc system on which these elections were run prevents an evaluation of the real influence of the Communist Party.

them once again to join his government of national unity. He obtained the support of Jorge Mañach but not that of Dr. Grau. Two years later, on July 24, 1942, he brought two Communist ministers, Juan Marinello and Carlos Rafael Rodríguez, into his cabinet. They were the first Communists to serve in any Latin American government.

The facts which we have just recalled speak for themselves and are easy to put together. The José Martí National Library in Havana has the complete lectures and reports of Blas Roca, and many other Communist texts. Even before the Communist Party itself became legal, its press was tolerated by the authorities, and devoted much space to the concerns of the antifascist front. The facts relating to the legal life of the Communist Party are moreover reported at length in the ten volumes of the *Historia de la Nación Cubana,* which is extremely well documented, though slightly colored in favor of Batista.[34] But a more up-to-date and complete analysis of the Communist alliance with Batista has never been written.

For example, we have consulted the *Manual de Capacitación Cívica,* published in 1960 for the special use of Castro's militants; 50,000 words are devoted to history, but the main story ends in 1934, the rest condensed to less than two hundred fifty words. In 1967, the Political Directorate of the Ministry of Defense published a much more ambitious historical handbook: it was meant to be a kind of Marxist history of Cuba from the pre-Colombian times onward. It runs to 611 pages but devotes a mere eight lines to the events following the revolution of 1933–34. This should be enough to show that Cuban historians have written very little indeed about the interval between the failure of that revolution and Fidel Castro's victory a quarter of a century later.

This silence reflects their extraordinary embarrassment in the

34. The *Historia de la Nación Cubana* (Havana 1952) was published by a loose group, led by Ramiro Guerra y Sánchez, historian and author of the classical *Azúcar y población en las Antillas* (Havana, Cultural S.A., 1927) .

The Communists and the Revolution

face of Communist dealings with Batista. If the president so valiantly supported by the Communist Party had completely withdrawn from politics at the end of his mandate in 1944, they would doubtless have been able to justify Communist participation in his government by playing down his fascist and repressive tendencies during the years 1934–36. But the early panegyrics of the Communists reaped an ironical harvest when the fascist of 1934 was resurrected with a vengeance in 1952. Then the speeches of Blas Roca and of all those of his comrades who had so volubly praised the noble life and example of this fine man, of this leader with his "roots deep in the people," this "living symbol of the revolution of 1933," began to look like so many sick jokes, so many symptoms of a pathological form of political myopia. In Havana, they prefer to pass the whole matter over in stony silence.

Still, silence is not necessarily golden, and I have the feeling that this kind of discretion does nothing but harm to the Communist "old guard." It ought to be made clear that most of them really did not have the least idea of how their party became involved in so perilous an enterprise. Many have told me that in their opinion the key to the whole problem lay not in Havana but in Washington: Roosevelt ordered Batista to collaborate with the Communists, and the Party took advantage of this fact to strengthen its organization and to gain what concessions it could for the working class. This naïve story cannot fail to amuse those who are in the least familiar with the history of the New Deal; at no time was Roosevelt a pro-Communist nor did he put the least pressure on anyone to rally behind the extreme Left. Not even Roosevelt's most vehement opponents, not even McCarthy and his witchhunters, have ever accused him of playing this kind of double game. There is not a scrap of evidence to support the view that the Cuban Communists were singled out for Roosevelt's generosity.[35]

35. Robert Merle, in his *Moncada, premier combat de Fidel Castro* (Paris, 1965), remarks in passing on the events preceding his main story. This is how he describes Roosevelt's "beneficial" effect on Cuban politics:

No wonder, therefore, that the more intelligent of the old guard, like Carlos Rafael Rodríguez, produce a completely different explanation. According to them, all the misfortunes of the Cuban Left were due to the uncritical pro-American attitude of Dr. Grau, who refused the hand the Communists held out to him. "Division was the Achilles heel of the Cuban Left."[36] Now this was a disease that afflicted socialists throughout the world, but in Cuba the rift became unbridgeable just as soon as men like Grau San Martín concluded from the failure of the 1933 revolution that no change on the island was possible without the good will of the United States. From then on they bent over backward to get into Washington's good graces, and what better way of doing that than proving their anti-Communist sentiments? Hence every attempt by the Communist Party to form a common front with them was doomed to failure from the very start.

Though apparently more coherent, this explanation stands up no better to serious scrutiny. First of all, the speeches of Blas Roca demonstrate that the Communist Party had ceased to be anti-American by 1936, after which time it gave as many accolades to Roosevelt as any other Cuban party. Washington therefore did not regard the Party as a threat, and the Americans do not in fact seem to have been unduly worried by the

---

"So Roosevelt is a liberal? Then so is he [Batista]. So Roosevelt has declared war on Japan after Pearl Harbor? So did Batista. Roosevelt is an ally of Soviet Russia? Batista has brought a Communist into his government."

Even supposing Batista to have been a faithful disciple of his American master, it ought to be stressed that Roosevelt himself never called a Communist to serve in *his* administration. Far from it, he had the leader of the U.S. Communist Party, Earl Browder, thrown into jail (Atlanta, 1939), and he never dreamed of signing an electoral pact with the Communist Party. Moreover, none of the other Latin American countries adopted a *Batistiano* attitude toward the Communists. Hence the whole thesis is rather childish and, in any case, completely unsubstantiated.

36. This phrase occurs in a manuscript of Carlos Rafael Rodríguez entitled, *La Revolución Cubana y el período de transición,* which he was kind enough to lend to me. It will appear in print soon.

The Communists and the Revolution

flirtation between Batista and the Communists. Why then should they have withheld from Grau what they so freely granted "their man in Havana"? Finally, their failure to reach agreement with Grau does not really explain why the Communists should have felt impelled to sign a pact with Batista. Between the slogans *solos contra todo y contra todos* and *con todo y con todos,* between complete isolation and promiscuous union, there is a definite limit which simple prudence should have discouraged the Party leaders from overstepping.

Still, Carlos Rafael Rodríguez was quite right when he spoke of the fragmentation of the Cuban Left. Even a European accustomed to seeing this phenomenon in his own continent is amazed by the stage it had reached in Cuba. It is enough to mention that during the elections to the Constituent Assembly, there were at least five parties claiming to represent the Left, and that almost every one of them contained as many different factions within its own ranks. Dr. Grau San Martín, who became the standard-bearer of the Left opposition in the wake of the anti-Machadoist struggle, had the greatest difficulty in keeping this tendency in check, and apparently spent most of his time concluding or breaking agreements with one or the other dissident element. However, all strands of the non-Communist Left were in agreement on one point at least: they would not underwrite Batista's putsch of January 1934.

The heterogenous structure of the Left coalition contributed to its distrustful attitude toward the Communists. The anti-Machadoist camp included a large number of right-wing "revolutionaries"; and the Left was haunted by memories of the Cuban soviets. Reports from Europe, in particular from France and Spain, seemed to indicate that the Communist parties were the chief beneficiaries of all attempts to set up popular fronts. Blas Roca said as much in his speeches to the Cuban comrades. No wonder then that the "bourgeois wing" of the Cuban opposition became increasingly apprehensive: even without Blas Roca's indiscretions it tended to overestimate the importance of his party. The radical Left, on the other hand, distrusted the

Guerrillas in Power

Communists for quite different reasons: the Party had not only grown lukewarm in its struggle against the government, but had underwritten Batista's hateful regime. In return for permission granted them to demonstrate their solidarity with Spain, they were ready to make concessions to the usurper in home affairs. This conciliatory attitude, coupled with intransigence toward the Left, could only increase the fears of those who remembered how the Communist Party had changed sides at the crucial moment of the anti-Machadoist strike. Would the same situation repeat itself once there was a trial of strength with Batista? Had not Blas Roca endorsed the remarks of José Díaz, the Spanish Communist leader, according to whom the chief enemies of humanity, and indeed of civilized society, were the fascists, the Trotskyites, and the "undisciplined"? And who were these "undisciplined" in Cuba if not the revolutionary Left?

Hence it was not so much the pro-American policies of Dr. Grau—which were not shared anyway by all members of the coalition—that explained Left reservations with regard to Communist advances, as memories of the bloody days of August 1933. In short, the Communists were both too much to the left and too much to the right to gain the support they sought. And that is precisely why Dr. Grau's coalition put the Party in an impossible position, first calling for a "single revolutionary party," then turning a deaf ear when, against all expectations, the Communists agreed to all his demands. In the face of such tactics the Communists would have needed far greater skill, clarity, and determination than they could muster, and above all a far greater ability to come to terms with the progressives and anti-imperialists among the "petty bourgeois revolutionaries"; these were precisely the qualities the Party had lacked since its inception.

It is equally true that when Batista made overtures to Dr. Grau, the coalition did not immediately fall to pieces. But then, Dr. Grau had only agreed to meet the ex-sergeant in 1938 and on condition that Batista hand over power to him. In

94

the end a "compromise" was reached: the electorate would be consulted after the National Assembly had made arrangements for a fair referendum. And Batista did, in fact, scrupulously observe all clauses of his agreement with Dr. Grau—he granted an amnesty and restored the autonomy of the university—save for holding presidential elections by universal suffrage. And so Dr. Grau chose to remain in opposition until Batista honored his promises in full. And when he did, in 1944, Dr. Grau's patience was rewarded: he was elected president of Cuba.[37] But it is worth repeating that Dr. Grau's intransigence was not so much the result of his own strength of character— once elected he showed that he had never been a man of

37. Dr. Grau San Martín obtained 65 per cent of the votes cast, and so won a telling victory over the *Batistiano* candidate, Salagrida, and his Communist supporters. J. Arnault in *Cuba et le marxisme* surpasses himself in trying to justify this electoral defeat and the strange alliance between the Communists and one whom he himself was forced to call a conservative:
"Faced with Grau's refusal to adopt a resolute anti-fascist position, at a time when the Second World War was not yet over, the Communists decided to support Salagrida. But so rife was corruption under Batista's presidency that many electors preferred to vote for the opposition candidate. This electoral failure in no way reflected a decline in Communist influence among the working class" (p. 45).
We have seen that, as far as Jacques Arnault is concerned, the Party emerges triumphant from any test, no matter what its conduct. But how was it possible to accuse Dr. Grau both of being pro-American and also of refusing "to adopt a resolute anti-fascist position" during the Second World War? Jacques Arnault's dialectical prowess enables him to brush this historical obstacle aside. In the same chapter he writes: "After Grau's fall [in 1934] persecution against the workers' movement was greatly stepped up. Batista, having gone over to the imperialist camp, assumed greater and greater powers. . . . Repression was fierce." Next: "During the presidential elections of 1940, the Communists participated in a democratic socialist coalition which supported Batista's candidature." Arnault sees no need to explain any of the reasons that persuaded the PCC to fall in behind this particular candidate. Later, when discussing the 1952 coup d'état, he compares Batista to de Gaulle and speaks of the confusion caused, in their respective countries, by the return to power of these two generals. One does not have to be a Gaullist to realize that these two men had nothing in common apart from their military rank. In particular, de Gaulle did not start his military career by smashing a general strike, or by assassinating opposition leaders.

principle—as a sign of the hatred all good revolutionaries bore Batista for his treachery of January, and for his bloodthirsty campaign of persecution which had cost the lives of Antonio Guiteras and thousands of others.

The ex-sergeant could not fail to notice the rising tide of opposition, and he realized that he could not continue to run a rebellious country at bayonet point. After all, he had personally witnessed Machado's downfall and the days of the great popular terror. Moreover United States interests no longer favored a simple policy of repression in Latin America. Thanks to Roosevelt, the American trade union movement had achieved, for the first time, a position of real importance, and it now strongly opposed persecution of workers anywhere within the United States' sphere of influence. Batista was therefore in urgent need of popular support, and this he could only obtain by enlisting the help of at least one opposition party. It was his instinct for self-preservation rather than orders from Washington which led him straight to the Communists, once he had received a telling rebuff from the followers of Dr. Grau.

The Communist Party was prepared to take part in these maneuvers because it too was trying desperately to break out of its isolation and form the anti-fascist front ordained by the Comintern. But how was it to form this front with Dr. Grau's Left, when all its overtures were coldly rejected, or with the heirs of Guiteras—those "implacable rebels"—or even with the neo-Marxists of the former *A la Izquierda Estudiantil* who looked upon themselves as a predominantly anti-American organization? How could the Party possibly get involved with allies such as these, at a time when Moscow was at pains to discourage any manifestations that might offend Washington?

With Batista, things were much simpler. He did not ask the Communists to repent of their conduct in 1933; he was far too concerned with justifying his own. Furthermore, he was a mulatto and thus an anti-racialist and an anti-Nazi; and that was what really counted. Finally, he raised no objections to the setting up of a national trade union organization, the Confederation of Cuban Workers (CTC), thus giving the Communist Party control of an important section of the community. What did he ask in return? Very little, it seemed; the Communists were to drop the subject of his bloody past, and to dwell instead on "his deep popular origins"; they were to provide the social harmony so needful to the war effort, and finally, they were to keep up the attacks against the opposition. Both sides stood to gain from this new arrangement, and the Communist Party could hardly have anticipated that Cubans would one day conclude that, in the name of anti-fascism, the Party had signed a pact with the worst fascist in their country's history.

Once committed to a man like Batista, the Communists had of necessity to take further steps down the same slope. The cost had been dear in 1933 and, despite appearances, would be even dearer in 1938–44. All the Party did then was to add to the confusion and ideological retreat of the Cuban Left, on which it depended far more than it was ever able to realize. A few figures may serve to illustrate its rapid decline after the Batista pact: in 1942, according to official statistics, the Communist Party numbered 87,000 members; in 1952, on the eve of Batista's new coup d'état, that figure had dropped to 29,000 and in 1959 at the time of Fidel Castro's victory, it was down to 7,000. In 1939, the Communist Lázaro Peña was elected general secretary of the newly founded CTC by a huge majority; by 1947 the Communists were already in a minority within the trade unions, and in 1959 at the First Congress of the CTC following the Revolution, there were only 170 Communists among the 3,240 delegates.

True, the Cold War and the great anti-Communist offensive of the United States during the '50s made the Cuban Party's task an extremely difficult one. And to win, the Communist Party would have needed a great many allies and a good deal of foresight. It was lacking in both, and by collaborating with Batista, it threw away what few trump cards it had ever held. For a better appreciation of how the Party paved the way for its own defeat, we must quickly pass on to another delicate and even less known topic in its history: that of its total commitment to Browderism.

Earl Browder's promised land

"Earl Browder, leader and guide of the United States Communist Party, and the most formidable political brain in America, has taught us that while the world itself changes rapidly, relations between different social strata alter but slowly. Everything that lives and grows must evolve, and so must everything that dies and rots away." This was how Blas Roca sang the praises of Earl Browder in 1938, by way of acknowledging the latter's elevation to the post of general secretary of the Communist Party of the United States.[38] The arguments of this new leader could not yet be said to have sprung from a "formidable brain," but Cuban Communists already seemed very impressed. For the next seven years, from 1938 to 1945, they would take every available opportunity to refer in respectful tones to the thoughts of the head of their fraternal party in the United States.

This allegiance was clearly not the result of Browder's strong personality, nor of the importance of his contribution which, in retrospect, strikes one as being tenuous in the extreme. However the Popular Front policy of the Comintern and later the overriding demands of the Second World War forced Communists in Latin America to kowtow to U.S. policies as well as to attach a position of prime importance to their comrades in that country. Thus while European Communists were able to join popular fronts without abandoning their own standpoints, the Latin Americans found it necessary to indulge in ideological gymnastics of a singular kind and to reverse most of their previous conclusions. They described fascism as the "ultimate form

38. In his address to the Tenth Plenary Assembly of the Central Committee, on July 18, 1938.

of monopoly capitalism" but proposed to fight it at the side of the Americans, the leading monopoly capitalists in their part of the world. And they proposed further to struggle for social changes at home, even while Cuba remained completely under the thumb of U.S. big business. Altogether these policies were so many attempts to square the circle.

Unable to reconcile the irreconcilable, they decided to support unconditionally the wartime alliance between Russia and America. Their conduct would not only help to preserve social harmony but would show Washington that Communists could be reasonable men, capable of making a useful contribution to the running of a stable free-enterprise society, in full conformity with the spirit of Roosevelt's New Deal. Thanks to the wise example set by the Cubans, the American President would surely wish to enlist Communist support for his wider plans to improve the life of mankind.

In fact, the Cuban Communists carried on as if their country were nothing less than an integral part of the United States. They worried about U.S. internal stability, prosperity, and the strength of America's armed forces. Yesterday's wolf had apparently turned into a vulnerable sheep that was bravely leading a threatened flock. At the same time they kept clamoring for the rapid rearmament of their own island. Thus, during a now famous meeting on November 12, 1938, Blas Roca demanded "powerful guns, troops to defend our shores and block the way of the Nazi invaders." Such proposals from members of the Communist movement may strike us today as unbelievable, and we wonder what possible contribution this sort of propaganda could have made to improving the average Cuban's attitude toward Washington in general, and to their own army, led by the infamous General Batista, in particular.

The Axis countries admittedly did pose a grave threat to the entire American continent. For though no one in Berlin or Tokyo ever dreamed of invading countries so staunchly defended by the U.S. fleet, Nazi agents in Latin America were counting on the prevalent anti-Yankee feeling when launching

99

all kinds of schemes and plots designed to cut off America's chief source of raw materials. We must not forget that the outcome of the Second World War mattered to all mankind and that a victory for Hitler would indeed have had dire effects on the whole world. But did that mean that the Communists perforce had to turn a blind eye to all other problems? Could they not at the very least have demanded a guarantee from the United States that relations between the two Americas would be radically revised after victory had been won? Was it really necessary to go to extremes and treat all those who still dared to raise the question of their country's exploitation by the United States, or simply looked forward to a social revolution, as *agents provocateurs* or even as Nazi spies?

True, the mistakes of the Latin American Communist parties were not so much the result of their blindness as of Stalin's skillful designs. The Soviet leader had realized as early as 1936 that Roosevelt was a sincere and implacable opponent of fascism; moreover Roosevelt was the only man capable of bringing the United States into the war against Russia's chief enemy, Hitler Germany. For though Japan threatened America more directly, Roosevelt's remarkable political acumen had led him to see that the vital front, even as far as his own country was concerned, ran through Europe. The strategists at the Foreign Office in London were all counting on a Russian-German confrontation, to kill two birds with one stone, but the American leader did not take too much notice of these pointless and indeed dangerous expectations. As far as he was concerned there was only one thing for it: Hitler had to be stopped before he was in a position to turn on the United States. For this, Roosevelt earned Stalin's full support, and the cooperation of the Latin American Communist parties as a pledge of Soviet good will.

Still, in Europe as in Asia, Stalin could not turn Communists into Social Democrats overnight, the less so as resistance work encourages radicalism and the use of revolutionary methods. Russia could partly dismantle this time bomb in the name of coexistence, but not only was she incapable of defusing it completely, she did not even wish to do so lest she be robbed of a potentially useful political instrument in the postwar period. Moreover, while Stalin liked to appear as a moderate and reasonable man, he did not really want to be compromised as an out-and-out revisionist. He had already dissolved the Comintern, so that no one could any longer accuse him of directing "a huge international conspiracy"; he had no further need of this old warhorse for keeping foreign Communist parties in check. Yet when Roosevelt, at Teheran, tried to draw him into a discussion about the brave new postwar world, Stalin hedged and asked instead for assurances about the Second Front and the future partitioning of Germany.[39] On the other hand, he raised no objections to the endorsement by North and Latin American Communists, whose future had never inspired him with great faith, of Roosevelt's great dream of international harmony. As long as the Soviet Union was protected, it was too bad if foreign comrades had to commit what was virtually political suicide.

In any case, the Cuban Communist Party, now reduced to a mere auxiliary in a great national, and basically conservative, coalition, was destined to pay heavily for this privilege. True, it obtained considerable advantages for its working-class members: guaranteed employment, an eight-hour day, and a wage increase —but since none of the fundamental problems of the country had been solved or even raised, these advantages proved neither durable nor even relevant to the real plight of the Cuban masses. Worse still, the new concessions strengthened conservative trends in a country with a poverty-stricken and chronically unemployed peasantry, and a hypertrophied service sector made up of small shopkeepers and a vast army of corrupt officials. The Communist Party could keep telling the people *"por que y para que participan los comunistas en el gabinete,"*[40] but it could not tell the

39. See the Proceedings of the Big Three meetings as published in *Mezhdunarodnaya Zhizn* (Moscow, 1961) .

40. "Why and for whose sake the Communists have joined the Cabinet"— the theme of a national education conference held in Havana on March 26, 1943.

101

whole truth nor convince anyone. It was at this point that Earl Browder came to the rescue.

On December 12, 1943, a week or so after the meeting of the Big Three at Teheran,[41] he took the opportunity of a meeting at Bridgeport, Connecticut, to develop a new thesis: in future, all conflicts and social problems within the United States would have to be solved by peaceful compromise; continued struggles at home could only serve to weaken world unity, the importance of which had been fully recognized at Teheran. On January 10, 1944, at Madison Square Garden in New York, Browder delivered an even more sensational speech, which was reproduced in full by the Communist press in Havana, under the significant title: UNITED STATES COMMUNIST PARTY CHANGES ITS NAME.[42]

"Before Teheran," Browder was reported as saying, "the whole world wondered whether the coalition between the United States, Great Britain, and the Soviet Union would survive the defeat of the common enemy, or if these three countries would again go their separate ways, thus inaugurating a new period of revolutionary agitation and international struggle, culminating in a Third World War. Teheran has reassured all those who believe that it is impossible to fight a war as allies unless there is agreement about the future. . . . Humanity has risen to a new level of intelligence. Capitalism and Communism have already begun to march hand in hand toward the peaceful collaboration of tomorrow. This broad policy, pursued in the interests of all, also imposes an obligation on all of us to reduce to a minimum, and if possible to eliminate altogether, every form of violence in the life of every country. . . . I have long reflected on this matter and have come to the conclusion that the people of

41. The Teheran Conference, attended by Roosevelt, Churchill, and Stalin, took place on November 28–December 2, 1943. The Western version of that meeting has come to us chiefly through Sir Winston Churchill's classic memoirs, *The Second World War*. The Russian version was published in 1965 under the title of *Dokumenti teheranskoi i krimskoi konferentsii rukovoditelyei triokh vielikih dzhergyav* (Moscow, Gosizdat).

42. See *Fundamentos*, theoretical journal of the PCC, February 1944.

The Communists and the Revolution

the United States are subjectively unprepared for a socialist transformation of society. In proclaiming such an objective, far from uniting the nation, we merely foster divisions that can only profit the most reactionary forces. So as to sow confusion in the democratic camp, the reactionaries are fighting their election campaign [the presidential elections of November 1944] under the banner of free enterprise; we Marxists must not fall into their trap by proclaiming the opposite message. . . . We declare quite openly that we are ready to contribute to the effective running of free-enterprise capitalism, lest the marvelous development of our economy be slowed down after the war."

After an analysis of the economic problems besetting the United States and branding the evil of unofficial strikes, Browder went on to say that there were some who believed that aid to underdeveloped countries was a flagrant denial of the principles of free enterprise. But this apparently thorny problem was easily resolved: the United States government need only render as much foreign aid as the interests of American exporters allowed. As for the wage question, it must be settled by an intelligent income policy, i.e. by keeping wage increases proportional to productivity.

Finally, Browder proposed the dissolution of the Communist Party; the traditional two-party system of the United States did not allow it to play an effective role. A new Communist Political Association (based on the same old hierarchical principles as the old) would no longer nominate special candidates for public election; its members would be content to work within the two existing parties, "which form two great institutionalized channels," and support "every decent and progressive" measure. "We are about to follow the line of problems instead of the line of parties."

In Havana, Communists greeted Browder's speech as a godsend. Until that moment, they had followed their own government rather diffidently, and against strong opposition from the rank and file. Now quite suddenly Browder had given them the perfect theoretical justification for all their compromises with

Batista. Everything they had done to cement social peace at home had been for the very best, and had contributed not only to peace between the great powers, but also to the future of the whole of mankind. By fostering the national unity of all Cubans they had added a brick to that marvelous new world built on peaceful agreements, on harmony between different classes and social systems, and no longer on revolutionary struggle and wildcat agitation. Moreover Cubans, like Americans, were clearly quite unprepared for a socialist transformation of society. Hence, had the Communist Party proposed such a transformation, it would simply have added grist to the reactionary mills. In the circumstances, it had done the only decent thing, and could now congratulate itself on its foresight and on the wisdom of its moderation.

We have simply let the facts speak for themselves, or rather we have summarized the innumerable speeches delivered by Cuba's leading Communists as collected in a pamphlet with the significant title of *A la luz de Teheran* (In the Light of Teheran) .[43] The Cuban Communist Party had endorsed every one of the fundamental theses put forward by Earl Browder, "our great American comrade," except for one: there was no intention to transform the Cuban Party into an "Association of Communists." But then the Cuban political scene was so crammed with political parties great and small, that it would have been ridiculous to speak of a traditional two-party system. Still, so as not to be left out on a limb completely, the Party nevertheless agreed to change its name to *Partido Socialista Popular,* a label to which it stuck to its bitter end—in 1961.

All these innovations did not go entirely unchallenged by the Cuban, or for that matter the U.S., Communist movement. In New York, the well-known Party leader, William Foster, had long fought against Earl Browder, while in Havana, César Vilar, one of the founders of the Party, squarely accused Blas Roca, Aníbal Escalante, Juan Marinello, and Carlos Rafael Rodríguez—the four principal Teheranists—of suffering from

43. Havana, February 1944, PCC publications.

petty-bourgeois delusions. The ensuing debate reached great heights of sophistication, as some argued that the name determined the cause, and the rest took the opposite view. The issue was settled with near-Solomonic shrewdness by Juan Marinello, poet and president of the Party, who declared that "the name makes the cause provided the cause makes the name."[44]

The leading group carried the day, and at the Second National Assembly of the PSP, in September 1944, Aníbal Escalante tried to apply the thesis of Browder, *el gran americano,* to the particular problems of colonial countries. "With Teheran, the world has entered a new historical phase; in this unusual situation we must try to apply unusual solutions, or else we would not be Marxists." Cuba could face the future with great economic confidence because she was certain to benefit from the "economic difficulties of the other continents ravaged by the war. Sugar production having fallen off everywhere—from Europe to Java—Cuba had the duty and privilege of supplying the world market with this essential product." And while faithfully collaborating with the United States in the spirit of Teheran, Cuba had the right to ask the United States to make "some voluntary sacrifices" in revising the mutual trade treaty and in giving Puerto Rico its freedom.

The Assembly instructed Blas Roca to send a "Letter to Earl Browder," asking him to use his good offices with enlightened capitalists in the United States, and to persuade them to give the "good neighbor" policy an even more progressive look. After congratulating the North American comrade on the brilliance of his writings and on the success of his recent book in Cuba (twenty thousand copies were sold within four months), the Communist Party went on to declare that good relationships between the two Americas would not grow automatically; Communists had a duty to fight resolutely against all obstacles the reactionary forces tried to place in the path of victory.

While they were debating the future of the world and of their

44. See Carlos Rafael Rodríguez' article, *"De la Liga Comunista al Partido Socialista Popular,"* in *Fundamentos,* February 1944.

own hemisphere, the Cuban Communists lost the elections: Dr. Grau formed a new government. True to its faith in national unity, the Party immediately declared its readiness to support the new *Auténtico* administration, and recalling its former (fruitless) negotiations with the "revolutionaries" now in power, wished them success in their present task. As a token of good will, the Communists even offered the government the collaboration of the trade unions—80 per cent under Communist control. And so, in February 1945, Havana witnessed a "historic" breakfast, unique in the annals of the country: the Employers' Association entertained the leaders of the CTC (the Confederation of Cuban Workers) in the presence of cabinet ministers. Lázaro Peña, the leading Communist trade unionist, drank a toast to the "new era in the history of humanity." Blas Roca described the occasion as "a transcendental act." All the speeches were collated in a pamphlet that was widely distributed, bearing the resounding title of "Collaboration Between the Employers and the Workers." For final perfection and so as to dispel any remaining doubts, the Party also sent out a sort of catechism composed of questions by a skeptical rank-and-file member, and reassuring replies by his far more knowledgeable leaders.

Collaborationist euphoria was still at its peak in Havana when quite suddenly, in April 1945, the thunder of condemnation crashed down on the head of Earl Browder. Contrary to what one might expect, the noise did not come directly from Moscow—Stalin, true to the promises he had made upon dissolving the Comintern on May 22, 1943, kept up the pretense of complete indifference to the activities of foreign Communist parties. In any case, he could not himself publicly disown Browder and his collaborationist doctrine without alarming the Americans or casting doubt on his good faith as a member of the Great Alliance. The attack was accordingly launched by one of the leaders of the French Communist Party, Jacques Duclos, and might have been taken as the expression of his personal views, or even as the beginning of a polemic between two Marxist theorists. In fact, the French Communist Party had for a long time enjoyed the status of an elder in the Muscovite church. Its

106

The Communists and the Revolution

leader, Maurice Thorez, had just returned to France after spending the entire war in the Soviet Union, and there is every reason to think that the article of Jacques Duclos published in April 1945 in the *Cahiers du Communisme* was dreamed up in its entirety by the Kremlin.

Jacques Duclos accused his American comrades of three unpardonable sins: 1) of liquidating the only independent party of the U.S. working class; 2) of propounding revisionist theories about the disappearance of the class struggle in each country and throughout the world; 3) of spreading dangerous and opportunistic illusions by presenting the purely diplomatic procedures of the Teheran Conference as a new Communist platform. Duclos concluded his indictment by pointing out that most Communists had not been taken in for one moment by Browder's revisionism, with the notable exception of some parties in Latin America, particularly those of Cuba and of Colombia (the latter having changed its name to Democratic Socialist Party).

Earl Browder was quick to hit back. He thanked Duclos dryly for his interesting contribution, but recalled that the Communist International had ceased to exist and that consequently he was the only fit person to formulate the policy of the party he led. This was an idle boast—his cause had already been weighed in Moscow and found wanting. In any case, the Popular Socialist Party of Cuba had no intention of following its mentor into a political wilderness, or indeed of putting up any kind of defense for the most recent phase in its tortuous history. Duclos' article hit them like a bolt from the blue and, in July 1945, when they published his attack on Browder, they merely added a commentary by Blas Roca, with such weak excuses as: we did not, after all, dissolve our party; we merely spoke of a *tendency* for the class struggle to disappear; we did not really entertain any opportunistic illusions. Blas Roca admitted that they had been far too uncritical of the Communist Party of the United States, but added that Browder's opinions had even been applauded by a number of outstanding Marxists in the Soviet Union. He was careful not to mention them by name, and the rest of his case was equally unsubstantiated. Six months later, the rout of the PSP was complete. At its Third Assembly in January 1946, members vied with one another in beating their breasts; speaker after speaker mounted the platform to confess his sinful ways. Yet the Party leaders remained at their posts, and at the end of their deliberations published a document with the brave title "To Battle!"[45]

But to what battle? Battle against whom? With what allies? Could the Party really start from scratch, forget its alliance with Batista, the years of Browderism, and resume its great anti-imperialist and anti-capitalist battle of former years? It was utterly compromised and completely isolated; only a small band of the ever faithful, a minority with a religious turn of mind, was prepared to follow its latest twists and turns. The "utter incomprehension" of most Cubans now forced the PSP to live completely under the wing of Moscow, to place its few remaining hopes in the success of the U.S.S.R. Now the Soviet Union had just entered the era of Zhdanovism, of wholesale repression and of Russian superpatriotism. In the circumstances, it took a great deal of courage to preach these strange doctrines in Cuba, but there was little hope that they would produce any response. As the mouthpiece of an alien world, the PSP was forced to vegetate on the fringe of Cuban society, in an atmosphere of cold hostility.

Life in that atmosphere was exceedingly uncomfortable. The Cold War was now at its height, and the ruling *Auténticos,* anxious to find absolution for their leftist trends of former days, beat the anti-Communist drum all the more loudly, directing their attacks chiefly at the Communist trade unions, the last strongholds of the PSP. And they succeeded in smashing them with criminal violence,[46] after encouraging political gangsterism

45. See Resolutions of the Third National Assembly of the PSP, held in Havana, on January 24–28, 1946.
46. Many trade union leaders were assassinated by gangsters in the pay of the government. The most famous, Jesús Menéndez, leader of the sugar workers, was killed in 1948.

108

and completely demoralizing the country. The hopes born during the glorious days of August 1933 had survived all storms and tides, all the ups and downs of a divided Left—until the advent of the Grau government. Its failure struck a mortal blow to a great tradition. "A frustrated revolution produces caricature revolutionaries," Fidel told me quite simply when describing the atmosphere he found in 1946 at the University of Havana when, at the age of nineteen, he began his studies and took his first steps in politics.

"Constitutional legality" and violence

"History," wrote Ortega y Gasset, "proceeds by generations." Cubans often apply that maxim to their own past. They speak very highly of the revolutionary generation of the '30s, sadly of the hopeless generation that took over, and enthusiastically of the next, which rediscovered the path of victorious revolution under Castro. This is obviously no more than a rough and ready guide: a generation does not arise fully armed, like Minerva from the head of Jupiter. The generation without hope had close links with the generation of the '30s, and without either the Castroists could never have become what they are. In short, the "lost children" of the middle generation represented a tradition and a potential that political circumstances and the lack of leaders simply caused to fall into temporary disrepair.

There is no doubt that between 1934 and the fall of the constitutional republic in 1952 the rebellious Left practiced violence for the sake of violence. Those "stunted revolutionaries" in rival cliques whom Fidel discovered at the University of Havana in 1946 were armed to the teeth but no longer very revolutionary. They harked back to their libertarian traditions but it was not in the name of the great ideas that they killed or banded together. An armed group must needs replenish its ammunition, recruit new fighters, obtain financial backing. Survival becomes an end in itself, particularly when the situation prevents any positive line of action. Each year, these "revolutionaries" would piously celebrate May 8, the anniversary of Antonio Guiteras' death, only to resume their battles for the monopoly in the sale of duplicated lecture notes immediately afterward. They held rich students to ransom, traded in diplomas, completely undermined the work of the FEU (*Federación Estudiantil Universitaria*) and, for good measure, terrorized the teaching staff. Common gangsters? Yes and no. Some undoubtedly were just that; others were dupes; but most were simply rebels, venting their spite on a mediocre and corrupt society. Moreover, terrorism in its various forms had always flourished in Cuba; it was not the invention of these young people. The guardians of the law, in particular, were in the habit of employing paid killers, whose recklessness increased as they continued to go free, gaining "experience." Even during the '20s, under the "liberal" Alfredo Zayas, it was rumored in Havana that all crimes on the island could be traced back to the presidential palace. Zayas' successor, Machado, went one better: he sent his killers abroad as well, and publicly took credit for the assassination of Julio Antonio Mella in Mexico. And when Batista came to power in 1934, he beat all records in this field; he very discreetly promulgated a law that enabled him to pass the death sentence on any person denounced by the police.

Violence by the authorities and violence by the opposition had thus become part of the normal political struggle in Cuba. But after the fall of the short-lived Grau-Guiteras government, the opposition was forced to work under conditions that left little room for constraint. No one today would want to justify its bloody *tiroteos* (skirmishes): they involved far too many innocent victims. But it would be idle to deny that their violence sprang from that "crisis of a whole nation," from that very crisis respectable politicians were so anxious to sweep under the carpet. It is in this context that we must read the curious history of the so-called "action groups."

Demoralized by the overthrow of the Grau government, the Cuban Left succumbed to what some observers have called a

The Communists and the Revolution

case of "geographical fatalism." Cubans, like Mexicans and Latin Americans in general, had long had a strong feeling that they were much too far from God and much too near to the United States.[47] The "realists" among them had always contended, since the end of Spanish rule, that the island must simply strive for home rule inside the North American Union. José Martí had challenged this thesis, but when Cuba achieved independence, an entire class of *compradores,* seeking nothing but immediate profit, continued to clamor for what they so euphemistically called "autonomy within the American realm." And after 1934, the Left, even its most intransigent members, came to hold that Cuba could not hope for any more. They did not shout this fact from the rooftops, but in practice they dropped their anti-imperialist demands. Jorge Mañach summed it all up very neatly when he said that no one could make a revolution at the very mouth of the Mississippi without the United States vomiting its warships onto the island.[48] No one tried to refute him; all parties were agreed that Cuba must resign herself to American tutelage; all she could possibly ask for was some of the trappings that usually went with the American way of life, to wit, democratic institutions. In fact, from 1935 onward, the Cuban opposition, Communists included, never asked for anything better.

And so Cuba became the theater of a great democratic charade that lasted for nearly fifteen years (from 1935 to 1952). The celebrations were only just marred by a few skirmishes backstage. The front was littered with the same old props: Cuba had remained a country of shocking social contrasts. The rural areas were poverty-stricken and unemployment reached the fantastic level of 25 per cent of the total labor force. True, the expansion of Havana had helped the country's recovery in the '30s, and the rise of sugar prices during the Second World War

47. The Mexican president Porfirio Díaz (1830–1915) had exclaimed: "Poor Mexico, so far from God, so near to the United States!"
48. Quoted by Raúl Roa in his classic *La Bouffa Subversiva* (Havana, 1936).

111

enabled the treasury to build up reserves of foreign credits. But even then, economic development continued to lag behind population growth.[49] The chief concern of Cuba's statesmen was to control the sugar production so as to cause a rise—or at least no drop—in the world sugar price.

But how could anyone possibly hope to run a "liberal" democracy against a background of glaring inequality, and with a degree of social injustice that favored nothing so much as corruption? In Havana, people said that the 1940 constitution resembled a beautiful virgin: she was lovely to behold, but no one could savor her charms. Most of the clauses restricting the despotic powers of the rich had never been applied, and it was clear that they would remain dead letters unless there was a radical change in Cuba's relationship with the United States. In the early days, the Communist Party had gone out of its way to demonstrate that the corruption of politicians and governments was not a matter of chance, that it did not depend on the immorality of certain ministers but on the system as a whole. And then almost overnight, the Party had become the most eloquent and uncritical champion of the system.

Only *los violentes* now perturbed the national symphony, but their *tiroteos* were no substitute for reasoned social arguments. From the very start their weakness had been the direct consequence of their special links with one of the legal parties. The action groups sprang up in 1934, after Batista's "great betrayal," at a time when the prestige of Dr. Grau was at its height. The latter was extolled as the only honest revolutionary president, as a true patriot and a friend of youth, one who had been brutally deposed by the dregs of the army in the pay of foreigners. Members of the *Directorio* and a host of young sympathizers accordingly engaged in clandestine struggle, their eyes hopefully turned to Miami where the ex-president had sought refuge. Dr. Grau had just founded a new party with the same name that

49. Julio Alienes y Urosa claims in the book from which I quoted earlier that Cuban economic growth rarely exceeded 2 per cent per annum during the entire existence of the Constitutional Republic (1940–1952).

The Communists and the Revolution

José Martí had once bestowed on his: the Cuban Revolutionary Party. To this glorious name he even added the adjective *auténtico* lest anyone doubt the fact that he was authentically engaged in the struggle against tyranny. His armed partisans in Cuba fully expected that, like Martí, he would one day return to the island and expel the hated tyrant.

Dr. Grau himself never entertained such rash ideas. He contented himself with sibylline pronouncements, and left the task of interpreting his intentions to whomever it pleased. In truth, he was just another demagogue, and one too mediocre to have the least ideas of his own. Had he stayed on the island, he might well have continued to live in the shadow of the anti-Machadoist revolt, sharing the radical views of his former companions. But in Miami he heard quite a different tune, and his democratic soul readily succumbed to the new siren strains. And so the great war of liberation was never launched; when Dr. Grau returned to Cuba it was quite peacefully, in a U.S. plane, after Batista had signed the 1938 agreement on the restoration of "constitutional legality."

This "happy ending" did not quite satisfy the action groups in the *Auténtico* Party, which had suffered savagely from Batista's repression and had lost its best fighters. They completely failed to understand how their great idol could lend support, in exchange for a few vague promises, to a regime born of a military putsch. In consolation, they benefited from the general amnesty that was part of the new agreement and could henceforth function with complete impunity inside the university.[50] Dr. Grau had lost some of his prestige, but he nevertheless remained Batista's only opponent of any weight—the Communists, as we saw, had meanwhile joined the dictator's camp. And so the action groups as a whole decided to stay loyal to their leader. This was an inevitable but fatal step; a revolutionary

50. University autonomy was restored by Batista as early as 1937, as a token of his good faith. In 1940, it was made a fundamental law of the Republic.

113

movement that has strong ties with a party as unrevolutionary and as unscrupulous as the *Auténticos* was bound to degenerate, as indeed it did soon afterward. Recruitment presented no problem. The university itself was an unending source of members, because the new generation felt, as keenly as its predecessors, the futility of living in a society incapable of guaranteeing it even a minimum of human dignity. The workers' suburbs and the unemployed also provided their quota of volunteers. All were ready to fight, albeit the targets seemed hard to define. Batista had confined his shock troops to the barracks; his chief henchmen were now officers, and he had few adherents outside the army. To fight Batista therefore meant taking the army barracks by storm, no easy task at a time of peace and national reconciliation. The only government supporters at which one could hit out with relative impunity were the Communists. They were numerous at the university and busied themselves in all spheres of social life. True, they too had their strong-arm squads, led by the formidable Rolando Masferrer (of whom we shall have occasion to speak again), yet they were more vulnerable than the army. And so the action groups gradually became the shock troops of an anti-Communist crusade. This role did not suit the more politically conscious among them who, at the beginning of the '40s, quit this questionable struggle, leaving the field to more violent and less politically radical men. The result was internal conflict, and the emergence of clans, each swearing blind obedience to a leader. Such "movements" would have caused a scandal in most democratic countries; in Cuba people preferred to keep silent about them. The Communists were the only ones to protest and to insist that Dr. Grau, as leader of the opposition, denounce his terrorist gangs. But Dr. Grau demurred; he felt that the action groups might prove useful to him later, the more so as he had his doubts about Batista's real intentions. He preferred to keep a reserve army capable of replying, in case of need, to a new wave of government terror. It was not until he came to power in 1944 that the groups began to constitute a threat to Grau himself; now the guardian of law and order, he decided to disband them.

The Communists and the Revolution

Elsewhere such draconic measures would have triggered off a crisis; in Cuba the problem could be solved quite simply, and to the satisfaction of all concerned. The only truly national industry—that is, the only one completely under Cuban control—was the State. It put ministers in control of considerable funds, which they could use to build luxury villas or to create additional jobs for their relatives, friends, and sympathizers. It was largely thanks to this generous arrangement that Havana was so prosperous. The appetite of the *Auténticos* had been further whetted by their long sojourn in the opposition, where they had been forced to make do with mere crumbs. No wonder therefore that, in 1944, the new ministers set about their business with a will, dipping their hands so deep into the state coffers that their zeal took even the oldest experts by surprise.

The Minister of Education, José Manuel Alemán, for example, had the distinction of being described as the perpetrator of the "greatest theft of the century":[51] he transferred the total funds of his ministry to Florida, and invested them in enterprises that proved to be far more profitable than national education. Now this type of man was tailor-made for buying off the leaders of the university action groups. His colleague in the Ministry of Labor, Carlos Prío Socarrás,[52] used the funds of his department to subsidize "revolutionaries" while they rid the trade unions of the "Communist yoke." Finally, the Ministry of the Interior found permanent jobs for many action group officials whose experience in strong-arm tactics made them natural candidates for the police force.

The Grau government worked discreetly, of course, careful not to offend the parliamentary opposition, or to challenge the ideological basis of the action groups. At no price must these young idealists be driven into the arms of less accommodating

51. The title of an article in the *American Mercury* (February 1952) by Sam Boal and Serge Fliegers. They told in some detail how Minister Alemán loaded all the departmental funds onto trucks for transport to Florida. I am quoting from *Juventúd Rebelde,* January 5, 1969.
52. Carlos Prío Socarrás succeeded Dr. Grau as president of the Republic in 1948.

guides. The two main groups were therefore encouraged to preserve the same rhetoric with which they had fought against the "rotten regime." The first, the *Movimiento Socialista Revolucionario* (the MSR), was led by Mario Salabarria, the second, the *Unión Insurreccional Revolucionaria*, by Emilio Tró. Unfortunately for Grau, they continued to fight each other mercilessly; indeed the two leaders were such sworn enemies that they were determined on mutual extermination even when both of them had become high police officials.

Into this explosive environment there burst, in 1946, a forceful young man, brimming with energy, sure of himself, and determined to make himself heard. Fidel Castro was not the usual freshman; from the very start, his dynamic qualities were apparent to all his fellow students. He immediately gained a circle of supporters (and they are proud of it to this day), young men who admired his oratory and his obvious powers of leadership. Fidel was the son of a fairly well-to-do farmer, but quite the opposite of a spoiled child. He had only just enough money to get by, i.e., he was one of that group of students who must use all their ingenuity to supplement their allowance. But the *dolce vita* did not interest Fidel in the least, and he despised all those who pursued it. He was a man of action, a patriot in the tradition of his native Oriente, a man with a passionate interest in politics.

Fidel rarely speaks of his parents, but one day in 1961, he made the following public confession: "I have been shaped by the worst of reactions, and have wasted many years of my life in an atmosphere of obscurantism, superstition, and lies."[53] It was obviously not in the Jesuit colleges at Santiago or Havana that he was given a taste for nonconformist thought and acquired a taste for politics.

Fidel Castro looked like the sort of student destined to join one of the action groups. He was determined, knew how to handle a gun, and his political zeal, coupled with his lack of

53. Fidel's address to young intellectuals on June 30, 1961.

theoretical training, ought to have driven him straight into the arms of those who spoke about a future insurrection while contenting themselves with the distribution of offices in the student federation. But Fidel had quite different ideas; from the very start of his student career he showed a singular capacity for living out the experiences of his generation without falling prisoner to them.

Mario Salabarria's *Movimiento Socialista Revolucionario* quickly realized that this ambitious individualist might become dangerous, and decided to get rid of him before it was too late. Fidel had a miraculous escape from an ambush, and approached the *Unión Insurreccional Revolucionaria,* the only group capable of keeping his enemies at bay. But he refused to surrender his independence or submit to UIR discipline. Instead, he made the best of a bad situation and took full advantage of his close contacts with a large section of a youth movement engaged in pseudo-revolution. And though he himself was far too intelligent to be drawn into such follies, the Communist paper *Hoy* nevertheless saw fit in 1947 to denounce him as a gangster.[54] For the past twenty years, all his enemies have vainly tried to dig up evidence in support of this charge. In fact, Fidel was to distinguish himself a few years later by his scorching denunciations of gangsterism; moreover, his first contributions to the journal *Alerta,* and his first appearances at the bar, were in defense of victims of pseudo-revolutionaries in the pay of the police.

Fidel has never been one to take to adventure for adventure's sake; his student comrades, even those who have admitted that they failed to appreciate all his great qualities, are unanimous on that point. But despite his obvious prudence and a fine sense of discernment quite unusual in one so young, he was unable to avoid all the snares set by demagogues skilled in exploiting youthful generosity. In the spring of 1947, when these men called for volunteers to liberate Santo Domingo from the Trujillo dictatorship, Fidel was one of the first to join up. The

54. Copy missing from incomplete collection in National Library.

target had been extremely well chosen. Of Cuba's three national heroes, José Martí, Máximo Gómez, and Antonio Maceo, the second was a Dominican, who had come to Cuba solely in order to rid the island of the Spanish yoke.[55] Young Cubans felt that they owed a great debt of gratitude to Máximo Gómez' homeland. And for the more politically conscious among them, the Trujillo regime was the incarnation of evil; its very existence was a blot on the reputation of Latin America. In the circumstances, what could have been simpler than to direct the fury of young Cubans from the continued injustice prevailing in their own country to the festering cancer of Trujilloism?

The whole campaign was organized in the name of the MSR, but Fidel's independence within the UIR was so well known that he was allowed to join the expedition. Mario Salabarria, in any case, was keeping in the background so as to disguise the real nature of the whole enterprise. One of the three main leaders of the expedition was Rolando Masferrer, who had fought in the Spanish Civil War, was a leader of the Young Communist League, and was later put in charge of the Communist Party's strong-arm squad. At the time of the expedition, Masferrer was only twenty-nine years old but already a man steeled in battle and intrigue. His idealism had evaporated over the years, but not his liking for violence. He had left the PSP in 1945, founded his own paper, the *Tiempo en Cuba,* and made new friendships with men the world over who knew how to take care of themselves in a corrupt and hypocritical world. And since he was able and intelligent, he seemed cut out for success.[56] Still, in 1947 he lacked the power to impose himself

55. General Máximo Gómez distinguished himself during the first phase of the war, and José Martí made him commander in chief of the Cuban army. Together they issued the Montecristi Manifesto after the resumption of hostilities in 1895. After victory, General Máximo Gómez refused to meddle in the politics of a country in which he was a stranger. Cubans treat him as a national hero and also admire him as a pioneer in the art of guerrilla warfare.

56. Rolando Masferrer is an outstanding illustration of the moral decadence of a certain type of revolutionary. He became a senator under

as commander in chief on the small liberation army, and so had to share power with two *Auténticos,* namely Eufemio Fernández and Manolo Castro. Eufemio, another expert on violence, had been in the thick of every battle waged by the action groups. Manolo Castro,[57] president of the FEU, was a friend of Minister José Manuel Alemán, from whom he was able to obtain financial backing for the expedition, over and above the subsidy of 350,000 dollars voted by President Perón of the Argentine.

At first everything went according to plan. Lest they inculpate the Cuban government, the "liberators" pitched camp on Cayo Confites, a reef almost halfway between Cuba and Santo Domingo, and so barren that no country had bothered to lay claim to it. A simple flat rock, one kilometer long and a little narrower, this Cayo could not boast a single tree. There was no escaping the sweltering heat or the tropical downpours. Worse still, clouds of flies and mosquitoes plagued the 1,500 freedom fighters throughout their stay, so much so that veterans of the war in the Pacific declared that life on Cayo Confites was far more unbearable than jungle warfare against the Japanese. The younger expedition members, such as Fidel, were suddenly brought face to face with all the horrors of the soldier's trade in a tropical climate.

All this did not discourage them, however. They kept training meticulously and patiently and wondered what battles they would have to wage in other parts of Latin America, once Trujillo had been defeated. All were agreed that the liberation of Nicaragua from the Somoza regime came next on the list, followed by the overthrow of all the remaining dictatorships on

---

Batista and ended up with an army of professional killers—"Masferrer's Tigers"—who distinguished themselves by their counterrevolutionary deeds. He later made his fortune and emigrated to Florida, where he took part in the CIA preparations for the Playa Girón landing in 1961.

57. The more honest of the two, Manolo Castro, was killed soon after his return from the expedition, in the middle of Central Park, Havana. His killers were never found, or even sought. It is said that he was drawn into the adventure without realizing all the implications, and eventually became a witness who knew too much.

the continent. They decided to call their small band the American Army of Liberation.

As far as the first battle was concerned anyway, everything was prepared: the suicide battalion bearing the name of Antonio Guiteras would land in the enemy capital and draw Trujillo's fire. The three remaining battalions, bearing the names of Máximo Gómez, José Martí, and César Augusto Sandino,[58] would profit from this diversion to attack the city from the flanks and encircle the enemy. Each battalion was being trained for its special task and, after sixty days of intense preparation, the troops were anxious to move out.

But the order for the attack did not come. There were negotiations for further contingents of volunteers, for air cover, and there was talk of the purchase of a ship specially equipped for the landing. And while the expeditionary forces were kept waiting, life on the reef became increasingly unbearable. Food, at the best of times strongly seasoned with insects, disappeared; tempers grew increasingly frayed, and thefts, feuds, and even *tiroteos* became a common occurrence. Discipline declined from day to day. And still the phantom boat did not turn up.

The Grau government which at first was only too delighted to see so many young hotheads leave for foreign parts, had suddenly begun to have second thoughts. Havana was rife with rumors as to the real intentions of the leaders of the expedition: they were said to be in contact with ambitious politicians and planning a coup d'état. The name of Minister Alemán was on everyone's lips. Nothing of all this was certain, nothing could be proved, but all things being equal, nothing about the rumors was improbable either. In the circumstances, President Grau decided that there was no harm in taking precautions. In any case, he thought it highly imprudent to place so many guns in the hands of young men who worshiped the memory of the great liberators. The commander in chief of the Cuban army, General

58. César Augusto Sandino, a Nicaraguan revolutionary, has become a legendary figure following his resistance to U.S. occupation of his country in 1928. It took the Americans six years of war to best him.

Pérez Damera, received orders to disperse the men on Cayo Confites. The official leaders of the expedition protested as a matter of form, but offered no real resistance.[59]

Carlos Franqui, who was present on Cayo Confites, half as a *franco-tirador,* and half as a journalist, has told me that Fidel, furious at the orders to disperse, proposed to Juan Bosch, who was also present on the reef, to recruit a group of fifty men and to wage guerrilla war on Santo Domingo with this small band. Bosch declined to fall in with the plans of this young man who had only just celebrated his twentieth birthday.

It is easy to imagine Fidel's state of mind when he returned to Havana in October 1947, after having wasted three long months. Adding insult to injury, some of his friends now informed him that he had fallen for a gigantic hoax; the whole affair had been staged by Mario Salabarria, leader of the MSR and subsequently head of the Police Investigation Department, for the purpose of tricking and liquidating his old enemy Emilio Tró, the leader of the UIR and now Director of the Police Academy. Salabarria had carefully kept a few shock detachments back in Havana and, one evening, had ordered them to attack the villa in which he believed Tró lived alone. In fact, Tró had prudently retained a well-armed guard of his own, and there ensued a gigantic battle, worthy of Chicago during its heyday. This was too much even for tolerant Cubans, and the government was forced to imprison Salabarria, the victor of this bloody feud. The two leaders of the action groups thus disappeared more or less noisily from the scene.[60] But the scandal rebounded on the *Auténticos;* both gangster-revolutionaries had been friends and protégés of *Auténtico* ministers and even of the president himself.

And so the year 1947 ended on a mixed note of farce and tragedy; the liberation of Latin America had collapsed on the

59. Rolando Masferrer simply gave an interview to *Bohemia* (October 12, 1947) deploring the fact that "the chief of the army had decapitated the Dominican revolution."
60. Though gangster warfare soon returned, as we shall show below.

shore of Cayo Confites, and the old revolutionary tradition of the *Directorio* had turned into an ignoble story of gangsterism. Fidel, disturbed, looked elsewhere. In April 1948, he joined Alfredo Guevara and two other comrades on a trip to Bogotá in Colombia, where he attended a conference of Latin American students. This meeting, organized chiefly by young Peronistas, began very badly: the Argentinian delegates concentrated all their fire on Great Britain and had few complaints against the United States, whereas the Cubans took the opposite view. This lack of a common language once again emphasized the scope and the depth of the divisions besetting the American continent.

The conference was about to fizzle out when suddenly, on April 9, an extraordinary event shook the whole of Bogotá: a hired killer had murdered Jorge Eliecer Gaitán, leader of the Liberal Party and a great champion of the poor, right in the center of the city. A few hours later, Bogotá was a blazing inferno: a furious mob seemed intent on destroying every building and so destroying the established order. In fact, the *bogotazo*[61] was not yet a revolution, it was only the first episode in a civil war that, twenty years later, still goes on in Colombia. But it drove home to Fidel the extraordinary violence smoldering just beneath the apparently peaceful surface of Latin America, and showed him its social roots: desperation and hunger. He came to realize that the fight for moral right and justice must be coupled to the fight for social betterment. This discovery left a deep mark on him. His anti-imperialism had become part of a social philosophy.

On his return to Cuba, he immersed himself in the sociological

61. On the day of this popular explosion, a conference of the Organization of American States was due to be opened in Bogotá. The U.S. press immediately accused the Communists of a plot and, carried away by its own enthusiasm, spoke of the execution of priests and other acts of "red vandalism," conveniently forgetting the real cause of the events: the assassination of Jorge Eliecer Gaitán, leader of the Colombian Left. But as Jules Dubois, a writer no one can call a pro-Communist, has explained, not a single priest was murdered in Bogotá, nor was there the slightest evidence of a Communist plot. (See J. Dubois: *Fidel Castro*, Mexico, Grijalbo, 1959.)

and political texts published by the Mexican *Fondo de la Cultura Económica*. He read Lenin's *State and Revolution* and some Marx as well. Although he was not tempted to join the PSP, he had already made friends with Communist students whose sense of discipline and organizational skills he admired. With them he founded the 30th of September Movement,[62] an anti-imperialist student league. "How many anti-imperialists do you think attended the University of Havana at that time?" he asked delegates to the Latin American Communist Party Congress in 1964. "Well, all in all there were thirty of us—including the Communists."

In fact, Cuba—three years after the end of World War II—was still smitten by its chronic disease, the corruption of public life. For some, politics meant the greased palm, for others a continuous campaign against the thieves in public office. One has only to page through the files of *Bohemia,* a weekly with a very large circulation (250,000 copies), to get the feel of this kind of atmosphere. The column headed "In Cuba" was each week crammed with cases of corruption, gangsterism, political assassinations, and public immorality on the grand scale. The editor, Miguel Angel Quevedo, made no comments; he simply published factual accounts and photographs of the victims. The result was altogether horrific. For the rest, the paper was rather humdrum. International reports neatly reflected American clichés about the Cold War—in that respect, *Bohemia* was quite indistinguishable from any run-of-the-mill Texan weekly. Sensational reports, copied faithfully from the American press, painted the Soviet Union in the blackest colors, likening it to Nazi Germany. The United States was constantly held up as the great champion of liberty. Evidently part of this approach was due to pressure from the North American business community, which no Cuban journal could escape—advertising revenue, so essential to the running of a free press, is easily turned into an

62. So called in honor of the great student demonstration of September 30, 1930.

instrument of blackmail. But that was by no means the whole story: *Bohemia* was simply preaching the pro-American doctrine which the Left had done so much to foster during the war.

To this anti-Soviet campaign, the Communists replied with extravagant praises of Stalin and the U.S.S.R. Communist propaganda hit a new low during this period of Zhdanovism and international peace congresses. In Europe, the resulting doubts were slightly allayed by memories of Stalingrad, and of the great part Communists had played in the Resistance movement, but the Cuban Party had had no hand in these events and consequently could take no credit for them. And so it stewed in its self-created ghetto, while the whole island slipped into the American orbit. Meanwhile the young members of the Anti-Imperialist League were thrown back on themselves, had to dig deep beneath the propaganda lies to discover the truth about Latin America and with it the anti-American zest of the '30s.

Their voices went largely unheard. Eduardo Chibás, an *Auténtico* senator from Oriente and a former leader of the *Directorio,* sick of the corruption he saw all around him, had just raised the banner of revolt against his own party. "Enough of corruption, enough of injustice, *vergüenza contra dinero!*"[63] he kept repeating in his weekly radio program. He caused a split in the ranks of the *Auténticos* and, in October 1947, founded the Party of the Cuban People, which he called "Orthodox" to stress his strict adherence to the ideas of José Martí. His emblem, a new broom, showed what he was about. His speeches might have come straight from the *Alma Mater,* the old anti-Machadoist paper of the *Directorio.* He issued the same appeals when he called for a fight against the thieves in government, in the name of honor, and a fight against exploitation and poverty, in the name of justice and moral dignity; and his speeches showed the same lack of clarity when it came to methods of radical change.

True, Chibás was not up against a Machado, a caricature of a

63. "Honor before money!"

dictator supported by American banks, but against a good "independent" democrat, Dr. Grau. Chibás accordingly preferred electoral battle to dynamite. He seemed to symbolize the hopes of an entire generation which at last saw a chance for decent government. The rise of the new party was spectacular. In 1948, at the end of his term in office, Dr. Grau made way for Prío Socarrás, and still the Ortodoxo Party continued to grow. In less than three years it had become the most important Cuban party, and Chibás' new broom spared no one. He accused the president himself and Minister Alemán of being involved in the shadiest of deals. Unable to support these allegations with solid evidence, and threatened with a libel case, Chibás committed suicide on August 5, 1951, during one of his weekly radio broadcasts. He ended his final address with these words: "People of Cuba, awake, this is my last warning!" The shot which put an end to his life rang out through thousands of Cuban homes. There was a furious outcry. People came out en masse to enroll in the Ortodoxo Party, which was now certain of winning the next year's presidential elections. One of its parliamentary candidates was young Fidel Castro.

But the radicalism of the Ortodoxo Party, though much watered down, was more than the rulers of Cuba were prepared to swallow. Rubén Martínez Villena summed it all up when he said: "To get rid of gangsters, you need dynamite." The elections of June 1952 never took place; nine weeks before the appointed date, during the night of March 10, 1952, General Fulgencio Batista organized a new *golpe,* once again, needless to say, so as to restore "order and democracy." Next morning, Cuba woke up under a dictator.

The "Old Guard" under the hammer of revolution

Fulgencio Batista's second *golpe* was a marvelous illustration of Karl Marx's famous sally: historical facts and personages occur twice; the first time as tragedy, the second as farce. In 1934, the ex-sergeant had only been able to crush the revolutionary move-

125

ment by means of a blood bath. Eighteen years later, in 1952, he returned to power without firing a shot—after a carnival night, and with the help of a handful of soldiers. The ease of his victory took him as much by surprise as it did the rest of Cuba. President Prío was quite strong enough to defend his government; he preferred not to use his powers and slipped quietly away to Miami.

Who then carried Fulgencio Batista to the presidential palace for the second time? Could a small group of officers in the Columbia barracks really have imposed their will on the country? The Communists would later try to demonstrate that the *madrugazo* was the work of much wider social forces. According to them, it was the big landowners anxious for large reductions in the sugar crop (in 1952 the harvest beat all records and threatened to bring prices crashing down) who felt that only a strong man could impose *their* will on the small growers and on the workers likely to suffer from the proposed cuts. In other words, Batista's had been a preventive putsch meant to stem a hypothetical social crisis. Perhaps so. However, in 1952, Cuba was doing relatively well economically, at any rate as well as could be expected in a country afflicted with a chronic structural disease, i.e., with a permanent unemployment rate of 25 per cent. In contrast to 1933, there was no threat of revolution this time. The trade unions were meek and paralyzed by "mujalism,"[64] the Communists reduced to isolation and impotence.

64. Eusebio Mujal, a Trotskyist turned trade-union leader, first in the service of the *Auténticos* and later of Batista, was a union boss on the American model. He amassed a fortune but nevertheless defended, and often with great skill, the wage claims (though not the political aspirations) of his members. "Mujalism" hence came to stand for the type of trade union attitude that ends in the complete depoliticization of the workers. Opinions as to its consequences differ widely. Maurice Zeitlin explains in *Revolutionary Politics and the Cuban Working Class* (Princeton University Press, 1967) that, according to a 1962 survey, the great majority of Cuban workers was in favor of the Revolution, but a number of Castroist leaders have told me that mujalism helped to deflect the industrial proletariat—a relatively small section of the Cuban underprivileged—from active participation in the struggle and affected their attitude even after the victory of the Revolution.

126

The Communists and the Revolution

Only the Ortodoxo Party threatened the power of the *Auténticos,* but the *Ortodoxos,* too, were a bourgeois, radical-democratic party, solely concerned with purging the corrupt administration.

In fact, Batista's *golpe* was made possible chiefly by the extreme rottenness of the state. Barely six days before the coup d'état, a young advocate, Fidel Castro, painted a convincing picture of its degradation in the columns of *Alerta.* Castro had just laid charges against President Prío before the Audit Office, and his indictment began with the following words: "I am appealing to the Tribunal in the name of our homeland. Cuba, now torn by fratricidal strife, is moving toward its own destruction, is fast becoming a gambling den, a refuge for lawless men; she turns to you, in desperation, in the hope that Your Honors may yet forge a miracle and save her from constitutional and moral collapse. . . . The sole cause of the government crisis and the sea of blood is unbridled enrichment at the expense of the state. Attacks on a bank, or any other private institution, immediately mobilize all the resources of society—public opinion, the police, the tribunals. However, thanks to the inexplicable lack of a sense of social preservation and collective awareness, the continuous misappropriation of fabulous sums of public money causes no outcry. In the long run the consequences are fatal: bloodshed, demoralization, anarchy, and ruin."

Fidel was particularly incensed that, despite the scandal of 1947, gangsters should once again be operating, and on an even greater scale. The new president, Prío Socarrás, had passed a famous "Law against Gangsterism" (Law No. 5 of November 1948), but all he had done to implement it was to get the action groups to sign a truce. This truce, Fidel claimed indignantly, had not been ordered for social or humane reasons, or in the belief that repression is futile. No, it was one of the most scandalous events in the history of civilized society. Prostituting his high office, the president had capitulated unconditionally to the fratricidal groups and had bought public peace at the price of shameful concessions. Castro did not stop at general accusa-

127   E*

Guerrillas in Power

tions; he gave details of the ruses by which members of the
various action groups were enabled to draw salaries from the
various ministries without rendering any services in exchange.[65]
In addition, the presidential palace granted 18,000 dollars per
month to various groups in the form of six hundred private
fees.[66] "Without this money," Fidel concluded, "there would be
no assassinations. The revolvers with which all the killings are
done are paid for by Prío. The killers are protected by Prío. I
charge him before this tribunal with responsibility for our national tragedy, even though I may have to pay with my blood
for following the dictates of my conscience."[67]

Prío did not react to this attack, just as he did not react a
few days later to Batista's armed challenge. But then the other
political parties did not react very much more forcibly either.
At the time of the *golpe,* a group of students presented themselves at the palace to implore the president to resist. When
nothing came of this, they published a declaration of principles
in *Bohemia,*[68] bearing a motto taken from Martí: "Students are
the bulwark of liberty and its most loyal defenders." The manifesto went on to proclaim: "We shall not return to our studies
while the Constitution is being violated. . . . We call upon all
parties, organizations, and democratic groups to close ranks with
us in this noble crusade for the Republic. We exhort all students,

65. Here is a list of the fictitious appointments offered to the various
groups: Comella's group, 60 jobs; Revolutionary Executive Tribunal, 120
jobs; Insurrectional Revolutionary Union, 250 jobs; Colorado Group, 400
jobs; Masferrer Group, 500 jobs; Policarpio Group, 600 jobs. Altogether
more than 2,120 monthly "pay" packets were handed out by the Ministries
of Health, Labor, Interior, and Public Works. The leaders of the groups and
their closest associates were able to put quite a sizeable number of wage
packets into their own pockets. Thus one Manuel Vilma drew 30; Guillermo
"El Flaco" drew 28; Pepe "El Primo" drew 26; "El Boxer" drew 26; and so
on. These gratuities were all handed out by Señor Casero, secretary in the
Ministry of Public Works, on the express orders of the president of the
Republic.
66. Fidel Castro also accused President Prío of using soldiers to tend his
private estates, and worked out how much this piece of fraud cost the
treasury. Eduardo Chibás had made the same accusation two years earlier.
67. See *Alerta: "El derrumbe constitucional,"* March 4, 1952.
68. See *Bohemia,* No. 32, March 23, 1952, p. 54.

128

The Communists and the Revolution

workers, peasants, intellectuals, and public officials to raise their voice with ours, for it is the voice of the people and hence of God." This appeal, which was signed in the name of the FEU by about twenty students—including José Antonio Echeverría, who later founded a new *Directorio*—made a great impression, but did little else. Everyone in Cuba had grave apprehensions about the future, but no one was prepared to step out of turn. Miguel Angel Quevedo, editor of *Bohemia,* summed up the widespread anxiety when he wrote: "This regime will give the people nothing but persecution, death, and misery."

The Communist Party, too, roundly condemned Batista's putsch, adding a meticulous analysis of its alleged international and internal causes.[69] But having lived in a political wilderness for years, the Communists could not make their voices heard, for which they now blamed the passivity of the masses. This time there was no reference to Batista's "profound popular roots." The Cold War had started, and Batista was now unmasked as a puppet of the Americans, a man who had broken off diplomatic relations with the Soviet Union, a cynical anti-Communist, a gangster who raised the red scarecrow as a means of stepping up his reign of terror. But feeling that every cloud has a silver lining, the Communists called for the creation of a national democratic front that would topple the dictator and incidentally put an end to their own isolation.

A vain hope, seeing that the democratic parties were far more anti-Communist than anti-*Batistiano,* and did not have the least intention of compromising themselves with a partner who would have reduced to nothing what little influence they still had in the United States. Instead, they kept reminding the Americans of the former alliance between Batista and the Communists, trying to convince them that, if they really wanted to save the island from the Reds, they were betting on the wrong horse. This type of propaganda also worked inside Cuba, for Com-

69. See *Fundamentos,* April 1952, p. 431: *"El madrugón del 10 marzo tuvo un largo proceso de gestación"* (*Análisis de la comisión ejecutiva del PSP*).

munist protests that disunion among the anti-fascist ranks only served the dictator's darkest designs went completely unheard: the PSP, however well-founded its arguments, had lost the ear of the old Left and did not even suspect the existence of new forces. And so it continued to work for a popular front within the existing legal framework, when the struggle against Batista now called for a far more radical approach.

The *Ortodoxos,* although Batista's putsch had cheated them of certain victory at the polls, chose to keep silent. They were stricken with paralysis, completely crushed by their misfortune. They had never seen further than their noses, did not know what to do now, and, worse still, were beginning to crack up from within. The heady scent of power had brought into their ranks a host of timeservers, men quite unprepared for a prolonged new spell in the opposition. Moreover, Batista kept tempting many away by protesting his liberal intentions, swearing that his sole concern was the restoration of order and constitutional government. He promised to hold elections, admittedly at an indefinite future date, and gave his officers formal instructions to avoid bloodshed at any price. Life in Havana had, in fact, greatly improved since the reign of the *Auténticos.*

Only the young *Ortodoxos* were beyond such temptations but, lacking determined leaders, they were forced to act individually. Fidel Castro was one of the first to do so. On March 24, 1952, he protested formally to the Court of Constitutional Guarantees against the Batista coup d'état, and called upon the Emergency Tribunal to order the arrest of the usurper. In a long and legally polished document, he showed that Batista ought to be sentenced to more than a hundred years in prison for violations of a whole series of laws. "If, in the face of such flagrant acts of treason and sedition," he concluded, "the Tribunal fails to judge and punish, how can it ever sentence for sedition or rebellion any citizen who rises up against this illegal regime, born of treachery? To do so would be flying in the face of the most elementary principles of impartiality or justice. . . . Logic tells me that if these tribunals have any justification Batista must be punished, and if he is not, if he remains head of the state, president, prime minister, senator, civil and military commander, holder of executive and legislative power, master over the life and property of all citizens, then clearly these tribunals have ceased to exist, or have been subverted by him. Is this the terrible truth? If it is, let the honorable judges say so, let them take off their robes and resign their office. The worst thing they could do would be to keep silent, to resign themselves to a tragic situation, one that is absurd, devoid of logic, standards, sense, glory, honor, or justice."

The Court of Constitutional Guarantees rejected the appeal of advocate Fidel Castro, on the grounds that "the revolution is the fount of law." The Emergency Tribunal ignored his complaint completely. Castro himself could not have expected anything else. What he was trying to prove to the young *Ortodoxos* no less than to himself was that all attempts to get justice done through the courts were quite futile. He, for one, had decided to burn his boats. To him and to his entire generation, the revolution—the true revolution, the one he felt was needed to get rid of the dictator and to escape from the impasse into which the traditional opposition had got itself—had become the sole fount of justice and law.

His had not been an easy choice. For years past, he had fought against violence, which in Cuba had become synonymous with political degeneracy; moreover, he was deeply influenced by his legal training. But he had come to realize that violence was unavoidable now; the failure of his court case was clear proof of this, if such proof were still needed. But violence must help to break the vicious circle of Cuban politics: in the past, the young had fought and sacrificed themselves on the altar of democratic liberty only to find themselves saddled with a new dictator after yet another *golpe* or a new *cuartelazo*. All that had to change. Castro accordingly gave the word "revolution" a new meaning: though he did not yet call himself a socialist, by 1953 he had come to realize that revolution was far more than a return to the *status quo ante*.

131

This conviction forced him to act outside the parties, even outside the *Ortodoxos,* with whom he nevertheless remained associated for some time to come.[70] He had lost faith in the possible radicalization of the traditional forces, the two most important of which—the *Auténticos* and the *Ortodoxos*—although unalike on the moral plane, had proved themselves equally ineffective in action. As for the students, they were still profoundly under the influence of the action groups, and Castro had no intention of addressing himself to them. Instead he was determined to forge a new instrument of revolutionary struggle, and we shall see below how precisely he tackled this task.

There remained the problem of his relationship with the PSP, an established party like the rest but dedicated in principle to social revolution. One of its leaders told me that in May 1953—two months before the attack on the Moncada fortress—Fidel Castro passed by the Party library and asked to see him. "He didn't make much of an impression on me," this leader confessed, and he still wonders whether Fidel had come to make a deal or to discover what action the Communists themselves were planning to take. In any case, my informant did nothing about it; the conversation never got off the ground and for good reason: not even the most convincing arguments could at

70. The formal break between Castro and the *Ortodoxos* did not take place until March 19, 1956. But all along Castro had acted as an independent agent, engaging in polemics with the party and with its Youth League, and it was only gradually that he severed his ties with them. On August 16, 1955, he sent the Party Congress a message in which he declared: "The July 26th Movement does not constitute a mere trend inside the party; it is *the* revolutionary instrument of Chibasism,' with deep roots in the base of the movement." When the final break came, Castro accused the *Ortodoxos* of having adopted an opportunist line and of having succumbed to factional strife. He declared that the July 26th Movement was the real heir of Eddie Chibás, "an *Ortodoxo* who did not take his orders from the *latifundistas* like Fico Fernández Casas; from sugar kings like Gerardo Vásquez; from speculators in the stock exchange; from industrial or commercial magnates; from rich lawyers, provincial potentates, or political bosses. . . ." See Jules Dubois: *Fidel Castro* (Mexico, Grijalbo, 1959), pp. 95–97. Dubois was subsequently attacked by Castroists as a CIA agent, but at the time he was president of the Inter-American Press Association and a declared opponent of Batista. His highly informative book is, however, remarkable for its political naïveté.

132

that moment have persuaded the Party to call for armed struggle.

Castro therefore decided to go it alone. He recruited men who, like himself, had had more than enough of Batista, and who were sickened by the meekness of the opposition.[71] At first they all met in an apartment in the Vedado suburb of Havana; each member of the group would bring along or propose new recruits. Thus Jesús Montané, an accountant in the Cuban branch of General Motors, introduced Abel Santamaría, who was to become Castro's right-hand man. Another member brought along Nico López, a young worker who was to become the third in command. Together they decided to strike at the earliest possible moment, certain that a quick show of force would trigger off a general uprising on the island. They refused to take notice of the general apathy; according to them public opinion was fiercely hostile to Batista and the people were only waiting for a sign before coming out into the streets. They accordingly decided to attack the Moncada fortress in Santiago de Cuba, in Oriente, the most rebellious of all the provinces. While one group, disguised as soldiers, would seize the barracks themselves, others would capture the Palace of Justice and the local hospital; yet another group would cause a diversion at Bayamo. Then a radio appeal would be broadcast to the nation at large.

Castro selected 170 men from 1,000 candidates, but explained

71. This is how José Ponce, one of the rebel commanders, has described his own conversion: "It was in the park one evening that I made the acquaintance of Pepe Suárez, who told me what was going on. He spoke to me about Fidel, told me that he was young, that he had new ideas, and that the Movement had no links either with the past or with present-day political schemers. Then I told him: 'That suits me fine. Please keep me informed.' I remember one Saturday morning he came and told me: 'Ponce, wait for me tomorrow: we're off to Havana.' That's all he said to me." (See Carlos Franqui: *Le livre des douze* [Paris, Gallimard, 1965], p. 15.) And here is the story of Juan Almeida, a black mason who later became one of the leaders in the Sierra Maestra: "It was on the university hill that I met Fidel. . . . The first guns I ever saw were the ones he put in our hands. He started talking about the Revolution, told us what it all meant, and explained the meaning of progress and that a coup d'état is merely a step backward. He said that the young must band together, that they were a living force, that he was counting on those who had never compromised with the past" (*op. cit.* p. 16).

his precise plans to only a few of them. Arms were bought and paid for by the rebels themselves: Jesús Montané resigned his post and handed Castro all his savings; others sold their homes or their small family businesses. They arranged to meet on a farm in the Siboney district near Santiago. On the eve of July 26, 1953, Fidel distributed uniforms and arms and briefly addressed his troops. He gave those who wanted it the chance to withdraw: almost everyone stayed with him.

Then Castro's trucks made for Santiago decked out in gay flags—it was carnival night. The group led by Raúl Castro, the first to arrive, quickly seized the Palace of Justice. The second, commanded by Dr. Muñoz, and including Melba Hernández and Haydée Santamaría, occupied the hospital with no greater difficulties. But the assault on the Moncada barracks failed. The result was a massacre, not so much in battle, as by torture and cold-blooded murder. One of those put to death was Abel Santamaría, whose eyes were torn out and handed to his sister. Fidel, Raúl, and a few others made good their escape, in broken ranks, into the surrounding mountains. A week later, exhausted by hunger and fatigue, they allowed themselves to be taken prisoner; their lives were miraculously saved by a sympathetic officer. Later, Fidel explained how this experience had taught him that the mountains provide outstanding shelter, but only to men who have been trained and equipped to survive in them.

The captured men were brought before the Military Tribunal in September 1953; two days afterward, the court decided to hear Fidel's case separately. He was tried behind closed doors on October 23, in a small ward of the Santiago hospital, and chose to defend himself. His defense plea, "History will absolve me," was to become the charter of the future July 26th Movement. Fidel was sentenced to fifteen years' imprisonment in a penitentiary on the Isle of Pines.[72]

72. For Moncada, see particularly Fidel Castro: *History Will Absolve Me* (Cape Edition No. 23, Jonathan Cape, London, 1968); *Haydée habla del Moncada* (Havana, Instituto del Libro, 1967); Carlos Franqui, *op. cit.;* and the accounts of Celia and Haydée in Robert Merle, *op cit.*

The Communists and the Revolution

The failure of the Moncada attack was not the end, but the beginning, of the Castroist campaign. Batista was forced to drop his mask of the honest man anxious to re-establish law and order. He now unleashed a campaign of ferocious repression, decreed a state of emergency and re-introduced censorship. Then, a few months later, no doubt so as to calm his American protectors—two successive U.S. Ambassadors, Gardner and Smith, were his personal friends—he promised that elections would be held in 1954. He hoped that his old rival, Dr. Grau San Martín, would act as official opposition candidate thus lending the elections a minimum of credibility. The old leader of the *Auténticos* played along for a bit, but a few weeks before the poll he withdrew from the competition, certain that the die was cast.

In fact, Moncada forced not only Batista, but the entire opposition, to take a clear stand toward Fidel Castro. On the remote Isle of Pines, he had become a national figure of considerable renown; everyone knew that in his prison cell he was spinning the threads of a new political network. His friends seemed to be everywhere, and everyone was convinced that, sooner or later, Batista would be forced to release him. In May 1954 this strange prisoner even succeeded in producing a cabinet crisis: in an open letter, the secretary to Hermida, the Minister of the Interior, denounced his chief for having attended a secret meeting with Castro on the Isle of Pines. The secretary, Rafael Díaz Balart—Fidel Castro's brother-in-law, but a supporter of Batista nonetheless[73]—was forced to tender his resignation, and so was the minister himself.

Fidel was released from prison in May 1955, as part of a general amnesty. Journalists were waiting for him at the gates, and accompanied him all the way to the capital by boat and train. At Havana station the crowd gave him a triumphant reception. Fidel moved to Vedado, not as a repentant prisoner

73. Fidel was still a student when he married Mirta Díaz Balart, by whom he had one son, Fidelito. She asked for a divorce while Fidel was a prisoner on the Isle of Pines.

rejoicing in his freedom but as a revolutionary leader who announced, *urbi et orbi*, that the struggle was about to be resumed. A few months later he left for Mexico, but not without first promising an armed return to liberate the island. The movement he left behind was embryonic, but his message had already captured the imagination of many. Those who had been with him at Moncada did their utmost to rejoin him abroad.

In Mexico, Fidel did not allow himself to be forgotten. He lost no opportunity of addressing young or old, of placing flowers on monuments to the heroes of the Mexican revolution, of calling for solidarity with enslaved Cuba, of collecting funds. In fact, he acted as the leader of a fraternal nation on an official visit, certain of returning to a governmental palace temporarily occupied by intruders. The Mexican police had a hard time keeping up with this whirlwind of a man, who turned up everywhere, and aroused curiosity wherever he appeared. In addition to his vast public activity, Fidel Castro also engaged in semi-clandestine work to recruit, equip, and train an armed contingent capable of driving the intruder from Cuba.

Recruitment for the future guerrilla force posed few problems: young men rushed the house of María Antonia, a Cuban exile in Mexico who was acting as hostess to Fidel and his staff. A Cuban-born ex-colonel of the Spanish republican army, Alberto Bayo, gladly agreed to train the volunteers, though he had to do it very quietly—Mexico, despite, or perhaps because of, her traditional violence, found it difficult to tolerate armed strangers on her territory.

But the real problem did not lie there; it was of a political nature. The Cuban dictator, too stupid to grasp Fidel's grand design, had readily fallen into the latter's trap. He no longer attacked the *Auténticos* and the Communists—as he had done on the morrow of Moncada—but concentrated his fire on the July 26th Movement, thus greatly enhancing its popularity. Fidel was jubilant: "This is the worst mistake of his life."[74]

74. Quoted in Jules Dubois, *op. cit.*

But the rest of the opposition was unwilling to accept Fidel's leadership. Some, and particularly the old *Ortodoxos,* accused him of mythomania and opportunism, and alleged that his "flight to Mexico" had disqualified him from the leadership stakes.

This type of negative publicity did not suit Fidel, who was anxious to enlist the direct support of the entire nation. While his own movement was still weak, particularly during his imprisonment on the Isle of Pines, he had warned his comrades against having anything to do with the *Auténticos* or the rest. "Any pact with them would be a grave ideological deviation," he wrote to Haydée Santamaría, to Melba Hernández, and later to Dr. Faustino Pérez.[75] As late as January 1956, he sent a hard-hitting article to *Bohemia.*[76] It was entitled *Frente a todos* (We stand alone) and told his critics a number of home truths. But at the same time he let it appear that a dialogue between all patriots was a matter of urgency. Soon afterward he had a series of meetings with representatives of the various groups; he even saw ex-President Prío, whom he had previously accused of a whole series of crimes.[77]

These dialogues proved rather abortive. Only one organization took a positive view: the *Directorio Revolucionario.* This student movement, which had earned its laurels during the '30s, was resuscitated in 1955 by José Antonio Echeverría, a young

75. Faustino Pérez, like Armando Hart and a great many other Castroist leaders, began his political career soon after the coup d'état in the ranks of the National Revolutionary Movement (MNR) founded by García Bárcena, a professor of philosophy and a veteran of the '30s. That is why none of them participated in the Moncada attack or rallied to Fidel until they realized that Bárcena's attempt to subvert the army was bound to fail.

76. Published on January 8, 1956.

77. The meeting between ex-President Prío and Fidel Castro took place in September 1956 at McAllen, Texas, on the Mexican border. Fidel went to Reynosa on the Río Grande, and lacking a U.S. visa, crossed the border illegally, dressed as a worker. According to another version he swam across the river. Later the *Auténticos* spread the rumor that *Granma* had been bought with their money. Faustino Pérez has denied this categorically; he told me that the money was collected in Havana from a very large number of people with very small earnings.

Catholic. Like his predecessors, he did not want the movement to remain confined to the university. Hence, while he jealously kept control of his learned enclave and did not allow anybody, not even the July 26th Movement, to gain a foothold in it, he tried to carry political action from the campus into the streets. In December 1955, for instance, the *Directorio* gave full support to the striking sugar workers, and, in general, it behaved as if it were the sole guardian of the revolutionary tradition of the '30s. Even though the members of the *Directorio* were not completely disinterested in what would happen after Batista's overthrow, they gave priority to immediate action. Their relationship with the July 26th Movement was therefore an alliance of fighters and not of politicians.

In September 1956, José Antonio Echeverría went to Mexico, where in the name of the "young revolutionary generation" he and Fidel signed a joint action pact and an appeal to the nation. The *Directorio* continued to remain an independent body but remained loyal to its promises in Mexico; it fought Batista passionately and with skill. Moreover, and this was not its least merit, it rid the universities of the last vestiges of gangsterism, the evil that had infested them for so long.

The relationship between the Communist Party and these two "violent" movements constitutes a chapter in itself.[78]

At the time of the Moncada attack the PSP, on July 25 and 26, was busy with a semi-clandestine national conference in Santiago. The dictator was therefore quick to blame them for what he called this "criminal incident" and to hunt them down.[79] The Party leaned over backward to refute the allegation; its

78. The *Directorio* fought against Communist ideas at the university on the ground that these allegedly turned the students from their prime objective, the struggle against Batista. Hence, the *Directorio* did its utmost to prevent the formation of Communist cells, and its quarrel with the PSP became so bitter that it culminated in the Marcos Rodríguez drama (see pp. 285–286).

79. Batista's police never bothered about the consistency of its accusations—at the same time it also accused Prío and Sánchez Arango of having fomented the revolt. They, too, denied the allegations and disowned Castro's action.

leaders explained that they had been in Santiago by chance, for the sole purpose of celebrating Blas Roca's birthday. And to drive their innocence home even further, they issued violent denunciations of Castro's adventurism. One of the members of the PSP's Political Bureau, Joaquín Ordoqui, distinguished himself above all the rest by the intemperance of his vituperations.

Seven years later, in 1960, Blas Roca was to tell the Eighth National Assembly of the PSP that, seen in perspective, July 26, 1953, marked a decisive turning point in Cuban politics, and this for three reasons: "Because it brought on to the political stage young partisan leaders determined on revolutionary action and infused with revolutionary ideas; because it demonstrated that armed struggle constitutes a prime lever in the destruction of tyrannies; because it forced Batista to unmask himself."[80] Unfortunately this "great perspective" cruelly eluded the Communists at the moment when they most needed it. For in August 1953 when, after the shock of the revolt, the PSP decided to examine the situation more calmly, it arrived at conclusions that were no less damning than the first. In a special "Letter to Militants"[81]—the Party paper *Hoy* had meanwhile been banned —it characterized the Moncada assault as "a putschist attempt, a desperate form of adventurism, typical of petty bourgeois circles lacking in principle and implicated in gangsterism." Needless to say, this line of argument did little to make the Communists more popular among the young rebels.

Worse still, the Party developed and published theories on its formal opposition to armed struggle. "A putsch frightens the masses and hence paralyzes them completely." The Moncada attack had only helped Batista, and this at precisely the time he was finding it impossible to meet the wave of wage claims, and when it was essential not to give him the least pretext for anti-Communist and anti-working class repression. And because Ba-

---

80. See Blas Roca: *The Cuban Revolution: Report to the Eighth National Congress of the PSP of Cuba* (New York, 1961) , p. 41.
81. See *Carta de la Comisión Ejecutiva Nacional de PSP a todos los Organismos del Partido,* August 30, 1953 (mimeographed) .

139

tista was aiming chiefly at the destruction of the Communist Party, the primary task of all true democrats was to defend that party and to press for its recognition. Beyond that, there was a most urgent need for a national democratic front; since the forces of repression were now directed at the entire opposition, it was essential to close ranks; beyond that the democratic forces must get up petitions and do everything necessary to ensure greater freedom for the people and the revision of Batista's electoral roll, which was particularly disfavorable to the Communists.

This was not a particularly ambitious program, even if it included, as always, a long list of reforms for which the whole of Cuba was crying out. The chances of a pact between all the "democratic" parties were as slight after Moncada as they had been before, but the PSP preferred this to union with the "violent" men whose actions they abhorred. In any case, the Communists could not help feeling anxious about the growing popularity of the July 26th Movement, particularly during 1953–56. Castro's triumphant reception on his return from prison, and the solicitude of all the other parties, indicated clearly that the Castroist specter would be extremely difficult to exorcise. And certain Party leaders, recalling the "errors of the '30s," had begun to ask themselves if Castro might not perhaps be a new Antonio Guiteras; an Antonio Guiteras no longer isolated but transformed into a leader of men, a builder of revolutionary forces, a man of the hour, a revolutionary organizer on the grand scale pursuing clear-cut aims. We know that the whole question was thrashed out by the top brass of the PSP, but we cannot tell to what effect since the clandestine Communist press did not breathe a word about these discussions. Still, according to reliable witnesses, the anti-Castroist line[82] was at-

82. Under the repressive regime of 1953, the Political Bureau of the PSP, formerly comprised of ten people, was reduced to an inner circle consisting of Blas Roca, Aníbal Escalante, Joaquín Ordoqui, Severo Aguire, and Manuel Luzardo. Since Blas Roca was out of the country most of the time, actual control passed into the hands of Aníbal Escalante.

tacked by two influential leaders, namely Osvaldo Sánchez and Carlos Rafael Rodríguez. The absence of Blas Roca[83] and the problem of taking disciplinary measures under clandestine conditions, joined to news of the dramatic de-Stalinization campaign in the U.S.S.R., forced the PSP to relax its habitual rigidity. The Party line remained unchanged, but Communists, as individuals, were free at last to make personal contact with the Castroists.

Mexico was teeming with Cuban Communists at the time. Some, more or less estranged from the Party, were former university comrades of Fidel's, such as Alfredo Guevara; others, such as Lázaro Peña, were trade unionists; still others were former friends of Raúl Castro's. There was a great deal of coming and going between the house of María Antonia and "Communist headquarters" in Mexico. Fidel, we have already said, was ready to have discussions with anybody; he had never been one to tremble at contact with a Red. But neither he nor the Communists were anxious to draw attention to their irregular meetings; Castro because he did not want to compromise himself with the PSP, and the Communists because they had no authority to negotiate, however unofficially.

Instead, the Communists simply informed *el doctor* Castro of the Cuban workers' mood following the sugar strike of December 1955, and gave him their views on the spread of popular discontent. Castro in turn informed them of his projects and of the date of his proposed landing. In his opinion, the situation was so tense, particularly in the towns, that his arrival would cause an explosion, not only in Santiago—where an uprising was being organized—but even in Havana and the rest of the country. The Communists did not share his optimism and advised him to prepare the ground more carefully. So much we know—the rest is pure speculation.

Fidel obviously did not want to wait. He had formally committed himself, for had he not declared: "We shall be free men

83. In 1955–56, for instance, Blas Roca spent a whole year in Peking.

this year or else we shall be martyrs"? Come what may, he was determined to land in Cuba before the end of 1956. The suspense he had created by his announcement served him as a formidable psychological lever:[84] all Cubans held their breath as they awaited the outcome of his great historical wager. Meanwhile he was being harassed by the Mexican police who seemed unwilling to tolerate the presence of his small army for much longer.

On November 26, 1956, when an old tub, the *Granma,* set sail, the last phase in the struggle against Batista was begun. On December 2 the rebels disembarked, or rather foundered, as Raúl Castro and Faustino Pérez put it, a few hundred yards off the Cuban coast. They had been expected two days earlier, and a few miles farther, on a quiet beach at Niquero. Celia Sánchez[85] had brought up the camouflaged trucks that were to drive them to the small barracks they expected to take by assault. Supporters in Santiago and Manzanillo had donned the uniforms of the July 26th Movement preparatory to their onslaught on the Batista forces. But at the appointed hour, Castro and his men were still at sea, and a two days' journey away from Cuba. Venerable old *Granma,* designed to carry eight persons in comfort, did miracles braving heavy weather with eighty-two men on board. No one could blame her for being so slow or for shipping so much water. In any case, the trucks waited vainly in Niquero, and the uprisings in Santiago and Manzanillo were crushed well before the expedition arrived. Worse still, Batista's army had got wind of Castro's impending arrival and had strengthened the coastguard patrols.

84. When Castro announced his impending arrival on November 15, 1956, Colonel Bayo was outraged at this lack of military discretion. But Castro told him: "I want everyone in Cuba to know that I am coming. I want them all to trust in the July 26th Movement. That is part and parcel of my strategy" (Dubois, *op. cit.* p. 113). In fact, the first peasant the rebels met following their defeat in Alegría del Pío recognized Fidel immediately.

85. Celia Sánchez Manduley, the daughter of a doctor from Manzanillo, was working in Oriente with Frank País; later she came up into the Sierra and became Fidel's chief collaborator both during and after the Revolution. At present, she is a minister of state.

The Communists and the Revolution

Exhausted by seasickness, the eighty-two men on *Granma* had to swim ashore after abandoning their provisions and part of their equipment. They then had to struggle across an interminable mangrove swamp, stumbling over tangled roots in the stagnant salt water. Batista's air force discovered them there, and keeping them under constant watch, directed the search by local army units. Three days later, when the rebels believed that they could at long last afford to take a few hours of rest at Alegría del Pío, the government forces launched a surprise attack and only just failed to exterminate them. Batista hastened to announce that Fidel had been killed and his expedition liquidated. He himself came to Alegría del Pío to thank and reward his valiant soldiers.

But Fidel and about twenty of his companions made good their escape to the Sierra Maestra.[86] "Now the days of tyranny are numbered," Fidel told his comrades. A few weeks later, on January 17, 1957, the guerrillas attacked the small barracks of La Plata, thus informing the country at large that the report of their death was—as Mark Twain would have put it—highly exaggerated. A month later, Herbert Matthews of the *New York Times* interviewed Fidel in the Sierra, and thus once again gave Batista the lie. The dictator had obviously cried victory far too soon, and his boasts now turned sour on him. No one could have told just how strong the guerrilla force really was, but the mere fact that *el doctor* Fidel Castro could survive unscathed in the Sierra and even receive members of the foreign press, drove home to all Cubans the utter impotence of their "strong government."

The story of Castro's guerrilla band is now legendary. The reminiscences and above all the diaries of Che Guevara, the letters of Fidel, the writings of Carlos Franqui, the eyewitness accounts that are still being published—all enable us to reconstruct each step the guerrillas took, and give us a fair idea of daily

---

86. The twenty-two rebels captured at Alegría del Pío were tried together with the insurgents of Santiago. Among the dead was Nico López, one of Fidel's oldest comrades. It was López who had introduced Ernesto Che Guevara, whom he had known in Guatemala, to the movement.

life in the Sierra. Here we shall merely look at the direct political repercussions of the *foco guerrillero* in the Sierra Maestra.

From the start of the struggle, other political movements
seemed almost as convinced as Fidel himself that the question of
life in post-Batista Cuba had ceased to be a purely academic
question. By their very ability to survive in the mountains, the
barbudos had proved that the days of the tyrant were numbered.
A government forced to bombard its own territory and which
even then cannot eliminate a small band of rebels, is a spent
force. Everyone now wanted to deliver Batista the *coup de
grâce,* ostensibly for the good of Cuba, but in fact so as to pull
the best chestnuts out of a fire lit by Fidel Castro.

The unexpected activities of President Prío's *Auténticos* and
by Aureliano Sánchez Arango's Triple-A movement was the most
typical, if the least fruitful, reaction of this type. They suddenly
declared their complete solidarity with the guerrillas, and their
readiness to sign any sort of agreement with them. But instead
of supplying the guerrillas with arms and money, they used all
their vast resources to build up armies of their own. They even
hired Colonel Bayo to train their men for a *Granma*-style landing on the northeast coast, and filled their clandestine arsenals
in Havana to bursting point. But their base in Miami was
riddled with Batista's spies and, as was only to be expected, all
their attempted landings ended in tragic failure.[87] Fidel was not
taken in by them and criticized their activities unmercifully:
"Ever since this nation has risen up in rebellion no one has
sent it a single gun. . . . While our unarmed peasants have to

87. In May 1957, a group of *Auténticos* trained by Bayo and led by
Calixto Sánchez White landed in northeast Oriente province, with a considerable supply of guns and ammunition, for the purpose of opening a
second front in the Sierra Cristal. This venture, known as the Corinthia
Expedition (so called after their yacht) ended disastrously in an ambush,
from which only ten members managed to escape. In August 1957, Cándido
de la Torre, acting for the Triple-A Group, and Colonel Bayo left from
Miami on Prío's yacht *Blue Chip* which they had loaded with arms. They
were intercepted by the Mexican police. Later de la Torre made a successful attempt to land arms in Cuba, but the police seized the entire store.

watch their houses being burned down and their families being killed, Cuba is full of hidden arsenals which have never been used to kill any of Batista's minions, and which simply wait for the police to stumble upon them. Their owners apparently wish these arms to be used against the rebels, hoping that the tyranny will somehow collapse by itself." In short, Fidel was accusing the *Auténticos* of preparing for battle, not only against Batista but also against his own men.

But Fidel would not be drawn; he would not dissipate his forces on two fronts. He accordingly kept up his official contacts with the *Auténticos;* his accusations were simply intended to make them think again and more particularly to win over some of their rank-and-file members. He continued to reject compromise with them or anyone else and even disowned his own representatives in Miami, who on November 1, 1957, signed a "Joint Opposition Document." He had not yet won the war, but felt strong enough not to put his future victory in pawn. His tactics proved to be correct; the other movements did not dare to denounce him openly, and several prominent *Auténticos* and *Ortodoxos* even rallied to his cause.[88]

The only other force that thought itself strong enough to take immediate advantage of Batista's growing weakness was the *Directorio Revolucionario.* On March 13, 1957, while Fidel's guerrillas were still taking their first steps in the Sierra, José Antonio Echeverría's men attacked the presidential palace in force. Their leader seized Radio Reloj and, at the precise moment when his comrades broke into Batista's office, announced the end of the dictator and of his hated regime. But as luck would have it, Batista had just gone to take a brief rest in another part of the building and the assailants found themselves in an empty room. They were unable to search the entire palace —the guards had meanwhile been alerted and were counterattacking in force—nor could they leave the building: police

88. Among them Raúl Chibás, brother of the founder of the Ortodoxo Party.

reinforcements blocked all the entrances. Most of the assailants were massacred on the spot.

José Antonio Echeverría was one of those butchered by Batista's henchmen. The official order was no longer "no bloodshed at any price," as it had been in 1952, but "no prisoners at any price." Even moderate critics of the regime, men who had had no part in the attack, were dragged out of their houses and shot outside the city boundaries. One of them was the lawyer Pelayo Cuervo, whose only crime was that his name was found in Echeverría's papers. Batista's terror lasted for several days.

The Castroists, who had known in advance of Echeverría's plan and had not approved it, now expressed their full solidarity with the victims of repression, and have ever since honored March 13 as a great date in the history of the Cuban Revolution. Those few who managed to escape with their lives—Faure Chomón, in particular—were gradually able to rebuild their organization, and at the beginning of 1958 even set up a *foco guerrillero* of their own in the mountains of Escambray. Their attitude was in striking contrast to that of another group, the Second National Front of Escambray, which operated in the same mountains and was led by Eloy Gutiérrez Menoyo:[89] the locals referred to them scathingly as *comevacas* (cow eaters). In addition to the signatories of the Miami pact and the independent guerrilla forces, there were the Communists—as active as ever in their isolation. What precisely did they do after the *Granma* landing and during the final phase of the war? The moment we ask this question, even today, the facts become clouded by passion. Some people tell you brusquely that the Communists did nothing at all, that they were far too concerned with the preservation of their own party machine. In support of this allegation they cite a series of curious facts: when the Party president, Juan Marinello, obtained a chair in the University of Havana in November 1958, he apparently sent a copy of his

89. Gutiérrez Menoyo tried to land in Cuba in 1965 to establish an anti-Castroist front. He was arrested three days later and is now in prison.

poems to the Minister of the Interior in the Batista government with a cordial dedication; *La Carta Semanal,* the clandestine weekly of the PSP, allegedly reached all subscribers quite openly through the post; the number of Communists who had suffered from Batista's repression was very small indeed.

These allegations go back to the early post-revolutionary period, when the whole moderate wing of the July 26th Movement —and Catholic opinion as well[90]—tried to stop Castro's move toward the Left and dwelled at length on the misdeeds of the PSP and the Soviet Union. In a documentary film made at that time, and sponsored by *Bohemia,* the commentator explained that the crowd, wildly cheering Castro's victory, could not restrain its fury against Batista's men or the Marxists, who were apparently tarred with the same brush.[91] Other commentators hinted at collusion between the Communists and their former ally, Batista. Attacks by the clandestine PSP press on Castro were duly reproduced to remind the readers, no less than Fidel himself, of the duplicity of his detractors of yesterday.

The Communists were quick to take up the challenge. In August 1959, the thirty-fourth anniversary of the Party, Aníbal Escalante—who had led them throughout the last phase—presented his version of the events: "At the time of the *Granma* landing, our Party took immediate steps to support the insurrection . . . and to transform it into a veritable revolution. But the attack did not develop according to plan and so the Party concentrated its efforts on breaking the grip of the tyrant and on saving what remained of the *Granma* expedition. We were practically alone in this fight and our efforts were crowned with success. By mobilizing the masses, we were able to hold Batista's forces in check, thus giving the rebels time to withdraw into the Sierra Maestra. Bit by bit, the rebels then gained the understanding and support of the local peasants—particularly of the Com-

90. See *Bohemia* throughout 1959, and especially the articles of Father Angelo del Cerro and Andrés Valdespino.
91. I was able to see this documentary in 1968, by courtesy of ICAIC, the Cuban Cinema Institute.

147

munists among them—and this enabled them to survive and to recruit new members. Thanks to its excellent strategy and guerrilla tactics the armed movement finally won over the masses and could always rely on our Party. We too, like Fidel and his comrades, were fighting for the salvation of our country. The decisions of the Party leadership in February 1958—which were preceded by active support for the armed movement— were not the beginning, but only the seal on, our participation in the civil war against tyranny. Our Party fought on two fronts: armed struggle and nonarmed mass action. Among those who deny our participation in the war are quite a few honest men who misunderstand the facts, simply because, for tactical considerations, which still apply, we were forced to keep our contribution secret. Today we can merely say that our Party acquitted itself with honor, that hundreds of Communists responded to the call and joined the ranks of the rebels; that our detachments fought in all the provinces; that the rebel command found our militants courageous, faithful, and disciplined soldiers; that our organizations distinguished themselves by aiding the rebels; and finally that during the historical invasion of Camagüey and Las Villas our action committees harassed the enemy and sabotaged his transport, not at random but in accordance with the directives of the only staff capable of directing the general struggle: the staff of the Sierra Maestra."[92]

This page merits being quoted at such length if only because it is a real masterpiece of innuendo. Without mentioning a single fact, Escalante makes it appear as if Castro and the PSP were linked by bonds of steel, and that tactical considerations alone forced him not to reveal the details. Only because the Communists sacrificed their lives generously and silently, did their exploits remain unknown to all but a few initiates bound by an oath of secrecy. These claims were as unsubstantiated as they were impressive. But they were also vague enough not to run the

92. See Aníbal Escalante: *"La Conmemoración del 34° aniversario del Partido"* in *"Año de la Liberación," Fundamentos,* August 1959.

risk of being disproved with hard facts. In short, Escalante built up a new fable to support his claim that the Party had always been right, had always acted in the best possible way. But to prove this theory, the alleged partner in the conspiracy ought to have confirmed at least part of the claim. In fact, the Castroists confirmed nothing of the kind.

And so, at their national congress of August 1960, the Communists were forced to change their tune. Blas Roca in person led their chorus of collective self-criticism. The Party, he let it appear, had not mobilized its forces because it had failed to grasp the profound significance of Fidel Castro's revolutionary strategy. "That was our mistake."[93]

This confession ought to have been welcomed by all those who had been linking the Communists with Batista. But by then many of them had left for Miami where they found it more profitable to allege that the Communists had been in league with Castro instead. By an odd reversal of roles, they now defended Escalante's thesis, even improving upon it while giving evidence before various U.S. Congressional Inquiry Committees. All the old stories about Batista's association with the Communist Party were suddenly dropped and allowed to fall into oblivion. The result was a web of contradictions so dense that the uninitiated were bound to become trapped in it.

For their benefit, let us simply mention a number of established facts. To begin with, the Communists were in opposition right through Batista's overt dictatorial phase—the Cuban no

93. See Blas Roca's report to the Eighth National Assembly of the PSP in August 1960, in which the following passage occurs:
"We rightly foresaw, and greatly looked forward to, the prospect that in response to conditions created by the tyranny, the masses would organize and eventually engage in armed struggle or popular insurrection. But for a long time we failed to take any practical steps to hasten that prospect, because we believed that these struggles, including a prolonged general strike, would culminate in armed insurrection quite spontaneously. Hence we did not prepare, did not organize or train armed detachments. . . . That was our mistake. Fidel Castro's historical merit is that he prepared, trained, and assembled the fighting elements needed to begin and carry on armed struggle as a means of destroying the tyranny."

149

less than the international situation prevented any *componenda* (compromise) between them and this "American puppet." But though they were intransigent opponents, they did not for a moment believe in the possibility of a Cuban revolution. Throughout, they remained Popular Frontists, advocates of a broad anti-fascist union, built on the model designed by the Seventh Congress of the Comintern. If need be, they were ready to play second fiddle in such a coalition. Socialism was not on the cards, and hence it was idle to proclaim it the goal of the present struggle.

Within this narrow frame, they did their utmost to maneuver and to adjust their tactics. At first, they looked upon the Castroists as simple adventurers, or at best as deviationists undermining the unity of the democratic forces. But after the *Granma* landing, which helped to transform the July 26th Movement into a political force whose importance could no longer be denied, the Popular Front had clearly begun to include the Sierra. Only in 1958 did the Party accordingly take the weighty step of making direct contact with the Sierra, long after all the other opposition forces had done so. But having once taken it, the Communists forged some ties with the guerrillas, particularly during the final phase of the struggle.

The various phases of this conversion can be retraced meticulously. At the time of the *Granma* landing, only a handful of Communists believed in Castro's success. When Escalante wrote: "We took immediate steps to transform it [the Castroist insurrection] into a veritable revolution," he clearly meant: "We were forced to join in a struggle whose outcome looked extremely dubious." And so the Party took no steps to help the men on *Granma* and kept away from Santiago and Manzanillo where uprisings in support of the landing were being planned.

In 1957, the urban branch of the July 26th Movement made tremendous headway, as we can tell from a whole series of spectacular actions in Havana and Santiago. These were greeted with enthusiasm by the Communist rank and file, but the leaders still refused to take the plunge. They frowned particularly on the *Frente Obrero Nacional* (National Labor Front), founded by the Castroists and led by David Salvador, an ex-Communist, and they mistrusted the overt anti-Communist tendencies of some Castroist propagandists[94] and disliked their glorification of armed struggle. In fact, paralyzed by doubts, the Communist Party spent the entire year of 1957 sitting on the fence.

It was not until February 1958, during a meeting attended by most of the Party leaders, that the decision was taken to send Carlos Rafael Rodríguez to the Sierra, and to offer support—"on certain conditions"—for the general strike the Castroists were busily organizing. We could say a great deal about these "certain conditions," but the fact is that the official Communist attitude to the July 26th Movement had suddenly become far more positive. The clandestine Communist press, above all the Communist youth organ *Mella,* issued appeal after appeal in favor of the coming strike and exalted the new-found unity of the workers. Ten years later I was shown the faded pages of this modest, mimeographed paper; former members of the PSP will produce it for anybody with great pride, as irrefutable proof of their party's genuine change of heart. However, the strike of April 9, 1958, which the Castroists expected to topple the Batista regime, turned out to be a failure. Nor is there any evidence that the Communists joined actively in this decisive battle on the urban front. "That was because rightist leaders

---

94. The Castroists were prepared to grant their local groups considerable freedom of speech which, in certain parts, assumed a sharp anti-Communist tone. The Miami group in particular excelled in this sphere. As an example, we need merely quote this pearl from the *Sierra Maestra* published in Miami: "Fidel Castro, educated in a Catholic School in Santiago, has never left the faith and always keeps a Catholic chaplain by his side, a man who has even fought with him in the Sierra. Nor is it possible to suspect of Communism one who is the son of a landowning family with vast estates and other interests in Oriente province. . . . As everyone can see from the magnificent photographs, published by *Bohemia, Life,* and *Time,* Fidel always wears a gold medallion of the Virgin over his heart. Have you ever seen a Communist wearing such a medallion?" (From: *"Fidel Castro no simpatiza con los comunistas"* in *Sierra Maestra,* official organ of the July 26th Movement in exile, June 1958, No. 5.)

151   F

of the July 26th Movement in Havana did not want us," PSP veterans will tell you. "They presented us with a *fait accompli,* and did not invite us to play any part at all in the actual preparation of the strike." In fact, the Castroists could not— nor wished to—sign a pact that would grant the Communists unearned privileges in the hour of victory, which, they firmly believed, was about to strike. Moreover, their idea of a general strike was quite incompatible with the Communists': the July 26th Movement put much greater stress on a spectacular show of military strength in the heart of Havana than on the organi- zation of factory cells. At 11 A.M., while the radio invited all workers to leave their factories and offices, 2,000 armed men pre- pared to storm various strategic points in the capital. If they had succeeded, Batista would most probably have been taken prisoner or been forced to escape. In other words, the Castroists did not expect the masses to lead the revolution, but merely to lend their admittedly crucial support to what was predominantly a military action. It goes without saying that the men who or- ganized that action were unlikely to entrust its organization to a Central Strike Committee, as the Communists demanded. At that point, they felt entitled to unconditional support, and this the PSP was not prepared to grant.

Paradoxically, the failure of the strike led to a closer under- standing between the Castroists and the Communists. This time, Fidel's men did not put up a blind defense of the methods they had chosen. In fact, the strike issue had been the subject of serious disputes within the July 26th Movement. Fidel, like the men in Havana, believed that victory was just around the cor- ner; and when things went wrong he was one of the first to ad- mit it. Later the movement went so far as to contend that it was impossible to win any battles in the towns, where the main forces of repression are always concentrated. But first they called a meeting in the Sierra for May 2, 1958—a meeting Che Guevara has called "decisive."[95] On that occasion he attacked Faustino

95. See Ernesto Guevara: *"Una reunión decisiva"* in *Obra revolucionaria* (Mexico, ERA, 1967), p. 237.

The Communists and the Revolution

Pérez and David Salvador for their inability to collaborate with the Communists. In other words he presented the PSP as the victim rather than the guilty party of the April *fracaso*. And, not unexpectedly, his particular reading of the events was warmly welcomed by the Communists.

It was then that Carlos Rafael Rodríguez went up into the Sierra Maestra. He has told me that on the eve of his departure in the spring of 1958, he and Osvaldo Sánchez were seen by Aníbal Escalante, who briefed Rodríguez on what line to take with Castro. To make doubly sure, he thrust upon him a long memorandum, crammed with instructions for the July 26th Movement. It contained "advice" on the best means of conducting the war, on running the country, on the correct attitude toward the other political forces, and on international politics. The whole thing was written in the classical, authoritarian style. When they left, Sánchez,[96] a staunch advocate of friendship with Castro, was almost in tears: "Everything is lost, he will never put up with this. We are moving toward a new split." A broad grin appeared on Rodríguez' face: "Don't give it another thought. I haven't the least intention of bringing any of this up with Fidel; I am going to the Sierra to listen to him, to hear what he expects of us, and not to ram our policy down his throat."

When I was told this story in 1968, Escalante had just been sentenced to a long term in prison for reasons that had no direct connection with his political past—as we shall see below. His former companions were not particularly sorry for him; each recalled the unspeakable arrogance that had made relationships with him so difficult. Some of them, though, told me in private that the chief credit for the Party's "conversion" to Fidelism in 1958 must go to Escalante. He was secretary-

---

96. After the Revolution, Osvaldo Sánchez was generally taken for a tool of the Soviet Union. A high-up in the Cuban police force, he was killed on January 9, 1961, during a mysterious shooting: apparently failing to identify his helicopter, Cuban soldiers opened fire, fatally injuring Sánchez and his two companions.

153

general at the time, and the Communist Party being what it was, no one could have forced him to change the line. Escalante, according to them, even took grave personal risks when he threw his entire weight behind the Castroists.

Oddly enough, these two versions are not contradictory. Aníbal Escalante had come to realize that the July 26th Movement was moving toward certain victory, and so decided to jump on the Castroist bandwagon before it was too late. But not for a moment did he think that the man whose cause he was at long last prepared to underwrite would encroach upon the acknowledged Communist preserve: the construction of a socialist society. To him, Fidel Castro was just another Nasser or Kassem, who needed a leg up lest he slide down the fatal slope that led straight into Washington's open arms. The thought that the fire of battle had forged a new revolutionary vanguard, capable of transforming the entire social scene, did not even occur to him. It was in this sense that we may say that the tacit but indisputable alliance entered into by Castroists and Communists during the final phase of the struggle was founded on a deep misunderstanding.

In any case, in the spring of 1958, the PSP gave its militants leave to collaborate with the July 26th Movement. The Communists even organized their own resistance movement in Las Villas, and later placed it at the disposal of Che Guevara, who had just led his victorious columns into that province. They were also fighting on the "Second Front," in the Sierra Cristal,[97] where some of them—Armando Acosta for example—reached the rank of major, the highest in the rebel army. These eleventh-

---

97. In March 1958, Fidel Castro sent his brother Raúl, at the head of a column of sixty-seven, into the mountains in northeast Oriente, the Sierra Cristal. This Second Front, bearing the name of Frank País, a hero of the movement killed on July 30, 1957, at Santiago, proved extremely successful. Raúl Castro was able to recruit more than 1,000 fighters and, in the final phase of the war, controlled an area of some 6,000 square miles. He even had his own airplanes and arrested local U.S. citizens as hostages to stop further bombardments; the United States was, in fact, supplying rockets to Batista, despite repeated promises of nonintervention.

The Communists and the Revolution

hour acts did not topple Batista, but they did help to heal the old rift, and encouraged the guerrillas to look more kindly at collaboration with the PSP. In the final phase of the war, the Communists apparently tried their old method of infiltration, but, unable to propose an alternative policy, they simply got on with the struggle against the common enemy.

But it is worth repeating that the Communists themselves never thought that they were contributing to the birth of a new type of socialism in Cuba, or that they were being overtaken by a movement which, according to doctrine, was quite unfit to lead a socialist revolution. At no time, either before or after Castro's victory, did they try to force him into a more radical posture; indeed all their publications show that they tried to do the very opposite: to moderate the reforming zeal of the *barbudos* lest they came into head-on collision with the United States. Thus in January 1959, in an open letter to President Urrutia, they simply called for the restoration of the Constitution of 1940, for agrarian reforms, for the lowering of the voting age, and for a return to proportional representation. They also asked for a resumption of diplomatic relations with the People's Democracies, but at the same time stressed Cuba's vital need for friendly relations with, though not subservience to, the United States.

All this was in line with their general attitude and with the overall strategy of the Soviet Union. At the beginning of 1959, Nikita Khrushchev was already preparing his visit to the United States, and accordingly expected Communists throughout the world to foster the idea of coexistence. The last thing the U.S.S.R. wanted just then was for Cuban Communists to take revolutionary steps that might give America cause to doubt Russia's good faith. There was nothing, of course, to prevent Communist participation in a purely patriotic enterprise, in ridding Cuba of a corrupt regime. Indeed, according to Moscow, the current troubles in the Third World and the violence they engendered were two important subjects in the impending dialogue with the other superpower "responsible for the maintenance of peace in an atomic age."

Castro's plan

We can now give fairly precise answers to some of the questions we have asked about the role of the Communist Party during the Cuban Revolution: the Communists neither fostered it nor were even among its leading advocates. This failure on their part cannot be ascribed to a local deficiency, to some "tropical" deviation, but must be seen as the direct result of unquestioning adherence to the Soviet brand of Marxism-Leninism. It was this loyalty which blinded the PSP to the specific conditions and the real potentialities of a semicolonial country such as Cuba, and which on the wider plane is still responsible for the notorious impotence of the Communists in the Third World. The history of the PSP and of its counterparts elsewhere forces one to ask himself if any political organization with the same structure, the same approach, the same political logic, and the same close ties to the U.S.S.R. can ever be the right instrument for creating a socialist society. This problem is not altogether new: it was brought up a long time ago by the reformist wing of the labor movement and by left-wing critics of the Stalinized Comintern. But, in the past, critics could be silenced with the argument that the only revolutions to triumph over capitalism were those led by Communist parties. This argument no longer applied. The Cuban Revolution had been the first to triumph *without* or even *against* the Communists, so that its victory forced the labor movement to re-examine its premises. At present, this problem is the subject of keen debates between those who, in the past, forgave the Communists so many of their mistakes in the name of efficiency, and the younger generation which is disenchanted with them.

Hence the great interest in Castroism, in this new recipe for making revolutions regardless of—indeed often in direct opposition to—the theories and organizational panaceas of Moscow.

The Communists and the Revolution

Having succeeded where others had failed, Fidel Castro was seen as the pioneer of a new revolutionary method disencumbered of all the heavy ideological luggage and dead weight of the classical Bolshevik movement. Paradoxically, quite a few European pro-Castroists have turned against this interpretation; they now contend that, far from being a model of anti-ideology and anti-organization, Castroism is a form of pure Leninism forged in the fire of guerrilla warfare.[98]

All in all, it is very much simpler to explain why the Communists failed to make a revolution in Cuba than to agree on the factors that enabled Fidel Castro to do so. Moreover, this difficulty is not just confined to foreigners ignorant of the facts; many of those who participated in the events take equally irreconcilable views of the past. If some of them have changed their opinion it is not because they are trying to falsify history, postrevolutionary developments have borne down on their intellectual and political thinking. Their changes of mind demonstrate that no victorious revolution ever takes the correct historical view of itself. Instead it looks upon its origins as a kind of crucible from which the noble elements can be extracted and the base ones cast out. This selective approach is fostered by the magnitude and didactic needs of the postrevolutionary struggle and by the desire to remain true to one's own past. This is particularly true of Cuba, since few revolutions have had to pass through so many phases in so short a time as the Castroist Revolution has.

Before examining the original Castroist program and deciding how much of it was achieved, we must run ahead of the events and look at the sources of the most recent controversies. We saw in the last chapter that the Cuban Revolution until April 1961 called itself humanist, left-wing nationalist, and democratic, and never bothered to justify itself in terms of what was still an alien, socialist doctrine. Indeed, Castroists felt no need for a

98. See Mario Sabbatini: *"Ideologia della rivoluzione cubana,"* special issue of *Ideologia,* Rome, 1969.

narrow ideological framework. Despite the cracks that were fast appearing in the old anti-Batista façade, the *guerrilleros* were determined to express the aspirations of all Cuba and not just of the working class. It was only in 1961, on the eve of the invasion by anti-Castroist forces, when the threat of civil war no longer left anyone in doubt about the loss of national unity, that Castro first spoke of a socialist revolution and appealed to the workers in town and country to rise up against a class enemy who was trying to hand Cuba to the North American imperialists.

In other words, it was the treachery of the big landowners and of so many other bourgeois elements that first drove home to Fidel Castro the social implications of his original platform. Even then he remained convinced that he was merely fulfilling the promises he had made during the Moncada epoch and that not a single one of the reforms he had promulgated—and which so outraged the possessing classes—was contrary to the spirit and the letter of his great plea: *History Will Absolve Me.* By enlisting the aid of the CIA against this program, certain anti-*Batistianos* had shown that they had always been opposed at heart to all social change, and that the workers and peasants were the backbone of the Revolution. From that realization to the conviction that his program had been socialist from the beginning was only a short step, which Fidel took with as much sincerity as alacrity to the applause of his Communist allies. Overnight the proletariat was turned into the hero of the Revolution while the *guerrilleros* and the urban resistance fighters were relegated to a subsidiary and purely transitory role, turned into more or less passive pawns.

It was the desire to provide his revolution with a socialist identity *a posteriori* that caused Fidel Castro to deliver his astonishing speech of December 2, 1961. While admitting his mistakes and bourgeois prejudices, he declared that he had always been a Marxist-Leninist at heart. At the same time, some of his comrades who were even less entitled to that label claimed they had all the time been Marxists without knowing it,

158

while others declared that they had never been anti-Communist and were therefore open to conversion. This period, known officially as the sectarian one, benefitted no one except the Communist old guard, which, not without reason, believed that it was about to inherit the Revolution. However, by March 26, 1962, Fidel had had enough of the Communist stranglehold on the administration of his country; he had Aníbal Escalante replaced and sent to Moscow. The missile crisis in October 1962, and the general disappointment at the Russian attitude greatly accelerated the process of Castroist disenchantment with the "orthodox proletarian" version of their past. There was never the least question of returning from socialism as such; the Castroists were simply determined to rehabilitate the real champions of the Revolution: the *guerrilleros* and the anti-Batista resistance fighters in the towns—all of them radical revolutionaries but not Communists.

The credit for this change must go largely to Ernesto Che Guevara, who never stopped proclaiming the exceptional nature of the Cuban experience and the importance of the lessons it had taught all Latin America about the role of guerrilla warfare. Soon after his departure from Cuba in 1965, his writings and speeches became the basis of the third official interpretation of the Cuban Revolution. It is by far the best known, not only because it is the most recent, but also because it has been widely publicized in Régis Debray's *Revolution in the Revolution.* According to this version, the Cuban Revolution was the culmination of an entirely new socialist revolutionary process, one that was as distinct from bourgeois reformism as from Leninism, Trotskyism, and Maoism. In its vanguard were the *guerrilleros*, men without a special class identity but the only ones capable of expressing—or of awakening—the needs of the exploited in countries devoid of both a genuine bourgeoisie, and also of an advanced proletariat.

This new approach was in open conflict with the general views of Latin American Communist parties and with the coexistence doctrine of the Soviet Union. It set itself the goal of fostering

159   F*

revolutions throughout the subcontinent, and hence of creating two, three, many Vietnams as the only effective answer to the global offensive of the United States. In Cuba itself it exalted the virtues of the men of the Sierra: disinterestedness, self-sacrifice, austerity, and discipline. The role of the men of the Llano, on the other hand, was played down: except, of course, for the martyrs among them, all of them had apparently been tainted by the bourgeois character of city life.

Which of these three versions, all drawn up in the post-revolutionary era, is the most accurate? Are all three different facets of one and the same truth, or are they completely incompatible? To answer these questions we can do no better than look at the factors that presided over Castro's political development.

In 1952, Fidel Castro was a young lawyer and the Ortodoxo Party had put him forward as their parliamentary candidate. He was to the left of that party, but by and large he was not so much a revolutionary as a champion of the moral radicalism of Eddie Chibás. Hence his arguments with the party leadership immediately after Batista's coup d'état were not so much based on ideological as on tactical differences. While the others contended that the whole country had been lulled to sleep by Batista's liberal and constitutional promises and was not ready for immediate action, Fidel believed that Cuba needed no more than a signal to rise up in revolt. He suspected that the Ortodoxo leaders were using popular passivity as an excuse for their own affliction, so well-known in the history of Cuban radicalism, the failure to make their actions fit their words. He accordingly decided to strike by himself.

Castro's choice in no way implied a conversion to terrorism, militarism, or putschism. His aim was not to end Batista's *golpe* with yet another *golpe,* but to prepare a genuine mass uprising. To that end he launched his attack on the Moncada barracks in Santiago, relying on the traditional revolutionary response of Oriente province. On July 23, 1953, he wrote the manifesto to the nation which he proposed to read over the

160

radio after the success of his venture. In it he declared that "this revolution is inspired by the ideas of José Martí and adheres to the revolutionary programs of *Jóven Cuba,* of the Radical ABC Party, and the Ortodoxo People's Party of Cuba."[99] He promised to restore the 1940 Constitution and was, in fact, proposing to install a party he could not possibly hope to lead. His name did not even figure in the manifesto.

His companions shared his disinterestedness, his hopes, and no doubt his uncertainties as well, or so Haydée Santamaría suggests when she writes: "Those who attacked Moncada had no fear of death; their only fear was to be misunderstood, to be taken for a group of lunatics. Our aim was to get a reaction from the people, to make them exclaim: 'Look, they have succeeded or failed, but in any case they fought for our sake.' "[100] And seen in that light, the Moncada assault was not a complete failure. For though the people did not rise up, they did not think Castro a fool. Everyone seemed to grasp the meaning of his sacrifice, first and foremost Batista himself, who at once dropped his liberal mask.

But then Fidel himself suddenly decided to change his strategy. He remained convinced that the people wanted a revolution, but he felt that he could no longer rely on their spontaneity, that more than a detonator was needed to trigger off a national explosion.

The second phase of Castroism began with Fidel's *History Will Absolve Me.* This plea, intended not for Castro's judges but for the nation at large, went considerably beyond the teachings of Eddie Chibás. In it, Fidel drew a devastating picture of Cuba's social misery and pointed an accusing finger not only at the corrupt practices and despotic acts of the old regime but also at the social injustices perpetuated by the great landowners and by the country's dependence on foreigners. His was a radical reformist program, in the broadest sense of the word. It was

99. *Manifesto a la nación de los asaltantes al cuartel Moncada,* Section VII (Revolutionary Archives; Havana).
100. See *Haydée habla de la Moncada,* Havana, Instituto del Libro, 1967.

ambitious in its aims but completely vague as to its means. Fidel's ambiguity was not intentional; he expected to be taken at his word that he would get to the end of his road and would somehow keep all his promises. The only thing that mattered for the moment was that this program should galvanize the nation and help to create a new force: the July 26th Movement.

"Without a mass movement there can be no revolution," he wrote to Haydée Santamaría and to Melba Hernández[101] from his prison on the Isle of Pines. He went on to give detailed instructions about propaganda and recruiting methods; estimated the cost of pamphlets to be sent to all sections of the population, suggested what attitude the movement should adopt toward the other opposition groups—in short, he neglected no detail that could contribute to the building of the new movement. "We need a hundred thousand young militants, a hundred thousand workers, a hundred thousand women."[102] He was asking a great deal of his young companions, and though he failed to reach his target, he nevertheless got considerable results. It was at this period that such veterans of the MNR as Faustino Pérez and Armando Hart joined the July 26th Movement, and that the particularly active Santiago group of the *Acción Nacional Revolucionaria* led by Frank País and Pepito Tey made common cause with the Castroists while retaining their independence. In 1955, on the point of his final break with the Ortodoxo Party, Fidel declared in Mexico: "What else is the July 26th Movement but the revolutionary spirit of the *Ortodoxos?*"

The guerrilla project matured at the same time. It was meant to be a sort of complement to that of the political movement. Fidel was still convinced that the Batista regime was highly unstable, and he was, in any case, not predisposed to a long, purely political, struggle. He therefore decided to establish a sort of military *cum* political counter-government in a relatively

101. His letter to "Melba y Yeye" is dated June 19, 1954.
102. *Ibid.*

sheltered part of the country, a government that, by its very existence, would keep the country in a state of permanent agitation. It would encourage the whole nation to resist, and so help the urban movement to hasten the decay and eventual collapse of the regime. The whole operation was not so much meant to be military as it was political. The movement would have to fight in order to survive in the Sierra Maestra, but it would also establish a permanent dialogue with the people and would unmask Batista, facilitating the task of all his enemies.

However, the Castroist program was off to a bad start. *Granma* arrived two days after the beginning of the insurrection in Santiago, during which Pepito Tey and many other leading figures were killed; the expeditionary corps itself was decimated in Alegría del Pío, and those who managed to escape took twenty days to reach the Sierra Maestra, and were, in any case, too few in number to engage in the kind of military operation Castro had intended.[103] When Frank País first went up into the Sierra to review the situation with Fidel, the outlook was so grim that he advised an immediate return to the mainland and the planning of a new expedition.[104] Castro would not hear of it; with a further fifty men from Santiago he could hold on where he was. Frank País sent them on March 14, but not all of them stayed. Young men from the towns found the nomadic life of the *guerrilleros* hard to bear, and few local peasants were

103. On January 17, 1957, the *guerrilleros* attacked a small barracks in La Plata and seized ten guns. But this was only a minor victory and did not create the necessary degree of national enthusiasm.

104. This is what Haydée Santamaría had to say about their meeting: "Frank . . . said to me: 'Yeye, we must find a way of getting Fidel out of here; he must be persuaded to go to a Latin American country where he can reorganize the movement. . . . If he stays on here, he may easily get killed and we can't afford that luxury.' But when we reached Fidel's place, both of us were tongue-tied. Then Fidel said: 'Look, the soldiers down below are firing at us, but they don't dare to come up. If you could only get me bullets and guns, I promise you a real battle in two months' time.' Neither Frank nor I knew what to answer. He spoke with so much conviction." See Carlos Franqui: *Cuba: le livre des douze* (Paris, Gallimard, 1965), p. 60.

prepared to follow the example of Guillermo García and join the small band. It was not until June 1957 that the battle of Uvero brought the Castroists their first military success.

In December 1956, one of the *Granma* survivors, Faustino Pérez, left for Havana to give the Llano movement some fresh encouragement. On leaving, he advised Fidel: "Dig in and don't budge on any account; the only thing that matters to us is to keep you alive. You are the symbol of the revolution; we shall do the rest in Havana."[105] But Castro was not at all inclined to hide. He continued his campaign even though, at the time, the urban front was by far the more important and the *guerrilleros* had agreed to play a subordinate part. It was the cities which supplied the *guerrilleros* with arms, money, information, and provisions, and from start to finish the vast majority of the *guerrilleros* were recruited in the towns.[106] It was the towns which, in February 1957, launched a great publicity campaign in favor of the Sierra, inflicting serious

105. When Faustino Pérez left for Havana, he is said to have left behind twelve *guerrilleros*—the legendary twelve; however, that number seems to have been purely symbolic. The *Granma* expedition counted eighty-two, twenty-two of whom were captured and sentenced in Santiago. The number of dead has never been made public, possibly because it is difficult to establish on account of defections. Those who got away from Alegría del Pío made their way to the Sierra in four groups: 1) Fidel, Faustino Pérez, and Universo Sánchez; 2) Che Guevara, Almeida, Ramiro Valdés, Chao, and Benítez; 3) Camilo Cienfuegos, Pablo Hurtado, and Pancho Gonzáles; 4) Raúl Castro, Ciro Redondo, Efigenio Ameijeiras, and René and Armando Rodríguez. Calixto García, Julio Díaz, Luis Crespo, Calixto Morales, and Carlos Bermudes joined them separately. When all of them were reunited with Fidel, Pablo Hurtado was lying ill in a farm (and was taken prisoner) and César Gómez had surrendered. The twelve were therefore twenty at this point, but they immediately dispersed again. At what stage then were there twelve? We know that at the battle of La Plata there were seventeen—at least thirteen *Granma* men and the rest young peasants.

106. Facts and figures on the numerical and social composition of the guerrilla movement are extremely hard to establish. It seems clear, however, that there were never more than two hundred and eighty resistance fighters at one time in the Sierra Maestra and that the national figure, even including last-minute recruits who were particularly numerous in the Second Front, never exceeded two thousand. From start to finish, townsmen accounted for at least 60 per cent, and according to other estimates, for 80 per cent of all *guerrilleros*.

blows to Batista's prestige.[107] Finally, and above all, the men of the Llano waged a fairly efficient political and military campaign of their own.[108]

Toward the end of July 1957 the urban resistance movement suffered a severe setback: Frank País, the irreplaceable "David," was killed by the police in Santiago. The workers replied with a general strike in Oriente, but when the July 26th Movement tried to extend this protest to the rest of the country,

---

107. The most successful publicity stunt was Fidel's interview with Herbert L. Matthews on February 17, 1957. It was arranged by the urban resistance movement, which managed to smuggle *The New York Times* correspondent into the Sierra, and its effect was increased by the *guerrilleros* themselves who greatly exaggerated their striking power. This is how Manuel Fajardo tells the story: "When Ciro [Redondo] advised us of Matthews' arrival, Fidel told us all to act like real soldiers. I looked first at myself, and then at the others, at our worn-out boots, tied up with electric wires and full of holes. But we managed it somehow; I went ahead of the column, and we all marched in step. As Fidel was talking to Matthews, Crespo arrived. Raúl took him aside and then sent him to Fidel: 'Major, we have made contact with the Second Column,' he said. Fidel explained to Matthews that we constituted the staff of the First Column, and that all the other columns were scattered throughout the area. In fact, what Matthews saw before him was the entire rebel army." See Carlos Franqui, *op. cit.* p. 80.

108. Acts of sabotage by the urban branch were often highly spectacular and attracted notice far beyond the frontiers of Cuba. One can easily imagine the effect on tourists or on American businessmen of attacks that deprived Havana of electricity and water for three days, or of the burning of Rancho Boyeros, the international airport. However, their boldest stroke was the capture, in December 1957, of the Argentinian racing driver, Fangio, who was kept a prisoner for forty-eight hours. This "disinterested" kidnapping revealed to the whole world that Cuba was in the grip of a veritable civil war. It is more difficult to tell what part the Castroists played in the Cienfuegos naval uprising on September 5, 1957, which turned out to be an event of the greatest national importance. It would seem that the conspirators were in close touch with the local resistance movement and more particularly with Dr. Osvaldo Dorticós, but their action was not, apparently, part of a nationally coordinated plan. It would be a grave mistake to underestimate the fighting climate created by the July 26th Movement. It gave rise to innumerable independent uprisings all of which proved annoying, if not dangerous, to the regime. The most notorious example was the attack on the Goicuria Barracks in Matanzas during April 1956. All the assailants were massacred, and many of them have not been identified to this day. Very little is known about their political affiliations.

165

it failed badly, no doubt because the strike had taken it by surprise. Even so, the idea gained ground that the regime could be toppled by industrial action, as in 1933. While continuing to harass government troops and provisioning the Sierra, the men from the Llano accordingly began, with Fidel's blessing, to make preparations for the great April strike of 1958. Some of the other *guerrilleros* were less enthusiastic: Che and Raúl Castro, in particular, were afraid that a Llano victory might produce a stunted revolution and one that would escape the control of the July 26th Movement. But Fidel did not share their fears: he wanted Batista overthrown as quickly as possible. He trusted in his lucky stars and in the dynamics of the events, and felt that he was strong enough to take charge when the right moment had come.

But the April strike proved a failure as well, and paradoxically it was Batista himself who now displaced the nerve centers of the Castroist movement from the cities into the Sierra. He struck first at the men of the Llano. Then, believing that his adversaries were completely demoralized, he launched a major offensive against the *guerrilleros*. In May 1958, fourteen infantry battalions, with air cover, artillery, and even naval support, moved in on the small Sierra enclave, defended by 280 men. And, incredible though it may sound, the defenders turned the tables on Batista, inflicting 1,000 casualties and taking 500 prisoners during two months of continuous fighting. "We have passed beyond the guerrilla phase to go on to positional warfare,"[109] Fidel said of his new strategy. The guerrilla movement now ceased to be a mere branch of the movement, a mere complement to the urban wing; indeed it was no longer a guerrilla movement in the proper sense of the word. It had become transformed into a rebel army, engaged in military operations of the classical type.

109. See Fidel Castro's order of the day, August 1958, entitled *"Parte sobre la ofensiva,"* in which he declared: *"la guerra de guerrilla habia dejado de existir para convertirse en una guerra de posiciones y movimientos."*

The Communists and the Revolution

With the weapons he had captured, Fidel was able to arm more than 800 men, divided into six columns. Raúl Castro, who had opened up the Frank País Second Front in the Sierra Cristal, commanded a further 1,000 men. Castroist resistance centers or *focos* were set up in the province of Las Villas, where *guerrilleros* first made their appearance in the Sierra de Escambray, and to a lesser extent in the province of Pinar del Río. It was all no more than a beginning, but already the enemy had lost his nerve. Many government soldiers preferred aiding the rebels to fighting for a dictator whose days were clearly numbered. Unfortunately, the zeal with which they tried to demonstrate their new loyalties was to prove a graver threat to Fidel Castro than their erstwhile hostility.

The great offensive of the rebel army reached its climax during Christmas 1958. On December 24, Che Guevara's column occupied Sancti Spiritus, a town on the central road from Havana to Santiago, and immediately advanced on Santa Clara, the capital of Las Villas province. A few days later it made contact with Cienfuegos' column outside that town. At the other end of the country, Raúl Castro came down from the Sierra and laid siege to Guantánamo. Fidel himself moved into Palma Soriano, some thirty miles from Santiago, and prepared a new Moncada attack, this time with incomparably greater resources than in 1953. But on December 27, General Cantillo, the commander in chief of the government forces in Oriente, asked for talks with the rebel chief in order to "avoid unnecessary bloodshed." He arrived next morning by helicopter and offered Fidel more than a truce: he himself would organize a military revolutionary movement in support of the *guerrilleros*. Fidel was rather suspicious; he explained to Cantillo that he wanted Batista captured alive, and that he was utterly opposed to a palace revolution. The general accepted every one of Castro's demands, whereupon Fidel agreed to postpone the attack on Santiago for a few days. Cantillo left fully satisfied, but instead of returning to army headquarters, his helicopter took him straight to Havana.

167

Guerrillas in Power

The founder of the "military revolutionary movement" was obviously playing a double game. He intended to smuggle Batista out of the country and then to form a neutral government, a sort of "peace cabinet" that would quietly slow down the dynamic of the revolution. And, in fact, he was wholly successful in carrying out the first part of his program: on New Year's Eve Batista and his principal henchmen made their getaway to the Dominican Republic. An old magistrate named Piedra then agreed to head the transitional regime that was to be imposed upon the country within the next few days. But that was as far as it went. Despite the general's precautions to keep Batista's departure a secret, next morning all leading papers brought out special editions to inform the country of what had happened. *Bohemia* produced a profusely illustrated issue on the evils of the dictatorship and sold a million copies.

Fidel Castro at once denounced Cantillo's treachery and called for a general strike, to continue until such time as the army placed itself unreservedly at the service of the revolutionary regime. He announced that the July 26th Movement had appointed Manuel Urrutia president of the republic, and ordered his troops to resume the offensive. They met with no resistance; on January 2 the columns of Raúl Castro and Hubert Matos entered Santiago, and that same evening Fidel delivered his first great speech in that city. The men led by Camilo Cienfuegos and Che Guevara did not reach Havana until January 5. Thus for a whole week the situation in the capital was dominated by the strikers. Not all their leaders were members of the July 26th Movement, and the men of the Llano would never have been able to seize power if the *guerrilleros* had not come to their help. On the other hand, the rebel army would not have been strong enough to carry the capital or topple the old regime without a powerful strike movement. In the final phase of the struggle it was therefore the combination of a military arm (the *guerrilleros*) and of a political arm (the urban movement) that ensured the final victory of Fidel Castro and his revolution.

168

The Communists and the Revolution

In less than four years the July 26th Movement had succeeded not only in overthrowing a despot but also in kindling great hopes for a better society. The slogan M.26.7 that sprang up on every wall symbolized the resurgence of a country which had been thought of as an amorphous mass by its former political leaders. The hopes of the immense majority of Cubans had become bound up with the name of Fidel Castro and no other force, revolutionary or otherwise, could challenge his right to represent and lead the Revolution. The men of the *Directorio* tried to do so; they seized the presidential palace and the University of Havana, and barricaded themselves inside. Their revolutionary credentials were beyond question: they had participated in the struggle from the very beginning and they were indirect heirs to the glorious *Directorio* of the '30s. Hence Camilo Cienfuegos and Ernesto Che Guevara could not possibly try to dislodge them by force, especially as the students had seized large quantities of arms and ammunition in the barracks of San Antonio, and as their leaders, Faure Chomón and Rolando Cubelas, were young but determined military commanders. The problem could only be solved on the political plane, and even here only by Fidel.

The ease with which he resolved this problem provides us with a remarkable illustration of the weight of his moral authority and the measure of his popularity. He entered Havana on January 8 and, after passing in triumph through the enthusiastic city, delivered his famous plea for unity in the Columbia Barracks. "Can we have forgotten what happened after Machado's fall in 1933? One of the greatest ills to attack the revolutionary forces was the proliferation of groups squabbling among themselves. And what happened as a result? Batista came to power and remained there for eleven years!"[110] Fidel went on to declare that, from the beginning of his campaign, he

110. All quotations from this speech are taken from *Discursos del Dr Fidel Castro Ruz, comandante en jefe del ejército rebelde 26 de julio* (Oficina del Historiador de la Ciudad de la Habana, 1959).

had been determined to prevent any repetition of that disaster: "That is why I always thought that all of us ought to be united in a single organization. . . . Then the people could express their wishes through a vast and powerful body which would avoid the terrible consequences of the proliferation of revolutionary groups." He assured his audience that he had not set out with the idea of proclaiming his own movement the sole candidate for the great task of uniting the people: "Ours or any other, provided only that we remain united." But it had happened that "our movement was the first to join battle, the first to show that victory was possible, the first to use the new tactics and the new strategy which led the Revolution to triumph." He did not belittle the others; he paid homage to their martyrs and their sacrifices, but he added that "the role of the July 26th Movement in this struggle has been glorious indeed" and that, as a result, it was now privileged to speak for the majority of Cubans. The masses were so enthusiastically behind the July 26th Movement that one was entitled to wonder (Fidel made a point of not mentioning the *Directorio* by name) : "*¿Armas para qué? ¿Para luchar contra quién?*" ("Arms for what? To fight against whom?") And he concluded: "No one can win a war against a united people." That same evening the semi-dissidents of the *Directorio* applied spontaneously for membership in the July 26th Movement.

Fidel's call for unity was no mere tactical ploy—he had always been a champion of a united front. Thus while still a prisoner on the Isle of Pines he wrote: "The attempt by José Martí to reconcile all the great leaders of the struggle for independence, each with his own history, his own fame and his own achievements, was a work of love, of understanding, and of infinite patience on the part of the only man capable of accomplishing this miracle. I am convinced that without this effort Cuba would still be a Spanish colony or a mere Yankee province. . . . I have far greater admiration for José Martí's gigantic, heroic, and silent attempt to draw all honest Cubans into the struggle

170

than for all the achievements on the battlefield that grace the pages of our history."[111] And since José Martí with his "infinite concern" for unity had always been Fidel's model, Fidel had good reason to be pleased with the students' response to his plea. All the conditions seemed ripe for the transformation of the July 26th Movement into one vast body capable of absorbing not only the *Directorio,* the PSP, and the remnants of other revolutionary groups, but also a large number of sympathizers new to the political struggle. All the conditions, that is, save one: Fidel's wish to bring this about.

The facts speak for themselves: the July 26th Movement has never held a national congress or a deliberative conference at any other level. Early in 1959 a few hundred civil and military leaders met privately in Havana, where they witnessed a violent clash between Fidel and Raúl Castro. That is all we know about it; no minutes have ever been published and verbal reports grow more confused as the years go by. What is certain, however, is that no further meetings were ever called. The slogan M.26.7 was still written on Cuban walls and still graced the front page of *Revolución;* but that paper had started as the official organ of a popular movement which, though its leaders are in power, had ceased to exist as such. The men from the Sierra and the Llano, who represented Castroism and spoke in its name, were as well known as ever, but no one could tell you where and how they make their decisions. Moreover, it was in their ranks that the main political cracks had appeared soon after the Revolution, simply because postrevolutionary developments took them utterly by surprise. Thus three episodes left a profound mark on Year One of the Cuban Revolution: the defection, in July, of Díaz Lanz, commander of the Castroist army and chief of the air force; the enforced resignation, on July 17, of President Urrutia, who had been brought into office by the July 26th Movement; and the trial, on December 14, of Hubert Matos, one of the military chiefs in the Sierra.

111. See Fidel's letter to Luis Conte, dated August 14, 1954.

Some people declare that it was precisely because of these developments that Fidel made no attempt to reorganize the movement: he knew that the divisions had grown too deep. Others claim that many of the divisions could have been avoided if only the July 26th Movement had adapted its organizational methods to the needs of the postrevolutionary period: it was because they were left to their own devices and experienced rather than caused events that the former leaders of the Castroist movement became uncertain of their purpose and began to fight one another. As against this, the upholders of the first thesis argue that the defections were inevitable once Fidel took measures against the bourgeois class which, until then, had mistaken him for a run-of-the-mill democrat. But whatever the rights and wrongs of this argument, it remains a fact that the disappearance of the July 26th Movement is an important element in the history of Castroism and one that is extremely difficult to interpret.

What precisely was the July 26th Movement? How could it become an essential weapon in Castro's revolutionary arsenal when it was so weak and diversified? Ernesto Che Guevara wrote several years after the Revolution that the July 26th Movement was *"algo nuevo, muy difícil a definir,"* something new and difficult to define.[112] And, indeed, how is it possible to define a movement in which men as different as Che himself and Hubert Matos fought shoulder to shoulder—to mention but one case of glaring political incompatibility. Tempted as we are to think in European terms, we may conclude that the July 26th Movement was simply a nationwide anti-fascist front, strongly resembling the national resistance movements that sprang up in most parts of Europe during the German occupation. Nothing could be more mistaken, for while the European movements were made up of politically homogenous groups which agreed on a common program and on the means of realizing it at various phases of the struggle, the Cuban *algo nuevo*

112. See Ernesto Che Guevara: *El partido marxista-leninista* (1963) in the anthology of his writings (ERA edition, Mexico, 1967) , p. 564.

was based neither on closed organizations nor on the acceptance of a common program or tactic.

I have tried to find out precisely what made the movement tick during its most glorious period, and, as a result, I now have a far better appreciation of Armando Hart's complaint: "You in Europe have a tendency to underestimate the role in history of great personalities." In fact, the only executive organ of the July 26th Movement that functioned perfectly from beginning to end was Fidel Castro himself. As for the rest of the collective leadership, they distinguished themselves by the scarcity of their meetings and by their abstention from any political activity worthy of the name. They met on two occasions: the first time in February 1957, after the disaster of Alegría del Pío, when the chances of successful guerrilla warfare still seemed very slender, and again in May 1958, after the failure of the April strike, when the future of the Llano movement looked particularly somber. It was to the second gathering that Che referred in 1964 in an article entitled *A Decisive Meeting*,[113] from which it

---

113. *Una reunión decisiva* was first published in the weekly *Verde Olivo* on November 22, 1964 (Year V, No. 47), and was immediately included in most versions of Che's *Reminiscences of the Cuban Revolutionary War*. No date was given. In reality, the article was first drafted in 1958; this fact throws a great deal of light on Che's evolution during the postrevolutionary period. A simple example must serve to make this point clear. In the final text, Che attacks Nico Torres (the successor of David Salvador as leader of the *Frente Obrero*) for his reluctance to collaborate with the "Stalinists," and even protests that this epithet should have been applied "to the comrades of the PSP" in the first place. It is very unlikely that Che would have referred to members of the PSP as comrades in 1958. But by 1964 he had come to believe that revolutions in Latin America called for 1) Communist participation in the struggle and 2) the concentration of political and military power in the hands of the *guerrilleros*. In other words, *Una reunión decisiva* was meant to show the correctness of the new thesis by means of an historic example that, in my opinion, does not in the least lend itself to this sort of interpretation. In particular, Che exaggerates the importance of relations between the July 26th Movement and the PSP, and makes too much of the disagreement between the Sierra and the Llano on the subject of the April general strike. The reason he calls the meeting held after the failure of this strike a "decisive" one is simply because it allegedly voted to concentrate all power in the hands of a single leader, Fidel Castro. In point of fact: 1) the PSP was a marginal force and did not unreservedly rally to the resistance; 2) a whole series of

incidentally appears that Che and Raúl Castro did not even belong to the national executive of the July 26th Movement. It would be an even greater waste of time to look for documents dealing with the organization of lower party levels or reporting the political views and discussions of ordinary members. In the Sierra Maestra, you could learn your politics by individual discussions with Fidel, Che, or Raúl, if you happened to be part of their circle.[114] But it was also quite possible to emerge from

---

documents, including letters by Fidel to Faustino Pérez before and after the strike, prove quite clearly that the strike was not the result of a unilateral decision by the Llano group, but was demanded by the Sierra; 3) Fidel's powers were barely increased by the "decisive meeting" for the simple reason that he had always personally appointed and dismissed all officials, both in the towns and in the mountains. For the rest, Che's article tells us a great deal about his own relationship with the leaders of the Llano movement. We learn, for instance, that he attended the "decisive meeting" at the request of Faustino Pérez who was anxious to thrash matters out with his chief critic. But Che was not even a member of the national leadership of the July 26th Movement, which at the time consisted of Fidel Castro, René Ramos Latour (Daniel), Faustino Pérez, Vilma Espin (Debora), Nico Torres, Luis Busch, Celia Sánchez, Marcelo Fernández (Zoilo), Haydée Santamaría, David Salvador, and Enso Infante (Bruno). Che's criticisms of the urban movement are, in fact, a testimony to the importance of the Llano. In August 1957, immediately after the death of Frank País, Che asked Fidel to send him to Santiago where he proposed to take over País' job. In his letter, which was first published in Europe by *Il Manifesto* (Rome, December 1969, No. 7) Che wrote: "We must send someone to Santiago who is a good organizer and who has close links with the Sierra. In my view, the right person is Raúl, or Almeida, or Ramiro, or even myself. (I say so without false modesty, but also without the least wish to press my own claim.)"

114. The fact that men like Che, who had strong political views even before joining the guerrilla force, should have exerted a considerable influence on those who worked by their side need not surprise anyone. It is said, for example, that Camilo Cienfuegos was "made" by Che, and that Raúl Castro, for his part, "made" a number of Cuban leaders, particularly during the Second Front period. And it is a fact that the austere, difficult, and dangerous life of the *guerrilleros* created very solid links of friendship. But the men from the Sierra received most of their political training *after* the Revolution, when Castroism assumed a more clearly defined political and ideological expression. On the day of victory the human material from the Sierra was politically immature, even on the admission of many veterans, and this explains why so many *guerrilleros* later defected.

guerrilla warfare without a shred of political education. At no time did the July 26th Movement run a political training school, or organize branches and cells.

In the towns again, clandestine activity necessarily stopped the movement from leading a normal political life: the entire organization was highly militarized and disciplined to respond quickly to orders from the top.[115] However, because they were forced to keep in contact, and to devote part of their efforts to recruitment, the men of the Llano were undoubtedly more likely to discuss the future of the Revolution and politics in general than their comrades in the mountains. It follows that they were also more likely to fall prey to the confused anti-Communist ideas that were particularly widespread in the towns. [116]

115. The urban movement consisted of three wings: the militia, commanded by René Ramos Latour was responsible for all para-military actions; the *Resistencia Cívica,* led in Havana by Manuel Ray, consisted chiefly of middle-class liberals and was chiefly responsible for gathering information, collecting funds, and locating hiding places for the militants; the *Frente Obrero,* led by David Salvador, operated on the industrial front. In addition, there was the *Frente Estudiantil* or Student Front, but this had to take second place to the *Directorio Revolucionario* which was much stronger at the university. All three (or four) branches enjoyed considerable autonomy, and the urban leaders of the July 26th Movement (above all Faustino Pérez and later Marcelo Fernández) were no more than coordinators. They kept in permanent touch with the Sierra, and most of them made the perilous trip to the mountains quite regularly. It was in the course of one of these visits that Armando Hart was arrested at the end of 1957 and forced to spend the rest of the war as a prisoner on the Isle of Pines.

People have often wondered about the exact numerical strength of the urban movement because, in Cuba as elsewhere, victory helped to inflate the number of self-styled veterans, particularly in the towns where clandestine conditions were such that no registers could be kept. If we accept the figure supplied by the July 26th Movement on the total number of people killed by Batista (20,000), we are bound to conclude that the movement counted many tens of thousands of members, on the grounds that the Castroists were the most active resistance fighters of all and that the survivors outnumbered the casualties. But both the premises and the conclusions are open to challenge.

116. The men of the Llano maintained excellent relations with anti-*Batistiano* Americans and hoped to make use of their services in stirring up

Guerrillas in Power

The July 26th Movement was thus the personal creation of Fidel Castro. It was he who helped to bind together brave men of differing views and to fire them, as well as the entire country, with new energy and the spirit of self-sacrifice. Castro alone could have smoothed the many cracks that disturbed the even façade of the movement. He reassured and encouraged people wherever he went, and according to a popular saying would gladly have met the devil himself if only the movement could have profited from the encounter. True, voices were raised quite early against his determination to solve every problem by himself; some critics even said quite plainly that it would have been much better if a number of decisions had been made collectively. Fidel at once promised to change his style, and the critics—who were also his best friends—left him reassured; they had need of his genius, his human warmth, and his optimism.

It is quite unfair to accuse Fidel Castro of duplicity: he at no time promised different things to different people, not even in private. He is neither a time-server nor a wicked schemer. He believed most sincerely in his doctrine which, unsystematic though it may be, nevertheless reflected Cuba's deepest aspirations so often deceived but never forgotten. He believed with all his heart in the ideas he had put forward in his *History Will Absolve Me*, and it was this program, no more and no less, that he repeated to, and that was apparently acclaimed by, all in public and in private. Europeans who are accustomed to more clearcut social and political divisions may find this story incredible, but they should not forget that the ideological vacuum C.

U.S. public opinion against the dictator. The further task of persuading these Americans that Fidel Castro was the only man capable of restoring genuine democracy to Cuba fell above all to the émigré branch of the July 26th Movement in Miami and New York and to a lesser extent in California. The importance of this branch was such that Fidel saw fit to send Haydée Santamaría to Miami in 1958, with orders to take charge personally. It should be noted in passing that the very controversial Miami pact of November 1957, which Fidel at once denounced as a reactionary maneuver, bore the signature, in the name of the July 26th Movement, of Lester Rodríguez, one of the men from the Sierra.

The Communists and the Revolution

Wright Mills discovered in Cuba after the Revolution was one of very long standing. Here the hold of the United States was very much stronger than in the rest of Latin America and necessarily stamped all political values, beliefs, and actions. At the time of the Cold War, people in Cuba as elsewhere spoke glibly of a free world and of democracy, even though democracy on the island had never been more than a caricature, and though the existence of the Batista regime within the "free world" made an obvious mockery of the term. The result was more than confusion: it amounted to an incurable disease, to a split between political verbiage and reality. Fidel Castro himself was a product of that split society; if not he would never have been able to draw up a radical program that opened the door to far-reaching social changes while ignoring the ideological distinction between pro-Americans and anti-Americans, between pro-socialists and anti-socialists. No political manipulator, no strategist from the outside (even from Latin America) could, in my view, have shown the same sensitivity to popular feeling. Fidel succeeded, not because he was "a Bolívar who has read Lenin," as my friend Saverio Tutino has put it,[117] but because he was one of the veterans of Cayo Confites, one who had shared all the political experiences of his generation. He knew how to transcend the limits of these experiences, how to place himself one step—but only one step—in front of his countrymen, who could thus follow him without too much difficulty.

What, in fact, were Fidel's precise ideological affiliations during the anti-Batista struggle? I have reread his personal letters and all his public declarations. The picture that emerges is of a man deeply attached to the moral doctrine of Eddie Chibás, a man with an open mind instead of a clear-cut creed. In 1953, he told the judges of the Santiago tribunal, who took him to task for his ownership of Marxist books: "Nowadays, only ignorant men can dispense with socialist literature." This does not make him a socialist in disguise. His reply must be

117. See S. Tutino: *L'Ottobre Cubane* (Turin, Einaudi, 1968) , p. 399.

taken quite literally; he wanted to say no more. In June 1958, the Castroists obtained irrefutable proof that the United States was supplying Batista's air force with rockets from Guantánamo, although the Americans had promised in March 1958 to suspend arms deliveries to the government of Cuba. Raúl Castro immediately arrested a number of U.S. citizens in Moa, and announced that he would keep them as hostages as long as the bombardment of civilians with American bombs continued. The affair caused a scandal in America, where people seemed more incensed about the fate of the hostages than about the broken promises. At the time, Fidel wrote to Celia Sánchez: "When this war is over, a much longer and more important war will begin for me, the war I shall have to wage against the Americans. I feel that this is my destiny."[118] It was still José Martí who dictated these words and not Lenin: Fidel had neither adopted Lenin's definition of imperialism nor is there even the least evidence to show that he was moving in that direction.

His determination to fulfill his destiny and his lack of ideological preconceptions are, in fact, the only continuous aspects of Fidel Castro's political career (as he himself never tires of stressing). If he had indeed been the disguised Marxist-Leninist his enemies claim he was, he would never have been able to convince that wing—probably the majority—of his movement which, though not pro-American in the strict sense of the term, was nevertheless very strongly influenced by the democratic rhetoric of the "free world."[119] On the other hand, had he merely been the radical democrat others make him out

118. This letter to Celia Sánchez is dated June 5, 1958.
119. According to some reporters, "anti-gringo" sentiments were much less widespread in Cuba than in most Latin American countries, but they were not completely unknown. Thus in 1955 when the U.S. government wanted to build a canal across the island to cut the distance between New Orleans and South America, there was so much indignation in Cuba that the scheme had to be abandoned. Those protesting against the Yankee attempts to cut their island in half included some of the most vociferous champions of the "free world." Anti-American feeling was apparently much stronger in the provinces than in Havana.

to be, he would not have been able to maintain close and friendly links with that growing circle of those who, without being pro-Communist, had begun to fear the paralyzing effects of the kind of anti-Communism the United States was trying to foster.[120] The double appeal of his program—libertarian and therefore democratic; radically reformist and therefore tending toward socialism—helped Fidel to succeed where anyone setting out with a rigid doctrine would surely have failed. Che Guevara was quite right to say that "the foremost, most original, and perhaps the most important single factor to render the Cuban Revolution so exceptional was that natural force that goes by the name of Fidel Castro.[121]

In the light of postrevolutionary developments we may well wonder whether this exceptionality did not perhaps hide the germs of future schisms and grave problems. It is a sad but undeniable fact that Fidel's "infinite concern" for unity did not give rise to the least attempt to create a collective leadership or to discover ways and means of establishing a truly democratic rank-and-file organization. Neither interested him, not because he was afraid of losing his personal grip on the country (there was no one to dispute that) or because he had reason to be afraid of the rank and file (he was more popular than ever) but simply because the problem of the relationship between the revolutionary vanguard and the masses, or of the role of the vanguard in arousing the class conscience of the proletariat, passed him by. Fidel Castro was not trying to build a socialist society. He had no need of "all these hypotheses"; he had a single objective: to overthrow Batista and to prevent a return to the *status quo ante*.

Just before coming down from the Sierra Maestra, he still declared that he did not seek a leading post in the new

120. If I were pressed to give a political definition of the most radical wing of the July 26th Movement, I would say that it was anti-anti-Communist. But in prerevolutionary Cuba that was radical enough.

121. See Ernesto Che Guevara: *Cuba: excepción histórica o vanguardia en la lucha anticolonialista* (1961).

administration; his aim was simply to restore the democratic rights enshrined in the 1940 constitution. Now according to that constitution the minimum age of the president of the republic was forty years, so that Fidel would have been legally disqualified from holding that post before 1967. Nor did he want to become prime minister; the titles he had borne in the Sierra were enough for him: general secretary of the July 26th Movement, and commander in chief of the rebel army. He accordingly moved into the Hotel Habana Hilton and sat back while a government composed chiefly of men from the Llano and other leading anti-*Batistianos* took power.[122] Only three of Castro's military chiefs were included: Humberto Sori-Marin, Augusto Martínez Sánchez, and Faustino Pérez.[123]

This legalistic approach pleased the radical wing of the Castroists no more than the personality of the new ministers did; it seemed as if Fidel was making a gift of his revolution to men who cared little for the social objectives of the July 26th Movement. Hence the clash between Raúl and Fidel during the only official meeting attended by the leaders of the movement; hence also the alleged attempt by certain "hard liners" supported by the PSP to proceed to an immediate distribution of land, without waiting for an agrarian reform law that might never

122. Thus Professor Roberto Agramonte, a former Ortodoxo candidate to the presidency of the republic, became minister of foreign affairs. Llano members of the new government included Armando Hart (education), Enrique Oltuski (communications), Manuel Ray (public works), Luis M. Busch (secretary to the president of the council), and Luis Orlando Rodríguez (interior). Dr. Regino Botí and Dr. Raúl Copero Bonilla, two sympathetic experts, were put in charge of the departments of economics and commerce respectively.

123. Major Humberto Sori-Marin was put in charge of implementing the agrarian reforms drawn up in the Sierra and introduced even during the period of guerrilla warfare. He was replaced by Major Pedro Miret on June 14, 1959, and later tried for high treason and executed (April 16, 1961). Major Augusto Martínez eventually took over the Ministry of Labor and retained this post until 1965, when he tried to commit suicide and disappeared from the political scene. As for Faustino Pérez, he resigned on November 26, 1959 (see below) and later became minister of hydraulic works. In the spring of 1969 he was demoted and appointed director of a hydraulic plant in Sancti Spiritus.

come.[124] Fidel reacted very strongly to this attempt to force his hand, but the conflict quickly died down when it became obvious that Fidel was as determined as anyone else to promulgate the reforms he had promised the peasants. Nor did he intend to make a present of his revolution to anyone; it was just that he had no need to be in the government to control it. He could rely on the support of the people at large, and on his army, the only *de facto* executive in the country. It did not take the ministers long to appreciate this fact and it was at their insistence that Fidel agreed to become head of the government on February 12, 1959. The former prime minister, Miró Cardona, stepped down and readily accepted an ambassadorial post in Madrid.

The enthusiastic acclaim of the masses and the devotion of most of his companions combined to strengthen Fidel in the conviction that he alone was able to lead his people forward. It was this conviction and not personal vanity that persuaded him to continue governing the country, always on a temporary basis, in the same way that he had previously led the July 26th Movement. Most Cubans were delighted; they asked nothing better than to follow a man who had already rid them of their greatest evil, and now promised to stand up to threats from the United States. Others, particularly among the politically educated, began to have some difficulty in following him; the choice before them was no longer the simple Manichean alternative of the prerevolutionary epoch: the good cause of the revolution *versus* the evil cause of the dictatorship. More subtle distinctions, previously hidden, had now come to the fore. Thus some began to ask just how far Fidel intended to go in his conflict with the Americans and in his attempt to nationalize

124. This whole story is based on hearsay and must be treated with the utmost reserve. It would seem that in Oriente, and especially in the region held by the Second Front, Communists in search of popularity helped "impatient" Castroists to distribute the land summarily, while Fidel, properly, wished to introduce serious agrarian reforms based on less demagogic considerations.

industry and agriculture, and since Fidel was quite unable to tell them, he began to treat them as so many public nuisances. He was ready to explain everything to the people afterward, but he increasingly lost patience with those who asked too many questions in advance. It was for that very reason that the persistence of even so rudimentary an organization as the July 26th Movement became an obstacle in his path: he no longer needed any intermediaries in his dramatic dialogue with the people.

At the beginning of July 1959, the first of a series of defections shocked the July 26th Movement: Major Pedro Luis Díaz Lanz, a leading militant from Santiago and an intrepid aviator—the first to land his plane in the Sierra Maestra (in 1958) and responsible for thirteen out of the fifteen arms drops to the *guerrilleros*—had fled to the United States. As the head of the Cuban air force he was, of course, greatly sought after by various U.S. Senate commissions and welcomed in the name of "pure" (i.e., democratic as well as anti-Communist) Castroism. In fact, Díaz Lanz was a young adventurer; the wider he opened his mouth the more obvious his lack of political discernment. He was clearly not the man to step into Fidel's shoes, though his mere presence in the United States did help to highlight the fact that all was not well in Havana.

On July 16 when Cubans opened their *Revolución,* they learned an even more stupefying piece of news: Fidel had resigned his premiership. The announcement took even the staunchest Castroists by surprise; Fidel had told no one in advance and had gone personally to the printing office to compose his *renuncia.* He filled in the rest when he delivered a blistering attack on President Urrutia before the television cameras. Cubans were told that their president, though not exactly an accomplice of Díaz Lanz, had nevertheless gone to the brink of treason; any further collaboration with him was out of the question. Even as they listened to Fidel some hotheads were itching to rush to the presidential palace and—as Raúl Castro put it—to extirpate this obstacle on the road to revolution. But this was not what Fidel wanted; a *golpe* of the Latin American type was not at all his style. He was out to force a resignation by popular request. And this is precisely what happened: the people put enormous pressure on a man who, it later transpired, had in any case tendered his resignation several times during the previous few months. Fidel now tried to hand the presidency to Miró Cardona—who was quite ready to accept the honor, but would probably have forced Castro to enact the same play all over again a few months later. Luckily, Che and several other military leaders intervened at this point and persuaded Fidel to choose Osvaldo Dorticós Torrado, a man of the Left.

In October, another far more personal tragedy struck at the Castroist ranks. Hubert Matos, the former commander of the Antonio Guiteras Column (Column IX), was arrested in Camagüey, where he had been military governor ever since the Revolution. A small farmer from Manzanillo, Hubert Matos had joined the men of the Sierra in March 1958, rather late in the struggle. To make up for it, he had contributed a large stock of arms obtained by his own resources. More highly educated than many of the *guerrilleros,* but less open to radical ideas, he had nevertheless gained the confidence of Fidel, who had rewarded him with the highest rank in his army and appointed him head of the column that was among the first to enter Santiago. Hubert Matos became one of the most popular leaders from the Sierra and as such was put in charge of Camagüey, a particularly "delicate" province because it had always been the fief of the great landowners. As a staunch anti-Communist, he immediately called for a ban on the PSP, which brought him into direct conflict with Castro, who apparently saw no objection to entrusting Communists with some of the most important administrative posts. Finding himself a voice in the wilderness Hubert Matos tendered his resignation and advised several of his collaborators to do likewise. On October 21, Camilo Cienfuegos, another popular hero, went personally to Camagüey to arrest Matos and escort him to Havana. Matos offered no resistance, but indignantly protested that he was no plotter. On December 14, at the end of a dramatic trial, in which Fidel himself gave evidence for the prosecution, Hubert Matos was sentenced to twenty years' hard labor.

The Matos affair caused a government crisis: on November 26, 1959, Faustino Pérez and Manuel Ray tendered their resignations in protest. Eighteen months later, Faustino Pérez rejoined his old companions in the battle of Playa Girón, while Manuel Ray had become one of the leaders of the anti-Castroist expedition. By all accounts, Pérez had merely resigned in an attempt to change the course of the Revolution, while Ray had merely joined the Revolution to fight it from within. No one should be surprised that a process of social transformation as radical as the Cuban should have produced such violent differences. A revolution can hardly be expected to please everyone, especially in Cuba where many people met every radical measure with cries of dismay reminiscent of nearby Florida. What was at stake was not simply class privilege, but also old habits of thinking and deeply anchored beliefs and prejudices. Not everyone who left Cuba was a *latifundist,* capitalist, or inveterate pro-American; many became "Americanized" in spite of themselves, often from fear of the consequences of a conflict with the United States. Were all of them incurable? It is difficult to judge, and it seems an oversimplification to say they left because they had to leave. The problem of introducing radical measures in a country as unprepared for them as Cuba can only be solved equably if everyone is given the chance of developing with the revolution, in a genuinely collective and democratic process. In Cuba, the qualitative jump was too great for everyone to make with no springboard other than the wisdom of Fidel Castro. Moreover, the peculiar methods he adopted deprived the country of a large number of trained men who might otherwise have stayed on to make a considerable contribution to the Revolution.

Fidel Castro will often tell you: it is five times more difficult to develop a country after the revolution than to seize power. He

The Communists and the Revolution

does not hesitate to illustrate this thesis by the example of his own practical errors, all due to his lack of experience. But this is not really the point. The reason it is five times more difficult to build a socialist society than to seize power is the failure to create a genuine socialist outlook even while the struggle is still being waged, or to establish popular methods of running the new society. Socialism has no chance of success unless, in the very fire of action, at the very point of social explosion, a move is made toward the solution of the delicate problem of the relationship between the masses and the political leadership. Now the search for this solution was never part of the Castroist scheme. True, without Fidel, Cuba would be like the Dominican Republic, but this does not alter the fact that Fidel's method—the only possible one, perhaps—is the basic cause of his greatest difficulties. A people that says: "If Fidel is socialist, so are we," is not really mature enough to build a socialist society; it has only just been admitted to the rank of builder's apprentice.

This provides the answer to my last question: why did Fidel see fit, at least for a time, to rely so completely on the PSP, and to entrust so many responsible posts to Communists? It was simply because he had rushed headlong into nationalization without bothering to set up the rank and file or administrative machine needed for running the increasingly important state sector of the economy. He could count on the blind allegiance of most of his companions, but these were only a small group and one, moreover, that because of its youth and special training, lacked political competence and administrative skills. The Communists were not a very large group either, nor did they excel in political wisdom or radicalism, but they were supposed to have a keen sense of organization and discipline, two qualities that Fidel thought essential at the time. They were also advocates of a hierarchical power structure, in which socialist ideas and plans are dispensed to the people from above, and were accustomed to taking the sagacity of their leaders for granted. In addition to all these "qualities," they had powerful

185

allies in the East, and powerful allies were what Castro needed more than anything.

In his dealings with the Communists, too, Fidel Castro stands cleared of the charge of opportunism. He had come to believe in a socialist revolution with as much sincerity as, in the Sierra, he had believed in his *History Will Absolve Me*. His plans had changed under the pressure of events, but Fidel Castro had remained the same. He was still the same visionary, felt the same passion, and had never lost his integrity, albeit his strategy had become socialist and anti-imperialist in the Leninist sense of the term, and hence apparently closer to that of the Communists. He accordingly welcomed the PSP with open arms, as unexpected recruits to his new Sierra Maestra: Socialist Cuba. He even believed that they would cause him no greater trouble than had his young *guerrilleros*. The rest is another story, and one in which Cubans were no longer the sole protagonists.

The Russians arrive

The Soviet-Cuban tie-up

Being small and tubby, Nikita Khrushchev found his arms a little too short to encircle the huge Fidel Castro in a Russian bear hug. However, carried away by his expansive nature and Ukrainian humor, he caught his *barbudo* friend in something like a wrestling hold, pressed his head hard against that vast chest and burst out laughing, conscious no doubt of the comical situation. Fidel, in his best olive-green and sporting his tie for state occasions, could not help laughing heartily either. This was in September 1960, in the middle of "enemy" country in New York; and people in America, half shocked, half terrified, angrily attacked the UN for giving the "Reds" this chance of making a public demonstration on U.S. territory. In Cuba, by contrast, the photographic record of this great bear hug was about to be plastered on walls everywhere as a symbol of Soviet-Cuban friendship.[1]

1. Khrushchev and Castro gave each other their first bear hug on September 20, 1960, at the Hotel Theresa in Harlem, where the Cuban delegation

187

Guerrillas in Power

Other progressive leaders also took part in the famous Fifteenth General Assembly of the United Nations, but Fidel was clearly Khrushchev's favorite. Before each session opened, the Soviet Prime Minister would make a point of crossing the Assembly hall, where the delegations are seated in alphabetical order, to give him a demonstrative welcome. "Fidel Castro is not a Communist; but he will be one in two years, thanks to American pressure," he told reporters delightedly, as if it were all a foregone conclusion. Castro seemed not the least disturbed by this prophecy. Since his previous visit to New York in April 1959, he had come a long way. He no longer accused the Soviet bloc of suppressing freedom nor repeated his old slogan, "No bread without liberty; no liberty without bread." Though he did not admit to being a Communist, he let it be understood that the decision was his alone: he challenged the Monroe Doctrine and denied that the United States had the right to prevent Cuba from choosing its allies or principles.

Khrushchev's attitude toward Cuba had changed no less spectacularly during the previous twelve months. On his 1959 visit to the United States he had said nothing at all in defense of the Cuban Revolution, and had remained quite unperturbed when his hosts attacked Cuba from a narrow anti-Communist standpoint. Until November 1959, Russia had not even thought it necessary to keep a Tass correspondent in Havana. It was only after February 1960 that things began to change: Anastas Mikoyan, the Soviet vice-premier, visiting Mexico at the head of a Soviet industrial exhibition, agreed to take his wares to Havana as well. He thus became the first Soviet leader to see the *guerrilleros* in power. Favorably impressed, he signed a limited but generous trade agreement with them.[2]

---

was staying. But we cannot positively assert that the famous photograph was taken then, since the same thing happened when Castro visited the headquarters of the Soviet delegation, and again at the UN meeting.

2. By this agreement Russia undertook to buy 425,000 tons of Cuban sugar in 1960 and to increase this quantity to a million tons in the following year. In exchange the Soviet Union agreed to sell Cuba a limited quantity of oil and to lend it $100 million at 2.5 per cent per annum.

The Russians arrive

In truth, the Soviet Union was busily signing such agreements with many countries of the Third World, including pro-Western ones, as a token of her intention to make the Russian presence felt more widely. In Havana, Mikoyan was careful to say nothing even vaguely anti-American. Indeed, after his return the U.S.S.R. was in no hurry to re-establish diplomatic relations with Cuba, a gesture that would have alienated no one. Soviet "penetration" of Cuba was clearly both modest and extremely discreet.

Three months later this attitude had changed completely. Beginning in May 1960, all Soviet speeches included some laudatory remarks about the Cuban Revolution, while Moscow newspapers printed rapturous articles about the country. On July 9, 1960, Khrushchev took his pro-Cuban sentiments one stage further still: backed by the threat of his ICBMs, he firmly requested the United States to keep her hands off the island. Never before had he addressed America in such terms, or reacted so strongly in defense of a country not under direct military threat.[3] The hugs he lavished so ostentatiously on Castro in New York set the seal on a friendship that had flourished after a mere five months. What precisely had happened?

One possible explanation was that the Cuban Revolution had meanwhile grown far more radical. Another was that Alexander Alexeev, the Tass correspondent in Havana, had become convinced that the Castroists had genuine progressive aspirations.[4] Lastly, America's refusal to grant Russia even a limited right to trade with Cuba was something the Soviet Union could not tolerate.

In the circumstances, Khrushchev's attitude was perfectly

3. The Soviet Union had already used the missile threat in 1956 against Britain and France, when they attacked Egypt. But that time there was a real war, whereas in July 1960 there had been no mention of an American or even a "patriotic" invasion of Cuba.
4. In June 1962, Alexeev became Russian ambassador to Cuba, replacing Kudriavtsev. This promotion was probably due to his great popularity in Cuba, but might also have been an indication that Alexeev, who had been in Cuba since 1959, was sent there, in the first place, in more than a purely journalistic capacity.

189

logical, and in April 1961 when he saw a chance of making a big show of Soviet solidarity with Cuba, he seized it. The battle of Playa Girón had roused strong feelings in the U.S.S.R., as it had elsewhere in the world. Khrushchev had bombarded Washington with notes of protest which, according to the Russians, prevented direct U.S. intervention. The victory of Playa Girón now became as much a Russian as a Cuban triumph, and was suitably played up as such in the Soviet press. And yet, Moscow preserved a frigid silence when Castro described his revolution as a socialist one. In the flood of articles and speeches commemorating the "common" victory, not one word, not one allusion, was devoted to Castro's newly chosen political path.

The Russians, it is said, were most annoyed that they were faced with a *fait accompli;* Castro's decision had been quite unilateral and he had not bothered to consult anybody. True, Faure Chomón, the Cuban ambassador in Moscow, had gently prepared the ground with his speech of March 13 in which he had referred to Cuban revolutionaries as "we Communists"; but then everybody had taken this for a slip of the tongue. Moreover, the PSP paper *Hoy*[5] had printed the word "Communists" in quotation marks, and a figure of speech was hardly the proper way in which to inform a friendly country of a major political change. The Russians in particular would have liked some explanation before sending messages of congratulation to the new sister republic in the Caribbean.

But Russia's ambiguous attitude toward Castro persisted for almost a year, which showed that more than mere etiquette was involved. For twelve months Havana kept extolling socialism, while Moscow pretended not to notice. Cuba always had had a good press in the U.S.S.R.; the island was well liked, but not enough to bracket it together with the rest of the "socialist world." Official Soviet phraseologists were at all times careful to speak of "the U.S.S.R., the People's Democracies,

5. Report in *Hoy* (March 14, 1961) of Faure Chomón's speech on the occasion of the fourth anniversary of the attack on Batista's presidential palace by the *Directorio Revolucionario.*

The Russians arrive

and Cuba," the last constituting a unique category falling neither in the capitalist camp nor yet wholly in the socialist bloc.

It should not be forgotten that since its foundation in 1919, the Communist International had been a highly select "club," with very strict rules and regulations. No outside leader or political movement had the right to call itself "Communist" without express permission from the club secretary. Whoever aspired to this title had first to submit his candidature for approval by the International, and give pledges as to his future good behavior.[6] After the dissolution of the Comintern in 1943, the whole procedure lost most of its practical significance, as there was no longer a central body capable of verifying the credentials of possible candidates. Since, moreover, no party had asked for admission to the club since that time, the problem had remained purely academic—until the Cuban episode, that is. Now Cuba was not entirely unknown in the Communist world. A Leninist party, properly accredited by the Comintern, had been established on the island for the past thirty-five years, and according to accepted ideas, was the only one entitled to lead the working class and the people forward to socialism. In reality that party had never led anyone; it was not in power now, nor could it boast a single minister in a government that had just proclaimed itself a Communist one. The accepted rules demanded that Fidel belong to the PSP, the only official Communist Party, or that he remain one of the "non-aligned" who, that September 1961, were holding their congress in Belgrade. Moscow quite clearly favored the second solution. Then, one fine morning on April 11, 1962, the unsuspecting Russians learned from a lead editorial in *Pravda* that the Cubans were also working for

6. The original constitution of the Comintern incorporated twenty-one points governing doctrine, organization, and internal discipline. These empowered the leaders of the Comintern to choose, and where necessary to replace, the ruling groups in the various Communist parties; and in fact the Comintern, especially during the first years of its existence, openly intervened in the internal affairs of several member organizations.

G*

socialism, just as they themselves were. From that day on, Comrade Fidel Castro acquired full membership rights in the international Communist family, and Cuba ceased to be a special category in the Soviet phrase book. Procedural problems were solved with astonishing facility, the more so as there was not a single Communist Party to raise objections. To crown it all, the decision was taken two weeks after the dismissal of Aníbal Escalante, one of the chief leaders of the old PSP (we shall return to this later) . What, we may ask again, had happened?

It is immediately obvious that Cuba followed a far less tortuous course than the Russians, whose "absenteeism" in 1959, revolutionary frenzy in 1960, hesitations in 1961, and fresh bout of intransigent anti-imperialism in 1962 were not simply due to changes in the Cuban situation.

A more careful examination of the timetable of Soviet-Cuban relations shows that Nikita Khrushchev was playing his Cuban cards so as to score points in the difficult game with both his enemies in Washington and his comrades in Peking. Let us look more closely at what happened during the Khrushchev phase in Soviet history. At the end of 1957, when Khrushchev succeeded in beating all his rivals in the race for Stalin's succession, and became both prime minister and Party secretary, a Soviet rocket placed a satellite—Sputnik—in orbit around the earth; shortly afterward, a Russian, Yuri Gagarin, made the first space flight in history. These exploits astounded the Russians as much as they did the rest of the world. Russians suddenly discovered that, despite all the mistakes they had committed during the "personality cult" era, their country was a long way ahead in technological progress and defensive capacity. The U.S.S.R. was no longer a "beleaguered fortress": her ICBMs secured her against all attack.

Thus, the reign of Khrushchev began auspiciously: the international prestige and self-confidence of the U.S.S.R. were greater than ever before, and the new prime minister was determined to make the best of this propitious state of affairs. A pragmatist, Khrushchev was more interested in the scientific and technological revolution that was apparently taking place in Soviet industry than in questions of doctrine and Party history. "We have said enough about Stalin's misdeeds; let us now roll up our sleeves and work for socialism 'with butter,' " his speeches to the Russian people seemed to say. He was convinced that a new era was at hand; that Soviet society, by its very nature, was best fitted to apply the latest technological inventions to production. The Soviet Union did not have to reckon with the archaic selfishness inherent in the capitalist system; here there was no fear of unemployment and hence no brake on the development of automation; and here universal education was helping to turn out an impressive number of trained technicians. According to Khrushchev, the U.S.S.R. had at long last reached the point where it could reap the maximum benefit from the socialist foundations laid by those who had had to be "sacrificed" to the early five-year plans. Nor did he speak merely as a technician, or "technocrat"; he was equally interested in improving the quality of life. He promised the Russian people more leisure time, higher education, and more time for cultural pleasures not within the reach of workers in other industrialized countries. Now the road to the good life could only be pursued through rapid economic success.

In order to grease the wheels of the ponderous centralized economic system, Khrushchev started a whole series of administrative reforms. He set up relatively autonomous economic regions—*Sovnarkhozes*—and even split the Party apparatus into two branches, one specializing in agriculture, the other in industry. At the same time he appealed to the pioneering spirit of the young, calling upon them to play their part in turning the immense virgin lands of Soviet Asia into one vast granary. Lastly he intended to gear the educational system more closely to industry, so as to turn out the maximum number of young specialists capable of breaking production records. At the beginning of 1959, he launched a seven-year development plan which would enable the U.S.S.R. to outstrip the most advanced capitalist countries. Two further seven-year plans would suffice to give Russia an abundance of wealth that would before 1980 enable it to put into practice the Communist principle of "to each according to his needs." The world-wide repercussions of such a victory would be incalculable.

Nor would the U.S.S.R. stand aloof from the rest of the world—as it had in Stalin's day. Russia needed the widest international exchanges of information to stimulate scientific and technological progress at home. Its goal was peace without terror or ruinous arms races. And it hoped to get all this because it had so much to offer in exchange. Its military power counterbalanced that of the imperialist countries, and hence served to discourage all expansionist attempts. It could engage in peaceful competition with the West, especially in the Third World. The Soviet Union accordingly offered the great powers peaceful coexistence, an end to all wars, including local ones, and a guarantee that all small countries could develop along lines they themselves had freely chosen. Khrushchev became the traveling salesman of this reassuringly peaceful new Russia, a Russia wide open to a "dialogue" with the "great," and unselfishly ready to help the "small." His efforts went a long way toward increasing the popularity of the U.S.S.R. and its influence on Western opinion.

Today we know the sequel. The Soviet Union did not surpass the American level of production in 1965, and will not reach the age of Communist abundance in 1980. In 1964, Khrushchev fell, and his successors, far from searching their consciences, have simply stopped making promises. Their only ambition seems to be to keep power in their own hands. Faced with a worsening social, economic, and political situation in their own country as well as in their whole camp, they have once again had recourse to repression at home, or to tanks, as in Czechoslovakia. Compared with their rigidity and political mediocrity, Khrushchevism appears in retrospect as a great breath of fresh air.

But Khrushchev's attempt was doomed to failure, for reasons that have since become quite evident. He tried to deliver the Soviet people from their paralyzing "father complex" by show-

194

ing them that they had built a magnificent socialist society, not thanks to Stalin, but despite him. To listen to him, one might have thought that the U.S.S.R. had, in record time, closed the enormous gap between it and the most industrialized capitalist countries; had already become a perfectly just and healthy society ready for a rapid advance to Communism. That is why he apparently felt entitled to promise astounding economic progress, followed by the automatic liquidation of all the remaining sores introduced into the healthy body of the U.S.S.R. by his predecessor.

This assessment was quite false. To begin with, during the past three decades, the Soviet Union had not been led by the "highly democratic and combative" Communist Party, but solely by Stalin. Hence if Soviet achievements were all Khrushchev alleged, they would in fact have redounded to the credit of Stalin, and the "de-Stalinization" campaign would have been slanderous, to say the least. In 1931, ten years before Hitler invaded the U.S.S.R., Stalin had declared: "We are fifty to a hundred years behind the advanced capitalist countries. We must catch up within ten years or else we shall be crushed."[7] And when the test did come in 1941, the U.S.S.R. was already powerful and industrialized enough to emerge victorious from its test. It was this very fact that gave rise to the myth of Stalin's infallibility. The only means of overthrowing him was to challenge the quality of the society he had built up by such harsh methods. The point was not so much that victory would have been far less costly had Stalin been a better man, but that his "victory" meant breaking the socialist promises of the October Revolution.

Khrushchev did not wish to say this, nor indeed could he do so, and that was precisely why his de-Stalinization campaign was a sham. Worse still, by drawing up so triumphant a balance sheet of the preceding epoch, he was led into making new promises he could not possibly keep. In fact, the breakthrough

7. J. Stalin: *Sochinienia* (Works), Vol. 13 (Moscow, Gosizdat), p. 39.

into space in no way proved the health of the Soviet economy. On the contrary, like all Stalinist successes, it was obtained at the price of enormous sacrifices, sacrifices that threw economic and social life completely out of gear. Far from being on the ascendant, the Soviet economy was running out of wind, and it was an illusion to think that the throttling political and social pressures accumulated over the decades could be eliminated in a hurry. In short, by staking everything on rapid economic progress, Khrushchev was merely repeating Stalin's old wager, but under even worse conditions—the mystique was no longer there.

Khrushchev himself was not, of course, entirely fooled by his public optimism; it did not take him very long to realize that he had built his hopes on economic sand. That is precisely why he came to attach so much importance to coexistence with the West: disarmament would enable him to switch over vast sums to the civilian sectors of the economy, and the resulting psychological boost was bound to stimulate the energies of the Soviet people. In retrospect, it is thus easy to see why, from a certain moment onward, an international thaw became his top priority, and why in this sphere he reacted with the impatience and fury of a desperate man.

Here, too, the reasons for his failure are quite clear today: it sprang chiefly from the equivocal view the Soviet leaders took of their world role. The U.S.S.R. was not only a great power, but continued to present itself as the spiritual fountainhead of a revolutionary family. The Western nations were only too happy to welcome "good old Russia" into the concert of industrialized nations, but in return they expected it to refrain from making anti-capitalist speeches and to behave like any other conventional country. They would have liked its conversion to be frank and complete, would have liked the Soviet Union to join into common aid projects designed to maintain the status quo in the underdeveloped countries. While Khrushchev would have been quite prepared to follow this line quietly, he could not renounce his Communist rhetoric, which after all was his title deed to power, and which was inseparable from

196

the myth of the socialist nature of Soviet society to which he ardently subscribed.

In short, Khrushchev did not wish to appear before the world as a man suing for peace at any price. He was forced to "theorize" his policy of coexistence with the explanation that it would prove profitable not only for the U.S.S.R., but also for the world labor movement. This declaration rather alarmed Western leaders, according to whom it cast some doubt on the sincerity of the Soviet statesman.

Nor was Western opinion the only thing Nikita Khrushchev had to worry about: ever since 1945 the U.S.S.R. had ceased to be the only socialist fatherland. By its side, and partly thanks to its victory in the Second World War, there now stood a whole group of countries, great and small, some more advanced than the U.S.S.R., some terribly backward, but each with its own social reality, needs, and external conflicts. To preserve monolithism in so heterogeneous a family, Stalin himself, despite the reputation of infallibility he enjoyed in the Communist camp, had been forced to make systematic use of terror and purges. The reader will remember his excommunication in 1948 of the Yugoslav Communists and his pitiless persecution of the "national deviationists" in the People's Democracies right until the end of his life. Needless to say, Nikita Khrushchev lacked the authority to run his camp in this manner. In 1956, when revolts broke out in Poland and Hungary, he reduced them to silence, but promised that he would never again interfere in the internal affairs of any country. By a solemn declaration of October 30, 1956, the Communist Party of the Soviet Union granted each country in the Eastern bloc the right to pursue its own path to socialism.

Clearly this was easier said than done. Because of the diversity of the countries concerned, and the inadequacy of the doctrinal "cement" uniting them (it had crumbled during the de-Stalinization process), the new policy, if applied to the letter, would inexorably have given birth to several Communisms, all equally legitimate and all based on special interpretation of

Marxism-Leninism. That would have been the end of Communist monolithism on the international scale, and also inside each party—something neither Khrushchev nor the leaders of the People's Democracies wanted at any price; their fear of any form of debate or democratization was the sole link uniting them all. Nevertheless there were two defections, one negligible: Albania, the other so great that it became the nightmare of all the heirs to the old school: China.

Egalitarian, leftist, and anti-bureaucratic ideas did, of course, exist in China even before de-Stalinization, and Mao Tse-tung would surely have chosen his own road even had Stalin been alive. He would never have waited for the Kremlin to grant him leave to go his own way. However, in the new circumstances, the U.S.S.R. was completely powerless to do anything about his "heresy"; it had renounced all legal arguments against it. At most it could beg Mao not to go too far in search of his "shortcut to Communism," and warn him of the dangers to which any precipitate actions might expose China.[8] This warning went unheeded; in 1958 Mao's China virtually abandoned the Soviet road to socialism. As a result, the two Communist giants drew further and further apart, if at first without public recriminations. But though both quoted the same "classical" sources and proclaimed themselves true Communists, their aims and objects became more incompatible by the day. The dangers of this situation could no longer be warded off by summit conferences, and the specter of a final split henceforth haunted both Khrushchev and Mao Tse-tung.

This affected the Soviet prime minister more than his rival. He was traditionally, and at least titularly, *primus inter pares* in the Communist family. A split with China would highlight his inability to preserve the unity he had been bequeathed by the Third International and undermine his prestige and au-

8. The Soviet Union undoubtedly intended to mobilize world Communist opinion against China, and to that end intended to hold a World Communist Party Congress in November 1960. We shall have more to say about this below.

thority, to mention only the purely personal implications of this disaster. Moreover, he could not allow Mao to parade before the world Communist movement as the true heir to the revolutionary tradition, as the more implacable opponent of imperialism. Hence Khrushchev's hands in his negotiations with the West were tied.

That there was a left opposition in his own ranks was fairly widely known; and this undoubtedly provided him with a lever in his dealings with the West. Left pressure might well drive the Soviet Union, if not toward Maoism, at least toward greater intransigence. Khrushchev accordingly let it be known that if no agreement were reached, he might quickly be replaced by someone less taken with the idea of an East-West dialogue. His unofficial spokesmen lost no opportunity of stressing "the dangers of a return to Stalinism" and their arguments were eagerly taken up by the world press.[9]

But then his economic plans became bogged down by the country's bureaucratic inertia, and Khrushchev was forced all the more to support peaceful coexistence. At the same time, he was less than ever in a position to satisfy the demands of his Western partners—partly because of increasing Maoist pressure on his left, partly because of the threatened breakup of the Communist camp. It was in this complex situation that a new actor appeared on the stage—Cuba.

9. During the UN session of September 1960, I attended a number of cocktail parties at which unofficial Soviet representatives—journalists and junior diplomats—kept referring, off the record, to the "Stalinist folly of the Chinese" and to their desire to push the world into war. At that time I blamed the vodka, which was flowing in unlimited quantities, but later I realized that all this was part of a well-staged campaign, aimed in this atmosphere of well-oiled conviviality at convincing Western opinion of the urgent need for an agreement with Khrushchev. It might be mentioned that the mystifiers succeeded in mystifying themselves. Unable to treat the Chinese arguments seriously, Khrushchev did his best to pillory them as Stalinist warmongering. In reality his own political line was far closer to traditional Stalinism than Mao Tse-tung's, and he knew perfectly well that the Chinese, far from seeking war, were merely objecting to his dreams of achieving a political, economic, and ideological truce between the two blocs.

Guerrillas in Power

At first, Khrushchev was not very interested in Cuba: his campaign of friendship with the West was proceeding very satisfactorily. He compared world politics to a cabbage, with Soviet-American relations at the center. In 1959, the "outer leaves" had been pulled away, and on September 14, there he was, in Washington, about to get down to the heart. He was full of optimism about the outcome of his historic journey, the first visit any Soviet leader had paid to the United States. At the end of his tour, on September 26 and 27, he spent forty-eight hours at Camp David in almost continuous discussions with President Eisenhower, pleading for new rules in the international game. Eisenhower did not say no; he agreed to call a summit conference in Paris in May 1960 where America, Great Britain, France, and the Soviet Union could discuss the whole matter.

Khrushchev then left, full of optimism, and made straight for Peking, intending to secure his "left flank." On October 1, the anniversary of the Chinese revolution, he made a speech before Mao Tse-tung and five thousand guests at a great banquet in the People's Palace. In it, he not only defended his conception of coexistence—this was expected—but went on to attack all those backward elements who refused to grasp the need for change in the nuclear age. He insisted that war was no longer possible, that Eisenhower wanted peace and that just a few "militarist cliques" in the United States still clung to the obsolete idea of imperialism. His hosts kept a stony silence. For the first time, they refused to mark the occasion of a visit by the leader of a fraternal party with a special communiqué. They did not disavow Khrushchev publicly, nor did they propose to obstruct him, but their very silence proclaimed louder than words that they gave his policy little chance of success.

On May 1, 1960, two weeks before the opening of the Paris conference, a U-2, an American spy plane, was shot down near Sverdlovsk in the heart of continental Russia, and its pilot taken prisoner. The Soviet premier was, it seems, convinced that this violation of Soviet air space had been organized by those "American militarist cliques" for the sole purpose of embarrassing their

200

own president and of marking their opposition to his talks with the Reds. Khrushchev accordingly allowed the Pentagon to become trapped in a mesh of lies and then, on May 5 presented the Supreme Soviet with incontrovertible proof of American culpability. Logically, President Eisenhower should now have repudiated the military clique, if only to clear his own name. Instead, he argued that America had a perfect right to fly over Russia if this was demanded by U.S. security. This was a far cry, indeed, from the spirit of Camp David, and from coexistence between the two superpowers.

Despite this slap in the face, Khrushchev attended the Paris conference, trying vainly for four long days to drag some kind of apology out of Eisenhower. He had doubtless counted on the English and French to disavow Eisenhower's extraordinary doctrine. But "Western solidarity" was clearly too great to be shaken by arguments about the inviolability of national air space or breaches of international law. On May 18, before returning empty-handed to Moscow, Nikita Khrushchev called a press conference at the Palais de Chaillot, determined to tell the world what he thought of Eisenhower.

The Cuban Revolution was then seventeen months old, seventeen months of bitter struggle with the United States. Khrushchev had not referred to this fact until then, but at the Palais de Chaillot he suddenly chose to stress the prime importance of a revolution which, if nothing else, showed that America was powerless to hold up the march of history. "The dawn of progress breaks even over the Americas, over the heads of the imperialists who will be no more able to stop it than to prevent the rising of the sun!" he cried, and went on to glorify the "struggle of the Cuban people for independence." It is possible, given the internal developments of Cuba, that sooner or later he would have made such a speech anyway, but the timetable shows clearly that the U-2 incident and the failure of the Paris conference accelerated this development. On May 7, 1960, came Eisenhower's first refusal to apologize for the spy plane; on May 9, 1960, Moscow re-established diplomatic relations with

Havana and sent warm messages of congratulation on the Cuban Revolution; on May 15–18, 1960, Eisenhower refused once again to apologize; on May 18, 1960, Khrushchev made his speech at the Palais de Chaillot, dwelling at length on the Cuban problem.

It is an old habit of the great powers to show concern for small countries fighting their rivals. Khrushchev's determination to exploit the sensitive issue of Cuba against Eisenhower was therefore quite in the cards. But what he said suggested that he had more in mind than a purely verbal offensive. The Cuban Revolution had shown that the United States was extremely vulnerable in Latin America—which was of course the reason for American hatred of Castro. What would happen if the Soviet Union were to use all its enormous resources in support of revolutionary movements on that continent? Were not the discussions at the Palais de Chaillot a warning to the Americans? Did they not herald a new Soviet strategy, based no longer on a search for agreement with the West but on massive aid to international revolution?

In any event, this was how the speech was interpreted in Havana, where it was greeted with jubilation. Peking responded quite differently; it refused to be bought off with vague threats against the aggressors or to allow Khrushchev to extricate himself so cheaply from the failure of his policy. The Chinese demanded self-criticism in the approved style, and wanted Khrushchev to admit that international revolution could not be achieved by compromise. They chose to say so openly in June 1960, a month after the Paris fiasco, to the Communists who had found themselves in Peking together with the delegates to the Congress of the World Federation of Trade Unions. It was still a message meant purely for family consumption and was delivered behind closed doors, luckily for Khrushchev; a public polemic with Peking following so closely on the heels of the Eisenhower rebuff would have been a major disaster for him. He decided there and then to secure his flank and, almost providentially, the "Cuban affair" came to his aid, as significant coincidences in the timetable show.

202

The Russians arrive

The Central Committee of the Communist Party of the Soviet Union was due to meet on July 11, 1960, ostensibly to "approve the policy of the First Secretary of the Party." In reality, Khrushchev intended to submit a series of measures calculated to reduce the Chinese leaders to silence. Rather than engage in fruitless discussions with them, Khrushchev proposed to teach them a severe lesson by withdrawing all economic aid, stopping all deliveries—even those already paid for—and recalling all Soviet technicians who were still working for the Peking regime. In other words, he was anxious to declare an economic blockade on China, much as Stalin had done with Yugoslavia in 1948. In his view, an "economic lesson" would soon force Mao to get back into line, thus obviating disciplinary action on the political level. The scheme was risky—if the Chinese refused to capitulate, the whole thing might easily rebound on the Soviet Union. For how could Russia possibly justify before the international Communist family the use of such harsh measures against a country with full rights of membership? And a meeting of all Communist parties was scheduled for November 1960.

On July 6, 1960, five days before the "Chinese Meeting" of the Central Committee in Moscow, Eisenhower cut the balance of the Cuban sugar quota for 1960 (some 700,000 tons). The two events were probably quite unconnected, for, despite the "brilliance" of his intelligence services, the American President knew absolutely nothing about what was happening on the Sino-Soviet front. But his action gave the Soviet rulers a golden opportunity to demonstrate the full measure of their internationalist sense of solidarity. On July 9, the Soviet Union agreed to buy all the Cuban sugar the United States refused to take, or might refuse to take in future. The U.S.S.R. further undertook to give Cuba all the economic aid she might need and, in order to discourage American aggression, declared that "figuratively speaking," in this era of intercontinental missiles, she could hit back at the United States as easily as if they were next-door neighbors.

The following day, July 10, during a mass meeting in front

Guerrillas in Power

of the presidential palace in Havana, Che Guevara thanked Khrushchev for his unprecedented gesture of international good will and declared: "Cuba is a glorious island in the middle of the Caribbean, protected by the rockets of the mightiest power in history."[10] Communists the world over were equally enthusiastic, marveling at this show of strength by the Soviet Union. In Moscow, a three-line communiqué stated baldly that the Central Committee of the Communist Party of the Soviet Union had unanimously approved Nikita Khrushchev's policy. Inserted as it was between dispatches describing the enthusiastic reactions to the declaration of July 9, this news item gave the impression that the Central Committee had done no more than approve the First Secretary's Cuban policy, when, in fact, it had given him the go-ahead on launching his grand anti-Maoist campaign.

In all probability, the Soviet hierarchy would have followed Khrushchev's lead in any case; after all he was still in control of the Central Committee. However, the Cuban affair gave him an unexpected internationalist alibi. Who could call Russia a self-seeking big power, now that she had unhesitatingly thrown her entire weight behind a small faraway island that was not even socialist? Chinese allegations that Khrushchev was a revisionist would not, at that time, have been received very sympathetically in the Communist world. And this was just what Nikita needed —he had few other successes with which to impress foreign comrades in November 1960. For, far from capitulating, China had compiled a mighty dossier against him, and had forced him to buy her silence with major concessions at the conference table. The Cuban affair helped him to conceal the magnitude of his defeat. Without it, the final document adopted by the Conference of Eighty-one Communist Parties would undoubtedly have shown that he had failed to obtain family backing for his policy of peaceful coexistence. After his speech of July 9 and bear hugs with Castro in New York, those passages of the

10. For the complete speech see *Collected Speeches of Che Guevara,* edited by Laura Gonzáles (Italian edition) , *op. cit.,* p. 810.

204

text concerning the necessity of intensifying world revolutionary struggle, the condemnation of Yugoslav revisionism, and the de-nunciation of America as "world policeman" no longer looked as if they had been forced upon him. It appeared as if Khrush-chev himself, wishing to ride two tigers at once, was still un-decided which suited him best.

But this impression was totally false: not for an instant did Khrushchev believe that the Soviet Union could do anything other than strive for agreement among the great powers. His country needed disarmament and peace; it was suffering too much under the Cold War, was too scarred by the disappoint-ments of the Stalinist era, and had become too depoliticized to endure another major political battle on the world scale. It matters little whether Khrushchev himself had lost faith in world revolutions or whether he realized that his compatriots had done so, for the practical consequences were the same: Russia must at all costs cling to the hopes of the Camp David period. It was for that reason—and especially after the Kennedy administration had taken over in Washington—that he must have begun to fear that his Cuban involvement might pull him in unwanted directions. The machinery he himself had set in motion was no longer under his sole control—Washington and Havana had begun to manipulate the levers as well.

The Americans, for example, were utterly alarmed by the press conference in the Palais de Chaillot. True they had been describing Castro as "some kind of Communist" all along, but only so as to undermine his authority at home, as a pretext for getting rid of him without trouble. But they had realized that he was neither a "Soviet agent" nor even vaguely connected with Moscow. After Khrushchev's speech, however, they were haunted by real fears that Cuba might, in fact, become a "base for Communist subversion" in their own hemisphere, and this was a threat they were ready to meet with the utmost severity.

Eisenhower's decision to cut the balance of the 1960 Cuban sugar quota reflected this irrational fear. As a form of economic pressure it was quite pointless: first, because Castro had warned

205

Washington that he would hit back by nationalizing American estates worth far more than those miserable 700,000 tons of sugar; second, because—to take a cynical view—it was very much in America's interest to leave the sugar question pending until next year, and then take Castro by surprise when he had a new crop on his hands. On July 6, 1960, everyone still thought that Eisenhower had merely fired a warning shot, that things would quickly settle down again. President Frondizi of Argentina at once offered his services as a mediator, and Castro agreed to wait one month before taking reprisals against American companies on the island. But the Soviet declaration of July 9 was more than Washington was prepared to stomach. Eisenhower now refused to back down, lest the world conclude that he had flinched at the mere mention of Russian rockets. And so Frondizi's mediation attempt came to nothing; Castro nationalized most American estates in Cuba, and the chances of reconciliation looked dim to both Washington and Havana. In January 1961, a few days before leaving the White House for good, Eisenhower broke off diplomatic relations with Cuba.[11] He left his successor a poisonous legacy: a small army of anti-Castroists trained by the CIA.

By then it was much too late to convert the Castroists to neutrality, as Khrushchev tried to do; they were determined to find not only new allies but a wider historical framework for their revolution. Throughout 1959, Cuba sought, and not unsuccessfully, support in Latin America and the Third World. And then the Russians suddenly gave them everything on a silver platter: the socialist model, the possibility of participation in an international anti-imperialist crusade, the promise of help

11. He did so on January 3, 1961, twelve days before John F. Kennedy took over in the White House. In an editorial in its Sunday edition of January 8, 1961, *The New York Times* wrote that American patience with Cuban propaganda lies about an imminent U.S. invasion was exhausted. Eisenhower himself was fully aware that this invasion was in fact being planned and, if we can believe Victor Bernstein and Jesse Gordon's excellent account published in *The Columbia University Forum* (Autumn 1967), even the editors of *The New York Times* were in the know.

and defense—in short, everything they had been seeking else-where. To be sure, they took all the Russians' promises at face value, and conveniently dismissed Khrushchev's continued pro-fessions of faith in coexistence as polite diplomatic chatter. Some observers were amazed at this rather selective Cuban interpreta-tion of Soviet politics, but Havana had only two things to say: 1) "We know the Russians by their deeds, and leave the inter-pretation of their motives to our common enemies," and 2) "We are friends enough not to ask the Russians indiscreet questions." And events seemed to bear the Cubans out: the simplest explanation for the speed and extent of the Soviet com-mitment was a wish to see "the sun of revolution rise as quickly as possible over Latin America and the rest of the world."

On the other hand, not being used to the ways of the Com-munist fraternity, the Cubans had every right to think that, if they were told nothing, it was simply because there was nothing important to tell. It so happened that Ernesto Che Guevara was in Moscow in December 1960 at the very time of the World Communist Congress. He had many friends among the dele-gates in general, and the Cuban PSP delegation in particular. How could he have believed that no one, not Aníbal Escalante or anyone else of the inner circle, would bother to keep him informed of disputes and disagreements, if there had been any? He made no distinction between dyed-in-the-wool Communists and others; a revolutionary among revolutionaries, he had no ulterior motives himself, and did not think it possible that others might.[12]

12. I was told by one who went with him to Moscow that Che Guevara really knew nothing of what went on during the Congress. This may seem odd, seeing that the Congress was full of dramatic ups and downs and—as we now know—its fate hung in the balance to the very last moment. The Albanian delegate, Enver Hodja, accused Khrushchev in full session of the worst crimes, calling him a "starver of the people" and, to all intents and purposes, a counterrevolutionary. The Chinese wanted his speech pub-lished in full; as may be imagined, the Russians wanted the very opposite. The Italians, for their part, thought it absurd that the final document should contain a new ban on Yugoslav Communism, when all the Communist parties of Europe, led by the Russian, had such excellent relations with

Guerrillas in Power

The Cubans were obviously naïve, so much so that their candor began to cause Moscow serious embarrassment. Thus Havana kept on waving Khrushchev's "imaginary rockets" of July 9, 1960, under the noses of the Americans, explaining to Latin America and the whole world that the Russians intended to fight a revolutionary crusade by their side. It was doubtless at Khrushchev's personal insistence that they agreed to attend the conference of nonaligned countries in Belgrade in 1961, though they had little or nothing to say to this heterogeneous family. Cuba was now well along the "socialist" road, and all it now wanted was victory for its side. Khrushchev, who would rather have avoided a trial of strength with the United States, did not find the Cubans easy partners. But it was too late to go back on the promises he had made.

From his point of view, the whole Cuban affair was a nightmare. To begin with, it was an embarrassment on the diplomatic level: to reach a détente with the West, Khrushchev had to eliminate any "hot spots" over which the two blocs might clash. Now Cuba was just one more source of discord, and one that was exceedingly difficult to keep in check since Castro, who was not of the "old school," did not accept the discipline of the Soviet camp and interpreted its strategy as he saw fit. Secondly, Cuba was a military embarrassment: the Soviet Union had committed herself to defending an island more than 6,000 miles away and at the very gate of the United States. The poorest strategist in the world would not have chosen so unfavorable a ground for a showdown. Soviet superiority in conventional

---

Belgrade. To the very last day, no one knew whether the Chinese would agree to sign the final document. The head of the Albanian delegation even left Moscow before the end of the Congress, leaving the signing of the document to a minor official. Incredible as it may seem, this squabbling family was as determined as ever to keep its family secrets from the outside world, and this was true even of such men as Che Guevara, for all that he and his like were progressive, revolutionary, and friends of the socialist bloc. These conspiratorial methods were partly responsible for eventually turning Che, one of the warmest supporters in Cuba of the Soviet Union, into one of its severest critics.

arms was canceled by distance. The threat of "shadow rockets" harmed the world prestige of the Soviet Union: it made a mockery of Khrushchev's protestations of peace, and did not really frighten the Americans, who knew full well that no great power would commit nuclear suicide in defense of a limited foreign objective.

Thirdly, Cuba was a doctrinal source of embarrassment: by admitting young revolutionaries who were unorthodox and full of fervor, Khrushchev was bringing into his camp a possible source of further dissension at a time when he had his hands full with internecine quarrels. Castro might not have had any clear-cut "heretical" ambitions; but fighting as he did in the front line of the anti-imperialist struggle, he was perforce driven to question the possibility of peaceful coexistence, thus playing straight into the hands of the Chinese.

Last but not least, Cuba was an economic embarrassment: the Soviet Union had underwritten the development of a country whose tastes, needs, and economic structure had been molded by the Americans. Cuba was to be a showcase of Soviet efficiency in Latin America, when in fact it was the last country in the world to make good use of Soviet foreign aid.

In this connection, it is worth pointing out that in 1960, when the Russians came to the rescue of the Cuban Revolution, their sense of solidarity was in direct proportion to their total ignorance of the situation and problems of that country. "The Russians did not come here overburdened with facts: most knew very little more about us than the few poems Mayakovsky had written during his visit to Havana in 1924; and they could only tell you that Castro had a beard. They knew just about as much about us as Christopher Columbus did when he landed in Cuba." This I was told by one of Castro's collaborators, a man who had helped to show the first Russian "pilgrims" around the island.

But, it may be objected, did not the Cubans derive great benefits from Khrushchev's involvement? Where else could they have found so effective a counterweight to American pressure?

Guerrillas in Power

Those who defended the "objectively revolutionary" historical role of the Soviet Union always came back to one question: "What would have become of Cuba without the Soviet Union?"

Rather than engage in this kind of speculation, we shall try to show what really happened to Cuba after her entry into the Soviet camp. It is a story that can be written without the use of the conditional. It proves quite clearly that a marriage contract whose terms are not plainly set out deceives both parties, and that the resulting union is a disaster.

A factory is like a woman . . .

"A country of the happiest prospect," Mayakovsky had exclaimed, moved by Cuba's beautiful landscape, its giant palms, and tropical flowers. But his first flush of enthusiasm did not survive a visit to Vedado, the new "American" quarter of Havana.[13] For every man in a white suit with a cigar in his mouth, he found a whole army of beggars ground down by poverty, dejected, and helpless. Gay Havana with its bright lights was a hell for anyone forced to live on its fringes. The Soviet visitor's poetic indictment was not exaggerated; as to its essence, most Cubans could have added something of their own.

Being geographically so close to Florida and wishing to imitate its pleasures and compete with it as a tourist center, Cuba had tried to emulate the "American way of life." And though only a minority of *compradores* had the means to live in this style, it was their way of life that generally determined the wants and priorities of the whole island. The average yearly income per head (set at 400 dollars at the time of the Revolution), the number of cars (over 300,000), and the number of television sets (over 500,000) gave the world and Cubans themselves a false picture of their wealth. These statistics merely disguised the

13. Vedado was built immediately after World War I, during a time of intense speculation known as the "million dollar waltz." Later, following the sugar boom in World War II, an even more exclusive suburb, the Country Club, sprang up farther to the west of the old city.

gross disparities between the conspicuous riches of the few, the grinding poverty of the many, and the wish of those in the middle to "stay in the race."

It was this reality that shaped the economic structure of the country. To pay for her imports, many of which were luxury goods, Cuba was forced to concentrate on certain of her exports —sugar growers were granted every conceivable privilege in accordance with the principle "no sugar, no country." They had the right to work the best land to death, and to create unemployment in order to draw on seasonal labor; they were given all sorts of government grants and credits to equip and modernize their factories. Apparently only thus could they compete on the open market. In fact, the resale price of Cuban sugar was among the lowest in the world.

There was the same concern for the tobacco growers who, luckily, could work with less expensive capital equipment. The nickel mines were completely in the hands of Americans, whose strategic needs determined the fluctuating output. Yet U.S. interests saw fit to build one of the most modern metal plants in the world, at Moa, in Oriente province—"just in case." Coffee, the fourth most important export, enjoyed less protection, despite the fact that the annual surplus of more than 40,000 tons represented a considerable source of foreign exchange. Altogether, exports earned Cuba some $800 million a year; given her size and population, this was enough to incite the jealousy of any developing country.

Nor was that all. The clamor for consumer goods stimulated the growth of a whole range of light industries. In general, these were branches of big American firms which found it profitable to use cheap local labor; in addition, the proximity of the United States and the absence of any real tariff walls between the two countries served to make Cuba part and parcel of the U.S. market. This meant that goods produced on the island had to be able to withstand competition from those imported directly from America. They were moreover produced under the same license and with the same technical resources and leadership. Thus the Cuban "Goodyear" tire was as good as any tire made in the United States; "Procter & Gamble" detergents from Havana washed as white as American detergents; and much the same thing could be said of textiles, man-made fibers, the General Motors shops, Coca-Cola, condensed milk, etc. Cuban factories may have been much smaller than their U.S. parent firms, but their standards were as good in most respects.

There were exceptions, of course. Part of the consumer goods sector was equipped with obsolete machines discarded by U.S. factories; these machines were acquired by Cuban concerns with government credits during the boom of the '50s, when buildings sprang up like mushrooms in Havana. The cement industry was another backward sector. Three large factories were built or modernized at the time of the boom, in Mariel, Artemisa, and Santiago; together they had an annual potential of 960,000 metric tons, though before the Revolution, output never exceeded 743,200 metric tons, i.e., 76.4 per cent of total capacity. But this was due more to fluctuating demand than to technical incompetence.[14]

Cubans have never had a taste for statistics, hence it is difficult to draw up a balance sheet showing what the Castroists inherited from their predecessors. They estimate investments in new industries during the period 1954–58 at $462.4 million,[15] but they never made a complete inventory of all the factories and other properties they nationalized in 1960, the value of which has been put at about $1 billion.[16] Americans and Cuban émigrés naturally protested that this figure was far below the

14. Paradoxically, Cuba had a building boom at the height of the anti-Batista struggle. Some of the big hotels in Havana, the Hilton and the Habana Riviera, went up in 1957–58. Building was considered the safest and most profitable investment; but there was little attempt to rehouse the poor peasants and people living in shantytowns. Hence fluctuations in the demand for cement.

15. Figures submitted by the Cuban delegation to the International Symposium on Industrial Development in 1957.

16. In *Cuba Socialista* (No. 13, September 1962), the value of U.S. property alone is given as $965 million.

true value, to which Havana riposted that Cuba had not yet been fully reimbursed for "the enormous sums the Americans had siphoned out of the country for more than fifty years."

For all that, economists friendly to Cuba have pointed out that few countries were able to cast off foreign domination and emerge as relatively unharmed as Cuba did. According to them, the Cuban Revolution was born with a silver spoon in its mouth; it came into a considerable and completely unimpaired fortune. The civil war had been short and had done little damage, even in the countryside; and it had in any case passed the towns by completely. Industrialists had not expected nationalization and had gone on stocking and servicing their factories right up to the end. Precious foreign funds, no longer "diverted" as under the old regime, had continued to flow into the treasury from the main exports, especially sugar and tobacco. It was no accident therefore that the blaze of neon signs in Havana was as dazzling after Castro's victory as it had been before: there had been nothing to upset the smooth running of the economy, and, in that respect, the situation in Cuba differed from that of other countries immediately after a revolution.

This remarkable continuity enabled the Castro regime to concentrate its efforts on the redistribution of wealth in favor of the *humildes,* the victims of the old regime. The Revolution wished to be humane not only in words but also in deeds; and its first care was to improve the quality of life of the poorest. In this connection, one of its first measures was highly symbolic: the most exclusive beaches and amusement parks were thrown open to everyone, and placards invited people to give more thought to leisure in general and to the pleasures of the seashore in particular. And yet nobody felt that future stability was being sacrificed to present enjoyment or that precious resources were being wasted, simply because no one had a real grasp of the overall economic situation. In the main, the economy still functioned *por la libre* (without restrictions) . The flow of goods into the market was uninterrupted; national reserves of foreign currency kept growing; and consumption kept on rising.

213

Cubans seemed to have very good reason for asserting that once a country is freed from foreign overlordship, it finds itself automatically on the road to general prosperity.

Russians visiting the island at this point were only too happy to endorse Mayakovsky's view that Cuba was "A country of the happiest prospect," and this time they did not say so tongue in cheek. The poor in Cuba had not yet vanished from the landscape; but they were the first to declare their confidence in the future. The existence of a whole range of light industries seemed to guarantee—with even more certainty than in the U.S.S.R.— a rapid improvement in the standard of living. The richness of the Cuban soil greatly impressed many Soviet visitors: "Here one has only to spit on the ground for something green to pop up," said Timur Gaidar enviously, no doubt thinking of the recalcitrance of his native soil. Havana, with its shops full of the latest gadgets, its streets lined with American cars, its airconditioned restaurants, and its swimming pools, beaches, and parks, showed the whole world that socialism could go hand in hand with gaiety and still prosper.

To be sure, Cubans intended to modernize their country. Heavy industry would put an end to unemployment and to dependence on imports for basic industrial equipment. Their ambition seemed neither exaggerated nor unrealistic, even though they had virtually no native sources of energy (reserves of petroleum were far too small to meet the country's needs). There was iron in Cuba, as well as nonferrous metals, particularly nickel. Less favored countries such as Japan had become big exporters of finished steel, even though they had to import most of the raw materials. Cuba lacked technicians, but Russia could easily repair this deficiency. After all, the Soviet Union had built gigantic steelworks in India, a country much poorer than Cuba.

A few months after the great nationalization wave of October 1960, things began to take a turn for the worse, and supplies became rather unpredictable. This was clearly the result of the American blockade, but the Castroists, anxious to deny the effectiveness of this "criminal enterprise," preferred to attribute it to cuts in production from the end of 1960 up to the Playa Girón invasion, during all of which time the country had been in a state of alert. They accordingly continued to see the future through rose-colored glasses, the more so since they could look forward to the benefits of a planned economy. Before 1961, they had looked upon nationalization as a reprisal against American economic aggression, but after April of that year they warmly welcomed a life free of capitalist waste and the uncertainties of blind competition. Why, for instance, was it necessary for a host of small factories to make different brands of soap and spend ridiculous sums on advertising, when their products were identical in quality? All that advertising did was to make soap too expensive for a large part of the population. Surely it was much more rational to combine these factories into one single *empresa consolidada*,[17] one that could afford to lower the price and hence bring soap within the reach of all Cubans, including the poorest. "This is precisely what socialism means: revolutionary power and planned organization of the economy," the country's new rulers proudly asserted.

Soviet and Czechoslovak experts, who had arrived in great numbers, took care to foster this optimism. Yet their own system of planning was in process of revision at home, and some of the visitors expressed astonishment that no echo of their discussions should have reached Havana to dampen the Cubans' enthusiasm. But there was a good reason for this: the Cubans were still discussing the general principles of planned economy and not the complex practical problems that would have to be solved in due course. When it came to planning, the Cubans were mere beginners, learnedly discussing such topics as the monopoly in foreign trade which, until the summer of 1960, had been left in the hands of a whole number of more or less parasitic private

17. For the *empresas consolidadas* see Che Guevara's collected essays in Laura Gonzáles (ed.) : *Scritti, Discorsi e Diari di Guerriglia, 1959–1967* (Turin, Einaudi, 1969) . See especially pp. 489–505 and 507: *Regolamento organico della Empresa Consolidada.*

companies. The experts from Eastern Europe were right in contending that, at the stage of development Cuba had reached, some form of planning, however rudimentary, would be a considerable step forward; there would be time enough to point out the dangers lurking behind a rigidly state-controlled economy. Furthermore, the Achilles heel of the Soviet planning system lay in its inability to stimulate agriculture and consumer industries. Now it was just these fields that the Cubans considered their forte: they could produce convincing figures to show that agricultural production had risen markedly since the Revolution. Hence there was good reason to hope that, owing to the particular assets of their country, their overall plans might work equally well. What point was there in discouraging them by talking of problems that had arisen elsewhere and under quite different historical conditions?

Russian and Cuban optimism thus came together and reinforced each other. "Veterans" of Eastern socialism and their young Caribbean disciples vied with one another in making happy forecasts. Cubans already saw themselves enjoying a Swedish standard of life, convinced as they were of Russian generosity and the efficiency of the planning "clock." For the Russians and the Czechs, a socialist country had, and needs immediately to have, a very high growth rate. That, to them, was a dogma, forged during the Stalinist era. The two points of view thus combined to predict an imminent "economic miracle" in Cuba. For once, moreover, the conjunction of quite exceptional circumstances seemed to favor a young socialist country, so much so that the planners did not hesitate to assign it truly miraculous objectives.

Early experiences did not confirm these forecasts. The summer of 1961 started off badly: shortages spread to almost all staple products, and reached markets in small quantities and at irregular times. So as not to favor those who did the least work and therefore had the most time to wait for deliveries, every Cuban was registered at a shop and had to make do with what happened to be available. This was rationing, even if no one yet dared to call it by its name.

216

The Russians arrive

Ernesto Che Guevara, then Minister of Industry, was apparently the first and the only one to be seriously worried by this development. He had no doubts about the value of the plans, even less about the basic choices that faced the country; but he was worried by the poor labor discipline, by the low returns and shortcomings he noted in all sectors of the economy. In private he frankly admitted that Cuba was in the midst of a "production crisis." His comrades did not agree with what they thought was an unduly grim view of the latest developments; they even attributed it to the exacting character of Che, who would have liked to see all administrators and workers live and act with the same admirable efficiency that he himself brought to everything he did. The Communists of the old PSP, who were busily trying to establish a monopoly in administrative key positions, even started a whispering campaign against "that leftist" Che Guevara. Fidel Castro agreed with them in theory if not in practice; according to him the shortages were purely temporary and, in any case, the direct result of an increase in demand caused by his new social policies. But he had no intention of disowning Che or of breaking with him. Instead, he summoned all his economic experts—some 3,500 people in all—to a meeting in Havana on August 26, 1961. At the start of this National Convention on Production he put an end to all possible controversy by stating categorically: "The Revolution faces no crisis in production; far from it, production has never stopped rising."

And that was that. Fidel now gave the floor to Regino Botí, president of the *Juceplan*[18] and Minister of Economy, who ex-

18. The JUCEPLAN (*Junta Central de Planificación*) was inaugurated in 1960 with the help of Soviet and Czechoslovak economists, but did not really get going until February 1961 under the presidency of Regino Botí. Botí, the son of a well-known poet, was professor of political economy at the University of Santiago and represented Cuba on the UN Economic Commission for Latin America until the Revolution. Thereafter, he became Fidel Castro's economic adviser and later minister for economic affairs. He was removed from his post as planning chief in 1964 by President Dorticós, and the Ministry for Economic Affairs was abolished. At present he is a government adviser but holds no portfolio.

plained how production would go on rising during the next four years. The rate of economic growth would vary between a lower and upper limit of 10 per cent and 15 per cent per annum respectively. By the end of the four-year plan, Cuba would be the most industrialized country in Latin America; she would have the highest per capita consumption of steel, electricity, cement, petroleum, and tractors.[19] Light industry and agriculture would develop *pari passu*. By 1970, Cubans would use as much cloth, as many pairs of shoes, as Swedes, and their consumption of food would also be on a level with that of the advanced countries of Western Europe.[20]

Other economic experts now followed Botí to the platform. They gave details of their departmental plans and talked very frankly about their worries and temporary difficulties. In this connection, the palm went to Che who, in a highly matter-of-fact way, drew up a balance sheet of mistakes, made both in his own ministry and in all other sectors of the economy: agriculture, public works, foreign trade, food supplies, etc. "You have greeted me with prolonged and warm applause," he said, "but I feel that you have done so as accomplices, not as consumers." According to Che, the overall balance of the economy was favorable, but it could have been much better still. "For it is clear that there are many weaknesses and many flaws in our productive machinery. It may be possible to justify some of them; but the important thing is not to look for justifications but to prevent mistakes from recurring."

Che alleged that the managers of most *empresas consolidadas* were indifferent to the quality of their goods and accused them of "total lack of foresight." He gave many examples, some of which may cause us to smile, but all of which cast some light on the situation. "There is at present a shortage of toothpaste.

19. According to Botí's figures, Cuba would be producing more than 2 million tons of cement, 700,000 tons of steel, and 5,000 tractors a year. Consumption of electricity per head was to double.

20. According to Botí, by 1965 each Cuban would consume more than 60 kg. of meat, 192 liters of milk, and 197 eggs per annum.

The Russians arrive

Let us see why. Production of toothpaste was stopped for four months, but there were considerable stocks, so no one was particularly worried. Only when the reserves began to run out, and no raw materials were coming in, did those responsible become galvanized into action and begin the hunt for the various raw materials. A consignment of calcium bisulphate arrived, but proved of inferior quality. Undeterred, the comrades in charge of production rolled up their sleeves and succeeded in making a toothpaste pleasing to the eye and as clean and white as any, but which hardens after a while [Applause]. Comrades, do not clap. They did not do it on purpose, and I warn you that in four months' time people are going to object because we are selling them stones in tubes. . . . Somebody has just handed me a note: 'It is not at the end of four months but at the end of five weeks that the paste turns hard.' Buyers should therefore make sure to use it within a month of purchase."

Che Guevara claimed that the new managers lacked initiative and were prepared to throw anything on the market. New factories could not work properly without reserves of raw materials, accurate statistics, and strict discipline. Furthermore, since "socialism is not in conflict with beauty," the quality and pleasing appearance of products should also be taken into consideration. Everybody applauded such sensible remarks, and the floodgates of criticism and self-criticism were thrown wide open.

As we read these obviously sincere remarks, so many years later, we cannot help seeing that they, and the rest of the discussion, were really about side issues. Some facts had been brought into the open, but there was no serious analysis of basic problems. The speakers did not hesitate to denounce the guerrilla methods still used by administrators. Fidel spoke of a *comandante* who had closed a fishing harbor in the north as a military precaution for two weeks, though it was never clear precisely what landing he anticipated. In any case, no trawlers had been able to leave harbor and the fishermen had been deprived of their livelihood. Later Fidel was to assert that more guerrilla fighters had been killed on the roads in requisitioned cars than had fallen during the battles in the Sierra. Che, for his part, thought it insupportable that any *capitancito* should be able to requisition trucks and skilled labor without a thought for the harm he caused to industry. Civil servants seemed equally beyond public control, at least until a superior stumbled upon their malpractices.

Many speakers contrasted these flagrant abuses of authority with instances of popular initiative. Here, workers at a sugar factory had succeeded in making their own spare parts;[21] elsewhere a mere nightwatchman had informed the administration that three trucks were used to deliver milk on one street at half-hourly intervals, when one could easily have done the job. Other details of varying importance showed that the Cuban masses had been won over to the Revolution and were only too willing to play an active part in its administration and development. In Cuba, it was impossible to speak of lack of political awareness or of apathy—the very stings that were poisoning the social foundations of the Eastern European socialist countries. To be sure, Cubans lacked the political education needed to run their country efficiently, but was this a reason for considering them so much clay in the hands of young leaders who themselves were not the world's greatest political or administrative experts? And yet, during the three days of the National Convention on Production, no one so much as raised the question of popular democracy or workers' control of the factories.

Another astonishing attitude was reflected in the absolute refusal of the delegates to discuss the reason for the fall in quality, or simply in production, in certain branches of industry. When speaking of toothpaste, Che had said nothing about the raw materials, which had come from Poland and were of much poorer quality than those used before by the Procter & Gamble factory. Assuredly, those responsible should have waked up earlier, instead of waiting until the stocks were exhausted; but when all

21. As a matter of fact, the sugar industry could boast many more instances of worthwhile popular initiative and fewer breakdowns than any other. All sugar mills—*ingenios*—kept going except for brief interruptions.

was said and done, they would still have produced "stones in tubes." Even now, seven years later, Cuban toothpaste has an annoying tendency to refuse to come out of its tube. Problems of this type have appeared everywhere, in all factories forced to make do with raw materials that do not meet their technological needs.

The young Minister of Foreign Trade, Major Alberto Mora,[22] nevertheless reminded the conference that few countries in the world were so dependent on imports as Cuba. All the country's products, including even sugar, involved the use of foreign products. Thus a *zafra* of 5 million tons of sugar called for more than $20 million worth of foreign equipment. "Imports represent about 25 per cent of our GNP and to pay for them, including transport costs and international charges, our exports must reach nearly 33 per cent of our GNP." Now 73.5 per cent of these indispensable imports used to come from the United States, which in return took 74.5 per cent of Cuban exports; the remaining foreign trade was largely with countries in the American orbit, while trade with the East was practically non-existent. In 1959, immediately after the Revolution, imports from socialist countries still amounted to less than 2 million pesos; in 1960 they reached only 136 million pesos; but in 1961 they quadrupled dramatically to account for more than 580 million pesos. The list of Cuban imports included some 30,000 different products and raw materials—from oil and cotton down to screwdrivers and packing materials. So great a redeployment of trade had never before taken place in so short a time, and Major Mora had every right to cite this fact in mitigation of the errors committed by his ministry. But to hear him speak, one might have thought that everything would be put right again within a few months: Cuban buyers would be able to specify their precise needs and the suppliers in Eastern Europe would deliver everything in perfect order and on the dot. The Major

22. Alberto Mora, the son of one of the martyrs of the attack on the presidential palace in 1957, was one of the youngest ministers in the Cuban government.

thus reduced the problem to one of organization, when it was something altogether different.

Economically speaking, Cuba had been part and parcel of the United States, and having cut that tie, the island was forced to graft herself onto a bloc which, apart from being totally different, was already afflicted with its own specific illnesses. The operation would at best have caused a great deal of pain, even if all those concerned had given proof of great foresight and clarity of mind; in the absence of both, it became a source of enormous waste and disappointments, with wide repercussions on the economic and political relations between the new partners.

Two technical aspects—which, incidentally, were not raised at the August convention—are enough to show the difficulties to which this "grafting" process gave rise. Cuba had virtually no harbor installations and lacked warehouse space for large-scale trade with countries across the Atlantic. Supplies from the United States had normally come by ferryboat from West Palm Beach in Florida or by "sea trains" from New Orleans. Proximity to the source of supplies and frequency of delivery had made it unnecessary for Cubans to invest great sums in harbor facilities. The international port of Cuba had been New Orleans and not Havana.

The number one priority, in these conditions, should logically have been the construction of equipment and buildings for the quick unloading and storing of goods from Europe or Asia. It was no longer possible to expect supplies in small quantities: a ship from China could hardly be expected to spend two months at sea in order to discharge what little edible oil Havana could consume in a day. It had to carry the whole 50,000 tons ordered by the Cuban Ministry of Foreign Trade. Now, it was only just before the arrival of the ship that the consignees realized that so great a quantity of oil had never been brought into their country and that there was nowhere to store it.[23] Solids did not

23. The soya oil in question was finally put into crude oil tanks which had previously been cleaned. On this subject see Edward Boorstein: *The Economic Transformation of Cuba*, p. 69.

pose the same difficulties, since most could be stockpiled in the open. But heat and humidity did not improve the quality of products kept under such conditions.[24]

Later the Cuban authorities alleged that responsibility for these costly mistakes must be laid at the door of the Czech experts who had worked on the development plan. Since Czechoslovakia is landlocked, these men must have simply overlooked the need to set aside money for harbor installations. This story caused much laughter after the event, and was always told as proof of the weakness of economic theories divorced from practical life. True enough; but the plan itself was hatched neither in Prague nor in Moscow. Was it possible that the practical Cubans had been so mesmerized by their Eastern comrades as to forget that their country was an island?

The second "technical" aspect was closely linked with the first: the Cubans ordered raw materials or complete factories from the East in the apparent belief that all products going by the same name must necessarily have identical qualities. No time was taken to get full particulars, no experts were available to test samples. It was only after delivery, when the factory yards were cluttered with raw materials or machines, that people tried to adapt these precious commodities to the specific needs of Cuban industry. Quite often these attempts came to nothing. But the money for the goods could not be refunded, nor could they be returned to the sender.

Similar disappointments cropped up with complete factories, ordered on trust and in a hurry. During one of the regular meetings Che held at his ministry,[25] he admitted that the canning factory bought in Poland at the then market price em-

24. It should be added that poor postal communications between Cuba and the Eastern bloc did not make the distribution of these goods any easier. Factories often complained about the nondelivery of raw materials or machines that had been "sun-bathing" in the ports of Havana or Santiago.

25. The discussions between Che and his colleagues were taken down and published (in Vol. VI of his works) for the private use of political and economic leaders. I was allowed to examine them but not to take them out. Che's remarks are therefore quoted from memory. The meeting mentioned here took place on July 19, 1962.

ployed 270 workers to produce what, in a Western-style factory, could be done by only 25. The Minister of Industry and other leaders were completely taken aback by the technological backwardness of the Eastern bloc, despite the fact that most of them had visited the "continent of marvels." For a long time they even treated as potential counterrevolutionaries all those many technicians who dared to assert that Russian jeeps or trucks looked like twenty-year-old American models, and that Russian tractors were not the equal of the Caterpillars once imported from the North, except on the invoice. Later, when the Cuban leaders were forced to take stock of their early mistakes, they had to admit that their pro-Soviet attitude had prevented them from seeing a truth that was staring them in the face. Unfortunately, many leading Cuban technicians had not waited for this admission, and had left instead to swell the ranks of exiles in Miami.

Was all this inevitable? Regino Botí—who is no longer a minister—explained to me good-humoredly that the balance sheet is not nearly as bad as people believe. They tend to forget the extraordinary difficulties in the Cubans' path: "A factory is like a woman. You have to know her thoroughly, intimately, if you want to get on with her. Now we knew nothing at all about our latest factories. Every worker or technician was confined to his particular corner; only the American owners knew the delicate mechanism that made the whole thing tick. Just take one example with which I am familiar: at Bayamo we took over a condensed-milk factory, a branch of a large Connecticut concern. It was literally run by remote control from the head office. When there was a breakdown, the technician simply phoned Connecticut and told them what he thought had gone wrong. He was told at once what to do about it, and he simply followed instructions, without having to bother his head about theory. If this did not do the trick, a plane would arrive four hours later with a team of specialists. After nationalization, we could no longer phone for help, and the few technicians who might have been able to deal with minor faults had gone. Soviet experts came to the rescue, but knew nothing about the factory's hidden secrets. Worse still, they brought no spare parts and were not about to set up a factory especially to produce them. And so we had to learn the whole thing from scratch: it has taken us years to find out the real secrets of this fine but mysterious plant and how to service it. Even now we don't always know exactly what is what.[26]

"Similar problems arose almost everywhere," Botí continued. "No sooner had we filled one breach, than we had to face a far more serious one in another sector. Our public transport system —buses, trains, trucks—ran short of spare parts, which could only be found in the United States. We tried to put Russian engines into General Motors buses, but without success; we would also have had to change the automatic transmissions for Russian manual ones. Only one trained engineer stayed behind in the big textile factory at Ariguanabo in Havana province; only one mechanic was left to do the servicing in the American automated glass factory; and so on. And yet we managed to continue manufacturing our chief exports—sugar, tobacco, and nickel; in fact, we have not done too badly, especially with regard to the last. And we generate more electricity than was available at the time of the Revolution."

All in all, according to Botí, the Cubans had not done at all badly. In spite of their eagerness to set new records for economic growth, they made no really absurd investment, although a fair amount of waste could have been avoided by postponing some of their projects. Objective factors helped to lower the efficiency of existing industries and hence contributed to the growing scarcity of the winter of 1961. In effect, seven months after the great "National Convention on Production," on March 13, 1962, Fidel Castro was compelled to introduce a severe rationing system covering most essential products—from meat and milk to textiles, shoes, soap, and detergents.[27] The shortage of consumer

26. The factory at Bayamo, once a branch of American Nestlé, was capable of processing 400 tons of milk a day; its present output is no more than 250 tons.
27. The rations fixed on March 13, 1962, were as follows: meat, 3/4 lb. per week; chicken, 2 lbs. per month; fish, 1 lb. per month; vegetables, 3½ lbs. per week; rice, 6 lbs. per month; beans, 1½ lbs. per month; milk,

goods had direct repercussions on agricultural production which, moreover, had been hit by a drought. Small peasant proprietors, who still numbered more than 50 per cent of all those engaged in agriculture, had no great incentive to produce surplus food when there was little to buy in the towns.

To deal with this whole series of disappointments, the Cuban leaders introduced sweeping administrative reforms, abolishing certain ministries and creating others, moving the managers of the *empresas consolidadas* from pillar to post, and constantly enjoining the workers to keep discipline. But the Castroists had not, in principle, given up hope of rapid economic growth and industrialization. In speeches, they continued to promise prosperity in the near future and called on the workers to fight for the rapid realization of this goal. Only later, in 1963, did they admit that their lack of experience had cost them dear; they had wasted much time and energy, simply because they had gone by appearances and had allowed unfounded optimism to get the better of them. And so Cuba started on the long road to modernization almost three years later than she should have done.

Cuban self-criticism had clear overtones of reproach toward the comrades and friends from Eastern Europe. But the time for polemics had not yet come, nor even for reflection on the fundamental causes of the technological and human failings of Soviet society. On the contrary, there were explanations about the harsh conditions in which the Soviet Union had been forced to develop, isolated and facing a hostile world; that she still could not meet the demands of her huge internal market and hence could not worry too much about the quality of her products. But these explanations had ceased to carry much conviction. How could people believe that Russia was about to overtake the United States, when they had seen Russian engineers staring open-eyed with wonder at American factories in Cuba?

1/5 liter per day for adults, 1 liter per day for children under seven. See Dudley Seers: *Cuba, The Economic and Social Revolution* (University of North Carolina Press, 1964) , p. 35.

The Russians arrive

Moreover, in their first rapture, the Cubans had signed contracts for the purchase of factories from Eastern Europe in exchange for sugar or on credit.[28] Now, brought up as they had been to make something of a fetish of modern technology, they found it difficult to swallow the idea that they had to pay high prices for things not worth the money. "A developing country," Che explained, "must never import obsolete equipment; for this means mortgaging the future and sacrificing long-term needs." True, better than three more years of sad disappointments, especially in politics, were to pass before Che, in a great speech at Algiers, saw fit to criticize Soviet ways of doing foreign trade,[29] but as early as 1962, his remarks at meetings of the Ministry of Industry had begun to betray his profound disillusionment with the U.S.S.R.

The Russians, for their part, also had reason to complain of their Cuban friends. They had never realized how under-equipped their new partners really were—nothing had led them to suppose that there was even a lack of facilities for receiving their aid. This, and the everyday difficulties of practical collaboration, led them to become deeply disillusioned. "The bride never told us that her dowry was mortgaged," they said in bitter jest, after having established that the keys to Cuba were lodged in the United States and not in Havana. American managers were the only ones with enough know-how to run Cuban factories; American institutions the only ones familiar with the climatic and geological nature of the various provinces. These were some of the terrible aftereffects of fifty years of semi-colonial domination. When the Revolution started, Cubans

28. In 1961, Cuba sold to the Soviet Union and its partners 4 million tons of sugar at 3.95 cents per pound and an unspecified quantity of nickel, tobacco, and coffee; 80 per cent of these products were paid for in goods, and the remaining 20 per cent in convertible currency, to allow the Cubans to buy various materials unobtainable in Eastern European markets. Arms deliveries were accounted for separately, and after the missile crisis of October 1962, the Russians stopped demanding payment for them.

29. Che Guevara's speech at Algiers (February 1965) in the Maspero edition, *op. cit.* p. 265.

227

were as little familiar with their own homeland as their new friends from faraway Europe.

Hence many of their worst misunderstandings and difficulties. The Cubans had asked for aid to diversify their industrial output, to reduce their dependence on sugar crops, and to replace imports with homemade goods; they expected to start off from a fairly high level. Unfortunately, they had failed to notify their partners of their lack of trained staff to run even the existing factories; or of the extent to which their agriculture had been marred by a long and exclusive reliance on sugar.

"Our plans were unrealizable," one of the European advisers to the *Juceplan* explained to me later, "simply because we were working with completely fanciful data. We were asked to establish the maximum growth rate of an economy, without being given exact information about its productive capacity, the availability of labor, the mineral resources, the possibility of replacing sugar cane with new crops—in short, without any information. And then, when breakdowns occurred, in one sector after the next, we were asked for engineers to get the semi-automated cold drinks factories going again, as well as for agricultural experts who could teach peasants to grow onions—just as if we had a whole reserve army of experts on tap, all of them specially qualified to deal with Cuba's problems. No other developing country gave us so much trouble. In Cuba, people expected miracles. Everyone felt entitled to throw up his hands in indignation when an inexperienced engineer failed to make quick repairs to an automatic cable in the nickel factory, or when some agricultural expert was unable, on the spot, to pick the ideal place for starting the cultivation of something that had never been grown in this climate."

The embittered experts would not admit that they might have taken more trouble to find things out for themselves, or to prevent breakdowns before it was too late; nor would they admit that they should have anticipated differences between the advanced practices of their own highly industrialized societies and the more traditional approach of Cuba. In fact, their mis-

228

The Russians arrive

takes were the direct result of their mistaken intellectual and political training, which prevented any real exchange of ideas with their young revolutionary hosts and inclined the experts to push for excessively rapid development (in accordance with habits they had acquired at home). It was not that they lacked good intentions—rarely had Russians or Czechs been so captivated by a new revolutionary country. Here they could relive the heroic experiences of their forebears. But on the professional level they were specialists in the strictest sense, specialists in clearly defined sectors of the various branches of industry; they were as alike as two peas to those engineers in the condensed-milk factory at Bayamo who knew nothing beyond their own particular corner, and for the rest had to call the head office. At the least sign of trouble, the engineers from Eastern Europe, too, got in touch with their head offices in Moscow, Prague, or Berlin; but these, unlike their American counterparts, were in no hurry to reply. The Soviet experts were plainly not expert enough to act with that "American efficiency" the Cubans expected of them, while the head offices in the faraway European capitals were too set in their bureaucratic ways to consider the time factor which was often of crucial importance to Cuba.

In fact, even if they were not personally responsible for all the errors in the planning or direction of the Cuban economy during this period of "socialist takeoff," the missionaries from Eastern Europe had a far greater responsibility than they cared to acknowledge. They brought with them a conception of economic construction that disregards the human (and even economic) cost of accelerated growth. They were so used to waste at home that the fanciful orders or ill-conceived projects of the Cubans hardly shocked them, and certainly not enough to do anything about them in time. How else explain the fact that they allowed orders for outmoded factories to pass without comment, factories for which raw materials were even in short supply? The Cuban buyers in Havana could plead inexperience and protest their absolute confidence in Eastern

229

Guerrillas in Power

Europe, but their Soviet or Czech advisers ought surely to have known better, however inadequate their general training may have been.

Collaboration between the Eastern bloc and Cuba highlighted the defects—and especially the extraordinary clumsiness—of the Soviet economic machine. Quite unexpectedly, it showed how irresponsible the Russians and their allies really could be (sending over raw materials without bothering to find out whether they were usable; selling manufactured goods totally unfit for the Cuban market, etc.) and how irrational was their method of looking for specific solutions, when what was needed was a thorough study of the basic problem. Thus the Russians set up special sections in their institutes of science, metallurgy, and agricultural science which, with incredible slowness, and at great cost, examined Cuban difficulties as they arose. According to a number of skeptical Cuban observers, the U.S.S.R. would have saved money and trouble if she had bought Cuban sugar with convertible currency, thus allowing Cuba to satisfy her needs in Western Europe or Canada, instead of investing in expensive research projects that rarely came to anything.

In any case, Eastern aid did not please the Cubans, who began to criticize it more and more openly; nor did it please the Russians, who spent so much money that they had some grounds for alleging that "Caribbean socialism" was positively ruinous. In fact, both parties in this veiled dispute had cause for complaint, though each had the very best intentions in the world. The Cubans could have shown that the goods sold them by Eastern Europe at world market prices were very much inferior to those they could have bought elsewhere. The Russians could have proved with figures that these products cost them more than they charged and that they subsidized the economy of the island twice over: first by giving credit and then by selling high-cost products at a loss. The resulting recriminations, one side shouting "stinginess" and the other "ingratitude" proved a source of constant discord in Russo-Cuban affairs.

But it was too late for a divorce; both parties were by now

far too involved with each other. All the same, in 1962 Khrushchev tried to find a way out which, had it been successful,
might have made things easier, politically and economically, for
the Soviet Union no less than for her Cuban protégé. In my
view, it is with this fact in mind that we must look at what has
become known as the "missile crisis."

The consequences of mini-Stalinism

The fact that the Castroist Revolution was now taking its cue
from the Soviet Union affected not only the economy, but all
spheres of Cuban life. This became apparent to me during my
second stay in Havana, in July 1961, when a trip to Latin
America enabled me to visit again, this time without professional commitments. My friends and acquaintances gave me a
warm welcome and we continued our discussions just where we
had left off three months earlier.

Havana was still something of a paradox: a big city straddling
two historical epochs. The old billboards of Braniff and Eastern
Airlines still boasted the former comfort of flights to New York;
there was a great deal of traffic; neon lights blazed; jukeboxes
played American hit tunes. But, a step away, rousing posters
called upon the people to rally to socialism, militiamen stood
guard before public buildings night and day, while others
mingled with the crowd that filled La Rampa, 23rd Street, in
Vedado every night. The big casinos had shut down, but this
was taken so much for granted that it evoked no comment. The
cabarets, on the other hand, were still doing well, and had added
a number of revolutionary themes that seemed most surprising
in such places.

It was in spots such as these that the paradox of Cuban socialism struck the European visitor most forcefully. There was, for
instance, the dinner in honor of Yuri Gagarin on July 27,
1961. The late dinner at the hotel Habana Libre was not, as I
had fully expected, followed by long speeches of welcome; instead the curtain rose on a stage to the right of the "presi-

dential" table and we were told that artists from the Tropicana Cabaret would perform numbers specially written for the famous cosmonaut. At once an enchanting troupe of dancers rushed onto the stage: the blondes, who wore the hammer and sickle, appeared to be exceptionally light on their feet, and seemed almost to touch the stars; the brunettes, wearing the stars and stripes, tried in vain to copy them. The blondes then put out their tongues at their unhappy rivals. There was a roar of applause for this demonstration of Russian superiority in space over the United States. The whole thing ended with a wild dance on the theme *Cuba si, Yankee no!* to the accompaniment of much head-wagging and hip-wriggling. The Cubans could barely keep in their seats as they encouraged the dancers with shouts and hand clapping before finally joining in their chorus of *Y viva la Revolución!* The Russians from Gagarin downward seemed rather torn between admiration for this fine display of feminine beauty and their doubts as to the socialist character of the performance. They clapped politely, without getting to their feet, determined not to let themselves be carried away. As for the Chinese, present in equal numbers, they remained quite impassive at their end of the table; their eyes were closed, and from what one could tell they were sleeping peacefully.

"Socialism with the *pachanga*" was certainly far from dead, but Cuban daily life had changed a great deal since April 1961. To begin with, shortages were visible everywhere. There was a lot of standing in line in Havana and the big shop windows were virtually empty except for portraits of the Cuban leaders. My friends and guides made no attempt to hide the fact that food had become hard to get. Of course, all of them repeated Fidel's explanation that the shortages were purely temporary, and due, in any case, to a steep rise in purchasing power: "If the rest of Latin America had redistributed incomes in favor of the *humildes* as we have done here, they, too, would have little left in the shops. Our only problem is to increase production so as to meet a demand we have ourselves created." And my friends had not the least doubts that the whole problem would be solved within a few months, if not within weeks.

232

The Russians arrive

Then they would wax indignant at the way Americans pursued their wicked policy of starving Cuba and preventing her from buying supplies on nonsocialist markets. They were astonished at the extent to which even liberal papers in Europe were prepared to make allowances for Kennedy: "How can they admire this 'enlightened' President, when his chief distinction is a determination to crush a little country like ours?" They gave me example after example of American attempts, by a mixture of blackmail and bribery, to stop European or Latin American suppliers from delivering even such peaceful articles as food and medical supplies.

And they had no words bad enough for those of their own party who, in these difficult times, had deserted to the enemy in search of an easy life. For there had been many deserters among the veterans of July 26. Some had started to leave as early as 1959, at the time of the first trial of strength with the United States. In the early period, only the privileged classes of old or well-known right-wingers had taken the path of exile, but once socialism was officially proclaimed, these refugees were followed by others who, in the past, had protested their strong support for the social reforms accomplished by the Revolution. Why had they decided to leave?

It seemed that they could not swallow a number of repressive measures that the CIA plots had brought in their wake. Thus the Bay of Pigs invasion had been followed by a wave of arrests in Havana and throughout the country: a hundred thousand, it is said. Many of the suspects were innocent, and were of course released, but the security police had been given increased powers and this was enough to disturb a great many Cubans. For all that, the runaways, by deserting instead of fighting for what they thought was right, greatly facilitated the task of those who were anxious to regiment the whole country.

Nor was that all. Many of those who had left alleged that the old leaders of the PSP were getting more powerful by the day. They said that they would happily have supported Cuban socialism, but not the Soviet kind Blas Roca and his friends represented. And on the surface, the facts seemed to bear out

233

their allegations: Communists of the old school were solidly entrenched in both the local and also the national administration. In his speech of July 26, 1961, Fidel Castro explained that it was thanks to their basic unity of purpose that the mass of revolutionaries had banded together in the ORI, the Integrated Revolutionary Organizations. He gave no details about the composition of this new movement or when it would hold its first congress, but everybody in Havana knew that the old PSP formed the backbone of the ORI, that Aníbal Escalante was in charge of organization, his brother César of propaganda, Carlos Rafael Rodríguez of economic matters, Edith García Buchacha of culture—and that they were all Communist leaders of the old school. People even had the impression that Fidel Castro and his supporters from the Sierra were willing to play second fiddle to this old guard. There were some disconcerting aspects about the whole business, and these did nothing to increase the popularity of a revolution that needed popular support more than ever.

My informants, all of them devoted followers of Castro, put most of the blame on the "weak" comrades in their own ranks. It was the vacillation and lack of staying power of these men that had compelled Fidel to rely more and more on PSP militants; they, for one, were unlikely to flee to the United States and their loyalty to the Revolution was beyond question. Some of those to whom I spoke were all the more bitter for having relations or friends among the "lukewarm." One of them said to me: "When we were all in the underground, I should never have dreamed that some of my comrades were potential traitors, and that I would have to work with the kind of men we used to despise for their lack of revolutionary imagination." He continued to hold the PSP in low esteem and was certain that its dogmatic cadres would be incapable of running the country intelligently. Still, he acknowledged that Fidel had no choice, that one had to work with the PSP, and possibly even under its direction.

The time had not yet come for an objective analysis of the breakup of the old anti-Batista front. Everything was explained in terms of personalities: this one was a bit of a coward even in the old days; that one had not fought well in the Sierra; a third had a suspicious liking for the easy life; yet another was a revolutionary in words only, and so on. I must admit that I never found such explanations very convincing.

It is of course possible that defections from the ranks of the July 26th Movement did drive Fidel Castro into the arms of the PSP: he could no longer play the supreme arbiter between the various factions in his vast coalition movement, simply because the right flank had deserted en masse. If all his old associates had stayed on and accepted the necessity for Cuban socialism, the influence of the PSP would undoubtedly have been greatly reduced. But the reasons which had prevented the deserters from accepting Castro's socialist aims had nothing to do with questions of character. Cuba's ever closer links with the Soviet Union did much to speed up the process of disintegration, driving a good number of waverers over to the other side. In addition, as soon as pro-Soviet sympathies became the touchstone of revolutionary fervor, those who had spent a lifetime praising the U.S.S.R. were likely to be taken for the best revolutionaries, while all those—whether of the Left or the Right—who had criticized the Soviet Union for one reason or another, automatically became suspect. Now, even if Cuba was at no time the kind of police state the Soviet Union had been under Stalin, those under suspicion did not have an easy time of it. As a result, they tended increasingly to get out, leaving the field to the old hands in the PSP.

At all events, the mass promotion of the Communist old guard greatly affected Cuba's political climate. It was precisely this fact that constituted the main and the most unpleasant difference between my first and my second stay on the island. In April 1961, the stage had been held by Castro's disciples, most of them young men, who, having just discovered the benefits of socialism, were trying to win one over with arguments that though often lacking in skill were never anything but frank and spontaneous. Three months later the "experts on Marxism-

Leninism" of the old Communist school had taken over; hence-forward only they had the right to interpret the past and put forward plans for the future. They had a most difficult time of it since, as we saw, it was dogmatic blindness rather than tactical errors that had lost the PSP the support of the Cuban masses in the pre-Castroist era. Moreover, the Communists were well aware of their general unpopularity, and were therefore afraid to trust any but "tried and true" comrades, or members of their own narrow circle. Hence as soon as one of them was given a job in the administration, he would quickly slip in a host of friends, partly for sectarian motives, but mainly because these were the only people on whom he could rely.

The repercussions were particularly ominous in the economic sphere. Excess of originality was assuredly not the Communists' greatest sin: they knew the Soviet tenets on industrial organiza-tion by heart and stuck to them through thick and thin. Who-ever dared to make the least critical suggestion was treated as a potential enemy or, at best, decried as a simpleton incapable of grasping the deeper profundities of Marxism. Though the Communists were honest—no one to my knowledge has accused them of misappropriating public funds—nobody thought much of their administrative skills. My informants may have had a grudge against them, and I was ready to make allowances for their prejudice, but the countless cases of administrative incom-petence they quoted sounded genuine enough. To be sure, no one can say with any certainty that the more rapid promotion of the Castroist rank and file would have made for a better ad-ministration. Yet there is little doubt that when the old PSP took charge of Cuban industry, it became an obstacle to all original research on the role of the trade unions and on rank-and-file participation in the control and management of the economy.

Needless to say, the Communists posed an even deadlier threat to intellectual life. To them the Cuban situation was quite in-tolerable. How could a country that called itself socialist and wished to form an integral part of the Soviet bloc allow ordinary bookshops to display heretical works that were bound to embarrass and offend all the comrades who had rushed over from Eastern Europe to the aid of the Revolution? Quite apart from the works of Trotsky, all the books banned in the Soviet Union —from *Doctor Zhivago* to Kafka and Joyce—were spread out provocatively for all to see. The occasional blue-jacketed editions of the Moscow Foreign Publishing House could barely make up for such outrages. And it was the same with the cinema: people lined up to see trashy French and Italian films and obstinately stayed away from Russian masterpieces. And to crown it all, if a film from Eastern Europe happened to be a success, it was most often a Polish one or some other unorthodox production denouncing the evil side of socialism.

And so the Communists asked for a free hand to bring some sort of order into this cultural and ideological jungle. That this task proved inordinately difficult was due not simply to the bad habits of their Americanized fellow-countrymen, but also to the ideological crisis that was then gripping Russia herself. The "good old days" of Zhdanovism were a thing of the past. Edifying works in praise of Soviet heroes had become scarce even in Moscow, where the leading writers had begun to sail into the aberrations of the "personality cult" and, to get past the censors, were penning esoteric works full of allusions incomprehensible to such outsiders as the young Cubans. The other great achievements of "proletarian culture"—from genetics to socialist realism in painting—were faring no better. It was, of course, possible to dig up a few diehards of the old school in Moscow, but their works would have been poor examples to hold up to the new Cuban socialists.

The cultural leaders, foremost among them Mrs. García Buchacha, would have liked but were unable to supply their country with socialist culture imported from Russia in ready-made, easy-to-digest form. On the other hand, they were certain about what books Cubans must *not* be allowed to read. This explains the sad business of the *Lunes de Revolución* in the summer of 1961. *Lunes* was the cultural supplement of Carlos Franqui's

Guerrillas in Power

daily, *Revolución*. It first came out in March 1959, and had always managed to combine revolutionary fervor with respect for cultural values. The paper was edited by young men: Guillermo Cabrera Infante,[30] the editor in chief, was barely thirty. His second in command, Pablo Armando Fernández,[31] was even younger, and so were Heberto Padilla[32] and José Alvarez Baragaño,[33] all of them poets and completely devoted to the cause of the Revolution.

The weekly supplement discussed such topics as avant-garde art and the aspirations of the modern Left. Trotsky's writings on art and revolution were deemed worthy of presentation to the Cuban public, and the space devoted to André Breton showed the group's attraction to surrealism. Yet they did not neglect the *Communist Manifesto* either, or the works of the great Bolshevik era, from John Reed and Mayakovsky to Isaac Babel. On January 18, 1960, on the sudden death of Albert Camus, they dedicated a whole issue to his writings; three weeks later, on the occasion of Anastas Mikoyan's visit, they published a special number on the Soviet Union, its films, theater, and litera-

30. G. Cabrera Infante (born 1929) was the film critic of *Carteles*, a magazine that ceased publication in 1960. After editing *Lunes* from 1959 to 1961, he became cultural attaché in Brussels and then chargé d'affaires. He was relieved of his diplomatic post in 1965, and left Cuba for London. His collection of short stories *Así en la paz como en la guerra* is well known and has been translated into fourteen languages; and his novel *Tres tristes tigres* won the Biblioteca Breve prize in 1964.

31. Pablo Armando Fernández was born in 1930. He spent some time in the United States and returned to Cuba after the Revolution. He has traveled widely, especially in Russia and China, and after the disappearance of *Lunes* was cultural attaché in London until 1965. He has published several volumes of verse, including *Toda la poesía* (1961), *Himnos* (1962), and *Libro de los heroes* (1964). His novel *Los niños se despiden* won him the Casa de las Américas prize in 1967.

32. After the suspension of *Lunes*, Heberto Padilla worked for some time in Prague and Moscow, as a journalist and representative of various Cuban publishers. In 1968, he received the UNEAC prize for his collection *Fuera de juego*. This earned him the fury of a host of Cuban sectarians, who loathed his independence of mind and the great talent that made Padilla one of the best poets of his generation.

33. José Alvarez Baragaño, born in 1937, died of a heart attack in 1962.

238

ture. When Sartre came to Cuba a month later, they published his *Ideology and Revolution* together with a lengthy interview.

It would be unfair to say that *Lunes* followed no line: it was, in fact, a voice crying out against commercialized culture and a powerful means for the dissemination of neglected leftist classics. Moreover, it published fundamental studies of the history of the Cuban Revolution, and some of the most important works of Fidel Castro, Ernesto Che Guevara, and Camilo Cienfuegos. One possible objection was that *Lunes* did not express clear editorial views on the often contradictory articles it printed. But all the Cuban leaders acknowledged that it met a specific need of a new generation, eager for knowledge and quite capable of making up its own mind. According to Ernesto Che Guevara, *Lunes de Revolución* was a striking contribution to Cuban culture.[34] And Fidel Castro described *Lunes* as "a worthy attempt to give expression to three similar things: revolution, the people, and culture."[35]

To foreign visitors, the circulation of *Lunes* was a revelation. It had as many readers as the daily *Revolución,* and eventually sold 250,000 copies. Surveys showed that readers of the daily newspaper also read the cultural supplement carefully. Sartre and Simone de Beauvoir expressed their astonishment; conversations in all parts of the island had shown them that, thanks to *Lunes,* many ordinary Cubans knew more about Picasso and avant-garde art than did a good many Frenchmen.

But it was precisely these qualities that earned *Lunes* the strictures of the Communist old guard. Could a young and heterodox group be allowed to publish whatever works it chose —including even those banned in other socialist countries? And furthermore, could it be allowed to operate independently of the Party leadership? The sooner a stop was put to this scandalous state of affairs, the better.

On June 16, 1961, Carlos Franqui and his protégés were invited to a discussion at the National Library in Havana. They

34. See the birthday issue of *Lunes de Revolución,* March 1960.
35. *Ibid.*

were told nothing about the purpose of the meeting and they expected a small, friendly gathering to discuss certain minor differences between them and their country's cultural leaders. Instead, they found themselves in a large hall, at a meeting attended by almost all the country's intellectuals, great and small. They had to face a board of inquiry chaired by Mrs. García Buchacha and made up chiefly of PSP leaders; and they were addressed in a manner far more suited to a court of law than to an intellectual debate. They were accused of splitting the ranks of the Revolution, a serious crime at a time when unity had become a matter of life and death. They were accused of lacking a proper socialist perspective, of hankering after Western culture, and, more generally, of upholding dubious cultural trends. A terrible indictment, all told.

However, the whiff of Zhdanovism their accusers exuded proved so offensive to a number of intellectuals not part of the *Lunes* group that they jumped to the defense of Carlos Franqui and Pablo Armando Fernández; Roberto Fernández Retamar[36] and Lisandro Otero[37] were but two who spoke up for them. They all declared that loyalty to the Revolution was perfectly compatible with the defense of avant-garde ideas and that they did not accept authoritarian definitions of socialist culture.

To be sure, a number of well-known intellectuals, including Alejo Carpentier who had previously supported and even praised *Lunes de Revolución,* were careful to take no part in the debate. Some others, such as the poet José Alvarez Baragaño, were even ready to indulge in self-criticism for their contributions, and confessed that their supposed errors had been due to

36. Roberto Fernández Retamar studied and taught in Paris, London, and Yale. His published works include *Historia antigua* (1964), *Poesía reunida* (1966), and an anthology of the works of the Che Guevara. He is the present editor of *Casa de las Américas.*

37. Lisandro Otero, son of a well-known journalist, worked on *Bohemia* and fought with the July 26th Movement in Havana. Publisher of *Revolución* since 1959, he has published his discussions with Sartre and has written several novels, including the controversial *Pasión d'Urbino.* He is vice-president of the Cuba Council for Culture.

their bourgeois origin. But on the whole this Communist attempt to bring the intellectuals to heel met with so much resistance that it could not be brought to a successful conclusion at that time. Two further meetings were called. At last, on June 30, 1961, Fidel Castro intervened personally to sum up the proceedings. His speech reassured the intellectuals. Fidel declared straightaway that the Cuban Revolution had not the least intention of imposing a cultural line on artists. There was no desire to limit the freedom of research or expression of anyone on the side of the Revolution. "Within the Revolution, complete freedom; against the Revolution, none." This formulation might have looked rather vague, seeing that Fidel failed to say who would decide the issue, but the intellectuals had almost unbounded confidence, not in Fidel's liberalism—the word was applicable—but in his passionate interest in new ideas and avant-garde experiments. All things considered, they thought he was on their side. His Marxism-Leninism was the same as theirs; not that of Mrs. García Buchacha.

For all that, publication of *Lunes de Revolución* was stopped, not because the paper had been guilty of crimes against the Revolution, but because Fidel decreed that it was improper for so small a group to have so powerful a weekly. He asked all writers and artists to combine their efforts in starting a big cultural weekly, and to that effect a Union of Writers and Artists was founded in August 1961. It exists to this day, but has never produced a journal—it does, however, put out a run-of-the-mill magazine called *Unión,* whose small circulation is a measure of their lack of originality.[38]

In short, the meetings at the National Library ended in com-

38. Another victim of these meetings was the film *PM,* which was not allowed to be screened. Some said it was too sexy, others that it featured too many Negroes, and yet others that it gave quite the wrong impression of Cuban life and merely provided the enemy with ammunition. In fact, when a copy of the film was discovered abroad, no counterrevolutionary organization rushed to buy it, and neither did American television, doubtless because *PM* does not lend itself to anti-Cuban propaganda.

promise. The intellectuals had won a certain respite, but lost one of their main weapons in the cultural field. The PSP was content as well, for it had no wish to capture *Lunes* or to set up its own cultural and political journal. However, it was determined to prevent intellectuals from having anything to do with politics and ideological questions; in a pinch, they might be permitted to paint abstract paintings or write esoteric novels, but no more.

The public debate on the history and uniqueness of the Cuban Revolution was cut short in much the same way. Here, too, the old guard wanted at any cost to force the facts into the classical mold, no matter how reluctant the facts or those who had participated in them. Oddly enough, Fidel Castro raised no objections, even though the PSP version of recent events was an indirect criticism, not so much of him personally—for that was still unthinkable—as of his revolutionary activities. Rumor even had it that Fidel had summoned his old Sierra companions one by one to tell them: "Dear Jorge, or Pablo, or Jesús, you fought well in the guerrilla war and your revolutionary spirit is beyond question; but you must admit that you are really neither a politician nor a soldier. You must learn to be one or the other; only then can I give you an important job in the Party or the army, or wherever you wish." Jorge or Pablo or Jesús were thus forced to choose between enrolling in the School for Revolutionary Education or in the military academy, both of which were completely under the thumb of the PSP. In both, Sierra veterans were taught that the front line of the anti-Batista struggle had been manned by the workers in the factories, under the leadership of the PSP. Thanks to them, and to them only, the *guerrilleros* had been able to outflank the enemy. And so the Cuban, like all other socialist revolutions, once again bore witness to the decisive role of the working class and its vanguard, the Communist Party.

Details in support of this audacious version of history were produced. While Communist victims of Batista's repression were held up as great leaders, martyrs from other movements were al-

The Russians arrive

lowed to sink into oblivion, as if their deaths had been quite accidental. There was even a black joke going around Havana that the *Granma* expedition had really been led by Blas Roca who, for security reasons, had decided to put on a false beard and call himself Fidel Castro.

But these jokes had ceased to make anyone laugh, and I myself had the distinct impression that Cuba was rapidly being turned into a Stalinist quagmire. My Cuban friends, on the other hand, though apprehensive about what was happening around them, declared that Fidel had absolutely nothing to do with it. To me, their complete trust in the man from the Sierra seemed a bit sentimental. Castro must have known full well what was happening; after all he still traveled all over the country and spoke to all sorts of people. One cannot suppose that he knew less about current developments than myself, a mere visitor, almost a holiday-maker.

I was deeply pessimistic on leaving Cuba, certain that all these mini-Stalinist aberrations were taking place with Fidel's full knowledge, and that he would not be able to set things right even if he wanted to. I felt that Cuba was taking the easiest road downhill, faithfully copying the Soviet method of running economy, police, information services, and even intellectual life. Enthusiastic speeches in praise of the superior morality of Soviet society had made way for blind imitation of the Russian example, despite storm signals that even Soviet sympathizers were quick to discern.

My disappointment was all the greater in that I had come from Latin America, and had just seen what great hopes the Cuban Revolution had raised everywhere. Cuba had become the symbol of freedom through victory over the United States. Its effects were felt everywhere. This potentially great movement had not yet assumed a clear-cut political form, had not yet become institutionalized. It was more a state of mind in search of a way, and all eyes were fixed on Cuba.

The United States, which in March 1961 had set up the Alliance for Progress to direct Latin Americans away from the path of revolution, was now forced to recognize that the status quo could no longer be maintained in Latin America. As more news about the poverty and destitution of Latin America filtered through, an ever larger number of responsible Americans realized that things had to change, and change quickly. And as everybody else knew, President Kennedy's generosity was in direct proportion to his fear of Cuban influence. Quite suddenly he was promising money and reforms; was heralding the reign of justice and democracy. And in return he asked for nothing more than a break with Havana. Lázaro Cárdenas, the ex-president of Mexico, told me in his house at Apatzingán that this immoral attempt to buy off the conscience of Latin Americans was doomed to failure from the start. "We do not believe that America will send us manna from heaven, or that she is capable of changing anything at all on our continent. There can be neither a revolution nor reforms without a struggle against the United States, as the people know only too well."

The Cuban example had proved that the United States was not invincible and that a revolutionary state could afford to grant more freedom and progress in conditions of independence than could any other regime. It was this kind of prospect that especially fired the imagination of the young, who had no interest in the old controversies of European Communists. They were sick of speeches about the comparative standards of living of Soviet and American workers; all these abstract questions left them cold, as did promises of peaceful coexistence, and of international cooperation and disarmament. In other words, they shared none of the concerns of their own Communist parties. They had their own ideas about Cuba, because what had happened there had a direct bearing on their present and future situation, and made sense to them here and now.

Unfortunately, my stay in Havana had given me the impression that, in future, they would get nothing from Cuba but a dreary flow of stereotyped propaganda in the Soviet style. The language of the Cuban Revolution was becoming stilted, and its vision impaired by official Communist myopia. The big July 26th celebrations in Havana had been attended by a full

244

complement of veterans from the various Latin American Communist parties. Everyone had treated them with the respect and deference due to true Marxists. All political and even technical exchanges had to have their approval. A young Latin American who wished to work in Cuba had first to get permission from his own Communist party. Yet all these parties survived on the fringe of society, much as the PSP had in Cuba. All of them were victims of Stalinism, and had been sacrificed on the altar of the Great Alliance during World War II. And the more isolated and powerless they were, the more uncompromisingly pro-Soviet they became. In the end their blindness was touching and pathetic, for it was imposed upon them by the very people whose wisdom and merits they extolled. As for Cuba, with its host of young and imaginative allies on the Latin American continent, it was nothing short of suicide to forge exclusive bonds with such small and calcified groups.

In Havana I made the acquaintance of a Chilean Communist in his fifties, whose vaguely Polish name escapes me. He told me in all seriousness that, thanks to their enthusiasm and the natural wealth of their country, Cubans would catch up with Bulgaria in five or six years at the most. This seemed to him the very height of ambition, Bulgaria having apparently made remarkable progress and set up an especially attractive form of socialism—for an agricultural and backward country. To question the relevance of Bulgarian socialism would have been as pointless as trying to convince a bishop of the virtues of profligacy.

A week or so later, in Mexico, at the home of the writer Fernando Benítez, I tried to express my qualms with an account of what had happened to *Lunes* and *PM*. My friends showed concern, but implored me to try and see matters in proper perspective: "Do you think that any Latin American prime minister has ever bothered to sit down with intellectuals as Fidel Castro has done? Here newspapers and films are banned without the least discussion or explanation. In Havana the reins of power are in the hands of such men as Fidel and Che, men who are neither sectarian nor enemies of culture. So long as they

245

are in power, there is no fear of Cuba turning into a banana republic, nor, for that matter, into another Bulgaria." All the same they agreed to inform the Cubans of their fears about the resurgence of the PSP and about official links with Latin American Communist parties.

C. Wright Mills, who was spending the last year of his life in Europe, was of the same opinion. Despite his illness, he wanted to go to Havana to plead with Fidel Castro. He hoped to bring with him intellectuals who were respected in Cuba and could not be suspected of anti-Communism. He believed that what was needed was not so much to attack Castro or to question his choice of socialism, as to sound the alarm against too close an identification with Eastern Europe. But Wright Mills' proposed tour never came off—several European intellectuals replied that his proposed mission was premature since nothing serious had happened; others thought it was much too late and that Castro's latest alliances would henceforth govern his behavior in all political and cultural matters. Not wishing to go by himself, Mills gave up the whole plan. Meanwhile what scraps of news reached us from Cuba during the latter half of 1961 served merely to confirm our worst fears.

On March 8, 1962, the composition of the National Directorate of the ORI was announced in Havana. Previously this organization had functioned in a somewhat mysterious fashion, and no one outside could have told you who precisely were its leading officials. Now it was officially made known that its 25 members would be made up of 13 delegates from the old July 26th Movement, 10 from the old PSP, and 2 from the old *Directorio*. Now, given the suspect leanings of some of the veterans of the July 26th Movement such as Raúl Castro, it looked very much as if the Communist old guard would have the upper hand in the new organization. The whole thing was no great surprise to anyone.[39]

39. The twenty-five leaders were: Fidel Castro, Raúl Castro, Ernesto Guevara, Osvaldo Dorticós, Emilio Aragones, Blas Roca, Carlos Rafael Rodríguez, Augusto Martínez Sánchez, Aníbal Escalante, Faure Chomón,

The Russians arrive

But five days later, on March 13, 1962, a dramatic event took place on the steps of the University of Havana, during the commemoration service to the martyrs of the attack on the presidential palace. One of the leaders of the Young Communist League read out the "Testament" of José Antonio Echeverría, which was widely known in Cuba, and contained a few passages about God and religion. When the young Communist now chose to secularize this testament by omitting all references to religion, Fidel Castro leaped out of his seat and lodged a violent protest, enraged by this lack of respect for a dead comrade. Yet it was common knowledge in Havana that the Schools of Revolutionary Education and even official and semi-official newspapers of the ORI had begun to rewrite recent history in an even more outrageous fashion, without Fidel Castro batting an eyelid. Consequently his present rage was quite out of proportion to the provocation; one possible explanation was that it proved the final straw, the final insult by outsiders who thought they could do with the Revolution as they pleased.

This impression was quickly confirmed by later events. On March 26, Fidel addressed the nation on television and passionately denounced Aníbal Escalante, the secretary of the ORI. According to Fidel, Escalante had forced Cuba into a sectarian straitjacket, and so had many of his subordinates in the provinces. All of them were displaying an incredible degree of arrogance, though all of them had crept under their beds during the fight against Batista.

The speech hit Cuba like a bombshell, and Havana suddenly recovered some of the revolutionary fervor of January 1959. Friends reported this holiday atmosphere with unreserved delight—Fidel had fully deserved their trust, after all. "Didn't we tell you that he would put things right sooner or later?" Others went even further and tried to prove that the Cuban

---

Ramiro Valdés, Haydée Santamaría, Severo Aguire, Flavio Bravo, César Escalante, Joaquín Ordoqui, Lázaro Peña, Manuel Luzardo, Ramón Calcines, Juan Almeida, Armando Hart, Sergio del Valle, Guillermo García, Osmani Cienfuegos, Raúl Curbelo.

Revolution was much too healthy, much too strong to be infected by the sectarian virus. It had taken the Revolution a whole year to get rid of it, but what was a year when measured against history? Suddenly people everywhere spoke quite openly and freely about the misdeeds of the Escalante era, now baptized the mini-Stalinist phase. Escalante having discreetly retired to Moscow, everything in Cuba would quickly be put right again.

And yet, a close reading of Fidel Castro's speech showed that his attack had been directed at the secretary and not at the bureaucratic system that had enabled this man to act as he did. Moreover, Escalante's own friends were quick to back Fidel up and to heap abuse on their old leader. Blas Roca, in a spirited article in *Cuba Socialista*,[40] rejoiced at the fact that anti-Communists and anti-Russians would be disappointed, since the new party had emerged from its latest trial stronger than ever, and more certain of its historical mission. And while heaping praise on Fidel Castro, Blas Roca did his utmost to reduce the episode to a lapse on the part of one who, according to him, had shown suspicious signs of deviationist tendencies even in the past. Not a word of blame, however, for the system that had grown up in Cuba under the aegis, or at least with the active participation, of Aníbal Escalante.

Fidel had given his country a respite, just as nine months earlier he had granted the intellectuals a measure of liberty in their own field. He allocated responsible posts to men more attractive to the rank and file, men who could speak their language. His warning shot also helped to make Communist leaders in various parts of the administration less arrogant than they had been. All this was greatly to the good and showed that Cuban society had, in fact, developed strong antibodies to the Stalinist virus. But it provided no answer to the structural problem of a society planned and managed from the top, without control or real participation of the masses,

40. *Cuba Socialista*, May 1962.

a society that stifled original ideas and hence the emergence of real socialism.

Unable to introduce more sweeping changes, Fidel Castro simply indulged in a fresh, but necessarily evanescent, burst of badly needed optimism. As a result, the Cuban mini-crisis became a reflection of the Communist crisis at large. The Cubans, like the Russians, had to change their international posture. This was probably the cause of the new Soviet-Cuban honeymoon in the summer of 1962, the prelude to the Cuban missile crisis.

The missile crisis

Both principal actors in the "Cuban missile crisis" have disappeared from the political scene. John F. Kennedy was assassinated in Dallas in November 1963 and Nikita Khrushchev was removed from power and reduced to silence in October 1964. But their "reconciliation" after the thirteen dramatic days of October 1962 opened a new chapter in Russo-American relations of which we have not yet heard the end. Neither the missile crisis nor its spectacular conclusion would have been possible had Soviet society revealed its true nature after the death of Stalin. It is conceivable that there would have been a closer understanding, even without this trial of strength between Moscow and Washington, but that trial undoubtedly speeded up and reinforced the process Khrushchev had initiated the moment he came to power. Cuba was the stake in, or rather the pretext for, a confrontation between the two superpowers. For this very reason, the affair of the Soviet missiles cannot be understood by reference to Cuba alone. What happened in Washington and Moscow was equally important.

The American version is by far the better known—victors tend to be more talkative. Some of John F. Kennedy's former associates such as Ted Sorensen[41] and Arthur Schlesinger,

41. Theodore Sorensen: *Kennedy* (London, Hodder & Stoughton, 1965).

Guerrillas in Power

Jr.,[42] have described the crisis in detail. More recently, the friends of the late Senator Robert F. Kennedy have published his clear and concise version of the events.[43] Robert F. Kennedy played a major role throughout the missile crisis; he was his brother's closest adviser and was able to follow his reactions and motives throughout the long trial they endured together, day after day, hour after hour.

It all began on October 16, 1962. That day John F. Kennedy was given incontrovertible proof that the Russians were installing ground-to-ground missiles in Cuba. He spoke of it first to his brother Robert, then at 11:45 summoned to the White House a number of high staff officials and experts in Soviet and Cuban affairs. The experts were all stunned by the news. Civil and military leaders had believed all along that the Soviet Union would never risk such an adventure, not least because the Russians had given them repeated reassurances, both public and private.[44] A few weeks earlier, Dobrynin, the Soviet ambassador in Washington, had handed Robert F. Kennedy a personal message for his brother in which Khrushchev stated that he would do nothing that might embarrass the President during the autumn election campaign.[45] It was on the strength of these

42. Arthur Schlesinger, Jr.: *A Thousand Days: J. F. Kennedy in the White House* (London, André Deutsch, 1965).

43. Robert F. Kennedy: *13 Days: The Cuban Missile Crisis* (London, Macmillan, 1969).

44. On September 11, 1962, the Tass agency transmitted a lengthy declaration by the Soviet government to the effect that the Soviet Union had no need for bases abroad, since its ICBMs already enabled it to strike any part of the world. This was meant to be a reply to Kennedy who, a week earlier, had announced that he would do nothing against Cuba so long as there were no offensive weapons on the island. The Americans allege that the first missiles arrived in Cuba on September 8, four days after Kennedy's warning and three days before the Tass agency's solemn declaration.

45. On November 5, 1962, Americans went to the polls to elect both a new Congress and one third of the Senate. These mid-term elections were of crucial importance to Kennedy, who had come to power two years earlier with a very slender majority and was eager to demonstrate that his popularity had risen. People in the Kennedy circle promised that, once given confirmation of his mandate, he would make a start with the more

250

assurances that, on September 4, Kennedy was able to refute the arguments of the Republican Right, led by Senator Homer E. Capehart, which had called for direct military action against Cuba. Then, on October 16, aerial reconnaissance photos showed beyond a shadow of a doubt that the Russians were hurriedly constructing launching pads for their ground-to-ground missiles.

Kennedy summed up his thoughts to his brother, saying that if he did not take some action now, he would pay politically. The problem was what action to take. Kennedy asked the small group he had chosen to receive the news first to form an ad hoc committee. All the meetings of what became known as the "Ex-Comm" (Executive Committee of the National Security Council) were held in secret, with complete freedom of discussion. Formalities went by the board; people said what they felt, and sometimes changed their minds from one meeting to the next or even in the course of a single session. There was a clear division of opinion. On one side were the "hawks" who called for immediate military action against Cuba on the grounds that only a surprise attack could completely eliminate the offensive weapons on the island. During one meeting Robert Kennedy passed his brother a note saying: "Now I know how Tojo felt when he was planning Pearl Harbor." But the President refused to side with the hawks, even though they were in a majority on the committee.

Instead he opted for the arguments of the "doves," as did his brother Robert and Defense Secretary McNamara. According to them, the United States must not place before the Russians the alternative of either sacrificing their Cuban ally and their honor, or else launching a suicidal atomic attack. The door should be left open and the Soviet Union allowed to retreat without losing face. McNamara, for long the champion of the

---

liberal policies he had set his heart on. The Russians had been informed of this, and one must see Khrushchev's message and his desire not to embarrass the President in this light. Khrushchev, in effect, felt that Kennedy had more important things to do than keep an eye on Cuba, and that this was an eminently suitable moment for installing his missiles.

251

theory of selective retaliation,[46] quite naturally felt that military action against the Cuban bases was premature. As for Robert F. Kennedy, he was apparently one of the few to have moral scruples. He insisted that a great country such as the United States could not mount a brutal attack on a small island without grievously damaging its image throughout the world.

On October 22, John F. Kennedy addressed the nation at large. In a television broadcast he explained that the Russians had lied to him and that he was now forced to fence Cuba in, to prevent further deliveries of offensive weapons. From now on all ships bound for the island would be intercepted on the high seas and searched by the U.S. Navy, and this would continue until such time as the Soviet Union removed her missiles from Cuba. Kennedy's decision immediately received full backing from the Organization of American States (OAS) and from America's chief allies on the other side of the Atlantic, the first to offer his support being General de Gaulle. This made the whole affair something of a joint crusade and gave it a semblance of legality.

But world opinion was not so easily convinced as were the allied leaders. Communists, in particular, mounted a large-scale campaign against "the American lie,"[47] and their arguments

46. Robert McNamara's idea was diametrically opposed to that of John Foster Dulles, who, as Secretary of State in the Eisenhower administration, had advocated "massive and instant retaliation." Now Dulles' ideas were quite inapplicable since, in practice, the United States was as unwilling to launch a total war as the Soviet Union. Robert McNamara accordingly decided that America must instead be able to take whatever limited and gradual countermeasures were demanded by local conflicts. It was owing to him that the Kennedy administration created the Green Berets and similar forces whose specific task it was to fight Communists and revolutionaries on their home ground. In sum, he believed that America should be in a position to export counterrevolution without running the risk of starting a conflict among the great powers.

47. There were mass demonstrations against "the American lie" especially in countries with very strong Communist parties. In Milan, a young demonstrator by the name of Giovanni Ardizzone was killed during a scuffle with the police, and the city was paralyzed by a forty-eight-hour protest strike.

252

The Russians arrive

gained currency even in liberal circles. The United States had lied so often about Cuba, especially during the Bay of Pigs invasion, that people now refused to believe even in photographic proof of Russian missiles. The Canadian prime minister, John Diefenbaker, went so far as to express the fear that the blockade of Cuba might lead to an ideological break between the United States and the rest of the world. Washington was not indifferent to these criticisms. Khrushchev, for his part, refused to confirm the presence of missiles on the island and sent Kennedy a very angry letter denouncing "American piracy and the folly of degenerate imperialism." Zorin, the Soviet representative at the United Nations, was no less obdurate and refused to answer Adlai Stevenson's charges in the Security Council. All he said was: "I am not before an American court of law." Tension rose by the hour; the press gave news of Soviet and Allied troop movements in West and East Germany and along the whole frontier between the two blocs. Strangely enough the Chinese, usually so quick to protest against Yankee imperialism, were the only ones to make no comment.

In Washington, the Ex-Comm was in constant and tense session. American intelligence services reported that work on the Soviet bases in Cuba was being speeded up. Despite increased air reconnaissance, it was impossible to tell whether some of the launching pads were fully operational. Meanwhile Soviet ships kept sailing toward Cuba. Khrushchev obviously had stronger nerves than his opponents: he even allowed himself to be photographed at the opera, all smiles, as if nothing at all were amiss. Yet all the while the two superpowers were digging in their heels, and it seemed certain that they would come to blows. The U.S. Navy remained under orders to search Soviet ships bound for Cuba and, in case of resistance, to escort them to an allied port. The Soviet ships, on the other hand, were under orders to repel all search parties and resist the American "pirates." An explosive incident on the high seas seemed only a matter of time.

The "hawks" once more took the offensive. They thought it

absurd to leave the initiative to the Russians and called for immediate action against Cuba. Preparations were made for an invasion of the island which, according to Pentagon calculations, would cost the American army 25,000 dead. But the "doves" stood firm and President Kennedy once again sided with them. He decided to wait until the Russian ships reached the quarantine limits, fixed by the Navy at 500 miles from the Cuban coast. It was expected that contact would be made on Wednesday, October 24, between 10 and 11 A.M. Were it to come to a naval battle, the Americans were certain of gaining the upper hand; the bulk of their fleet was concentrated in this part of the world, whereas the Soviet vessels had no more than a submarine escort. But a victory at sea would be hollow unless the Soviet ships dragged into United States ports could be shown to be loaded with missiles. If they were carrying nothing but "powdered milk for Cuban babies"—as Kennedy himself feared —the operation would merely serve to turn America into a laughing stock.

The clash never took place. The Soviet ships prudently turned back just before reaching the American check point. Only the tanker *Bucharest* sailed on—Kennedy had given orders that it was not to be intercepted, as he was certain it carried no war materials. But to show that he had meant what he said all along, he had a neutral ship bound for Cuba boarded and searched on the high seas.

Let us leave the American version for a minute and note that the Russian change of tack on the high seas corresponded to a change of tactics by the Communist propaganda machine. Gone were the denunciations of the "American lie"; the keynote now was peace and "the dangers of atomic war." World opinion, though thankful for Russian prudence in the Caribbean, continued nonetheless to be deeply shaken. Was Russian acquiescence not proof positive that the Russians had, in fact, been sending missiles to Cuba? And people become more and more suspicious of the Soviet attitude in the whole business.

Even Party supporters were unhappy. Thus on October 25,

The Russians arrive

when the Franco-Cuban Friendship Society organized a big solidarity meeting chaired by Professor Charles Bettelheim at the Palais de la Mutualité in Paris, the hall was only three quarters full and most of those who came were non-Communist, middle-class intellectuals. And a similar drop in militancy could be observed everywhere, not least in Latin America. Instead of being indignant, as they had been during the first few days of the crisis, people felt dazed when it was brought home to them that this time the biggest liars had been the Russians (and by extension, the Cubans), not the Americans. The shock was the more painful in that nobody could understand why the Soviet Union should have behaved in this way, and how she could have allowed herself to be caught in the act by President Kennedy.

On Friday, October 26, what uncertainties remained about the missiles vanished completely. The Soviet prime minister, in a personal letter to President Kennedy, admitted that nuclear weapons had been set up in Cuba, and went on to ask that neither country take any irreparable steps. To reassure the American President, he explained that these fearful weapons were under the control of Soviet officers and hence could not be used against the United States, even accidentally. This was his way of telling the President that serious people do not cause mischief and can quickly reach an understanding. The Cubans, who were to be officially excluded from the coming negotiations, next day shot down an American U-2 to show that they were as determined as ever to have their say. The crisis nearly started all over again, as the "hawks" called for strong reprisals. But President Kennedy kept his head.

Events once more rewarded his foresight: on October 27 and 28, Khrushchev wrote two further letters which put an end to the whole affair. In the first, the Soviet prime minister proposed a sort of global bargain: the Russians would remove their missiles from Cuba if the Americans would do the same with their bases in Turkey. In the second he agreed to the dis-mantling—under international control—of the Cuban bases in exchange for a simple American promise not to invade the island. On the advice of his brother Robert, John F. Kennedy took no notice of the first letter but gave a favorable response to the second, which suited him perfectly in any case. As a sportsmanlike gesture he congratulated the Soviet opponent on his "prudent and statesmanlike conduct," and asked his own colleagues never to speak of victor and vanquished when referring to this crisis. He realized that, at the cost of sitting for thirteen days on the edge of the atomic abyss, he had gained much more than the mere removal of Soviet missiles from Cuba.

But this fact is carefully omitted from all American versions of events. The "doves" who happen to have written most of the books on the crisis haughtily assume much of the credit for its happy outcome. Thanks only to their level-headedness, America attained her objective and caused right and justice to triumph without striking a blow. Without them, and especially without the Kennedy brothers in the White House, it would have been impossible to prevent a surprise attack on Cuba and therewith unquestionably a third world war. Their books unwittingly give a terrifying picture of the American power elite, bursting with incredible arrogance[48] and encouraging the belief that American bombs and the American Navy would be enough to impose a Pax Americana on the world. For this elite, might was the only right; hence it is hardly surprising that it should have called for the bombing of Cuba, much as it later caused the bombing of another small country, Vietnam. One can only hope that, at the cost of unspeakable suffering and sacrifices, the Vietnamese have brought home to this elite the limits to its murderous powers.

Another striking fact about American writings on the missile

48. The term "arrogance of power" was later used by Senator Fulbright for the title of a book in which he criticized American policy in Vietnam. However, Robert F. Kennedy has claimed that, during the missile crisis, Senator Fulbright supported the idea of a surprise attack on Cuba. The case of the Senator thus tends to show that experience of defeat is the only remedy against this arrogance. However, one must give him his due; he was among the first to be cured.

crisis is their substantial lack of political insight. Why did the Russians risk setting up missile sites in the Caribbean? What was their purpose? Why did they retreat? Why did they not put pressure on the weak links in America's defensive system in Asia or Europe? One looks vainly for answers to these questions in the writings of Robert Kennedy and other Americans intimately involved in these events.

At most, they tell us that Khrushchev was trying to alter the balance of power between the two giants, but even here they do not bother to explain why he should have seen the need for this. They themselves had long since ceased to believe that the "Communist devil" wanted to subjugate the "free world" at any price. In fact, they neither criticized Khrushchev's Communism nor attacked him personally. Robert Kennedy assures us that, throughout the crisis, his brother was certain that "Khrushchev wanted peace."

Khrushchev, if one is to believe them, was simply a bad psychologist, with little understanding of the American mentality. As early as June 1961, after their meeting in Vienna, Kennedy told James Reston of *The New York Times* that he felt Khrushchev thought him immature—because of the failure of the Bay of Pigs invasion—and was convinced that America could be made to retreat on all fronts.[49] And so Kennedy determined to be firm to show Khrushchev his error; he refused to make any concessions or even to negotiate about Germany's frontiers; in 1961 he sent a large team of "advisers" to South Vietnam where U.S. forces had just suffered their first casualties; and he stepped up the pressure on Cuba. But all this apparently failed to convince Khrushchev that America was determined to defend her interests abroad. It was this error of judgment that led him to make the mistake of sending rockets to Cuba in 1962. This is as far as the American accounts go—officially, at least. The

49. This story was first made public by the Senate Republican Policy Committee on the Vietnam war (1967). See: *The war in Vietnam* (document prepared by the staff of the Senate Republican Policy Committee, released in Washington, D.C., on May 2, 1967), p. 39.

whole thing is so unconvincing that even as staunch an ally as Harold Macmillan has remarked that the missile affair remains "still scarcely explicable."[50]

Unfortunately, the Soviet version of the events is no more helpful. During the past few years, the Russians have sat by with folded arms while the Americans brought out a whole series of revealing books on the actions of the Soviet leaders, ministers, and ambassadors during the crisis. Their very silence would seem to corroborate the truth of U.S. allegations, compromising not only to Khrushchev—since removed—but to many others who still hold down their old jobs. What is more, these American books give the lie to the only official Soviet version, issued immediately after the crisis, first by Kosygin and later by Khrushchev.

Kosygin, then vice-premier of the Soviet Union, was the first to speak out, less than ten days after the removal of the missiles had been agreed by both parties. His remarks were meant for the inner circle of the Soviet Communist Party and government, assembled for the annual celebrations of the Bolshevik revolution, on November 6. The Cubans, he said, had asked the Soviet Union for missiles because they feared for the safety of their country. But the guarantees since given by President Kennedy made it unnecessary to keep these weapons in Cuba. The Soviet Union had taken very great risks to achieve this result. Fortunately everything had turned out for the best, and everyone could face the future with optimism.

"Was it really necessary to give in? Yes, it was well worth it. . . . The peace of the world was at stake. If nothing else, these mutual concessions, at a time when thousands of people were threatened with the horrors of nuclear war, proved that socialism and capitalism can live together in peace, provided they stick to peaceful competition. . . . We must now remove the problems that give rise to this type of tension."[51]

50. See Macmillan's foreword to the English edition of Robert F. Kennedy's book.

51. The text of this speech was printed in *Pravda* (November 8, 1962). Despite Soviet insistence it has never been published in Havana.

The Russians arrive

The reader will notice that all these remarks were forward-looking, as if the "tension" in the Caribbean was a thing of the past, no longer worth mentioning. But things were not nearly as simple as that. The Cubans, for one, refused to accept an agreement that had been signed over their heads. And then the Chinese suddenly sprang to life, organizing demonstrations in support of Castro, and publishing articles in which they accused the Kremlin of having followed an "adventurist and capitulationist policy" in the Caribbean. Such disgraceful behavior put the Chinese in mind of "the treachery perpetrated by German Social Democracy on the eve of the First World War." This was not the first time, they continued, that a great workers' party with a glorious tradition had made a mockery of internationalism and betrayed its historic mission.

On December 12, 1962, when Nikita Khrushchev took the floor before the Supreme Soviet, his main concern was to rebut the Chinese attack. He added nothing substantial to what Kosygin had already said, but stressed the fact that the Soviet Union had saved Cuba from attack by the Americans. "We solemnly declare that the Soviet Union has firmly stood by revolutionary Cuba and continues to do so. Let no one think that our country will ever leave the Cuban Revolution in the lurch. The Soviet Union will fulfill its promise to help Cuba and will not leave her undefended."[52] After this, he refuted the arguments of

52. The Russians did not merely publish Khrushchev's speech in *Pravda* and all other newspapers, they had it printed as an advertisement in about ten Western newspapers. In France *L'Express* had the honor—and the good fortune, financially speaking—of being chosen as the medium for this publicity stunt. The editors suggested to the Russians that the text be broken up with pictures to make it easier for readers unused to the austere manner of presentation practiced in Moscow. But this proved impossible because no one dared to take the slightest liberty with the sacrosanct prose of the First Secretary of the Communist Party of the U.S.S.R. The text was reprinted in its entirety exactly as it had appeared in *Pravda*. This, to the best of my knowledge, is the only time the Russians have chosen so expensive a way of making their point of view widely known, particularly in a country like France in which the Communist Party has ample funds and unreservedly defends the Soviet Union. Clearly they were anxious to reach a wider, "bourgeois" public and explain to them that the U.S.S.R. was firmly committed to peace and in no way countenanced Chinese warmongering.

259

Guerrillas in Power

Peking in the customary Soviet fashion; i.e., without naming the opponent or producing his real point of view. "Imperialism is no longer what it was when it ruled the whole world. . . . But we have no wish to triumph at the cost of millions of dead. If we are forced into war, to war we shall go; but meanwhile, we shall do our utmost to prevent it." This speech would of course have been more convincing had the missile sites been installed by the belligerent Chinese and dismantled by the peace-loving Russians. In the event, this speech took in nobody but the ill-informed in the Soviet Union itself or Communists abroad who had something to gain from Khrushchev's pro-American attitudes.

It was quite some time, however, before the basic inconsistencies in the Soviet argument became plain for all to see. True, Khrushchev's account of the facts seemed tenuous from the very beginning. He had said nothing about the unorthodox methods used to get the missiles into Cuba, or about the sudden negotiations with Kennedy over Castro's head. However, in the absence of more detailed information, it was impossible to reject his version out of hand. Throughout the summer of 1962, the whole world had after all been given the impression that the Americans were getting ready to invade Cuba: even America's Atlantic allies had been seriously alarmed. One need only glance at the liberal British press of that period to realize the extent to which America's obsessive anti-Castroism shocked public opinion and made people fear the worst.[53] In these circum-

53. London newspapers unanimously approved the stand of the British government when it refused to bow to American pressure to cut off trade with Cuba. This same stand, however, came in for severe criticism in the United States even from such liberals as James Reston. The Sunday *Observer* in answer to Reston printed a scathing editorial reminding him of the futility of the slogan "my country, right or wrong" and denouncing anti-Cuban obsession in America. James Reston then hit back. He mentioned the emotional ties linking his fellow-countrymen with Cuba and recalled that even Thomas Jefferson had expressed the view that Cuba was the country he would most like to see included in the United States. Reston's arguments in no way convinced the *Observer* which unceremoniously called him back to the present and asked him not to hide behind the authority of

260

stances, it was quite conceivable that Cuba might have called on the Soviet Union for help, and that faced with this situation Khrushchev might have decided to risk everything so as to prevent an attack on Cuba. In that case, he would have found the outcome of the crisis entirely to his satisfaction: his only aim had been to save Cuba, and save her he did.

But this story no longer holds water today, when we can read Castro's disclosures and the memoirs of many of the Americans involved in the crisis. Castro, though deeply incensed, refrained for a long time from embarrassing his Soviet allies by challenging their version of how the missile affair had started. However in February 1963, during a dinner given for Claude Julien of *Le Monde*, he asserted that far from asking the Soviet Union for missiles to defend Cuba, Moscow had foisted them on Cuba for the purpose of "strengthening international socialism."[54] Later that year, Castro, in a long interview with Jean Daniel—now editor in chief of *Nouvel Observateur*—gave more details about how the Russians had warned him that America was about to invade the island and that the only way to stop them was to build missile sites.[55] In the conversations I myself had with

---

the great men of the past. This polemic, clear evidence of a difference of opinion between American and British liberals on the subject of Cuba, was republished in *L'Express* on October 25, 1962, after the start of the missile crisis. At that time, however, people still found it difficult to credit American allegations about the presence of Soviet missiles on the island.

54. Claude Julien's interview with Fidel Castro was published in *Le Monde* (March 22, 1963). American press agencies at once gave a summary of it that was thought in Havana to be needlessly sensational; Castro immediately issued a denial. However, he made it plain from the start that Claude Julien was in no way responsible for the American exaggerations; and, more important, he never denied having uttered the key phrases we have quoted.

55. The account Castro gave Jean Daniel is worth quoting at length because it shows in great detail (never denied by either Havana or Moscow) how the Russians managed to persuade the Cubans that America was about to launch an attack on them:

"Six months before the missile sites were set up in Cuba we already had a mass of information about renewed preparations by the CIA for an invasion of the island. . . . Then one day Khrushchev's son-in-law, Adzhubei, came on a visit here, on his way to the United States where he had

Guerrillas in Power

Castro several years later, he again emphasized that the initiative had come not from him but from Khrushchev. Then again, from reading such books as Robert F. Kennedy's one can see that the Soviet premier's explanation was hollow. He knew full well that the United States was not plotting to attack Cuba; indeed what strikes one so forcibly in the Senator's account is the extent to which Russia and America were already in league. Thus Gromyko, the Soviet foreign minister, had come to the White House on October 18, 1962, to give Kennedy assurances about Castro's intentions, explaining to him that Cuba was not interested in exporting her system to other Latin American countries and, like the Soviet Union, wanted only peace. And Dobrynin, the Russian ambassador, who was on excellent terms with Robert F. Kennedy, publicly minimized the danger Cuba represented in Latin America. To hear these discussions one might have imagined that the representatives of the two superpowers were the heads of two giant businesses with con-

---

been invited by Kennedy's associates. As soon as he arrived in Washington, Adzhubei was received by Kennedy. They spoke mainly about Cuba. A week after this interview we in Havana got a copy of Adzhubei's report to Khrushchev. It was this copy that started everything off. What did Kennedy say? Take note, because it is very important. He said that the United States found the new situation in Cuba intolerable and that the American government refused to put up with it any longer; he added that peaceful coexistence was seriously compromised by the fact that Soviet influence in Cuba had altered the agreed balance of power. Then," here Castro emphasized every word, *"Kennedy reminded the Russian visitor that the United States had not intervened in Hungary.* This was clearly a demand for Russian nonintervention during the projected invasion. The word 'invasion' was of course not used, but Adzhubei drew the same conclusions as we. . . . What were we to do? How was the invasion to be thwarted? We found that Khrushchev shared our worries. He asked us what we wanted. We replied, do anything that will convince the Americans that an attack on Cuba is tantamount to an attack on the Soviet Union. Upon this basis we began to think it through. Various things were possible, a declaration of common interest, an alliance, conventional military support. The Russians told us that they had a double concern: to save the Cuban revolution and therewith the honor of the socialist world, and at the same time avoid a world war. As far as they were concerned, the threat of conventional retaliation might not be enough to persuade America to think twice before invading Cuba" (*L'Express,* December 1963).

siderable mutual interests, two concerns that, for all the competition between them, were determined to keep order in the market. This complicity did not exclude lying—such tricks are after all common practice in the business world no less than in world politics—but it did exclude a frontal attack by one partner on the other. Both competitors could use ruses, disagree on a number of points, even clash here and there in the world political arena—as in Germany, for instance—but they were basically in agreement not to come to blows and they kept each other informed of their plans.[56]

The more one learns about the missile crisis of 1962, the clearer it becomes that Khrushchev lied to everybody. First of all he lied to Castro (as Castro and his followers understand it), emphasizing the need to strengthen international socialism in order to defend Cuba against U.S. invasion and to foster revolutions throughout Latin America—when, in fact, no U.S. invasion was being planned and when Khrushchev had not the least intention of supporting social uprisings in the Third World. He also lied to Kennedy whom he had promised not to embarrass during the 1962 election campaign and to whom he had given his word never to send offensive weapons to Cuba. To top it off, military experts have proved that, from a purely strategic point of view, a missile base in Cuba would have changed nothing in the Russo-American balance of power and would not have given the Soviet Union even a short-term advantage.[57] Why then did the Soviet premier run such risks for such miserable stakes?

56. Having found out during the missile crisis that their communications were not fast enough, the Russians and Americans decided in 1963 to install a "hot line" between the White House and the Kremlin.

57. One does not need to be an expert to realize that Polaris-type missiles carried by submarines are more difficult to detect and destroy than those the Russians installed near San Cristóbal in Cuba. Now the Russians do have nuclear submarines. Moreover, it is well known that the Americans themselves had come to appreciate that fixed launching pads are exceedingly vulnerable and that they had accordingly—even before the missile crisis—decided to dismantle them in Turkey and Italy. Finally, had Soviet missiles, fired from Cuba or from a submarine, struck the United

Guerrillas in Power

The answer must be sought inside the U.S.S.R. and in the ever more obvious contradictions of its de-Stalinization policy. Today, seven years after the event, we know more about what happened, and it is in the light of our new knowledge that we must view the "mysterious affair" of the Russsian missile sites in Cuba.

In October 1961, a year before the Cuban missile crisis, the Twenty-Second Congress of the Communist Party of the U.S.S.R. was held in Moscow. On the surface it introduced nothing new in internal affairs: it endorsed the elimination of the long-since toppled Stalinist old guard (Molotov, Kaganovich, et al.) and the expulsion of Stalin's remains from the mausoleum in Red Square. Khrushchev repeated his promise to achieve Communism in the Soviet Union before 1980, and proclaimed that the U.S.S.R. was no longer a proletarian dictatorship but, in view of the disappearance of social distinctions, had become the "state of the entire nation."

Clearly, therefore, the Congress did no more than elevate an existing policy to the rank of an official doctrine. It turned out to be the swan song of Khrushchevism: the Soviet leadership realized that Nikita's economic projects had become bogged down in insuperable difficulties. His seven-year plan had fallen behind, and the economic growth rate, instead of increasing, had been dropping ominously since 1958. Behind the scenes, Soviet economists had begun to whisper about reforms based on a return to market mechanisms and a greater measure of managerial independence. Needless to say, not an echo of these discussions was heard from the platform of the Twenty-Second Congress. Instead, Khrushchev launched a fresh attack on Stalin, as superficial and full of contradictions as the first. Five years

---

States, there would have been reprisals not only against the firing base but against the Soviet Union herself. It was therefore absurd to believe that these weapons could be used in a local Cuban-American conflict without affecting the U.S.S.R. It could also be noted that both superpowers claimed to have enough nuclear arms to destroy 80 to 90 per cent of the other's population in the first twenty-four hours of a nuclear war. In these circumstances, it is difficult to see how an advanced missile base could in any way have increased Russia's pre-emptive power.

earlier, at the Twentieth Congress, it could still have been argued that such attacks were a genuine prelude to a real de-Stalinization campaign, that Khrushchev had every intention of going beyond mere words to improve the machinery his predecessor had bequeathed him. But after 1961, it was no longer possible to entertain such hopes. For at the Twenty-Second Congress, Khrushchev was at the height of his power and could have spoken his mind, and yet he chose to say nothing new and, in particular, failed to revise his triumphant estimate of the kind of society Stalin had created. In short, his attacks on Stalin had been mere expedients that cast grave doubt on the sincerity of his promise to produce Communism by 1980.

Small wonder that, even at the Twenty-Second Congress, Brezhnev, Kosygin, Podgorny, and many of Khrushchev's other protégés, apparently had lost faith in his "subjective promises." The Soviet elite was, of course, grateful to Khrushchev for stabilizing the Soviet power structure during the difficult transition period following Stalin's death, and for his introduction of the rule of law in place of Stalin's terror. Still, they did not want to be held responsible for his impetuosity, for his gigantic economic gamble, and for his fruitless attempts to run with the American hare while hunting with the Chinese hounds. They blamed Khrushchev for the growing gap between his fine Ukrainian oratory and his failure to produce any real results at home or abroad. They knew that time was running out, that at the next Congress something more was needed than a rehash of the same old speech; that Stalin's remains could not be kicked out of the mausoleum twice in a row.

And so, though the Twenty-Second Congress endorsed his line, Khrushchev was not a real victor. He realized that the only way in which he could regain the confidence of his comrades was to bring off some sort of dramatic coup. And since no miracles were possible on the home front, he decided to stake everything on a grandiose international scheme. It was to that end that, at the Twenty-Second Congress, he forced through the expulsion of the Albanian Communist Party, thus flouting a resolution

265

adopted by the Conference of Eighty-one Communist Parties in 1960, and openly provoking the Chinese. This was a calculated gesture, meant to convince the world in general, and the United States in particular, that he was serious about coexistence and that he would make a clean sweep of his Stalinist critics wherever they might be found.

Kremlinologists in Washington ought to have been quick to see that this was the precise import of the expulsion of the tiny Albanian Party. But even if they had done so, even if they had realized that Khrushchev was desperately anxious to achieve a reconciliation, the fact remained that Washington was not in nearly as great a hurry as Moscow. The Americans were quite prepared to mute their anti-Soviet propaganda and to treat the U.S.S.R. as a "responsible power," but they were chary of the rest of the Communist camp, and quite particularly of Cuba, that focus of revolutionary infection in their own hemisphere.

It was in order to remove that irritation that President Kennedy decided to seal off the island behind a veritable *cordon sanitaire*. When that happened, Castro could obviously not sit by with folded arms, and the more the Russians asked him to proclaim his faith in "peaceful" coexistence the more the words stuck in his throat.[58] On January 31, 1962, when the United States forced the expulsion of Cuba from the OAS,[59]

58. A case in point was the interview Fidel gave Adzhubei and Satiukov in January 1962. The Soviet journalists were, respectively, chief editors of *Izvestia* and of *Pravda* and formed part of Nikita Khrushchev's "backstairs government." They normally accompanied him abroad and were regular members of his immediate entourage. They were attending an international conference in Havana and tried to persuade Castro to follow the Soviet line. It seems they were successful, or so the reports published in both their newspapers suggested. Four days later however, *Revolución* published the Cuban version of the same interview, which differed considerably from the Russian. It contained whole passages about the need for revolutionary struggle and proclaimed, *inter alia*, that "no coexistence is possible between the exploited masses of Latin America and Yankee monopoly." See *Revolución,* January 30, 1962.

59. It was at Punta del Este, near Montevideo, that the Americans obtained OAS approval for the Alliance for Progress in August 1961 and that they pushed through Cuba's expulsion in 1962. We shall say little more about

The Russians arrive

Castro called a mass meeting and got it to pass the Second Havana Declaration, with the henceforth celebrated *leitmotif:* "The duty of every revolutionary is to make revolution." This call even succeeded in influencing some Latin American Communist parties, formerly pro-Russian and convinced of the virtues of coexistence. The Venezuelan Communist Party was the first to engage in armed struggle and its example was about to be followed by others. What could Khrushchev do in the face of this development? Castro was "legitimate," so to speak, and Moscow had no wish to become involved in a war of words with him. It was, of course, his example that had inspired the Venezuelan Communists—his example and the firm belief that Khrushchev stood solidly behind him.

In addition, the economic blockade added greatly to the burdens of the Soviet Union. Moscow was forced not only to send more goods to Cuba but even to provide the currency needed for trading with what few countries were still willing to deal with Cuba. All this greatly displeased the People's Democracies, and even good Soviet citizens had begun to complain about what they called the "Cuban waste." Khrushchev was increasingly criticized for being more interested in Santiago de Cuba than in Kharkhov. "Cartierism"[60] was far from being a purely French

---

the Alliance for Progress since, on looking back, it is clear it was nothing but an attempt to throw dust into the eyes of Latin Americans and had not the slightest influence on the real course of events. But one gets some idea of the extent to which Latin America sympathized with Castro when one notices that even governments closely dependent on Washington were reluctant to support this American attempt to isolate Cuba. Thus, the expulsion of Cuba from the Organization of American States in January 1962 was passed by 14 votes to 6, which satisfied Kennedy on the procedural level. It remains a fact, however, that the six countries which voted against the motion—Brazil, Argentina, Mexico, Chile, Ecuador, and Bolivia—make up two thirds of South America and represent four fifths of its population.

60. Cartierism, so-called after Raymond Cartier, who contended that France had a duty to aid its own "backward areas" before helping the Third World, has become the symbol for a certain sort of short-sighted egoism rife in wealthy societies. In the Soviet Union and the East European People's Democracies Cartierism had to take the form of a whispering campaign. It was most common in countries closest to the West such as

phenomenon; it had adherents also in the Soviet Union who, if
they could not express their views in a Russian counterpart
of *Paris-Match,* nonetheless found other ways of making their
views felt.

However—to continue this comparison—there was one difference between France and the Soviet Union. The Russians felt
that the world was ignoring their enormous military strength
and hence did not grant them enough diplomatic influence.
Their discussions with partners in the Russian bloc, including
the Chinese, gave proof of this attitude. They would seize
every opportunity to ask, "What would become of you if you
had to defend yourselves against imperialism without the Red
Army behind you?" They were prouder of their guns and rockets
than of anything else, politics included. From the beginning of
1962, boasts of military strength increasingly became the main
theme of their speeches. They felt aggrieved that the United
States neither acknowledged nor made allowances for Soviet
might. "If America wants coexistence, she must agree to coexistence in all parts of the world," Russian diplomats told
me in Paris, a few weeks before the missile crisis started.

This phrase undoubtedly holds the key to the entire missile
affair. To the Russians it seemed obvious that America did not
want global coexistence; hence she had to be made to accept it,
not by means of interminable discussions or demonstrations
and petitions—no, the era of peace conferences had long since
passed—but by a show of strength on America's very doorstep.

At the time, Russia herself had no territorial ambitions—
the claim of some political commentators that she intended to
annex Berlin is completely without foundation. All Russia
wanted was to force the world to recognize East Germany,
which would have gone a long way toward guaranteeing the
stability of her protégé. Nor had she the slightest wish to export

Poland and, later, Czechoslovakia. But the same state of mind was evident
in the Soviet Union where you could hear people say that Russia would
be a very wealthy place if only it stopped wasting its substance on "black
and yellow princelings."

revolution, as the Western powers knew full well. Hence there was only one reason for threatening the United States: to force it to accept coexistence on a world scale. This would also serve to convince everyone that world peace was the result of Soviet power and not of Soviet concessions to a stronger adversary. And Khrushchev, in fact, made no secret of this.

In a sense, therefore, the dispatch of missiles to Cuba was an exaggerated expression of the kind of political thinking that went on in Moscow. The operation was bound to fail, simply because the world was other than it appeared to Khrushchev. America's goal was the defense of specific interests; and a psychological shock in the Caribbean, painful as it might have been, was hardly likely to change these goals. It may be taken for granted that even without the discovery of Soviet missiles in Cuba and their forcible return to the Soviet Union, Kennedy would not have agreed to "worldwide coexistence," if this involved the resumption of diplomatic and trade relations with Castro under pressure, or the recognition of East Germany. Hence a Russian victory would merely have served to intensify the struggle between the two power blocs, thus hastening a return to the Cold War. However, all this is mere speculation.

What we can be certain about is what followed from the *American* victory. Khrushchev's capitulation in October 1962 fatally undermined his position in the Kremlin; the Cubans even claim that Khrushchev lost his majority in the Politburo while the crisis was still in progress. If that is so, it would explain his precipitate retreat. However, as no one in Moscow has published a diary like Robert Kennedy's, we have no means of knowing what happened on the other side of the barricade during those terrible thirteen days. However, when Khrushchev said in passing on April 23, 1963, that he would not be in power forever, he was clearly hinting that his days in the Kremlin were numbered.

During this final period, he had, in fact, been ousted. He had just enough time to sign another treaty with the United States and Great Britain banning atmospheric nuclear tests and to complete the break with China. Unable to bring about a reconciliation with the United States, flags flying and to the tune of the *Internationale,* he did what he had to do more discreetly and without fuss: he desisted from embarrassing the Americans any further, and declared his intention to avoid anything that might endanger world peace. This "wise" policy, which his successors are following to this day, has neither resulted in grand universal harmony nor prevented new conflicts—as in Vietnam —into which Russia was drawn against her will. The world seems determined to prove that international affairs are far more complex than the heirs of the October Revolution can find it in themselves to believe. They suffer what changes do occur as they would natural catastrophes, and repeatedly warn anyone who will listen of the dangers of a new confrontation. Given what Russia has become, no other outlook or policy is likely to come from her. And the Soviet lead will only be followed by those who, in their turn, have given up all hope of effecting a radical transformation of society. Many Communists have quite happily accepted this change of front, just as they accepted Khrushchev's strange behavior during the missile crisis. But for the Cubans, unmarked as they were by the terrible afflictions of that family, the great Soviet turnabout was a grave blow with dramatic consequences.

With the Russians, for want of anything better

On Monday, October 29, 1962, when *Revolución* announced the removal of the Russian missiles, it also made it plain that the heyday of pro-Soviet fervor was over. The one-time organ of the July 26th Movement made no protest against Khrushchev's unilateral action or against his manner of reaching an agreement with Kennedy without even informing the Cuban government. *Revolución* simply gave prominence to Fidel Castro's five conditions for a fair settlement of the crisis[61] and at the same

61. These five conditions, or "five points" were: 1) an end of the economic blockade and all other forms of economic pressure by the United States;

The Russians arrive

time printed a telling series of photographs glorifying the Cuban struggle from the time of José Martí to that of Fidel Castro. This was as much as to say: "We have fought a whole century for independence and revolution and we shall go on doing so." There was no reference to friendship with the Soviet Union or to world socialist solidarity.

The Cubans, who had learned to read between the lines, at once grasped the profound significance of this sudden recall of their revolutionary tradition. For almost two years official propaganda had played down this very aspect, doing its utmost to minimize the difference between Cuban and more orthodox revolutionaries, by stressing that both were part and parcel of the same international Communist movement. This had caused a great deal of confusion, but it bore witness to Castro's determination to bring Cuba into the socialist bloc, and to bridge the gap between the men of the Sierra and the comrades in the PSP. Hence when it recalled the feats of the only radical branch of the movement, *Revolución* was challenging this whole approach, at home no less than abroad.

Six months after the Escalante affair, Khrushchev's turnabout had completely destroyed what prestige the Soviet Union and the Communist old guard still enjoyed in Cuba. Two years had seen "free and completely frank" collaboration (the words are Fidel Castro's) give way to mini-Stalinism. And then, in October 1962, the Russians simply dropped Cuba like a hot potato. This was more than the country could stand—people who had only just managed to get rid of their old prejudices suddenly found their worst suspicions confirmed. The most disappointed of all were undoubtedly those who had put the greatest trust

---

2) an end to all such subversive activities as the parachuting of arms, the infiltration of spies and saboteurs, and the training of mercenaries on U.S. territory or on the territory of its accomplices; 3) an end to pirate raids from U.S. bases and from Puerto Rico; 4) an end to all violations of Cuban air and maritime space by North American planes and warships; 5) the liquidation of the American naval base in Guantánamo and the return of occupied territory to Cuba.

in the Marxist-Leninists of the PSP and in the internationalism of the Soviet Union. However, this was not the time for self-criticism. Cuba was still in danger and this time she stood almost alone against the American giant. It was essential to close ranks and Cubans needed no orders from on high to do that. Anywhere else the defection of a powerful ally would have caused panic, possibly even despair and demoralization; in Havana people just kept smiling, hiding their bitterness behind the determination to resist to the end. The Revolution had suddenly recovered its purity and drive; the heavy mortgage to Russia no longer weighed them down.

"Nikita mariquita—lo que se da no se quita,"[62] *"Pim pam fuera—abajo Caimanera,"*[63] chanted the militia as they marched, abusing Khrushchev for leaving them in the lurch and repeating the old slogans against U.S. occupation of Cuban territory. This was a spontaneous popular reaction—the Cuban press had still said nothing against the Soviet Union. What was perhaps even more remarkable was how little effect two years of official pro-Russian policy had had on a country that had never wished to forfeit its independence and had resisted all attempts at brainwashing. No public opinion polls were taken during this period, but anyone who was in Cuba at the time will tell you that there was a most striking resurgence of popular support for Fidel Castro and that everyone, except for a small minority of old Communists, wished for a clean break with Russia.

This climate of opinion was just what Fidel Castro needed: it was his trump card in the three-cornered conflict with Russia and America. He had no means of preventing the Russians from removing their missiles, which in any case had remained under Soviet control. Nor could he force the United States to leave Guantánamo or to agree to his other four demands. But he was determined not to give in, wherever the choice

62. "Nikita, you little braggard—what one gives, one gives for keeps."
63. "Pim pam out—down with Caimanera." Caimanera is the Cuban name for U.S. headquarters in Guantánamo Bay.

was up to him. Thus he would not hear of international control over the dismantling of the missile bases. Even before the exchange of letters between Kennedy and Khrushchev, the Americans had demanded the right to keep the island permanently under surveillance, not only in order to ensure that it would not become a base for attack but also by implication to drive home the limits of Cuban sovereignty. Fidel simply told them that anyone trying to check on Cuba would have to come in battle dress. "This is our final reply to all projects for inspection of our country."[64] On this point he was quite adamant, as he was convinced that America had only one reason for insisting on international control, namely, to demoralize the Revolution by the presence of foreign inspectors.

As Fidel Castro did not know the precise terms of the agreement reached by Kennedy and Khrushchev, nor how determined they were to force Cuba to toe the line, he had no means of telling what the effects of his intransigence were likely to be. He expected a trial of strength and for at least forty-eight hours thought that a break with Moscow was inevitable. The Russians might at any moment inform him that, in view of the tightening of the American blockade (which according to Kennedy was to remain in force until Cuba agreed to an inspection), they could no longer send supplies to the island. Even worse, America had stated that her promise not to invade the island was dependent on prior inspection. Until then she reserved the right to do as she wished. Castro was thus taking a calculated risk; but he preferred this to the certainty of political and moral defeat.

He made no bones about the choice before him, for though he made no public statements on the subject, he mentioned it to enough people to ensure that everyone in the country knew all about it. During several evenings, he had discussions with

64. Speech on October 23, 1962, the day following President Kennedy's announcement that Cuba was "in quarantine."

students at the University of Havana, where he had served his own political apprenticeship. This choice of a meeting place was unquestionably symbolic; and what he said was fully in the spirit of Moncada and the *Granma* expedition: "We may die, but we shall not surrender our freedom!" No official account of these evenings at the university has been published; what happened was revealed by "inspired" indiscretions. Saverio Tutino, the *Unità* correspondent, one of the few foreigners to attend these meetings, had this to say: "One night Fidel told the students that they must be prepared to tighten their belts and perhaps even to die. Cuba might soon become an abandoned island without oil and electricity. But she would go back to primitive agriculture rather than accept loss of sovereignty by agreeing to territorial inspection."[65]

According to Tutino, many of Castro's followers were tempted to make "the supreme sacrifice—to go down with the ship in order to save revolutionary principles which would one day be taken up by others on the same road to universal democracy."[66] But Fidel Castro was not of their mind. For all his wounded pride and his deep resentment of Khrushchev's behavior, he remained a practical politician, determined to save his revolution. For that very reason he refrained from slamming the door in Russia's face; he is even reported to have said during one of his university gatherings: "We shall not make the same mistake twice; we shall not break with the Russians after having broken with the Americans."[67]

His first public speech, on November 1, 1962, was characteristic of this attitude. Three quarters of it was devoted to a very lively account of his meeting with U Thant who had come on behalf of the UN to ask for Cuban agreement to the inspection demanded by America. Fidel reported his refusal in considerable and frequently ironical detail, without once mentioning the fact

65. See Saverio Tutino, *L'Ottobre Cubano* (Turin, Einaudi, 1968), pp. 46–47.

66. *Op. cit.*, p. 46.

67. See André Suarès, *Cuba, Castroism and Communism* (Cambridge, Mass., M.I.T. Press, 1967), p. 175.

that Khrushchev had given his blessing to the inspection and had even asked U Thant to get on with it.[68] Not until the last part of his speech did Castro touch on the Russian problem: "One must admit that certain differences—*discrepancias*—between the Soviet and Cuban governments have appeared during the crisis. But this is not the place to air them; nor this the time to allow our enemies to profit from our differences. We shall discuss these matters with the Russians at government and Party level. We shall discuss in the light of reason and principle all the problems that require discussion. But first and foremost we are Marxist-Leninists and friends of the Soviet Union. No rift must appear between the Soviet Union and Cuba."[69]

This could have been taken for a "moderate" stand, especially abroad where one of Fidel's more spectacular explosions had been expected. But in Cuba, people remembered his warmly pro-Russian speeches only too well, and took his declaration as clear confirmation of the general impression: "Fidel agrees with us and will not stand for it." In Moscow, where it was never published, Castro's speech had the effect of a cold shower; it was interpreted as a veiled threat aimed at Khrushchev. Despite their Chinese and Albanian experiences, the Russians were still not accustomed to having "foreign comrades" issue public invitations to discussions "in the light of reason and principle." But since they were in no position to act the injured party, they sent Havana their most skillful negotiator, Anastas Mikoyan. Mikoyan was thought capable of selling refrigerators to Eskimos, but above all he was famed for his friendship with Cuba, for had he not been the first Soviet statesman to make contact with the Castroists?

His stay—the vice-premier of the U.S.S.R. spent a total of

68. Almost immediately after reaching agreement with Kennedy, Khrushchev asked U Thant for UN help in implementing it. The UN Secretary-General was forced to remind him of the need for Cuban approval, a detail that had completely escaped the Soviet Premier. It appears that U Thant himself mentioned this to Fidel Castro during his fruitless visit to Havana. This revelation was not likely to alter the bitter feelings Castro reserved for the Russians at that time.

69. Fidel Castro's televised speech of November 1, 1962.

twenty-four days in Havana—had all the elements of a vaude-ville farce set in an embassy. Nothing was lacking: slips of the tongue, malentendus, crossed lines between Fidel and Mikoyan, and pinpricks behind the scenes. It is said that, to the Cubans' first question, "Why did you negotiate with the Americans with-out keeping us informed?" Mikoyan replied, "There was no time," but that his Russian interpreter, doubtless because he had little Spanish, translated this as "There was no need." At this, Castro, who was already disgruntled, gave vent to his indigna-tion. According to some he went red as a beet while accord-ing to others he turned quite pale. In any case, to spare himself further insults, the Cuban prime minister decided there and then to wash his hands of the special envoy of the Soviet prime minister. He did run across him on November 6, at the Soviet Embassy, where a crowd of some two hundred people had gathered to celebrate the forty-fifth anniversary of the October Revolution, but after that he found that he could not spare Mikoyan a single minute.

And so Khrushchev's envoy had to make do with much less lofty contacts, and the Cubans obligingly invited him to take part in the "Week of Solidarity with the Revolutionaries of Venezuela" or to meet students at the University of Havana.[70] Mikoyan had no choice: he could not leave Cuba empty-handed because he knew, perhaps even better than Castro, that the Russian story of the missile crisis would have collapsed like a house of cards had Fidel chosen to publish the truth. To top it off, on November 15, 1962, the Peking *Jenmin Jih Pao*

70. By all accounts Mikoyan's great political and oratorical skill showed to advantage during his meeting with the students. No top-level Cuban leader accompanied him; nor apparently had anyone warned him that the students were in a particularly militant frame of mind and very much against the Soviet decision to remove the missiles. Mikoyan threw himself to the lions, but emerged unscathed thanks to a "leftist" speech full of generalities and warm praises for Castro and the Cuban revolutionaries. He is reported as saying that he had spent forty-five years of his life at the University of the Revolution, but that he had learned a great many new facts during his last ten days in Cuba.

The Russians arrive

("People's Daily") published a lead story on the missile affair. Mikoyan, who had been waiting for ten days for his first private discussion with Castro, had the opportunity of reading this indictment, reprinted verbatim in the Cuban press without comment. If he needed more information, he could easily have found it in the unofficial daily *El Mundo* which, thanks to its excellent Peking correspondent, Goldberger (a Chilean Communist), gave daily reports of Chinese reactions to the Cuban missile crisis. And in case the Cubans had failed to notice that the Soviet Union and America wanted to impose a new "Munich" on them, the Peking dispatches hastened to inform them of just that fact.[71]

Mikoyan thus found himself in a most unenviable position. To reverse the present current of opinion, he would have had to deliver patently anti-American speeches and make "revolutionary" commitments to Cuba, at a time when his country's official policy required that he do neither. His mission was to persuade Fidel Castro to accept international inspection of the island and to stop beating the anti-Yankee drum. This was the more essential as the missile crisis was far from settled; Kennedy was maintaining his quarantine of Cuba and was now demanding not only that the Russians take back their missiles, but also that they remove their IL-28s, light bombers now suddenly included in the list of offensive weapons threatening U.S. security. Each day brought Khrushchev's envoy some new surprise, and forced him to ask for more and more concessions from the Cubans, who so far had granted him nothing.

71. In their arguments with the Soviet Union, the Chinese made endless references to the Munich agreement of 1938 between Germany, Italy, France, and Great Britain. In his speech on December 12, 1962, Khrushchev retorted by accusing the Chinese of warmongering: "Only those who want a thermonuclear war can speak of a Munich in the Caribbean." To this Peking replied on January 15, 1963: "We have never contended that avoidance of thermonuclear war in the Caribbean constitutes another Munich. What we are resolutely opposed to is the sacrifice of the sovereignty of a country [Cuba] on the altar of imperialism. It is this type of total compromise we mean when we speak of a second Munich."

Guerrillas in Power

All the same, he succeeded in breaking the ice, and when he was called back to Moscow by the death of his wife, the Russo-Cuban atmosphere had grown a great deal warmer. To be sure, Fidel Castro had not accepted UN or Red Cross control of the island, and the Russians, in order to fulfill their promises to the Americans, had been forced to agree to inspection of their own ships carrying the missiles back to the Soviet Union.[72] But Mikoyan had paved the way for fresh negotiations and so made it possible to patch things up just in time.

This success was not due solely to the extraordinary skill of the Vice-Premier of the Soviet Union.[73] The upheaval of October 1962 had presented Castro with a *fait accompli* which left him little choice. He had learned that the Soviet Union was not "the greatest military power in history" (Che's phrase) and that Khrushchev's missile threat of July 9, 1960, had been nothing but propaganda: the Soviet Union could not impose her will on the United States and, in any case, did not want to start a war over Cuba. By removing his missiles, Khrushchev acknowledged implicitly that the era of spheres of influences was not yet over, and that the United States was still the "law" in her own hemisphere. This meant that Cuba would henceforth have to rely for her defense on political rather than military weapons; her aim must now be to achieve separate status within the U.S. sphere. The Russians could help by putting their diplomatic resources at Cuba's disposal, and this, after all, was something to be grateful for.

For the time being no other power or group of countries

72. The Soviet ships allowed low-flying U.S. Navy helicopters to pass over and count the number of missiles on them, after Russian sailors had removed the covering tarpaulins. This explains why people in Havana joked about a Russian strip-tease in the middle of the ocean.

73. Anyone referring to the personal talents of Anastas Mikoyan and of his skill in getting the dialogue with the Cuban leaders going again ought also to mention the role played by Ambassador Alexeev, who made Mikoyan's task very much easier. Alexeev was very popular in Havana and when he learned of the removal of the missiles, at the height of the crisis, he is said to have wept unashamedly before the Cubans. The Cubans were touched by this spontaneous and not very diplomatic exhibition on the part of the Soviet Ambassador.

could offer Cuba anything to equal even this limited protection. The several non-aligned nations did not constitute a united force, and most of them had, in any case, condemned the setting up of the missiles. The big Latin American countries, especially Brazil and Mexico, which had sided with Cuba in the past and were still linked to her by a sort of unwritten agreement to resist the foreign overlord, had openly opposed "Soviet intervention in the Western hemisphere." Presidents Goulart and López Mateos even bore Castro a personal grudge: they accused him of lying to them on the eve of the crisis. Even if we think this accusation no more than a convenient excuse for their defection to the side of the United States, it remains a fact that Castro had not bestirred himself sufficiently to retain their support.

Kennedy himself left no one in any doubt as to his determination to liquidate the Castro regime. To begin with, he was in no position to exploit the differences between Moscow and Havana. American public opinion was violently against Castro, the "warmonger," and would have frowned on any attempt to arrive at a compromise solution in the spirit of coexistence, or even to give him breathing space. Those Western countries—Great Britain, Canada, and to a lesser extent France—which had exercised some restraining influence on Kennedy now supported him without qualification.

Beyond that, progressive movements, which in other circumstances might have been able to put pressure on their governments, had themselves been completely demoralized and split by the crisis. This was especially true in Latin America. Fidel Castro told me later that the prime object of his refusal to allow inspection teams on the island was to give the revolutions in Latin America another chance, and to prevent the complete collapse of the pro-Cuban camp.[74] The dispute between Havana and Moscow was to lead to an undeclared split between the

74. "It was our refusal to allow any sort of control in Cuba that saved our own revolution and prevented the demoralization of the revolutionary movement in the whole of Latin America," Castro told me in an interview I later published in the *Nouvel Observateur* (September 20, 1967).

official Communist parties and the great mass of pro-Castro sympathizers. During the preceding two years Castro had placed far too much reliance on the extreme left of Latin America and, thanks to his friendly relations with Khrushchev, had to some extent been able to mobilize support for revolutionary ideas with a distinctly Cuban flavor. The ambiguous atmosphere of the post-Stalin era had favored him; even the old hands of the Comintern did not know whether or not Moscow had approved the ultra-revolutionary appeal of the Second Havana Declaration—whether the declaration formed part of the complex strategy of the Soviet Union or was something the Cubans had dreamed up themselves. But on October 28, 1962, all uncertainty vanished, and the sheep and goats returned to their respective folds. The Communists were henceforth to have time for nothing but the "defense of the peace" or "the struggle for coexistence." Their great hero was Khrushchev, the man who had saved humanity from thermonuclear war, and not the pigheaded Fidel Castro who stood in the way of a great peace treaty between the two blocs. Even if they forbore to criticize Cuba directly, the Communist parties were not prepared to fight with her against the wishes of the Soviet Union.

And so Fidel Castro had no option but to make up with Khrushchev. He did not do so cap in hand, did not agree to toe the Soviet line blindly. For, if Castro needed the Soviet Union, the Soviet Union had even more need of him. At no time was the preservation of the Cuban Revolution more indispensable to the Russians than immediately after the missile crisis. Without it and without Castro's corroboration of the Russian story about the origins of the missile affair, Khrushchev would have been completely defenseless against his Russian and international detractors. Only Castro could "prove" that the dispatch of these weapons to Cuba had been no mere adventure, and their removal no abject surrender, without quid pro quo, to an imperialist enemy stronger than the Soviet Union. Khrushchev had not only his remorseless Chinese critics to contend with; he also had to put heart into his own patriotic party bosses, whose na tional pride had been deeply hurt by the retreat. And so Khrushchev, who had treated Castro as a pawn on the world chessboard, was now at his pawn's mercy.

In these circumstances what was Castro to do? Ought he to seize the opportunity and give Khrushchev a lesson in internationalism, at the same time showing the world Communist movement that the policy of coexistence was a pernicious fallacy? Or should he do the best he could for Cuba and start afresh with the Soviet Union on a more advantageous footing? For Castro there were no two ways about it; he would negotiate with Khrushchev, this time without illusions as to the "disinterestedness" and "superior morality" of Soviet man. Whatever he might say in public about the unshakeable bonds which united Marxists-Leninists the world over, after the Cuban missile crisis Castro no longer identified himself with the Eastern bloc. Experience had removed all illusions about the "continent of marvels," about its unity (the Chinese and the Russians were henceforth to tear each other to pieces quite openly), and about its capacity to provide a scientific interpretation of Marxist doctrines. Cuba had to seek her own road to socialism, in the context of Latin America, her great continental fatherland and her natural ally against the United States. There was no longer any talk of Russia's superior wisdom; all that Cuba could now hope for was a modus vivendi with the Soviet Union, one that best suited the political and economic interest of her own revolution. "Until the end of October 1962, we worked with Khrushchev freely and with complete confidence," Fidel Castro later told Saverio Tutino, leaving the subsequent nature of his relations with Moscow to the Italian's imagination.[75]

Contrary to what one might have expected, the economic and not the political points at issue were the most difficult to settle, and it was over these that negotiations between the Soviet Union and Cuba dragged on for months. The preceding years had taught the Russians that they had overestimated their ability

75. See Saverio Tutino, *op. cit.*, p. 15.

to help Cuba. They naturally blamed the Cubans for the poor returns on Soviet investments, for their lack of organizational talent, for the low productivity of their workers, for agricultural deficits, and for other "calamities" suffered by the Cuban economy. And they had come to appreciate that no amount of technical aid or financial aid would cure these ills. What they had already supplied was much more than they had originally bargained for. The Cubans, for their part, observed that much of the obsolete Russian equipment neither met their needs nor enabled them to get out of their economic difficulties, which the reader will remember proved especially serious at the beginning of 1962. Many of Castro's followers thought all of it was Russia's fault, and did not look with favor upon the Russian (or Czechoslovak) technicians who had come to help them. They too thought it senseless to increase imports from the Soviet Union and so to step up investments that made the country poorer instead of richer.

In short, both partners wanted a new type of economic collaboration, but could agree neither on what had gone wrong in the past nor on the best remedy for the future. And so negotiations became completely bogged down until one day *Le Monde* published the interview between Fidel and Claude Julien. It will be remembered that it was in this interview that Castro claimed he had never asked Khrushchev for missiles. The effect of this statement was as swift as it was decisive: the Russians invited Fidel Castro to Moscow and more or less promised to agree to all his demands. This visit was something they undoubtedly welcomed from a diplomatic point of view as well; nevertheless, the rashness of Castro's statements greatly hastened the visit and must have contributed to its success.

It should also be mentioned that Fidel's protracted stay (from April 27 to May 23, 1963) was a complete triumph for the Cuban leader: not since the end of World War II had such huge crowds filled the streets of any Russian city to welcome a foreign statesman or comrade. All in all, Fidel seemed more popular in Russia than Khrushchev and all the other Russian leaders put together.[76]

Upon his return to Cuba, Fidel Castro, now a decorated hero of the Soviet Union, made an important announcement: Cuba was going to step up sugar production, but from now on the *zafra* would be much less backbreaking—Khrushchev had promised to send Russian machines to take the place of human labor. This optimistic announcement gave his audience a foretaste of the island's new economic policy; Cuba was about to renounce her dreams of industrialization and give priority to agriculture —to sugar, stock farming, coffee, and citrus fruits. The Soviet Union, for her part, would help to mechanize farming and provide a stable export market for Cuba's surpluses. Thanks to this policy, Cuba would rapidly overcome her supply problems and build up the reserves of foreign currency she needed for her eventual industrialization.

In brief, the two countries seemed to have arrived at a mutually satisfactory arrangement. As long as Cuba was being blockaded, it was clearly of paramount importance to cut food imports to the minimum; the Soviet Union for her part was far better at supplying trucks and tractors—and, it was thought, cane-cutting machinery—than at setting up new industries in a

76. Castro's visit was a diplomatic success for Khrushchev as well, though not enough to halt the decline of his own popularity. Giuseppe Boffa, the Moscow correspondent of *L'Unità* and a great admirer of Khrushchev's, spoke amusingly of this in his *Dopo Krusciov* (Turin, Einaudi, 1965), p. 19: "Castro was a sort of legendary figure. Whenever he and Khrushchev appeared together (as they almost always did) the Cuban always had the best of it. Castro was young, handsome, tall, and bearded like a prophet; Khrushchev was short, squat, old, bald, and bespectacled. Castro spoke in a high-sounding foreign language, improvising as if he were in the pulpit, waving his long arms and radiating the heat of his own eloquence. Khrushchev preferred to read speeches written for him by his secretaries; he delivered them in a monotonous voice, and occasionally stumbled over difficult words. Castro still seemed to the Russians to be a passionate son of a wild people touched with the magic of the Sierra. Khrushchev was a statesman from the Kremlin, powerful, aloof and forbidding. Such comparisons between the two men were made everywhere in the Soviet Union."

country accustomed to American standards of technology. There was thus good reason for believing that Moscow and Havana were about to become the very best of friends all over again.

Within Cuba herself, this new friendship had repercussions far beyond the economic sphere. Immediately after the missile crisis, Fidel Castro had come to the conclusion that he no longer needed ideological go-betweens in his negotiations with Russia. The Communists of the PSP had probably proved a greater disappointment to him than even Khrushchev: at the crucial moment they had supported the views of the Soviet Premier against his own. Fidel felt that he could no longer trust them, and denied most of them any further part in the negotiations with the East.[77] Now, given the importance of foreign relations to the very survival of Cuba, a demotion of this sort, though only partial at first, was bound to become total in time. On the other hand, having become reconciled with the Russians, Castro could not allow continued attacks on the Soviet Union—as we saw, there had been a particularly violent outburst of criticism after the removal of the missiles. For this reason, Castro took the newspaper *Revolución* severely to task immediately after his return from Moscow and, in due course, put an end to its existence.[78]

77. Carlos Raphael Rodríguez, the only Communist leader to join Castro in the Sierra Maestra, retained his trust because (as people said in Havana) "he had behaved properly" even during the missile crisis. But there was no other PSP veteran in the delegation to Moscow. Instead, the old guard of Castro's own movement—Faustino Pérez, Marcelo Fernández, Efigenio Ameijeiras—appeared at the head of various missions, both to Moscow and to Peking. All these men had been brought out of virtual oblivion, not to say semi-disgrace, immediately following the October crisis of 1962. As we saw, Fidel Castro took not a single Old Communist with him on his own visit to Moscow; instead he was accompanied by Emilio Aragones, Sergio del Valle, Guillermo García, Regino Botí, Raúl Curbelo—all from the July 26th Movement.

78. In his speech of June 4, 1963, Fidel Castro bitterly complained of the way *Revolución* had reported his visit to the Soviet Union. In his view, the paper had no right to make certain minor incidents public; by doing so it had given proof of a lack of seriousness and responsibility. Castro went on to cite *Pravda* as an example of good journalism, claiming in all seriousness that it was the best newspaper in the world. At first people thought he merely had a grudge against Juan Arcocha, Moscow correspondent of *Revolución* and a former friend and fellow student at the University of

He also resisted attempts by Faure Chomón to drag up the old story of Communist misbehavior during the anti-Batista struggle,[79] and urged all members of the July 26th Movement to

---

Havana. But it became clear soon afterward that it was *Revolución* as a whole that Castro disliked for its independent approach and its continual harking back to the libertarian spirit of the July 26th Movement. For this, Carlos Franqui was peremptorily relieved of his post as editor in chief of the paper he had founded. In 1964, *Revolución* and *Hoy* were amalgamated and replaced by *Granma,* which is still the organ of the Cuban Communist Party. It appears to be trying to imitate *Pravda,* no doubt in the hope of becoming the second-best newspaper in the world.

79. Faure Chomón, former leader of the *Directorio,* had managed to collect overwhelming evidence against Marcos Rodríguez, a Communist student in the University of Havana, who had apparently denounced the four survivors of the attack on the presidential palace to the Batista police on April 20, 1957. The four (Fructoso Rodríguez, Juan Pedro Cabro Servia, Joe Westbrook, and José Machado) were brutally murdered. The *Directorio* had suspected Marquitos Rodríguez all along because he knew the hiding place in which the four were later discovered, but they were unable to produce any proof. Marquitos himself moved to Mexico where he is said to have confessed his crime to Joaquín Ordoqui and Edith García Buchacha, the leaders of the PSP. Both allegedly offered him their protection and helped him to obtain a scholarship in Prague. The informer allegedly also explained his treachery by saying that he wanted to rid the *Directorio* of anti-Communist elements, and so help to set up a united front at Havana University. He also claimed that he was provoked beyond measure by jibes of the men he later denounced, to the effect that Communists were good only for the distribution of anti-imperialist leaflets and no use in revolutionary activity. Finally, he alleged that he had not foreseen that the police would murder them on the spot. However it may be, he kept his secret well, and after the Revolution quietly served in the Cuban diplomatic corps (in 1962 he served in the Cuban embassy in Prague). Then he was arrested for reasons that seemed quite unconnected with the 1957 affair. It was at this point that he must have asked for help from his protectors in the PSP, and that his letters came into the hands of Faure Chomón. There were a number of dramatic confrontations, including one at the presidential palace, with Joaquín Ordoqui and Edith García Buchacha who denied any knowledge of Marquitos' crime. There was a public trial, in the course of which Faure Chomón accused the PSP of moral responsibility for the murders. According to him, Marquitos' treachery was simply the bitter fruit of Communist sectarianism. Fidel Castro also appeared at the trial and read the court a lengthy report of his own examination of the accused. This report revealed contradictions in the testimony of Marquitos (who himself said nothing throughout the entire trial). Fidel declared that he was convinced that though the defendant was guilty, his crime could not be laid at the door of any political party. Finally he asked that no political capital be made out of the cowardice of a misguided

drop their old quarrels with the PSP; instead they ought to devote their energies to achieving greater administrative efficiency.

In fact, after having at one stroke got rid of both the Communist old guard and its critics, Castro found himself more and more isolated and forced to gather ever greater powers in his own hands. The new concentration on agriculture strengthened his position even further—Castro had always been more interested (and it seems more competent) in this field than in industry.

Indeed, the new line and the greater role of Fidel Castro in it seemed to imply a return to the early days of the Cuban Revolution. As in 1959–60, the men from the Sierra once more formed the hard core of the government, with Fidel, popular and unconventional as ever, as the dominating and driving force. The world outside was told time and again that "the people preferred it this way." They had the utmost confidence in Fidel, and had always distrusted the ORI government riddled as it had been with PSP members.[80] All the same, it was an illusion to imagine that a mere reshuffling at the top would suffice to wipe out the effects of three turbulent and dramatic years.

In 1963 the group from the Sierra and Fidel himself were no longer the enthusiastic, open-minded avant-garde they had been in 1960. Two unforgettable events had happened since then, two events which had marked them for all time. First there had been the break with the United States, and the ensuing internal

---

young intellectual, lest the resulting indignation strike at the roots of the Revolution. Marcos Rodríguez was sentenced to death and shot. Faure Chomón never mentioned the affair again, and is still a minister in the Cuban government. After having this case ruled out of court, Joaquín Ordoqui and Edith García Buchacha were again arrested in December 1964 and are still in prison. They apparently played some minor part in this unfortunate affair and were made to pay for it, but in such a way that their crime could not be laid at the door of the party they once led.

80. The PURS (United Party of the Socialist Revolution) took over from the ORI in 1963 and itself made way for the Communist Party of Cuba in 1965. There is not a single member of the old PSP in the Political Bureau of this party, which has still to hold its founding congress.

crisis which had shattered the unity of the anti-Batista front. "The Sierra" itself had been split, and each member had been forced to decide where he stood in relation to a Communist alliance. Next came the crisis in Cuba's relations with the Soviet Union. This had been the more dramatic as Cuba's future had by then been settled: she must needs stay in a camp to which she was bound neither by political tradition, nor by any measure of real trust.

And so Cuba started on that long road to "solitude" which Fidel would describe as her fate one day in 1967, when he deliberately twisted the old slogan, *"Cuba no está sola."* It was of course only a relative and temporary isolation. To escape from it, Fidel counted on two factors: success by a superhuman effort on the economic front, and the creation, in record time, of a popular consciousness capable of sloughing off old habits, of combining Communist with unorthodox ideas. To accomplish this task, Fidel had to stake everything on a combination of individual freedom and initiative with maximum centralization—on the fierce enthusiasm of the young, on the acquiescence of the old, and on harsh discipline. These together were to ensure the transformation of agriculture, the birth of a new state, and the development of victorious guerrilla units in the Third World.

When I returned to Cuba in 1967 it looked to me as if this effort was about to pay dividends. Cuba's prestige was at its height, and when Fidel declared at Santiago on July 26, 1967, that *"Cuba está sola,"* only a little bitterness could be detected beneath his faith in forthcoming victories. He was optimistic about the island's economic take-off, and he knew that Che Guevara was about to create new Vietnams in Latin America and that his example was inspiring the youth of the entire world.

A year later, most of his forecasts had been proved wrong and there were no dividends to collect. Was this new series of setbacks the direct result of a great tragedy (Che's death) and unfortunate climatic conditions (the drought)? Or was it rather inherent in the rash gamble of 1963, when Fidel decided to retain his freedom while preserving his ties with the Soviet Union?

287   K*

Part two

"A Cuban heresy?"

The "Year of Heroic Vietnam"

I returned to Havana in July 1967, six years after my first stay. In the interval I had had few contacts with Cubans. Most of my time had been spent in preparing a tour of China, which I eventually visited in 1965, and then I was busy writing my book on this, the other face of Communism. When I finally left for the Caribbean, I was still full of the passionate debates on the "great proletarian cultural revolution." I, like everyone else in Europe, had not forgotten that in this year of grace, 1967, the Cubans, too, were making gigantic efforts to leave the well-trodden paths of traditional Communism. Their line, although far less radical than the Chinese, seemed inseparably linked to an event that was about to upset more than one modern dogma —the war in Vietnam.

That war had demonstrated before all the world that the "great American democracy" thought nothing of engaging in

291

blatant aggression against a small country, one of the poorest in the world, and seemed not to care in the least about its liberal image or its traditional anticolonial and anti-imperialist professions. Many people had come to feel that the United States was not at all concerned with placating Moscow, particularly now that the missile crisis had shown that America was so much more powerful than the U.S.S.R. Thus the Pentagon had felt free to order the systematic bombing of North Vietnam, an integral part of the Eastern bloc, at the very time that the Soviet prime minister, Alexei Kosygin, was visiting Hanoi, and the Soviet Union had apparently been unable to do anything about the affront. Since February 7, 1965, it had seemed very much as if the United States were the only true superpower left, that no rival could challenge its dominance. For Cuba, the development boded ill; any day now the island might be next on the list of American targets for military invasion.

Nor was that Vietnam's only lesson. Another was that the Americans, their vast military and technical superiority notwithstanding, had failed to break the resistance of the National Liberation Front in South Vietnam or to demoralize the people of North Vietnam. Far from being able to establish their *pax Americana,* they were fast losing ground, were being humiliated, and were almost held up to ridicule by the tenacity of their Vietnamese adversaries. And so, instead of demonstrating, as they had hoped to do, that "wars of liberation" were things of the past, they had proved that they themselves were quite impotent when faced with this type of attack.

In Cuba, the Castroists had adopted the habit of giving each year a special name; it was thus that 1967 became the "Year of Heroic Vietnam." Cuba thus marked its complete identification with the Vietnamese people; just as the Vietnamese resistance movement was helping Cuba's own survival so the island would do its utmost to aid Vietnam. This feeling of solidarity was reflected by the very close alliance between Havana, the NLF, and Hanoi. The North Koreans joined the alliance as well, because they too felt threatened by the U.S. military build-up, and because U.S. intervention had caused a new situation in the

"A Cuban heresy?"

Communist camp: the war in Southeast Asia had, in fact, speeded the break between China and the U.S.S.R., infusing it with strong emotions. American aggression in Vietnam had not so much changed their respective attitudes toward the United States as emphasized the differences between them. Thus Moscow looked on the war as a regrettable but purely temporary diversion on the great road to peaceful coexistence, while Peking felt that it proved the utter impossibility of coexistence with imperialism, a leopard that would never change its spots. Lacking a common view as to the nature of the enemy, the two great Communist powers could not agree on a common war aim, nor did they trust each other enough to coordinate their actions. They came to Vietnam's aid separately, in piecemeal fashion, and at the same time indulged in the most vicious mutual recriminations, each accusing the other of working for the American aggressor. Every Communist country and party now had to choose between Moscow and Peking; it was no longer possible to ignore that they stood for two diametrically opposed concepts of the revolution and socialist strategy.

Once again, most of the People's Democracies and most Communist parties sided with the U.S.S.R. Only one—Rumania—tried to profit from the internecine struggle and to wrest major concessions from Moscow while standing coolly on the sidelines.[1] The Vietnamese, the Koreans, and the Cubans refused to commit themselves to either side—they were concerned only with keeping America at bay, although for different reasons. Thus, the Vietnamese, unable to survive without Soviet military aid, had been longing to part company with Moscow without being driven into excessive dependence on Peking;[2] and the North

1. During the missile crisis, Rumania had informed Washington very discreetly that it intended to be neutral in case of a wider conflict. Later, the Rumanians skillfully tried to gain the confidence of both the West and Peking. Rumania was the first Communist country to receive an American President, when Richard Nixon visited Bucharest on August 4, 1969.
2. Since 1960, when it took up the struggle, the South Vietnamese National Liberation Front had had to contend with Nikita Khrushchev's reluctance to see the conflict spread. Until 1965, the Soviet Union almost

Koreans, who had been saved by the Chinese and had followed Mao Tse-tung's antirevisionist line for a whole decade, were still not prepared to start a cultural revolution of their own or to declare themselves staunch Maoists.[3] The Cubans, finally, felt ill at ease about all aspects of this fratricidal war and were anxious, above all, to preserve the independence of their island.

The history and political attitudes of each of these three countries were so different that it was difficult to lump them together under the label of the Third Communist Front. Their courageous stand had nevertheless earned them the allegiance of a broad spectrum of the revolutionary Left that was unwilling to follow blindly in the footsteps of either Peking or Moscow. However, this section of the Left did nothing, or next to nothing, to organize an independent movement; it simply called on all genuine anti-imperialists to rally under the banner of "Victory to Vietnam."[4] Even this restricted program, perfectly justified by the circumstances, offended both pro-Russians and pro-Chinese.

---

completely ignored the South Vietnamese resistance movement and had had increasingly strained relations with Hanoi, which was following the Chinese line. After the Gulf of Tonkin incident, in August 1964, when the Americans ordered reprisal raids against the North, Moscow's reaction was noticeably soft. Immediately after Khrushchev's fall, the new leaders tried to improve the situation and sent Kosygin on a special mission to Hanoi. It was during this visit, on February 7, 1965, that the Americans took a new step in escalation, ordering the regular bombing of North Vietnam. The Soviet Union then promised to send defense equipment and, in fact, stepped up supplies considerably. The Vietnamese accordingly refused to underwrite the Chinese allegation that the new team in the Kremlin was no better than the old. In an interview he gave delegates of the Italian Communist Party in May 1965, the secretary of the North Vietnamese Communist Party Le Duan said that Khrushchev had asked the Vietnamese to stop the war, irrespective of the plight of their comrades in the South, and that he had threatened them with economic reprisals if they refused. Kosygin proved much more understanding.

3. During the Korean war (1950–53), China was the only country to aid the Korean Communists. This intervention completely changed the military situation, so much so that the Americans have been forced to concede that this was the first war they failed to win.

4. Supporters of the "Victory to Vietnam" campaign set up worldwide Vietnamese aid committees, which were often frowned upon by the local Communist parties.

"A Cuban heresy?"

The first preferred to call for peace rather than victory in Vietnam and suspected that the more militant section was trying to resurrect the Cold War, or involve them in a trial of strength with the United States; the second, although fully prepared to accept the idea of a struggle to the death in Vietnam, believed that victory could not possibly be achieved with the participation of the Soviet Union, now a mere accomplice of the Americans and irredeemably lost to the cause of revolution. By expressing their common hostility to the nonaligned Left, Moscow and Peking merely drew more attention to it and thus helped to make its viewpoint more widely known.

Nor did the paradox end there. By weakening the Eastern bloc, the conflict between China and Russia greatly encouraged American arrogance in Vietnam and so worked to the detriment of Cuba and North Korea. At the same time, these victims of American aggression gained so much moral prestige that the official leaders of the two Communist camps no longer dared criticize them, let alone exert economic or political pressure on them. Any socialist country that dared to speak ill of the Vietnamese would at once have been discredited by the entire Left. The Cubans and Koreans, too, were untouchable, even though they were not just then fighting in the front lines.

Certain of this immunity, the three small Communist countries could thus permit themselves the luxury of challenging the authority of both Moscow and Peking with complete impunity. However, their common concern persuaded them to proceed with caution. In 1967, however, the Cubans apparently grew tired of the whole game. They now rose up against that "petrified and dogmatic" form of Marxism that was preventing Communist parties in Latin America from harnessing the immense revolutionary potential of their continent. The Cubans did not seem at all concerned about the anti-Soviet implications of this indictment, as it was common knowledge that all these parties were unconditional supporters of the Moscow brand of Marxism-Leninism. The U.S.S.R. remained unruffled. It did not rush to the defense of the faithful in Venezuela or Guatemala nor even break its silence when the Castroists went on to castigate Soviet flirtation with reactionary governments in Latin America; thus the Cubans dared teach the U.S.S.R. a lesson in internationalism.

In private, Soviet sources did not, of course, hide their disgust at what they chose to call "that Caribbean viper in our bosom." A leading intellectual from Moscow, who visited Havana shortly before I did, had declared quite brazenly that Cuba had turned Stalinist, an unpardonable crime to his mind, but a rather ludicrous accusation to all those familiar with the political background of the plaintiff. In any case, it was quite certain that neither he nor any of his colleagues was going to ask *Pravda* to print a single line about this forbidden subject.

Few people in Europe could have told you anything about the repercussions in Cuba of Castro's latest heretical offensive. In February 1967, *Granma* had published a remarkable study of socialist bureaucracy and, incidentally, shot a poison arrow at all those Eastern-European countries guilty of carrying their evil practices into Cuba.[5] This might, of course, have been no more than an isolated attack. In any case, Cuba remained uncharted territory to most Europeans—even the greatest political experts seemed taken aback by developments on the island. After the missile crisis they had gained the impression that Fidel Castro was anxious to reach agreement with the U.S.S.R. in order to make the best of a bad job, and, if need be, to use Khrushchev's good offices to improve relations with the United States.[6] They did not for a moment believe that Cuba had lost

5. The text of this study, which appeared in four issues of *Granma*, has been reprinted in leaflet form by *Obra Revolucionaria* (Havana, 1967). It was published in Italy under the title of *Contro il burocratismo una battaglia decisiva* (Milan, Feltrinelli, 1968). In Havana the study is widely attributed to Armando Hart, a member of the Political Bureau of the Cuban Communist Party, but the fact that it was unsigned suggests that it represented the views of the entire Cuban leadership.

6. This view was encouraged by a series of good-will gestures Fidel Castro made toward the United States and, above all, by his remarkable interview (published in *The New York Times* of July 6, 1964) on the possibility of improving relations between the two countries during the next five years. The Americans, for their part, seemed to be clamping down on the activities

its independence and had become one of Moscow's satellites, but they did think that Fidel had a great need for breathing space, for taking temporary shelter from the raging international storms. The departure of his alter ego, Che Guevara, only helped to strengthen this impression.

Ernesto Che Guevara had left Cuba in the spring of 1965, because, as he put it, "other nations of the world call for my modest efforts."[7] On October 3, 1965, Fidel had read this farewell message to the assembled Central Committee of the newly formed Communist Party of Cuba. A facsimile of the original text was published by the entire Cuban press.[8] Those who knew Che, also knew that he was one of those rare political birds who are incapable of telling a lie, even for tactical reasons. The warm tone of his letter was enough to convince them that there had been no ideological rift between the two leaders of the Cuban Revolution.

But the news was too spectacular for public opinion abroad to accept at face value. The Americans, who were convinced of the shrewdness of their CIA, would not admit that a political leader of such importance could have left Cuba for one of the most explosive regions in the world without their knowledge. They declared that if Che was working underground, it was in the literal sense of the word—in a Castroist dungeon or worse.[9] They thus fed the imagination of political fiction writers, who immediately constructed a full-length romance on the life-and-death struggle that was being waged in the Cuban leadership.

Nevertheless, Che's departure caused some dismay even among

---

of Cuban refugees in Florida and, while not calling off their economic blockade, had begun to adopt a more conciliatory, or at least a less threatening, tone toward Cuba.

7. From Che Guevara's farewell letter to Fidel Castro, *Reminiscences of the Cuban Revolutionary War* (New York, Grove Press, 1969), p. 262.

8. The publication of the facsimile helped to disprove all those who had claimed that no one had ever seen the original text of Che's letter to Fidel.

9. According to *Le Monde* (October 11, 1967) a spokesman of the CIA said of Che's disappearance: "Yes he is underground, six feet under the ground."

those who, as friends of the Cuban Revolution, did not heed the dark tales about the physical liquidation of the former Minister of Industry. They were perturbed to see the removal of one who, having been a staunch advocate of close alliance with the U.S.S.R., had recently adopted an increasingly intransigent and critical attitude toward the Soviet model of socialism. On February 25, 1965, while speaking in Algiers just a few weeks before he left Cuba for good, Che had delivered a remorseless attack on the Soviet approach to commercial relations among socialist countries and on Soviet ideas about aid to the Third World.[10] Never before had a Communist leader in office dared use such language about the Soviet Union when his country had neither broken with, nor been excommunicated by, Moscow.[11] Now Cuba, far from breaking with Russia, had just sent a high-powered delegation—led by Raúl Castro and Osmani Cienfuegos—to a Communist conference called by the Russians and strongly attacked by the Chinese.[12] All this suggested that in his Algiers speech Che might have been expressing a purely personal point of view and that his departure from Cuba might lead to a closer alignment between Cuban and Soviet strategy. Leo Huberman and Paul M. Sweezy expressed grave apprehensions of this view in *Monthly Review* and were not the only ones to do so.

It took no less than two years to dispel these fears completely. In April 1967, when OSPAAAL (The Organization for Solidarity Among the Peoples of Africa, Asia, and Latin America) pub-

10. We shall return to this speech, delivered as part of a lecture tour on mutual aid among African, Asian, and Latin American countries. The speech itself can be found in his *Oeuvres*, Vol. III (Paris, Maspero, 1968).

11. After 1948 (i.e., after they had been expelled by Stalin), Yugoslav Communists protested loudly about the scandal of the so-called "mixed companies" set up by Moscow immediately after the Second World War for the express purpose of exploiting the newborn People's Democracies. The Albanians after 1961 and the Chinese after 1963 also published bitter attacks on Soviet methods of commerce with their countries. But none of them opened its files on the subject until they had officially broken with Moscow.

12. This conference is discussed in greater detail on pp. 301–303.

lished in Havana a message from Che, which bore all the hall-marks of his inimitable style, the very fact of its publication constituted a political event of primary importance. This is what Che had to say:

"It is a painful fact that Vietnam, a nation embodying the aspirations and hopes of a completely forgotten world, is tragically alone. Ironically, the solidarity between the progressive world and the people of Vietnam resembles the solidarity between the *plebs* and the Roman gladiators. Instead of merely hoping for the success of the victim of aggression, we must share his fate, follow him into death or victory. . . . American imperialism is guilty of aggression; its crimes are immense and cover the entire world. That much we all know. But equally guilty are all those who, in the hour of decision, have been slow to declare Vietnam an inviolable part of the socialist world. Doing so might well have exposed them to the risk of a world war, but it would also have forced the American imperialists into the open!"

After denouncing the failings of the great socialist countries—or more precisely of the U.S.S.R. since it alone had sufficient resources to "declare Vietnam an inviolable part of the socialist world"—Che went on to call on Latin American revolutionaries to create "two, three, many Vietnams" on their own continent. That, to his mind, was the only effective method of helping the Vietnamese. It was both illogical and immoral to allow them to fight the American Goliath single-handed. Creating new Vietnams was also the only means of freeing South America from the Yankee stranglehold. Revolution necessarily involved armed struggle—guerrilla warfare at first, followed by a full-scale popular war on the Vietnamese model. Che made it clear that this path would be thorny, full of sacrifice and destruction. The Americans would never again allow themselves to be caught napping as they had been in Cuba; they would not hesitate to use the sophisticated weapons of destruction they were currently deploying against Vietnam. But if thirty million Vietnamese could keep an ultramodern war machine at bay, then two hundred million Latin Americans ought to do considerably better.

The most important thing was to begin the struggle, not to be afraid of sacrifices, and not to waste time on vain fratricidal discussions, on a war of insults and mutual recrimination.

Che thus dismissed both the Russians and the Chinese, maintaining that their differences and disputes must not be allowed to stand in the way of the anti-imperialist struggle. Latin America was ripe for revolution; hence, it was imperative to start the fight and to force the rest of the world to declare itself for or against the revolution. Che seemed convinced that the pro-Soviets as well as the pro-Chinese in the Western hemisphere would thus be forced to support the common cause and that their masters in Moscow and Peking would have no choice but to come to the rescue—albeit reluctantly as in Vietnam. His message to OSPAAAL was thus a veritable charter of the Third Communist Front, a charter the Cubans immediately made their own and advanced with all the power at their command. No text since Fidel's *History Will Absolve Me* had been so widely read on the island. Guevarism was presented as a brilliant summary of Castroist thought on the international scene. All speculations about differences between the doctrines of Che Guevara and Fidel Castro now ceased. Ernesto Che Guevara, the great man of action, was simply putting into practice, somewhere in Latin America, the ideas common to all his old companions of the Sierra Maestra.

Fresh light had been cast on his departure from Cuba. Che had simply left so suddenly after the first bombing of North Vietnam because the Castroists knew that time was pressing. Despite its tragic destiny, Vietnam had the great advantage of being far from the United States and close to China, Vietnam's immense hinterland. But what if the Americans decided to bomb Cuba? It was idle to count on rescue by the U.S.S.R. The time for illusion had passed. It was no longer July 1960 when Che had proclaimed that Cuba was protected by the greatest power in history. The Soviets would try to limit themselves to sending material aid as they were doing in Vietnam, but in Vietnam they did not have to run the gauntlet of the American blockade.

"A Cuban heresy?"

The best solution for Cuba was to open a second front in Latin America, and the sooner the better. It was by spreading their cause to the rest of the continent that revolutionaries in the Western hemisphere could wage a fight on the Vietnamese scale. And who was better qualified to lead them in this enterprise than Che?

I was told all this as soon as I arrived in Havana. After reading his message, Cuba was living quite literally under Che's sign. Everywhere his giant portraits stared down, and immense billboards proclaimed his slogan in black on red: "We must create two, three, many Vietnams." Cubans were most indignant to learn that his message had not been published either in Moscow or in Peking. What better proof was there that, while invoking the isolation of Vietnam, Che had also been thinking of Cuba and the lack of sympathy and understanding toward Cuba of the big Communist countries? The silence of the Russians surprised them less than that of the Chinese, who as partisans of wars of liberation, ought to have declared their full support for the armed struggle Che was waging in the mountains of Latin America (no one was told precisely where). I gained the impression that it was chiefly about the Chinese attitude that my Cuban hosts wanted to speak to me, in the mistaken belief that I had been made privy to the most intimate thoughts of the leaders in Peking.

In fact, no Chinese official had mentioned Cuba during my entire stay in their country. I was, however, told by Latin Americans who had flocked to Peking in very large numbers that the Maoists were still unhappy about Cuban participation in the International Communist Congress of March 1, 1965. Perhaps this is the place to say a few words about this famous meeting. After wasting a great deal of ammunition fighting the Chinese head on, the Soviet Union decided in February 1964 to assemble Communist parties from all over the world for the express purpose of expelling China from their international brotherhood. This suggestion was not greeted with any degree of enthusiasm even by Communist parties traditionally devoted

301

to Moscow. One of the most famous Communist leaders in Europe, Palmiro Togliatti, the general secretary of the Italian Communist Party, wrote in a memorandum to Khrushchev that the proposed conference would do more harm than good.[13] The Cubans were apparently of the same opinion and asked Moscow not to count on their support. Then, on October 15, 1964, Khrushchev fell from power. It was rumored that his removal was at least partially due to his peremptory attempts to advance the date of the proposed Communist congress to December 15, 1964. Immediately after Khrushchev's fall, Chou En-lai arrived in Moscow to be present at the forty-seventh anniversary of the October Revolution, and a thaw in Sino-Soviet relations seemed to be setting in. President Dorticós of Cuba, who was also in the Soviet capital, is said to have done his utmost to reconcile the two estranged brothers.[14] But the Chinese demand that the whole conference be canceled was not granted. The Russians, whose prestige was too bound up in the conference, were prepared only to promise that no ban on China would be pronounced.

13. The Central Committee of the Italian Communist Party formally rejected the Soviet suggestion in April 1964. When Moscow persisted, Palmiro Togliatti went to Russia at the beginning of August but was unable to meet Khrushchev, who was touring Soviet Asia. Togliatti then took a holiday in Yalta, where he jotted down a number of points he intended to discuss with the Soviet leader. Struck down by cerebral thrombosis a few days later, he was never able to meet with Khrushchev. After his death, the Central Committee of the Italian Communist Party decided to publish his notes, which first appeared in *Rinascità* on September 4, 1964, and were reprinted in full by *Le Monde*.

14. President Dorticós had left Cuba for a tour of friendly countries in October 1964 and arrived in Moscow from Cairo on October 15, the very day that Khrushchev fell. Since none of Russia's friends and allies had been told anything about the palace revolt in the Kremlin, Dorticós had the bad luck of singing Khrushchev's praises just before leaving Cairo and of arriving in Moscow when Nikita no longer ranked a single line in the Soviet press. His visit, therefore, began in a chilly atmosphere, which the Cuban delegation tried to improve by hinting that their country had never been particularly enamored of Khrushchev and that they hoped for a more promising political line from the new team. That is why Dorticós thought it best to prolong his stay in Moscow and why the Cuban Communist Party decided to be present at the March 1st conference.

"A Cuban heresy?"

The Russo-Chinese thaw would have been of short duration in any case, as the two countries did not see eye to eye on anything. The Moscow meeting simply became a test case and precipitated the break. I was in Peking at the time and saw the language of the Chinese change abruptly on March 1, 1965, the day seventeen of the twenty-six invited parties assembled in Moscow to prepare for the great meeting. The Maoists now declared that Khrushchevism without Nikita Khrushchev was even more abominable revisionism than with him, and must be fought by all good revolutionaries. Their fire was directed equally at all the foreign Communist parties who had lent themselves to this sinister farce. Moreover, Peking was unlikely to forget that while the Italian Communist Party had kept to the Togliatti line, asking that the conference be called off, the Cubans had aligned themselves with the Russian delegates.

In the interview he granted me on March 17, 1965, Chou En-lai discussed the Moscow episode at some length, but made no specific reference, even in private, to the Cuban stand.[15] Other Chinese officials were just as discreet; not one of them criticized Cuba in my presence. True, they had nothing good to say about Cuba either. The Castroists were quite obviously not on a par with the Albanians, irreproachable Marxist-Leninists to a man, or with the Vietnamese, rightly admired for their anti-imperialist fight. Even so, the Castroist myth seemed to have retained its place in the popular imagination. I witnessed quite a few public displays glorifying the struggle against imperialism, and, almost invariably, in the front ranks were bearded figures, apparently representing the Cuban *guerrilleros*.[16]

Latin American visitors to Peking, however, explained that there was no importance attached to this detail. All bearded men were not necessarily Cubans. As Communists who had

15. The text of this interview was published simultaneously on March 26, 1965, in the *Nouvel Observateur* and in the *New Statesman*.
16. Very often these displays were enacted during mass rallies in Tien An-men Square in Peking. One was held in February 1965, after the start of the American bombing of Vietnam, and another in May 1965, after the landing of U.S. Marines on Santo Domingo.

303

broken with their parties, my informants clearly did not feel kindly toward the Castroists. Most had lived in Cuba when Soviet Russia was still being treated as a knight in shining armor and they now assured me that Fidel's alleged neutrality in the Sino-Soviet conflict was pure sham. According to them, the Cubans gave the Russians every chance of spreading their revisionist ideas, but were most reluctant to offer the Chinese similar facilities. A number of Latin American militants who had called at the Chinese Embassy in Havana once too often had even been confined to remote regions of the island or expelled from Cuba. My informants scoffed at all those who believed that Fidel had his stomach in Moscow but his heart in Peking. In their opinion, Castro's heart too was fully pledged to the Soviet Union because, being a petty bourgeois himself, he was perfectly at home with the upstarts who were running the U.S.S.R. Birds of a feather flock together, they said, adding that the presence of Raúl Castro and Osmani Cienfuegos at the Moscow conference had not surprised them in the least.

Their sectarianism and their bitterness were clear for all to see. This attitude colored their every remark, and whenever we spoke about events I knew something about they did their utmost to give them a *doctrinaire* twist. As members of a dissident fringe at home, they were desperately anxious to gain Chinese support and thus pretended to be more Maoist than Mao himself. I could not be at all sure that their anti-Castroist arguments were the faithful reflections of the thoughts of the Peking leaders. I also thought it unlikely that Che Guevara would try to recruit these pro-Chinese militants for his Latin American campaign.

There were, however, genuine differences between the true Chinese and the Cubans, and at the beginning of 1966, they exploded. This time it was started by Fidel Castro who, in a speech on January 2, 1966, accused the Chinese of trying to make political capital out of their rice deliveries to Cuba.[17] The

17. In his speech (published in *Granma* on January 2, 1966, and later in pamphlet form by *Obra Revolucionaria,* Havana, 1966) Fidel did not bother

"A Cuban heresy?"

Chinese immediately published a completely different version of the matter, and expressed astonishment that the Cuban premier should have seen fit to air in public commercial differences that were about to be settled amicably.[18] They explained further that part of their rice was earmarked for the Vietnamese, who, needless to say, were on the priority list. Accusations and counteraccusations were bandied about wildly; in the end all restraints were thrown to the wind, so much so that Fidel Castro called Mao a senile idiot and invited his own compatriots not to put up with leaders who had passed the sixty mark. After that age, he claimed, people were more inclined to act irresponsibly. He himself was thirty-nine at the time.

Peking did not follow Castro into the higher realms of personal abuse, but merely harped on its initial point that no socialist country has the right to stop another socialist country from distributing political material. China herself did nothing to prevent the Cubans from doing so in China. In the commercial field China had given Cuba a great deal of help and had scrupulously observed all the agreements she had signed. She was now genuinely unable to increase rice deliveries to Cuba; there simply was not enough to go around. The Cubans remained unconvinced as they had reliable information that China was selling large quantities of rice to Japan. And there matters remained until April 1966 when news of the cultural revolution broke on an unsuspecting world. Then *Granma*, the official

---

to disguise that his anger at the Chinese had other causes as well. Thus he revealed that, the year before, he had asked the Chinese ambassador to stop distributing propaganda material from Peking, but his request had fallen on deaf ears. His latest complaint was not that the Chinese were trying to cut rice deliveries, but that they refused to increase them, which in Fidel's view came to the same thing—Cuba's demand for this staple food was increasing from year to year. He stressed the fact that Cuba was quite prepared to pay for the extra rice with increased sugar supplies.

18. The Chinese reply was published in the form of a laconic communiqué in Number 3 of the *Peking Review* of 1966. Its tone was defensive and showed that China was unwilling to launch a frontal attack on one of the three Communist countries that were not committed to the Moscow line. However the quasi-anonymous character of the reply only served to add fuel to Castro's flames.

305

organ of the Cuban Communist Party, quite gratuitously coun-
seled the Chinese not to turn themselves into a laughing stock.
This was a final anti-Maoist attack, the last explosion, followed
by silence from both camps.

To my great surprise I found that in July 1967 my Cuban
hosts hardly recalled this episode. Instead they praised what they
were kind enough to call my sympathetic and understanding
book about the Chinese and told me that Fidel Castro himself
had read it with great interest. Their National Council of Culture had even published a chapter[19] in pamphlet form and intended to bring out a complete Cuban edition. Like myself,
they did not declare themselves unconditional supporters of
everything that was done in China, but they were keenly interested in certain key postulates of the Chinese experiment—
its egalitarian approach, its refusal to use material incentives.
Beyond that, they were tremendously impressed by the political
fervor of the Chinese. They told me, the Chinese are plainly
far better revolutionaries than the Russians, and they kept coming back to the same questions: "Why do they refuse to treat us
as full comrades? Why do they ignore Che's message and our
concepts of revolutionary struggle in Latin America?"

This preoccupation struck me as a most curious political fact.
For while China would not tolerate anyone calling for coexistence in a world dominated by the American imperialists and
was therefore Cuba's ideal partner, Havana still had closer links
with Moscow than with Peking, even though the Cubans seemed
to have lost any faith in their ability to change the prevailing
Soviet line. In fact, the breach between Havana and Moscow
was much deeper than Cuban pronouncements abroad seemed
to suggest. The language used by the Castroists at home was full
of phrases reminiscent of Chinese arguments. They used the
term revisionism as an obvious reference to the U.S.S.R. and its
allies abroad. Even merchandise from eastern Europe was com-

19. Chapter IV, "The Elusive Proletarian Culture," in K. S. Karol: *China, the Other Communism* (London, Heinemann, 1967).

monly described by this title. Thus on my first day in Havana I learned that revisionist trucks were of very poor quality, or that anyone using revisionist blades needed no shaving cream—his tears would be quite enough. But it was chiefly the Russian idea of peaceful coexistence that angered the Cubans. On that subject they disagreed; every advance Moscow made to Washington during this Year of Heroic Vietnam struck them as a fresh affront and outrage. They could not find words strong enough to express their disgust at Kosygin's meeting with Johnson and other American leaders at Glassboro.[20] To crown it all, immediately after smiling at the *bombardadores* of Vietnam, the Soviet prime minister had gone on to Havana hoping, said the Cuban man in the street, to receive a certificate of good revolutionary conduct. But he was sent away empty-handed; Fidel absolutely refused to sign a joint communiqué at the end of the visit, the only one a Soviet prime minister had ever paid to Cuba.

Clearly, the Soviet Union had lost the love, and even the respect, of this island, and Peking's star was in the ascendant. But the Cubans neither wished, nor could they afford, an open break with Moscow. They assured me that this was not sheer opportunism by saying that their revolution was not so calculating as to give way on matters of principle. Even at this late stage, they showed their determination to win the Russian people over to the side of the Latin American revolutionaries. The U.S.S.R. would have to change its policy and play an active part in the creation of those "two, three, many Vietnams" that would

20. After the Six-Day War (June 6–12, 1967) the prime minister of the U.S.S.R. attended a special meeting of the United Nations in New York to discuss the Middle East. Anxious to meet the American President, but not prepared to go to Washington, the Soviet leader agreed to a meeting at Glassboro, halfway between New York and the U.S. capital. For forty-eight hours, on June 26–June 28, Kosygin was in conference with President Lyndon Johnson, Secretary of Defense Robert McNamara, Secretary of State Dean Rusk, and other American leaders. No official communiqué was issued after this meeting, which is said to have been conducted in a most cordial atmosphere.

inevitably spring up during the next two years, or else become utterly discredited in the eyes of the world socialist movement. And if many Cubans had no illusions as to the choice Moscow would make, they nevertheless felt that they owed it to Che and to all the Latin American guerrilla fighters to continue exerting patient but unyielding diplomatic pressure on the U.S.S.R. "Our Vietnamese and Korean comrades, whose revolutionary honor is beyond all doubt, are advising us to follow this very line, to be firm and yet refrain from provoking the Soviet Union unnecessarily." Havana obviously liked to see herself in the role of spokesman for the three nonaligned Communist countries. The Cubans would have loved to be understood by China, their great potential ally, but no signal came from Peking. Neither the Vietnamese nor the Koreans were in any position to act as go-between with the Maoists; they found it difficult enough to live with Chinese intransigence as few of them were wholeheartedly in favor of the "great proletarian cultural revolution" with its challenge to the entire heritage of the world Communist movement.

The Cubans had begun to realize that differences with the U.S.S.R. over international strategy lead slowly but inexorably to a critique of Soviet society in general and in particular of the Soviet model of socialism. They said so quite openly, and though the world knew little about their innovations, they were certainly ambitious. I myself did not discover their "heresy" before I set foot on the island; its full import struck me during an exciting drive from Havana to Santiago de Cuba, the capital of the remote province of Oriente, where Fidel Castro was due to deliver a speech on July 26, 1967.

The heritage of Ernesto Che Guevara

Renato Guitart. . . . Who was this frail young man, whose portraits had been pasted up everywhere for the July 26th celebrations? I thought that I had learned the names of all the great heroes of the Cuban revolution on my previous visits, but neither the name nor the face of Renato Guitart was in the least

familiar to me. Major Jorge Serguera, nicknamed Papito, came
to my aid: "We, too, were told very little about Renato and the
other martyrs of Moncada until now." He said it very quietly,
without any ill feeling toward those doctrinaires who had kept
Cubans in ignorance of their real past. But his remark was obviously aimed at these men. Clearly, what few attempts were
made to rehabilitate the non-Communist branch of the revolutionary movement after the sectarian period and the missile
crisis, and to do justice to those who had died in battle while
the Communists made speeches about a national democratic
front, had not gone far enough. It took renewed tension with
Moscow and a new guerrilla war in Latin America for Cuba to
give Renato and his comrades their full due. Castroists did not
spell this story out in so many words, but anyone familiar with
Latin American affairs knew what it was all about. Serguera
seemed convinced that this was the most effective manner of attacking the orthodox without causing a permanent breach. The
Major said this with a touch of that highly individual humor I
had had occasion to appreciate the evening before.

In July 1967, the Cubans had invited the Parisian *Salon de
Mai* to an exhibition of their work in Havana. This project
had first been promoted by Carlos Franqui in 1964, soon after
he had left the editorial staff of *Revolución;* however, it was
three years later that he was finally promised support by Cuba's
cultural authorities. In art, no less than in the case of Renato
Guitart, a new theory was clearly at work. Socialist realism on
the Russian model had never had many followers in Cuba;
however, by inviting the *Salon* and by widely publicizing their
tour, the Castroists were giving official blessing to the kind of
art on which other socialist countries had resolutely turned their
backs. Worse still, the Cubans now declared that the only truly
revolutionary and progressive art was art that did not allow
itself to be fettered by petrified Marxism. Apart from the *Salon*
they had also invited surrealists and members of other schools
abhorrent to the U.S.S.R. My own qualifications in this field
were very slight but Carlos Franqui insisted on including me in
his list, assuring me that as far as he was concerned, the great

cultural congress must under no circumstances remain confined to painters.

Barely had we stepped into the Nacional, the most Cuban of the big hotels in Havana, when we were all invited to a highly original soirée, a sort of revolutionary happening. On an immense scaffolding erected before the Cuban pavilion, in the center of Vedado, some sixty painters of different nationalities and schools were busily painting a collective fresco before the large crowd that had massed into the nerve center of the city. To keep up the crowd's interest and to divert them during dull moments—the painters were making very slow progress—dancers from the Tropicana enacted revolutionary scenes on a special stage in the middle of the street. The purpose of the whole display, we were told, was to bring the people closer to culture, and to judge by the vast throng and its enthusiasm, this object had been fully attained.

Those of the invited guests who were neither artists nor dancers were gathered on a small lawn with an excellent view over both the painters' scaffold and the dancers' stage. While we were talking to leading personalities in the cultural life of Havana, we could see the painters flourishing their brushes and paints and watch the dancers coming and going in the wings. The display continued without a break; vivid and picturesque visual impressions flourished during the entire evening.

Toward midnight, while the excitement was at its peak, a Cuban army major beckoned me to his corner of the lawn and told me, gravely, that he wanted to speak to me. As if it were the most natural thing in the world, he immediately launched into the subject of China, the U.S.S.R., and the problems of the European Left. My questioner was none other than Jorge Serguera, better known as Papito, then director of ICR (the Cuban Radio and Television Institute) ,[21] and despite his youth

21. ICR plays a considerable role in Cuba, thanks to the paramount importance of radio and television in the life of most Cubans. It is said that the Castroist Revolution was the first revolution in history to be televised.

—he looked thirty at the very most—he had a long and distinguished revolutionary past.[22] Nor did he only ask me simple
questions; but, having lived so close to the heart of events and
being a close collaborator of Fidel's, he had much to tell me in
his turn. Since that evening in Vedado was too brief for an ex-
haustive discussion of all subjects of mutual interest, I was only
too delighted when, a few days later, Papito proposed that I
join him and Major Jesús Montané on a trip to Santiago, where
everybody, including the *Salon de Mai,* was to gather for the
July 26th celebrations. A drive with these Castroist veterans appealed to me very much more than an organized tour with
European intellectuals whom I could visit in Paris any time I
liked. I asked for Carlos Franqui's opinion, and he readily approved my choice.

Our caravan set out on July 20. It was made up of three well-
restored American limousines; nonetheless, it was thought best
to drive in close convoy for mutual aid in case of breakdowns.
The Italian Communist deputy, Rossana Rossanda, the Spanish
writer Jorge Semprun, and his French wife, Colette, constituted
the other members of the international team accompanying the
ten civil and military colleagues of Majors Jorge Serguera and
Jesús Montané, better known as Chucho. Chucho, a veteran of
the Moncada attack and of the *Granma* expedition, was the new
minister of communications and a member of the Central Committee of the Cuban Communist Party. Though he had played
a most impressive part in the Revolution, he led our safari
without putting on great airs. Despite his olive-green uniform
there was nothing martial about Chucho's manner or bearing.

Cuba is a long, narrow island; the distance between Havana
and Santiago is close to 600 miles. Luckily the central highway,
the *carretera,* is an excellent road; it can be covered in less

22. In 1956, Jorge Serguera, then a young lawyer, was one of the defense
counsels for the *Granma* contingent. Later he joined the guerrillas in the
Sierra Cristal, i.e., in Raúl Castro's Second Front. After the Revolution he
became, in quick succession, public prosecutor, military governor of Camagüey, and finally ambassador to Algeria and to the Congo.

than twelve hours without too much strain. We left Havana a week before the July 26th celebrations because Montané and Serguera had business to settle in the province and also because they had very kindly offered to show us some of the achievements of the Revolution. Lisandro Otero, vice-president of the National Council of Culture, was also traveling with us. Thanks to him we were able to visit theaters and libraries, museums, and places of artistic interest in every major town we passed. We also made many long stops to see special economic projects, the so-called Fidel plans. Most were large farms engaged in intensive cultivation, which relied partly on volunteer work. Here the Cubans were trying to develop completely new crops by taking full advantage of the favorable climate. They seemed equally if not more concerned about the social aspects of the Fidel plans; it was in these oases of progress that they hoped to produce their *hombres nuevos,* new men, true idealists who would scorn all material incentives and who would live by genuine Communist standards. The regime did everything in its power to facilitate this task, and Montané and Serguera were anxious to make sure that their particular departments had not been remiss in any way.

They were also keen to draw our attention to the warm human relationships, characteristic of the Castroist style, they had with the local officials and the farmworkers. They seemed to be on familiar terms with everybody and were received most cordially wherever they went. Our timetable was highly elastic with the result that it was sometimes well past 2 A.M. when Montané and Serguera would meet the local comrades. No one looked in the least disturbed by the improvised nature of these nocturnal meetings, no one seemed to have been pulled out of bed, nor did anyone display obsequious respect toward the men from Havana.

All the Party offices where we spent our nights were teeming with men in olive-green. These offices, most of them nationalized villas, were busy centers of local political life. Even when our guides had no official business to discuss, the local leaders would come along for friendly chats during and after meals. I was

312

struck by the extreme youth of all these men, a fact that had surprised me during my previous visits. Now, six years later, this country was still being run by a sort of New Wave of the young.

The fleeting nature of our visits did not allow us to tarry at any one stop, or to make anything like a detailed study. We were, however, able to admire some major agricultural successes. In Vanao, for example, in the vicinity of Trinidad, we were shown strawberries, asparagus, and good eating apples—all crops that were not previously grown in Cuba. We also visited a banana plantation, which had grown up near Cienfuegos on soil that had been covered with *marabu,* a tough shrub that had to be cleared with bulldozers. Walking a few miles under a hot sun, we were shown banana plants bearing their first fruit. The men in charge of the plantation, and all the agricultural experts, pointed them out proudly, almost with surprise at their own success.

The star attraction, however, was the great training school at Topes de Collantes, in the Escambray Mountains. More than seven thousand students, four hundred teachers, and as many administrators live and work in this isolated spot, which can only be reached by jeep. The school, named after Manuel Ascunce Domenech,[23] represents the second phase in the Cuban system of training revolutionary teachers. When they are fifteen to sixteen years old, these pupils spend their first year at Minas del Frío, in the Sierra Maestra, under Spartan conditions. Only those who have passed the first, grueling stage graduate to Topes de Collantes. They stay for two years, taking crash courses in their chosen subjects. They are subjected to strict disciplinary rules, and must work on the land and participate in a variety of strenuous sports. But they live in a modern building that has nothing guerrilla-like about it; it was a sanitorium before the Revolution. They spend their fourth and last year at the Makarenko Pedagogical Institute at Tarara, near Havana, and

23. Manuel Ascunce Domenech, like Conrado Benítez, was killed by counterrevolutionaries from Escambray during the literacy campaign of 1961.

do their practice teaching in the capital. The director of Topes, Manuel Ruá Rodríguez, and his assistant, Carmen Hernández, told us about the advantages of this intensive and diversified program of training in the mountains and stressed that most of the pupils came from poor peasant homes. Many of the staff were ex-pupils, though the greatest number of graduates by far worked among the peasants, helping in the literacy campaign and trying to set a revolutionary example wherever they went.

Topes de Collantes, like the two other institutes of the same level, is a coeducational school, with girls constituting close to 50 per cent of the pupils. Like the boys, they are expected to study, work, and exercise at an intense rate. The school day is very long; it begins at 6 A.M. and ends at 10:30 P.M. There is only one rest day per week and a one-month holiday per year. The number of pupils who drop out is very small indeed. On the other hand, the number of applicants is so large that the buildings need to be extended all the time. We watched some of the new blocks going up during our visit; nearly two million dollars have been spent on new constructions, and our guides assured us that national education figures very high in the Cuban budget.

While we were debating the pros and cons of this method of training a new generation of Communists, Montané and Serguera attended a technical discussion on possible improvements of the telecommunication system and tried to discover the best spot for a television relay station. No one was wasting time. During all our stops, the program was the same—working sessions and inspections for some, and revolutionary tourism, as Serguera called it, for the rest.

After leaving the provinces of Matanzas, meaning massacre,[24] and of Las Villas, with Trinidad a veritable museum-city from the Spanish colonial period, we descended into the great plain of Camagüey, the Texas of Cuba. It had earned this nickname,

24. The Spaniards are said to have slaughtered some twenty thousand parrots on the spot where the city of Matanzas later rose up. According to other sources, the victims were Indians, not birds.

rather unflattering to anyone familiar with the United States, because its *vaqueros* and Texan cowboys are very much alike and also because stock-breeding has been practiced here for centuries. Vast herds of cattle roam about in search of pasture and water, and all the *vaqueros* have to do is drive a fixed number of them to the abattoirs from time to time. But, in contrast to Texas, Camagüey has cattle of the very poorest quality. The Zebu strain of that region is remarkable only for its low milk yield—less than half a gallon a day—and for the poor quality of its meat. Thus Cuba used to import beef from the United States, while its own prairies teemed with some six to seven million Zebus, i.e., with nearly one Zebu per inhabitant.[25] When devising their new agricultural policy, the Cubans decided to activate the idle, or underused, capital locked up in their livestock. They imported Holstein, Brown Swiss, and other strains renowned for their milk and meat yield, with the intention of crossing them with Zebus and breeding a new race, both resistant to the climate and also highly productive. And so the glorious period of independent cows, left to fend for themselves, came to a sudden end in Camagüey, and also in Oriente, the next province. We were shown artificial insemination centers and could inspect very impressive F-1 crosses between Holsteins and Zebus. Lisandro Otero proved to be quite unexpectedly erudite on all matters of breeding livestock. He talked with great authority and assurance about the origin and characteristics of each cow—and there were quite a few—we came across in the prairies of Camagüey.

25. Stock-raising under the old regime seems to have been somewhat more advanced than my informants in Camagüey suggested. Intensive breeding of Creoles, which were apparently much more productive than Zebus, was practiced well before the Revolution. The report that the Cuban delegation submitted to the FAO in 1967 ("Agricultural and Livestock Production in Cuba") did not give precise figures on the importance of livestock and meat production in Cuba before 1959. From *Bohemia* of August 8, 1969 (No. 32), we may gather that in August 1967 Cuba had 7,171,962 horned animals, of which 4,049,866 were on state farms and 3,122,096 were owned by individual farmers.

Guerrillas in Power

In the historical province of Oriente, the cradle of Cuban independence and the home of Fidel Castro, it was Papito Serguera who became our chief instructor. He had been born there, had studied at Santiago, and had been a friend and comrade of the famous group led by Frank País and Pepito Tey. It was Tey who had first drawn his attention to Nicolas Lenin.[26] Beyond these reminiscences, Serguera was able to tell us a great deal about sugar. His father had been manager of one of the biggest mills in the country. After lecturing us at length on cane sugar, which is particularly important to the economy of Oriente, he told us that his father's archives had yielded a great deal of interesting information on the political machinations and internal differences of the *latifundist* class. These documents apparently threw a great deal of light on the political and social background of Batista's putsch in 1952, and Papito regretted that he lacked the time to prepare them for publication.

Major Chucho Montané also had quite a few things to tell us about Oriente, from where he had helped mount the attack on the Moncada barracks. He could even complement his own reminiscences with his wife's, Melba Hernández, who, with Haydée Santamaría, had represented Cuban women during that epic struggle. But human witnesses are notoriously frail, and Chucho Montané gave us to understand that Cuba can boast as many versions of these events as there are survivors. The differences hinged on minor details, but they were big enough for him to question his wife's version. He even told us an amusing story about the ups and downs of this family debate, thus adding a lot of gaiety to one of our collective meals.

We never ate in restaurants. When we left one stop, party

26. Pepito Tey, one of the earliest Castroist martyrs, was killed at the age of nineteen during a street battle in Santiago, on November 30, 1956. Shortly before his tragic end, he had informed Serguera, "You know, all we have been saying about revolution was said long before us by somebody called Nicolas Lenin." Curiously, Vladimir Ilyich Lenin is known throughout Cuba as Nicolas Lenin; this is also how popular Communist texts refer to him.

officials in the next were informed of our impending arrival and just how many of us they could expect. The menu rarely varied from generous helpings of roast chicken or steak. In Cienfuegos, however, we were treated to a copious and excellent meal of grilled lobsters. No kind of ceremony presided over our collective repasts. From the very start we formed a harmonious group, and all of us were soon addressing one another by first names.

This persistent good humor did not, however, mean that we did not have serious discussions. They continued throughout the trip and were often very heated. Having lost touch with Cuban developments over the past few years, I had a great deal to catch up on—Che's latest economic theses, the real reasons for his attacks on the U.S.S.R., and, last but not least, the promulgation of plans he had devised just before his departure. I was rather intrigued to hear Papito Serguera seize every possible opportunity to attack the persistence of commercial standards in postrevolutionary societies in general, and in the Soviet Union in particular. At first, I thought that his diatribes against the Moscow revisionists and their Stakhanovite incentives were merely his personal views, but then he told me that this anti-revisionist passion had been communicated to him by Che himself. It was under Che's influence that he had come to realize that commercial mores were irreconcilable with socialism. As we drove along, he would miss no opportunity to illustrate his point, to show how greatly superior moral incentives were to financial rewards. At Vanao, for instance, we were presented to young girls proudly bearing the title of Vietnamese women; they had earned it by self-denial and devotion to their work. No amount of money could possibly have given them the same satisfaction, Papito assured me. All this encouraged me to delve into the writings of Ernesto Che Guevara, essential reading for anyone interested in "the Cuban heresy."

In 1961, Che had been deeply worried about what he called the crisis of Cuban production. But at the time he was still firmly convinced that the system of management and planning imported from the U.S.S.R., via Czechoslovakia, would one day enable his adopted country to run the economy with clockwork precision. He simply blamed the crisis on his own comrades' failure to grasp and apply the finer details of this infallible plan. Ever unsparing of himself, Che had made a thorough study of the whole subject, down to mathematics. Moreover there was no doubt that Cuban economists had made serious mistakes. But precisely because he concentrated on this single problem —unavoidable in a country suffering from a lack of economic experts—Che seems to have neglected the shortcomings inherent in the very principle of a plan set up by a small number of specialists acting on the orders of political leaders answerable to no one. Far from being able to predict, at any given moment, the economic potential of the country or the needs of the population, such a system, as practiced by the U.S.S.R. and the People's Democracies, tends to act as a brake on production. The 1956 Polish revelations on the moonshine[27] plans of this type had not apparently shaken Che's confidence in the reliability of the clockwork he had imported from the East. What he and his comrades did instead was to make sure that no young Cuban economists would henceforth complete their studies in Poland, a country far too much to the right, if not revisionist in the literal sense of the word.[28]

In 1962, people in the Soviet Union itself, the originator of socialist planning, heard highly revealing discussions on the subject of economic reforms. Reading between the lines of the works of Professors Nemchinov, Trapeznikov, and Liberman,[29]

27. Wladyslaw Bienkowski's article on the incredible planning aberrations during the Stalinist period was first published in the Warsaw *Przeglad Kulturalny* No. 43 (October 23, 1956) and was reprinted in a special issue of *Temps Modernes*, February–March 1957 (No. 132–133).

28. Thanks to the work of Professors Lange, Bobrowski, Kalecki, Brus, and other less widely known economists, Poland was generally recognized as having one of the best schools of economics in the world, and certainly the best in the socialist camp.

29. When Professor Nemchinov, the former vice-president of the Soviet Academy of Sciences and founder of the Econometric Institute in Novosi-

"A Cuban heresy?"

to mention only the best known theorists of the reform movement, Che was bound to conclude that the Soviet Union, too, was in the throes of an economic crisis, albeit no one dared call it by its proper name. In particular, the reformers showed that, during the first few years of the latest Seven Year Plan (1959–65), the national growth rate, far from enabling the U.S.S.R. to overtake the United States, had begun to drop alarmingly.[30] Soviet investment was, however, incomparably greater than that of most capitalist countries; it accounted for considerably more than 25 per cent of the gross national product. But because it was too diversified or too concentrated in the priority sectors—opinions on this subject differed—Soviet investment proved singularly unproductive. Moreover, the quality of Soviet products was so poor that factories were crammed with unsold stock, while industries continued to clamor in vain for equipment and while the population clamored for consumer goods. As a result, the U.S.S.R. had to pay an infinitely greater price for economic progress than her Western rivals, and the

---

birsk, died in 1965, Professors Trapeznikov and Liberman became the foremost spokesmen of the economic reform movement in the U.S.S.R.

30. The annual growth rate of the national income in the U.S.S.R. (between 1958 and 1963) was:

1958	12.5 per cent
1959	8.0 per cent
1960	8.0 per cent
1961	6.8 per cent
1962	5.7 per cent
1963	4.1 per cent

The corresponding figures for Czechoslovakia, during the same period, were:

1958	8.0 per cent
1959	6.0 per cent
1960	8.3 per cent
1961	6.8 per cent
1962	1.4 per cent
1963	−2.2 per cent

See Charles Bettelheim: "Le problème des prix dans les pays socialistes d'Europe," taken from *La Pensée*, No. 133 (June 1967) and No. 134 (August 1967).

standard of life had become needlessly depressed. It was impossible to improve matters by increasing the rate of investments even further as the resources of the country were already stretched to the maximum. Also, the curative effect of such a remedy seemed doubtful.

What then did the reformers propose? They declared that the old methods of planning and management were no longer fitted to the needs of the Soviet economy, which had grown far too large and complex to be run in the way it had been during the phase of rapid industrialization. The Gosplan (the State Planning Center) and the ministries responsible for the various sectors of the economy were no longer able to supply enterprises with the precise guidelines needed for the smooth implementation of the overall plan or for the best utilization of available resources. The reformers demanded greater autonomy for all enterprises, even in matters of finance. This would enable them to arrive at answers the Center could no longer give on their behalf.

The new system would help the most dynamic enterprises to fit their supplies to the prevailing demand, to make profits, and to reinvest these directly in new plant. Some experts even suggested that exchanges between the various enterprises should, as far as possible, dispense with planning mechanisms, and rely instead on the law of supply and demand. This part of the proposal, which would have made nonsense of all forms of central planning, was, of course, thrown out of court: all enterprises were still expected to deploy their extra initiative within the framework of a central plan, and could only collect bonuses for exceeding the production targets set from above. Only in the consumer sector would the market be allowed to play a somewhat more important role. The range of consumer goods would be increased and buyers were authorized to patronize those factories that made some effort to improve the quality of their goods. Modest though these innovations were, the reformers hoped that they would produce a psychological shock among the leaders of industry, who now had a material interest in the

320

success and profits of their particular enterprises. The reformers
did not, in fact, disguise the fact that they looked upon financial
incentives as the best means of ending shortages and of making
more rational use of what had proved to be a rather unproductive labor force.

This project, which enjoyed the patronage of Kosygin, came
up against the entrenched habits of the Soviet bureaucracy, and
was not adopted until 1965, after three years of behind the
scenes discussion.[31] It did not abolish central planning, did not
turn profits into the mainspring of Soviet economic life, as some
Western commentators have alleged, and was not incompatible
with the traditional Soviet principle of "to each according to
his labor." For all that, the reforms were not nearly as trivial
as other critics have claimed. They marked a first step away
from the path the U.S.S.R. had followed ever since the creation
of its system of planning and economic control.

In the past, the Soviet leaders had sometimes admitted that
they still lacked the precise scientific techniques needed for the
formulation of absolutely perfect plans. Their country was still
too underdeveloped for that. All the central authority could do
under the circumstances was to collect and analyze the greatest
possible relevant data and to formulate its directives accordingly.
Quite often there were major reorganizations at the top; the
last, in 1957, involved the division of the country into
Sovnarkhozes (regional economic councils), which, by being
closer to the national pulse, promised to reduce some of the
worst planning errors. The ultimate goal of Soviet economists
was to improve planning techniques to the point where they
would allow the maximum exploitation of all available economic resources for the benefit of the community as a whole.
That goal had remained unchanged and, with the dawn of the
age of computers, this goal seemed closer than it had ever been.

31. The reforms were adopted by the Central Committee of the
Communist Party of the U.S.S.R. in September 1965, and ratified by the
Twenty-third Congress of the Soviet Communist Party in March 1966.

However, such were the practical effects of the new reforms that, when they finally came, the whole Russian economy was thrown into reverse. For the first time the Soviet leaders decided to hand down fewer directives to the rank and file, to keep less rigidly to the science of planning, and to place much greater reliance in more spontaneous and less controllable regulators, e.g., in the market. Even though these reforms were relatively mild and covered no more than a limited sector of the economy, that of consumer goods and services, they represented a qualitative jump out of the past and heralded much more radical change for the future.

One of the fathers of Soviet planning, Professor Strumilin, once said that "the ideology of the planner is an integral part of the plan."[32] The Soviet leaders had always proclaimed that all their managers had been trained in Red universities, that all of them had reached their positions primarily because they were good Communists. And now the reformers were claiming quite brazenly that these same "Bolshevik officials" had been guilty of a lack of initiative and that the only way to remedy the situation and to get them to work for the general good was to stimulate them materially; i.e., to grant them special privileges, higher incomes, and greater authority over their subordinates. This tacit admission, even among the Soviet elite, that appeals to the political consciousness had fallen on deaf ears necessarily had severe repercussions on the whole of Soviet society, on its attitude both toward work and in life. In the past, Soviet leaders had made a great point of associating productivity bonuses with appeals to social ideals. Nor had they hesitated to use threats and force against all those who did not allow themselves to be stimulated either morally or materially; but this attitude poses quite a different problem and merits a volume to itself. The new reforms revealed to what a large extent the Russians even at the top had already grown deaf to

32. See Czeslaw Bobrowski: *Formation du système soviétique de planification* (The Hague, 1956), p. 55.

political or moral appeals. The reforms merely served to accelerate this process by encouraging Soviet citizens to indulge their selfish preoccupations.

In the People's Democracies, the economic reforms were greeted with acclaim, almost with fervor. It was not that people were hoping for an economic miracle; no one had any illusions on that score. But "liberalization," as the reforms were described in Eastern Europe, suddenly put the Muscovite seal on all the many reform projects devised and discreetly practiced since 1956. By contrast in Cuba, Che Guevara, who smelled a revisionist rat in all Polish and Hungarian reforms, was not ready to accept the great liberal *volte face,* even if it now bore the Kremlin's own *imprimatur.* Perhaps he would have been less intransigent, and less disrespectful of Moscow, had the whole economic debate not been brought into the open during the very year in which the missile crisis had served to discredit Khrushchev and the Soviet Union.

In an interview with Sam Russell of the London *Daily Worker* on December 4, 1962, Che stated quite bluntly that he disapproved of the Soviet premier. In fact, the published text was said to have been watered down considerably lest Soviet-Cuban relationships be given too severe a jolt. People also remarked on the fact that Che, the chief Cuban negotiator with the Eastern bloc in 1960, had chosen to be absent during the new economic negotiations with Moscow; therefore, it was not until May 1963 that he had apparently learned of the terms of the new Russo-Cuban agreement, drawn up entirely by Fidel and Khrushchev. Many people believe that he strongly disapproved of Fidel's agreement to concentrate on the agricultural sector. According to them, Che, as champion of industrialization, could not possibly have agreed to this particular choice. But I have looked at all his speeches on the subject at meetings of the Ministry of Industry and have been unable to discover the slightest shred of evidence in support of this thesis. It is nevertheless true that once the choice had been made, his ministry lost much of its hold over the economic life of the country, especially as the sugar industry was transferred to a special ministry, newly created. Che nevertheless remained a member of the Political Bureau and one of the most influential leaders in all Cuba. Hence it was as a man wielding full authority that he attacked the Russian reforms in a searching theoretical essay entitled "Reflections on the Cost of Production as a Basis of Economic Analysis for Enterprises Run on a Budgetary System."[33]

In this essay Che tried to show that, in a socialist system, or in a system moving toward socialism, all such concepts as profitability, value, or even merchandise, have very different meanings from those prevailing in a capitalist system and therefore could not be invoked to justify reforms of a liberal type. He developed this point even further a month later when he published a study on the budgetary system of financing enterprises.[34] He declared that in a socialist state all enterprises must fit into a wider frame of the service of society at large. Nationalized means of production represent social assets and not capital that a particular factory can acquire so as to increase its own production and profits. In a country like Cuba, with a relatively low level of industrialization but one of the best communication systems in the world,[35] no technical obstacles stood in the way of centralized control of industry. Now since this sector must be treated as a whole, every enterprise ought to be considered as a workshop in the national enterprise and not as an independent unit whose profitability must be evaluated in isolation. Moreover, for Marxists, a product has an exchange value only because of its sale in accordance with the laws of capitalist dis-

33. See: "Consideraciones sobre los costos de producción como base del análisis económico de las empresas sujetas a sistema presupuestario" in *Nuestra Industria*, No. 1 (Havana, June 1963) .

34. "Sobre el sistema presupuestario de financiamento" in *Trimestre* (Suplemento del Directorio financiero) , No. 7 (Havana, July–September 1963) .

35. The leading American telecommunication companies had used Cuba as a testing ground and, upon leaving, bequeathed her a network that in some respects was better than any in the United States. Many of the new techniques tested by Americans in Cuba on a small scale had not yet been introduced in their own country.

"A Cuban heresy?"

tribution. But in the case of a single, state-owned enterprise, there could be no question of "sales" or "exchange values." Bookkeeping and economic calculations could serve no other purposes than improved planning and more effective running of the whole economic machine.

Che also had many, far less theoretical reasons for rejecting the ideas of the socialist reformers. In Cuba much of the land had remained in private hands, while the cities teemed with petty bureaucrats. The state had been a kind of national industry under the old regime. These men would have been the first to profit from a socialist market economy. Hence the reforms, far from encouraging the most progressive elements, would chiefly help those who were expert in filling their own pockets and who had done relatively well even under the old regime. Now, to Che, the Revolution stood primarily for social justice, for repairing the criminal neglect of the *humildes,* that enormous unemployed and semiliterate mass of yesterday. Granting financial autonomy to Cuban enterprises, far from repairing old injustices, would only serve to perpetuate them. Cuba's industries were adapted to the old, unfair pattern of consumption that the Revolution had sworn to eradicate. Cuban industry was in desperate need of redirection, not of stimulation by market mechanisms. True, consumer tastes had not been transformed during the short postrevolutionary period, but that was no reason for titillating them further at the cost of shortages in resources and manpower. In the old Cuba even the working class, skilled workers in particular, had been relatively privileged with respect to all those who had no work at all or were only allowed to work sporadically. Thus even if financial autonomy went hand in hand with democratic workers' control it would not lead to greater justice, because financial autonomy would simply favor those who had enjoyed a long head start.

However, Che did not list all these specifically Cuban factors to claim that his country was the exception to the general rule; he challenged the very rule of the reformers. His attitude may seem to be paradoxical. He was, in fact, defending a system im-

325

ported from the U.S.S.R., which was now considered ineffective by its originators. But this paradox was only superficial. The Soviet reforms were the result of specific political and social developments in the U.S.S.R., which Cuba had never adopted. This is reflected in Russia's and Che's respective attitudes to the crucial question of incentives. Ernesto Che Guevara put forward a number of startling ideas, which Cuban revolutionaries fervently embraced in 1967, the year of their disaffection.

In Che's view, massive recourse to material incentives was quite incompatible with the social aims of the Revolution because it put selfish greed before concern for the common good. It was bound to create new social inequalities and lead to the collapse of the revolutionary consciousness of the masses. Now it was precisely this revolutionary consciousness that, according to Che, was the greatest asset of a socialist society. Without it all attempts to build a new and better world were doomed to failure from the outset.

But Che even refused to admit that financial incentives could bring purely economic advantages to a socialist country. According to him, the desire for profit could only act as a powerful lever in a capitalist society, where money is the basis of all privilege. In postrevolutionary Cuba, by contrast, enrichment was no longer an aim in itself. Financial incentives held no greater attraction for the workers than the *Pastorita,* a Cuban lottery with prizes too insubstantial to appeal to the more ambitious, or to shake the rest out of their indifference.[36]

True, Che fully realized that the old mercantile mentality had not been eradicated and that some sections of the population remained deeply attached to money. He also recognized that the educational standard of the Cuban workers, and above all of the new proletarians, was not yet high enough to enable them to take charge of the complex machinery of a centralized economy. These were obstacles inherited from the past. Che regretted them

36. See: Che's letter to Mestre in *Reminiscences of the Cuban Revolutionary War* (New York, Grove Press, 1969).

but was unwilling to let them deflect him from his main purpose. He remained firmly convinced that productive relationships could outpace productive forces and, conversely, that every compromise would have to be paid for with political setbacks and economic failures.

Though he always tried to substantiate his views with detailed and clear-cut arguments, Che failed to convince many of his own comrades. Some, like Carlos Rafael Rodríguez with whom he had already quarreled in 1961, were highly impressed by the reformist endeavors of Eastern Europe. Others, like Major Alberto Mora, who could not be suspected of pro-Soviet sympathies, believed that Che was ignoring Cuban dependence on external trade, which, as always, was governed by the law of supply and demand. Finally, such eminent Marxist economists as Professor Bettelheim had intervened in the debate to point out that even socialist plans must be geared to actual levels of productivity, at least during a long transition period, when they had to refer constantly to price and credit mechanisms, which, in their turn, demanded the most careful assessments of the profitability of all sectors of the economy.[37]

Che answered his critics with three extremely hard-hitting papers: "On the Concept of Value," "Bank, Credit and Socialism," and "The Meaning of Planning."[38] All these questions were discussed quite openly, without any of the taboos customary in other socialist countries, at bimonthly meetings of the Ministry of Industry. Here Che insisted that his point of view was in

37. Major Alberto Mora's article, entitled *En torno a la cuestión del funcionamento de la ley del valor en la economía cubana en los actuales momentos,* was first published in *Comercio Exterior* No. 3, 1963, and was subsequently reprinted in *Nuestra Industria,* No. 3, 1963. Professor Bettelheim's *Formas y métodos de la planificación socialista y nivel de desarrollo de las fuerzas productivas* appeared in *Cuba Socialista,* No. 32, April 1964.

38. Che's answer to Bettelheim was published in *Cuba Socialista,* No. 34, July 1964, and was called *La planificación socialista, su significado.* Che's other studies, *Sobre la concepción del valor* and *La banca, el credito y el socialismo,* appeared in *Revista Económica,* No. 3, October 1963, and in *Cuba Socialista,* No. 31, March 1964. See also: Ernest Mandel's *Le grand débat economique,* in *Partisans* No. 37 (Paris, 1967).

strict accordance with Marxist tradition and, on the purely formal plane, he was probably correct. I shall not cite what arguments he culled from Marx and Lenin, but shall instead quote the conclusions of Professor Vlodzimierz Brus, who is considered an authority in the field and cannot be suspected of partiality since he is a champion of reform in his native Poland. "The theoretical and ideological attitude of the revolutionary movement used to involve the firm conviction that a socialist economy must be a centrally planned economy, not only in general, but in all its particulars, and that market mechanisms are so many foreign bodies in a socialist economy that need to be tolerated for a time, but must be eliminated as soon as possible and with the utmost energy."[39]

However, in this whole debate there was a major gap which genuine Marxists might have been expected to close. Neither Che nor his opponents had come to grips with the problem of political power in, and the political organization of, all those societies where centralized or reformist experiments in planning and economic management were taking place. The "classics," which both sides so assiduously quoted, had never equated socialism with mere economic efficiency; i.e., with economic control by a small group deciding, in the name of the people, on the best way of organizing work and leisure. One can look in vain to Marx for this concept of permanently delegated political and economic authority. On the contrary, for Marx the entire transition period toward socialism and Communism was characterized by the direct participation of all workers, free at last, in the running of communal affairs. Even for Lenin, the founder of the theory of the proletarian vanguard party, Soviet power still came before electrical power. This problem was also behind the great debate on socialist accumulation that shook the Soviet Union in the twenties, and in which Preobrazhensky clashed bitterly with Bukharin, at a time when Stalin's dictator-

39. Vlodzimierz Brus, *Problèmes généraux du fonctionnement de l'économie socialiste* (Paris, 1969), pp. 45–46.

"A Cuban heresy?"

ship already prevented the problem from being aired in full.[40]
But, in 1963, the protagonists of the new debate, both in Moscow
and in Havana, were behaving as if "Soviet power" had become
a reality and that the whole problem no longer concerned them.
The silence of the Soviet Marxists could, of course, be explained
by political conditions in the U.S.S.R., and particularly by
memories of the unhappy lot of all those who had spoken up
in the past. Moreover, any professor of economics, be he
reformist or not, risked having his academic career cut short
if he ventured too far into the forbidden realm of politics. But
what about Havana? The Cubans had not, after all, been subjected to decades of terror and doublethink, and must surely
have realized that their institutions were still in a state of flux.
Their silence was very difficult to explain.

Che had, it is true, written some fine pages on the dialectical
unity between Fidel and the masses, a unity that enabled the
leader of the Revolution to engage in a permanent dialogue
with his nation. He had added that those who had never had
direct contacts with the Cuban experiment could not possibly
hope to grasp the full splendor of this phenomenon. But
during meetings at the Ministry of Industry, Che himself was
quick to deplore the lack of workers' participation in the social
life of their enterprises. He admitted, although implicitly, that
the system did not yet offer the masses enough opportunities to
manage their own affairs. In reading these texts the foreign
reader gains the clear impression that Che's analyses were lacking
in depth. This made itself felt even before the debate on
incentives when he spoke of the role of the trade unions in a
socialist country or when he called technicians and administrators the "backbone of the economy."[41] In fact, he seems to

40. The most important parts of this polemic have just been published in
Italy by Lisa Foa who, in her preface, reconstructs the political background
and also mentions Kamenev's prophetic speech to the Fourteenth Congress
of the Communist Party of the Soviet Union. See: *L'accumulazione socialista*,
Editori Riuniti, 1969.
41. Che's speeches and writings on trade unionism and related problems
can be found in Laura Gonzáles, *Ernesto Che Guevara, Scritti, discorsi e*

have misunderstood a crucial problem in the history of the workers' movement, namely the need and the right of workers to decide things for themselves, to determine their own fate under all circumstances. Revolutionaries certainly do not approve of the kind of narrow trade-union mentality that holds sway in certain labor organizations, but what they set out to do is to inspire these organizations with a greater political consciousness, to make them more socialistic, not to suppress them. It was only during the Stalinist period in the U.S.S.R. that the leading group, the Communist Party, tried to consolidate its own power by reducing the trade unions to mere pawns, a sort of sub-bureaucracy charged with supervising the implementation of plans decreed from on high.

In Cuba, despite the Mujalist corruption that was rife among trade-union leaders during the years preceding the Revolution, the Confederation of Workers (CTC) could boast a more revolutionary tradition. We need only recall the clashes of the '30s or the sugar strikes of 1955. The trade unions, now fully won over to the Castroist cause, were therefore in an excellent position to make a major contribution to harmonious but dialectical relations between the rank and file and the leaders of the new regime. But in order to play that role they would have had to preserve their autonomy and the right to express and defend the claims of their members. Che preferred to take shelter behind two myths, both of them imported from the U.S.S.R. First, after the Revolution, the workers should have no interests other than the acceleration of production in accordance with the overall economic plan; and second, the revolutionary leaders know best how to interpret the thoughts and needs of the working class, from which they themselves have sprung.

In so doing, Che had adopted, perhaps unwittingly, an old Stalinist slogan—*kadry ryeshayut vsyo* (the cadres decide everything). What is astonishing is that, even after his period of

---

diari di guerriglia (Turin, Einaudi, 1969). See particularly pp. 491–523 and p. 561.

330

enthusiasm for the U.S.S.R. was over, he never re-examined his premises and that he never wondered about the real causes of the crisis in Eastern Europe. Che apparently believed that the Russians had no other choice but between bad reforms and true socialism. In fact, as long as the political system remained unchanged, the only alternatives were technocratic reforms or the status quo, which in Russia meant increasing economic stagnation accompanied by complete political apathy. There was yet another possibility, of course, one that Che apparently overlooked. The state might have become a kind of sorcerer's apprentice by granting greater independence to the leaders of their various enterprises who, unlike the anonymous central planners, were in direct contact with their workers. That might have unleashed a bout of genuine trade-union activity and possibly even a revival of rank-and-file political activity. And as events in Czechoslovakia were to show in 1968, once such a revival starts, it is practically impossible to contain it within trade-union limits. The entire political system comes under attack.

Che did not envisage this possibility, nor did he greatly concern himself with the social and political aspects of life in the East. However, he did feel deeply anxious about the economic future of the U.S.S.R. Though he mentioned this to no one except his closest colleagues in the Ministry of Industry, he was fully convinced that the reforms were merely a prelude to the restoration of a type of market economy based on competition and thus not greatly different from that prevailing in capitalist countries. He paid his last visit to Moscow in the winter of 1964 and took the opportunity to broach the matter with Soviet economists and students. But aware of his quick temper, he studiously avoided public confrontations, preferring frank discussions with a handful of young people whom he invited to the Cuban embassy. Some of his guests asked him whether he did not think that making industrial enterprises responsible for their own solvency meant forcing them to adapt themselves to consumer demand and so to become more efficient. Che replied, "I cannot tell how this system would work in the

Guerrillas in Power

U.S.S.R., but as for the system itself I know it only too well. It was used in Cuba before the Revolution and is widespread in the foremost capitalist countries. And frankly, what you tell me about the profitability of enterprises under a market economy is neither a novelty nor a great secret. Capitalism knows all about this type of profitability. There is just one snag in this system; when all enterprises vie for profits, you have unrestrained competition followed by anarchy and finally by an irresolvable crisis. Then there is nothing to do but to make a revolution and thereby restore reason to society."[42]

Such an assessment ought to have gone hand in hand with a political analysis since the reforms were not the brainchildren of a handful of young economists, unfamiliar with Marxism, but were favored by the Kremlin, the *destacados marxistas rusos,* as Blas Roca had so fondly called them. How was this possible fifty years after the October Revolution, in an industrialized country, one that had firmly laid down the material foundations of socialism? Che did not provide the answer. He did not repeat as his own either the Trotskyist thesis of the bureaucratic degeneration of the U.S.S.R. during Stalinism or the Maoist thesis of the seizure of power in the Kremlin after the Twentieth Congress of the Communist Party by a new revisionist and bourgeois class. He simply expressed his bitter hostility to the current choices of the Soviet Union—to her desire to compromise with the United States, to her economic reforms and theorizations about the need for material incentives and the persistence of social inequalities under socialism, and finally to her attitude toward more militant Communists and the Third World.

But he never allowed himself to fall into the trap of sectarianism or purely negative criticisms. All his writings evince an extraordinary faith in the ability of men to overcome their

42. When Che visited Moscow in 1964, the Soviet debate on the reforms was not yet over. His young visitors must therefore have been referring to a project that involved much greater autonomy than the one finally adopted in September 1965. It is likely, however, that Che would have objected even to the watered down version.

prejudices and their selfishness, a firm belief in mutual aid and the possibility of building a more just world. He said he suffered deeply "each time that an injustice is committed anywhere in the world,"[43] and this came across in, and gave a breadth to, all his writings, revealing a human warmth that put him head and shoulders above the cold calculators in Eastern Europe. He may not have been the greatest Marxist theorist, but even when he spoke of the most highly technical problems, it was impossible not to be moved by his passionate desire to fight for the liberation of all the exploited and humble of this earth, and by his vision of a free and fraternal society. Even more than in the debate on incentives, Che's idealism could be felt tangibly in his last public lecture, in Algiers, where he made a fervent appeal to the U.S.S.R. and to the rich socialist countries to abandon their selfish practices of international trading—practices no better than those of Western capitalist exporters—and to come to the aid of the Third World and their poorer comrades. This is what he said:

"How can one describe as mutual benefit the sale, at world market prices, of raw materials produced with infinite suffering in the Third World, and the purchase, at world market prices, of machines produced in the great automated factories of today? If we make this kind of comparison, then we are forced to conclude that the [rich] socialist countries are, to some extent, accomplices in the crime of imperialist exploitation. One might argue that the volume of trade with underdeveloped countries represents an insignificant percentage of the foreign trade of socialist countries. That is absolutely true, but does not in any way alter the immoral character of this type of exchange.

43. In his reply to María Rosario Guevara, of Casablanca, who had asked for his family history to establish whether they were related, Che said, "I don't think you and I are very closely related, but if you are capable of trembling with indignation each time that an injustice is committed anywhere in the world, we are comrades, and that is more important." See *Reminiscences of the Cuban Revolutionary War* (New York, Grove Press, 1969) .

Guerrillas in Power

The socialist countries have a moral duty to end their tacit complicity with the exploiting countries of the West."[44]

But Che did not content himself with asking the Eastern bloc to do just a little better than its Western rivals, to be just a little more generous. He declared quite openly that, in his view, the development of countries on the path of liberation must be paid for by the established socialist countries. "We are saying this without the least intention of blackmailing anyone and certainly not for effect, but simply because it is our deep conviction. There can be no socialism without a transformation of consciousness leading to a growth of fraternal feeling, not only among socialist societies themselves or societies moving into socialism, but also internationally, toward all people suffering from imperialist oppression."

This moving appeal, which had little chance of being heard in the U.S.S.R., revealed the quintessence of Castroist thought. Fidel did not personally participate in the economic debate, but is said to have underwritten Che's thesis from the very start. More pragmatic and more diplomatic than his Minister of Industry, he was apparently anxious to keep doctrinal differences with the Soviet Union from erupting too violently, consoling himself that Cuba could follow her own road to socialism regardless of reformist tendencies within the Soviet camp. It was only when disagreement with orthodox Communists on the subject of Latin American guerrilla warfare and coexistence in general could no longer be ignored that he threw the entire weight of his authority openly behind the Guevarist "heresy." His speech of September 28, 1966, was already full of recriminations against those who had "nothing but pesos in their heads," and thereafter he did not bother to hide his preference for moral incentives.[45] During my tour of Cuba, I found quotations from Che and Fidel plastered on the same posters and insisting on the same priorities —support for the Latin American guerrilla fighters and the creation of socialist man in Cuba.

44. This speech has been referred to on p. 227.
45. See Fidel Castro's speech of September 28, 1966, in *Granma*.

"A Cuban heresy?"

Our traveling companions mentioned it all with great pride, explaining that their revolution was not afraid of the very grave risks involved in upholding internationalist principles, come what may. One had only to turn on the car radio to find that these risks were not exaggerated. A flood of anti-Communist propaganda, broadcast from powerful stations in Florida, assailed one's ears at all times. The enemy from the North continued to threaten the island, accusing it of "hooligan" behavior in Latin America—apparently the "gorillas" in power and the U.S. Marines had a monopoly on good manners on that continent—and promising Cubans the moon and the stars, all the benefits of the greatest consumer society in the world, if only they chased the Castroist criminals out of Havana.

"We have no means of jamming these broadcasts," Serguera told us. "But then the only people to pay any attention to them are the *gusanos*,[46] reactionaries who are getting ready to leave our country. What we are doing is making sure of the quality and variety of our own programs, so that no decent Cuban will be tempted away by the choice fare Florida offers between successive propaganda bulletins. It leaves us with a bill no other socialist country has had to pay, and, remember, we are infinitely poorer than our enemies in the North or our rich friends in Europe."

This may serve as an illustration of some of the difficulties involved in trying to build socialism ninety miles from the shores of the United States. Our friends went on to stress the fact that this proximity rendered Cuba much more vulnerable than China, despite the constant threat American escalation in Vietnam posed to the latter. Cuba, they believed, deserved even greater credit than China for championing viewpoints unostentatiously, which estranged her from her Soviet allies. "Our people realize many things without our having to spell them out. They know what is right in international politics and what are the fundamental problems of socialism. When you speak to

46. *Gusano*—literally an earthworm; the Castroist name for counterrevolutionaries.

335

simple people, you will see that they are well informed even about the Sino-Soviet dispute, on which subject we prefer to publish nothing, and that they can distinguish between good revolutionaries and bad."

My companions did not disguise the fact that in Cuba, too, there were problems and contradictions. The country was passing through a difficult economic period and supplies were beginning to dry up. The reason we avoided restaurants was simply that they served nothing or next to nothing. In the village bars en route it was idle to hope for a cool drink, let alone a cup of coffee. There were no market stalls either, which struck us as highly surprising since private small holdings and farms still supplied more than half the country's produce. But we were told that small peasants, just like state farms, have to sell everything through the official channels.

Hardly had we arrived in Santiago, when "our" Cubans disappeared. Serguera said in a confidential whisper that Armando Acosta, one of the few *comandantes* to have sprung from the old PSP, had just been replaced, and that they had to elect a new Party chief for Oriente province. Our international team meanwhile made for San Pedrito where we took up quarters in one of the new blocks of apartments that had been temporarily allocated to foreign visitors before being turned over to their permanent tenants. Since we were among the first arrivals, we could enjoy the Carnival longer than most. It all started a few days before July 26 and we were told that it was one of the most popular festivals in all Latin America. The reader will remember that Fidel Castro had chosen this day to attack the Moncada Barracks in 1953 because the whole population was busy singing and dancing in the streets.

Santiago is without doubt the most torrid city in Cuba. Its narrow streets hold the heat like a furnace. Cafés with air conditioning are much rarer than in Havana, and there is never a breath of wind. I cannot for the life of me imagine what demon was responsible for holding the Carnival here, in midsummer, at a time when you can hardly breathe even at night. But the ardor of the Cubans seemed in no way checked. From nightfall on everyone was dancing in every part of the town, and quite particularly in La Trocha, a long street that was nightly transformed into a sort of permanent ballroom. Blacks were particularly dominant in the province of Oriente, and they helped to make this Carnival a festival of Afro-Cuban song. The rum, now reserved for export, did not flow in buckets, but beer was all that was needed anyway. Toward dawn, the dancers formed up for a final procession and walked down La Trocha to the devilish rhythm of the conga, improvising couplets as they went along. This was the climax.

Except for Rio de Janeiro, this is the only such carnival to survive. It is truly an unforgettable experience, but one that the foreign visitor does not necessarily wish to repeat night after night. Semprun and I asked Serguera to show us some of the other sights during the two days before the great political event of Fidel Castro's speech on July 26. He was kind enough to organize a lightning tour of the *Granma* landing site, close to the Playa Colorado, of the Agrotechnical Institute near Manzanillo,[47] and of Nicaro, one of the two largest nickel plants in Cuba. Its location and external aspect made it look like a scene from an Eisenstein film. It was a red landscape studded with huge palms with a monumental factory shrouded in metallic dust; in short, a giant Putilov works transplanted from Russia into the tropics.

Once the first surprise had worn off, the Party secretary and various trade-union officials took us into the factory and treated us to a homily on the Cuban nickel industry. They spoke with justified pride; in this field, the Revolution has truly worked miracles. Not only had Cubans proved their ability to run Nicaro (and Moa which is completely automated), but they were even manufacturing their own spare parts and had in-

47. We inspected the Institute cursorily because we arrived late in the evening, exhausted by our pilgrimage to the Playa Colorado. The Institute is, however, a highly impressive place. It trains some twenty thousand agricultural technicians, including adults, and runs a gigantic experimental farm.

troduced various improvements to step up production.[48] Nicl
earns Cuba a great deal of foreign exchange; it will, sooner
later, form the backbone of an up-to-date industry capable
exporting large quantities of stainless steel.

Having learned all this, we were invited to a discussion
social problems in the local trade-union office. Did the work
participate in management and control, we wondered? We
there any forms of collective life? Our guides were surprised a
embarrassed by these questions. They delivered the tradition
sort of lecture on the socialist nature of the nationaliz
industries, all of which had been running like clockwork ev
since the capitalist exploiter had been chased out, which was
that apparently mattered to the overjoyed workers. Sempr
and I had heard this story far too often in Eastern Euro
not to be disagreeably surprised. These trade-union leaders we
no older than our traveling companions, and yet the two d
not seem to speak the same language. In Nicaro we hea
hackneyed phrases that would not have been amiss in the mou
of a Czechoslovak official during the Novotny era.

We came to the problem of wages. The differences struck us
being enormous. Engineers earned up to seventeen hundr
pesos a month while the average worker took home no more th
one hundred pesos. Seeing our obvious astonishment, the tra
union officials went on to explain that engineers were few a
far between and that they had to be paid a great deal becau
they did essential work. In any case they were being pa
historical wages; i.e., wages agreed on before the Revolutio
However, newly trained engineers were no longer paid at th
rate. They earned from three hundred to four hundred pesos

48. In 1957 Nicaro produced a record 20,180 metric tons. After t
Revolution this figure dropped to 14,521 tons in 1960 and to 14,222 in 19
Then there was a spectacular upsurge: 14,460 tons in 1964; 18,300 tons
1965; 19,653 tons in 1966. Our guides added that the figure would once aga
rise well above the 20,000 ton mark in 1967.

49. As far as I could gather, the average salary of an engineer w
1,200 pesos, or twelve times that of a worker. The factory employed so
3,200 workers and 60 engineers.

"A Cuban heresy?"

Did the workers have no wage claims or other industrial demands? "How could they when they all know they are working for the people? They are utterly content." What useful part did the trade unions play, in that case? "They inspire the masses to work even harder and so contribute to the progress of the Revolution."

And that was that. Just to test them we asked what they thought of the Sino-Soviet conflict. "Ah, you had best put that sort of question to our comrades on the Central Committee. We don't bother our heads with such things. And you, too, would do much better if you had a look at the new houses and furnished apartments we are providing for our workers." We went, admired, and then left on the jam-packed road to Santiago. When we tackled Papito Serguera, Chucho Montané, and the rest, they simply insisted that the views we had heard at Nicaro were completely unrepresentative of Cuban opinion, and promised to take us to meetings with more politically advanced workers. And that was that again.

It was not at all surprising that the road to Santiago was so crowded. Half of Cuba seemed intent on spending the night in the city. Columns of trucks and cars, filled with young and old people, peasants and schoolchildren, were all slowly converging on the capital of Oriente to hear Fidel speak. I had seen a similar migration on the eve of May Day, 1961, but now I had the clear impression that Cuba's transport pool must have greatly increased since then. The square leading to San Pedrito, a district which had been readied to hold a crowd of several hundreds of thousands, was black with people when we reached the special platform for the invited guests about two o'clock in the afternoon. Fidel did not start his speech until six o'clock; he and the other Cuban leaders had been listening to the baseball match between Cuba and the United States, part of the Pan-American games in Canada. The assembled multitude found this a perfectly good reason for being kept waiting, especially since Cuba won the match.

It was that evening that Fidel told the enthusiastic crowd

339

that Cuba now stood alone. *Cuba está sola.* He did not accuse
the socialist camp of abandoning his country in so many words,
but no one failed to observe that he did not once pay the usual
tribute to the Soviet Union. He spoke of simple things, in a
familiar matter-of-fact tone, almost mockingly criticizing mistakes in Cuba, frankly admitting the persistence of many
everyday annoyances. But he did all this merely as a prelude
to a rousing call for a more intense effort of socialist transformation and for greater vigilance against profiteers who
behaved as if the Revolution had been made for their particular
benefit. "The most difficult thing is not the capture of Moncada,
but to carry the Revolution through after victory," he declared.
And he hinted that if it were to succeed, Cuba would have to
find a new form of socialism.

Next he turned to American imperialism, to its barbarous
assault on heroic Vietnam, of the increasing threat it posed to
Cuba's future. But abroad no less than at home all that was
needed was perseverance and courage. *De l'audace, et encore
de l'audace et toujours de l'audace.* And looking at this vast,
cheering crowd, with its revolutionary slogans and banners, with
its bearded tribunes, few could have had any doubt about their
determination to answer the Castroist call. Gigantic portraits
of Che Guevara dominated the square and an ocean of streamers
proclaimed the gist of his message. Conspicuous by their absence
on the platform were Communist notables from Eastern Europe
or Latin America, or any of those who during the July 26th
celebrations of 1961 had pleaded so passionately that Cuba
turn herself into a second Bulgaria. The Revolution had come
a long way during the past six years. In this Year of Heroic
Vietnam, Cuba was determined to speed up the creation of
hombres nuevos at home, to give maximum support to Vietnam
abroad, and above all to demonstrate its solidarity with Ernesto
Che Guevara, in the great battle he was waging somewhere in
Latin America. Cuba might be *sola,* but she was clearly not
lacking in Guevarist determination this July 26, 1967.

340

"A Cuban heresy?"

A lesson in the Sierra Cristal

The foreign guests at the July 26th celebrations had little time to meditate on Fidel Castro's speech. There were two thousand of us, all due to leave for Gran Tierra at dawn for the official opening of a new village, followed by a meeting with the leader of the Cuban Revolution. We had no idea just where or what Gran Tierra was supposed to be. All we had been told was that it was a plateau in the extreme southeast of the island, near Baracoa where the first Spanish colonizers had landed centuries ago. For the rest, our shepherd and guide, Carlos Franqui, told us nothing, though he did hint that the drive was likely to prove rather uncomfortable.

That was an understatement if there ever was one. We started out at 3 A.M. and reached our destination at 5 P.M., covered with red dust, aching all over, and completely worn out. After following the main road to Baracoa, we had suddenly swung into mountain tracks that had never before been churned up by a procession like ours. Most of us were in bad humor or too tired to admire the new houses and school complex that were about to be inaugurated in this neglected region. Only Michel Leiris and Marguerite Duras, as always bubbling over with optimism and vitality, declared that they had had a most enjoyable ride.

Hardly had we recovered, and taken a good shower, when we were invited to a play, a speech by Fidel, and a rustic meal to be crowned by a discussion between Fidel and the European contingent. I do not remember anything about the play staged by Lisandro Otero, who was fresh as the morning because he had just arrived by helicopter, and his National Council for Culture; but I do recall Fidel's speech. "No doubt you think we are a little mad to have brought you here and to have made things so uncomfortable for you," he began. "But you see, we wanted to show you that Cuba is more than just Santiago or Havana, that it is also this desolate stretch of country, a stretch few foreigners have ever seen and that we ourselves hardly know." The

341

Guerrillas in Power

intellectuals applauded; suddenly every one of us was wide awake and grateful to Fidel for this chance of seeing "the other Cuba." The rest of the speech was devoted to the ever-present underdevelopment, a sore that only revolution could heal. Castro spoke of the good will of the FAO experts and of their inability to change anything in the Third World, where hunger and economic backwardness were the direct results of neo-colonial exploitation.

After dinner, which was served under the stars by a staff that had obviously come from Havana, I took what I intended to be a brief nap in one of the new housing estates that, once again, stood waiting for their permanent tenants. But I was so tired that I slept right through the discussion with Fidel. I woke up only when my companions returned, all of them enchanted by their personal encounter with Castro. I rushed into the big village square, then completely deserted, hoping against hope that I might yet catch a glimpse of the Cuban leader. Luckily the Cuban ambassador to Paris, M. Castellanos, was also taking the air. He seemed to be looking for someone, and that someone happened to be me.

At one end of the village, stretched across the steps of a small house, Fidel was eating oranges. He rose, an enormous silhouette in the semidarkness and, by way of a greeting, offered me a fruit. We sat down on the stone steps, in all simplicity and some discomfort, and he began to speak to me in a low voice, as if he were afraid of waking the village. Yes, it was true, he had read my book and wanted to discuss it. The day's drive had not tired him in the least and the late hour—it was now well past 2 A.M.—apparently did not daunt him. Author's pride helped cure my own fatigue and we talked amicably for at least half an hour.

Suddenly his voice rose: "Listen to me. The Chinese may be doing interesting experiments, but we are trying to go much farther than they have. Money remains at the core of their social program, even though its sights are set on equality, while the Russians deliberately encourage differences in income. We

342

intend to get rid of the whole money myth, rather than tamper with it. We want to abolish money altogether." For a moment, I was completely dumbfounded. Then, collecting my wits, I ventured to remark that I had noticed large wage differentials in Nicaro so that money had not seemingly lost its appeal even in Cuba. But Fidel was not in the least put out. "You simply cannot imagine the glaring inequality that used to exist in our country before 1959. We have already done away with many privileges and inequalities, and our aim is to get rid of the rest. But we are not prepared to level down by cutting high wages. Instead we try to create the kind of social atmosphere in which no man works just for money, in which the very idea of personal enrichment has lost its appeal. Education, social security, electricity, water, telephone, and sports are already free. We supply our workers with houses and furnished rooms without charge. In 1970, we propose to abolish all rents. And we shall continue along this path until one day—nearer than you may think—food and clothing will also be supplied *gratis* by the state.

A soldier brought us Cuban grapes, the first to be grown here. We paused, and afraid that this might be my one and only chance of talking with Castro, I decided to ask for his views on other topics, although I found the present one most absorbing. I now asked him about Russia and the situation in the Middle East. In last night's speech he had clearly disapproved of the cease-fire. Castro, though very critical of the Soviet Union, apparently did not object to her stand in the Arab-Israeli conflict. The Egyptians, the Syrians, and the Jordanians ought to remember the time-hallowed saying—help yourself and heaven will help you. The Russians could not possibly be expected to fight other people's battles, but if the Arabs had continued the war, the U.S.S.R. would simply have had to come to their aid. "Just look at Vietnam," he said in conclusion.

I asked him what he thought of Kosygin, whom, by all accounts, he had received so coldly a few weeks back. To my surprise, he told me that he found the new Soviet prime minister much more sympathetic than Khrushchev. "That man really had no principles," he added. Then, turning to Latin America, he said he felt highly optimistic. The guerrilla movement was making excellent progress, particularly in Bolivia and Colombia.

Dawn was breaking and still we had not finished. Suddenly Fidel said, "I am not at all happy about this rambling conversation, but if traveling in a jeep does not bother you, please join me on a tour of the Sierra Cristal. We shall make for Pinares de Mayari, a great new model farm, and on the way we can chat at our leisure." After the truck ride, a jeep held no terrors for me, and I jumped at this chance. My only fear was that I might be late again if I returned to bed, but Castro assured me I should not be forgotten.

There were some thirty of us who left Gran Tierra with Fidel the next morning at about ten o'clock. He drove the first jeep himself because, according to some, he was the only one to know exactly where we were going; according to others, because he hated dust in his face. By his side sat Guillermo García, the first peasant to join the guerrilla movement in the Sierra Maestra and now a leading member of the Political Bureau and the new provincial leader of Oriente. We took turns in the back seat; in the morning, the "Anglo-Saxons"—Stokely Carmichael and Julius Lester; in the afternoon, Ambassador Castellanos and myself.

Leading Castroist officials followed in other jeeps. This was my chance to catch a close glimpse of a great many people I had only read about in books. One of these was Major Faustino Pérez, the former head of the Llano, which was the urban section of the July 26th Movement. Pérez had organized the controversial strike of April 1958, had helped Fidel to build up his nationwide underground movement, and had sailed with him on *Granma*. They call him *el médico* and today he is a member of the Central Committee of the Cuban Communist Party and the minister of hydroelectric works. He surprised me by his youthful simplicity, his frank open face, his imperturbable bedside manner. He was truly the model of "the quiet man," a type found in all resistance movements. Looking at him, no one would have suspected that he was responsible for many of the bombs that shook Havana between the winter of 1957 and the summer of 1958. We spoke about this between two stops as if we were old comrades. The mere fact that I was Fidel's guest was enough of a testimonial.

Then there was Castro's close friend, Celia Sánchez. She had organized the *Granma* supporting operation and had been one of the few women to fight in the Sierra. Celia was completely at ease with her old companions and joined them on all their trips across the mountains and plains of Cuba, proving each time that the weaker sex is not necessarily the less Spartan. A minister now, she continued to do her routine work during our drive. Twice a day, an army helicopter would land close by with urgent messages to be dealt with on the spot by her or the rest of the ministerial team in our expedition.

And there was no lack of ministers among us. There was Ramiro Valdés, the redoubtable Minister of the Interior, a historical figure if there ever was one, Jorge Risquet, Minister of Labor, and a host of lesser lights in the Castroist Pantheon. Unfortunately I had little chance of talking to any of them, for when I was not in Fidel's jeep, I sat beside my protector, Papito Serguera, or else joined Faustino Pérez.

In the villages we passed, no one seemed in the least surprised at our sudden arrival. Fidel spoke to the people as one intimately familiar with all their special problems, and it seemed quite obvious that he had been there shortly before. "Fidel," a peasant woman shouted, running up to the jeep. "You promised us water and the well has come, it's true, but the electricity still doesn't come up all the way, and so our pump doesn't work. Just look where the wires stop, more than a kilometer away. ¡Mira al kilómetro!" "And are you incapable of bringing it up yourselves?" Fidel shouted back. "Isn't there a Party member in your village? Have you no women's association?" And a long wrangle began. "You see," Fidel told me as we were leaving. "We are a tiny country. This has a lot of drawbacks but it also has one great advantage; we can get to know one another." He was delighted to let me see on what friendly terms he was with ordinary men and women everywhere.

We passed through Guantánamo and had barely reached the Sierra Cristal when a tropical thunderstorm hit us. In no time at all, the road was a sea of mud. The first jeep managed to get through, and the second just barely, but the others were completely bogged down. We took counsel in the torrential rain. A young man in uniform, nicknamed Chomi, jumped into the first jeep and took off at great speed while two majors went in search of oxen to pull us out. The rescue operation was performed with speed and efficiency. Chomi returned just as quickly. Not far from us he had discovered a disused building site where we could spend the night. I wondered what our efficient Chomi did when he was not engaged in reconnaissance work. "Don't you know?" Papito Serguera asked me with obvious surprise. "He is the rector of Havana University. His real name is Miyar; he is an excellent *médico* and used to work in these parts."

When we arrived at the site, hot coffee was waiting for us, and people were rushing about everywhere. Soon afterward a rustic meal was served and, miraculously, the electric lights went on. All of us ate with great relish, and no one seemed to have the least wish to retire. The majors, most of them veterans of the Second Front, were in excellent humor, delighted at this unexpected fresh chance of roughing it on the ground. They clearly felt much more at ease here than in their ministerial offices. Fidel himself told me that he was not all that fond of Havana, that he had the soul of a peasant and liked to live with nature—if only to change it, he added with a smile.

Next morning, breakfast was cooked by soldiers who had rushed to our aid. Immediately afterward, Fidel led me to a map of Cuba pinned to the wall, and amid general silence, delivered a magisterial lecture on Cuban agriculture. He showed me what areas were cultivated before the Revolution; cane sugar accounted for more than 50 per cent and pasture for most of the rest. Coffee, tobacco, rice, and cotton were grown on a very

346

small scale. Many fields used to lay fallow. After the Revolution, the first job had been to diversify agriculture on the existing farmlands. The result had been disappointing; sugar production had dropped, and part of the livestock had to be sacrificed. At present cane sugar production had climbed back to its old place and had probably spread to new fields. All in all, sugar now covered more than one and a half million hectares, and in 1970 Cuba would be able to produce ten million tons of sugar per year, almost double the old average.

Beyond that, ranches were now being irrigated and treated with fertilizer and so, for the first time, afforded good grazing for quality cattle. "We had to start from scratch and ignored the advice of all those international experts who told us to grow maize as cattle food. Maize takes up a lot of room and is not an economic proposition on our island. As you know, we have always had a large number of cattle, but our cows have never been good milkers. Even now milk is still being rationed. But we have set up more than two thousand artificial insemination centers. Soon we shall have three thousand and then everything will begin to change for the better. We have a new breed of cows; you have no doubt seen some of our F-1s. Because of them, we hope to produce four million tons of milk per day in 1970. By 1975 we ought to have passed the thirty million mark. Just think of it, thirty million tons of milk per day in a country that will have just over nine million inhabitants! You can see, there is nothing utopian about our plan to hand out free milk to everybody. And thanks to our F-1s, we shall also have very large quantities of meat for export."

There followed an account of developments in the citrus industry. The Isle of Pines alone could outproduce Israel and all the North African countries put together. On top of that, two hundred and fifty thousand hectares would be set aside for coffee, 220,000 hectares for rice, 120,000 hectares for cereal crops, 100,000 hectares for other fruit, 65,000 hectares for cotton, and 65,000 hectares for tobacco. Modern ranches and timber plantations would take up a further 5,000,000 hectares. With this plan,

Cuba would become the world's leading sugar exporter, the second greatest coffee exporter, and an important supplier of meat, citrus, and other fruit. After 1970, Cuba would export an annual $1,600,000,000 worth of produce after reserving 60 per cent of her output for her own market. "Just think of that," Fidel said before he sat down.

I wondered about the outlets for this fantastic crop. Agricultural products are notoriously difficult to dispose of abroad. "But no," Castro replied. "We have no worries on that score because we are not just sellers like the rest. We don't want to amass gold and dollars like so many Latin American plutocrats; we shall be only too happy to take goods in exchange. We are the ideal partner not only for socialist countries but also for Western Europe. It is not by chance that the volume of our trade with France and England keeps increasing all the time. They even give us credit, which shows that they must have complete confidence in our solvency."

"Agreed," I said. "But aren't you afraid that the Russians, say, might one day refuse to buy your sugar, with the result that you would be forced to throw vast quantities on the open market and thus cause a terrific drop in world sugar prices?" "We have no fears on that score either. There is no reason why the Russians should not buy Cuban sugar when consumption in the U.S.S.R. is a mere third of what it is in Western countries and when their own sugar used to sell for three times the price of ours.[50] Of course, political factors may come in, but so far the Russians have never resorted to economic blackmail. Nor would they find it comfortable to join the American blockade of our island."

Next we discussed the internal problems posed by such vast increases in agricultural production. "You are deliberately opt-

50. When I checked these figures in Paris, I found that Fidel had been mistaken: sugar consumption in the U.S.S.R. was 37 kg. per inhabitant in 1967, as against 32 kg. in France, and 33 kg. in Germany. On the other hand, sugar consumption in Britain (50 kg.) and in Sweden (44 kg.) was higher than in the U.S.S.R.

ing for extensive agriculture at a time when you already seem to be short of manpower and are forced, each year, to mobilize the people during the sugar harvest." Fidel seemed surprised at this objection. It obviously showed that all intellectuals think in abstract ways. He pointed this out without the least bitterness. He was simply trying to make me look at things that were obviously staring me in the face. "We are about to create a socialist form of agriculture, a type of farming unknown anywhere else in the world. We have hundreds of thousands of young people anxious to take their place in the fields wherever they may be needed and regardless of sordid commercial calculations. We are training tens of thousands of agricultural engineers and are determined to equip them with the best available tools, including cane-cutting machines which we have not yet given up hope of obtaining. We will turn this nation into a nation of technicians, second to none. Why then talk of a lack of manpower or suggest that we are incapable of tending our fields?"

Everyone was full of admiration. Many of those present seemed to be discovering truths they had never even suspected. Doubtless that was a superficial impression on my part, but none of the Cubans present uttered a single word, not even when it came to the technical details. Fidel was now anxious to supplement his lecture with practical demonstrations and shepherded us from one village to the next, stopping at a host of road works and experimental fields, and talking to all manner of people. The Sierra Cristal was still a singularly underdeveloped stretch of country. In some respects it looked even more barren than Gran Tierra where they were increasingly growing mountain coffee.

It was hot again, and when we stopped for light refreshments in a largish village, there was no drink to be had at any price. And so we made for the hospital, where the staff was kind enough to serve us large glasses of delectable lemonade. I had noticed that most of the peasants in the Sierra Cristal were tending their own fields, and I asked whether there was not

349

perhaps a contradiction between the widespread survival o
private property and the ban on private sales of produce. I
all the peasants were indeed filled with collectivist and dis
interested ideas, why then did they fail to form family co
operatives? If, however, like all peasants, they remained attached
to their land and to profit, was it not obvious that they would
prefer to sell their crops directly rather than through the
official channels?

Again Fidel thought my arguments intellectual and abstract;
he had obviously failed to explain the real meaning of mini-
plans in the private sector. He made good this omission during
dinner, starting off in a rather rhetorical way. "You don't seem
to like individual peasants, do you? Perhaps you think I ought
to have mowed them down?" Then, reassured of my kindly
nature, he sailed straight into the problem. A vast private
sector in agriculture did not, admittedly, make planning any
easier, but experience had shown that cooperatives were no
solution. "What precisely is a cooperative? It is a conglomeration
of individual farms. If just one or two families are hostile to us,
they can quickly sway all the rest. Cooperative ownership is not
socialist ownership. It may even help perpetuate private property, though in a new guise, and become an obstacle to genuine
socialization. I don't get the impression that this problem has
been solved in the other socialist countries."

After a pause, he continued. "We do not favor cooperatives,
but we are also anxious not to antagonize our small peasants
by behaving like sectarians and by continually talking about the
class struggle in the villages. We prefer to make arrangements
that are advantageous to all parties. We supply our peasants
with fertilizers, equipment, and even with volunteers to work
their lands. In exchange, we only ask them to grow what crops
the country most needs. As you see, this allows us to modernize
agriculture while keeping our peasants happy by buying all their
crops at guaranteed prices."

So far so good, I thought, but surely this system is bound
to favor the peasantry at the expense of the rest of the

population. And, in fact, although the Second Agricultural Reform of 1963 served to reduce the size of private holdings, individual peasants were left in possession of farms of up to 47 hectares (116 acres) and by European standards, at least, that was a fair amount.[51] But I put my question as diplomatically as I knew how, trying not to appear too antipeasant. Fidel admitted that, for the time being at least, the peasants must be allowed to earn money. Oh, no large fortunes were involved, and the purchase of new land was forbidden by law so that the overall social structure of the country was not seriously dislocated. And there were two main reasons why in the long run his policy was bound to lead to the liquidation of private farming.

"A socialist agriculture is being developed so quickly that the law of supply and demand must eventually work to the detriment of the private sector. For example, almost 80 per cent of our coffee is currently being produced by private cultivators, and we have agreed to pay them high prices to encourage productivity. But we are about to grow hundreds of thousands of hectares of coffee on state farms. In 1968, we intend to plant a type of coffee that likes the shade of fruit trees and will, so to speak, become a subproduct of fruit farming. For that purpose we have set aside some 75 square miles of land, just outside Havana. Tomorrow it will be the small peasants who will be forced to follow our lead if they want to sell their coffee. And it will be the same with other crops. At the same time, we shall guarantee everyone the benefits of the kind of distributive economy I have described. Do you really think that tomorrow the sons of our peasants will still want to run the risk of farming outmoded family holdings?"

His next argument was even more remarkable. Massive state

51. The first agricultural reform in May 1959 did not affect farms of less than 30 caballerías (i.e., about 400 hectares). But on October 4, 1963, the Second Agricultural Reform reduced to 5 caballerías the size of individual farms. Since that date, 70 per cent of all land in Cuba is managed by the state.

M*

intervention by way of the mini-plans was bound to transform the old relationship between the peasant and his land. "He may remain a landowner and pocket his profits, but he no longer makes any real choices. He can see an army of enthusiastic young people, working hard for the sake of the country and living communally by his side. All this is bound to change the entire character of rural life." Fidel advised me to see all this for myself at San Andrés, near Havana, where a pilot plan had recently been started.

During our drive we met a host of young people returning to their villages from the Santiago celebrations. Fidel often stopped to pick up hitchhikers—thus obliging Guillermo García to cling to the outside of our jeep—and subjected them to a friendly form of cross-examination. All were the children of small peasants and all hoped to become agronomists after studying in one of the special colleges. Fidel insisted, "Are you sure you don't want to work your own land? Wouldn't you like to grow what you like and sell it where you like?" The young never wavered. "No, not at all; private business doesn't interest us in the least." Fidel glanced around to see if I had taken it all in.

The first questions he invariably put to peasants were: "How many children do you have in school? Where do they study?" Most had a son at boarding school or a girl in a special college, often in a distant province. Their answers verified the explosive growth of education in Cuba. Under the old regime the children of these poor peasants could never even have dreamed of big schools and degrees. However, this was not the real purpose of Fidel's demonstration. He was, in fact, preparing the way for his final argument.

On our travels we had usually come across small peasants. Occasionally we would see someone on horseback, evidently more prosperous than the rest, as if to illustrate by his very presence that inequalities persisted in the Cuban countryside. I was told that some of them were not even covered by the mini-plans, and if they spoke to Fidel with respect, they clearly did not bear him any great love. Castro was fully aware of that,

352

but immediately told me that most of the sons of these rich peasants were studying at politically advanced institutes in the towns. "Just leave it to them, they will carry the Communist virus into their homes. They will infect entire villages with it." And he repeated that family farming in Cuba was absolutely doomed. It would collapse under the joint impact of social and material progress and the growing political consciousness of the young.

At long last, we arrived at Pinares de Mayari, the great plateau dominating the mining districts of Nicaro and Moa. According to Fidel, it was a region that was destined to become a major industrial center within a few years and would give employment to some 250 thousand workers. But Pinares had not been designed only as a market garden for this future Pittsburgh of Cuba. Here twenty-five thousand hectares of citrus, vegetables, and timber were tended by seven thousand young volunteers, most of them girls. They were fed, housed, and clothed at the state's expense, and their wages were not dependent on their output. True, each one was expected to work to a norm, but that was merely for purposes of rationalizing the overall plan, not for wielding a whip over them. Pinares was therefore a model experiment on the social no less than the agricultural plane.

Fidel liked the place tremendously, especially since he had been born in this region and had helped create this gigantic estate from nothing. As an adolescent he had loved riding on horseback across this plateau, savoring its sweet air and perfect climate. The experts had confirmed his impression. Pinares de Mayari is the ideal place for growing crops that do not like too much humidity or tropical heat. Large irrigation works have been set up, and the Academy of Sciences has added a fine research station to look into the full potential of the soil. It was in one of the Academy's chalets that we made a long stop and feasted on mangoes and gigantic watermelons.

The man in charge of Pinares de Mayari, Señor Ruiz, thirty years old and in olive-green, told me that the youngsters were full of communal ideas and so keen on the work that they had devised a most unorthodox form of punishment. Slackers were not allowed to work for a day or two and had to spend all their time on the beach. This type of ostracism had apparently proved extremely effective, but when I asked whether the community itself ordered such sanctions, Señor Ruiz told me that the final decision was taken by the head of the labor brigades, often after consultations with him. To my great surprise Fidel did not seem to know anything about this pedagogical innovation, but instead of commenting on it, he now preferred to dwell on the differences between the old generation and the new. "Those who grew up under the old regime have been stamped by the ideals and values of a commercial civilization. We used to live in the shadow of the United States and were contaminated by them. We were poor, of course, but don't forget that in America, the poor, too, behave like mini-capitalists. And Cuba was no exception. But for the past eight years we have been making a small cultural revolution of our own, aimed at eliminating every last vestige of the old mentality. And it is with the young that we are succeeding best. It is they who will see our socialist projects through. We have put them in charge of vast experimental tracts; the Isle of Pines, once famous for its penitentiary, is now an island of youth, and, believe me, it will be the first truly Communist island in the world."

Did this mean that some parts of Cuba would enter the age of abundance before the rest? Not at all. According to Castro, society never progresses in a straight line. In Cuba, as in all underdeveloped countries, society was still far too heterogeneous for the appearance of a uniform political consciousness. "Reformists," Fidel explained, "used to point their fingers at the most backward of our people and declare that it was impossible to change this illiterate mass overnight. That was their excuse for doing nothing at all—a scientific excuse if you like. True revolutionaries refuse to accept this opportunistic premise; they do not despise the people, no matter how illiterate they may be, and experience has shown that they have good reason to trust the people. But revolutionaries must set them an example. And

354

what else was the Sierra Maestra if not an oasis and model of revolution? And, he added, Communist oases would have to be established all over Cuba, each acting as a kind of locomotive that would pull the backward out of their rut sooner or later. Under present conditions, such oases could only be formed by young people living communally and being fed, housed, and clothed by the state. "What possible importance could such people attach to money?" Castro asked, as if to emphasize that his economic ideas were anything but utopian.

By then we had reached Holguin, our last stop. After a farewell dinner, Carmichael, Lester, and I were supposed to take the plane back to Havana. Castro intended to continue his tour for a few more days in order to devote some time to his Cuban companions whom he had rather neglected for our sakes. Needless to say, we had not spoken only of Cuba's agriculture, but had also referred to Russia and China, to Communist movements elsewhere, and to the struggle in Latin America. We had spoken of Che, of his Algiers lecture, and his attack on socialist trading practices with the Third World. Fidel had grown less diplomatic as he got to know us better; he no longer bothered to disguise his apprehensions about the Eastern bloc. At times, I even gained the impression that he felt he was running a sort of race against the clock while trying to build a buffer against possible conflicts with Moscow, or an intensified U.S. blockade. True, he did not believe that Cuba could live forever in splendid isolation, but to listen to him one might have thought that, in two years' time at the latest, Cuba would have enough agricultural reserves to survive a prolonged siege.

Fidel had no wish to provoke the Russians. Hence it was agreed that I would not report any remarks that the highly sensitive Russians might consider offensive. He also expressed the hope that I would not enlarge upon the Cuban dispute with China in 1966, or upon the reservations he had expressed about their cultural revolution. To avoid any misunderstanding, we decided to meet again before my departure, so that I might show him, if not the definitive form, at least the essential sections of my report. Some of our discussions, particularly those we had

Guerrillas in Power

had at Holguin, had been recorded by Chomi Miyar for my benefit. But I have never been able to lay my hands on those seventeen reels, and during my last fifteen days in Havana, I had no time to write down long notes about our tour while everything was still fresh in my memory. I felt instead that I ought to spend as much time as I could at the Latin American Solidarity Congress which had just opened in Havana. Moreover, the news of my familiarity with Castro had spread like wildfire, with the result that all doors had been thrown open to me, and I wanted to take full advantage of this to meet other Cuban leaders who might help me fill in the details in the bold picture Fidel had painted. Foremost among these men was Osvaldo Dorticós, president of Cuba.

Communism, not just socialism

"What in your view, is the goal of our revolution?" This question sounded odd in a country where the word revolution has been on everyone's lips for nine years. It was, however, what I was asked by the Cuban president, Dr. Osvaldo Dorticós Torrado, in a tone of voice that made it clear he had thought a great deal about the answer.

An advocate, and a senior member of Fidel's team, though he was only forty-eight, Dr. Dorticós, with his glasses, small moustache, and grave voice, looked the typical academic. He is clearly not a Castroist like the rest; he never fired a gun in the Sierra Maestra, is beardless, and does not wear olive-green. The militiaman's uniform he occasionally wears at mass demonstrations looks quite out of character on him. With his quick mind and quiet manner, he is obviously an intellectual and, indeed, his intimacy with socialist writings, from Marx to Gramsci, is extremely impressive. As leader of the civil resistance movement in his native Cienfuegos, President Dorticós did not meet Fidel Castro until after Batista's fall. Then he joined the government and was made responsible for the drafting of all the revolutionary laws. Six months later, when President Urrutia clashed with the Castroists and thus forced them to appoint a new head of state, Dorticós was chosen unanimously and has remained at his post ever since.

His high office and reserve seem to make Dr. Dorticós less approachable than the young guerrilla leaders, though he is a man of very great simplicity. He first received me on August 12, 1967, in the impressive setting of the new presidential palace with all the usual protocol. But after we had been talking for a short while, he proposed to pay me a visit in the Hotel Nacional after dinner. He proved extremely punctual, and we kept talking until well into the night. And Osvaldo Dorticós was indeed worth listening to. Not only was he the head of state and a member of the Political Bureau of the Cuban Communist Party, but he was also the chairman of *Juceplan* (*Junta Central de Planificación*), the country's chief economic planning authority. In a sense, he has taken Che Guevara's place as the top theorist of Cuban Communism. This alone puts enormous responsibilities on his shoulders. His approach is quite different from Castro's. Thus while Fidel likes tangible facts and uses isolated achievements to justify his dreams of a great future, Dorticós is more inclined to stress the general processes governing particular developments.

For our first meeting, I had prepared a list of questions about Cuba's economic situation. During my tour with Castro, I had been fed a host of data from memory. Figures had been thrown at me with such speed that I could never have remembered them, and even if I had, there were no published statistics against which I could have checked them. Moreover, we had chiefly spoken about agriculture and had skimmed over the broader economic issues and long-term priorities. Despite the giddy round, I had nevertheless discerned that the picture was not all light and happiness. I hoped that Dorticós might help me to put things in broader perspective, and it was in answer to this request that he had fired his question about the goal of the revolution at me.

"We are about to build Communism," he said, when he noticed my astonishment. "The aim of our revolution is not to build a socialist state, but to move with minimum delay toward

357

full Communism. It is pure illusion to think that Communism will come automatically, just as soon as all the conditions are right. We have to prepare for it here and now, by partial transformations of our society." This was said with some gravity, slowly, as if he was inviting me to reflect on it; it also sounded like an echo of Fidel's views on the evils of money and the need for Communist oases. Dorticós admitted that his remarks ran completely counter to Soviet doctrine, which held that the socialist phase was bound to be very long, and that it was sheer folly to imagine that Communism could be achieved before a host of economic and social conditions had been satisfied.

"Well, yes," Dorticós declared. "We have our little heresy," and he granted that there were fundamental differences between the Cuban view and the Russian. He added that he was trying to produce a more satisfactory elaboration of his theory for the very purpose of meeting possible Soviet criticisms. Without wishing to be dogmatic, he felt that his view represented the correct interpretation of Marxist thought.

Marx and Engels had outlined a future society in which man would be able to throw off his economic shackles through the collective ownership of the means of production. Only then would he cease to be an alienated and repressed creature, and could he begin to develop his whole personality. Progress during the capitalist phase had laid the foundations for the eventual emergence of a new society, at the same time creating the social class best suited to serve as its midwife. That class was the proletariat. But, according to Marx, the step from economic exploitation to freedom could not be taken on the day of the revolution; it called for a brief transitional phase, and this was precisely what he had meant by socialism. During that phase, the state, now enjoying the support of the immense majority of the people, would establish the dictatorship of the proletariat in order to frustrate attempts to restore the old order. It would also speed the social accumulation of wealth needed for the emergence of a Communist society in which all classes or class distinctions will have disappeared.

358

"A Cuban heresy?"

Unfortunately, no revolutions had come to the most highly industrialized capitalist countries. They had occurred in parts of the world in which capitalism was too weak to defend itself, especially in semifeudal Russia and in economically backward China. This was a development Marx and his contemporaries had never foreseen. Russia under Stalin tried to obtain the accelerated rate of production which alone could provide the material foundations of socialism, by the creation of a monolithic state. In a sense Russia had succeeded; after all the U.S.S.R. had become one of the world's leading economic powers. But the further it developed along this path the less interested it became in the transition to Communism. Thus, even when the future of the U.S.S.R. was once again thrown open for discussion under Khrushchev, the debate focused exclusively on future prosperity, as if the abundance of consumer goods was the only problem to solve.

Ever since 1962, President Dorticós went on to remark sardonically, Russians have spoken less and less of Communism and more and more about profits and the restoration of market mechanisms. He repeated Che's criticism and added that some theorists in the East were trying to use the new reforms as a justification of perpetual socialism. For them, socialism was not simply a halfway house between capitalism and Communism, as Marx and Lenin had claimed, but a third system with its own mode of production and thereby capable of permanent survival.

How could the Russians possibly justify this bizarre conclusion? Could they still invoke capitalist encirclement? Did one really have to wait for the age of abundance before changing social relationships in the U.S.S.R.? That is precisely what the Russians claimed, and to men like Che or Dorticós their arguments sounded so unconvincing that they began to suspect the Soviet Union had turned into just another oppressive society which though socialist in name had completely failed to live up to the great promises of its revolutionary founders.

True, the Cubans kept these thoughts to themselves and,

Dorticós added, many of them even refused to admit the possibility that Communism might forever elude the land of the October Revolution. But the Eastern bloc had obviously lost interest in revolutionary ideas; genuine Marxists were now asking themselves new questions about the real nature of Soviet society. For a revolutionary country like Cuba, this was no mere academic problem. Cuba must in no way be caught in the same trap. It was for that very reason that Cubans had gone back to the fundamental teachings of Marx in the hope of discovering possible remedies and solutions.

Dorticós' explanation may seem odd since Marx had never anticipated the revolutionary transformation of an underdeveloped country, and therefore could not possibly serve as a guide to Cuba, which lacked big industries and a class-conscious proletariat that alone could usher in radically new productive relationships. According to Dorticós, however, to pose the problem in these terms was a sign of dogmatism; it showed attachment to the letter and not to the spirit of Marxism. Marx had fixed the final goal and explained the nature of the future society; the rest was simply a matter of discovering the right means. And the more appropriate the means the more quickly the ends would be attained.

This was the real meaning of the "Cuban heresy" and the basis of Castro's every economic, social, and educational decision. The chief asset of the Cuban Revolution was an overwhelming popular wish for a change, or else the old regime could never have been overthrown, no matter how class-conscious the revolutionary vanguard. Now this asset had to be put to work, and the best way of doing that was to keep widening the circle of people who wanted to adopt a Communist style of life. It was essential to explain to all citizens the meaning of the profound social changes that had already been introduced. The good example of a few, a radical form of political education, and skillfully applied economic changes, however small, were bound to create a general climate of opinion compatible with Communism.

"A Cuban heresy?"

We returned to the problem of material incentives. "From each according to his abilities, to each according to his needs," is a basic principle of Communism. A truly Communist society, Dorticós contended, will have put an end to all forms of exploitation, to commercial relationships of every kind. But as Fidel put it, a country like Cuba, which suffered from "a heritage of misery heaped up over the centuries," was much too poor to meet all its needs. It could not dispense with money, or level incomes, or eliminate private greed by decree. But it could and must realize that all these things are so many blots on the revolutionary escutcheon, shameful vestiges of the past. Men must be shown that life is more than a rat race to the top, must become suffused with fraternal ideas and must be given a larger vista of humanity. In the short run, this policy might well prove less economically efficient than one based on monetary rewards, and therefore more in line with old habits. But would it not be far better to make a costly long-term investment than run the risk of perpetuating the evil social values implicit in the old mentality?

Clearly it would be dangerous to impose norms of conduct that strained existing attitudes too far. The only result would be economic paralysis. What was needed was a fair balance between the desirable and the possible, always giving priority to the first. In Cuba many people clearly would be working for money and pursuing selfish aims for a long time to come. But the number of more fully integrated people seeking fulfillment in the great social liberation movement would keep growing steadily until, one day, they would be the overwhelming majority. In the long run, therefore, their work and devotion would be the determining factors in the economic transformation of Cuban society at large.

President Dorticós went on to tell me that Che's plans for a centralized economy and an industrial sector that did not have to balance its books were beginning to be put into practice. This did not simply reflect an administrative preference for simpler calculations, but was the immediate application of true Com-

361

munist standards. Cuba used to be the kingdom of bookkeepers; if they were given their way they would enmesh the whole country in a web of financial red-tape that would forever mask the real situation. On the other hand, because of the excellent system of telecommunication and the technological progress, Cuba was wonderfully placed to make quick computations of her material resources and of the man-hours needed to fulfill a particular task. As any Marxist plan must be built on labor value and not on exchange value, Cuba's industries could be treated as a single factory in which movements of goods do not call for banking operations, and accounting can be reduced to the keeping of minimum records for statistical purposes.

This system, I was told, was being used already; needless to say it could not be applied in a day, and clearly it involved grave risks and unknown dangers. But the first results were highly promising and, according to President Dorticós, as soon as enough practical data had been gathered, Cuba would be able to formulate a new and precise theory of management. He thought preliminary results might well be published early in 1968, but during a subsequent interview he declared that this project had had to be postponed for several months.

As I listened to President Dorticós, I was struck by the similarities between his thesis and that of the Maoists, though he never once referred to them by name. Mao Tse-tung had been the first to raise the problem of the transition to Communism, in 1957, just as he had been the first to express his anxiety, and for good reason, about the state of Soviet society. True, his analysis differed in many ways from the Cubans'. Mao Tse-tung did not question Stalinism or suggest that the choices made in the Stalinist era were responsible for the subsequent developments he deplored; yet the Chinese had gone much further than anyone else in questioning the Soviet model. They had attacked the very pillar on which the social system of the Soviet type was built; i.e., "the perpetuation of the socialist phase," and with it the bureaucratic structure and the persistence of political privilege, Mao seemed determined to avoid these

362

pitfalls in China, no matter what the cost. To his mind, Soviet institutions merely served to keep a new aristocracy in power and to mask its despotic rule. This at least, seemed the obvious meaning of the cultural revolution, and even if one could not predict its long-term results, it represented an unprecedented rupture with the traditional methods of the "dictatorship of the proletariat" of the Stalinist type.

Neither Fidel nor Dorticós wanted to broach this subject. They felt, in any case, that Cuba was in a completely different position. Here, postrevolutionary society was still young and highly flexible and so had no need of Communist re-education. What Cuba had to do was to encourage the emergence among the masses of the "new man," to promote the kind of life and mentality that alone could help Cuba to take the great step from socialism to Communism. Naturally Cuba, too, could not afford to slacken its assaults on bureaucracy, and as President Dorticós told me, this was precisely why Fidel was determined to combine his prime minister's job with that of leader of the opposition. Fidel kept in direct touch with the people and whenever he turned up in Havana he made a point of badgering all official bureaucrats who had caused unnecessary suffering or delays. He expected other officials to adopt the same methods, to head the opposition in their own departments.

It was on this somewhat droll note that our brief review of the Cuban "heresy" ended. What President Dorticós had told me had all been perfectly logical, except perhaps for his last remarks. The claim that Cuban society was elastic seemed to be contradicted by the existence of a chain of command based on the Castroist military tradition and, I thought, on certain dogmas imported from the East during the period of pro-Soviet intoxication. Nor was I altogether convinced that all the ministers and officials were heads of the opposition keeping bureaucracy in check. Who, I wondered, was there to keep an eye on the ministers themselves? An old English proverb states that the proof of the pudding is in the eating. Now the practice of Cuban socialism fills one with certain apprehensions, even those of us who are ready to grant it every possible extenuating circumstance; after all, the Cuban Revolution has had to stand up to an enormous degree of subversion from the United States. We shall return to this point, but first let us hear what Cubans think of the revolutionary struggles in Latin America, why they treat these struggles as their most important contribution to international Communism in 1967.

The "fundamental path" of OLAS and Fidel's great hope

"The history of Cuba is the history of all Latin America." Beneath portraits of Simón Bolívar, Máximo Gómez, José Martí, and Ernesto Che Guevara, this slogan fluttered in luminous letters on an immense banner, directly opposite my room in the Hotel Nacional. It set the tone for the conference of the Latin American Solidarity Organization (OLAS), which opened on August 4, 1967, in Havana, and which, according to the Cubans, was to mark a milestone in the history of their continent.

The slogan and portraits watched over me all the time I was reading a highly absorbing 159-page pamphlet, the *Informe de la delegación cubana a la primera conferencia de la OLAS* (the report of the Cuban delegation to the first OLAS Conference), which I had been handed together with fourteen volumes of documents on the social, economic, and political background of the Latin American States that had sent delegates to this crucial meeting.[52] Curiously, this Cuban report, although

---

52. Before the previous OLAS meeting, in January 1966, Havana had played host to the Tricontinental Conference, which as its name suggests was attended by delegates from all parts of the Third World. This conference decided to set up OSPAAAL (the Organization of Solidarity between the Peoples of Africa, Asia, and Latin America), with headquarters in Havana, and to publish a bimonthly paper called *Tricontinental* (banned in France in June 1968). The Cubans, however, had grave misgivings about the long-term usefulness of OSPAAAL and accordingly abandoned the idea of convening a second conference. They preferred to concentrate on the problems besetting Latin America and attached incomparably greater importance to the OLAS Conference.

364

written by Castroists, did not begin with an account of the famous machete charge or any other great event in Cuban history, but with the battle of Carabobo on June 24, 1821, which had resulted in the birth of Venezuela and Colombia. At one point in this battle, Bolívar's troops had begun to flinch under the concentrated onslaught of the massed Spaniards, and when one Pedro Camejo, covered with blood, had run up to Bolívar and sprung to attention, the Liberator had said contemptuously: "I can see that all the cowards are taking to their heels." "No, General, I have come to take my leave of you because I am dying," said Camejo and dropped dead at Bolívar's feet. He was an illiterate black soldier, and after victory Bolívar declared him a national hero.

What precisely was this story supposed to prove? Why did the Cubans put it at the head of their report? A little reflection told me that it was a pointed lesson in Guevarism. The authors were recalling, first of all, that in South America at least, the fight against the colonial oppressor was the business of all the people. Simón Bolívar had set out to liberate not only Colombia, but an entire continent. In this fight he had enjoyed the support of all social classes, including such illiterates as Pedro Camejo. The other great strategists of South American independence had had the same broad vision of the struggle for freedom because, like Bolívar, they all realized that Latin America was one, and would not prosper until it was fully united. According to the authors of the *Informe,* this fundamental fact had never changed, not even as the result of "balkanization" in the latter part of the nineteenth century. The fourteen-volume report was meant to prove with UN and UNESCO statistics and even with documents culled from the most unexpected North American sources that Latin America had always had a homogeneous political, economic, and social climate. The alleged divisions or antagonisms between the various Latin American nations were nothing when compared with this great unifying factor.

The Cubans did not deny the existence of national peculiarities on their continent, but they were more concerned to dwell on the common condition of all, if only to stress the fact that the Revolution, too, was indivisible. The same disease calls for the same cure; and, since the subcontinent as a whole was sick of North American exploitation, the revolutionary medicine had to be applied on the continental scale. To Cubans, the OLAS Conference was the first step in that direction. Their views were rooted in the great internationalist tradition of the labor movement, and yet were called heretical and opposed by all orthodox Communists. In fact, ever since the Twentieth Congress of the Soviet Communist Party in 1956, all Communist parties had adopted the view that each national situation calls for its own solution, that each party must take the path to socialism that best suits local conditions. The Chinese, although critical of the Twentieth Congress, had agreed with the orthodox on this particular point; they declared their formal opposition to the regionalization, as they called it, of Communist strategy. The Cuban proposals were therefore neither academic nor innocuous. For if the Communist parties of Latin America said yes to Havana, they would automatically have to say no both to Moscow and to Peking.

To convince them, Cuba could not simply harken back to the glorious battle of Carabobo; luckily, the Castroists were not short of other arguments either. To begin with, their own history had been typical of that of America as a whole. In the North no less than the South, European settlers had wiped out most of the indigenous population. The only difference had been that those who had chosen the North were for the most part pioneers, filled with the ideas of an up-and-coming bourgeoisie, while the South had the even greater misfortune of being colonized by backward and anachronistic aristocrats, scions of dying empires. Early in the nineteenth century, Simón Bolívar, the Liberator, had declared that the business of the North was to pillage the South. José Martí had gone even further: he had warned all Latin Americans against the monster from the North. Meanwhile the economic, and sometimes the military, violation of free societies south of the Rio Grande had continued unchecked, striking all with the same plague, spread by a single exploiter feeding on their impoverishment. And this, the Cubans argued, had caused a unique situation, one that, despite the Twentieth Congress, called for a united reply.

The ground having been thus prepared, the Cubans produced their second heretical proposition: Latin America lacked the basis for a peaceful transition to socialism. They made not the slightest adverse allusion to the historical Twentieth Congress, but even the most naïve reader was bound to conclude that the Cuban thesis was a clear disavowal of the chief theoretical and strategic discoveries of Nikita Khrushchev and his successors. In fact, at the Twentieth Congress, the Soviet leaders had declared that the new balance of power between the East and the West had so radically changed the nature of the international class struggle that some countries now had every chance of introducing socialism by peaceful means, without violent revolution. Needless to say, they were careful not to stipulate what countries they had in mind, but most Communist parties seemed to believe that the remarks applied to them. Latin American Communists, although numerically weak, were no exception to this rule. The Cubans now proposed to shake them out of this illusion and to reconvert them to the gospel of violent revolution.

To crown it all, they did not even call for a return to the Leninist doctrine popular before the Twentieth Congress. Lenin, it will be remembered, had bitterly attacked the Populist and Social-Revolutionary parties for contending that, since czarist Russia had a vast peasant majority, the peasants alone were capable of leading the struggle against oppression. Lenin, following Karl Marx, told them that the only truly revolutionary class was the proletariat; hence, only a proletarian revolution could be a truly socialist one. He invited his opponents to take a more dialectical view of historical developments. Capitalism, and with it the proletariat, was growing apace everywhere, including Russia, while the importance of the peasantry was decreasing no less remorselessly. It followed that the revolution must be led by the working class. Even the Chinese later defined their revolution in these terms despite the fact that three quarters of their troops were poor peasants.

The Cubans, on the other hand, were contending, without

367

saying so explicitly, that Latin America could have no proletarian revolution for the simple and excellent reason that the proletariat was far too weak and was unlikely to increase its proportional strength without a massive new dose of industrialization. Now the Americans were making quite sure that this would never happen. They kept draining off the natural resources of the subcontinent, investing little or nothing in other sectors of the economy, and flooding the whole of Latin America with their manufactured goods. Their capital stayed abroad only just long enough to get the process of exploitation going. This helped to bring ruin to the countryside but not to create new industries. It also drove a mass of dispossessed peasants into the urban centers, increasing the army of the subproletariat, the semiemployed who eked out an existence, although no one knew how. At the same time, the local bourgeoisie, handicapped from the start of the race between the North and South, had become so tied to the U.S. purse strings that they had long since abandoned any hope of ever playing an independent economic and political role. It followed that the exploited of all classes of Latin American society had but a single enemy—Yankee imperialism.

The authors of the *Informe* continued that in these conditions it was idle to expect the proletariat to liberate the subcontinent from its frightful misery. Nor was it reasonable to speak, as the Communist parties did, of a progressive alliance between this virtually nonexistent proletariat and a national bourgeoisie that had nothing national about it. "Let us be done with the phantom they call the national bourgeoisie. In Latin America that bourgeoisie has never existed nor can it possibly exist in the future." The Cuban attitude was as clear as it was peremptory.

The Castroist argument was cogent enough, in all truth. The thesis of the peaceful transition to socialism could be applied, at best, to highly industrialized democratic countries, in which the workers, as the majority of the electorate, had the chance to change the established order through the ballot box. This applied at least in theory, though it had never happened in

368

practice. But who could seriously believe in that possibility in Latin America? To whom could the Communists' peaceful and parliamentary hopes be attached in countries where elections were rarely, if ever, held, and where violent military putsches succeeded one another with monotonous regularity? When it comes to the history of wars of liberation in the nineteenth century, people can argue at length. But the history of the democratic movement in Latin America leaves no room for argument; it is a long tale of complete failure. Without dwelling on the past, on, say, the unhappy fate of Jacobo Arbenz in Guatemala, we need only look at the Latin American scene after the formation of the Alliance for Progress in 1961. The aim of this great Alliance was to foster democracy and modern ideas on the subcontinent, but its only practical results were a series of military *golpes*, of which Arturo Frondizi in the Argentine and João Goulart in Brazil were the most conspicuous victims.[53] In these circumstances, it was odd, to say the least, that Communist parties should have persisted in clinging to hopes that even President Kennedy's advisers, the sponsors of the Alliance for Progress, had long since abandoned.

The Castroists, for one, were determined to dispel these democratic pipe dreams. They, who had so often been accused of pragmatism, now used Marxist doctrines to beat the Communists, those self-confessed apostles of Marxism-Leninism, at their own game. They explained that the national bourgeoisies had failed to give the political lead, not because they were traitors, but simply because they lacked the necessary material basis. In Latin America, the great North American companies had monopolized all the real wealth and local businessmen had nothing but left-overs. No modern bourgeoisie with reformist aspirations could flourish in these circumstances, which encouraged nothing so much as the general degeneration of political mores. Ought

53. In April 1962, Argentine officers overthrew the legal government of President Arturo Frondizi, and two years later, in April 1964, Brazilian officers did the same to President João Goulart.

369

one to fold one's arms before so unhappy a spectacle? The Cuban
answer was no. Latin American degradation had produced an
enormous army of dispossessed who must form the basis of the
revolutionary movement. And revolution was clearly needed on
a continent where the very idea of a peaceful transition toward
socialism had become laughable.

But how was the revolution to be ushered in? Was it enough
for the Communist parties simply to change their old line? The
authors of the *Informe* did not even bother to make that suggestion; they quite obviously felt that Communists could no
longer play a decisive part in any Latin American revolution.
And so they simply invited them to join in an insurrection led
by others. Their attitude reflected Castro's old conviction about
the role of the PSP. Even if the Communists had wanted to lead
the armed struggle in Cuba, few people would have followed
them. Of course no one wanted to speak the harsh truth, least
of all now that all freedom fighters were ostensibly part of the
same family, fighting under one flag. And so the Castroists
simply asserted that the Latin American revolution could not
follow the old Leninist scheme, i.e., could not start from the
towns where the proletariat was strongest and where the Communist parties had their deepest roots. Instead, guerrilla centers
would have to be set up in the remote mountains, from where
the revolt would spread to all classes of society, thus gradually
breaking the stranglehold of the army and state. In other words,
all Latin America was invited to emulate the Cuban example.

But who would play the part of Fidel Castro and set up
these centers of insurgence? Who would lead the revolutionary
movement? Who would coordinate its plans with those of the
resistance movement in the towns? The Cuban *Informe* kept
discreetly silent on these delicate matters. It contented itself
with declaring that the guerillas must lead themselves, that they
must not be allowed to become military appendages of any
political organization in the towns. From this, the more percep-
tive reader of the *Informe* could not but conclude that in the
first place, the Castroists were reluctant, for diplomatic reasons,

to insist that the Communists change their doctrine and strategy and, moreover, agree to play second fiddle to the guerrillas. Secondly, they might conclude that Fidel's part would be played by Che Guevara who had already set up a guerrilla center somewhere in Latin America and would take charge of the overall military and political campaign.

Having thus lit up the stage and allocated the parts in Latin America, the authors of the *Informe* ended their document with a solemn declaration: they were not merely well-intentioned advisers to, but active participants in, the Latin American revolution. The status quo on the subcontinent was as unacceptable to those who were already liberated from the yoke of imperialism as it was to all those who still felt its full weight. Cuba refused to have any truck with the dishonest slogan of peaceful coexistence, and felt that it had a duty and a right to come to the aid of its struggling comrades, just as the Yankees came to the aid of their "gorillas." This final declaration set a seal on the entire Castroist "heresy."

The Cuban *Informe* was remarkable for its lucidity, its cutting style, and the boldness of its message. In short, it redounded in all the qualities that are so lacking in run-of-the-mill Communist texts. But it was above all a masterpiece of political innuendo. Not once did it mention the U.S.S.R. or China by name, even while assailing every one of Moscow's and Peking's pet theories. Not once did it call a spade a spade, or attack the Latin American Communist parties. And yet, no one was left in any doubt about its heretical and offensive nature. Aside from questions of doctrine, it was common knowledge that relations between the Castroists and the Latin American Communists had become strained. Some claimed that this had started immediately after the missile crisis, when Fidel was outraged by the pro-Khrushchev attitude of local Communist parties. According to others, things had not gone wrong until 1964, when all the Latin American parties met in Havana. It was on that occasion that Fidel delivered an astonishing autobiographical address, which he allowed me to read but which has not yet been published. It was movingly simple and honest and delved deeply into his own past, his trials and tribulations, during and after the Sierra Maestra epoch. He explained how his strategic concepts and his political consciousness had grown in battle; that experience and contact with reality alone were the true schools of revolutionary science. Without setting himself up as an example or challenging the theoretical knowledge of his Latin American comrades, he asked them to open a new, Latin American front. Only in that way would they find the answers to the problems they had vainly tried to solve for decades.

His speech obviously contradicted the doctrine of peaceful co-existence, the illusion that the Third World could attain socialism by the usual democratic paths. He asked no one to disown Moscow; on the contrary, he reaffirmed his hope that the struggle within the Communist movement would soon cease. But each country must be allowed to devise its strategy without fear of recriminations or excommunications. Unfortunately, the Soviet leaders had taken public issue with the so-called Maoist heresy, and he sincerely deplored their methods of arguing with the Chinese.

Fidel had asked Che Guevara to take the text of this speech to Peking, in the firm hope that his militant stand and call for unity might be seen to fit him for the role of mediator.[54] We know that this did not happen, and I had the clear impression that the Maoists were amazed at, rather than convinced by, the public confession of the Cuban leader. I was also unable to discover the precise reaction of Latin American Communist parties,

54. Ernesto Che Guevara arrived in Peking on February 3, 1965 and, according to Cuban sources, was given the cold shoulder. He was unable to meet Mao Tse-tung or any other leading Communist. But Chinese reserve had nothing to do with Castro's speech; it was solely due to Cuba's decision to attend the Moscow Congress. The Russians had made this known to the Chinese in a letter dated November 24, 1964 (during the thaw in the great polemic), and on December 12, 1964, *Pravda* announced that the date of the preparatory meeting had been fixed for March 1, 1965. Now since Che was not in Peking in his private capacity, but as head of an official delegation, he had to bear the brunt of Chinese anger at what they considered the unholy alliance between Havana and Moscow.

but I assume that their training had not specially fitted them to appreciate this type of speech.

In any case, Fidel's address failed to inspire the delegates, who adopted run-of-the-mill orthodox resolutions, let alone persuade anyone to set up guerrilla centers. On the contrary, the Communist Party of Venezuela, which had been deeply involved in armed struggle until then, suddenly decided to reverse steam. It did not do so in order to spite Fidel, but because it doubted the chances of victory, and worse still, was losing control of its own comrades in the mountains. The Venezuelan guerrilla movement was not exclusively made up of Communists; it also included young militants of the MIR (Movement of the Revolutionary Left), of the URD (Republican Democratic Union), and even dissidents of the AD (Democratic Action, the party in power since 1958). Together they constituted an independent political force, with its own president, Fabrizio Ojeda, and its own commander in chief, the Communist Douglas Bravo. The Party, true to its monolithic conception, took a dim view of this situation: first it censured Douglas Bravo for his alleged breach of discipline, and later had him expelled.[55] At the same time it began to look favorably on a return to more peaceful and legal activities.

Fidel Castro had been alerted to these developments by his friend Fabrizio Ojeda for whom he had long had a warm regard[56] and who, a mere seventeen days after sending a special

55. The Communist Party of Venezuela began to lose interest in armed struggle toward the end of 1963, after it had vainly called for a boycott of the presidential elections that swept Señor Leoni into power. Douglas Bravo, then a member of the Political Bureau, disagreed with its attempt to make peace with the new president and, in 1965, he and other champions of continued guerrilla warfare signed the Iracara Manifesto. This led to his expulsion from the Political Bureau and from the Central Committee of the Communist Party of Venezuela. His expulsion from the Party itself came after Fidel Castro's attack on the Communist Party of Venezuela (in 1967).

56. Fabrizio Ojeda, one of the leaders of the non-Communist Left, was president of the *Junta Patriótica,* a body that overthrew the dictator Pérez Jiménez in 1958. Elected a deputy on the URD (Republican Demo-

373

message, on June 21, 1966, was murdered by the Venezuelan police. The circumstances of his arrest looked highly suspicious and suggested treachery. True, Fidel had no proof and could not make a public charge, but his fury against the Communists in Caracas mounted considerably. Thus, on March 13, 1967, a misunderstanding about a plot, approved by representatives of the Venezuelan *guerrilleros* in Havana and disapproved of by the Communist Party of Venezuela, was enough for Fidel to include a bitter tirade against the Venezuelan Communist leaders in his annual address. The Venezuelans replied without mincing their words either, but failed to reply to any of Fidel's charges. The latent conflict between the Castroists and the orthodox Communists had turned into a head-on clash.

One month after Fidel's Venezuelan speech, an explosive book appeared in Havana. It was entitled *Revolution in the Revolution?* and its author was Régis Debray. He was a young French university lecturer, who had come over to teach at the Faculty of Philosophy in Havana, and was ostensibly expressing his own views. But in Havana everybody knew that he had written his book after long private discussions with Fidel Castro, who had himself revised and corrected the proofs. The mere fact that it was given so much publicity in Cuba set an official seal on it and guaranteed it an international audience. Debray's book said quite plainly what such official documents as the *Informe* had only been able to hint at, more or less diplomatically, in the sort of code known only to the initiated. Régis Debray made it clear from the start that he would not beat around the bush;

---

cratic Union) list, he remained a member of the coalition government until 1961. He visited Cuba several times between 1960 and 1962, and struck up a great friendship with Fidel Castro. Soon afterward he resigned from his party and from Parliament and joined the guerrilla movement. He was arrested, but managed to escape from prison. On June 17 or 18, 1966, he was recaptured at Caracas, following a denunciation. After prolonged torture by the technical branch of the Judicial Police, the "special" branch, he died in prison, allegedly by his own hand. But this official version was too familiar to convince anybody. Fabrizio Ojeda was either tortured to death or shot in prison.

his main purpose was to persuade other comrades to ask the right questions and to find the answers for themselves.

What precisely did Régis Debray have to say? He explained, first of all, that all Communist parties, be they pro-Soviet, pro-Chinese or Trotskyist, had failed in Latin America for the simple reason that they had tried to impress the European or Asian ideas of revolution upon a continent where quite different conditions prevailed. He castigated all these parties for their doctrinaire attitude, their bureaucratic structure, their sectarianism, and a whole list of further errors and omissions, all enumerated in his book. Debray's conclusion was that none of these heads without a body was in any position to build a guerrilla force or to lead it from faraway urban bastions. Now the guerrilla force, according to Debray, was the nucleus of the people's army, and hence the arm of a revolutionary party in embryo: "Any guerrilla movement in Latin America that wishes to pursue the people's war to the end, by transforming itself if necessary into a regular army and beginning a war of movement and positions, must become the unchallenged political vanguard with the essential elements of its leadership being incorporated in the military command."[57] Here then was a clear answer to a question the *Informe* had only just touched upon. Régis Debray was inviting Communists of whatever trend to take their orders from the guerrilla force, and to do so without discussion.

Then, dwelling on the very harsh conditions of guerrilla life, Debray went on to stress the need for selecting physically strong and resourceful military and political leaders: "In Latin America, wherever armed struggle is the order of the day, there is a close tie between biology and ideology. However absurd or shocking this relationship may seem, it is none the less a decisive one. An elderly man, accustomed to city living, molded by other circumstances and goals will not easily adjust himself to the mountains nor, to a lesser degree, to underground activity in

57. Régis Debray, *Revolution in the Revolution?* (London, Pelican Books, 1968), p. 108.

the cities. . . . A perfect Marxist education is not at the outset an imperative condition. That an elderly man should be proven militant and possess a revolutionary training is not, alas, sufficient for coping with guerrilla existence especially in the early stages. Physical aptitude is the prerequisite for all other aptitudes. This is a minor point of limited theoretical appeal, but armed struggle appears to have a rationale of which theory knows nothing."[58] The Cuban Revolution had demonstrated the need for, and the effectiveness of, this type of selection. Fidel had entrusted political responsibility to those who had proved their tenacity in the mountains. Debray said: "It was worth the risk: Raúl Castro, Che Guevara, Camilo Cienfuegos, and scores of officers are today in the political leadership of a proletarian and peasant revolution."[59]

Régis Debray obviously knew that armed revolutionary struggle was not an invention of the *Granma* crew in 1956, but he also knew that other countries, far from delegating maximum responsibility to the physically fit, had done their utmost to keep the young well under the thumb of the old politicians. He himself quoted Mao Tse-tung's dictum that "politics direct the gun" and General Giap who, although a soldier himself, had written: "The first fundamental principle in the building of our army is the imperative necessity of placing the army under Party leadership, of constantly strengthening Party leadership. The Party is the founder, the organizer, and the educator of the army. Only its exclusive leadership can permit the army to hew to a class line, to maintain its political orientation and to fulfill its revolutionary tasks."[60] Debray thus realized that Lenin, no less than Trotsky, Ho Chi Minh, and Mao Tse-tung, believed that the political sector must invariably prevail over the military. The modern revolutionary movement must challenge this tradition, a tradition based on no sacrosanct prin-

58. *Ibid.*, pp. 101–102.
59. *Ibid.*, p. 90.
60. Giap: *Geurre du peuple, armée du peuple* (Paris, Maspero, 1965), quoted in Régis Debray, *op. cit.* p. 95.

ciple, which had arisen in situations that differed radically from those existing in Latin America. Here the guerrilla movement alone had a legitimate claim to political responsibility and political power.

How could this heresy be justified? By "the class alliance which it [the guerrilla force] can alone achieve, the alliance that will take and administer power, the alliance whose interests are those of socialism, the alliance between workers and peasants. The guerrilla army is a confirmation in action of this alliance; it is the personification of it. When the guerrilla army will seize the prerogatives of political leadership, it is responding to its class content and anticipating tomorrow's dangers. It alone can guarantee that the people's power will not be perverted after victory. If it does not assume the functions of political leadership during the course of emancipation itself, it will not be able to assume them when the war is over, and the bourgeoisie with all necessary imperialist support will surely take advantage of the situation."[61]

In support of this thesis, Régis Debray cited the conflict between the men of the Sierra and those of the plain. Had the July 26th Movement been led by the latter, the revolution would never have gone beyond the bourgeois stage, because "any man, even a comrade, who spends his life in a city is unwittingly bourgeois in comparison with a *guerrillero*. . . . The best of comrades from the capital or from abroad—even those assigned to important missions dedicated to their work—fall prey to this difference which is tantamount to objective betrayal. Many of them know it. When a guerrilla group communicates with city leadership or its representatives abroad it is dealing with "its" bourgeoisie. Even if such a bourgeoisie is needed—as an artificial lung is needed in moments of asphyxia—this difference of interests and milieu must not be lost sight of; the two worlds do not breathe the same air. Fidel Castro had this experience and did not hesitate, even at the risk of being left alone during

61. Régis Debray, *op. cit.* pp. 108–109.

Guerrillas in Power

very difficult moments, to repudiate 'his' bourgeoisie, which was given to making unprincipled alliances."[62]

Debray also tried to demonstrate that, in Latin America, there could be no question of establishing stable Red bases, as Mao had done in China, or even of waging a war on the Vietnamese model. Least of all was Latin America suited to European methods of struggle by means of strikes or mass demonstrations. True, he did not deny the need for propaganda and even affirmed that the guerrilla fighter must set up his own radio station. But, in the last resort, it was his arms that counted: "The best propaganda is a successful military action."

This very brief summary suffices to show that if Régis Debray wanted to start a controversy, he could have done no better than publish his book. Unlike the more prudent Fidel Castro, he rode roughshod over most of the accepted theories of the international labor movement and in doing so, incidentally produced a new version of the history of the Cuban Revolution.

However, by the time the OLAS Conference opened, Régis Debray was no longer in Havana. Soon after the appearance of his book he had left for Bolivia where he wanted to discuss his ideas with Che Guevara. He was arrested, tortured, and later sentenced to thirty years in prison for his criminal theory of guerrilla warfare. During that August of 1967, while the Hotel Habana Libre was playing host to revolutionaries from twenty-six Latin American countries,[63] all Cuba was filled with admira-

62. Régis Debray, *op. cit.* pp. 68–69.
63. I have been unable to discover reliable data on the precise composition of this conference. The Communist Party of Venezuela was not invited and the Communist parties of Brazil and Argentina refused to attend. The other Communist parties attended in force as did most other leftist groups, with the exception of the pro-Chinese Marxists-Leninists. The numerical strength and representation of the different delegations is, however, extremely difficult to assess, because of all the recent schisms that had helped to split the extreme Left of most Latin American countries. In Brazil, for example, there were then at least four Communist parties, while in the Argentine the largest party was said to be made up of people expelled from the official C.P. It is certain, however, that the two strongest Communist parties on the subcontinent, namely the Chilean and Uruguayan, were present at the OLAS Conference; the latter even sent its general secretary, Rodney Arismendi.

378

tion for Debray's conduct toward his jailers and everyone feared for his life.

In every conference, there are leaks and indiscretions; the OLAS Conference was no exception to this rule. Thus we learned that all resolutions had been passed unanimously, except the Cuban-sponsored one censuring the U.S.S.R. for aiding reactionary governments in Latin America, notably those in Brazil and Colombia. For the rest, the conference agreed that guerrilla struggle must be considered the fundamental path of Latin American revolution, though not necessarily the only one. The delegates also declared that the *guerrilleros* would fight under the flag of Marxism-Leninism, and that they would enjoy the active support of all revolutionaries. The thorny problem of the precise relationship between the *guerrilleros* and the politicians was not apparently resolved, or even discussed, but that was not surprising. The conference was asked to take its stand on the policies discussed in the Cuban *Informe* and not on Régis Debray's book. As we saw, the *Informe* had left the entire question open, in the expectation that an equable relationship between the *guerrilleros* and the political parties would be forged in the fire of battle. Debray's solution would never have been adopted unanimously; Latin American Communists were unlikely to commit political harakiri for the sake of a better future.

Fidel Castro summed up the message of the conference in the Chaplin Theater to a large audience of some five thousand invited guests, Party militants, and the entire diplomatic corps. Those Communist and other leaders who had participated in the OLAS deliberations sat at the presidential table, under a banner that boldly proclaimed the Second Havana Declaration: "The duty of every revolutionary is to make the revolution."

Fidel declared himself highly satisfied with the work of OLAS; in his opinion we were witnessing the birth of a vast movement which would sweep the continent in irresistible waves (*olas* is Spanish for waves). He affirmed that Cuba did not propose to found a new International; that it would not try to play the part of leader state. Cuba had simply put forward a number of new ideas and was happy to see that OLAS had adopted them

379

as their own. He pleaded that past differences be put aside as internal quarrels merely served to sap revolutionary energies. In the new movement, there would be room for everyone, and Cubans would never support one revolutionary faction against another.

After this long paean to unity, Fidel nevertheless saw fit to launch an attack on the Venezuelan Communist Party, exposing the opportunism and reformism of its leaders. He read out the highly insulting letter they had sent him in March 1967, and added that copies of it had been dropped by parachute, from Miami, by such notorious anti-Communist organizations as Alpha 66. He also accused the leaders of the Venezuelan Communist Party of plotting with Moscow and of trying to incite the U.S.S.R. to use economic reprisals against Cuba. The audience shouted its indignation with a mixture of boos and catcalls, and then rose to its feet when Fidel read his reply. At the presidential table, however, a good many officials sat on in stony silence.

This contrast became even more glaring when Fidel dealt with the question of Soviet aid to governments in Latin America hostile to Cuba. In their letter, the Venezuelans had claimed that Cuba had no grounds for complaint against the Soviet Union, since she herself maintained commercial relations with Francoist Spain and with Great Britain which, despite the decline of her empire, was still oppressing a fair number of people. Fidel was outraged at so much hypocrisy. Cuba had always upheld the principle of freedom of trade with any country; why else should it have protested so strongly against the U.S. blockade? But there was a difference between commerce and direct aid. All he objected to was that the U.S.S.R. should see fit to grant credits to countries that refused to enter into commercial relations with Cuba. He did not have time to finish his phrase; the hall, on its feet to the last man, broke into stormy applause, and heads turned toward the right, toward the Soviet ambassador seated in his balcony with the rest of the diplomatic corps. At the presidential table, too, there was prolonged applause, but I noticed that Rodney Arismendi, leader of the Communist Party of Uruguay, the most prominent of the orthodox delegates, and quite a few others, did not join in. I even had the feeling that some of them remained seated; at least they must have, unless they were as small as the Bolivian delegate, whom I could clearly see in his second row seat.

There was something highly unusual in this public demonstration of differences between fraternal delegates. Of course these differences bore on Soviet foreign policy and not on the fundamental path of the guerrilla movement, but could one really separate the two? Could one adopt the Cuban line for Latin America while embracing the Soviet doctrine of peaceful co-existence? The whole Castroist case was a direct challenge to the Twentieth Congress of the Soviet Communist Party and to the international strategy adopted by it, and Communist delegates to OLAS were sufficiently skilled in the art of deciphering official documents to have no illusions on that score. Moreover, they were all free to consult Debray's book, and that would quickly have dispelled any lingering doubts. How, in these circumstances could they possibly have voted for Cuba's "heretical" resolution and yet have hoped for Moscow's continued blessing? Indeed, the only remarkable fact to emerge from the conference was the display of courage that kept the orthodox wing impassive and defiant amid a large crowd of frenetically cheering Castroists. In the circumstances, it began to look extremely doubtful whether Latin American *guerrilleros* could continue to count on supplies and reinforcements from their comrades in the official Communist parties. More than one Cuban who realized that Che was depending, at that very moment, on the help of orthodox Communists in Bolivia, must have been filled with deep forebodings, that evening in the Chaplin Theater.

Next day we attended a farewell party in the presidential palace. Present were all those of us who had spent crowded weeks in Havana, Santiago, and Gran Tierra, and then again back in Havana at the OLAS meeting or in the corridors outside.

381

Guerrillas in Power

Fidel was in his element: he made scoffing remarks about American journalists who had remained unconvinced even after meeting the CIA saboteurs at a press conference; he shook hands with the Latin Americans murmuring words of encouragement, and embraced the Vietnamese. I had difficulty in forcing my way past men who had an infinitely greater claim on his time than myself, but I wanted to say good-bye to him. I had not spoken to him since our tour of the Sierra Cristal. He seemed surprised to hear that I was leaving on August 14, thought aloud about his timetable, then turned to Papito Serguera who was standing by my side: "Bring him to me on the 13th." Apparently he did not know where he would be that day, but according to Papito, I was not to worry on that score. Once Fidel had arranged a meeting he was sure to keep it.

Early on Sunday August 13, Papito led me to Havana airport where a special plane was warming up. We were not the only passengers. Juan Almeida and a number of officers, all of them historical figures, but whom I had not previously met, were already on board. It was only en route that I learned we were making for the Isle of Pines, and that this day was Fidel Castro's forty-first birthday.

Birthday or not, Castro was waiting for us in his jeep, as always. We had a quick breakfast in the villa where he had put up for the night, after opening a new dam, and then drove straight to an experimental farm. I was told that here, where citrus trees were now abounding, there was once nothing but boulders and stones. Not that Cuba was short of land and forced to cultivate every last inch of rock, but Castro had blown up these very stones and fertilized these very fields to show that even the earth must yield to man provided only that he treats it intelligently. "Communism is just that: man will use his creative gifts to master nature and share her fruits with his neighbor."

Then, after a long walk in the orange groves, it was time for lunch. José Llanusa, a former basketball and tennis champion, a man of impressive build, presided over our table; he is minister of education now and as such one of Fidel's closest collaborators,

382

for Fidel prizes education. He quickly brushed aside José's attempt to propose a toast. Fidel hates all such formalities. Instead, he returned to a theme he had broached during our last encounter: the importance of the subjective factor in the revolutionary process.

"Ideally, revolutions should be made when the objective and subjective conditions are perfectly balanced. Unfortunately, this happens too rarely; all we can say is that when the objective conditions are ripe but the revolutionary will is lacking, there will be no revolution. On the other hand, when the objective factors are not quite perfect, but the subjective will is there the revolution has every chance of success."

As for the OLAS Conference, he gave me to understand that he had been perplexed by some of the delegates' reticence on the subject of armed struggle. Things would be quite different if only they stopped being afraid of taking the slightest risk and stepped out of their dogmatic universe. He was even more astonished at their failure to analyze why their parties had become so many small sects quite incapable of harnessing the vast revolutionary energies of Latin America.

But was he not exaggerating the importance of the revolutionary will? Was he not oversimplifying or rather overpersonalizing what was a highly complex problem? After all, the European labor movement had produced leaders of great quality and had nevertheless failed to make a revolution.

He realized that full well. He did not question the worth of a Rosa Luxemburg, a Karl Liebknecht, or an Antonio Gramsci, and in his view there had been special reasons for their failure. He had just read Isaac Deutscher's trilogy on Trotsky and was familiar with the history of the Russian revolution. "I often wonder whether Lenin did not make a mistake in signing the peace of Brest-Litovsk," he said gravely. "Who knows what might not have happened, had the young Soviet republic taken the risk of waging a revolutionary war thus helping the Western proletariat to free itself." He spoke with the cool deliberation of a man whom the sad schisms of the Communist movement had happily bypassed, but who suddenly found himself deep in their grip because he had been brought face to face with very similar problems. Despite the existence of an enormous socialist camp, Cuba, like Russia after the revolution, was encircled by enemies, and like Russia placed her hopes in the outbreak of new revolutions, which alone could end her seclusion.

He realized that the aid he gave to the Latin American underground might unleash further American aggression against his country; indeed he foresaw that every *guerrillero* victory would increase U.S. hostility to Cuba and strengthen the hand of those hawks in Washington who considered the destruction of the Cuban revolution a prerequisite of maintaining the economic and social status quo in Latin America.

But he was prepared to run that risk, and all his comrades approved his decision because they knew their international obligations and their long-term interest. "Yes, the more I think of it, the more I realize how right Marx was when he said that there can be no real revolution until there is a world revolution. We are not stupid enough to believe that we can build a brave little Communist state in splendid isolation."

He often wondered why the Bolsheviks had not run the same risks; why they had allowed the Hungarian Communists and the German Spartakists to be crushed. I was deeply moved by his passion, but remarked that there had been at least one Russian attempt to export the revolution, and that it had ended in abysmal failure. In 1920 the Red Army had drawn up before the gates of Warsaw, and the Polish proletariat had not bid it welcome. It was essential to draw the lesson of this failure, namely that the Red Army was essentially a peasant force and as such ill-prepared to carry the flag of revolution across the European continent.

Fidel sat quite still, perhaps mulling it all over before making a reply. One of the officers profited from the silence: "The Warsaw fiasco was Stalin's fault." Fidel quickly took the cue. To him, too, Stalin was the very embodiment of evil; he assured me that even Khrushchev—no great internationalist—had reported things about Stalin that he would never have believed had they not come from the mouth of a Soviet leader.

384

"A Cuban heresy?"

"But then Khrushchev is not the most reliable of witnesses," I objected. "He was simply trying to save himself, and with him the whole Stalinist system. By blaming everything on one man, he was saved the bother of looking for the real roots of the evil." The silence that greeted my remarks told me that I had not made myself clear, and that I was being mistaken for an apologist of Stalin. So I quickly added that no one born in Poland, like myself, could have the slightest sympathy for the former Soviet leader. In 1937–38, he had exterminated the entire leadership of the Polish Communist Party and had ordered the Party itself to be expelled from the Comintern (the only case of its kind).

Fidel was appalled and took some time to recover from the shock. "But why ever did he do that? It really is monstrous." He kept repeating this phrase three or four times, raising his hands in obvious horror, overcome with indignation. Just then a tropical storm broke, and Fidel's exclamations were punctuated by thunder claps. He rose to make himself heard, his gigantic silhouette dominating this curious birthday meal.

"Very well," he said, "the Communist movement has a very long history; when one remembers its bitter past, one can't be astonished to see what it has become in some countries. But everything would have been quite different had Communists everywhere come to one another's aid, just as Cuba is trying to do. Unfortunately the imperialists seem to be the only true internationalists left. They know how to help one another and have no qualms about their counterrevolutions. For what is the war in Vietnam, if not a counterrevolutionary aggression on a world scale? Or what else is happening in Latin America, studded with American military camps, under permanent surveillance by the Pentagon and the CIA? And what do the other Communists do about it all? They content themselves with preaching peace, with singing hymns to the glory of coexistence, desperately searching their records for old and stereotyped resolutions about alliances with the national bourgeoisie. Sometimes I wonder what sort of world we are living in!" And he sat down again to finish his meal and to let us get on with ours. While

385

he had been speaking no one had taken a bite, perhaps to avoid making a noise, but more probably because everyone had been carried away by Fidel's passion.

The conversation now continued in calmer tones. "As you well know," Fidel said, "I do not wish to engage in polemics with the Chinese and I have even tried to forget all about our rice dispute of 1966. Before then, I was deeply impressed by their conduct and their high revolutionary morality, and the last thing I expected was that they would try economic blackmail on us. But all that is past history, and at present we try not to offend them. Still, it is a fact that the Chinese maintain contact with the Americans, though purely formally, at periodic meetings of their respective ambassadors. I am absolutely convinced that the Chinese ambassador does no more than press his country's legitimate claims. I do not believe for one moment that China is engaged in secret negotiations with the American imperialists. Even so, the Chinese have seen fit to maintain this channel of communication, no doubt because they think it may prove useful one day. For our part, we have no dealings with these gentlemen, nor do we want to have any. Ever again!"

He turned toward his companions as if seeking their approval. When all of them nodded agreement, he continued: "For eight years, the Americans have done all they can to destroy our revolution, to make life impossible for us. And now we keep getting messages from Washington: they will be only too happy to forget the past, to drop all their claims against us, to live with us in peace everlasting, if only we desert our Latin American comrades. These men do not grasp the first thing about revolutionary morality. They think that everything can be bought and sold for money, and they seriously believe that we shall sell our birthright for a mess of pottage. They must be out of their minds. We shall never accept peaceful coexistence on such terms. Our resources are small, for we are a small and underdeveloped country, but we shall fulfill our international obligations to the last letter and we shall never desert those who struggle for socialism in Latin America and elsewhere."

386

"A Cuban heresy?"

The meal ended on this solemn promise, loudly applauded by everyone present. The thunderstorm had now stopped, and Fidel invited me to take a brief walk. What he had said in the Sierra Cristal and again during this luncheon on the Isle of Pines made it absolutely clear that his and the Soviet positions were miles apart.

I asked if Cuba's material dependence on the U.S.S.R. did not severely hamper its freedom of expression and hence the revolutionary education of Cuban and Latin American youth. He said no, he did not have to make too many concessions, and Cuban dependence on Russia was more temporary than most people believed. "In one or two years' time we shall be able to look after ourselves; our exports will have become so diversified that we shall no longer be tied to a single market or a particular supplier. Meanwhile, our young people know what they have to do, even if we avoid an open clash with the Russians. We are not building socialism in complete silence as you may have come to think; we have our own way of explaining ourselves, and who knows but that Latin American Communists may listen to us as well."

Did he really believe that all those who had participated in the OLAS Conference would eventually take the fundamental path of the guerrilla movement? He was not dogmatic, but seemed optimistic. In his view, it did not matter whether they themselves took the path of revolution, so long as they placed no obstacles on it. "In Latin America, you see, all that is needed is a detonator; once it has gone off, the explosion will be so violent that not even armchair theorists will be able to keep out of the battle." We parted on these words. I left for Havana, he and his colleagues for a tour of the Isle of Pines, the workshop of Cuban Communism.

Che's death and the rise of controversy

October 8, 1967, was the darkest day in the history of Castroist Cuba. That day Bolivian Rangers, acting on orders from La

387

Guerrillas in Power

Paz, murdered Ernesto Che Guevara in Higueras, a godforsaken village in southeastern Bolivia. We know all about Che's last battle in the Yuro gorge; how, at the head of a tiny guerrilla band, he was surrounded, wounded, captured, and finally killed.[64] But when the news first filtered through, no one wanted to believe it. The Rangers had often claimed victory in the past only to swallow their words soon afterward. This time, they had admittedly exhibited Che's body to a group of journalists at Vallegrande, but they had whisked it away before his own father, who had flown in specially from the Argentine, had a chance to identify it. The whole world was therefore looking to Havana, hoping that Fidel might once again give the lie to the Bolivians. But when he did broadcast to the nation on October 15 it was only to tell them that "the death of Major Ernesto Guevara is a bitter certainty." He had arrived at this sad conclusion after examining photographs of the body and facsimiles of a few pages from Che's personal diary, released by the Rangers. There would be three days of national mourning, followed by a mass meeting on Revolution Square where the nation could pay its last tribute to their legendary hero.

64. Here is Castro's own account of Che Guevara's death: "Barrientos [president of Bolivia at the time of Che's death], Ovanda [Bolivian army commander in chief and leader of a successful coup in September 1969], and other top military chiefs met in La Paz and decided to assassinate Che in cold blood. . . . Major Miguel Ayoroa and Colonel Andrés Selnich, two Rangers trained by the Americans, ordered a noncommissioned officer, Mario Terán, to murder Che. Terán went in [i.e., into the schoolhouse in Higueras, where Che was being held] completely drunk, and Che, who had heard the shots that had just killed a Bolivian and a Peruvian fighter, seeing the brute hesitate, said to him firmly: "Shoot, don't be afraid." Terán left the room; and his superiors, Ayoroa and Selnich, had to repeat the order, which he finally carried out, firing his machine gun at Che from the waist down. The official tale that Che had died a few hours after combat was already in circulation; this was why his executioners gave orders not to shoot him in the chest or the head so as not to produce instantly fatal wounds. Che's agony was thus cruelly prolonged till a sergeant, who was also drunk, finally killed him with a pistol shot in the left side." See Fidel Castro's tribute in Ernesto Che Guevara: *Bolivian Diary* (London, Cape/Lorrimer, 1968), pp. 19–20.

388

"Che's death," Fidel told them on that occasion, "has struck a severe, a terrible blow to the revolutionary movement, has robbed it of its ablest and most experienced chief. But those who shout victory are shouting too soon. People who think that his death spells the end of his message, his tactics, his views on guerrilla warfare, his theses, are utterly mistaken. . . . Today, at the end of this meeting, as all of us render him homage, as all our thoughts are turned toward Che, as we look forward confidently to the future, to the final victory of the people, we all say to Che, and to all the heroes who have fought and have fallen by his side: Ever onward to victory!"[65]

Havana had never witnessed the like. In the dead of night, a solemn crowd stood stricken with grief. Who could put their feelings into words? They knew that, ever since his meeting with Fidel in Mexico, this great Argentinian had fought for their cause, had placed his immense talents unreservedly at their service, had run fantastic risks, and had gone to do battle in Bolivia for their sake. And it was not by chance that among those who fought by his side to the bitter Bolivian end were some of his old companions from the Sierra Maestra.[66]

Che's death was not only an emotional shock but also a grave political and theoretical setback for the Castroists. For even the optimistic note on which Fidel ended his tribute could not dis-

65. Text of Fidel Castro's homage as published in the French weekly edition of *Granma* (October 22, 1967).
66. In 1969, the Cubans revealed the identity of some of their compatriots who had fought by Che's side in Bolivia. These included: Captain Eliseo Reyes, called San Luis, who had fought in the Sierra Maestra when he was only seventeen and who, when he left for Bolivia, was a member of the Central Committee of the Cuban Communist Party; Major Antonio Sánchez Díaz, called Pinares, who had joined the men in the Sierra Maestra in 1957 and had also become a member of the Central Committee of the Cuban Communist Party; Captain José María Martínez Tamayo, who had joined the Second Front in Oriente in 1958, had entered the Argentinian guerrilla movement led by Jorge Ricardo Masetti, in 1963, and had gone to Bolivia in 1966 to prepare for Che's arrival; and Lieutenant Carlos Coello, also a veteran of the Sierra and Che's ordnance officer since 1959. "I feel almost as if I had lost a son," Che wrote when Coello was killed on June 26, 1967.

guise the fact that Che's disappearance meant a long delay in the final victory of the Latin American people on which Cuban revolutionaries had been counting so fervently. According to their credo, great personalities play a paramount and irreplaceable role in history. They even blamed European Marxists for not paying sufficient attention to this factor. "Can you imagine our history if Fidel had been killed in Moncada?" they had asked me in July 1967. True, defeat at Moncada had prepared the way for final victory in 1959, but then Fidel had survived to tell the tale.

The failure, temporary or otherwise, of the Bolivian guerrilla movement did, in fact, pose very serious problems for all Latin American revolutionaries. The Castroist theory of guerrilla warfare was not a tried and tested doctrine; it presented a relatively new challenge to the traditional methods of the anti-imperialist Left and had still to be proved in practice. Armed struggle had never been alien to the Latin American tradition it is true; and several guerrilla centers continued to exist in Venezuela, in Colombia, and in Guatemala. But lest the new attempts end in failure as they had in Bolivia it was most urgent to learn whatever lessons could be derived from that sad experience.[67]

For Latin American Communist parties, Che's death was the signal to a complete return to the official Moscow line. They had been afraid all along that, like the PSP, they might be faced with a *fait accompli*, that *el doctor* Che Guevara might repeat the exploits of *el doctor* Fidel Castro and make the revolution in their stead. They could, of course, have tried to seize the initiative from Castro, but armed struggle had no great appeal for them, especially as they were unwilling to deplete their

67. A special issue of *Monthly Review* (July–August 1968; Vol. 20, No.3) was devoted to Régis Debray and the Latin American revolution and to an analysis of the pros and cons of the Cuban guerrilla thesis. Though he was unable to see this issue in his prison in Camiri, Régis Debray wrote a long letter to the editors of *Monthly Review*, in which he explained the "collective nature" of his book, and answered a number of general criticisms. His letter is included in the French pocket edition of *Revolution in the Revolution?* (Paris, Maspero, 1969).

notoriously thin ranks in this sort of adventure. The result had been an amazing tightrope walk between reluctant support for the Cuban method and genuine belief in the superiority of the parliamentary path and peaceful coexistence. In most parts of Latin America, party unity had been badly shattered, and they must have been greatly relieved now that they could once again come together in rendering homage to Che's courage and spirit of sacrifice while silently burying his theories on the Latin American revolution. Only the incorrigible Argentinian Communists, long the most anti-Guevarist of all, could not refrain from blowing their own horn. Their great theorist, Ghioldi, insisted at this tragic hour, that his party had always been right.

In Europe, orthodox Communists reacted even more sharply. Writing in *Humanité,* Jacques Arnaud wondered just how Che Guevara had come to die in Bolivia and went on to insinuate that Fidel Castro must have sent him to his death: "On January 2, speaking of Che Guevara, Fidel Castro compared him to the phoenix which rises perpetually from the ashes. But could not this phoenix be put to rest somewhere for good?"[68] More circumspect, *Pravda* did not make such vulgar insinuations, but it nevertheless saw fit to reprint Ghioldi's boasts, an honor the Argentinian had never enjoyed in the past.

Fidel Castro was in no mood to take such lessons. The more he learned from the survivors of the Bolivian massacre, the more he was inclined to put moral responsibility for Che's death on

68. In his article, which *Humanité* published on November 17, 1967 under the title "Why Did Che Guevara Go to his Death in Bolivia?" Jacques Arnaud also gave a most glowing account of Bolivia's alleged prosperity: "As one crosses from Peru to Bolivia, the change is unmistakable; decent clothes, many more people wearing shoes, good peasant homes, an air of great Indian dignity all give one the feeling that these people are highly integrated into Bolivian society. In the streets of La Paz, the Indian is no vagrant; he is fully at home." In fact, a brief glance at the statistics suffices to show that Bolivia (with a per capita income of $165) is the poorest country in Latin America. Moreover such visitors as Francesco Rosi, the Italian film director, who saw the region in which Che's *guerrilleros* were operating, discovered a degree of peasant misery so unspeakable that he declared: "The Indians of Bolivia have been turned into outcasts of history."

the Communists in La Paz.[69] The old reluctance not to offend the orthodox Communists had given way to a sense of outrage that refused to be silenced. And, indeed, though the Cubans did not waste their breath on a Ghioldi or a Jacques Arnaud, they let the Soviet Union know what they thought of the Argentinian article in *Pravda*. The Russians sent their apologies for what they described as an editorial lapse, and one, moreover, that had not the slightest political significance. They had no desire to offend Havana; far from it, they were hoping that Fidel Castro would be present at the fiftieth anniversary of the October Revolution, for which Moscow was just making the most elaborate preparations.

This was an idle hope; neither Fidel Castro nor President Dorticós, nor any other well-known Cuban leader attended that celebration. The island was represented by its minister of health, Major Machado, who contented himself with placing a wreath on Lenin's tomb and spoke not a word at the Kremlin ceremonies. He left Moscow before the end of the festivities, ostensibly because he was afraid of missing the direct weekly flight of the regular line. His strange behavior drew the attention of the entire international press to the tension between the two countries. Thanks to inspired leaks, the press also learned that talks between Moscow and Havana on the renewal of the 1965 triannual agreement had broken down. Clearly, no love was lost between Cuba and the U.S.S.R., and Havana no longer cared to disguise the fact.

Cuba was just then making final plans for an International Cultural Congress. Its set theme, "The intellectual and the struggle for the liberation of the people of the Third World," had no obvious connection with the latest political developments, and the congress had, in any case, been decided upon

---

69. In his preface to Che's *Bolivian Diary* Fidel Castro accused Monje, leader of the pro-Soviet Communist Party, and Oscar Zamora, leader of the pro-Chinese Communist Party, of sitting back like cowards when the hour for action had struck, instead of joining Che as they had agreed to do. Che Guevara: *Bolivian Diary*, p. 13.

well before Che's death. The Cubans were happy to welcome so many leading intellectuals as possible allies against Moscow.

There were many reasons for this: first of all, intellectuals were highly sensitive to the deep humanity that spoke from Che's every utterance. He may have been a guerrilla fighter first and a sober economic planner, but Che always made it clear that only one thing mattered to him: the creation of the new man, fully integrated into his community and hence fully capable of expressing his true nature. His writings thus marked a return to the humanitarian ideas of Karl Marx, even though his arguments sprang less from a strict analysis of social and economic processes. For him the revolutionary struggle was itself an uplifting and liberating human activity; it enabled man to climb the ladder of perfection until, finally, he became whole.[70] Che had not taken this theory as far as he would have liked; his last book, *Socialism in Cuba*,[71] was only a brief draft. But in raising this subject at all, he posed problems that many intellectuals had been mulling over for years. Moreover, Che had shown that heroism was not the prerogative of men born in poverty and reared in despair under the yoke of colonial oppression, like the Vietnamese, the Chinese, or the Koreans. An intellectual himself,[72] an asthmatic since early childhood, he invariably fitted his own actions to his beliefs, as if to prove that such conduct was well within the grasp of all. And at the end of his life, his deep concern for a sick comrade, his sympathy for the very people who were refusing his helping hand, con-

70. In Che's *Bolivian Diary* there are quite a few references to the liberating effect of the revolutionary struggle on all who participate in it. But Che had spoken of this even earlier in his writings on the Sierra Maestra.

71. This small forty-eight-page book, published in Havana in 1967, was originally a letter to Carlos Quijano, editor of the Montevidean weekly, *Marcha*.

72. This is how President Dorticós has described Che: "A revolutionary intellectual, a man of books, a man of thought, a man of honor, a man of sacrifice, but above all a revolutionary, a Communist." From the speech of Osvaldo Dorticós of November 2, 1967, published in pamphlet form by the Cultural Congress of Havana.

trasted sharply with the cold cruelty of his killers. To men of intellect and passion, this counted for much more than any amount of dissertations on the correctness of a given strategy and helped to transform Che into a lasting witness to human greatness.

Moreover, many left-wing intellectuals from Europe had long been looking upon Cuba as a kind of spiritual home. It stood for an entirely new attitude, for the rejection of a life built on commercial standards, that had not degenerated into sectarianism or intolerance. After the regrettable but brief mini-Stalinist interlude—long since forgotten—the Cuban leaders had apparently forsworn any type of cultural dictatorship, and their encouragement of the free arts formed a striking contrast to the murky habits of the other socialist countries. In Havana, no one thought twice about publishing books banned in the East, or about importing films by Fellini, and when Blas Roca, in his official capacity of Party secretary, had tried to stop such films from coming in, he had been severely and publicly rebuked.[73] As far as painting was concerned, freedom had been complete long before Cuba extended her invitation to the *Salon de Mai*. "Our fight is with the imperialists, not with abstract painters," Fidel had told Claude Julien during an interview in February 1963.[74] Cuban journals, and especially those published under

73. On December 12, 1963, Blas Roca, then editor of *Hoy*, published an attack on Fellini's *La dolce vita*. He admitted that he had not seen the film but that "workers who had seen it felt that such films ought not to be shown in a socialist country." In his reply, Alfredo Guevara, the director of ICAIC (The Cuban Institute of Cinematographic Art), did not pull his punches: "To men like you," he told Blas Roca, writing in *Hoy* on December 17, 1963, "the public is made up of babies in need of a wet-nurse who will feed them with ideological pap, highly sterilized, and cooked in accordance with the recipes of socialist realism." Blas Roca beat a retreat on December 24; he no doubt realized that Alfredo Guevara's use of such strong language could only mean that he enjoyed the support of Fidel Castro, his old university friend. This controversy clearly went far beyond a simple debate between two film critics. See Angel Rama: *"En Cuba se polemiza"* in *Marcha*, Montevideo, March 6, 1964.

74. The same interview in which Fidel declared that he had never asked Khrushchev for missiles. See p. 261.

the *Casa de las Américas* imprint, had always been of the highest quality, and reading them, no one could doubt but that little Cuba was setting an example to the entire socialist family. It was refreshing that this small country, so exposed, so threatened, felt at liberty to prove to the whole world that socialism was not synonymous with intolerance and obscurantism.

Admittedly the "Cuban proof" would have been more conclusive if certain shadows had not appeared in the bright picture. During the summer of 1965, for example, the revolutionary authorities had started a cruel campaign against homosexuals. They did not encumber themselves with theoretical explanations or justifications but simply drafted "guilty" and suspects alike into UMAP (Military Units to Aid Production). Most of this contingent was made up of intellectuals—Khrushchev had already said that only a homosexual could be an abstract painter—and the purge at Havana University had been specially severe. But in contrast to what usually happens in socialist countries, the Union of Cuban Writers and Artists (UNEAC), far from applauding the wisdom of the political leaders, had sent them a very bitter letter of complaint. Fidel heeded their appeal and the UMAPs were dissolved. Still, the affair was bound to leave bitter memories, especially as the antihomosexual and puritanical obsession of the Castroists has not evaporated to this day.

Nor was this the only painful episode to cause concern for the perfect harmony between the Cuban leaders and the intellectuals. One could not but help feeling that in this deeply committed country, intellectuals, instead of being invited to play an increasingly important part in political and ideological activities, were gradually being driven further back into their own shells. After the first wave of enthusiasm when Cuban men of letters had done their best to come to grips with the economic, social, and cultural foundations of their revolution, they had somehow lost their original drive. Works on contemporary history, economic studies of the period of transition toward socialism, analyses of the new culture and its relationship to the masses became increasingly rare. Theoretical magazines such as

Cuba Socialista, which used to publish important papers, including the famous controversy between Che and Bettelheim, had ceased to appear; others like *Pensamiento Crítico* now concentrated on foreign authors.[75] The quality of the daily and weekly press seemed to be fast declining. The fact that Cuba was much freer than other socialist countries was poor consolation in these circumstances.

Echoes of the differences between the politicians and the intellectuals could also be discerned in the writings of some of the most authoritative sources. Che, for example, mentioned these differences in his *Socialism and Cuban Man,* but put the entire blame on the intellectuals:

"The frailty of many of our intellectuals and artists is the result of their original sin—they are not genuine revolutionaries. One can graft pears onto an elm tree, but one must first plant a pear to obtain the scion. New generations will be born untainted by original sin. The wider we spread our cultural net and our means of cultural expression, the greater the chance that we shall see the emergence of exceptional artists. We must make sure that the present conflict-torn generation does not pervert itself, and with it the generations to come."[76] But how does one widen the "means of cultural expression" and prevent the "present generation" from transmitting its sinful ways? How explain the well-known fact that many intellectuals, tainted though they may have been, participated in the Cuban Revolution and fought in the battle of Playa Girón? (It was not their fault that this battle lasted only three days.) There are many such questions one might have asked Che; his peremptory judgment

75. *Pensamiento Crítico,* edited by the youthful Fernando Martínez and a team of young philosophers and writers (Aurelio Alonso, José Bell Lano, Jesús Díaz, Thalia Fung, and Ricardo J. Machado) deserves particular credit for the discernment and courage with which it selects its foreign texts. It was the only Cuban journal to publish the famous resolution of the Central Committee of the Chinese Communist Party on the cultural revolution (August 1966).

76. Ernesto Che Guevara: *Socialism and Cuban Man* (Havana, 1967), p. 39.

showed that he had failed to look at the deeper reasons for the
withdrawal of intellectuals from politics. No doubt he would
have been forced to make good his omission sooner or later, for
to substantiate his thesis he would have had to analyze the power
structure prevailing in Cuba, and in socialist countries in general. Unfortunately, now that Che was gone it seemed unlikely
that anyone else had the quality or standing needed for reopen-
ing the debate on so thorny a subject. Fidel, though exceedingly
tolerant of intellectuals in their own particular spheres, clearly
felt no need to involve them in the theoretical elaboration of his
"heresy."

Nor did this flaw—real or supposed—in Cuban society seem
to bother many European intellectuals. For most, Cuba had retained its old appeal, especially by giving clear proof of its
solidarity with Vietnam and Korea at a time when the war in
Southeast Asia had helped to destroy a host of illusions about
American democracy. Few intellectuals were attracted by the
Chinese model, for though they refused to swallow the sensational stories about the cultural revolution supplied by the
Western and Soviet press, they were worried about its anti-
cultural aspects. As for the U.S.S.R., it had been losing good
will throughout the years by its obstinate defense of a cultural
doctrine that no one with the least critical acumen could approve. Intellectuals were sick and tired of shadowboxing with
these champions of proletarian culture. And now that Fidel
Castro, too, had grown tired of his fruitless dialogues with Moscow and the orthodox Communist parties, they were prepared to
overlook almost anything he might have done wrong.

Even while making preparations for the congress, the Cubans
had behaved in quite unprecedented ways. Thus, while they had
invited a number of Communist intellectuals from the West,
they had not, as custom dictated, done so through the respective
Party secretaries. And far from topping the list of guests with
the greatest possible number from the Soviet bloc, they had
asked the latter to send small contingents. As if it were the most
natural thing in the world, they had also invited notorious

heretics, ex-Communists, independent Marxists—all of them detested in Moscow. And yet Moscow could do nothing at all about these scandalous irregularities; Cuba was still on their official list of friendly countries. And so they sent a very small delegation, which was just what the Castroists wanted. For once Cuba had succeeded in making the best of her uncomfortable position.

Altogether more than five hundred intellectuals from seventy countries flocked to Havana. Bertrand Russell, Jean-Paul Sartre, and Ernst Fischer, unable to attend for health reasons, sent warm messages of support. Such famous European writers as Michel Leiris, Jorge Semprun, Max-Paul Fouchet, and Arnold Wesker; such renowned scientists as Pierre Lehman, Giovanni Berlinguer, Daniel Amati, and Jean-Pierre Vigier; such well-known painters as Matta, Lam, Pignon; such social scientists as Miliband, Hobsbawm, Guerin, Axelos—and the list is far from complete—mingled with prominent delegates from the Third World. Among these delegates, the Latin Americans and the Antillians, including Aimé Césaire, Julio Cortazar, and Benedetti, were the most widely represented. Nor was the congress remarkable for its composition alone; its agenda was no less extraordinary. Five working committees were to deal with five great themes: culture and national independence; the integral education of man; the responsibility of intellectuals for the underdeveloped world; culture and mass media; art, science, and technology. A very full program indeed. The Cuban organizers made it clear, right from the outset, that they were not interested in academic debates, but hoped for a concrete reply to the central question underlying the whole agenda, namely how the intellectual can best serve the Revolution. They did not shock anybody. On the contrary, the foreign guests had feared that, despite all their sympathy for the Castroists, they had been asked to Havana simply to demonstrate their solidarity with Cuba, to be put on public display in the usual Soviet manner. All of them were most agreeably surprised to find that nothing of the kind was intended.

"A Cuban heresy?"

Better still, in asking the intellectuals to deal quite openly with the problems of the Revolution, the Cubans were inviting them into realms that Communist parties had always considered their own preserves. Indeed, official Communists had invariably heaped abuse on these petit bourgeois hairsplitters and troublemakers as soon as any intellectuals had had the audacity to encroach on that preserve. Now, quite suddenly, the Cubans, heroic Communists though they were, had asked these same intellectuals to share in their most intimate deliberations and to provide the answers to their most pressing questions. Nor did the Cubans leave it at vague hints, for every time they denounced the failure of revolutionary movements in capitalist countries, every time that they attacked reformism or the spirit of compromise, they put the blame squarely on the orthodox Communists, and so exonerated most of those present. In the corridors, they gleefully repeated what was said to be a remark of Fidel's: "The leaders of the Communist Party are like football players trained for the 1924 championship, but nevertheless trying to carry off the World Cup in 1968."

Delegates from Eastern Europe were given every chance of defending their orthodox views: the procedure adopted by the congress guaranteed—and this was not the least of its novelties—absolute freedom of speech. All *ponencias* (resolutions) were included in the agenda without the slightest interference. In committee, you could discuss anything you liked from sex to bureaucracy, provided it had some small bearing on the problems of the Revolution. Now on most of these points, the delegates from the East had absolutely nothing to say, so that one gained the impression they had been invited for the express purpose of letting their eloquent silence bear witness to their theoretical vacuity and their lack of real interest in the problems of the Revolution. The rector of Warsaw University, a Russian film director, or a Czech professor, all holding Party cards, looked as strange at this congress as they might have at a meeting of the Ecumenical Council.

And the debates were extremely sharp at times, particularly

399

when it came to the Israeli-Arab problem, on which European intellectuals held strong views. The Cubans themselves presided over the most thorny sessions of each of the five committees, acting as peacemakers with great skill and tact.[77] At the end of the congress, when they committed the blunder of rewriting the text of the final resolution, the so-called Havana Appeal, as drafted by the First Committee, and were taken to task for it, they immediately called an extraordinary meeting at which they offered profuse apologies and made the necessary amends.[78] Politically unattached intellectuals, ex-Party members, and various minority Communists were delighted by this show of democratic fair play. Eastern delegates, on the other hand, were completely nonplussed by this unheard-of laxity. But the worst

77. When the Arab delegates demanded that Zionist imperialism be condemned as sharply as U.S. imperialism, many delegates felt that the final resolution would be weakened by the coupling together of forces that posed quite unequal threats on the world scale. By insisting on the joint condemnation of American and Zionist imperialism, the Arabs were thus threatening the unity of the congress. The Cubans who had not broken off diplomatic relations with Israel, and who were, moreover, critical of the Arab countries, both before and after the Six-Day War, were not prepared to see their congress reduced to a forum of discussion about the Middle East. At the same time, they did not wish to adopt a stand that might have looked biased to their Arab guests (there were no delegates from Israel). They accordingly appealed for help to the Vietnamese and North Korean delegates, and such was the prestige of these two that they quickly succeeded in calming ruffled tempers and in having the Middle Eastern obstacle removed from the agenda.

78. The text of the Havana Appeal was drafted by Ralph Miliband and Marcel Liebman, after long discussions (for reasons mentioned in the last footnote), and was finally adopted one evening before the congress closed. Next morning, at a general meeting which had to approve the resolutions adopted by each committee, the chairman read out the Havana Appeal in a version that its own authors had some difficulty in recognizing. Included, *inter alia,* was a new passage praising the example of Che Guevara and calling on intellectuals to turn into guerrilla fighters. Ralph Miliband immediately declared that these changes had been introduced without his knowledge. The delegates looked disturbed, and the Cubans at once got together with their European friends, and, after a few hours of consultation, called an extraordinary plenary session. José Llanusa, president of the congress and minister of education, personally presented his apologies for this incident and assured the delegates that the Cuban leaders would make good their error. Then Alejo Carpentier read out the true Havana Appeal and the whole episode was forgotten.

400

shock was still waiting for them. It came on January 12, 1968, when Fidel Castro explained the lessons of the congress before a large audience in the Chaplin Theater.

I knew this theater, for it was here that Castro had lashed out at Venezuelan Communists at the end of the OLAS Conference. At the time, I had already gained the impression that his audience of some five thousand tough militants had been egging him further into heresy, by greeting every one of his more critical remarks with loud ovations and prolonged applause. Fidel improvises all his speeches. He makes few notes, but usually takes along a couple of press communiqués to support his arguments and provide him with an occasional breather; for the rest, like all great orators, he allows himself to be guided by his public. This time he intended to make a tough speech, as he had told me a few days earlier, during a discussion of topics that need not delay us here. And, in fact, his public, including the five hundred delegates from the Cultural Congress, was fully expecting him to unburden himself to the Communists about their reaction to Che's tragic death. The overheated atmosphere of the Chaplin Theater was therefore charged with emotion as this speech of January 12 would surely be something those present would never forget.

Yet Fidel began to speak on a calm note. He examined American penetration in Europe and the resulting problems for Cuban trade with the Old World. He stressed the dangers American interference posed for the future of all nations, because rarely in the past had the world been brought up against "an enemy as universal as Yankee imperialism." But resistance, he continued, was growing stronger by the day. Then, taking a deep breath, he suddenly changed key: "To be quite honest, we must admit that, often before now, when it came to crucial world issues, to imperialist aggression and crime, it was the intellectual workers who showed the greatest militancy, who reacted with the greatest determination, and not those political organizations whom one might, in all conscience, have expected to give the lead." The audience, on its feet now, greeted this revelation with

401

a storm of applause. The next passage had an even more explosive effect: "On many occasions the so-called organized vanguard was found hiding behind the rearguard in the battle against imperialism."

This direct attack on the Communist parties—for what other "organized vanguard" could Fidel possibly have meant—obviously called for corroborating evidence. Fidel accordingly recalled the missile crisis of 1962, when it first dawned on him that Communists put the claims of the U.S.S.R. before the needs of the Revolution. He had already said so quite plainly at the final OLAS session when he had denounced that microfaction, that small group of Cuban Communists who had rallied unconditionally around Khrushchev and against their own country.[79] This time he preferred to sail into European Communists who, at the decisive hour, instead of mobilizing the masses, had demonstrated that their defense of peace was nothing but a cliché, and one, moreover, that helped to demobilize, to disarm the working class. "For if there had been actions, great or small, we should have known about them. Instead, we have the clear impression that their 'defense of peace' served only to lull the masses to sleep."

Fidel had an even more striking illustration, more striking because it was more recent: "Just who was it who tried to carry Che's banner to the rest of the world after his death? Who exalted his example in Europe? On whom did Che's death make the strongest impact? Not on the political organizations and parties, but on intellectual workers." Carried away by his own argument and by the ovation he received, Fidel now struck out at all those "who asked [like Jacques Arnaud] why Che went to his death, and who will never discover the answer, because they are incapable of dying like him, of being true revolutionaries like him." This was strong talk: after giving the intellectuals a certificate of good revolutionary conduct, Fidel now told

79. Neither at the OLAS Conference nor at the Cultural Congress did Fidel bother to name that microfaction, but on listening to him one gathered that he was thinking of the old PSP.

the Communists that they were utterly lacking in revolutionary qualities and, worse still, that these qualities would forever elude them.

Continuing in this vein, he read out a message to the Cultural congress from a group of Catholic priests, who had decided to follow the example of Camilo Torres.[80] Then he poured scorn on the dogmatic Marxists: "It is not one of the least paradoxes of history that, at a time when certain sectors of the clergy have seen fit to become revolutionaries, certain Marxist sectors have turned themselves into a pseudorevolutionary church. I only hope that by drawing attention to this fact I shall not myself be excommunicated, or delivered over to the Holy Inquisition.

"Nothing is more anti-Marxist than dogma and petrified thought. No one has a monopoly of ideas, and of revolutionary ideas least of all. No one is a repository of all revolutionary truths." This time Fidel no longer pretended to be speaking of Latin America and Latin America alone. He had taken a new step forward and was plainly asking all militants, and the intellectuals chief among them, to rise up against their calcified leaders. The time for sparing the feelings of these men was gone forever. Fidel did not hide the fact that he was counting on the emergence of a new, Guevarist generation, and that Cuba, like Vietnam, could set them an example. He could not have spelled out more plainly that a new age had dawned in the Communist camp.

Fidel's speech had a bombshell effect. The foreign visitors left Havana convinced that they had watched a milestone being laid in the history of the Communist movement, that they had at

80. Camilo Torres Restrepo (1929–1966), a former chaplain at the National University of Bogotá, and subsequently professor of Sociological Methodology, eventually joined the Colombian guerrilla movement (ELN, *Ejército de Liberación Nacional*) in 1965. As a Catholic priest at odds with the hierarchy, he explained his recourse to violence in several books which had a profound effect on young Catholics. He was killed in battle on February 17, 1966.

403

long last been offered a chance of making a real contribution toward building a better world. I shared their conviction, although I did not leave Cuba with the rest. I stayed on for another three months gathering further material for this book. Much of what I discovered, at my leisure and without official guides this time, I found gravely disturbing. For if Cuba was truly to survive its possible, or rather probable, expulsion from the Communist family and go on to set a real example to the young, it ought first of all to have put its own house in order, and small and underdeveloped though it was, have moved steadily forward toward a clearly defined goal. But was this truly the case? On what real foundations did the Castroist "heresy" rest?

V

"Hay problemas, hay contradicciones"

The Khrushchev machine and the giant zafra

Comparative studies of prices and wages in a young revolutionary country rarely reflect the true economic picture. Revolutions cause social upheavals on so large a scale that they make nonsense of all such analyses. The privileged of yesterday are suddenly forced to reduce their appetite, while others who used to eat practically nothing can at last enjoy their slice of the national cake. All this introduces some imponderables into the economic equation: the enthusiasm of the masses, their devotion to the cause, a relative lack of greed. Moreover, the revolution gives absolute priority to education, to free health service, and to a host of other elements which constitute a "guaranteed social wage" and help to transform the quality of life of the whole population. It is therefore a waste of time to try to compare the income and expenditure of a Cuban with those of his neighbors in Latin America, let alone with a European's.

405

This does not mean that Cubans now live in a universe apart, one in which our normal criteria do not apply, in which there are neither food shortages nor galloping inflation. All these are only too obviously present, and we all know the ravages they have caused in other postrevolutionary societies, not simply in economic terms but also with respect to ideological training, an area to which Cuban leaders attach much importance. It is therefore without the least "European malice" that I confess my great anxiety about the long lines outside the food shops in Havana and, in fact, outside shops of whatever kind. In principle, the rationing system guarantees the necessary minimum to all, and so brings a measure of equality to a society that used to be a great deal less fair than most. But the system of distribution leaves much to be desired; only the most patient, or the most cunning, seem capable of collecting their due, and then only after wasting a vast amount of time and energy. In short, Cuba has been suffering from a heavy dose of socialist inflation.

Cuban leaders have confessed their inability to reverse this trend. They have told me that they know its causes and that they can even predict when it will end; meanwhile they resign themselves to the inevitable. They added that the present inflationary wave was as nothing compared with the one Cuba had known during the first few years after the Revolution. At that time, the government had been too rash in redistributing incomes, and many had acquired "the habit of working less and earning more," as Fidel himself had put it.[1] The result had been a grave imbalance between supply and demand. At present, quite different mechanisms were at work. Since 1965, Cuba had been making massive investments in agriculture with the object of producing ten million tons of sugar in 1970 and of reaching a number of other, equally ambitious, agricultural targets. Un-

1. *El hábito de trabajar menos y ganar más.* See Castro's speech on September 19, 1964. He has used the same expression in more recent addresses.

fortunately nature does not allow herself to be forced; she yields her fruits in her own good time. Between the time of sowing a new sugar field and the first sugar harvest two years must pass— two years of applying fertilizer, weed killers, and starting costly irrigation schemes. Similarly, it takes time to breed a more productive race of cattle out of poor tropical herds. From the day the first pedigreed bulls are imported and artificial insemination centers are set up, until the day that the first cross-bred cows come into milk, at least three years have gone by. During all that time, vast sums of money have to be spent on equipment and wages, without any immediate returns. Hence the new imbalance and the inflation.

Now the ten million tons of sugar expected in 1970 ought to earn Cuba more than a billion dollars, and so enable her to fill her larder on the open market. From then on sugar alone would be enough to re-establish economic equilibrium, and Cuba would still have many other export products. The Cuban leaders concluded that Cuba must tighten her belt for a time— after all, what are four or five years in the life of a nation if the end result is the end of underdevelopment? Surely that was far better than spreading the process over many years in an effort to avoid inflation? An encircled country like Cuba could not permit herself the luxury of gradual progress, and, moreover, nothing has a more stimulating effect on the popular imagination than a gigantic struggle for a healthy future built on concrete achievements.

The ultimate choice, therefore, was a political one, and Fidel Castro has never tried to disguise this fact. Returning from his second visit to the U.S.S.R. on January 24, 1964, he explained the advantages that would accrue to Cuba from the new sugar agreement signed in Moscow: "This sort of perspective [he was mentioning the ten million tons of sugar for the first time] acts of itself as a mobilizing force, encouraging people to work harder and generating enthusiasm. This force is also needed for the development of a social conscience, since from now on the people will look upon each individual who does not bear his share of responsibility, who shirks his duty, does not bother to play his full part, as one who undermines the extraordinary possibilities of our country, one who acts against the interests of the whole nation."[2]

The 10-million-ton *zafra* was thus presented not as a simple economic objective but as a symbolic challenge to the entire nation. "Through it," Fidel declared, "we shall obtain the optimum development, the maximum expansion of our economy," and he went on to argue that sugar, which had been a curse under the old regime, would become Cuba's greatest benefactor. He addressed himself to a people who knew all about sugar cane, and who were not slow to grasp the tremendous advantages of the Moscow agreement, by which the U.S.S.R. undertook to buy 5 million tons of sugar from 1968 on, at a guaranteed price of 6 cents per pound. And Fidel pledged "the honor of the Revolution" to the fulfillment of this grand plan.

Henceforth, he would tolerate no meddling in this priority sector. Cuban economic plans are generally more elastic than readers of *Granma* are led to suppose, and the objectives of one year are sometimes postponed for the next; but no such laxity was ever envisaged when it came to plans for the 1970 *zafra*. It would be 10 million tons, not a pound less—Fidel repeated this often, before Cuba and the whole world. However, the sugar output, after taking a leap in 1965 (6,050,767 tons compared with 4,397,781 tons in 1964) had dropped back again in 1966 (less than 4.5 million tons), had risen to more than 6 million tons in 1967 and had dropped back once more in 1968 (5.1 million tons).[3] Hence there seemed some reason to doubt the chances of doubling the figure in a mere two years.

2. Speech delivered on January 24, 1964, and published in leaflet form by *Obra Revolucionaria*, No. 3, 1964, Havana, p. 16.
3. Cuban sugar production since the Revolution:

1959	6	million tons
1960	5.9	million tons
1961	6.8	million tons

"Hay problemas, hay contradicciones"

Before I could put this point to Fidel Castro, he came back at me with a battery of scientific explanations designed to confound his critics and to demonstrate the inevitability of his great sugar success. According to him the 1968 *zafra* had been poor because of a severe drought, and could not therefore be thought typical of the country's real potential. Moreover, a great deal of new cane had been sown in 1969, and this would produce a maximum yield in 1970.[4] More fertilizers and weed-killers were being

---

1962	4.8 million tons
1963	3.8 million tons
1964	4.4 million tons
1965	6.1 million tons
1966	4.5 million tons
1967	6.1 million tons
1968	5.1 million tons
1969	4.3 million tons (estimated)

For comparison, here are some sugar production figures from before the Revolution:

1913	2.3 million tons
1916	3.1 million tons
1925	5.3 million tons
1948	6.1 million tons
1952	7.2 million tons
1958	5.8 million tons

4. Sugar cane is a perennial plant, but its yield decreases from year to year, so that fields are generally resown every six years. According to Julio Alienes y Urosa (1950) the yield from one *caballeria* (33 acres) is as follows:

1st year	100,000 arrobas
2nd year	60,000 arrobas
3rd year	45,000 arrobas
4th year	35,000 arrobas
5th year	25,000 arrobas
6th year	21,176 arrobas

The old cane is preserved for six years simply because, throughout this cycle, the loss of yield is balanced by lower maintenance and other costs. According to Urosa, the second-year crop is the most profitable of all. Sowing and tending one *caballeria* of cane calls for an investment of $1,700, while maintenance after the first harvest costs only $360 per year. See Julio Alienes y Urosa: *Caracteristicas de la economia cubana,* p. 112.

It should be added that since Urosa published his work, Cubans have not only begun to make intensive use of fertilizers but have also introduced new varieties of cane (quick, medium, and slow growing) so that the old cycle

409

applied by the most up-to-date methods and, above all, reservoirs had been built to protect the crops against possible droughts. "We have even made a pact with the rain," Fidel assured me. In fact, if I were forced to place a bet, I would say that the *zafra* of 1970 would in fact attain the ten-million-ton mark.

But during my prolonged stay in 1968, I also saw the cost Cuba had to pay for it. The whole country has to live with what can only be called a sugar obsession. The *zafra* is no longer confined, as it used to be, to the one hundred days of the Cuban winter. Since 1968, it has been extended by several months, and we are told that the 1970 harvest will begin in July 1969 and finish in the spring of 1971! To obtain the anticipated ten million tons of sugar, the bulk of Cuba's labor force will have to be diverted for more than eight months and exert itself in arduous physical labor during the incredibly hot summer, during a season, that is, when no one ever dreamed of cutting cane in the past.[5]

This fact made me take a second look at Fidel Castro's sugar plan. To that end, I decided, first of all, to re-read his speeches on the subject, beginning with the television addresses he had given after his two visits to the U.S.S.R.—in April–May 1963

no longer applies. One thing, however, has remained unchanged: the cane still produces its highest yield during the first harvest. Now, in 1969, the Cubans planted more than 100,000 *caballerías* of new cane, which represents a record figure for a single year. More than 25 per cent of the new fields are irrigated and the cane may thus be expected to have a much higher sugar content.

5. The traditional 100 days of the *zafra* used to begin in late November, not for humanitarian reasons or in order to spare the *macheteros*, but because the cane has the highest sugar content during this period. Quite possibly, the introduction of a new variety of cane has removed this difficulty. It remains a fact, however, that the productivity of the labor force during the hot months, when the temperature easily reaches 40° C. in the shade, is bound to be severely impaired, the more so as the cane cutters are no longer famished seasonal workers forced to earn in a few months what they needed to keep them alive for the whole year.

"Hay problemas, hay contradicciones"

and again in January 1964. Castro spoke quite frankly of the human cost of so tremendous a leap in production by a country of only seven million inhabitants. Thus in his speech of January 24, 1964 (after his second visit), he declared: "It is impossible to increase our sugar production as long as we are forced to cut cane by primitive, unmechanized methods. . . . Without the proper machines it would be idle to anticipate a *zafra* of even eight or nine million tons."[6]

In these circumstances, how could he possibly be thinking of a still larger harvest? Fidel's answer was that the grave problem of mechanization was about to be solved with Soviet help:

"The Soviet government, and more particularly Comrade Khrushchev, have evinced special interest in this problem. Khrushchev has a great deal of experience in agriculture. He has a distinguished service record as First Party Secretary in the Ukraine, an agricultural region, and he has done a great deal of fighting in that area. After the Germans left, he reorganized the economy and agriculture of the Ukraine, which explains his extraordinary intimacy with agricultural questions and his knowledge of machines. And, remarkably enough, using what information he had on sugar cane and everything pertaining to it, Comrade Khrushchev was able to list the ideal characteristics of a machine for cutting and harvesting cane sugar. Everything in a single machine: cutter and reaper combined. And from that moment, there was never the least doubt that the problem would be solved technically. Immediate contact was made with the Ministry of Machine Construction and with agricultural engineers; a study group was formed on the spot, led by one of Khrushchev's personal assistants, a specialist in agriculture, who had come to Cuba with urgent instructions to construct that machine. Khrushchev himself has contributed a series of new ideas about the nature of this machine and these will prove extremely useful to technicians, engineers, and specialists. . . .

6. As quoted in *Obra Revolucionaria*, No. 3, pp. 6 and 14.

411

In short, we have decided on the complete mechanization of the cane sugar harvest in Cuba."[7]

Next day, every Cuban paper proudly announced that, thanks to Soviet cane-cutting machines, Cuba was about to be delivered, once and for all, from her annual nightmare. And, in fact, the Russians shipped one thousand of Khrushchev's machines to Cuba all at once, so convinced of Khrushchev's foresight that they did not even bother to make preliminary tests in the field.

Unfortunately they were mistaken. In Cuba, unlike the Ukraine, the ground is not perfectly flat, and the cane will not send up fresh shoots unless it has been cut in a special way. And Khrushchev's machine was too heavy, too clumsy, and quite unsuited to Cuban conditions. In other words, it caused nothing but damage: "It is a great destroyer; where it has been nothing will grow for a long time to come. . . ."[8]

Today Nikita Khrushchev's brilliant invention is nothing but a subject for bitter jokes in Cuba. I was not told whether the machines were sent back to the Soviet Union or left to rot in their sheds; in any case, none of them can be seen in the fields and, by all accounts, they could not even be used as substitute tractors or bulldozers. On the other hand, like everyone else on the island, I was able to watch sugar cane being cut—in the good old way, with machetes. Only reaping and transport have been mechanized (which of course eases the manpower problem considerably). At present the Cubans have themselves developed a prototype for another cutting machine which they have symbolically named *Libertadora,* but since their mechanical industry

7. Fidel's speech of June 1963, as published in *Obra Revolucionaria,* No. 15, 1963, Havana, p. 37.
8. Fidel Castro never again referred to Khrushchev's machine, but during a meeting on July 14, 1969, at the start of the ten-million-ton *zafra* he explained: "Cane is a very awkward plant; it does not grow straight like maize or rice. Cane lies down, particularly when its sugar content is high. Once the yield of a cane plantation exceeds 85 tons per hectare, the slightest wind will bend the cane over and mix it all up; to cut it on the ground, one must search for it among the leaves. Designing a machine that can lift the cane, cut it and strip the leaves is therefore an exceedingly difficult task." See *Granma,* French weekly summary, July 20, 1969.

is still in its infancy it will be quite some time before they can produce it in sufficient quantities to "liberate" anybody.[9] To obtain their ten million tons of sugar, the Cubans therefore still must rely on their muscles, on an enormous and prolonged feat of endurance. This, the most obvious and most striking facet of sugar production, raises the question of whether the vastly ambitious sugar plan does not threaten to throw the whole Cuban economy out of gear. Manpower, in a socialist regime, is the fundamental lever of development. If it is massively concentrated in a particular sector, common sense shows that it will be missing from others and thus impede their growth. Now, Cuba no longer has the old professional *macheteros* who can cut four to five hundred arrobas of cane per day.[10] These men have become independent thanks to the agricultural reforms or else they have moved to town in search of more regular and less strenuous employment. Some of them still respond to the annual appeal for a "people's *zafra*," and they still distinguish themselves at the task. But this contingent of *macheteros* is not large enough to produce even a normal harvest. The reader will remember that, in the past, whenever a particularly good harvest was expected, Cuba would recruit seasonal workers from Haiti or from Jamaica; her own labor force could not cope with any *zafra* greater than four to five million tons. It goes without saying that, since the Revolution, the import of foreign semi-slaves has completely stopped.

Who then cuts the cane? Much of the work is done by volunteers—soldiers and students. But these youthful enthusiasts are

9. In the same speech, Fidel had this to say on the subject of the *Libertadora:* "This is a complicated machine which still needs a great many improvements, and we cannot possibly order the construction of thousands of these machines before we are absolutely certain that they are not going to break down or cause us all sorts of problems."

10. Statistical evidence in support of the widespread belief that *macheteros* used to cut up to 500 arrobas (approximately five tons) of cane per day is extremely slender. I have been assured time and again that they did, though only by working a ten-hour or an even longer day. This used to be the classical case of exploitation under the old regime.

413

neither sufficiently numerous nor sufficiently expert to cope, and cannot, in any case, be pulled out of the universities, barracks, and workshops for the whole duration of the long *zafra* that is now being planned. Hence every factory or department is expected to send part of its labor force or staff into the fields, on a rotational system. During my stay in 1968, I was told that pressure was put on no one, that people were perfectly free to stay at their desks or factories, but that very few in fact took advantage of this. In any case the rota was fixed in such a way that no one was expected to work for more than two or three weeks in the sugar fields. All these "occasional *macheteros*" were paid full wages, and people who were poorly paid in the towns could even increase their income if they exceeded the norm.

That norm is now fixed at 100 arrobas per day—i.e., at less than 25 per cent of the alleged output of a good *machetero* before the Revolution. And yet, most of the casual laborers from the town seem to find it difficult to reach even that goal— Havana puts their average output at 60 to 80 arrobas per day. These figures (from official sources) set a problem in elementary arithmetic: if a 5-million-ton *zafra* called for 400,000 *macheteros* cutting some 400 arrobas per day before the Revolution, how many nonprofessional *macheteros,* cutting between 60 and 80 arrobas per day, are needed to bring in a ten-million-ton *zafra?* The result is clearly beyond the capacity of a country with a mere 7 million inhabitants. Luckily, the mechanization of at least part of the work and the extension of the *zafra* over a much longer period have introduced new constants, so that success in 1970 seems possible after all—needless to say, on condition that all Cubans take part in it, irrespective of occupation or status. It should be noted that, because the volunteers are paid their normal wages no matter how low their sugar output, the *zafra* is a major generator of inflation, and so helps to depress real wages.

Nor is that all. Sugar production calls for meticulous, almost clocklike, coordination between the cane harvest itself and the refining process. Cane cannot be stored; once it is cut, its sugar content keeps decreasing.[11] Hence it is essential to cut the exact amount of cane that can daily be transported to, and treated in, the refineries. If this is not done, the refineries do not work at maximum efficiency, and large quantities of sugar are lost. Now the 10-million-ton *zafra* has been computed on the assumption that the refineries will run at full capacity. But is it really possible to achieve this high degree of coordination with an unqualified labor force working on a rotational system, as the mood strikes it? In an official document submitted by the Cuban delegation to the FAO, it was admitted that Cuban agricultural laborers work less than eight hours a day on the average.[12] Fidel Castro, for his part, has declared that poor organization constitutes the Achilles heel of the Cuban sugar system.[13] Others have warned that unless there is a much higher degree of synchronization, sugar harvesting will inevitably fall out of step with sugar refining, so that an extra 10 to 15 per cent must be cut against probable wastage.

It was the occasional *macheteros* in a camp in Pinar del Río province who finally convinced me of the gravity of this problem. All of them were volunteers, and all of them insisted that the

11. Putting the sugar content of freshly-cut cane at 12 per cent, we obtain the following (approximate) figures:

	per cent
After the first day	11.65
After the second day	11.45
After the third day	11.30
After the fourth day	11.10
After the fifth day	10.85
After the sixth day	10.65
After the seventh day	10.40
After the eighth day	10.25
After the ninth day	10.00
After the tenth day	9.80

See *Fabricación del azúcar*, Havana, Editoria Pedagógica, 1965.
12. "Industrial Development in Cuba" in *International Symposium on Industrial Development*, 1967 (duplicated text), p. 106.
13. The entire Cuban press keeps harping on this fact, and special conferences have been organized to study past mistakes, above all those that caused the 1969 *zafra* to fall short of the set target.

zafra must take precedence over all other tasks. None could therefore be suspected of counterrevolutionary tendencies or of malice when they alleged that, even during earlier *zafras,* more than a million tons of sugar simply evaporated.[14] This state of affairs, they felt, would continue until such time as mechanization was complete, until the output of every machine could be calculated in advance and transport laid on accordingly. When that happened, they all assured me, thus echoing one of Castro's speeches, 20,000 workers would suffice to bring in the biggest harvest ever.

Meanwhile, they would continue to live in this somewhat primitive but well-aired camp (it was winter), sleeping on wooden bunks, eating healthy food,[15] and engaging in socialist competition with the neighboring camps. The record holder was a university professor from Oriente province, renowned for its cane cutters, and indeed he handled his heavy machete with impressive skill. He showed me the correct technique, and allowed me to try my own hand at cutting, after warning me that over-enthusiastic beginners often hurt themselves. The camp also had a women's dormitory, and I wondered how women could possibly do what, to me, was a back-breaking job. I was told that they were chiefly engaged on washing the cut cane, but that many of them were excellent *macheteras;* skill apparently counts for much more than brute strength.

Rather naïvely I asked if, in that case, it would not be much better to delegate the work to the most skillful, and leave the

14. In his speech of July 14, 1969, Castro himself admitted that poor synchronization and the ensuing drop in sugar content will lead to very considerable losses: "In a ten-million-ton *zafra,* 1 per cent in sugar content represents at least one million tons of sugar. In other words, if the average yield drops from 11.5 per cent to 10.5 per cent we lose one million tons." Fidel went on to say that in the course of the ten-million-ton *zafra,* breakdowns in the refineries would inevitably occur, and that, "as soon as problems arise at the refinery, the cutting must be stopped. To keep on cutting in these circumstances is the worst possible thing." See *Granma,* French weekly summary, July 20, 1969.

15. Our visit to the camp was unannounced; hence I do not think that a special lunch was cooked for us. We had soup, rice with meat sauce, fried bananas, yogurt, and—happy surprise—a cup of real coffee.

416

rest to get on with their usual jobs, where they would surely do much better. The professor gave me a broad grin, and I could have sworn he was about to launch into a lecture on the educational value of collective effort and camp life. But no, he simply explained that no other type of work could earn Cuba nearly as much foreign currency as the *zafra*. True, university research was useful in the long run, and the work of his colleagues from the Ministry of Education was important as well, but none of this brought in the dollars Cuba so desperately needed to re-equip her industry. By contrast, every arroba of cut cane brought in some of the badly-needed hard cash. Sugar still represents more than 80 per cent of Cuba's external trade; "Hence it is essential for us to do what we can in the canefields, unstintingly and regardless of our professions."

This was easier said than done: as we saw, by making a fetish of work that earns her foreign currency, Cuba runs the risk of seriously dislocating every other branch of her economy. But I did not wish to start a long argument with my *machetero* professor, especially as I had no figures with which to oppose his. However, I remained unconvinced.

To begin with, it is an elementary truth that one foreign currency is not as good as another; some are convertibles and can be used to buy goods in any part of the world, while others cannot be used outside their country of origin. The Cubans always think in terms of dollars, simply because their peso is officially worth one U.S. dollar. But barely a third of their exports earns them real dollars; the rest is tied up in barter agreements with the U.S.S.R. and her partners in the ruble zone. Like all countries, including those in the Soviet bloc, Cuba is anxious to increase her holdings of convertible currency; this would allow her to import a range of products and consumer goods she cannot buy with rubles—either because the Russians do not make them or else because the quality of their merchandise is inferior to that sold on the free market at the same price.

Cuba must obviously export to the ruble zone, from which she gets her oil and certain types of heavy equipment—notably turbines for her thermoelectric power stations—and long-term

417

credits. But if she is to raise her standard of life and modernize, she cannot restrict her purchases to that zone. In fact, it is only by importing more goods from the West that she can restore equilibrium in her home market, put an end to galloping inflation, and give her people a short breather after the hard effort of their current five-year plan.

The Cubans are sure, in any case, that if they had sufficient hard cash they could increase their trade with the rest of the world, despite the United States. "The ten-million-ton *zafra* will guarantee our country's second liberation," was how Carlos Rafael Rodríguez put it.[16] Now this takes us to the very crux of the problem: does sugar really constitute the ideal article for increasing trading with the West? This used to be the case in the past, but does it still apply today? Let us once more look at Fidel's speeches after his visits to the U.S.S.R., and see what he himself felt about the problems at the time.

When he launched his great plan in 1964, the price of sugar on the world market had just reached the record level of 12 cents per pound.[17] Fidel Castro was not blinded by this excep-

16. Quoted from *Bohemia*, No. 24, June 13, 1969.
17. The figure of 12 cents per pound is quoted by Michel Gutelman in his book *L'Agriculture socialisée à Cuba* (page 212), but this was the price ruling when the Soviet-Cuban agreement was signed (in January 1964) and not the average price for that year. According to the Sugar Year Book published by the International Sugar Council (London, 1966), the ruling sugar prices during the years following the Cuban Revolution were as follows:

	cents per pound
1959	2.97
1960	3.14
1961	2.70
1962	2.78
1963	8.29
1964	5.72
1965	2.03
1966	1.76
1967	1.99
1968	1.12

418

tionally high rate; he knew full well that the price of sugar had been unduly inflated by the marked decline in Cuban production, which in 1963 had fallen to its lowest level since 1916: 3,821,089 tons. If Cuba resumed intensive cultivation, her crop alone would suffice to end the temporary shortages and so cause a drop in world prices. Fidel also realized that the present boom was encouraging other sugar growers, and would lead to fiercer international competition. But he declared that such competition did not frighten him; Cuba was a better place to grow cane sugar than any other country, thanks largely to her climate and exceptionally fertile soil. Moreover, he saw no reason for restricting the production of a staple food at a time when large parts of the world had to go hungry. In brief, he thought there were sound political as well as moral reasons for increasing the *zafra*, irrespective of the world market price; if necessary, he would even cause a market crisis, thus demonstrating that a socialist country never stops production for sordid financial reasons, especially where food is involved.

And during the next few years, the market did behave in accordance with Fidel's more pessimistic forecasts. Sugar prices fell slowly but steadily, and by 1968 London was quoting sugar at a mere 30 to 40 dollars per ton. An agreement between producers and buyers improved matters slightly, but the prospect remains bleak. For some countries, such as Puerto Rico, Brazil, and Jamaica, this was a catastrophe, but one that did not cause an exploitation but merely increased their dependence on the United States which guaranteed the purchase of a fixed sugar quota at a preferential rate. Then, in October 1968, an international sugar agreement was signed in Geneva for the purpose of stabilizing the free market price or, as the Cubans called it, the "residual market" price. This agreement established a balance between export quotas and sugar prices and set a lower limit

---

Before signing her multi-annual agreement with Cuba in January 1964, the Soviet Union used to pay 4 cents a pound for Cuban sugar, based on the average price paid during the past few years. (Soviet sugar purchases began only in 1960).

419

of 3.25 cents per pound and an upper limit of 5.25 cents per pound. Cuba was granted a quota of 2,150,000 tons, the biggest for any one country. She was thus assured of a reasonable price for all the sugar left over after deliveries to the socialist countries, with which she had signed separate agreements, not covered by the Geneva convention.[18] Hence Fidel had good reason to think that his great *zafra* would yet earn him the convertible currency he was counting on.

On one point, however, Fidel's forecasts have gone wrong: he has been unable to mechanize the industry to the point that the giant *zafra* can be brought in by a mere 20,000 workers. This, as we have seen, was a major variable in his calculations, but it was not, unhappily, the only one; Cuban refineries are antiquated, the most modern having been built in 1927[19] and some so decrepit that they had to be pulled down after the Revolution. In these circumstances, it would have been difficult enough to force the *zafra* up to 7 million tons. Anything beyond that calls for enormous new investments (300 million dollars to produce 8.5 million tons; a billion dollars to produce 10 million tons).[20] It follows that the real choice before Castro was not one between unlimited production, at low cost, and artificially restricted production in accordance with capitalist practice before the Revolution. In fact, any increase in production beyond 7 million tons involves a radical transformation of Cuba's industrial structure. According to Huberman and Sweezy, the first million and a half tons above the 7 million mark would call for an investment of roughly 200 pesos per ton, while the next one and a half million would call for as much as 480 pesos per ton. The two economists went on to point out that other sectors

18. See *Granma*, French weekly summary, November 3, 1968.
19. Of the 152 Cuban refineries, 58 were built in the twentieth century, 90 in the nineteenth century, and 4 in the eighteenth century. The most up-to-date are the refineries in Salvador Rosales (Oriente province), built in 1927; in Candido González (Camagüey), built in 1926, and in Siboney (Camagüey), built in 1925. See *Cinco siglos de industria azucarera cubana* (Havana, Ed. Ped., 1968).
20. See Leo Huberman and Paul M. Sweezy: *Socialism in Cuba* (New York, Monthly Review Press, 1969), p. 175.

of the Cuban economy were equally in need of fresh investment, and that the 720 million pesos necessary for stepping up the *zafra* from 8.5 to 10 million tons were more than the total Cuban investment in all branches of the economy in 1963.[21]

True, when he decided to give absolute priority to sugar production, Fidel still had faith in the fabulous Khrushchev machine, and was therefore entitled to think that his experts in the Ministry of Agriculture had taken an overpessimistic view of the cost involved. Moreover, once the plan had been put into operation it was probably difficult to revoke it, for political no less than for economic reasons.

Nor should it be forgotten that investment in the 10-million-ton *zafra* would serve Cuba for many years to come. The Cubans have already increased the potential of their sugar refineries by 43 per cent; they have reorganized the ports of Matanzas, Cienfuegos, and Guayabal (in Camagüey), where an annual 6 million tons of bulk sugar can now be loaded straight onto ships; they have built new railway lines, roads, depots, repair-shops—and they have spent $465 million on fertilizing, irrigating, and otherwise improving. All this will remain, as will the bulldozers and heavy tractors supplied by Richard-Continental of Lyon for the nice round figure of $36 million (largely on credit), and the large fertilizer plant in Cienfuegos constructed by Britain for $60 million. The list of other investments is too long to include here; the Cubans have never disguised the fact that during the past few years they have been importing vast quantities of equipment from the convertible currency zone, almost exclusively for the sugar industry. This is what Fidel himself had to say on the subject: "We know perfectly well that we are short of many things. We know what the men and women of this country would like to buy. Nevertheless, during the coming years, we must confine investment to the essentials, and that means buying new machines. This is our guarantee of future abundance."[22]

21. *Ibid.*, p. 177.
22. Fidel Castro's speech of March 13, 1968.

But will a successful ten-million-ton *zafra*, in fact, ensure this great leap from austerity to relative abundance? Three quarters of the output is contractually earmarked for the Eastern bloc, and the two to three million tons left over for the free market are not enough to pay Cuba's debts in other parts of the world. The balance of payments with these countries was already in deficit to the tune of almost $100 million in 1967 (exports: $166 million; imports: $262 million) ; and since then the import of Western equipment has been stepped up considerably.[23] As the crucial *zafra* approaches, hard currency imports for the sugar industry grow bigger and bigger; even if there were an increase in world sugar prices, it would take Cuba several years to pay her creditors.

The reader might wonder why we have failed to include the 660 million pesos Russia will be paying for its share of the giant *zafra*. This raises a most interesting point. During his negotiations with Fidel in Moscow, Khrushchev told him: "Don't worry, we won't cheat you."[24] And, in fact, Russia agreed to pay Cuba what, at the time, was a very fair price for her sugar. However, from the outset many observers have expressed disquiet at the fact that, in order to meet her obligations to the U.S.S.R., Cuba should be forced to change her meager dollar reserves into rubles. For this is what is happening—in order to earn these rubles, Cuba has to invest vast amounts of hard currency in new plants and machinery.

23. The OECE statistics from which we have taken these figures are not up to date, and we are still awaiting complete records for the years 1968–69. But a few examples may serve to illustrate the general trend of Cuban purchases in the West. In 1967 total imports from France were $14.59 million, but in 1968 Richard-Continental alone supplied bulldozers and tractors worth $36 million. In addition, the Cubans have bought 1000 Berliet trucks at $25 million, and water pumps from Richier Benoto-Alta Pompe for a very large (but unspecified) amount. The same trend is apparent in trade with Great Britain, which sold Cuba goods worth $21.58 million in 1967; in 1968 Simon Carver began to build a chemical fertilizer plant which alone is worth $60 million. At the same time, British deliveries of irrigation equipment have gone up by leaps and bounds.

24. *"No vamos a engañarles."* See Fidel Castro's speech of January 24, 1964.

"Hay problemas, hay contradicciones"

Admittedly, the Russians can argue that they promised to buy no more than 5 million tons of Cuban sugar, and that they did not force Fidel Castro to produce twice that figure. If he decided to do so, it was for his own reasons, and no one could rightly blame the U.S.S.R. But this is a purely formal argument, one that completely ignores Cuba's desperate need for imports from the West. In fact, knowing that he would have to supply five million tons of sugar to the U.S.S.R. and more than two million tons to the other socialist countries (including one million tons to China), Fidel was forced to increase his target further in order to sell to the free market and gain convertible currency. He did not do it out of spite, but simply because the U.S.S.R. and her allies were unable to supply him with certain types of essential equipment, not to mention a wide range of less essential consumer goods. We have seen that these extra tons were precisely the ones that called for the greatest dollar investment.[25] In these circumstances, the Soviet Union really has

25. The figures that we cited after Michel Gutelman, Huberman, and Sweezy were based on preliminary estimates made by the Cubans in 1965. During the plan's execution these figures were evidently revised and we have reason to suppose that the budget of investment was increased rather than decreased. We make this inference from the experience of all socialist countries where, despite recent efforts to control investments, budgets are regularly surpassed and remain refractory to the "orders of the planners." In the Cuban case, where scarcely any attempt is made to economize or respect financial estimates, it would be more than surprising if the preliminary estimates of 1965 had been reduced along the way. Besides, the criticism that Edward Boorstein (author of *The Economic Transformation of Cuba, op. cit.*) directs simultaneously at Gutelman, Huberman, and Sweezy in the *Guardian* for July 26, 1969, seems to us ill founded. Boorstein himself does not cite any figures and is content to show that the Cubans canceled the construction of two new sugar centrals initially planned for and instead increased the expenditure for varieties of sugar cane that can be harvested in summer. Do the savings on the first project compensate for the expenses on the second? We do not know but have reason to doubt it. In the absence of official figures published by the Cubans, we are obliged to rely on the only existing figures—those of Gutelman, Huberman, and Sweezy. Moreover, Gutelman's book appeared in 1967 and the Cuban leaders had ample time to dispute his figures, his calculations, and his thesis, according to which the Cubans use sugar to transform dollars into rubles. If they have done nothing of the sort, it is because his thesis is difficult to refute.

no moral right to insist on her contractual rights, and on the superhuman sacrifices these entail for Cuba. Even forgetting the fiasco of the Khrushchev machine which upset all calculations from the start, the mere fact that Cuba has been forced to buy large quantities of equipment (tractors, trucks, and bull-dozers) from the West is a crushing indictment of Soviet industry, and one that Cuba is forced to make good with badly needed dollars.

No wonder that Michel Gutelman, a Belgian economist who has lived in Cuba and has studied the sugar problem on the spot, contends that the U.S.S.R. ought to pay for at least part of the sugar deliveries in convertible currency. This, he contends, would lead to the neutralization of those mechanisms which demand dollar investment for ruble sales. "Over and above the obligations of proletarian internationalism which impose a clear moral duty on every socialist country to help its less developed neighbors without exacting the full price, mutual interest alone, based on the division of labor in the socialist camp, would make sound economic sense of payment in foreign currency for part of the Cuban sugar imports."[26]

Employing René Dumont's estimates of the resale price of beet sugar produced in the U.S.S.R.—16 cents per pound—Michel Gutelman goes on to point out that the Soviet Union would still do good business by buying Cuban sugar in hard currency at six cents per pound.[27] Leo Huberman and Paul M. Sweezy[28] also claim that for climatic reasons and because of the nature of its soil, the Soviet Union is unlikely to reduce the cost of its sugar crop and ought therefore to be thankful for having found

26. See Michel Gutelman: *L'Agriculture socialisée à Cuba*, p. 214.
27. "To grow the five million tons due to her on Soviet soil—where the mean yield is 2.5 tons per hectare—the U.S.S.R. would have to deploy 200,000 hectares of land. In Cuba the same result can be produced on only 62,000 hectares." Michel Gutelman, *op. cit.*, p. 215.
28. Leo Huberman and Paul M. Sweezy, *op. cit.*, p. 77. The authors also contend, however, that Soviet sugar production has been increasing by an annual 13 per cent since 1960, probably reaching 9.6 million tons in 1965. This suggests that the Russians have no faith in the Cuban deliveries, since they would otherwise have grown more profitable crops.

"Hay problemas, hay contradicciones"

a partner like Cuba, favored by nature and capable of supplying agricultural products at a low price. Self-interest and internationalist aspirations alike ought therefore to convince the Russians that Cuban agriculture must be given every encouragement, even if Russia has to pay for it in dollars.

All these arguments presuppose a genuine division of labor in the socialist camp, when no such division has ever been part of their several plans. In fact, if the socialist countries were capable of coordinating their trade and general economic development, if each would specialize in a given field for the benefit of all, none would suffer a lack of foreign currency or a shortage of goods. The Cubans would not have been forced to invest their dollars in heavy or light equipment, because the socialist camp would have been able to supply it all, and the problem of payment in convertible currency would not have arisen in the first place. Unfortunately, such are present conditions in the Eastern bloc that it is as idle to count on a genuine socialist division of labor as it is to look for hymns of praise to Mao Tse-tung in the columns of *Pravda*.

In any case, the Cubans are no longer young enough or naïve enough to rely on the magic wand of the Soviet fairy. They try, like all members of the socialist family, to look after themselves as best they can. Perhaps in their next contract with the Soviet Union they will obtain better credit terms and higher sugar prices—not that the Soviet leaders have been filled with remorse about Cuba's difficulties, or shamed by Che Guevara's Algiers account of their uncomradely trading practices. They think of Cuba as a costly experiment, and they tell all those who care to listen that they have been pampering this ungrateful island, and that they can never recover their investments with any amounts of sugar, nickel, and tobacco Cuba may be able to send.

Fidel Castro told me one day that he was shocked to read in the pro-Soviet press that Soviet aid to his country had risen to a million dollars per day. He did not deny that his country was in debt to the U.S.S.R., but he assured me that full records had been kept and that they would be repaid to the last kopeck. No aid was involved at all; just ordinary business. "But even if they had come to our aid, if they had made us a free present of 356 million dollars per year—which they have not—why should they be boasting about it? What could be more natural for a great socialist country than to help a small island? What do 356 million dollars mean in the budget of a country like the U.S.S.R.? They give us nothing for nothing, and then act as if they were our greatest benefactors, as if they were showering us with gold!"

For Fidel Castro, dealings with the U.S.S.R. were decidedly no love affair, but a harsh necessity imposed by circumstances. Ironically, his great sugar plans only serve to bind him more tightly to his exacting partner. This is the great contradiction—and the essential problem—of the present situation. All the rest is its direct consequence.

One conscience or two?

Four hours of productive work per day was the national average in Cuba in 1966–68. This figure is not strictly official but has been mentioned at least once in *Granma*.[29] Moreover, though it is extremely difficult to establish the precise relationship between the possible and the actual man-hours, it is quite certain that absenteeism, poor discipline, and low productivity have for years been recognized as the real evils of the Cuban economy; neither appeals nor fines have been able to eradicate them. It is said in Havana that if there were a way of making every Cuban work the full eight-hour day the law demands of him, the situation would improve rapidly.

But why is it so difficult to discover this way? How can we reconcile the Cuban leaders' boasts about the deep commitment of the whole nation with complaints about low productivity? Fidel's own answer is simple:

"We are a people filled with enthusiasm and resolve, who at crucial moments are willing to lay down our lives, any hour, any day, anxious to perform the most heroic deeds at any minute.

29. In reporting the meeting of the Trade Union Congress (CTCR) in August 1966.

"Hay problemas, hay contradicciones"

But we are also a people lacking in constancy and courage, not at dramatic moments, but during each and every humdrum day. In other words we still lack persistence and are somewhat fickle in our heroism."[30]

And he named the chief cause of this temporary lack of virtue: underdevelopment. I heard him speak of it to the workers in the cement factory mentioned before, just outside Havana: "The English and the Germans have become famous for their punctuality, but when they were underdeveloped, I doubt if they were more punctual than we are."[31] And I could fill whole chapters with similar quotations from Fidel about the corrosive effect of underdevelopment on the behavior of his compatriots.

Underdevelopment was on everyone's lips. A great literary hit and a film based upon it were called *Memoirs of Underdevelopment*.[32] Both painted an unadorned picture of the survival in Cuba of some of the old mores. A minister or a Major will often be the first to point at a peasant dozing beneath a tree, or at a worker taking a rest beside his broken machine instead of trying to fix it. These, they will tell the visitor, are obvious consequences of underdevelopment. And after hearing this argument long enough, the visitor, too, often ends up by blaming all the troubles of Cuban life on this inherited plague. After all, he tells himself, similar blots on the social horizon can be found in every part of the Third World. It stands to reason that centuries of exploitation must distort and pervert the best human instincts.

Much of this is true, of course; yet this type of explanation is a gross oversimplification. For Cuba was never quite like the Congo, and since 1959, she has enjoyed the benefits of a progressive government, which ought to have stimulated her energies and given her people an immense thirst for knowledge.

30. Fidel's speech of March 13, 1968, as published in the French edition of *Granma*, March 24, 1968.
31. On January 5, 1968, in the presence of President Dorticós and most of the Cuban leaders. The speech was not meant for publication.
32. The author of this successful book, published in translation in the United States, was Edmundo Desnoes. The film was directed by Gutiérrez Alea.

427

Guerrillas in Power

Hence if Cuba continues to be afflicted by the worst symptoms of colonialism so many years after her great leap forward, the cause must surely be a decline in revolutionary fervor and not simply underdevelopment.

It is extremely difficult to draw Castroists into an unbiased discussion of this subject. To them the revolutionary spirit has never been as vigorous, as radical, as infective as it is at present. Their slogans covering walls from Havana to the most far-flung corners of the land, all proclaim it boldly: devotion to the common good, contempt for money, equality, a nobler style of life, the education of the whole man, a truly socialist outlook. In Cuba, you are told, you will not find the kind of deadly routine or the deep resignation that are so typical of socialist countries in Europe.

But facts are obstinate. Despite her progressive aspirations, Cuba, like Eastern Europe, continues to suffer from the insufficient output of her labor force. Paradoxically, the only country to be spared this impediment is China, which is, moreover, by far the poorest member of the socialist family. This cannot be solely due to the persistence of old habits, but must also spring from the moral climate reigning in all these postrevolutionary societies. If people fail to find in their everyday tasks, in the "daily and peaceful struggle for socialism," the same heroic incentives they experience at the height of revolution, then it must be because the new social relationships are such as to cause a loss of interest in communal affairs. The direct result is a subtle lack of enthusiasm, a waning interest in politics, a drop in productivity, and a growth of antisocial behavior.

In Cuba, as in Eastern Europe, low productivity is not simply a remnant from the past; it persists because the relationship between man and society remains defective, not to say bad. No amount of ultrarevolutionary slogans or socialist enclaves can disguise this fact; indeed, they merely serve to underline the striking contrast between hopes and reality. In Cuba, this becomes obvious the moment one looks more closely at certain facets of daily life.

428

"Hay problemas, hay contradicciones"

We shall not dwell on the inadequacies of a supply system that forces the people to stand in line for every item of food or clothing. In Havana, where the shops open at six in the morning, housewives have to spend their nights waiting outside. All the Ministry of the Interior does to help them is to issue the warning that unless they lock up their houses, they may find their possessions gone in the morning.[33] But no one apparently tries to improve the supply system itself, no one seems shocked by its failings. It is said that the officials in the Ministry of Home Trade have the safest posts in the whole country—no one is after their jobs—and this fact alone discourages initiative.

Consumer goods issued *por la libreta*—in exchange for ration tickets—are cheap, and within reach of all.[34] *Por la libre*, i.e., without ration cards, you can buy practically nothing, not even

33. This sound piece of advice to housewives was given by Minister Pedro Pupo Pérez, during a television interview, published in the international edition of *Granma*, of May 11, 1969.
34. Here, for example, are the prices of a number of rationed articles (one peso = one U.S. dollar; one centavo = one U.S. cent) :

Meat (first quality)	50 centavos per pound
Meat (second quality)	38 centavos per pound
Chicken	55 centavos per pound
Condensed milk	20 centavos per pound
Rice	19 to 21 centavos per pound
Lard	25 centavos per pound
Oil	23 centavos per pound
Macaroni	33 centavos per pound
Dried beans	14 to 16 centavos per pound
Coffee	96 centavos per pound
Flour	10 centavos per pound
Eggs	1 peso per dozen
Toilet soap	16 centavos per bar
Detergents	28 centavos per pound
Washing soap	15 centavos per bar
Toothpaste	50 centavos per large tube and
	30 centavos per small tube
Men's trousers	10 to 22 pesos
Work shirts	2.5 to 3.5 pesos
Underpants	1.1 to 2.75 pesos
Leather shoes	7.5 to 1.5 pesos

Guerrillas in Power

cigars or sugar.[35] Durable goods have completely disappeared from the official market. The rare Japanese or East European television set is earmarked for public institutions. There are no motor cars for sale since Cuba has not imported any for years, and the unofficial secondhand market was dealt a fatal blow when gas became rationed.[36] In practice, all essentials, from dishcloths to detergents, are sold in driblets *por la libreta.* All other goods—paint, for example—are quite unobtainable.

In these circumstances, what is the meaning of wage differentials? We have seen that the government refuses to level wages by pruning at the top and hence maintains relatively wide differentials. This, you are told, is essential if a host of nonpolitical technicians is not to decamp for greener fields. It also has the psychological advantage of showing people that their standard of living is not being reduced. But since wages have long since ceased to have the least relation to cost, it looks very much as if the whole wages structure belongs to the realm of pure fantasy.

In reality, things are much more complex than that; in Cuba, as elsewhere, it is better to have money than to be without. To begin with, there is still the luxury trade. High-class restaurants—the *Monseñor,* the *Torre,* the *1830,* the *Floridita,* and many less famous ones, still offer their clients excellent fare in ultra-chic surroundings, at prices that, in the past, only rich American tourists could afford. And taking the peso at its official value (1 peso = 1 U.S. dollar), a good meal costs as much as if not more than in the best restaurants of New York and Paris. Twenty, thirty, or forty dollars is the least a couple with average appetites must expect to pay. And yet long lines form outside these sumptuous establishments, waiting patiently as if they were outside a soup kitchen. So great is the throng

35. Sugar and cigar rationing was not introduced until 1969. The current sugar ration is 3 kilograms per month, and the cigar ration 4 per week.
36. Gasoline rationing was introduced on January 2, 1968, and at first the issue was fairly high. But the rations were reduced a few weeks later, and 90 per cent of Cuba's cars are old American ones, which are very heavy on fuel.

430

that telephone reservations can no longer be accepted; you have to be present in person at the time of place distribution, which takes place each day, several hours before meals are served.

It goes without saying that less elegant restaurants or simple cafeterias are besieged by even larger crowds. Though their prices, too, seem prohibitive when judged by the average wage, and though the clients must make do with whatever is put on their plates, bad meals costing at least five pesos are better than nothing at all.

There is yet another way of spending your money, the best way of all perhaps, though it calls for even greater perseverance: you can take up temporary residence in one of the big hotels, where meals are not generally served to mere passers-by. Therefore, if you want to dine in the luxurious Habana Libre or the Hotel Nacional or the Habana Riviera, you must first of all invest fifteen pesos a day for a resident's card. This is no waste of money, for it entitles you to the use of swimming pools, and to many services and distractions, and thus offers the citizens of Havana brief holidays on their very doorstep. And for many it is no great sacrifice to pay up to fifty pesos a day for these rare pleasures; after all the Americana on Miami beach is no cheaper.

Paradoxically, all this luxury has increased by leaps and bounds since Cuba launched its campaign for greater equality and the training of the *hombre nuevo*. There is no direct relationship between the two phenomena; Cubans do not frequent elegant establishments simply to demonstrate their refusal to scorn money. However, the contradictions of a system that rejects the idea of material incentives and yet preserves conspicuous waste in a period of national scarcity are obvious. I remarked on this to one of my guides during the summer of 1967, when the lines outside the restaurants and the hotels were still relatively short. "If we shared what is consumed by the gastronomic sector," I was told, "the difference to the general rations would be negligible. On the other hand, selling fairly small quantities of food at huge prices means removing hundreds

431

of millions of pesos from circulation and so eases inflationary pressures, which is surely to everyone's best advantage."

This sort of reasoning is of course quite spurious, even if one assumes that the government could have done nothing else to avoid inflation. It is an old rule that in periods of difficulty every party favors those classes which are most devoted and useful to it. While waiting for the ten-million-ton *zafra* and other projects to restore economic equilibrium, Cuba might therefore have been expected to reserve a greater part of her national cake for the most zealous and capable workers, for all those whose efforts go furthest to improve the situation. Since complete equality is not yet practicable, it is these people who ought to have received the surplus food that now goes to the luxury restaurants. But Fidel Castro does not accept this view; he refuses on principle to stimulate production by such capitalist tricks. But, in that case, why the wide wage differentials? And does it really make sense to pay most to those who work least, on the ground that they are the only ones backward enough to feel the pull of the peso? In practice, Castro's policy amounts to doling out money like water, and to sponging up the surplus with the help of a consumer's sector, inherited from the old regime, that is privileged above all others and typical of a mode of life and of tastes that are constantly denounced by the Revolution.

Who exactly are the privileged consumers of Havana? Is it true, as some Cubans claim, that ordinary people, too, can from time to time partake of such lordly feasts? I have been unable to gather precise data on the social origins of the people frequenting the big restaurants, but I must confess that this claim has disturbed rather than convinced me. For if a worker does indeed spend his free Sunday waiting in line for the privilege of wasting his weekly wage, his political consciousness—and his tastes—must have become seriously distorted. In any case, it is much more probable that the bulk of the clientele is made up of *rentiers*,[37] underemployed bureaucrats and black marketeers

37. The former owners of nationalized accommodation are paid an indemnity of up to 660 pesos per month, and some receive additional indemnities for their country properties, but precise statistics on this subject

"Hay problemas, hay contradicciones"

—people who have all the time they want to wait outside the *Torre* or the *1830*. Nor are they particularly grateful to the Revolution; they will readily tell you that things used to be infinitely better and, as far as they are concerned, they are probably quite right.

This brings us to the problem of the black market. It is not as conspicuous as the *Torre,* but no one can fail to notice that it is growing apace, despite heavy fines. It is a natural and inevitable by-product of scarcity coupled to the survival of a vast private sector in the countryside. A small peasant will never sell all his produce to the state, if only because he can buy nothing in the towns at official prices. If he does not find an advantageous market for what he creams off, he will keep it for himself, his family, and his friends. Fruit, vegetables, and greens, which are so scarce in Havana, are never absent from the peasant's table. Strict slaughter regulations do not prevent the constant increase of meat consumption in the countryside, to the detriment of the towns.

And there is no lack of private buyers, of people who are only too happy to pay the peasants considerably more than the state does. No doubt the ban on transporting more than thirty-three pounds of food per person, and above all gasoline rationing, hamper the mobility of speculators and so restrict the scope of this kind of trade, but they also cause a further rise in black market prices. All this contributes once again to keep the well-off—and the least productive—in a state of relative gluttony. And here too, there is a flagrant contradiction between Fidel's praiseworthy principle of *no hay a fusilarlos,* of not persecuting the small peasants, and his refusal to tolerate any kind of free market in the countryside; a contradiction that, in the long run, must turn against the regime. The small peasants continue to grumble although they are much better off than they ever were, and although they pocket considerable profits from the black market; the workers feel discriminated against and

---

are lacking. It is said that in Havana alone the number of *rentiers* is in the region of 100,000.

433

suspect one another of illicit trading. Paradoxically, it would have been much simpler for the government to organize a free market than to try controlling these underground machinations.

All these anomalies, which quite a few Castroists will acknowledge in private conversation, have never been discussed in public. I was assured that they would automatically disappear with the end of scarcity. But do they not rather help to prolong it, even to perpetuate it? Do they not harm the moral climate of the country? Do they not have the most adverse effects on the way Cubans work? The whole thing is a vicious circle, with dire economic consequences, and, worse still, with the worst effects on public morality: because it opens up a gulf between government doctrine and practice, it forces everyone to live by a double standard. I have good reason to be afraid of this phenomenon, for I experienced it myself in the U.S.S.R., during the Second World War.

On the purely political plane, that was the era of great popular enthusiasm and patriotic unity. The old slogan, coined during the period of in-fighting among the Bolshevik hierarchy —where Stalin is, there is victory—now came truly into its own. All of us were fighting on Stalin's side of the barricade, against a brutal invader, trying to halt the Nazi onslaught. Neither the end nor the means were in any doubt, and daily deeds of heroism were the rule not only at the front but also in all the factories.

But we were also living in a country where inflation and bureaucratic methods had led to a complete disparity between wages and prices. In 1944, I was a student at Rostov University, and my grant of 120 rubles a month[38] enabled me to eat, badly, in the canteen, to pay for my bed in the students' home, to buy (rationed) cigarettes, and to get what were supposed to be cheap seats at the movies from time to time.[39] All in all, therefore,

38. The grants were increased by annual increments. Thus while a first-year student received 120 rubles, fifth-year students were given up to 200 rubles.
39. I say "supposed to be," since in practice dealers would resell all the available tickets at fancy prices (up to twenty rubles per seat).

434

we students had few grounds for complaint. Most of us, moreover, were Red Army veterans despite our age, and had been sent to the university as a reward.

Yet the moment we stepped out of the cloistered environment of our alma mater, we discovered a strange world full of unsuspected pleasures. Rostov could not boast luxury restaurants or, for that matter, restaurants of any kind—each one of us was tied to his particular canteen. But there were two remarkable places where no one seemed to bother in the least about such humdrum things as rationing: the *kolkhoznyi rynok* (collective-farm market) and the *tolkuchka* (hustling). The *rynok,* as its name indicated, was supposed to sell the surplus of farm produce grown by cooperatives or individual peasants. In the event, most of this produce was quickly scooped up by resourceful housewives who, after procuring other ingredients (most of them rationed) turned it all into delectable borscht, succulent piroshkis, and a whole range of other equally mouthwatering dishes. They did the actual cooking at home, and then set up small stalls, keeping their pots warm under old blankets or on spirit lamps. Vodka, bread, and all the trimmings of a good Russian meal were freely on sale. It was not rare to see a high-ranking Red Army officer or a militia commander comfortably perched on a stool, savoring the excellent cuisine and complimenting the *khoziaika* (housewife) on her skill. The price was agreed in advance; the *khoziaikas* evidently did not do all this work for love or charity. In fact the payment they extorted was such that one might have thought it was perpetual payday in Rostov—at the *rynok,* two full meals and a couple of glasses of good vodka would just about swallow up a salesclerk's monthly wage.

At the *tolkuchka* you could buy a wide range of articles: clothes, furniture, and secondhand books (including officially banned works). And once the Red Army had marched into Germany, the number of products hit a new record, as every soldier sent a flood of trophies and mementos back home. Curiously, the increase in the supplies did not seem to depress the prices, which, as those expert in Marxism-Leninism never tired of assuring us, only went to prove that capitalist market criteria do not apply to a socialist system.

The authorities were perfectly aware of the real laws governing this murky sector of public life. For no one made any secret of the fact that, in the *tolkuchka*, you could also buy ration cards, special coupons, army coats, and God knows what else—rumor even had it that military medals and citations were for sale. The state tolerated it all, because it was quite unable to organize a more effective distribution system. One knew that this tolerance was purely temporary, that the authorities might clamp down at any moment, but everyone consoled himself that, after all, they could not throw everyone into jail. Meanwhile you just took your chance and made the best of your brief respite.

And so we all had our little private plans for "primary socialist accumulation" and were prepared to run the risks this entailed. And the state even helped us: it gave us travel permits two or three times a year, which enabled us to close the supply gap between town and country, or between one town and the next. Sometimes it even offered us the chance to round off our budgets with still fewer formalities. Thus port authorities in Rostov used to employ students for loading fish onto special trains. They paid us the official rate—a ruble an hour at the maximum—but recognizing the meagerness of that sum, they allowed us to walk out of the port, two or three times a night, *without being searched*. This made all the difference; we all wore coats with pockets deep enough to accommodate quite a sizeable number of fish. Commercially-minded housewives would buy them from us on the spot, and at very high prices.

We were never smitten with remorse. We lived our double life with a good conscience, and yet not one of us would have wanted to impede the war effort or retard victory by one day. Some even tried to produce a theoretical justification of what they called our efforts to improve distribution outside the normal channels. According to them, the planners in Moscow

"Hay problemas, hay contradicciones"

ought to congratulate themselves on our contribution, and bear it in mind when drafting their next set of annual plans. It would take me too long to list all the sophistries of our small circle of students in the science of Marxism-Leninism. But for those who are not fully familiar with the fourth chapter of the *Shorter History of the Communist Party of the Soviet Union*[40] our views might be summed up as follows: even in a socialist society each one must fend for himself, must rely on his wits and emulate those who work least and hence have the most time to fill their pockets—after all, some have bigger pockets than others. Above all, one must not expect too much of that unpredictable and vague entity known as the community. In short, we had all of us ‘fallen victim—more or less consciously, more or less openly—to a stunted form of individualism.

This type of social conditioning, this atomization of society, partly explains Russia's low productivity, even during the war, and the lack of protest against all the injustices that were visited, immediately after the war, upon the heads of a great many who had most contributed to Russia's victory. Our stunted individualism inoculated us against resentment, revolt, and political impulses. Someone who lives in an inexplicable world, who does not expect anything from others, cannot be surprised by, or object to, whatever tricks fate chooses to play on him. All he wants is to be left alone. True, such things as the *kolkhoznyi rynok* or the *tolkuchka* were not the only blots on the moral horizon of postwar Soviet society, but they alone suffice to demonstrate that the wrong sort of mentality does not vanish automatically with the destruction of capitalism.

The Cubans ought to have agreed with this conclusion; what other justification was there for their small heresy? But they were obviously reluctant to admit any similarity between their present situation and that of Russia under Stalin. They even protested

40. In this chapter, which used to be the Soviet bible, Stalin personally explained the true meaning of dialectical and historical materialism. These twenty pages formed the entire basis of our political studies at the University.

that young Cubans, the counterparts of my comrades in the University of Rostov, had a sovereign contempt for money, and could never be tempted by *langoustes au chocolat* at the *Monseñor* or by the questionable delight of staying in luxury hotels. Then, in the spring of 1968, Fidel Castro suddenly spoke out, not against these anomalies themselves, but against their most blatant repercussions. He launched a "Great Revolutionary Offensive" that was intended to mobilize the entire nation for land work; and this time he meant literally the entire nation.

This outburst had been coming for quite some time because, for all his talk about persuading the masses by setting them a revolutionary example, Fidel found it quite intolerable, unfair, and immoral that laggards should meanwhile be left to enjoy the fruits of other people's labor. And most of these could be found in Havana. Fidel had never loved this city;[41] to his mind it symbolized all the misfortunes of Cuban history, the unjust and scandalous character of her old economy and above all, the mercantile spirit he was determined to extirpate. Born in Oriente, he seems to have retained all his youthful pride in his native province, the cradle of Cuban independence, and with it a subconscious hatred of the capital's riches. In 1959, he had wanted to move the seat of government to Santiago, but it had proved impossible to administer the country from this remote city. Forced to spend most of his time in petit-bourgeois Havana, he became more and more allergic to the spectacle of its superficial prosperity. In his speech of July 26, 1967, he had already inveighed against "those itinerant purveyors of fried eggs and apple fritters"—particularly widespread in the old town— and had publicly exposed their immoral profit margins. The Revolution had not been made to keep such people in unaccustomed luxury, and Fidel promised revolutionary laws to put an end to this scandal.

41. Claude Julien mentioned Fidel's dislike of Havana in a book he wrote in 1960, before the Castroists embraced socialism. See Claude Julien, *La Révolution cubaine* (Paris, Juillard, 1961), pp. 100–101.

"Hay problemas, hay contradicciones"

But before taking further action, he decided to give the Havanese a last chance to redeem themselves: at the end of 1967, he invited them to build the *Cordón de la Habana*, to transform a vast zone round their city into an immense green belt: orange groves and coffee plantations, all complete with the most up-to-date dairy farms, and special centers for growing other crops. *"Para tomarlo, hay que sembrarlo"*—if you like coffee you have only to plant it, was the slogan of the day. *Granma* explained that Havana province, which represents slightly less than 30 per cent of the country's population, consumes almost half the agricultural output. This was neither fair nor reasonable. An extraordinary propaganda campaign was therefore started. In principle, the work was to be done by volunteers, but in fact, each factory and office was given its own sowing schedule, with orders to fulfill it come what may. Fidel spent New Year's Eve 1968 with volunteers in the *Cordón* to stress the importance of the work to be done.

And the people of Havana rushed out into the fields: many lived in tents for several weeks on end; others preferred to go out at dawn to return to their families at night. People were full of praise for the new scheme; it would cushion the capital against breakdowns in deliveries and above all it would enable her to withstand a possible break with the U.S.S.R. Fidel's speech on January 2, 1968, had lent much weight to the common rumor that such a break was imminent. Moreover, by introducing gasoline rationing, Fidel made it clear that Russia was applying pressure even now, and that the dignity of the Revolution demanded that Cubans tighten their belts. He did not say it in so many words, but a few days later *Granma* made a point of explaining that the cut in supplies was not due to shortages in the Soviet Union, where oil production had reached the record level of 300 million tons in 1967.[42] The obvious inference

---

42. *Granma* reprinted an article from *Pravda* on the progress of the Soviet oil industry, in a prominent place and without comment. This was evidently a highly effective way of showing how shabbily the Russians were

was that, for purely political reasons, Russia had decided to cut her supplies, and that there would be a shortage, not only of oil, but also of grain and of other produce. But thanks to her new *Cordón,* Havana would always have plenty of café au lait, fruit, and perhaps even meat. Some added: we also have cigars, in case our stomachs still rumble.

Foreign economists asked timidly if the *Cordón* was not likely to create fresh manpower problems, seeing that the ten-million-ton *zafra* had already depleted the urban labor force. They were told that their anxiety was quite unfounded; sowing and harvesting coffee and oranges were very simple tasks, which even schoolboys could perform, so that the men could safely be left to get on with the *zafra.* In any case, the *Cordón* had a social as well as an economic purpose; as the different strata were brought into closer proximity, distinctions between town and country were bound to decrease dramatically. Everyone in Havana appreciated this fact, and many were anxious to seize this chance of sharing some part of their lives with those who lived closest to nature.

It was in this light that we must look at the Great Revolutionary Offensive, launched by Fidel on March 13, 1968. "It must be admitted," he said on that occasion, "that bourgeois institutions, ideas, relationships, and privileges still persist among us. . . . We have always sought the best methods, have always tried to make life just a little richer every day, but there is no doubt that the old institutions have survived much longer than they ought to have done, that privileges have gone on for much too long. . . . This does not mean that the people of Havana are to blame; they have thrown themselves in great numbers and with incredible enthusiasm into the good work. . . . But there are many lazy people in the pink of condition, who take to their kiosks and run small businesses that enable them to make fifty

---

behaving. In fact, the U.S.S.R. had never claimed that it was short of oil. The main reason for the failure in deliveries was Cuba's adverse balance of payments, aggravated further by failure to reach the expected sugar target in time.

pesos per day, violating the law of the land and the laws of hygiene, while they watch truck loads of women go by for *el Cordón de la Habana.* . . . Many people wonder what sort of revolution it is that still allows such parasites to flourish after nine long years." Having stated the problem in these terms, Fidel revealed the results of a Communist Party inquiry into the extent and profits of private trade, and especially of the small bars, numbering 950 in Havana alone. All of them were guilty of bad revolutionary faith and were said to be frequented by asocial elements.[43]

And having pilloried these "parasitic upstarts," Fidel suggested that the people themselves might care to deal with them as they thought fit. Many Castroists did not hesitate to tell you (in private, in order not to tread on the anti-Chinese toes of the Russians) that here you had a Cuban version of the Cultural Revolution. And, in fact, the most active of them took direct action against these profiteers and asocial elements. Thus men from the television station invaded the *Funeraria*—a sort of café-cum-gallery that had sprung up toward the end of 1967 in an old funeral home on Twenty-third Street, in the center of Vedado, across the road from the broadcasting building. After first throwing out all the clients, they posted pickets with orders to stop anyone from entering. And yet the *Funeraria* had nothing private about it; on the contrary, it had been opened at great expense by the state, and a number of famous painters, including Edouard Pignon, who had come from Europe for the Cultural Congress, had helped to decorate it. But the activists found it intolerable that, whenever they looked out of their office windows, they should see young girls in mini-skirts and apparently carefree youth spending hours laughing and listening to music, as if they had nothing better to do. "We are not killjoys, we have no objection to people enjoying their leisure

43. In his speech of March 13, 1968, Fidel said not a word about the possible replacement of these asocial establishments by state-run shops and bars, and, in fact, nothing at all was done about the matter.

441

and amusing themselves, but at present Cuba has much more pressing and important tasks," Fidel had said, thus giving his blessing to the exploits of the television heroes.

During the first forty-eight hours of the Great Revolutionary Offensive, more than seven hundred meetings were called throughout Havana by trade unions, branches of the Communist Party, the Communist Youth League, and the Women's League, all demanding that the slackers be punished. There was little street violence, and physical attacks by the indignant people on speculators or idlers were extremely rare. The authorities had prepared lists of anyone operating in the private sector, and especially of those who did so without a permit (their number was said to represent a third of the total), and they themselves took quick and effective action. In less than a week, private trade had come to a standstill, not only in Havana, but in every Cuban town. According to the official figures published late in March 1968, altogether 58,012 stalls, shops, and private service establishments were nationalized, and large secret stocks of consumer goods were confiscated. In Havana alone, the authorities closed 16,634 private enterprises.

This figure included 9,179 craftsmen working on their own, with and without licenses. They were all invited to take their rightful place in the various factories. As for the illegal traders, a large body of them got together and offered to make good their past lapses with a promise of wholehearted collaboration with the authorities. The official figures tell us nothing about the precise number of people released for "more suitable" employment; they simply reveal that more than 50 per cent of the newly nationalized concerns had sprung up after the Revolution. In fact, 27 per cent of them had been started by workers who "have deserted their factories to turn into bourgeois egotists, and to accumulate riches by exploiting the very people from whom they had sprung."[44]

44. The figures and the quotation are taken from *Bohemia*, March 21, 1969, No. 12.

"Hay problemas, hay contradicciones"

Samples of the confiscated goods were shown on television; they were mostly spare parts for motor cars or television sets, linen, soap, condensed milk, flour, butter, perfumes, deodorants, and other products in short supply. Many of the traders had lived an extremely simple life, for fear that their neighbors would discover their crimes and become jealous of their good fortune. Others had lived off the fat of the land, flaunting their riches. But no matter what their attitude, all of them—according to the leader-writers—had modeled themselves on Julio Lobo.[45] The press dwelled on this point at great length, perhaps to emphasize the fact that the government was not really applying double standards in suppressing the private sector in the cities, while granting facilities to peasants working on their own behalf. "The peasantry is a productive class and is therefore a valuable ally of the revolutionary proletariat," Fidel had explained time and again, and *Granma* was not slow in recalling this very opportune message. And having done so, the paper went on to explain that Cuba was now "the socialist country with the largest nationalized sector!"[46]

But the Great Revolutionary Offensive had not simply been conceived for the purpose of eliminating petty profiteers; its major aim was to inspire the productive enthusiasm of the workers. "War on indulgence, on selfishness, on individualism, on parasitism, on vice, on exploitation; still more revolution!"— a mass of red placards proclaimed in bold letters. All workers were invited to fight this good fight to its happy conclusion. Even cabarets—which used to be encouraged because they suited the Cuban taste and temperament—were now closed.

In the future, no one would be allowed to remain inactive. Even prospective emigrants to America were mobilized: "Before joining imperialist society, they too must contribute their brick, their grain of sand toward the national edifice." A slogan that used to be famous in the U.S.S.R.—*"kto nie rabotayet, tot*

45. One of the richest men in Cuba before the Revolution.
46. *Bohemia*, No. 12, 1969.

nie yest" (those who do not work, do not eat) —was restored
to honor in Cuba. All future émigrés—or "Johnsons,"[47] as they
were called—would henceforth have to "earn by the sweat of
their brow the Cuban bread they consume before their departure."[48] The Cubans had few illusions as to the productivity
of these people, but their enforced stay on the land would help to
proletarianize Havana; and, in any case, no one could be allowed
to sit by with folded arms while others worked so hard.

The most spectacular innovation, however, was the new
method for reaching the fixed agricultural targets. Though the
word "militarization" was never used officially, the whole country was, in fact, reorganized on the model of its army. "Command
posts" led by members of the Political Bureau were set up in
every province to coordinate the great agricultural "battle."
Labor brigades were turned into battalions, each divided into
three squads, led by a major and a chief of operations responsible for discipline and work progress. As soon as a particular task, however small, had been completed, the command post
was informed and new measures were taken accordingly. If
necessary, reinforcements were sent to squads that had fallen

47. Since the beginning of the Revolution, the Cuban government has
allowed discontented elements to leave the country. However, the number of
planes available for this purpose proved quite inadequate after 1961, and
prospective emigrants found it increasingly difficult to obtain seats with the
regular lines. As a result there were more and more attempts to get away
by sea, a fact that anti-Castro propagandists seized upon with alacrity.
In 1964, Fidel Castro authorized the Americans to set up a "mini-airbridge" between Varadero and Miami to relieve the congestion. As a result
two flights a week still carry one hundred fifty emigrants to the United
States. Others leave the island on regular lines for Madrid and Mexico.
Nevertheless there are still many more candidates than places, so that there
is a long waiting list. In 1964 everyone whose name was on that list
automatically lost his job and had to live on his savings or private income,
but in September 1968 Fidel decided to change the whole system by sending
everyone on the waiting list to work in the fields. The Cubans themselves
have never published figures on the number of these candidates but
according to American sources, quoted by Huberman and Sweezy (*op. cit.*),
there are some 700,000 of them.

48. The last two quotations are taken from Fidel's speech of September
28, 1968.

behind. Motorized battalions were formed. As early as the
autumn of 1967 came a special "invasion brigade" named after
Ernesto Che Guevara. It was provided with giant bulldozers,
and tackled some of the most difficult tasks. The brigade was
under direct army control and served as a model for a host of
civilian detachments equipped with tractors and other agricultural machinery.

Assured of the help of this large army of workers, the
command posts kept setting more and more ambitious targets.
"New fronts" were opened in all the underpopulated and underdeveloped provinces; in Camagüey, for instance, 18,668 *caballerías* of fallow land were opened up for cultivation in 1968.
40,000 men of the regular army, 20,000 students from technical
colleges, and an unspecified number of volunteers from Havana
came to lend the local workers a helping hand. "The land battle
will be won in Camagüey," Raúl Castro proudly proclaimed on
May Day. As minister of defense, Fidel's brother did not seem
the most highly qualified person to pronounce on agricultural
problems. But according to experts on Cuban politics, he had
long held very strong ideas on the best methods of improving
labor discipline and individual output, on provincial priorities
and the desirability of particular crops. Raúl had apparently
first suggested the militarization of land work at a conference
in Santa Clara in 1966; at that time Fidel still preferred to
follow his own method of stimulating output.[49] It was only in

49. The only source of information about this conference is an article
by Saverio Tutino published in *Problemi del Socialismo*, Nos. 32–33
of 1968, from which I would like to quote the following passage
(pp. 974–975): "At the end of 1966, an agricultural conference was held
in Santa Clara and attended by the most important Cuban leaders. The
discussion was broad and frank. Raúl Castro proposed the immediate
adoption of measures to improve discipline. . . . Fidel then spoke at length,
as was his habit, criticizing bureaucratic methods but warning against
excessive pressure. . . ." Tutino also quotes extracts from articles published
by *Bohemia* (unspecified date) and signed by José Llanusa: "Raúl
interrupts and asks for permission to speak. 'For years we have been hearing
Fidel talk about the importance of technology and mechanization. . . . I
cannot imagine how he explains our failure to pay sufficient attention to
the way these machines work. . . . Far too many breaches of discipline have

445

the spring of 1968, when it became clear that the agricultural targets were nowhere near being reached, that Fidel apparently decided to give Raúl a free hand. Whatever the truth of this story, it reflects the conviction of many Cubans that, of the two brothers, Fidel is the more moderate and Raúl the more extreme.

In any case, once the Great Revolutionary Offensive had been launched, all Cuba's leaders spoke with one voice, exalting the great work, and presenting the results in terms usually associated with war dispatches. No matter whether it was the inauguration of a scheme for tapping the River Cauto, or the start of a new highway from Guane to Cienfuegos via Havana, the achievement was praised as yet another victory at the front, and the labor force as a heroic battalion.[50]

Havana had meanwhile been transformed into a typical army base. More than 20,000 people had handed their jobs over to their (previously unemployed) wives and had left to do battle in Camagüey. Factory workers who had reluctantly stayed behind joined Red Brigades and worked unpaid overtime for the good of the community. Selfishness and individualism, *Granma* affirmed, had been dealt a severe blow and were about to disappear altogther. Hotel staffs had voted unanimously against tips, those humiliating relics of the past, and quite a few banded together into a special labor brigade. War is war, and no one in Havana could be allowed to relax until victory was achieved at the front. One such occasion occurred in 1968, when the whole

---

come to our notice and it is quite obvious that we must take adequate measures to improve discipline and use what machines we have in a more rational way.' "

In point of fact, these extracts do not tell us nearly enough about the debate that is supposed to have shown whether it was Raúl or Fidel Castro who decided on the militarization of agriculture in 1968.

50. To quote just one example, on August 4, 1968, *Granma* (French edition), after declaring that the plan for a new Guane-Havana road had been personally drawn up by Commander in Chief Fidel Castro, went on to inform its readers that in July 1968 hundreds of men, "mounted" on powerful machines, had opened two labor fronts some eighteen kilometers from the Coloma-Pinar del Río road, the main front running east toward Havana and the other in the opposite direction toward Guane.

city celebrated the successful completion of the sowing program
for *el Cordón de la Habana*. Otherwise all forms of entertainment were frowned upon; you could not even get a glass of
beer when the dog days proved too trying; all the bars were
closed down. Services, inadequate in the past, became èven
scarcer: most hairdressers, electricians, shoemakers, cleaners,
private or recently nationalized, were sent out to plant coffee, to
sow cane or to pick oranges, and what few remained behind
could only meet the needs of a tiny minority. You had to reckon
on spending at least half a day in line if you were unable to
cut your own hair.

On September 28, 1968, the whole capital was invited to
Revolution Square to celebrate the anniversary of the foundation of the Revolutionary Defense Committees. Here Fidel told
a vast crowd that he was delighted with the results obtained so
far: "Today I can see an immense army, the army of a highly
organized, disciplined, and enthusiastic nation, ready to fulfill
whatever tasks it is set, ready to give battle to all who stand
in the way."[51] However, he admitted that there were problems;
ever since April 1968 a wave of sabotage had beset the country's
economy. Saboteurs had burned down a tannery in the Las
Villas province, a leather store in Havana, a chicken-feed factory
in Santiago, a chemical fertilizer depot in Manzanillo, a provincial store belonging to the Ministry of Internal Commerce in
Camagüey,[52] and so on. This time, Fidel did not accuse the
CIA, but laid the blame at the door of "parasitic elements"
inside Cuba, on people exasperated by the Great Revolutionary
Offensive. "It is only to be expected," he explained "that as the
revolutionary wave advances, the irritation and hatred of our
enemies will increase—the irritation of all those for whom the
Revolution is a curse. It is only natural that they should do their
utmost to undermine the work of the Revolution."

51. Speech on September 28, 1968, published in the French edition of
Granma on September 29.
52. Fidel also gave a long list of petty acts of sabotage, inter alia, in schools
and on building sites.

p*

Another matter, too, was worrying Fidel: the behavior of gay young people who were apparently flaunting their immorality in the very center of Havana. He attributed their lapses to several factors: relatives in Miami, parental neglect, and, often, "the negative influence on these determined youngsters of persons holding certain ideas and translating them into action." On all such counterrevolutionaries Fidel now declared war to the death: "The heads of all who try to destroy the Revolution will fall." As for the offending youth, it would be re-educated through work and military service: "Military law will apply to all youngsters over fifteen who are not engaged in studies. In future, they will be put into uniform. The law will have to be amended, but we already have army units composed of technical students, and these are splendid detachments with magnificent young people."

The tone of this speech was highly disturbing. It marked a decisive departure from the note he had struck during the early years of the Revolution, or even just a few weeks before the Offensive. For the first time, he was speaking with a kind of snarl. Militarism and repression had ceased to be exceptional measures; they had apparently become a permanent remedy for curing the recalcitrance of certain strata or the misconduct of a group of young people. Fidel even apologized for having given the mistaken impression that he was a liberal. In any case, his recent thesis that hostility between the forces of reaction and true revolutionaries must increase as socialism spreads had sinister undertones; Stalin had put forward the same arguments to justify his purges in the '30s. He had been the first to blame breakdowns in his five-year plans on saboteurs and enemies of the people (in that case, the Bolshevik old guard) and to accuse the Bolsheviks of trying to keep their besieged country in a permanent state of poverty and want, by deliberately fostering international tension. Fidel did not go quite so far in his speech of September 28, but he gave clear indications that he was moving in that direction.

Fortunately, the hardening of Fidel's line was not followed by new militarization measures. On the contrary, during the winter of 1968, the fever of the Offensive was allowed to abate. A crusade against refractory intellectuals started by *Verde Olivo*, the army weekly, died a sudden death.[53] On New Year's Eve, the bars and cabarets were reopened, ostensibly for a few days, but they are in fact functioning to this day. A minimum of entertainment is no longer deemed incompatible with the true revolutionary life, and appeals for austerity have become a little less insistent. True, the Great Revolutionary Offensive is not yet over, since the ten-million-ton *zafra* still calls for a great effort,[54] but Castro has obviously realized that further austerity measures would be nothing short of outright repression, and would have the most untoward effects on the economy.

In fact, he could not help noticing that the nation was rejecting the large doses of revolutionary medicine it was supposed to swallow. This recalcitrance had nothing to do with counterrevolution; it was simply that "education through land work" proved too one-sided a form of social education to be truly salutary. Some of his most devoted disciples, it is true, were only too happy to relive the heroic days of the Sierra and were stimulated by the chance to work side by side with tillers of the soil. But before one can appreciate this style of life, one must

53. In October 1968, the international jury of the Union of Cuban Writers and Artists awarded the annual poetry prize to Heberto Padilla and the drama prize to Antony Arrufat, to the dismay of the cultural authorities who greatly disliked these two non-conformists. They nevertheless decided to publish the prize-winning works, but added a critical preface that was the more questionable in that the authors could not reply. Even this was apparently not enough for *Verde Olivo*, which launched a vicious campaign against intellectuals, reminiscent of the Zhdanov period. One Leopoldo Avila, of whom I was told variously that he was an ex-communist, a young army captain, or a fictitious person, distinguished himself quite particularly in this campaign, so much so that many people came to fear the worst: an "anti-microfactional" campaign against intellectuals. The Padilla and Arrufat affair caused consternation among friends of Cuba, familiar with both the works and the character of the accused and hence unable to accept the views of the authorities, let alone Avila's vulgar attacks. Their protests were heeded in Havana: Heberto Padilla was left in peace but dismissed from his post.
54. The year 1969 was christened the "Year of the Decisive Effort."

449

already be a convinced revolutionary. For those who are not, cutting cane and similar tasks are only back-breaking, monotonous, and often repulsive jobs quite unrelated to social progress. Moreover, nearly 60 per cent of all Cubans came from the towns even before the Revolution; therefore, when doing their stint in the fields, they labored during the day at their agricultural tasks and at night returned to the discomfort of their tents, rarely, if ever, making the slightest social contacts with the peasants they were supposed to educate. The mobilization of an entire nation is an exceedingly difficult business unless the country is actually at war. Patriotic calls to agricultural battle are, at best, a form of moral pressure, and far too often lead to a sharp conflict between personal interests and social duty. Even in wartime, mobilization does not necessarily lead to the abolition of social contradictions—as witness the U.S.S.R. during the Second World War.

And, in fact, the economic results of the Great Revolutionary Offensive seem rather slender, at least if sugar production is used as a standard of comparison; the *zafra* of Summer 1968 to Spring 1969 yielded less than 4.5 million tons. Fidel blamed it all on poor organization. In other words, the authoritarian methods and the military measures attributed to Raúl Castro had failed to produce the desired effects. Admittedly, the Year of Decisive Effort was meant to prepare the way for the giant *zafra* of 1970, but one cannot help thinking that the agricultural squads and battalions must feel somewhat discouraged by the poor results their "decisive efforts" have produced so far.

The Great Revolutionary Offensive seems a form of blindness in the face of problems that could have been solved by more adequate political, economic, and social measures. Yet Castroist impatience with the continued unproductiveness and "backward mentality" of the population cannot really surprise anyone familiar with their terrible situation in the spring of 1968. Everything seemed to be turning against them: Che's death, strained relations with the U.S.S.R., the rift with Latin American Communists, and the alarming prospect of Nixon's victory at the polls. "Unfortunately, all our problems cannot be aired in public," Fidel confessed in his speech of March 13, 1968, "because we are a state and as such we must respect certain rules. In the complex and difficult world in which we live, certain things must remain unsaid. . . . All we ask of the people is to trust their leaders and their revolutionary government."

In short, the Cubans had every reason for closing ranks, for wishing to clear their economic hurdles in one brave leap. But the solutions Fidel chose were characteristic of his aristocratic conception of political power and leadership: the men who "know best," "deserve trust," and who have "opened up a vast new perspective to the people" in such a way that "the perspective itself constitutes a mobilizing force, a spur to work, and a source of enthusiasm."[55]

This conception is the basis of Fidel's views on social education, and of his attacks on selfishness and petit-bourgeois attitudes. It also explains his total refusal to admit that Cuba's political institutions might not be all they are cracked up to be, or that there is a lack of genuine rank-and-file democracy. Decrees against antisocial habits are common in socialist countries, yet they have never been able to change the behavior of the masses; at best they have led to nihilistic resignation.

Provisional institutions in perpetuity

On his return from Havana in 1960, Paul Baran[56] wrote that, "while all this [the Cuban system] is based at the present time on direct democracy in action, on the people's unlimited confidence in and affection for Fidel Castro, the time is not too

55. See Fidel's first speech on the great sugar program, quoted on pp. 407–408.

56. Paul A. Baran (1910–1964), professor of economics at Stanford University, author of *The Political Economy of Growth* and co-author (with Paul M. Sweezy) of *Monopoly Capital* (London, Monthly Review Press, 1966), visited Cuba on several occasions from 1960 to 1964. After his first visit, he wrote an essay to show that Cuba would necessarily take the path to full socialism. See Paul A. Baran: *Reflections on the Cuban Revolution* (New York, Monthly Review Press, 1961).

distant when it will become indispensable to create and develop institutions essential to the normal functioning of a democratic, socialist society." This, he went on to say, must be done with minimum repression and violence, and with the enthusiastic participation of the whole nation. At the same time, C. Wright Mills, also just back from Cuba, assured his readers that Fidel Castro was fully aware of the need to develop a system of more organic relationships between the government and the people.[57] Havana greeted the writings of these two staunch friends with a degree of satisfaction bordering on enthusiasm.

It would, of course, be unnecessary to recall these facts if so many Castroists did not still pretend that direct democracy, based on a dialogue between Fidel and the rank and file, constituted an end in itself and not just a step toward a genuine workers' democracy. Far from trying to develop "a system of more organic relations between the rightful government and the Cuban people," they tell themselves that this system already ·exists, indeed that it appeared in 1959–60, and that it has proved its worth ever since. Does that mean that Paul Baran and C. Wright Mills have misjudged the institutional needs of post-revolutionary Cuba? Fidel does not put it quite like that, as we shall see below. According to him, the course of events in European socialist countries shows merely what must be *avoided* on the road to proletarian democracy, and not how to get there. Faced with purely negative models, he has always been reluctant to surrender one prize for the mere shadow of another; he remains convinced to this day that it is far better to keep to his provisional institutions than to institutionalize bureaucracy.

And yet, even when one has made due allowance for all objective difficulties and for their obvious repercussions on the behavior of the Castroist leaders, one cannot but remark upon a most unhappy fact: the prevailing institutional interregnum constitutes an insurmountable handicap to the development of

57. See C. Wright Mills: *Listen, Yankee, op. cit.* p. 183.

all facets of Cuban life. An old Chinese proverb says that progress in history is like rowing against the current; as soon as you ship your oars, you do not stand still but are remorselessly swept back. And, indeed, it would be foolish to expect that after the evils of the "mini-Stalinist" period, after so many economic setbacks and broken promises, Fidel and his men should have been able to re-establish the direct and fruitful dialogue with the rank and file they enjoyed in the past.

This has been recorded for us by a host of enthusiastic visitors, Sartre, Mills, and Baran among them. They were impressed, above all, by Cuba's spontaneous and confident character. It was they who first spoke of direct democracy in Cuba, at a time when Castro was still far too busy practicing it to turn it into theory. The whole thing was in fact a new phenomenon, almost without precedent; Fidel was obviously not just trying to curry popular favor, or to set himself up as a great prophet; he was the mouthpiece of the *humildes,* and was determined to put an end to the social injustices from which they had suffered for far too long. "And if they ask you for the moon?" Sartre demanded. "If someone asked me for the moon, it could be because someone needed it," Fidel replied. Then, turning to Simone de Beauvoir, he added: "From time to time, it is true, they intimidate me. Thanks to us, they dare to discover their needs. They have now the courage to understand their suffering, and to demand that it be ended. In short, they are men. And what do we give them?"[58]

Fidel knew that he could not give the moon to those who asked for it, nor even satisfy their much more real needs here and now. All he wanted was to make them conscious of these needs, and to persuade them to join him in seeking a fair solution. Fidel and his small group of *barbudos* thus set themselves a task after the Revolution which Lenin had long ago assigned to the Communist Party in order to make the revolution: to infuse the masses with class consciousness from without.

58. *Sartre on Cuba* (New York, Ballantine, 1961) , p. 135.

453

Guerrillas in Power

In Cuba, however, the masses were not composed solely of workers and of poor peasants. Here an entire nation had suffered imperialist exploitation. It followed that every last Cuban had the right to participate in, and contribute to, the construction of a new, revolutionary society. And, in fact, quite early, a spontaneous intermingling between town and country took place in a kind of carnival atmosphere: while Habaneros proudly invited the *guajiros* to their homes, young citizens went out to live among the peasants and taught them reading and writing. Nobody had any definite recipes for the future, and no subject of conversation was taboo save one: no one must question the necessity of the Revolution. Fortunately this proviso only bothered a handful of Cubans to whom the free atmosphere all round was anathema in any case.

It might be objected that this general awakening of the masses was not direct democracy for, when all was said and done, Cuba had no Soviets or consultative assemblies; her citizens were merely invited to take a personal interest in the affairs of their resurrected nation. But Cuba was no totalitarian state either, not even a "dictatorship of the proletariat." All in all, therefore, the term "direct democracy" seemed a fair enough, though inadequate, description of a social system in embryonic form still trying to establish itself. Furthermore, a whole series of popular organizations had emerged in the wake of the first outburst of popular enthusiasm. There was the Militia, the symbol of a whole nation under arms; the various Committees for the Defense of the Revolution; the ANAP (National Association of Small Farmers) ; the revolutionary trade unions; and many others. No doubt Paul Baran looked upon all these as rudimentary expressions of the popular government of the future. They were halfway stages between that vague entity called direct democracy, which had infused them with life, and the kind of proletarian democracy that had still to be created and developed.

But what has happened since to this great dialogue between Fidel and the people? What has become of the rank-and-file organizations? Fidel has not changed; he still travels about a great deal and speaks to a lot of people, but no longer to help them "discover their needs"—they seem to know these only too well. He now demands their support for his great development plan which, according to him, is the only way to guarantee every Cuban's future happiness. Nor is their verbal agreement enough; he checks their sincerity by studying their behavior at work and by testing their revolutionary consciousness. At the same time he makes sure that his great plan is proceeding smoothly and tries to make allowances for unforeseen hitches. The result is a strange compound of purely technical discussions: "Why didn't you give the cows more fodder?"; "Just how much water are you using to irrigate this vineyard?"; Why the hell don't you get rid of those weeds in the potato fields?"; etc.; and political harangues: "As soon as this country stops being underdeveloped, everyone will get all the food and clothes he needs"; "Can you remember what happened to sick workers under the old regime? Today we can proudly say that no one need fear ruin because of illness"; "We used to be a nation of illiterates; tomorrow we shall be a nation of technicians"; etc. Fidel also tries to settle personal problems. Here an old man prefers to continue working in the factory and refuses to be pensioned off; there, another insists on his right to a pension, while his factory thinks otherwise.

Just once or twice, during my tours with Fidel, I was able to listen to more general complaints: "*Comandante,* we have been told that you are interested in agriculture, but have you really got any idea how they are bringing in the fruit and the vegetables this year?" There was quite a stir that time round Fidel's jeep; his aides were incensed by the provocative and insolent manner of the appellant. But Fidel let him finish, and then asked politely how he was managing his own farm (the man was a small peasant). In the end, he thanked him for his critical observations and offered him two cigars from his own box. The peasant left delighted, Fidel rather glum but not unduly disturbed. He knew, in any case, that all was not well in this region, and had some ideas on how to improve

455

matters. For such is his way—he does not waste his time on idle chatter but, wherever he goes, tries to suggest reforms and remedies, as if he were the only man capable of putting Cuban agriculture truly on its feet.

The foreign visitor is usually amazed by Fidel's closeness to the people and by his expertise in agricultural matters. But after a while he begins to wonder: why on earth must he bother with such a plethora of sheer trifles? Why enter into every petty administrative detail that any clerk is competent to solve? Why repeat endless generalities about underdevelopment, future plans, responsibility at work, etc.? These questions lead one straight to that institutional void which, to my mind, is at the very heart of the Cuban problem.

But before looking at this crucial matter, we might perhaps consider a few truths almost commonplace in their simplicity. The individual Cuban does not bring in a ten-million-ton *zafra;* he simply cuts cane on a small field under a particular section leader. The same is true of a nickel miner, or of a worker or peasant in any state enterprise. All of them work at special tasks allotted and supervised from above. They may be in total agreement with Fidel's great objectives, but if things are poorly organized in their small sector, they will work badly and finish up with doubts about the value of the whole project. They cannot tell Fidel, because they do not see him every day and also because workers everywhere are reluctant to complain about their superiors. Many console themselves with the fact that theirs is a purely local complaint, that other provinces do much better, and that things will come right in the end, but many more are profoundly skeptical. Yet whether they are skeptical or optimistic, not one of them can do anything about the organization or goals of the work he is doing, for there are no meetings at which people can air their grievances or make any real decisions. Sometimes, when a particular order is altogether absurd, a few rebels do succeed in having it revoked. I was told about a young Italian expert who convinced his co-workers, all of them volunteers like himself, that it was neither useful nor

456

revolutionary to sow cane on fields where everyone knew perfectly well nothing would grow. But to make his point, first he had to organize a strike, a feat that calls for considerable courage in a socialist country. There are some who are prepared to run that risk. Most prefer to do as they are told and to let their superiors take the blame.

Why can they not bring up all these technical questions, as well as others that have no direct bearing on production, during meetings of one of the many rank-and-file organizations that were once so dynamic? The answer is simple: these organizations have ceased to exist on anything but paper. They became mere puppets during the "mini-Stalinist" era, so much so that Cubans no longer boast about their workers' Militia[59] or about their Committees for the Defense of the Revolution. The latter now have a purely repressive function: they only spring into action when it comes to tracking down bad citizens or small traders, as for example during the Great Revolutionary Offensive. They have all been reduced to mere appendages of the *Seguridad,* or national police force, and have ceased to be genuine rank-and-file organizations. As for ANAP, its aspirations are pitiful and its prerogatives nebulous. The trade unions, however, do have a stake in the national pie. They are expected to stimulate productivity by fostering socialist competition among the workers. It has even been suggested that they be rechristened the "Movement of Historical Dates," because socialist competition is keenest on the eve of national celebrations. The FEU (the Federation of University Students) has become fused with the Union of Young Communists, ostensibly in order to debureaucratize it.

59. The Militia was replaced by a Civil Defense Organization under direct army control. Its aim is to teach the population elementary facts about civil defense through military training. While the latter is undoubtedly more professional than it used to be in the Militia days, the recruits have lost any sense of personal involvement. Nor is there anything of a "people's army" about the new organization; after each exercise the guns are safely locked up in the barracks. This is a far cry, indeed, from the time when Fidel was prepared to distribute arms "even to cats."

Guerrillas in Power

Cuban political life has thus been cut back to its most
rudimentary form. There is no hypocrisy on this subject in
Havana where, in contrast to Moscow, foreign visitors are not
subjected to painful discussions about the superiority of the
socialist method of elections over those employed in formally
democratic countries. In Cuba, no one is elected, or ever pretends
to be. Even the Communist Party has not yet felt it necessary
to fulfill its statutory duty of convoking a national congress.
All its organs, from the Central Committee down to the lowest
office, are appointed from the top by Fidel Castro and his
closest collaborators.[60] Admittedly, workers are invited to Party
meetings, and can even recommend candidates for membership
of the Cuban Communist Party. The final decision, however,
rests with the officials and the rank and file has, at most, a
consultative voice. The published facts on the present composition of the Cuban Communist Party are, moreover, far too
imprecise for any outsider to tell the relative proportion of
"recommended" and co-opted members.[61]

Some people have alleged that Fidel Castro has deliberately
lulled Cuban political life to sleep; that he has introduced a
vertical power structure for the sole purpose of assuaging his own
political appetite. I, for my part, am convinced that the present
situation has resulted from a process that completely escaped his
control. Fidel is its victim, not its master. He would dearly
have loved to conserve "the enthusiastic momentum of the
heroic phase of the Revolution" by the "disciplined participation of all." He has expelled all sectarians who blunted the
enthusiasm of the masses, together with all those who placed
too much reliance on it. He has chosen a most demanding way

60. Fidel announced the composition of the Central Committee of the
Cuban Communist Party on October 3, 1965. One day later came news of
the composition of the Political Bureau (Fidel and Raúl Castro, Dorticós,
Hart, Almeida, Ramiro Valdés, Guillermo García, and Sergio del Valle)
and of the Secretariat (Fidel and Raúl Castro, Dorticós, Blas Roca, Fauré
Chomón, Carlos Rafael Rodríguez).
61. According to official figures, the CCP has a total membership of 78,000,
with about 11,500 in Havana province.

458

of life for himself, rushing all over the country, explaining here, trying to keep up flagging spirits there, and preaching the virtues of disciplined action wherever he goes. But his achievements in the field are rather slim, especially compared with the tremendous effort he has put into them. The enthusiasm he kindles whenever he appears vanishes again soon after he leaves, and does not stand the test of the setbacks and hard realities of daily life. The discipline he tries to encourage is evanescent, and how, indeed, could it be otherwise in the absence of genuine discussions or any degree of real understanding? Worse still, many of his own interventions and decisions, made on the spur of the moment, show a great deal of confusion and do anything but alleviate the most pressing problems. A single person cannot be an infallible expert in all fields of technical endeavor, cannot be competent on questions of cattle breeding and irrigation, on the best method of cutting sugar cane and on the advantages of coffee plantations in the *Cordón de la Habana,* not to mention a thousand other spheres calling for special knowledge of the soil and of the political realities.

This is the point: the building of socialism cannot be the business of one man or of a single group of men, however well-intentioned. If the socialist ship is to come safely into harbor, everyone alike must take to his oars—a few men rowing up in front are not enough. This may sound like a slogan, but socialist democracy is not the kind of luxury people can only afford when everything else has been settled. Unless everyone pulls his weight, the leaders no less than the workers are exposed to an intolerable strain. In such circumstances, it matters little that great sacrifices no longer serve to enrich a minority of privileged people, or that the leaders are men of high integrity—and no one can say otherwise of the Castroists. The result is bound to be apathy and a general flagging of political interest.

Despite his eternal and proverbial optimism, Fidel cannot ignore these truths. Yet during all these difficult years, he has shown a marked preference for partial remedies, for remedies that do not involve a basic revision of the whole system. In

459

1967, well before attacking the small traders and the profiteers, he sailed into civil servants, many of whom he had chosen personally, but who had apparently ceased to play their full part in his great socialist project. At the time, an impressive anti-bureaucratic dossier was published in Havana, and the people were called upon to do "battle against bureaucracy." This battle, they were told, was as decisive as the one they had already waged against underdevelopment.[62] The dossier caused quite a stir abroad. It blamed European socialist countries for saddling Cuba, during the first years after the Revolution, with "certain administrative systems and certain forms of organization heavily infected with bureaucratism."[63] But its authors went much further than that. They declared that the bureaucrats, who in a capitalist state are a mere by-product of nationalization and mergers, have a distinct tendency, after a socialist revolution, to transform themselves into an autonomous class with special economic and political objectives. Che Guevara had written as early as 1963: "In a capitalist society, in which the entire state apparatus is in the service of the bourgeoisie, the importance of the bureaucracy as an independent organism is minimal. . . . it is sufficiently permeable to allow the passage of profiteers and sufficiently tight to catch the people in its net. But, after the triumph of the revolution, the evil of bureaucracy begins to proliferate mightily."[64]

In other words, Cubans had come to appreciate that popular rule—or if you prefer it, the new proletarian upper class—is quite unable to control and use the bureaucracy for its own ends in the way the bourgeoisie used to do. Under socialism, bureaucracy becomes an autonomous social force that poses a grave threat to the development of revolutionary society. "Bureaucracy engenders bureaucracy"; "Bureaucracy acts as a brake on revolu-

62. This dossier has been mentioned on p. 296, as one of the first "heretical" steps the Castroists took.

63. See *Contro il burocratismo una battaglia decisiva* (op. cit.) , p. 27.

64. See Ernesto Che Guevara: "Contra la Burocracia," in *Cuba Socialista*, No. 18, February 1963.

tionary action"; "Bureaucratization causes even greater damage than imperialism because it corrupts from within, attacking everything that is healthy and stable among the masses"; "Bureaucratic practices discourage the workers, sap their morale, and shake their confidence in the revolution"; "What could be more demoralizing for a worker or a peasant than to see problems he understands and is able to solve perfectly well by himself remain unsolved or botched up by bureaucratic officials?" As these quotations show, the Cuban champions of the fight against bureaucracy did not mince words.

Unfortunately, the anti-bureaucratic battle was reduced to two fronts: the particular composition of the administration and its style of work. Castroist anxiety on the first point was quite understandable. Cuba had inherited a vast army of officials, and despite all efforts to reclassify them, their number remained excessive for a small country desperately short of manpower. At the beginning of 1967, there were in Havana alone more than 74,000 administrative clerks earning more than 140 million pesos per annum. This was clearly too much. Young civil servants, and above all the Party members among them, were invited to work on the land, or perhaps at something less backbreaking, but in any case at something more productive than administrative paperwork. Thus a market in Havana was transformed into a factory for churning out anatomical models: human skeletons, arms, hearts, and other organs all made out of papier-mâché. Foreigners were urged to visit this strange factory; José Llanusa shepherded Leo Huberman, Paul M. Sweezy, and myself through its doors. All the former bureaucrats told us that they greatly preferred painting papier-mâché hearts red to blackening useless bits of paper in their offices. That evening José Llanusa also took us to a televized student quiz program, entitled "¿Quién sabes más?" After the final scores had been added up, the producer paid homage—at the minister's invitation—to the ex-bureaucrat producers of skeletons, for the remarkable way in which they were fostering the anatomical skills of the new generation.

461

Guerrillas in Power

But it was not the administrators themselves as much as their style of work that was prominent in the anti-bureaucratic campaign. The press, radio, and television never tired of explaining what qualities were expected of good officials and, in particular, how they ought to deal with the public. They must be "dynamic and vigorous," and must have no special ties with the bureaucracy at large. Next they must be neither too "soft" (i.e., trying to please everybody for the sake of peace or for demagogic reasons) nor despotic and unfair: " 'Softies' and despots alike are disqualified from playing a leading part in socialist construction."[65] Finally, they ought to discuss and examine all reasonable suggestions by the public, while being careful not to succumb to the typical bureaucratic disease of holding long conferences which merely wasted the workers' time and impeded smooth economic progress.

I found all this most intriguing. The Cuban leaders had obviously come to realize that in the absence of control by a "ruling class" the bureaucracy has an invariable tendency to act "on its own behalf." But to remedy this situation all they could think of was to increase the powers of the executive, instructing its representatives to "discuss and examine" the views and suggestions of the rank and file. Was this not one of those very contradictions the Cubans so bitterly deplored? The leaders thought otherwise. According to them, the mere fact that in 1967 they had definitely chosen political and moral instead of financial incentives constituted a departure from the old political climate. Officials of all grades would no longer be concerned with mere administration but would henceforth be devoting themselves to the "Communist education of the entire people." This called for exemplary conduct and left no room for bureaucratic practices. The style of work was bound to change automatically once the work of public officials was radically transformed.

65. This particular quotation appeared in a *Granma* article on workers' discipline (French weekly summary of May 19, 1968), but similar phrases appeared in the entire Cuban press.

462

"Hay problemas, hay contradicciones"

Mass organizations, too, were invited to take a keener interest in Communist education and, to that end, to strengthen their links with the Communist Party. In certain cases these links became so close that they led to the disappearance of the organizations themselves. This is what happened, for example, when the University Student Federation[66] merged with the Union of Young Communists. The latter group represented only 30 per cent of the student body, but being "in the vanguard of the fight," looked upon itself as the sole guarantor of the cause of proletarian democracy in the universities.[67]

In the name of "debureaucratization," Fidel thus proceeded to a further verticalization of political power, at the same time putting greater pressure on all top state officials. He gave them a

66. Founded in 1923 by Julio Antonio Mella, the FEU had always been deeply involved in the revolutionary struggle. The reader may recall that in March 1952 it was the only organization to call for the violent overthrow of the Batista dictatorship.

67. News of the fusion of the FEU with the UJC was announced in *Granma* (French weekly summary of December 17, 1967) by J. Vala, the outgoing president of the FEU, and was justified as follows: "There has never been and there never will be the slightest difference between the FEU and the UJC on the subject of objectives, the correct line or the best methods. In effect, there have never been and there could never have been contradictions between the FEU and the socialist revolution in whose fire the ideas of our young people, our students, are being forged. . . . The FEU has handed over to the university authorities several of its former administrative tasks which were bureaucratized by certain leaders of our organization. . . . Henceforth even those students who do not belong to the Union of Young Communists can aspire to the job of brigade leader, while the members of the UJC, who represent 30 per cent of the student mass, can hope to serve in all capacities. This is only logical, because it is to the vanguard that the most important tasks invariably fall. . . . Members of the UJC are the finest representatives of the Cuban student body, of the revolutionary student mass, of all those who are pledged to work by the side of our people in the construction and defense of socialism and Communism in our fatherland. . . . The secretary of the UJC will at the same time be president of the FEU, with the support of all university students. . . . In our view this represents a radical step toward socialist democracy. This step, which has rarely if ever been taken in the rest of the world, springs from the solid ground of our revolution, from absolute confidence in the masses. . . . The University Bureau of the UJC-FEU will devote itself to the training of the new man, of whom the most shining example has been Major Ernesto Che Guevara."

last chance to mend their ways; it was rumored in Havana that many of his closest advisers were urging him to proceed to the militarization of the whole country. But did this final appeal have the least chance of being heeded?

My fourth and longest stay in Cuba—from January to March 1968—took place a year, almost to the day, after the anti-bureaucratic campaign was first launched; that is, after a sufficient lapse of time for the "dynamic and vigorous" officials, men who were neither too soft nor too despotic, to prove their worth. Cubans, let us recall, are quite open with all their foreign friends. None of those who confided in me had ever been a *gusano*,[68] an enemy of the people, and none questioned the fundamental rightness of the Revolution. They spoke to me as they spoke among themselves, of particular facts, of regrettable lapses in certain sectors, of the shortcomings of certain officials and of their mistaken decisions. When you added up all these petty complaints you were left with a highly alarming picture of a system that I. Joshua has very aptly described as "authoritarian centralization coupled to anarchic decentralization."[69]

68. *Gusano*, "earthworm," was the name by which José Martí used to refer to unpatriotic people.

69. I. Joshua, a young French economist, and a pupil and collaborator of Professor Charles Bettelheim, worked in Cuba from 1963 to 1967. On his return, he published a paper in *Problèmes de Planification* (École Pratique des Hautes Études, Paris, November 1967) entitled "Organization and Productive Relations in a Transitional Economy." His view on authoritarian centralization *cum* anarchic decentralization, especially in Cuban agriculture, deserves to be quoted in full: "The annual plan for state-owned farms shows a clear lack of realism; it must be modified as it proceeds. An initial lack of realism is by no means the only reason for these modifications: unforeseen difficulties with the soil, climatic factors, the transfer of implements from one farm to the next, delays in preparing the fields, etc., all make some contribution. . . . Sometimes the changes are so numerous and so incisive that it becomes quite impossible to recognize the original plan. In this case you get 'extra plans,' 'operational plans,' or 'additional programs.' Now the proliferation of these operational or extra plans often means the end of any sort of planning, of all programs. . . . Every level (the national, the provincial, or the individual state farm) is brought face to face with a glaring contrast between the set objectives and the available resources. . . . They have two alternatives: they can either try to achieve all

"Hay problemas, hay contradicciones"

The sad result is that the party—or rather its leadership—keeps issuing orders and appeals, yet lacks the means of discovering whether its directives and exhortations are heeded or even

---

the objectives at once, or else establish some sort of priority among the objectives. If they choose the first alternative, they waste resources and a great deal of effort and accomplish only a part of the task. If, on the other hand, they establish an order of priorities (for example if they decide to concentrate first on bringing in all the green vegetables, then the potatoes, and finally the cane sugar) this also causes losses: the crops at the bottom of the list must often be written off. . . . The order of priorities is, moreover, purely subjective and local; it varies from level to level, from region to region, from moment to moment, etc. Nor is there any guarantee that a particular order of priorities is a *socially* valuable order, i.e., one that satisfies the economic and political demands of the country as a whole. . . . If the various levels establish their own orders of priority, we have decentralization, but of a completely anarchic kind. If, on the other hand, the lower levels do not establish their own order of priorities, we again have decentralization (since, faced with formidable tasks, each level will necessarily use its resources as it thinks best) . Now, this type of decentralization is just as anarchic as the first, as it causes heavy losses beyond the control of the higher levels. . . . Faced with this anarchic decentralization, the higher levels necessarily reply with sudden centralization decrees, and far too often purely mechanical and authoritarian. . . . They may succeed in imposing their own priorities on the lower levels but, under the given conditions, these priorities are often as arbitrary and subjective as those chosen by the lower levels themselves. Worse still, there is no guarantee that even this order is socially desirable, that it satisfies the economic and political needs of the whole. . . . Since the higher levels cannot impose their own criteria of allocating tasks in terms of an overall, socially coherent plan, they resort to the only means available to them: they give purely subjective orders. . . . This authoritarian type of centralization, which conflicts with the very organizational principle it is supposed to represent, rides roughshod over a host of prior decisions. Thus though manpower is supposed to be directed by the head of a particular farm, it is the *agrupación* which tells the state farm to concentrate its labor force on a given activity. And though the *agrupación* has the right to deploy its equipment as it thinks fit, the province may suddenly allocate the equipment for a particular task, irrespective of the program of the *agrupación*. In addition, though the farm leader is entitled to procure provisions in the state shop, some products will have been cornered by the higher levels in an attempt to impose their own order of priorities, now or in the future. . . . This order of priorities can at best guarantee the partial, momentary, and limited coherence, but not the general, overall coherence of the plan."

The author goes on to give detailed examples of how the system breaks down, and shows how this failure is the direct consequence of the general bureaucratization of the Cuban economy.

465

understood. And since, to Castroists of the purest faith, Fidel is entirely blameless at all times, they have to accuse one another or blame everything on the terrible failings of their omnipresent bureaucracy. "If only Fidel knew; if only we could tell him all about it"—how many times did I not hear phrases of this type from people who, in principle at least, had every chance of gaining the ear of their prime minister.

To make things even worse, most ministers have adopted Fidel's peripatetic style of life, so that it is extremely difficult to catch any of them in their offices. I had the impression that a good number of their subordinates, too, kept muttering under their breath, "If only the Comrade Minister knew; if only we could tell him all about it." Of course, all these men do not travel about for their own amusement; they lead an exceedingly strenuous and harassing life, for the sole purpose of settling a host of practical problems in the field. I was present when José Llanusa, the minister of education, personally inspected the work of the "country schools,"[70] and when he tried to solve the problems of one of the pupils. She was the daughter of a counterrevolutionary killed during the Playa Girón invasion, and was being ostracized by all her classmates. But how many of these affairs could have been settled by the local community, if only it had the necessary powers to do so?

It was not easy to discuss this subject with my Cuban friends. For some, the very term "democratization" had become synonymous with "economic reforms" on the Soviet pattern, and faithful disciples of Che that they were, they refused to consider it. Others told me that I was missing the forest for the trees, that what anomalies still persisted in Cuba could not prevent the country from moving forward toward an entirely new form of

70. The *escuelas en el campo* were set up in 1967 for the express purpose of enabling schoolchildren in the capital to participate in agricultural work while continuing with their studies by following courses broadcast over a special television channel. The pupils and their teachers spent six weeks at a time in these *escuelas* and their experience is said to have been extremely useful. According to Llanusa, most of the children would have liked to stay on longer and the parents did not seem to mind.

democracy. But the great majority referred me to Fidel himself; he was deeply concerned about the institutional problem, had very definite ideas on the subject, and was therefore the best possible person to enlighten me. In Havana there are no secrets —though none of my interviews with Fidel had been published, everyone knew that I had joined him on a *vuelta* of the Sierra Cristal, and that he was going to meet me again. Sometimes I was even told what subjects I ought to raise during these future meetings, so that I might return to my informants with precise reports on the thoughts of the *jefe máximo*.

In fact at the beginning of January 1968, soon after my arrival, Fidel had asked me to be present at the semi-public opening of a cement factory just outside Havana. This was to be followed by a long drive in his jeep. Fidel wanted to show me the work that was being done in the suburbs and had also promised to speak to me about other matters, next day at breakfast. And so, at 11 A.M. precisely, a car brought me to his very simple apartment on Eleventh Street, right in the heart of Vedado. His brother Raúl had come to join us and volunteered a great deal of interesting information on the prerevolutionary period. When Raúl stopped, Fidel declared that he did not like all these reminiscences: "What matters most is the present, the stage on which we are acting today." He accordingly invited me to join him on one of his next provincial tours, perhaps to the Sierra Maestra, the cradle of the Revolution.

Then came a series of false alarms. Fidel's friends kept announcing our imminent departure only to tell me, time after time, that it was off again. On January 24, 1968, all the most important Cuban leaders suddenly disappeared. I learned that the Central Committee of the Communist Party was meeting in plenary session. The conference was to last three days and was to be held *in camera*. Friends who were present merely reported that Fidel had delivered a remarkable ten-hour speech, one of the longest of his career, but they absolutely refused to tell me what about. At the time, the strangest rumors were circulating in Havana, especially in the Habana Libre, where I was staying.

467

Some claimed that there would be a rupture with the U.S.S.R.; others that Raúl Castro had been appointed prime minister, Fidel having decided to devote himself exclusively to agriculture and ideological problems; there was to be more rationing; a ban on marriages was imminent as part of the *zafra* recruiting campaign; Raúl Castro was about to join the Latin American guerrilla movement; and God knows what else. Most of it sounded like science fiction; it showed a truly exceptional credulity on the part of the Habaneros. In any case the suspense increased as the hours ticked by.

Finally, at noon on Sunday, January 28, 1968, almost thirty-six hours after the Central Committee had ended its deliberations, Radio Havana broke the silence. I found it a fascinating spectacle to see an entire city hanging on the words of a solemn-voiced announcer. When he had finished reading the historical resolution of the Central Committee, it was clear that all the rumors had been wide of the mark. Then why had the top brass locked themselves away for three days in absolute secrecy? They had apparently needed all this time and mystery for the simple act of expelling Aníbal Escalante from the Party. Escalante, together with eight other leaders of the old PSP, was to be handed over to the courts for the crime of "microfactional" activity.[71] Two other members of the clique, Ramón Calcines and José Matar were less compromised and hence merely expelled from the Central Committee.[72] The announcement came as a complete anti-climax. Aníbal Escalante had become a generally hated character during the "mini-Stalinist" phase, but after his replacement in 1962 he was stripped of all important functions; no one ever spoke of him and many of those who had

71. The other accused were: Octavio Fernández, Emilio de Quesada, Luciano Arguelles, Orestes Valdés, Raúl Fajardo, Luis M. Rodríguez Saens, Lázaro Suárez, and Marcelino Menéndez. However in addition to these eight "microfactionists," all of them members of the CCP during the Escalante trial, twenty-seven other "accomplices" not belonging to the new party were given long prison sentences.
72. Ramón Calcines was a former leader of the PSP; José Matar had only become a Communist after the Revolution.

not completely forgotten him believed that he was away in Moscow. The others accused had never been prominent personalities, and the few Cubans who knew them by name knew also that they had been kicked out of office well before the plenary meeting. The only surprising thing about the whole affair was the severity with which the authorities had obviously decided to arraign and punish a few dissidents, men who had lost any real influence long before.

Next, *Granma* published in installments a long report by Raúl Castro to the Central Committee on the misdeeds of the "microfactionists," the intervention of Carlos Rafael Rodríguez[73], and, finally, the charges preferred and the verdict of the First Revolutionary Tribunal: Escalante was sentenced to fifteen years' hard labor, and his accomplices to prison sentences ranging from three to twelve years. These documents made extremely painful reading, to say the least.

The prosecution had relied chiefly on questionable documents from the police files: records of telephone conversations, police denunciations, and "confessions" obtained after the arrest. The evidence also included photographs, published in *Granma* on February 3, 1968, showing Aníbal Escalante in conversation with some of the other accused outside his apartment and in several public places. The subject of their talks could not be read from the expression on their faces, and one wondered what precisely the courts could deduce from these pictures; since all the accused were known to be former members of the PSP, they must obviously have known one another and it was most unlikely that they would have tried to deny it.

---

73. Carlos Rafael Rodríguez put the full weight of his position as former leader of the PSP at the service of the prosecution. His evidence was given great prominence, no doubt so as to make it clear that the trial was not a blanket attack on all old PSP members, and to show that even former Communists disapproved of Escalante. Remarkably enough, Blas Roca, who as head of the old Communist Party was best qualified to pronounce on all the charges, chose to keep his counsel. He voted, like everyone else, but said nothing at all.

469

The prosecution, however, made a great deal of this "proof," in a desperate effort to establish a case which, to the eyes of incorrigible "legalists" like myself, remained completely unproven. Of what crime were Escalante and the others accused? They were said to have disagreed with Castro's domestic and foreign policy; to have held "pseudorevolutionary" (i.e., pro-Soviet) views, to have established a faction made up of former members of the PSP, and to have tried to influence the attitude of such friendly countries as the U.S.S.R., East Germany, and Czechoslovakia.

Their political past made them unlikely candidates for the "Castroist heresy." But was there a law against holding opinions of one's own, even the most unorthodox? In any case, the more rigid their ideas the less contagious they were. Were the Castroists really so afraid of the ideological influence of a discredited man like Aníbal Escalante that they had to stage a sham trial for the crime of holding the wrong sorts of opinions?

Escalante was not only charged with holding the wrong views of course; he was also accused of organizing a faction. It was on this point that the prosecutor of the Revolutionary Tribunal had concentrated the full fire of his indignation. But what statutory crime was the existence of a faction inside the Communist Party of Cuba? The courts are not there to enforce the constitution of a particular party. The ban on factions inside the Communist movement went back to Lenin's day. It may have been an error on his part or a proof of his great astuteness: in either case it was purely a Party matter. And if Fidel, despite his vaunted anti-dogmatism, chose to retain this particular dogma, he could always have brought Escalante before the Control Commission of the PCC. In principle, the state and the Party are not the same—in Cuba or in any other socialist country. No courts are competent to pronounce on factional or microfactional activity inside the Communist Party.

This fact alone makes nonsense of the whole Escalante affair, renders it absurd and virtually unique. Even during the notorious "Moscow trials" in the '30s, the prosecution never accused

470

"Hay problemas, hay contradicciones"

its victims of factional crimes. Instead, Stalin had all the alleged "Trotsky-Zinovievites" or "Bukharin-Trotskyites" impeached as agents of Hitler and of international imperialism. In fact, when he exterminated the Bolshevik Old Guard he was careful to disguise his real political motives by accusing them of the worst possible crimes against the Soviet State. The trial was inquisitorial and an enormous propaganda machinery used all the powers of religious persuasion to convince Soviet citizens and Communists at large, that the accused must be put out of the way for the sake of the world revolution and for the peace of good revolutionary minds.

Nothing of the kind happened in Havana; and I am the last person to hold that against the Castroists. On the contrary, it is to their credit that they did not accuse Escalante of collaboration with Hitler or the CIA; that they did not call mass meetings to explain why his "subjective disagreement" with the Revolution led him to commit the most heinous "objective crimes." Nor was the trial joined to a campaign in honor of Fidel's near-mystical infallibility. The "criminals" were not executed at the end of a trial, which, despite the severity of the verdict, was thus different even in degree from the Soviet precedent. The whole affair showed clearly that the Castroists, unlike the Stalinists, had not thrown all moral scruples to the wind, and that they refused to go beyond certain limits.

The Escalante trial also served to demonstrate that the Cuban leaders were making a mockery of their own judicial system. They sent to hard labor a group of opponents for a crime that did not even figure in the criminal code. This aspect of the trial made me feel particularly uneasy. Four of the five leading Cubans are lawyers: Fidel and Raúl Castro, Dorticós, and Armando Hart. They have said that they came to politics because they were revolted by the mockery of justice under the old regime. Hence they, more than anyone else, ought to have known what Cubans in general and the young in particular must think of a legal system that is bound so closely to the political executive. How ever could they have conceived the misbegotten idea

471   Q

of instructing the State Tribunal to try people for crimes that fell completely outside its competence? How could they possibly send a group of men to prison on nothing but spurious police evidence?

It was all quite beyond me. I wondered whether this whole legal tragicomedy might not simply have been staged because the accused had been guilty of real crimes against the state, crimes that Raúl Castro and the prosecutor of the Revolutionary Tribunal could not air in public for international reasons. If Escalante, for instance, had been a Soviet agent and had supplied the U.S.S.R. with Cuban defense secrets, this trial, however irregular, could have served as a warning to Moscow, as an oblique request to desist from such practices in future. Yet this interpretation had to be discarded at once; all the trial had done was to provide the Russians with political ammunition against "the Cuban heresy." In future, any orthodox parties anxious to suppress Castroist or other minorities could quote the precedent of Havana and order an "anti-factional" trial. Moreover, the spy hypothesis found not the least support in the evidence presented at the trial. True, there was mention of a few journalists or minor officials from the Eastern bloc whom these "microfactionists" had apparently contacted. But Raúl Castro had made a point of exonerating these men before the Central Committee and in public. He reiterated that Soviet experts were continuing to do excellent work in such delicate spheres as the security branch of his own Ministry of National Defense, and even singled them out for their exemplary conduct and for the great services they had rendered the Revolution.

On looking more closely at the evidence, one discovers another strange fact: the accused and their lawyers did not have the right to address a single word to the court, and the published documents contain no defense pleas of any kind. This irregularity was not a novelty in Cuba,[74] but this time the explanation

74. During the trials of Hubert Matos, in 1959, and of Marcos Rodríguez, in 1964, the Cuban press also published no defense pleas.

472

was not a desire on the part of the authorities to keep the "crimes" of the accused a state secret. In fact, Raúl Castro and the prosecutor made a point of listing every critical remark, including the most trivial, the accused had ever been heard to make. Everything was there: their protests against the *Salon de Mai* exhibition, their complaints against police surveillance, and their skeptical remarks about the ten-million-ton *zafra*. Cubans thus learned the whole truth from the prosecution, which did not even bother to refute the arguments of the accused. One wondered what possible reason there was for this strange method of spreading the critical views of the microfactionists. Did the authorities wish Cubans to understand that all such opinions were indictable, that henceforth all who expressed doubts on the giant *zafra,* or complained against police surveillance, would be clapped into jail?

Most of my Cuban companions had been accused personally by Escalante of holding the worst possible petit-bourgeois views. José Llanusa, Carlos Franqui, Celia Sánchez, Alfredo Guevara, Marcelo Fernández, and Major René Vallejo—each one had figured on his list of "bad revolutionaries." All of them, therefore, have good cause for resenting him, and were not perhaps the best people to give an objective account of the proceedings. I nevertheless broached the subject with Llanusa, at the end of a long walk in *el Cordón de la Habana.* He was nonplussed by my legalistic qualms: "We know Escalante only too well," he said, "for we saw him at work when he was in power. You may be quite certain that, had the roles been reversed, he would have had all of us shot. The people have had to suffer a great deal from his kind, and it is the people who are now clamoring for his head. But Escalante got off lightly, simply because Fidel is quite a different sort of man."

Carried away by the subject, Llanusa went on to speak at length about the crimes of the "mini-Stalinists" and about the personal outrages Escalante had committed against honest revolutionaries. The picture of Cuba in 1961–62 which he now painted seemed very much blacker than I had ever imagined, and I have no reason to believe that he was distorting the truth. Hence I merely inquired what guarantees there were that such outrages would never again be committed. "Our best guarantee against all forms of despotism, against all forms of injustices, is Fidel himself. He does not tolerate abuses of power, clamps down on all forms of antisocial conduct. Some of our best comrades, men who have done a great deal for the victory of our revolution, but who later tried to trade on that fact, have had their knuckles rapped severely.[75] For the rest, Fidel forbids all forms of police brutality even when it comes to questioning CIA agents caught red-handed."[76] "Very well," I said, "but apart from Fidel's person, what other, more institutional, guarantees are there against abuses by the state or even by the courts?" Llanusa took some time to think it over, and suddenly launched into a violent denunciation of the Stalinist terror. He apparently needed this preamble to explain that purges of the Soviet type were quite unthinkable in Cuba: "Here everyone is responsible for himself alone, and no one can ever be victimized or persecuted for being a friend or a relation of an alleged

75. Llanusa was referring to the so-called "dolce vita" affair which ended in the dismissal of Major Efigenio Ameijeiras, one of the "twelve" from the Sierra. Almeijeiras, a member of the Central Committee, and the former chief of the people's militia, was accused of loose behavior and removed from office.

76. Prisoners are no longer beaten in police cells, but more subtle methods of psychological and physical pressure are still in use, and not only against CIA agents. Thus prisoners are kept in tiny cells, prevented from sleeping, or prevented from communicating with their families. In fact, if unchecked, every police force will make rules of its own, and these will rarely be the most humane. At the time of my conversation with Llanusa, I had heard rumors on the subject, but I had no concrete facts to back them up. However, soon afterward, I learned the full circumstances of the arrest, detention, and fifteen-year prison sentence of Gustavo Arcos, a Moncada veteran and a former ambassador to Belgium. Arcos was subjected to iniquitous police methods before being sentenced for a crime that cannot possibly figure in the penal code: he was alleged to have said that Fidel was "crazy in the head" and to have sent part of his own earnings to émigré friends and relations. For these "crimes," he now languishes in prison—a semi-invalid who has never recovered from the wounds he received during the Moncada attack, fighting at Fidel's side.

474

criminal. Rolando Cubelas, for example, was more than a friend to me, he was a real brother. But, one day he got the idea of killing Fidel.[77] There was nothing for it: the Revolutionary Tribunal had to sentence him to twenty years in prison. All the world was aware of our friendship; it was common knowledge that we had been the closest friends. But no one so much as dreamt of inculpating me, or of challenging my right to remain a leader of the Revolution. Nor has any comrade ever been importuned because his parents have run away to Miami or because they were convicted for counterrevolutionary activities on the island."

"In Cuba," Llanusa continued, "we have always had a host of judges, advocates, and courts, but a lack of the most elementary justice. That has taught us that legal institutions do not provide safeguards against the worst excesses or against deliberate legal 'errors.' We are tackling the whole problem from an entirely new angle when we make sure that all officials treat every least citizen in an exemplary and humane way. We have told them quite plainly that even the slightest abuse of authority constitutes a crime against the Revolution, violates its principles, and will be punished accordingly. An official who nevertheless misuses his position, runs enormous risks, not least because he knows that his victims or their relatives have every right to put the record straight again. Of course, the last vestiges of injustice will only disappear when all our officials and our entire nation have become *hombres nuevos.* By then the whole question of crime and punishment will have become purely academic. Meanwhile we trust in our people, in our revolutionaries, rather than in the dead letter of the law or in so-called 'independent institutions.' " And he advised me to bring the whole subject up with Fidel, who would be able to explain better than he could

77. In 1966, Rolando Cubelas, a hero of the *Directorio,* and responsible for several famous attacks in Havana during 1956, later commander in the Sierra de Escambray, was sentenced to twenty years' imprisonment for an attempt on the life of Fidel Castro.

hope to do why revolutionary justice is far more effective and humane than purely formal justice.

Fidel explains his optimism

The list of subjects I wanted to discuss with Fidel became longer all the time, and still the promised drive had not materialized. Meanwhile the queue of foreigners waiting for a meeting with the *jefe máximo* grew longer as well. It included the editors of the *Monthly Review*, Leo Huberman and Paul M. Sweezy, the American anthropologist Oscar Lewis, and the Italian film director Francesco Rosi—just to mention some I knew personally. All of us waited patiently but did not waste our time. We could carry on sight-seeing or do research all over the place, because, as our guides put it, we were permanently "on tap," and Fidel knew where to find us at any moment. Early in March 1968 he at last invited me, not for a drive, but to a dinner on his experimental farm, his "mini-fundio," as he called it some fifty miles south of the capital. Llanusa offered to take me there in his car.

I would never have believed that I could ever feel cold in Cuba. Yet that evening a glacial wind, the *norte*, was blowing for all it was worth, while torrential rains blocked our progress along a deserted road. I was anxious, too, about what I knew would be a tough discussion with Fidel. My Spanish was only just good enough to expound fairly elementary ideas, yet I realized that, this time, I would have to step gingerly so as not to hurt the susceptibilities—real or imagined—of the Cuban leader. Llanusa sat silently by my side, worrying about the delay and the bad state of the road. When we finally arrived, at about 9:30 in the evening, the rain had stopped, but not the *norte*— the temperature must have been around 4 to 5° C.

Fidel received us in the Spanish manner, with a great show of friendship and hospitality, and then took us on a torchlight tour of his mini-fundio. He was particularly proud of his stable and of María-Rosa, or Rosa-Bella (I don't remember which), an F-1 cow that had beaten all milk production records. His coffee, too, had been exceptionally successful and we admired its splendor. All the while, I kept thinking of the most diplomatic way of putting my non-agricultural questions. At last, Celia Sánchez called us in for a simple but plentiful dinner. Fidel began by telling us about his meeting, a few days earlier, with a delegation from the Italian Communist Party.[78] But he quickly passed on to his talks with a Rumanian delegation which had surprised and delighted him. He was full of praise for Rumania's political maturity, yet I remembered only too well that during our *vuelta* of the Sierra Cristal he had been highly critical of that country. Apparently his latest criterion for sorting friend from foe was the prevailing attitude toward the U.S.S.R.; the Rumanians had proved more anti-Soviet than the Italians, hence they were obviously better. My role was limited to that of listener, but Fidel, astute as ever, must have divined that his love for Rumania left me rather cold. He continued anyway, but he seemed a little irritated, which did not augur too well for our subsequent discussions.

During dessert, I was delighted to see that René Vallejo had come to join us. He spoke English as well as he spoke French, and was the ideal person to get me out of any linguistic difficulties. Moreover, his ever-smiling face and good humor were highly infectious. Vallejo was a friend of C. Wright Mills and whenever we met, we would exchange reminiscences about him. The conversation became more relaxed, and I profited from the thaw to ask a few questions, carefully prepared en route, about Cuba's institutional problems. But Fidel was not one to wait for the end of long-winded perorations; he generally grasped their purport long before his interlocutor had done. "Ahay, no hay instituciones," he cut in this time, "no hay instituciones. . . . I quite agree, but just listen to me. . . .

78. This delegation, led by Giancarlo Pajetta, a member of the Political Bureau, stayed in Cuba February 17–21, 1968. No communiqué was published; both parties were anxious to keep the conversations private.

Guerrillas in Power

"Do you know how many true revolutionaries Cuba had at the time of the Revolution?" he challenged. "Well, there were less than one per cent! Just think of that, less than one per cent!" This time it was Fidel himself who insisted on taking us back into the past, on a guided tour of Cuban history since 1959, back to Year One of the Revolution. Fidel is didactic in private no less than in public. He prefers to repeat himself rather than leave room for the least misunderstanding. He now reiterated that in 1959 Cuba had witnessed a revolt by society as a whole against an inhumane and dictatorial regime. And he kept stressing the word *revolt*, lest I confuse it with *revolution*. "The people were for the Revolution," he continued, "and later they were for us and against the imperialists. All that is nothing but the truth. But what sort of revolution did they want? We ourselves, who had organized the guerrilla war, and who had helped to prepare the great national uprising, what did we really know about revolution? What means did we have to lead it to a successful conclusion? Well, I'll tell you: the people wanted a revolution because they hoped for higher wages, more consumer goods, abundance for all immediately, and so on. We ourselves knew little about the real possibilities of our country and we lacked a strong political organization. We had to learn everything and create everything from scratch. And we quickly realized that this is a small, poor, and underdeveloped country, unable to fulfill all the hopes and needs of our people here and now. Given these circumstances, should we have allowed the most highly educated, the most persuasive, those slightly more organized than the rest, to turn proletarian democracy to their own advantage, to grab a larger slice of the national cake? Or should we instead have told the people that before everyone can get a fair share, we must first of all pull together and produce the goods, looking in the meanwhile after those who are in greatest need, and not after those who can make the most noise?"

Fidel did not wait for a reply: he had solved this problem long ago. He was intent now, perhaps regretting the time that

478

was wasted when the millennium was apparently just around the corner. He told us the story of the bank clerks who, "good revolutionaries" that they were, firmly believed that after the Revolution they would all become bankers. He repeated that the working class was for the Revolution, like everyone else, but was not a truly revolutionary class and hence was unsuited to the role of midwife to a new society. In these circumstances, could anyone in his right mind really have handed over power to people whose only ambition was higher wages? Wasn't it better to launch a noninstitutional dialogue between the revolutionary vanguard and the people, encouraging everyone to pull his weight? "None of this fits in with the scheme of Karl Marx, I quite realize. But we transgressed against the laws of history by making our revolution in the first place. I suppose we shouldn't have made it?"

His defense of the Cuban Revolution did not stop at this bit of rhetoric. He also dealt with the thorny question of whether it is right to make a socialist revolution, even if the working class is not yet ready for it. But Fidel is not doctrinaire and the theoretical aspects of the problem do not really arouse his passion. He only mentioned them at this point because they were at the root of his practical differences with the Latin American Communists (and with orthodox Communists in general) and also because he had been cut to the quick by pseudorevolutionary dissertations on the petit-bourgeois composition of the Cuban leadership. In the heat of the moment he seemed to forget the original purpose of his argument, for he kept dwelling on the failings of the orthodox. "I often ask myself what sort of world these people really live in? What real substance is there to all their meaningless and stereotyped phrases? Isn't it senseless to speak of a petit-bourgeois revolution in Cuba, where we have done all we can to smash the bourgeoisie?" This time he paused for an answer, or perhaps he was simply catching his breath.

Fidel finds it difficult to sit still while he speaks. He moves about all the time, gets up, takes a few steps, sits down, stalks

479   Q*

back and forth, as if every argument were a kind of hand-to-hand struggle with a wily opponent. His expressive brown eyes remain fixed on his interlocutor and emphasize his words. He uses all the skills of the experienced lawyer—he takes advantage of the slightest weakness, sets traps, interrupts at just the right moment, keeps the initiative all the time. But he does it all so ingenuously, that few people can doubt his sincerity and candor. Thus during our previous meeting on Eleventh Street he had read me one of his letters from prison, written in 1953. He had obviously forgotten its content, and was delighted to rediscover the strength of his message. "That was well put, wasn't it?" he exclaimed with a mixture of satisfaction and self-mockery. He wanted to be admired, but he also accepted with good grace that some of his best effects were bound to fall flat. Sometimes a simple question was enough to make him exclaim: "Oh yes, that was more complicated than I thought." And he gave me a huge wink, that seemed to say: "If we couldn't exaggerate a bit, we'd all be the poorer for it." Sometimes, however, he would try to stick by his exaggerations. One day, for instance, he referred to one of his old companions in the July 26th Movement as a kind of vicar of Karl Marx in Batista's Cuba. But I happened to know the man, who had told me himself that his interest in politics was fairly recent. Fidel was quite unconcerned: "It doesn't matter what he told you; he's a modest man or else he has a short memory. I am telling you that he was a Marxist, perhaps a moderate Marxist, but a Marxist in his own way, just the same."

Fidel invariably monopolizes conversations, not because he refuses to listen, but simply because he thinks aloud and likes to answer his own questions. In the end, however, he always manages to get to the heart of the problem. His moral integrity, his sense of honor, his attachment to the simple virtues, invariably lead him there. But he makes his point by way of long monologues which, though fascinating to follow, are sometimes rather involved. He is decidedly not a political animal like the rest; I have never found another Communist or "bourgeois" leader to

480

compare with him. It is impossible, and in any case pointless.
to try to catch Fidel with his own arguments—he is the first to
admit that he has changed his mind. He will disarm you by ex-
claiming with obvious sincerity: "How many times have we
proved wrong!" And he does not just say so to disarm you; he
seems genuinely dismayed. For whenever things do not turn out
as he had hoped, he has had to reassess the situation both for
himself and for his companions. He has freely assumed this
crushing duty, and does his best to discharge it. Fidel is the most
active and most preoccupied of prime ministers in the modern
world. He would not have it otherwise, but sometimes, while
listening to his long explanations, one can sense his anxiety
about the final outcome. And it is perhaps this aspect of his
personality that makes him so fascinating.

Personally, I had no difficulty in following him when, pacing
about his freezing room, he explained with great feeling that, as
far as the Cuban leaders were concerned, the real difficulties only
began after the seizure of power. Socialist revolutions everywhere
had always had the misfortune of starting in places without the
material basis for socialist reconstruction. Lenin and Mao had
come face to face with this problem long before him. Once the
revolution has been made, the question of "Should we have
made it?" is, of course, purely academic. The only real problem
is the best method of clearing away the enormous obstacles on
the path to full socialism. How, with whom, and for whose sake
must revolutionaries run a society that refuses to live in the old
way, but is not yet ripe for socialist self-management?

When I put this question to Fidel, he replied in a way that,
though far from being "classical," was, in fact, much less heterodox and original than he apparently believed. The revolutionary
leadership, he said, must fulfill two parallel tasks: it must create
the material basis for socialism and it must foster the political
consciousness of the masses. And it must pursue these two tasks
simultaneously, simply because they are inseparable. Whenever
it can, it must give priority to the development of political
consciousness. It must also develop its noninstitutional dialogue

481

with the people, because it has no interests beyond their defense. This, he admitted, might not be the best formulation, but everything would have been much simpler if Cuba had had a powerful and class-conscious working class. In its absence, any attempt to organize relations between the rank and file and the leadership on pseudodemocratic lines would have had disastrous consequences. Fidel said that he did not like the fig leaves European socialist countries put on to hide their democratic nakedness. He told me how surprised and amused he was in 1960, when Eastern leaders whom he met at the United Nations urged him to hold "popular" elections. These men behaved for all the world like good American democrats, but with this difference: their idea of democratic elections was a single government slate which would receive 99.99 per cent of the votes cast, in accordance with socialist ritual. Fidel roared with laughter as he recalled the anxious faces of Gomulka and Novotny, who could not fathom why the stupid Cubans chose to scorn this beautiful democratic façade. The conscience of the world would have been appeased, and the socialist bloc would have found it much easier to defend Cuba against her detractors. But Cuba, Fidel said emphatically, would never lend herself to this kind of comedy; her people simply would not stand for it. In fact, they were not even bothered about holding any kind of elections; the very word had become discredited on the island. Once the nation as a whole had attained the level of consciousness of its vanguard, it would be time enough to change the prevailing power structure, and many other things as well. "Do you know how many true revolutionaries we have in Cuba today?" Fidel asked me, smiling with satisfaction. "Somewhere near 50 per cent of the entire population." And he sat down and left me to draw my own conclusion: since Cuba had gone halfway toward proletarian democracy in so short a time, his plans for the future should not be thought too Utopian.

In fact, this was not the conclusion I myself drew from my Cuban experiences, and I wondered if Fidel was not deluding himself about the real state of his country. I did not, of course, dare to put it as bluntly as that, and I considered making my point by oblique references to the Russian precedent. But I quickly realized that I would get nowhere by doing that; there was nothing Fidel liked less than comparisons between the Russia of yesterday and the Cuba of today. He would certainly blow up at me if I told him that his thesis bore a suspicious resemblance to Soviet theory at the time of the great industrialization campaign. In the U.S.S.R., too, they had said: Let us first create the material foundations and build up a socialist mentality; the rest will follow by itself. For men of Fidel's background, who had only discovered the Soviet Union after Stalin's death, the U.S.S.R. was a country of doddering bureaucrats who had nothing but "rubles in their heads." The Cuban leaders failed to appreciate that the U.S.S.R., too, had once had a revolutionary vanguard, composed of devoted and dynamic men who were not simply tools of the Stalinist terror. Dnieprostroy, Magnitogorsk, Komsomolsk, are monuments to the greatness and devotion of that vanguard. If, despite all that, the U.S.S.R. has failed to become a proletarian democracy, it is doubtless because the economic effort of a vanguard commanded from on high cannot inspire a whole country, let alone lead it forward to socialism. But this was too complex a bit of history to be used for scoring points against a seasoned debater like Fidel.

René Vallejo suddenly broke into my thoughts, interrupting Fidel, who was still expounding his reasons for feeling optimistic, to say that the cold had become unbearable. The room in which we were sitting was rustic and charming, but the *norte* whistled through its wooden walls as if through a strainer. It was no warmer inside than out, and we were not dressed for such Siberian temperatures. Vallejo suggested having "a little vodka, the best stuff the Russians ever sent us." Fidel, who kept moving about while he spoke, seemed to feel the cold less than anyone else. He declared that vodka does not really warm anybody (he was evidently lacking in experience) and voted for tea instead. Celia Sánchez put the kettle on immediately and proposed that we adjourn to the "salon" (another corner of the same room, and no more sheltered against the *norte* than the first). We did as we were told, having nothing better to suggest.

It was now long past midnight. Warmed and encouraged by several cups of tea laced with rum, I asked Fidel how it was that the general uplifting of the socialist consciousness in Cuba had not led to greater productivity, and how he could explain the general unconcern about such rumors as an imminent ban on marriages. He let me talk uninterrupted, and seemed to have some difficulty in grasping what I was getting at. The rum had not improved my Spanish, and trying to pack a maximum of critical observation into a single speech, I had obviously become quite unintelligible. I said to myself that I was using the wrong approach anyway—I ought to have spoken of the need for building up new institutions gradually rather than remark on the consequences of their absence. But as a wise Russian proverb has it: *"poslye draki kulakami nie mashut"* (don't show your fists after the brawl is over) and I can only report that my "critical questions" were not pointed enough to embarrass a man like Fidel Castro.

He said he was sorry I was leaving Cuba with unfortunate and superficial impressions: "It's all my fault. I ought to have taken you to the country, and shown you what is really happening here. But there you are, I was busy all the time, terribly busy. You spent too much time in Havana, that's your trouble. Because, believe me, you would have changed your tune had you seen how our people, particularly our young people, are setting to work in the provinces. All of them work *barbaramente,* I tell you, *barbaramente.*[79] So this is why I am so optimistic. If only you could see for yourself the magnificent effort of hundreds of thousands of volunteers, ready to go wherever the Revolution needs them. Nothing like this has ever happened before, nor was it even conceivable. How can we explain this new phenomenon, if not by an extraordinary increase in the

79. Like demons, extremely hard.

484

"Hay problemas, hay contradicciones"

level of political consciousness of our people, and of our young people in particular? And all you can tell me is that Havana is full of *bolas*[80] and that some people in the Hotel Habana Libre are afraid we might put a ban on marriages. But what can you do? Havana has always had a powerful *bola* industry. In parasitic towns throughout the world, especially where there are no other industries, this one grows up quite spontaneously. We are trying to change their gossiping mentality by creating *el Cordón de la Habana,* but, please remember, we have only just started."

I felt I had to jump to the defense of the Habaneros by explaining that there is an inversely proportional ratio between the number of *bolas* and the number of verifiable and fully documented press reports. I had learned in Eastern Europe that this ratio in no way depends on the level of industrialization. Moscow alone, for example, has more industries than all Cuba, but *bolas* are produced there by the dozen. The Cuban press has always been treated as black sheep, however, and Fidel merely seized on my remark to let fly at them. *Granma* was a very poor second best; he spoke of it as if he were an ordinary reader, forced to put up with it for lack of anything better. For his own part, he was doing his utmost to keep the nation informed not only by public speeches, but by such semiprivate interventions as I had witnessed in January 1968 during our visit to the cement factory. "I prefer such small get-togethers, because you get the chance to explain things, and people are not intimidated by television cameras or by flash bulbs. Unfortunately, I can't always say everything I want to in public. I would very much have liked to publish the speech I gave at the last meeting of the Central Committee, but the comrades thought it unwise. . . ."

He was obviously trying to tell me that his attacks on microfactional activities at that meeting had been directed at Cuba's socialist allies. Had I been right, after all, to think that the real truth of the Escalante affair had had to be hushed up for

80. Tall stories.

similar reasons? Fidel, who had often pressed me in the past to read some of his unpublished speeches, suggested nothing of the kind this time. And yet this last was the one speech I would have chosen above all the rest, had I been given the choice, or had I the impertinence to ask for it. Instead, I sat by silently while Fidel continued musing out loud on the need to keep the people informed and on the problems this posed under existing circumstances.

His tone had now ceased to be polemical; he no longer tried to allay my doubts and had stopped fixing me with his gaze. He seemed to be speaking to Celia, Vallejo, Llanusa, perhaps tacitly treating me as a witness to his country's present difficulties. He admitted quite freely that "the people are a little worried," and sadly shook his head. "We have many problems beyond our control. . . . We will have to fight hard for the next year or two, in order to turn the corner, to leave our difficulties behind us. . . . Next year we will have to organize not just a Girón week or a Girón month but a whole Girón year."[81]

I had the feeling that he spoke rather dejectedly, a little overwhelmed by the prospect of the general mobilization of a whole country, but I was quite wrong. Suddenly he began to walk about again, crossing the room, and addressing us as if we were at a public meeting. Cuba, he told us, had risen to unprecedented heights, her youth was extraordinary; in 1959, or even one or two years ago, he would never have believed that the people would respond so magnificently to the call for collective endeavor. "Yes, *hombre nuevo* is no longer an empty phrase, no longer a pipe dream! We have many *hombres nuevos* in this country! And it is thanks to them that we shall clear our hurdles, thanks to them that we have nothing to fear." He sat down again, and quite suddenly declared that the cold was unbearable; hot drinks alone would never keep us alive in this frozen room. Why not put the heater on in his Mercedes, and

81. Each year, Cuba remembers the Playa Girón invasion with a day of voluntary work. In 1967, it was decided to extend that day to a week of intense national effort.

"Hay problemas, hay contradicciones"

continue talking there? Vallejo remarked that we might just as well go back to Havana since it was now 2:30 in the morning.

The journey back was uneventful. Fidel returned to the problems of youth, in much the same terms he had used in the Sierra Cristal, and repeated that the young would all be *hombres nuevos* one day because they, at least, had not been contaminated. Among the "old ones," some were irredeemably lost and one could do nothing with them. I had the impression that, as far as he was concerned, the only social division that really mattered was the one between the "old"—he also called them the "underdeveloped generation"—and the "young," the new generation of disinterested men and women, all of them good technicians and fine workers. Before dropping me at my hotel, he begged me not to exaggerate the flaws in Cuban society. Things were tough just then, thanks to a chain of unfavorable circumstances, but the obstacles would be removed and things would improve much more rapidly than most foreigners believed. He quoted from memory figures about public investments, repeated his economic arguments, insisted once again on the Communist consciousness of the whole of Cuban youth. "Hurry up and write your book, because soon this country will be quite unrecognizable," he told me by way of farewell.

Next morning, when I was still half asleep, my Cuban friends surrounded me in the lobby of the much maligned Habana Libre. They were all dying to hear what had happened on Fidel's farm, and, in particular, if Fidel had dispelled all my doubts and answered all my criticisms. I reassured them because, in fact, the optimism of the *jefe máximo* is highly contagious. His account of current achievements and imminent changes—for what was a year or two when it came to "turning the corner"?—had had the effect of making me think that perhaps he had been right all along, that socialist democracy was within reach. There is nothing like a dinner or a *vuelta* with Fidel to help explain the optimistic mood of his entourage, and the devotion he inspires wherever he appears. For those, however, who do not have permanent access to this constant source of opti-

487

mism, reality quickly gains the upper hand. And then they begin to wonder whether Fidel's pedagogic conception of socialism is not closer to spiritualism than it is to Marxism, causing him to exalt an ideal of man rather than man in the flesh. "No one used to bother about the people"; "We must disabuse the people of their old ideas"; "We must help the people"; all these expressions spring incessantly from Fidel's lips. According to him, the people must be guided with a firm hand until they are fully adult and have all become *hombres nuevos*. The thought that they could be grown up already—and he himself claims that 50 per cent of them have already become "true revolutionaries" —does not seem to occur to him.

True, in its heart of hearts, every minority that has suffered prolonged isolation and the apathy of others and has had to run terrible risks in starting a revolution tends to have doubts about the real equality of all men and questions their inalienable right to govern themselves. Declarations of principle do nothing to alter this sad fact, whose consequences in other parts of the world are well known. It is always by reference to exceptional but real enough circumstances that the delegation of power by the rank and file to the top of the pyramid is justified. Fidel's originality is undeniable, even if his revolution seems to fit quite smoothly into the classic pigeonhole. And it is unfortunate that his very originality should figure so high on the list of Cuba's *problemas y contradicciones*.

His character is a mixture of fervor and profound pessimism, of contempt for the dangers and the material basis of life— whence his heroism—and bitterness toward what he considers "little things and petty sentiments." This, according to Herbert L. Matthews, is his share of Spanish transcendentalism.[82] It is said that during the trial of Hubert Matos he turned on the accused with: "But how on earth could you turn against the Revolution? What would you be without it? What is man if he

82. See Herbert L. Matthews: *Castro, A Political Biography* (London, Allen Lane, 1969).

has no goal beyond himself? A *desoladora nada!*[83] According to Fidel, the only thing that really counts is a man's purpose. And the duty of the revolutionary vanguard is to devise and impose this purpose. All his arguments betray an aristocratic spirit, a faith in the role of the elite, rather than trust in the converse of equals, in fruitful exchange of ideas between the rank and file and its leaders.

"What is life, if one does not give it for others, for the Revolution?" I heard him develop this view before two hundred workers, at the opening of the cement factory outside Havana. Some of the young people listened to him with obvious enthusiasm; the older ones had a distant look, or kept their eyes fixed firmly to the ground.

83. A pitiful nobody.

VI

The reckoning

Changing course

Fidel Castro's decision, late in 1968, to become reconciled to the U.S.S.R. hit Havana like a bolt from the blue. The year had begun with bitter attacks on the "calcified pseudo-Marxist church," and Fidel's new mood of forgiveness followed the Soviet invasion of Czechoslovakia, at a time when Russia's revolutionary credibility had hit a new low, and when even some of the most loyal Communist parties in Europe had felt bound to voice their disapproval of the latest "international action" by the workers' fatherland.

In their first surprise, many people believed that Castro's arm had been twisted by the U.S.S.R., and that his true motives could not be understood until the full story came out. Yet as subsequent events were to show, it was idle to hope for any such revelations: Fidel Castro's new policy was, in fact, the result of a perfectly obvious series of factors. It was rooted in Cuba's

490

The reckoning

internal *problemas y contradicciones,* in recent changes in the international climate, and, last but not least, in ideological adaptions to these events.

As we saw, the Castroist "heresy" began in 1965, in the face of U.S. aggression against Vietnam and Soviet failure to defend the frontiers of the socialist bloc. Cubans had begun to feel more insecure than ever before and this, together with their faith in the role of individual revolutionaries, caused them to react in an independent and highly unorthodox manner. To relieve U.S. pressure on the hard-pressed and isolated Vietnamese, Che Guevara tried to open up a second front in the rear of the enemy. This meant taking considerable risks, but, for the rest, it was neither a gesture of desperation nor a mad gamble. The war in Vietnam had produced an anti-American reaction throughout the world, and especially in Latin America, which had never bothered to conceal its hostility to the United States. The moment thus seemed highly propitious for triggering off a revolutionary chain reaction. Admittedly, Fidel no less than Che knew perfectly well that the United States would not stay on the sidelines, but they both had good reason to think that, since America had become bogged down in Asia, she would have difficulty in controlling a continental conflagration on so vast a scale. It was essential, however, to act quickly, to choose the most favorable terrain and to strike where the enemy least expected it. Cuba accepted that in doing so she might endanger her own existence, but all things being equal, she had a good chance of succeeding; in this way she might safeguard her future by much more reliable guarantees than the precarious Russo-American agreement of 1962.

This explains certain shortcomings in the preparation of the Bolivian war, and also in the very foundations of the Castroist "heresy." The time factor seemed paramount; the Cuban leaders felt they could not sit back while preparing perfect plans, but had to act immediately. The argument of "military victories" —as Debray called it—was certain to answer all questions pertaining to the organization, theory, and long-term perspective of

491

the Latin American revolution. According to the Castroists, there could be but a single distinction in the near future: that between the supporters of armed struggle and the reformists. Their whole tradition persuaded them to bet on one exceptional man, Che Guevara. He would act as a catalyst and create a new dynamic; he would forge, in the fire of action, the correct tactics and the right revolutionary strategy.

This highly unorthodox and—to the old Communists— noxious expectation was profoundly shaken by Che's death. The Castroists themselves admitted this implicitly when they affirmed that October 8, 1967, and July 26, 1953, marked two temporary setbacks, opening the path for new victories. But then, Fidel, after his abortive Moncada attack, had abandoned his initial approach and had begun to build the July 26th Movement. Therefore, after Che's death, it seemed equally urgent to find new answers to the outstanding Latin American problems, all of which had been shelved against the day of military victory. It now looked very much as if no new fortresses would fall unless a great deal of organizational spadework was done first.

Such preparation was far beyond the powers of the Castroists. The history of Cuba may have been inseparable from that of Latin America, but the two were not identical, and, in any case, Cuba was short of experts schooled in Latin American problems, and lacked efficient means of communication with the subcontinent. Moreover, she was no longer what she had been fifteen years ago, when a loose-knit group of idealists round Fidel had fought for her freedom; she now had a whole heritage to defend—her revolution and her newly-found Marxism. The island had been kept on a war footing, was prepared to brave North American reprisals in case of a continental conflict, but she was not ready to compromise her achievements by doctrinal disputes with other champions of Marxism-Leninism in Latin America. Any attempt to build up an "October 8th Movement," a continental equivalent of Cuba's own heroic July 26th Movement, but one that fought from the start under the red banner, would have meant stirring up all the sad past and reviving all

The reckoning

the theoretical wrangles of the international Communist movement, of which Castroism was now a part. And that was the last thing Fidel Castro wanted at this crucial stage.

And so he was forced to turn his back on what had been his paramount objective until then: a continental revolution. True, he continued to extol the virtues of guerrilla warfare, thus honoring Che's memory and justifying his own actions in the past. But the Latin American Solidarity Organization, founded with such solemnity in 1967, had virtually ceased to function, and its Havana secretariat had never even met. No fresh Cuban proclamations on the Latin American revolution had been issued since Che's death; instead *Granma* would, from time to time, publish resolutions by Guatemalan or Bolivian *guerrilleros* determined to continue the struggle.[1] No one, however, now spoke of victories in the near future—it had become clear that no anti-imperialist explosions were imminent south of the Rio Grande. The Cuban leaders did not shout this fact from the rooftops lest they demoralize their own ranks, but they were realistic enough to withdraw to defensive positions inside their "beleaguered fortress." They had clearly come around to the view that their survival depended on the eradication of underdevelopment at home and not, as they had thought in 1965, on a trial of strength in Latin America.

This forced withdrawal was the prelude to Castro's reconciliation with the U.S.S.R., which—for lack of an alternative—had remained his chief trading partner. Fidel could not, of course,

---

1. In January 1968, *Granma* published declarations by the Guatemalan FAR (Armed Rebel Forces) in the Sierra de Minas and by César Montés, to the effect that the *guerrilleros,* determined to continue the fight, had broken with the Guatemalan Labor Party (i.e., the Communist party of Guatemala). Later, on July 20, 1968, *Granma* published an appeal by Inti Peredo, a Bolivian Communist and Che's companion in arms. It was entitled "We Will Return to the Mountains! Victory or Death!" All these proclamations have since been published in pamphlet form, and many of them have been translated into foreign languages. Inti Peredo was killed on September 9, 1969, in La Paz, in an armed clash with the police. See French weekly summary of *Granma,* September 17, 1969.

acknowledge this publicly so soon after Che's death, nor did he have any wish to intimate to his demanding Soviet allies that he was trying to come to terms with them. On the contrary, he increased the stakes by a headlong flight into further heterodoxy. It is in this light that we must now read his speech to the Cultural Congress in January 1968, and his many references to the "new vanguard." We know that on that occasion he abandoned his traditional formula, "I speak for Latin America and for Latin America alone," to inveigh against the shortcomings and dogmatism of orthodox Communists in general. In so doing, he affirmed that his "Latin American dividing line" ran through the entire world; the courageous vanguard was everywhere up against pseudorevolutionaries who refused the good fight. But there was this difference from his earlier speeches: he no longer prescribed a clear-cut cure. His challenge to the orthodox had become broader and more annoying, but it was also vaguer and less dramatic. Fidel no longer asked them to subscribe to a precise guerrilla project, no longer presented them with a concrete choice.

The same vagueness marked his invitation to intellectuals, and to the new vanguard in general, to make a collective search for new ideas and new paths of revolution. When he declared that "no one has a monopoly of revolutionary truth," he had outraged the old Communist vanguard which, for the past fifty years, had pretended to be the sole guardian and true interpreter of the Marxist-Leninist doctrine. But a call to rebellion against them would only have had real meaning if Castro, the heretic, had initiated a public debate on the failures of the old orthodoxy. As it was, no one knew what to make of his great speech, simply because no one could tell at the time whether it was intended as an end in itself or as a prelude to a new political free-for-all. Then, three weeks after the Cultural Congress assembled, came the Escalante trial, and ten weeks later the Great Revolutionary Offensive of March 1968.

Now his meaning became clear: in opting for militarization, Castro had departed from his thesis on the need for introducing

The reckoning

elements of Communism during the present phase of socialist construction, and of initiating a genuine political and ideological confrontation with the orthodox. The Cuban leader gave the impression of having deliberately sacrificed the most original —and, to progressive opinion, the most fascinating—aspects of his experiment by suddenly slamming the door shut on all criticism, all genuine discussion, all forms of political dialectics. The authoritarian element had obviously gained the upper hand in Castroist theory as it had in Castroist practice. There was some hope that this might be only a temporary retreat, that when Fidel had told me to hurry up with my book because soon the country would be quite unrecognizable, the words might have hidden the promise that Cuba would soon become free for truly Communist and "heretical" initiatives. But one had to be quite an optimist to believe that, or to believe that the "great mobilization" would leave no clouds on the Cuban horizon. Fidel must also have realized that during the entire period of her "decisive effort," Cuba's hands would be tied; that she could not afford the slightest conflict with the U.S.S.R. or with any other trading partner. Hence, if Castro chose even greater vulnerability for a time, he must have done so quite deliberately, in the hope of shaking off the curse of underdevelopment once and for all. His gamble at home fully reflected his assessment of the international scene.

Now if this was indeed his analysis of the situation, he was in for a great shock. The year 1968 did not bring a gradual awakening of the "new vanguard" or a measure of calm to the world scene. On the contrary, crises and setbacks kept transforming relations between the two blocs and the political situation inside each one. These events did not follow a straight course; however, they revealed a failure on the part of the Castroists to interpret world realities, and highlighted the ideological contradictions of Cuban politics. Far from forcing international Communists to take a stand on Fidel Castro's vague heresy, events compelled Fidel himself to take a stand on a precise political development in the West as well as in the East, and this at the

495

worst possible moment from his point of view. Paralyzed by pressures at home, the Cuban leader reacted to each new blow by a choice of the lesser evil, passing it all over in silence or else offering theoretical explanations that revealed to all the world what had happened to his revolutionary ideology after ten years in power.

The year had begun most propitiously for the Cubans. There was, first of all, the incredible Tet offensive by the NLF, which few military experts would have believed possible. Vietnamese freedom fighters moved right into Saigon, attacked the U.S. Embassy, and held out for two long weeks in Hué, the second largest city in the country. This was a victory of the imagination by a small people over the blind technological forces of the greatest industrial power in the world. It showed the world that power was a relative concept, and encouraged the hopes of all who refused steadfastly to bend before a mighty but oppressive social order. Its repercussions were felt everywhere, in the United States no less than in Europe, where a wave of student revolts broke out and increasingly escaped the control of the traditional political forces. In Germany and Italy, the young came out into the streets and occupied their colleges, while chanting the names of Ho Chi Minh, of Mao Tse-tung, and above all of Ernesto Che Guevara, their great hero. Less of a theorist than Mao Tse-tung, less of a Party man than Ho Chi Minh, Che was an obvious idol —a youthful martyr whose great warmth and simplicity struck a chord in every young heart, and whose refusal to compromise with a society based on social injustice was an inspiration to all. And, needless to say, part of his radiance rubbed off on Cuba, the land of *his* revolution.

But the Tet offensive had other consequences as well, less obvious but no less important. It had proved that the United States could not possibly hope to win in Vietnam without starting a world conflagration, and so caused the balance in Washington to come down on the side of the doves. Local escalation had proved a failure, and for good measure had served to discredit America and to reveal her humiliating impotence. A major escalation, on the other hand, i.e., an attack on China, Vietnam's hinterland, involved too many risks and too many unknown factors. Far better, therefore, to beat a retreat and seek an "honorable" solution through Soviet mediation with Hanoi. And so the United States unconditionally—although by stages— called a halt to the bombing of North Vietnam, and put an end to the scandalous violation of the frontiers of the Eastern bloc. Moreover, Lyndon B. Johnson, the man who since 1965 had played fast and loose with all the rules of coexistence, had to remove himself from the presidential scene. The honor of the U.S.S.R. had been saved, and when Moscow did its utmost to foster American-Vietnamese talks, it looked very much as if the United States would be able to save its honor as well. In short, by their lone courage and sacrifice, the Vietnamese had succeeded in restoring the balance between the two superpowers.

Suddenly, in the month of May, just as American-Vietnamese talks were being started in Paris, the French student uprising took an incredulous world completely by surprise. A handful of youngsters, most of them members of left-wing splinter groups, had caused a social explosion without precedent in modern times. In France, as once upon a time in Cuba, a detonator had sufficed to trigger off a major crisis, on a scale the labor movement or its class enemies no longer thought possible in Western Europe. None of the orthodox forces knew what to do with a movement that was as unexpected as it was straightforward. Unhappily, the "new vanguard," which distinguished itself during the initial phase of the general confrontation, was unable to carry the issue to a successful conclusion, and gradually but inexorably lost the initiative to the old and more highly organized forces. Paris in 1968 was not Havana in 1959, and "revolutionary subjectivism" was obviously not enough to cause the revolution to triumph. For all that, the crisis had brought into the open the existence of explosive undercurrents beneath the calm surface of a great industrial country, undercurrents far too powerful to be dammed up with appeals to responsibility and talk of social harmony. The May events had drawn attention to

Guerrillas in Power

Europe's revolutionary potential; to that extent, they had borne out all those who, like Fidel Castro, had refused to submit to the status quo or to endorse foolish reformist schemes.

However, instead of rejoicing, Havana was deeply embarrassed. The Cuban press published news from France without comment, as if the whole affair, though interesting enough in itself, was of no particular concern to Cuba. Fidel Castro withdrew into complete silence which, to say the least, was most unusual, and Cuban student organizations—the UJC-FEU—did not even see fit to send a symbolic message of support to their comrades of the UNEF,[2] nor did the Cuban trade unions express their solidarity with the millions of strikers in France. This reticence on their part was especially astonishing in that anti-Castroists everywhere were quick to attribute the French revolt to Cuba; even the French Communist Party blamed it all on "those Guevarists," as if Ernesto Che Guevara had never been an acknowledged Communist leader or the member of the Politburo of a fraternal party. For good measure, the Gaullist minister of the interior, Marcellin, claimed that Havana had engineered a "student plot" in France, and by way of retaliation banned the Cuban journal *Tricontinental*. To add to the confusion, some left-wing Gaullists tried to co-opt Fidel Castro to their cause, claiming that the Cuban leader was really an enlightened nationalist, just like General de Gaulle, whom he was said to admire greatly.

Fidel's silence was therefore an uncomfortable one, and we may be certain that he himself was fully aware of its ambiguities. If he kept silent it was simply because he dared not speak out, for reasons of state as much as for ideological reasons. We have seen that, at this moment, Cuba could not afford the luxury of

---

2. The UNEF (*Union Nationale des Étudiants de France*) was the French equivalent of the FEU, and was particularly active during the May events. It is worth pointing out that Alain Geismar, the secretary of SNESUP (the National Union of University Teachers), who distinguished himself as an organizer of French student revolt, had attended the Havana Cultural Congress and had never concealed his pro-Cuban sympathies.

498

offending a single one of her trading partners. Gaullist France was supplying her with invaluable agricultural equipment, on especially favorable credit terms; a victorious left-wing opposition might well have turned out to be less sympathetic to the island, preferring to do the bidding of the Soviet Union which, like the United States, did not look with favor on any extension of Cuban trade with other countries. True, everything would have been different if the French revolt, escaping the logic of traditional politics, had led to the emergence of viable political forces, ready to embrace the Castroist ideal. But Fidel quite obviously lacked faith in the dynamics of the May uprising, or in the "new vanguard" that had started it all.

This brings us to the second reason for his silence. The French crisis had forced the political parties to clarify their position, to reveal their long- and short-term plans. This applied particularly to the French Communist Party, which had for so long been completely vague about its revolutionary and parliamentary aspirations, and which now ran the risk of losing out on both fronts. And so the French Communists came out quite unequivocally as a party of law and order, postponing their socialist aspirations to an indefinite future. Their stand was at once approved by the Russians, who concentrated their fire on the "hyenas" in the universities—now the common enemies of the Gaullists and the Communists. By contrast, Peking spoke of a new piece of treachery by the revisionists, and promised unconditional support to the rebels. The two great Communist powers thus reacted in characteristic ways, emphasizing the deep gulf between the orthodox forces now openly aligned on a purely reformist platform, and the new movement which refused to have any part of the prevailing social order. Now, its very origins and structure ought to have rendered this quasi-spontaneous movement far more palatable to the Cubans than to the Chinese, who had quite a different revolutionary history and who took a strictly Leninist view of the revolutionary role of the Communist vanguard. But then Peking looked upon the events in France as clear signs of a new crisis in the old pro-

Soviet labor movement, and quite naturally tried to use them to discredit the orthodox Communist parties. Had Fidel Castro remained faithful to the spirit and even to the letter of his appeal to the Cultural Congress, he ought to have adopted the same attitude.

But that was probably the last thing he wished to do. He had withdrawn from the Latin American field to avoid a head-on clash with the old pro-Soviet school on such basic matters as revolutionary theory and practice in his part of the world, and he had no intention now, five months later, in May 1968, of carrying the same debate so much nearer to the U.S.S.R. If he spoke up on France, he would be inviting a showdown with his most powerful backer. And so he kept quiet, even though his silence was a political betrayal and drastically reduced the credibility of his "Third Communism."

True, long after the May events, Cubans tried to regain some of the lost terrain by letting the world know that their sympathies had always been with the French rebels and not with their detractors. Thus, on July 26, 1968, at their annual meeting in Santa Clara, the secretary of the UJC-FEU for Las Villas province included the following passage in his long declaration of principles: "We know perfectly well that the world revolutionary process is indivisible, that the destiny of all peoples is one and that the enemy is one. . . . Today, while students in the most developed countries of Europe no less than in the most backward countries of America are braving bullets, repulsing the two faces of imperialism—the ugly face of underdevelopment and the deceitful face of capitalism—we, the Cuban students, who have been granted the privilege and the honor of participating in the construction of a new society, express our militant solidarity with them."[3] Fidel spoke immediately afterward, and was "delighted" to give his support to the declaration.

This accolade went totally unnoticed in France. No comment

3. See French weekly summary of *Granma*, July 28, 1968. The text of the UJC-FEU declaration was read out by a student, Antonio Castro.

The reckoning

was made at all, perhaps to repay Cuba for her silence in May. In any case, the main front of the student movement had moved from Paris to Mexico City, right at Cuba's door. In Mexico the signal for revolt was given on July 26, when the students organized a vast street demonstration in honor of the Cuban Revolution. They were dispersed by *grenaderos*,[4] firing guns and swinging clubs, and leaving more than ten dead behind them when they were finished. Next day all Mexican universities and high schools went on a protest strike. The students called for the restoration of all the rights inscribed in the constitution, for an end to police repression, and for the release of political prisoners, and their demands were taken up by the country at large, by a country that had far too long suffered under the despotic rule of the Institutional Revolutionary Party. People everywhere came out in the streets to demonstrate their solidarity with the students, and, one day in August, half a million of them marched in procession through the center of the capital, in answer to an appeal from the university strike committee. Mexico had not seen the like since the historical days of March 1938, when the entire nation had demonstrated its support for President Lázaro Cárdenas, and for his decision to nationalize the American oil companies.

This time, the ruling clique led by the former minister of the interior, now president, Gustavo Díaz Ordaz, was not disposed to heed the voice of the people. The result was a running battle, right under the eyes of the Cubans, whose response, once again, was an ear-splitting silence. If only this trial of strength had taken place anywhere but in Mexico, the one neighbor to have maintained diplomatic and economic relations with Castro's Cuba! Worse still, the only air link between Havana and the

---

4. The *grenaderos* are a special shock detachment, comparable to the notorious French CRS. The real number of its victims has never been discovered. According to the students themselves, the *grenaderos* make a point of disposing of their victims' bodies, thus effacing all traces of their efficiency.

subcontinent passed through the Mexican capital.[5] In the circumstances, taking a stand against Díaz Ordaz would have meant playing into the hands of the Americans, who had all along been pressing the Mexican government to make a clean break with Havana.

But the Mexican crisis, unlike the French crisis, could not be settled by political gerrymandering. To begin with, President Díaz Ordaz was quite unable to drum up enough support to beat his adversaries on the electoral plane. Moreover, he was in a hurry to put an end to all disorders, because in October he was to open the Olympic Games, in which he had invested fabulous sums. And so the climax was bloody: after pretending to make concessions to the students and authorizing an "informative gathering" to be held on October 2 in Three Cultures Square in Tlatelolco, he sent in tanks and shock troops who opened fire without warning on the 15,000 peaceful and unarmed demonstrators who had assembled there. There were more than 300 dead and 2,000 wounded after the Mexican army was done.[6]

Arrests ran into the thousands. Even the violent history of Mexico had known few episodes as bloody as this.

The students, their ranks decimated by repression on so vast a scale, were confident that the Tlatelolco massacre would cause an outcry throughout the world. And, in fact, Jean-Paul Sartre and Bertrand Russell called for a boycott of the Olympic Games, and had there been such a thing as a world conscience,

5. A weekly flight between Havana and Mexico is run by the Cubana Company. On their arrival in Mexico, all passengers are carefully searched and all "subversive" papers confiscated by customs officers. Understandably enough, many people prefer to avoid this gratuitous and unpredictable piece of interference, with the result that planes to Mexico are generally half empty. Latin American citizens have an added incentive to stay away: their comings and goings are registered, and their photographs filed—and not just for the records of the Mexican police either!—and they are often interrogated for hours, if not for whole days.

6. Officially there were only 35 dead, but *Le Monde* of October 3, 1969, basing its article on an inquiry by the Manchester *Guardian*, reported 300 dead and 2,000 wounded.

The reckoning

every civilized country would have heeded their appeal, would have shown its abhorrence of a government that used such vicious methods against students on the eve of a great festival of sport and youth. But the appeal fell on deaf ears in the West, in the East, and most surprising of all, in Havana. The Cubans, who in March 1968 had decided to withdraw from the Olympic Games in protest against the expected presence of South Africa,[7] saw no reason to make a similar gesture after the Tlatelolco massacre, no reason to demonstrate their solidarity with the thousands of young Mexicans who were being tortured in Mexican prisons for allegedly participating in a Castroist plot and for deliberately provoking the peaceful Mexican army. On October 19, 1968, the Cuban athletes filed past Gustavo Díaz Ordaz, just like their comrades from Eastern Europe. The Soviet prime minister, Kosygin, even sent the Mexican president warm wishes for the success of the great Olympiad.

To this day, Fidel Castro has passed no comment on the massacre, even though he previously (in his speech of January 2, 1968) saw fit to address a few friendly criticisms to the rulers of Mexico. Clearly this time any protest on his part would have gone beyond the limits of friendship, and this he could ill afford. He may have felt some qualms about a student movement with no clear-cut objectives and with which he had no direct links; or he may not have wanted to take a line different from that of the Soviet Union, so soon after his Czechoslovak "conversion." And it was indubitably this spectacular turning point which was the most remarkable event in a year so full of setbacks. Let us therefore take a closer look at the Cuban reaction to the historical crisis in Eastern Europe in 1968.

It was purely by chance that news of Prague's "new course" first reached Havana on January 6, the day on which I had

7. The invitation to South Africa was later withdrawn by the International Olympic Committee in the face of protests by Cuba, the African countries, and the East European countries. It should be mentioned that no Asian socialist country (China, Vietnam, or Korea) was represented at the Mexican Olympic Games.

breakfast with Fidel Castro and his brother Raúl. At the time, we exchanged a few generalities about the problems of Czechoslovakia, formerly the most highly industrialized country in that part of Europe, and the one richest in left-wing traditions. The name of Alexander Dubček, the new leader of the Czechoslovak Communist Party, meant nothing to any of us, nor could we tell what forces had helped him to oust his formidable predecessor, Novotny, head of the Party machine and in charge of the police. On the subject of Novotny the two Castro brothers had a great deal to say. For them, the man was the very incarnation of clinical mediocrity; they claimed that no country had swindled revolutionary Cuba as brazenly as Novotny's Czechoslovakia. Though they did not know Dubček personally, they were convinced that he could not be worse than his predecessor.

Until 1968, Czechoslovak affairs did not attract much attention in the Cuban press. The changes in Prague had not seemed sufficiently dramatic for anyone in Havana to get excited about. Only by the spring of 1968, when all Eastern Europe was humming with reports about Dubček's "new course," did *Granma* at last sit up and take notice. It did so with a degree of impartiality worthy of a Solomon, publishing attacks by the orthodox in Moscow, Pankow, and Warsaw side by side with explanations from Prague and Bratislava. On August 2, replying to an article that had appeared ten days earlier in Bratislava and had taken the Cubans to task for their neutrality, the Castroist mouthpiece countered with: "We have published all documents submitted to us by socialist press agencies, so that our people may know the different arguments before forming their own opinion on the Czechoslovak situation."[8]

8. On July 23, 1968, the Slovak paper *Pravda* published an article by Pavel Jurik, who contended that the Soviet Union was far more patient with Cuba than she was with Czechoslovakia and that the Cubans were wrong not to endorse Dubček's "new course." The article was therefore incoherent and its author confused: he found the Cubans "unjust and ungrateful toward the Soviet Union," but at the same time urged them to fall in behind Dubček's "ideas and his truths." *Granma* reproduced the text of this article, called it insidious, and replied with the lead editorial from

The reckoning

This, the only official Cuban statement on the matter, ended with the solemn declaration that Cuba would not allow anyone to "poison her friendly relationship with the people of Czechoslovakia."

Having been invited to form their own opinion, the Cubans, like the rest of the world, were stupified by the Soviet aggression of August 21, 1968. Clearly, none of their leaders had anticipated that sort of solution, so brutal a termination of what had apparently begun as a friendly debate between comrades. Preserving its habitual sang-froid the Cuban press contented itself, once again, with making a great show of impartiality. It published an obscure Soviet communiqué claiming that the Warsaw Pact countries had been called in by a number of important but anonymous comrades in Prague, anxious to check the counterrevolution, side by side with precise declarations by the Czechoslovak Communist Party and Parliament affirming that there had been no counterrevolutionary threat nor any appeal for help from anyone, and that their country had been the victim of downright foreign intervention. In the absence of special directions to the contrary, the Cuban reader was naturally inclined to believe the Czechoslovak version and to sympathize unstintingly with the unfortunate people of that country. Not surprisingly, therefore, Czech technicians in Havana were showered with solicitations and, greatly encouraged by this show of solidarity, they marched in procession through the streets in Vedado, shouting, *"Patria o muerte."* The radio announced that Fidel would address the nation on August 23 at 9 P.M.

He did this at a particularly dramatic moment. Havana was still without news of Dubček or Smrkovský, Černik or the other leaders, all of them arrested and taken to an unknown destination. The Czech Communist Party was holding a clandestine meeting in a factory on the outskirts of Prague and, while advising the people to stay calm, was considering the possibility

---

which I have been quoting. See French weekly summary of *Granma*, August 11, 1968.

of calling a general protest strike. At the same time it appealed for solidarity from Communists throughout the world—solidarity for a socialist victim of Soviet folly.

In the circumstances, it looked very much as if Fidel was making such haste in addressing the nation because he wanted to be among the first to heed this pathetic appeal. So convinced were most Cubans that he would do just that, that they behaved as if their leader had already condemned the U.S.S.R., as if the only remaining question was how hard he would hit out. That evening I was dining with a group of high Cuban officials on a brief stay in Europe. They insisted that all of us stay up for the actual speech, due to be broadcast at 3 A.M. European time, because that speech would open a new page in the history of the international labor movement.

Today everyone knows that if Fidel was anxious to speak that night, it was merely to stem the anti-Soviet mood of his party and people. Having sown doubts on the revolutionary credibility of the U.S.S.R. for so many years, he was appealing to a people with little love for the Soviet Union and none of the pro-Russian mysticism of more orthodox Communists. He was also addressing a nation with a maximum concern for national independence, for the sovereignty of small countries, one that could not but feel the strongest bonds of friendship with the fourteen million Czechs and Slovaks overcome by the Soviet colossus and its four acolytes.[9] And so Fidel had an exceedingly difficult task to convince them. While outsiders called his speech a manifestation of "revolting cynicism,"[10] many Cubans thought it the most pathetic and tormented performance of his entire life.

As a good lawyer, Fidel declared straight away that the Soviet alibi was worthless—Czechoslovak sovereignty had been violated without even a shred of legal justification. And he went on to

9. All the countries of the Warsaw Pact, with the exception of Rumania and, of course, of Czechoslovakia herself, took part in the invasion. Troops from East Germany, Poland, Hungary, and Bulgaria now stood on Czechoslovak soil.

10. See editorial in *Le Monde*, August 25, 1968.

The reckoning

say: "An entire nation has been exposed to the truly traumatic situation of foreign occupation, albeit by socialist armies. Millions of people have been placed before this tragic alternative: they must either remain passive in the face of circumstances that recall certain episodes of the past, or else they must make common cause with pro-Yankee spies and agents, and with other enemies of socialism."[11]

A wrong had been done to Czechoslovakia, but according to Fidel, it was only to prevent an even greater evil. "Czechoslovakia," he said, "had been marching inexorably toward capitalism, toward imperialism." And the whole trouble had apparently started with those bourgeois economic reforms which, though admittedly imported from the Soviet Union, had been applied so energetically by Prague as to undermine the whole socialist system—to the great delight of the imperialists. "Whatever earns the support and enthusiastic applause of the imperialist press, quite naturally makes me suspicious." And he went on to quote extracts from the West German and American press, all praising Czechoslovakia's new course. The main trouble had been that the Czechoslovak Communist Party, under pressure from intellectuals and other liberals, had forsworn the dictatorship of the proletariat.

In these tragic circumstances, the Soviet Union could not possibly sit by and do nothing while the imperialists snatched so valuable a prize from the socialist camp. To do so would have been highly prejudicial to the interests of the world revolutionary movement. Hence, Fidel concluded, the socialist bloc had been forced to violate international law, but in the name of "law even more sacred to all true Communists," namely "the people's struggle against imperialism." After this shrewd assessment of the Czechoslovak affair, the Cuban leader went on to declare that he would profit from the occasion to tell the Soviet

11. All the quotations are taken from a pamphlet entitled "Address by *Comandante* Fidel Castro on the events in Czechoslovakia," Instituto del Libro, Havana, 1968, and also from the French weekly summary of *Granma,* October 25, 1968.

Union "a few basic truths that I have been keeping to myself."
And he followed with a diatribe against the "weakening and
softening of the revolutionary spirit" in Eastern Europe, against
"indifference to, and ignorance of, the problems of the underdeveloped world," and the "tendency to favor commercial practices reminiscent of advanced capitalist countries." Fidel now
asked the Soviet Union to put an end to all these anomalies,
and to make an unequivocal promise that she would henceforth
come to the aid of any member of the socialist community,
above all the most exposed among them: Vietnam, Cuba, and
North Korea. He, for his part, was satisfied that Moscow had
come to see the "vanity of all idyllic hopes to improve relations
with the imperialist government of the United States," and that
the Soviet Union would cease to engage in "bourgeois economic
reforms which had had such disastrous effects in Czechoslovakia."

Cuban embassies throughout Europe made sure that this text
reached the widest possible audience, hoping to show by it that
Fidel had not endorsed the action of the U.S.S.R. uncritically;
that he had maintained his freedom of judgment even in a situation as delicate as the present one. In particular, the diplomats
tried to draw attention to his demands, and let it be understood that if the U.S.S.R. did not change her entire approach
quickly, Cuba might well have second thoughts about Czechoslovakia. But these arguments, intended to still the doubts, indeed to put an end to the confusion of European pro-Castroists,
were bound to have the very opposite effect in the long run.
Because, though the U.S.S.R. did not change her attitude in the
least, Fidel raised not another murmur of protest. On the contrary, since August 23, 1968, Havana has proved increasingly
understanding of the Moscow line.

It is, moreover, extremely difficult to believe that so shrewd a
politician as Fidel Castro could really have considered the invasion of Czechoslovakia a move in the Cold War between the
U.S.S.R. and the United States. In fact, from the very start of
the conflict in Eastern Europe, all the signs were that Washington had let it be known that it would not interfere in the

recognized Soviet sphere of influence. It was not by chance that
the Soviet leaders informed the President of the United States
of the impending invasion before they did any foreign Communist leaders, Castro included, and that after protesting
against the Soviet aggression as a pure matter of form, the
Americans should have hastened to declare that all this changed
nothing in their desire to improve relations with the U.S.S.R.
In the face of so much chivalry, what could the Soviet Union do
but respect the American wish to preserve the status quo in their
part of the world? Thus, if the Czechoslovak affair did nothing
else, it made it perfectly clear that "coexistence" meant the
continued division of the world between two superpowers.

This was hardly idyllic, but then Fidel Castro had not chosen
the Soviet Union out of love. His dislike of its politics, which
he had confessed to me on more than one occasion, could not
possibly have been changed—except for the worse—by the Russian reaction to Czechoslovakia's "new course." He may have told
his people that, after Czechoslovakia, the Soviet Union would
rally more strongly to the cause of international socialism, but
that he himself entertained this hope seems doubtful.

In fact, Castro's own reaction to the invasion was dictated
purely by political considerations. He believed that Cuba would
enjoy greater protection through continued membership in the
Soviet bloc—however "reformist"—than by strict adherence to
the principle of sovereignty for small countries. "We must learn
to face the political realities, and not give way to romantic and
idealistic dreams," he said in his speech. And, clearly, the
division of the world was a much more tangible reality than
any number of solemn declarations by the United Nations on the
inviolability of frontiers and universal peace. The fate of
Czechoslovakia following so close as it did on the heels of
Vietnam and of so many other acts of aggression, sufficed to
demonstrate this beyond all doubt.

Nor was that the whole story. The Soviet Union had not
offered to shield Cuba for purely altruistic reasons. It demanded
payment for services, and was in a good position to lay down
the terms. Fidel knew precisely what these were—he would

have to lie low for a long time to come, and he would have to shelve many of his dearest plans at home and abroad.

Was there no alternative, then? In principle at least, there was: the Cuban leader could have followed the Chinese in denouncing the "social imperialism" of the U.S.S.R. His voice had always evoked some response from the Communist family, now thrown into complete disarray by the Czechoslovak debacle. Thus, had he chosen this moment to expose the pseudorevolutionary myth of Soviet policy, his arguments—which he had built up over the years—would certainly not have fallen on deaf ears. But this would have meant challenging two superpowers at once, two giants who would show no mercy to an extremist Cuba allied to China. For that he lacked the courage, and perhaps even the means.

Nor was it realism alone that dictated his choice. In his heart of hearts, Castro agreed neither with China's cultural revolution nor with Czechoslovakia's new course; in his own way, he was genuinely behind the August invasion. True, he hoped for changes from the Soviet bloc, but not for changes initiated by uncontrolled and spontaneous forces. His greatest fear was that too violent upheavals might paralyze his allies, and leave Cuba to the mercy of the United States. Moreover, independent action by the rank and file was no part of his political program. His Czechoslovak speech had a ring of sincerity, simply because he was not altogether cynical, was not merely playing at power politics. In an odd way it may even be said to have been a kind of declaration of faith, and as such merits the careful attention of all those who wish to know how Fidel Castro conceived socialism in 1968, on the eve of the tenth anniversary of the Cuban Revolution.

A new honeymoon

Sudden political changes invariably pose serious problems, even in socialist countries whose masters do not take too much notice of public opinion. They throw the leadership—not to mention

The reckoning

the ordinary Party members—into utter confusion; experience has shown that every psychological crisis in the ranks of the socialist elite has unavoidable repercussions on society as a whole. After hearing Fidel's speech of August 23, 1968, few people familiar with Cuba's political atmosphere could have believed that he would go beyond certain limits in his reconciliation with the U.S.S.R. His return to the orthodox fold seemed even more improbable as his anti-revisionist fervor had waxed stronger during the long years of the "cold polemic"— the debate on Soviet-American coexistence. Every visitor to the island remembers the passion with which Fidel's closest colleagues vituperated against "those pseudorevolutionaries" responsible for so many setbacks the world revolutionary movement had suffered. To them, Fidel's support for the invasion of Czechoslovakia was a shock, tempered only by the fact that their leader had also repeated his attack on the "mistaken views of some European socialist countries."[12] And so while the Czechoslovak drama struck Cubans a painful blow, many came to see it as the consequence of terrible revisionist errors. A vast propaganda campaign was launched in the island to explain that, far from having surrendered unconditionally, Fidel had taken "very grave risks"—these were his own words—in telling the Soviet Union, at this grave hour in their history, "a few basic truths I have been keeping to myself."[13]

The Russians, for their part, adopted a guarded attitude; they put out no flags when Fidel endorsed their military intervention in Czechoslovakia. His speech was not even given a brief mention in *Pravda,* which in general opened its columns

12. In his speech of August 23, Fidel stressed the fact that he was criticizing the mistaken views of "certain European socialist countries, and not of all of them." He was careful not to be more specific.
13. "In town and country, on big estates and small hamlets, in the offices of the Committee for the Defense of the Revolution, the people gathered to study Fidel's speech on the events in Czechoslovakia, and to proclaim their Communist ideals more loudly than ever." Caption on a facsimile of Fidel's speech, covered with signatures by members of an enthusiastic audience, in *Granma,* French weekly summary, September 8, 1968.

to any foreign message that could be considered even vaguely favorable to the invasion. From this Kremlinologists concluded that the rift between Cuba and the Soviet Union had grown so wide that the Russians could not possibly consider it closed—even assuming they had wanted to—after a single gesture by Fidel Castro. The experts argued that the "heroic island" had lost the trust and friendship of the Soviet power elite, and that the Brezhnev team would think twice before allowing itself to be drawn into a fresh Cuban entanglement.

Yet less than a year later, Moscow and Havana were off on a new honeymoon. Nor was it merely a marriage between two independent states this time; the island was still resounding with echoes of Fidel's speech when a most surprising *ideological* rapprochement between Castro and the Eastern bloc was under way. And, unfortunately, the "basic truths" Fidel had addressed to the Russians on August 23, 1968, were uttered not so much for the first time as for the last.

From then on, whenever Castro wished to contrast his views of aggressive socialism with those of the "pseudorevolutionaries," he was most careful to specify that what he had in mind was Czechoslovakia, as if Prague were the only place where the revolutionary spirit had grown lax under the evil influence of bourgeois economic reforms.[14] As soon as the situation in Czechoslovakia was normalized, Fidel dropped all references to the "erroneous views" of his European allies.

In November 1968, Fidel received a delegation from the East German Communist Party with great ceremony; breaking a rule he had made after 1965 never again to sign a common declara-

14. In his speech of September 28, 1968, Fidel, referring to Havana's young layabouts, said that "these youngsters probably think they are in Prague," thus implying that the Czechoslovak capital was a hotbed of prostitution and immorality. Some contributors to the army journal, *Verde Olivo*, later used this argument against Cuba's nonconformist intellectuals whom they accused of searching for the *"dolce vita à la Prague."* During this whole period, the Cuban press published a stream of cartoons, direct attacks, and veiled insinuations against Dubček and his supporters. The palm in this anti-Czechoslovak race must certainly go to the satirical journal *Palante*, which published a cartoon coupling Prague intellectuals with Adolf Hitler and Wall Street bankers. (No. 45, August 29, 1968).

tion with orthodox Communists, he now put his name to a joint communiqué on the "necessity of fighting against all forms of revisionism and opportunism."[15] To Cubans, accustomed to lumping together Russians, East Germans, and the rest as "revisionists," this communiqué must have had a peculiar ring, especially as there was no official explanation of the reasons that had persuaded Fidel to scrap his old interpretations of revisionism and opportunism, in favor of the Russian one. But all that was only a beginning.

On January 2, 1969, before an immense crowd, Fidel drew up his balance sheet of ten years of revolution. He spoke of past achievements and present difficulties, of the great efforts that were still called for, and of the prospects for the future. Everyone present was certain that he was about to render the customary homage to the foremost organizer of a socialist economy in Cuba and to the great champion of Latin American revolution, Ernesto Che Guevara. Yet that day Fidel made no mention of either his former minister of industry, or of the Latin American *guerrilleros*. Instead, he ended his oration by expressing deep gratitude to the socialist camp and particularly to the Soviet Union for their aid and great show of solidarity. And he concealed his obvious embarrassment behind such phrases as: "In all fairness we must recognize that Soviet aid has been crucial for our country," or "Honesty compels us to

15. The East German delegation was led by Paul Werner, a member of the Politburo and Secretariat of his Party. Werner signed the communiqué on November 21, 1968 (see *Granma*, Spanish weekly summary, December 1, 1968), after touring Havana province in Fidel's company (see illustrated report, *Bohemia*, November 22, 1968). In this connection, it is interesting to note that, of all countries in the Soviet bloc, East Germany is the one that has most resolutely applied those "economic bourgeois reforms" which according to Fidel were at the root of all Czechoslovakia's ills. It is also a well-known fact that the opportunism of the leaders of the German Democratic Republic is equalled only by their Prusso-Stalinist arrogance. Incidentally, Ernesto Che Guevara, addressing a meeting at the Ministry of Industry on July 14, 1962, accused the East Germans of supplying Cuba with *porquerias* (garbage) instead of the promised factories. It was, in fact, this discovery which first made him wonder about the quality of deliveries from the Soviet bloc.

say that Soviet aid has been crucial during these decisive years."[16]

Even these stylish qualifications would eventually disappear from his speeches. Thus, in July 1969, when a Soviet naval squadron dropped anchor off Havana for the first time since the Revolution, Fidel, surrounded by an entire galaxy of leaders (including Blas Roca, suddenly brought back from oblivion), boarded the cruiser *Grozny* and went into raptures about the superior naval skills and unequalled revolutionary qualities of the Red sailors.[17] Soon afterward, the Cuban press as a whole praised the internationalism of the Soviet sailors, all of whom made a personal contribution to the ten-million-ton *zafra* by cutting sugar cane for half a day. The great prose devoted to this *hermoso gesto de solidaridad internacionalista* was singularly reminiscent of the writings in *Hoy* during the first Cuban-Russian honeymoon in 1961.

In other respects, too, the Cubans went out of their way to please their new allies. One month earlier, in June 1969, Fidel had revoked one of the rare collective decisions by the Central Committee (adopted during that very session of January 1968 which had voted to hand Russia's friend Escalante over to the courts) ; namely, that the Communist Party of Cuba would not participate in the world conference of Communist parties convened by the Soviet Union. In accordance with his new line, he sent Carlos Rafael Rodríguez to Moscow, ostensibly as an observer; Rodríguez delivered an important speech with this sonorous ending: "We declare from this tribune that in any decisive confrontation, whether it be an act by the Soviet Union to avert threats of dislocation or provocation to the socialist system, or an act of aggression by anyone against the Soviet people, Cuba will stand unflinchingly by the U.S.S.R."[18]

This oath of loyalty had the widest political and ideological

16. See Fidel Castro's speech on the Tenth Anniversary of the Revolution, *Granma*, French weekly summary. January 5, 1969.
17. See *Granma*, French weekly summary, August 3, 1969.
18. See *Granma*, French weekly summary, June 15, 1969.

514

implications; it went much further than a mere declaration of friendship with the U.S.S.R. The Chinese, as well as the Vietnamese, the Koreans, and other non-aligned parties had refused to attend this conference, precisely because its main object, as everyone knew, was to enlist support for a political—and perhaps even a military—crusade against Peking.[19] By sending Carlos Rafael Rodríguez and by having him proclaim his unfailing solidarity with the Soviet Union, Fidel had thus made a far-reaching political choice: unlike the Vietnamese and the Koreans he had decided not to sit on the fence between Moscow and Peking, but to side quite openly with the former. Not surprisingly, therefore, on October 1, 1969, during the twentieth anniversary of the Chinese revolution, no Cuban leader was found on the tribune in Tien An Men Square, while the North Korean president, Choi Yong-kun, the North Vietnamese premier, Pham Van Dong, and the president of the N.L.F., Huu Tho, stood right beside Mao Tse-tung.

The Soviet Union and its allies did not remain insensible to the latest Cuban gesture. They began once again to speak of the heroic island in flattering terms, and seemed only too happy to forget all about the heresies and the lack of discipline of the preceding years. *Pravda, Trybuna Ludu, Neues Deutschland,* once more resounded with glowing reports about the enthusiasm of the Cubans, their great achievements, and the radiant future

19. Neither the "Chinese question" nor Czechoslovakia were on the official agenda of that conference of Communist parties, several of which had made it a condition of their attendance that no internecine disputes would be aired. But from the second day of the conference, their wishes were completely ignored, and the Secretary of the Communist Party of the U.S.S.R., Leonid Brezhnev, saw fit to deliver a scathing diatribe against China. The Russians also did a great deal of lobbying and, in particular, tried to sound out the delegates' reactions to a possible pre-emptive strike against China's nuclear installations in Sinkiang. Anti-Chinese hysteria had reached such heights in Moscow that many Communist parties much closer to the U.S.S.R. than the Cuban had carefully avoided declaring their "unflinching" solidarity with the Soviet Union. No wonder, therefore, that the world press treated the presence and declaration of Carlo Rafael Rodríguez as Russia's chief political success during this conference.

that lay in store for them.[20] Out of delicacy, no East European envoy made reference to the lapses of the past, or to Castro's mistaken predilection for moral incentives (which he had never renounced). Cuba was praised as a good people's democracy, whose main purpose at the moment was to beat the sugar production records. On the occasion of July 26th celebrations in 1969, the leaders of the Warsaw Pact countries sent their good wishes to Fidel in terms they reserved for the best-loved members of the family. Even the strongly anti-Guevarist and anti-leftist French Communist Party, anxious not to be left out of this joyful reunion, sent the warmest greetings to the comrades in Havana.

Cultural and political exchanges between the Soviet Union and Cuba continued to grow, and other members of the bloc followed suit by sending delegations and experts to the island. Yet none of them seemed anxious to make Cuba any economic presents or to help it alleviate the cruel shortage of consumer goods that kept growing worse throughout 1969; like the first great love affair of 1961–62, the new honeymoon coincided painfully with a marked drop in supplies on the island.[21] There was no direct relation between the number of pro-Soviet speeches in Cuba and the cut in the rations, but for many Cubans who had not forgotten their leaders' complaints about the quality of "revisionist" merchandise, the concomitance of friendship with the U.S.S.R. and restrictions at home did not seem fortuitous.

But this time, unlike 1961–62, the Castroist leaders did not

20. East European press reports on Cuba invariably involved a number of falsifications. Thus *Trybuna Ludu* (December 23, 1969) ingeniously turned René Dumont's article in *Le Monde* (December 9, 1969) entitled "Cubans Find Time Hanging on Their Hands," into a paean of praise to the policies of Fidel Castro.

21. In 1969 bread rationing was introduced (50g per person per day), and several other rations were cut. To make things worse, the authorities had decided to hasten Fidel's plans for *El Cordón de la Habana* by forcing all peasants in the suburbs, and even people with kitchen gardens, to plant coffee, with the result that the stock of staple foods in the capital dropped to almost catastrophic proportions. René Dumont mentions this in his article, referred to above.

promise miracles as a result of the new friendship. Leaving little room for illusion, they mobilized the Cubans for the battle they themselves would have to wage against underdevelopment and poverty. And because this battle was intensified during 1969–70, on the approach of the ten-million-ton *zafra,* it seemed only natural that Fidel and his men should have spoken more and more about production and less and less about the simultaneous construction of socialism and Communism. All the traditional holidays (including even Christmas and New Year) were canceled, in an effort to help the workers to keep "their" promise to reach the great sugar target. *Granma* was now full of technical talk about production techniques and allied topics, repeating that Fidel was particularly concerned about reliability, discipline, and clockwork organization at work, and that he expected everyone to join in the pitiless struggle against sabotage, unpunctuality, and absenteeism.[22] In the immediate present, good *macheteros* were obviously more useful than *hombres nuevos.*

Indeed, the old "heretical" ideas were not merely put on ice; they were discreetly, but systematically, replaced by quite a different doctrine, namely that the building of socialism calls for a high investment rate coupled to low consumption, and for maximum technical and scientific knowledge; in short for economic growth in the quickest possible time. This line bore a suspicious resemblance to the doctrine of the Soviet Union at the time of forced industrialization and collectivization, and less and less to that which Che, followed by Fidel and Dorticós, had held up as the only way to spare Cuba the distortions to which a "certain type of socialism" was prone. Barely perceptible at first, the new doctrine became more and more obvious until, at

---

22. The struggle against absenteeism proved especially arduous in Cuba, where food was scarcer than money, so that the traditional stick no longer worked. The minister of labor, Jorge Risquet, cited this fact (see *Granma,* French weekly summary, August 17, 1969) as a justification for introducing "labor cards" (as from September 1969) on which all breaches of discipline would be noted with a view to possible prosecutions.

the end of 1969, it culminated in the official declaration that the Soviet model of the '30s was perfect for Cuba and that it was being applied at full speed.

Thus, addressing the graduation class of the school of political science and the faculty of sociology at the University of Havana on September 24, 1969, Armando Hart said: "We think that a serious study of the experience of the first proletarian state in history, the Soviet Union, is quite indispensable. We go even further than that, and assert that this experience is a decisive element in teaching us what we ourselves have to do. . . . The historical analysis and scrupulous study of developments in the U.S.S.R. will show us which are the cultural, technical, and organizational factors that have enabled the U.S.S.R. to make so prodigious a leap in production. . . . The Soviet success is explained first and foremost by the extraordinary conditions resulting from the socialization of the means of production, and especially from their collectivization in the late '20s and the early '30s. . . . The fact that a major proportion of the country's resources was invested in industry, and that the basic resources of the nation were used for socialist development and investment rather than for home consumption has been another, equally decisive, factor in the forward leap of Soviet production, so that if we study the Soviet path with a view to the better planning of our own, we are bound to conclude that the factors which presided over the unprecedented rise in production in the U.S.S.R. are the very same factors which our revolution stresses today.

"The raising of our cultural and technological level," Hart continued, "is an essential aspect of improved production and of a more efficient economy, and hence is one of our most important tasks. . . . Bourgeois propaganda is full of dogmatic, simplistic, and certainly false claims about cultural developments in the Soviet Union. . . . Apart from specific errors that might have been committed—and what revolutionary process is totally exempt from these?—there is no doubt that in a mere fifty years the U.S.S.R. has passed on from underdevelopment and

518

illiteracy to the peaks of science and technology, so that she
has become the undisputed technical and scientific leader of the
world."[23]

This frank statement—and the Cuban leaders were nothing if
not frank—would have gravely upset Moscow and its allies only
a few years earlier. For though the Russians themselves kept
stressing that they had become "the undisputed technical and
scientific leaders of the world" and even promised miraculous
advances in the future, they also wished to play down that whole
troubled period of the '30s which had helped them to reach
their high level of production and culture. Khrushchev's revelations, or rather semi-revelations, on that subject had left no one
in doubt as to the price the U.S.S.R. had been forced to pay for
these advances. The '30s in Russia—the Stalinist phase—were
not only marked by a rise in industrial production (and by a
grave recession in agricultural production), but also by coercion,
terror, and massive deportations, all of which have left deep
scars on the minds of Soviet man. Stalin's successors had no
desire to explain how it was possible for such crimes to be
committed in the name of socialism; so, after blaming the worst
excesses on Stalin's character defects, they invited their compatriots and their comrades abroad to look to the future and
to speak as little as possible of the past. Even the few Russians
still reluctant to agree to this obliteration of so fundamental a
chapter in Soviet history, indeed in the history of world Communism, were unwilling to argue that the Stalinist method of
"primitive socialist accumulation" had been a happy one; they
contented themselves with claiming that Stalinism had been historically unavoidable, a necessary evil in the dramatic and exceptional circumstances in which the U.S.S.R. found herself at
the time.

The Chinese even pretended that despite all her "errors,"
Stalin's Russia had evinced a far keener internationalist sense

23. See *Granma*, French weekly summary, October 5, 1969. Armando Hart's
speech has also been published in pamphlet form by Ediciones Cor, Havana,
1969.

519

than the "de-Stalinizers."[24] The Russians never argued with them on this point, simply because they did not want to rake over the ugly past. In private, however, they referred to all their left-wing critics as "Stalinists," particularly the Cubans whose stand between 1965 and 1968 they found most obnoxious. But in 1969, Castroist eulogies to the Stalinist model had suddenly ceased to bother them, and this for reasons we shall be examining below.

In any case, Soviet-Cuban ties grew ever stronger after Armando Hart's speech, and symbolic gestures of international solidarity followed one another in quick succession throughout the autumn of 1969. On November 6, Soviet diplomats and technicians, led by Ambassador Soldatov, celebrated the fifty-second anniversary of the October Revolution, by going into the fields and cutting sugar cane side by side with the Cuban leaders.[25] A week later, on November 12, when the Soviet minister of defense, Marshal Grechko, arrived in Cuba at the invitation of Raúl Castro, he, too, repaired to a cane field to do his little bit for the ten-million-ton *zafra,* this time by Fidel's side. In greeting him, Fidel declared: "All of us know, Comrade Grechko, that when you were in command of the Caucasian Army during the Second World War, you paid frequent visits to the trenches. That is why we should like you to look upon your stay in Cuba as a visit to a revolutionary trench, one in which, tools in hand, we are at this very moment fighting a decisive battle against the economic blockade."[26] In fact, even though the Americans had not lifted the blockade of the is-

24. The Chinese defense of Stalin was a rather unfortunate tactical move against Khrushchev and his team. In recent times, Stalin's portraits have grown rarer in Peking, and it does not look as if the Maoists are especially enamored of his charms, particularly now that attacks on the dictator have ceased in Russia. However, the negative effects of the Chinese attitude are still felt in France and in many other Western countries, where pro-Maoist movements continue to defend the authoritarian heritage of Stalinism, thus demonstrating their failure to appreciate how incompatible Stalinism is with the doctrine and policy of Mao Tse-tung.

25. See *Granma,* French weekly summary, November 9, 1969.

26. See *Granma,* French weekly summary, November 23, 1969.

land, Marshal Grechko had only come to Cuba because the
United States had grown less touchy about the island and was
not preparing a new assault on this "revolutionary trench."
Soviet naval squadrons and ministers of defense had previously
avoided Cuba, for fear of offending the United States. In 1969,
however, there was every chance that their voyage would not
scandalize Washington or rock the boat of Soviet-American coexistence.

The new Nixon administration hardly bothered to hide its
delight that the exuberant Cubans should have rallied to "wise
old Russia." It noticed with satisfaction the absence of references
to the Latin American guerrilla movement from Fidel's speeches,
in January 1969, on the occasion of the tenth anniversary of the
Cuban Revolution, and concluded that the door must be left
open for a possible resumption of diplomatic relations.[27] Some
Americans called for even bolder measures by the administration. The most important study of the whole subject appeared
in *The New York Times Magazine.* It was written by a former
official of the State Department, John Plank,[28] and declared
quite bluntly that the United States had an interest in resuming
contacts with Havana for the following three reasons: 1) to
eliminate a cause of tension and possible misunderstandings with
the U.S.S.R.; 2) to serve the general interest of the hemisphere
to which Cuba belongs geographically, historically, and cultur-

27. Replying to a question by Senator Aiken during a meeting of the
Senate subcommittee which had met to confirm his appointment as Under-
Secretary of State for Latin American Affairs, Charles A. Meyer said
that he personally was in favor of a resumption of the dialogue with
Havana. He said that, if after ten years of silence, the Cubans had some
interesting things to say, the United States would do well to listen. This
statement caused quite a stir, since in the past the U.S. Government had
posed several preliminary conditions to any such dialogue. One of these
conditions was a break with the U.S.S.R., a subject in which the Nixon
administration had clearly lost interest. Rumor even had it that American-
Cuban negotiations had already been started in some part of Mexico or in
Europe. See particularly the article by Herbert G. Lawson and Sidney T.
Wise in the *Wall Street Journal,* February 13, 1969, and the lead article in the
Miami Herald, March 27, 1969.
28. See *The New York Times Magazine,* March 30, 1969.

ally; 3) to initiate a system of economic integration and planning in the Caribbean for which such small countries as Barbados had long been clamoring. The writer accordingly advised the return to Cuba of the Guantánamo base—which would have lost any strategic importance—and suggested that the Soviet Union be asked to use its good offices in effecting a reconciliation. He added that he was convinced the U.S.S.R. would gladly accept the role of broker, and that Washington should not find it too difficult to grant what guarantees Russia might demand for the safety of the "Communist-Creole" regime in Havana.

This article, followed by many others of the same type, did not produce the slightest outburst of indignation in the United States; public opinion had by then become resigned to the continued presence of Fidel Castro. Moreover, the Cuban problem had long since ceased to be a source of discord between Moscow and Washington, so that the Soviet Union had no cause to fear that siding with Castro would draw her into unwanted battles.

At about this time, an unforeseen event in Latin America contributed further to smoothing out differences between Moscow and Havana. On October 2, 1968, Peru was the scene of a military *golpe,* in the traditional style, but one that placed in power a most atypical South American regime. To begin with the new team ordered the nationalization of U.S. oil companies, thus flattering the anti-American sentiments of the people. Then, in June 1969, they proceeded to agrarian reforms and to the abolition of many ancient taboos and privileges. On July 10, 1969, Fidel gave the new regime his public blessing: "It matters little," he declared, "that those who have started this revolution are a group of army leaders, many of them trained in the United States. If this revolution brings about a structural change, if it continues as an anti-imperialist revolution, if it defends the interests of the people of Peru, then it shall have our unqualified support."[29]

29. See *Granma,* French weekly summary, July 20, 1969.

The reckoning

This declaration, followed by many others in the same vein, was greeted with something approaching euphoria in Moscow, which, according to Adriano Guerra, the local *Unità* correspondent, saw it as a first step toward a general reconciliation between the Communist Party of Cuba and those of other Latin American countries.[30] For Moscow realized that by recognizing the revolutionary character of the Peruvian regime, Fidel Castro had implicitly gone back on his extremist stance at the time of the OLAS meeting. He now tacitly admitted that revolutions in Latin America did not depend on the prior destruction of the old military machine, and that this very machine could play a revolutionary role under certain conditions. Now, Latin American Communist parties had long ago spoken of this possibility; it was for this reason, and not because they were afraid of starting a guerrilla war, that they had apparently advocated a peaceful solution to the Latin American crisis. The same analysis had led the Soviet Union to render economic aid to Latin American governments irrespective of their political color or their attitude to Cuba.[31]

If Havana did not subscribe to these interpretations, it did not refute them either. And though the general tone of the Cuban press remained anti-Yankee and pro-*guerrillero*, the space it accorded to international events grew smaller and smaller.[32] This did not mean that Cuba's official line had changed but rather that, thrown back upon itself, the island was forced to pay more and more attention to home affairs. However, Fidel went to Rancho Boyeros airport on September 30, 1969, to welcome the fifteen revolutionaries that the Brazilian government had released in exchange for the kidnapped United States

30. See *Unità,* July 27, 1969.
31. One of many articles in this vein published in the European Communist press, was signed by R. Sandri, a member of the Central Committee of the Italian Communist Party, in *Rinascità,* October 5, 1969.
32. The only foreign country to retain the full attention of the Cuban press was Vietnam; solidarity with the NLF had never slackened on the island. On the death of Ho Chi Minh Cuba went into seven days' official mourning—longer even than after Che Guevara's assassination.

Ambassador. On that occasion he extolled the *guerrilleros'* action, and, though he did speak kindly of the Peruvian junta, made no reference to the possibility of "peaceful revolution" in Latin America.[33] Moreover, Che's writings continued to pour from the Cuban press and no attempt was made to cut out any passages that might have disturbed the new Cuban-Russian dream. In other words, the Cuban had not copied the Soviet method of rewriting history and expunging from the records any discordant voices. Unfortunately, this liberal attitude did not go hand in hand with any kind of public discussions, to the utter confusion not only of the man in the street, but also of the devout Party member, who could not help noticing a contradiction between Che's claim that the U.S.S.R. was copying the imperialists in her foreign trading practices and in her dealings with underdeveloped countries, and Fidel's recent hymns of praise. They must also have wondered whether Fidel's support for the Peruvian "revolution" did not fly in the face of the OLAS resolutions, and whether it was not time for Fidel to make it clear precisely how his new alliance with Russia was influencing his views on the Latin American revolution.

The development of Cuban-Soviet relations since the August 23 speech raised many other questions as well. It is a well-known fact that the Soviet Union refuses to recognize all forms of Communism other than its own; that it will not tolerate the least attempt by fraternal countries to give socialism a new face. How, under these conditions, could it possibly become reconciled to Fidel, immediately after he had uttered his great "basic truths," and after his declaration that he was as determined as ever to build a society based on appeals to the socialist consciousness of the masses and not—as the Russians advocated—on material incentives? How could there be any real agreement between Havana and Moscow when neither was apparently prepared to make concessions on so fundamental a point? The only possible explanation was that the question of incentives had suddenly lost its former importance, to the extent

33. See *Granma*, French weekly summary, October 5, 1969.

The reckoning

that, despite continued differences on this point, the Russians and the Cubans suddenly found that they were trying to build the same type of society—marked by the classical Soviet model. What then was the real meaning of Fidel Castro's Czechoslovak speech?

His appeal of August 23, 1968, rested on three pillars: 1) the Communist Party must exercise "the prerogatives of the dictatorship of the proletariat" until socialism and Communism were achieved; 2) the "socialist community" embodies the hopes of all struggling people and of the world revolutionary movement, and must be defended at all costs against external or internal enemies; 3) workers in socialist societies must be willing to make sacrifices to strengthen not only their own countries but also the socialist community at large.

After Armando Hart's speech, the striking similarity between this doctrine and that which held sway in the U.S.S.R. during the '30s became much more obvious than it had been at the time of Fidel's own address on August 23, 1968. When Fidel spoke, no one was prepared to believe that he was in fact pleading for the concentration of power in the hands of a supercentralized and monolithic bureaucracy, in the name of the dictatorship of the proletariat. After all, Fidel's well-known anti-Stalinism was based on familiarity with the most authentic Marxist analysts, Isaac Deutscher among them; it was neither superficial nor accidental. Fidel knew as well as anyone the real nature of the pseudodictatorship of the proletariat, personified by Stalin; he was aware of its failings. Moreover, he had told me several times that the Cuban Revolution was not a proletarian revolution. And yet, a careful perusal of his text proved beyond a shadow of a doubt that he had adopted the Soviet power thesis, although he still explained it so clumsily, mixing up essential notions and losing his way in a terminological maze, that the whole thing looked like a quick improvisation, in a moment of great confusion due to the Czechoslovak crisis.[34]

34. Thus Fidel Castro declared that the dictatorship of the proletariat was an essential function of the Communist Party. Now he must have known

Fidel's second "pillar" was even shakier. For several years he had been denouncing the Soviet policy of compromising with the enemy to the detriment of the world revolutionary movement. Che had expressed Fidel's own views when he showed that Vietnam was alone in its heroic struggle; he had gone to fight in Latin America without ever dreaming of asking the U.S.S.R. or its Warsaw Pact partners if they welcomed "two, three, many Vietnams." Yet less than a year after Che's death, Fidel was claiming that the Soviet Union and her four Warsaw Pact allies formed "a socialist community" embodying the hopes of the struggling masses. Why they and not China which, as Fidel himself had admitted in 1967, was far more revolutionary? Why they and not Cuba, which had simply been presented with the *fait accompli* of the Czechoslovak invasion but had never been consulted about it?

Fidel's use of the term "socialist community" was especially misguided as it led him to conclusions opposed to both the theory and the traditions of the international revolutionary movement. For had there been a true socialist community, it would not have had to impose its views on Czechoslovakia by force. By its very nature socialism is not for export, and certainly not for export under the rule of the bayonet. Real socialism can only be built by workers who have thrown off their shackles and are conscious of their collective purpose. There is no such thing as "a higher Communist right" to ignore this essential principle.[35] By sending its tanks into Prague, the

---

from his Marxist readings at the University of Havana that the dictatorship of the proletariat, as its name indicates, is a function of the proletariat, and not vice versa. In principle, the dictatorship of the proletariat is vested in the Soviets, i.e., in the entire working class. Though this principle has hardly been respected in practice, the U.S.S.R. has always preserved a formal distinction between the Soviets and the Communist Party. Moreover, even Stalinist rhetoric was invariably full of the leading role of the working class.

35. Thus when Stalin exported his type of revolution to Eastern Europe on the pretext of helping his struggling comrades, even he took good care to dress the People's Democracies up as genuine revolutionary states. However, the present situation in these countries demonstrates that exported socialism is not authentic, since twenty years after the birth of the Czechoslovak revolution it apparently has to be kept alive with tanks.

The reckoning

"socialist community" merely demonstrated—if there was still any need—that it was no community at all, and that it held all the traditional ideals of the labor movement in contempt.[36] Moreover, even taking the most cynical geopolitical view, one cannot help concluding that, far from strengthening its position, the occupation of Czechoslovakia has weakened the Soviet Union militarily—no less than politically and morally.[37]

Finally, in the third part of his plea, Fidel implied that if the revolutionary spirit has grown lax in Eastern Europe since the end of the Cold War, it is because the leadership has paid more attention to peace campaigns and material prosperity than to the fight against imperialism. He accordingly advised them, in their own interests and for the common good, to return to the old policy. He declared that "the masses will work much more enthusiastically and offer much greater sacrifices once they appreciate that the hard realities are such that only by giving priority to capital investments can the 'socialist community' hope to defend its achievements." Moreover, it is only by working for the country's good that they can apparently acquire the political consciousness needed to realize their Communist ideals.

36. The Soviet leaders, though unconcerned about a socialist consensus, were nevertheless far too intelligent to think they could find a theoretical justification for their act of aggression. They realized that only the Czechoslovak Communist Party could vindicate them by declaring after the event that it had asked for fraternal aid from the Warsaw Pact countries. It was in order to procure this retrospective alibi that the Russians put pressure on the Czechs to revoke all Party resolutions they had voted freely before and at the start of the invasion. After a year of unremitting endeavor —and thanks also to the continued presence of their tanks—the Russians seem at last to have attained their ends. There is little need to add that theirs was a Pyrrhic victory which fooled no one.

37. In several parts of the Third World the thesis gained ground that, even if the Russians had acted too harshly, they were entitled to defend the military and economic strength of their camp. This argument does not stand up to serious examination, simply because the strength of any country, and quite especially of a country that calls itself socialist, is measured by the determination of its inhabitants to defend it themselves and to work for its future. Now the invasion of Czechoslovakia has not only killed that determination inside Czechoslovakia but has completely demoralized the masses in the other socialist countries; they have come to realize that Russia will not tolerate the slightest move toward democratization, and that their future is bleak indeed.

But here, too, the historical experience of the Soviet Union disproves Fidel's claims. The '30s and the Cold War, rather than boosting the world revolutionary movement, turned it into a pawn in the hands of the Soviet leaders. Russia and the anti-imperialist movement suffered much more from this policy than their capitalist class enemy. Moreover in the U.S.S.R. itself, the external danger did nothing to stimulate the enthusiasm and class consciousness of the masses; why else was that period marked by a policy of conscription and deliberate terror? Even the socialist consciousness of the party vanguard turned out to be a somewhat tenuous affair. We must judge the tree by its fruits: if heroic work did indeed produce true Communists, the Soviet Union, having lived for decades under a regime befitting a "besieged fortress," would have been full of incorruptible *hombres nuevos*, instead of teeming with the "soft pseudorevolutionaries" of whom Fidel had complained not so long before.

But in his speech of August 23, 1968, he chose to ignore all these historical and theoretical facts, simply because he thought them irrelevant to the Cuban predicament. In 1968, a whole chain of circumstances, partly independent of his will, had led him to a dramatic decision: to militarize the whole island and to give absolute priority to the economic battle. Convinced of the correctness of his analysis, he tried to justify it, even to exaggerate it, in order to drive home to his people the absolute need for a "dictatorship of the proletariat exercised by the Communist Party."[38] It was for the same reason that he presented Cuba as a revolutionary trench in the great front held by the "socialist community," and that he tried to whip up the enthusiasm of the workers by telling them that every cane they cut was a blow struck in the common fight against imperialism. Throughout 1969, he continued to compare Cuban exertions

38. It is an odd commentary on the times that Fidel saw fit to vest in the Communist Party of Cuba, which had never even held an inaugural congress, the "function of exercising the dictatorship of the proletariat."

The reckoning

on the productive front with the most remarkable exploits of revolutionaries in other parts of the world.[39]

In any case, Fidel's new ideological platform was most reassuring for the Soviet Union. He was clearly defending a system of political power and economic priorities that contained automatic safeguards against the revival of heresies in Cuba. Moreover Castro's resurrection of the Stalinist doctrine helped to shine a tarnished image that several Russian leaders wished to restore to a place of honor in the U.S.S.R. and its satellites.

At the Twentieth and again at the Twenty-Second Congress, the Soviet leaders had suggested that it was best not to analyze the factors that had led to the "personality cult"; now they were once again mouthing the stale rhetoric of the past, glorifying what they had but recently chosen to ignore as passing all Marxist understanding. At first, their antics seemed no less surprising than Fidel Castro's speech of August 23, 1968. People asked themselves in dazed amazement precisely whom the Russians were trying to fool this time. After all, Soviet society was no longer what it had been during Stalin's reign of "steel and fire"; so there was no reason why Russia should once again adopt this blighted mystique. The affluence of the West had by then become the declared objective of Soviet citizens in general and of the Soviet elite in particular—an elite that enjoyed ever greater privileges and had become more and more imbued with "American" values. Edifying novels by Sholokhov and Fadeev about the "young guard" had become as alien to young Russians as they had once been to foreign readers: the new specter was no longer imperialism, but Red China. In these circumstances, the old Stalinist line about the great proletarian mission of Soviet workers could no longer serve even

39. A placard pasted on walls throughout Cuba proclaimed in bold letters: "*Como en Vietnam. Tenacidad, organización, disciplina, heroismo diario en trabajo. Diez años de lucha antiyanqui del pueblo vietnamito, diez milliones de toneladas de azúcar.*" (As in Vietnam. Tenacity, organization, discipline, heroism at work. Ten years of anti-Yankee struggle of the Vietnamese people, ten million tons of sugar.)

529

for the "true believers." Yet the leaders of the U.S.S.R., who did their utmost to hasten the depoliticization and bureaucratization of the masses, were themselves so morally bankrupt that the only justification they could hit upon for their system was the threadbare slogans of the Stalinist period.

The more glaring the contradictions, the greater the economic damage and the greater the need of the Soviet leaders to cling to an ideology long since surpassed by events and more incapable than ever of explaining real facts. In short, Stalin's successors became sorcerer's apprentices, creating a situation in which nationalism, race prejudice, and cynicism were again in evidence. To stem these disruptive forces, which grew inside the U.S.S.R. as well as in the rest of the Eastern bloc, the Soviet leaders forbade all discussions in the name of the Stalinist doctrine and tradition. It was this desperate defense of the status quo which finally drove them to military intervention in Czechoslovakia.[40] Any attempt to shake off the tutelage of the police

40. Throughout her own Stalinist period, Czechoslovakia had been the most conformist country in the entire bloc; not even the revelations at the Twentieth Congress of the Communist Party of the U.S.S.R. had been able to shake her out of her complacency. During the Polish and Hungarian uprisings in 1956, Prague had stood coldly aloof. Inflexible Stalinists therefore said of Czechoslovakia what Heinrich Heine once said of Holland: "When the world comes to an end, I shall go to Amsterdam, because down there, everything happens fifty years later." And it was because they set their faces so resolutely against the slightest change, that the leading Czechoslovak leaders reached a complete impasse and finally split up. This disagreement at the summit gradually enabled "unauthorized" groups to erupt onto the political scene; Czech intellectuals, workers, and students could at last declare openly that they had had enough, and set out to build "socialism with a human face," that is plain socialism, because there can be no real socialism with a bestial or semihuman face. But though their own experience had driven these men to reject the rhetoric of the old regime, it had not qualified them to prepare an alternative program. Paradoxically, Prague in 1968 suffered from the same ideological void—yet also enjoyed the same optimistic atmosphere—that C. Wright Mills encountered in Havana in 1960. It was against this background that a genuine rebirth of the Left eventually ensued, particularly among the working class. Given time, developments in Czechoslovakia would undoubtedly have encouraged a similar re-awakening throughout Eastern Europe, but, of course, supporters of the old order in Russia and in the rest of the Soviet bloc feared

and the Party did not seem possible, even, or perhaps particularly, in a country where the victory of genuine socialism seemed much more certain than that of the counterrevolution. They acted precipitately and with impunity, as they were certain of American complicity. But to justify their actions, they had to pretend that they had marched into Prague in the name of "proletarian internationalism" and not in order to maintain the division of the world between two superpowers. It was no surprise that after the invasion of Czechoslovakia, Stalinist rhetoric flowed even more glibly from the Kremlin, now supporting the limping doctrine of the "limited sovereignty" of socialist countries, in the name of the anti-imperialist struggle. This was their version of the "socialist community" so dear to Fidel Castro. Russians, like their adversaries—or rather like their competitors—in the West, knew perfectly well that the only battle this community would be waging was on the home front: in defense of the hegemony of the U.S.S.R. and of its leading group.

No longer able to invoke the dictatorship of the proletariat (the Twenty-Second Congress had "abolished" it in the Soviet Union in 1961), they produced a most ingenious alternative: on the occasion of the Lenin Centenary they introduced the concept that all socialist societies must be governed in accordance with the principle of democratic centralism; i.e., following the line adopted by Communist parties of the Stalinist type.[41] And,

---

nothing more than such a revival, which would certainly have questioned their right to power. It was this fear, and not the threat of a counter-revolution, which caused the Soviet Union and her allies to prefer military arguments to political persuasion in Czechoslovakia.

41. In 1970, the U.S.S.R. and all Communist parties celebrated the one hundredth anniversary of Lenin's birth. On December 23, 1969, *Pravda* published a long document, entitled: "Thesis of the Central Committee of the Communist Party of the U.S.S.R. on the One Hundredth Anniversary of the Birth of Vladimir Ilyich Lenin." The historical section of these theses seems to have come straight out of the Stalinist *Short History of the All-Union Communist Party* (*B*). But the fourth and final chapter, devoted to the "path to Communism," also contains some innovations that Stalin had obviously overlooked, for example, the application of the principle of

S

Guerrillas in Power

by a curious coincidence, at the very moment that Armando Hart was singing the praises of forced collectivization in Havana, Leonid Brezhnev, addressing a congress of kolkhoz delegates in Moscow, delivered an almost identical diatribe, although he admitted that a few minor errors had been committed during past attempts to implement this policy.[42]

Thus, by trial and error, the Cubans and Russians discovered in 1968 that they were defending one and the same political system, albeit in different parts of the world and under quite different conditions. As a result they drew close both ideologically and politically, and were able to chant with one voice the slogans from the past. In other respects, their second honeymoon in no way resembled the first. In 1961, they had come together somewhat by chance, in an atmosphere of great optimism, the Castroists believing that they had not only found a powerful ally, but also the socialist idea that ally was thought to embody. Cubans were ignorant of most of the theoretical foundations of socialism, of the way in which it had been misapplied by their new friends, and of the resulting crises. Later, when experience opened their eyes, they made great efforts to emerge from the

---

democratic centralism to all aspects of social life. It should be noted that when Russians speak of democratic centralism, they leave no one in any doubt as to their peculiar usage of that term: it means that orders from the top must be blindly obeyed at the bottom.

42. The rehabilitation of Stalin's policy of forced collectivization is the key to all recent attempts to paste together the torn shreds of the Stalinist ideology. Yet, immediately after Stalin's death and before the Twentieth Congress, the new Kremlin leaders were forced to admit that Russia's level of agricultural production was catastrophically low, and to promise the peasants a radical change. It was at this point that Khrushchev came out with his devastating revelations on the effects of Stalin's collectivization policy and denounced its incredible brutality and inefficiency. He even read the letters which Sholokhov had sent to Stalin in an attempt to draw the dictator's attention to the fact that his policy was not only unjust to the peasants but that it was seriously lowering the level of agricultural production. Abroad, such Communist leaders as Gomulka went even further and blamed collectivization for "certain deformations" of the Soviet system. In rehabilitating this entire policy, Brezhnev has clearly gone back on the line adopted at the Twentieth and Twenty-Second Congresses of the Communist Party of the U.S.S.R., and is once again glorifying Stalin's crimes (even though he still prefers not to mention the dictator by name).

532

ideological and practical snares of Soviet "socialism," while maintaining what had by then become indispensable economic relations with the U.S.S.R. In other words, their return to the fold in 1968–69 was not based on the same old naïve illusions but was the unavoidable consequence of their failure—perhaps temporary—to build a Cuban road to socialism. It was also a sad event, for Cubans had by then come to appreciate that their powerful European allies would do little to lighten their burden, and less for the Latin American *guerrilleros*. Russia in the '30s may not have been more revolutionary, but at least Stalin's professions of faith had still sounded credible enough to inspire a vast international following. In 1968, no one, not even Fidel's enemies, could seriously believe in the revolutionary intentions of Brezhnev's "socialist community"; and those who pretended to do so, like Fidel Castro, could only have been paying lip service under duress, and were certainly not taken in by their own rhetoric.

"The simplest thing, but so difficult to achieve"[43]

In 1970, all Cuba will witness a fiesta unlike any the island has ever seen. On about July 15, in Oriente province, the last arroba of cane will have been processed and the ten billionth kilogram of sugar produced. And just as soon as this stupendous feat is announced, the entire nation will explode with joy.[44] On the

43. Bertolt Brecht, writing about Communism ("*Kommunismus . . . ist das Einfache dass schwer zu machen ist*"). See Bertolt Brecht, *Gedichte,* Suhrkamp Verlag, Vol. 3, p. 67.

44. These lines were obviously written a few months before Fidel Castro made a speech on May 19th announcing that the target of ten million tons would not be reached. The carnival in Havana took place in spite of this relative failure because, as Castro himself declared, the blame could not be put on the Cuban people and men, who had worked for months, separated from their families, and deserved a big celebration. On July 26th, in the middle of this carnival, the leader of the Cuban revolution made an astonishing speech, full of self criticism, in which he described his country's economic situation in black colors indeed. He admitted that other sectors of the economy had paid a heavy price for the "sugar obsession" and that, as a result, industrial and agricultural output was actually lower than in 1968–69. The new figures show that I was too optimistic about the sugar

Guerrillas in Power

Trocha in Santiago, on the Rampa in Havana, people will dance day and night to the rhythm of Afro-Cuban bands, and in the intoxication of this supercarnival they are sure to forget all cares, past and present. This explosion is, so to speak, part of the whole plan; it is meant to set a glorious and memorable seal on a nation's devotion to the ten-million-ton *zafra*. But though planned well in advance, it will be spontaneous and sincere. All Cubans will be present, from Fidel who is devoting four hours each morning to cane-cutting (gone are the nocturnal discussions!) to the least *machetero* in uniform and dungarees. Even citizens who have not played a direct part in this great "machete charge" are counting the hours until the great day, because all Cubans have had to make sacrifices for the *zafra,* and all of them feel that their contributions merit some recompense, that something on the island must change after July 1970.

This feeling is not based on complex computations of the international buying power this bumper harvest will represent. For many months, Cubans have said little about this aspect of the *zafra,* have apparently forgotten its great economic benefits. Fidel himself has implied that its real importance is something quite different. For Cuba's balance of trade, half a million tons of sugar more or less is not a matter of life and death; the real reason why it is so essential to reach the fixed objective is that Fidel's personal honor and the integrity of his movement are at stake.[45]

The Cuban Revolution must demonstrate that it can keep its

---

prospects, but my basic analysis of the choices facing Cuba remains unaffected.

45. This is how Fidel himself put it in a speech in Santa Clara on October 18, 1969: "The ten-million-ton *zafra* represents far more than tons of sugar, far more than an economic victory; it is a test, a moral commitment for this country. And precisely because it is a test and a moral commitment we cannot fall short by even a single gram of these ten millions. . . . If, for example, we were to stop at 9,999,999 tons, we would undoubtedly have made a great, a most meritorious, effort, but we would have to tell ourselves that it was nevertheless a moral defeat. . . . Ten millions less a single pound—we declare it before all the world—will be a defeat, not a victory." See *Granma,* French weekly summary, October 26, 1969.

word, that it is capable of reaching the goals it has set itself. Posters everywhere proclaimed: *Palabra de Cubano: van: los diez milliones de toneladas van.* Which meant no more and no less than: "For once we shall do what we have decided." True, if there had not been quite so many unfulfilled plans in the past, Fidel would have had no need to create a great mystique round these ten million tons of sugar now. As it was, he felt in no position to face Cuba once again, explaining that yet another project had gone sour on him. And so he turned the 1970 *zafra* into a kind of national wager in which everyone's honor was involved, and used the most draconic measures to bring skeptics and slackers to heel. The *zafra* had, in any case, come to play so prominent a part in the life of the nation, that everyone was bound to be concerned. The victory on July 15 will therefore be a victory of an entire people. Through it, Fidel hopes to restore all the trust in his movement that has seeped away with the tide of unkept promises, and to build up enough fresh good will to see him through the next phase of his long march ahead.

What precisely is that phase? Cuba's economic plans for the years 1970–80 have not yet been published, but Fidel has revealed some of the highlights by hinting that, in the near future, Cuba will be self-sufficient in terms of rice and several other staple foods; that industrialization will be given a powerful boost (thanks to a spectacular rise in the world price of nickel) ; and that cane-cutting machines of the Henderson type will be built on the island. But, in fact, these economic objectives are not really Castro's chief problem.

To win his gigantic sugar wager, Fidel has had to pay so high a political price that one begins to wonder if he has not mortgaged the entire future of the Revolution. Industrial and military conscription; closer ties with the Soviet Union; the kind of "Communism" that prevailed in Russia during the '30s—all these are the direct consequences of his battle for the ten-million-ton *zafra*. The effects of decisions as dramatic as these will not disappear miraculously on the morrow of the great fiesta; the body politic has suffered too many bruises for that. Moreover, the ties binding Cuba to the Latin American revolutionary movement, essential for the island's whole future, have been gravely weakened by Fidel's return to the bosom of the U.S.S.R. It will be a very long time indeed before the harmony that prevailed during the OLAS period can be restored.[46] Fidel's about-turn of 1968 was bound to throw confusion into his ranks, especially those of the younger generation. And last but not least, his praises of the Stalinist model of socialism have greatly dimmed the radiance of the Cuban Revolution abroad, where the sad realities of Stalin's dictatorship and its sequels are only too well known.

True, Fidel has done nothing irreparable, but there are no signs that he intends to carry out any repairs. Possibly he is waiting for the end of the *zafra* before launching a new policy under a happier star, but this is mere speculation. In fact, no one can predict the outcome of the great sugar battle.

Nevertheless, there are two objective facts that Castro cannot afford to ignore for long. To begin with, the great majority of his nation is convinced that his pro-Soviet commitment and the

46. On January 15, 1970, *Le Monde* carried an AFP despatch from Caracas to the effect that Douglas Bravo, commander in chief of the Venezuelan *guerrilleros*, had published an attack on Fidel Castro and the present course of the Cuban Revolution. According to Bravo, the Castroists stopped aiding the Latin American revolution the moment they decided to concentrate on their own economic problems and to rally to the Soviet Union. It seems certain, moreover, that Carlos Rafael Rodríguez has had recent contacts with the Communist Party of Venezuela, which Fidel "excommunicated" three years earlier in his famous speech of March 13, 1967. Still, some members of an extreme left-wing party in Venezuela have taken exception to Douglas Bravo's act, no doubt because they objected to his carrying an internecine quarrel out into the open. But whether they express it in public or in private, there is little doubt that revolutionaries throughout Latin America share Bravo's misgivings. They were astonished at Havana's silence when their Mexican comrades were brutally murdered; they also could not see why Fidel's support for the Peruvian junta should have debarred him from speaking up on behalf of political prisoners in Lima, whose number include Hector Bejar, a man well known for his pro-Castroist sympathies, and the holder of the 1969 *Casa de las Américas* prize.

The reckoning

authoritarian policies on which he embarked in 1968–69 are no more than temporary expedients. Even if they are afraid to say so, these sentiments are common among them and constitute a crucial political signpost. Secondly, Cuba in 1970 is in no way comparable to Russia in the '30s—the island has no real need to jeopardize all its political and social objectives to steer an implacable course toward "primitive socialist accumulation." No amount of industrialization, no amount of accelerated growth can transform the island into an impregnable fortress. Cuba is not the U.S.S.R., and no one inside or outside the island can really believe that objective conditions force it to persist in a policy of military conscription and prolonged sacrifice.

True, Fidel has decided on an exceptionally high investment rate (to the detriment of consumption) and it is precisely in this sphere that he claims to have found it most useful to apply the Stalinist model.[47] But this decision bears on an immediate and limited objective: Fidel, unlike Stalin, cannot pretend that his policy is indispensable to the survival of world socialism. Between the mystique surrounding Stalin's slogan—"We have ten years in which to make up for a hundred years of backwardness. We must catch up or we will be crushed"—and the mystique Fidel has created around the *zafra—Palabra de Cubanos van—* there is a qualitative difference that is so obvious that we need not dwell upon it at length.

In short, Fidel would be taking unfortunate risks if, after July 1970, he made a fresh historical wager and tried to mobilize his tired country for yet another all-out productive drive. As he is far more prudent than his speeches suggest, and far more sensitive to the *vox populi* than his conduct during the last few months may indicate, he will probably prefer to use the trust a victorious *zafra* must surely earn him as a spring-

47. It should be noted in passing that the exceptionally high investment rate during the Stalinist period was something the planners had failed to include in their blueprint. It came in the wake of a whole series of political and economic blunders.

board for less perilous adventures. But what options are still open to him today, on the eve of Cuba's great national celebration?

Before we can answer that question, we must take another brief look at the strange zigzag course of the Cuban Revolution from the birth of the anti-Batista campaign in 1953 to the "second honeymoon" with the Soviet Union in 1968. What strikes one immediately is that Castro's methods and program have not, in fact, been in accordance with his declared aims, except during the first phase of the struggle. At that time, they sprang from a remarkably clear appreciation and profound analysis of the needs and potentialities of Cuban society under Batista. It was this close link with reality that enabled Fidel and his men to mobilize the masses and gain their enthusiastic support, to impress upon them the need for a new society, and to march forward in unison with them toward the achievement of genuine revolutionary goals. After victory, the objective and subjective factors prevented a renewal of this intimate bond between Castroists and the Cuban reality. Success invariably fills the victor with a sense of self-righteousness, particularly in a country such as Cuba where the absence of organizational skills among the rank and file was felt from the very start, and where the imperialist enemy forced the Revolution to adopt radical measures at a rate it would never have chosen otherwise. The new Castroist options were not yet understood by everyone. They seemed themselves subject to vacillation and incapable of galvanizing even that part of society that considered itself, or was inclined to consider itself, socialist.

Nothing could be more mistaken than ascribing these vacillations to an infantile disorder of Castroism: its petit-bourgeois origins. That the *guerrilleros* did not have a high level of political consciousness is an indisputable fact, but compared with the puerile pseudo-Marxist analyses produced by the Comintern and its offshoots, the empiricism of the *guerrilleros* was a breath of fresh air. The political fervor and open-mindedness of the Castroist team made up in good measure for

538

their theoretical and organizational shortcomings; they were all keenly aware of the political and moral problems on the horizon for socialism. The transition from the anti-Batistiano to the socialist phase could doubtless have been effected more painlessly and with fewer defections but when all is said and done the chances of the revolution remained remarkably unimpaired during this whole period of trial and error.

The first serious setback came in 1961, when Eastern Europe became the prototype of the socialist society the Castroists wanted to build in Cuba. From that moment, their program lost touch with reality; they came out with a completely illusory four-year plan which was to give Cuba a Swedish standard of living by 1965. Later, Fidel and his men attributed this costly error to their rather naïve faith in massive Soviet aid and in the capacity of the world socialist system to solve the specific problems of an underdeveloped country in the American zone of influence. There is, of course, some truth in this explanation; it ought to have made Castroists wonder how they could possibly have held such mistaken beliefs for so long. They allowed themselves to be carried away by dreams of a painless process of industrialization, of flourishing and diversified crops, simply because the idea of accelerated growth accorded with their general tendency to rush ahead. They had great difficulty in striking the right balance in a society as singular as theirs (both revolutionary and Americanized) and they had come up against the problems facing all who dare to brandish the Red flag "under the threatening mouth of the Mississippi." And so they persuaded themselves that quick industrialization was the cornerstone of Cuban socialism, and that everything else would follow in due course. There were many voices to warn them against the social upheavals their four-year plan was bound to create, but they refused to listen. All such advice, they claimed, was so much "anti-Communist prejudice." In any case, Cuba had no intention of following Stalin by sacrificing one or several generations on the altar of the plan. That is what Che told me in 1961, and I could even detect a sense of friendly rivalry in his remarks. He wanted Cuba to become a showcase of socialism, more attractive to Latin Americans than Russia. And he was persuaded that he held all the trumps, thanks to the riches of the island and the power of the "world socialist system."

Of course, the Castroists realized that they could not achieve all this without the help of friends, and so they deferred to their comrades in the PSP, those experts in Marxism who knew better than anyone how to mobilize the workers and track down counterrevolutionaries. This meant that the great industrialization project went hand in hand with a rise in sectarianism and the rapid disillusionment of the masses. A year later, in 1962, when shortages were severe and discontent rife, Fidel and his men at last realized that they had taken the wrong route, and called a sudden halt. Aníbal Escalante was denounced for his methods and promptly dispatched to Moscow, while the nation breathed a great sigh of relief. If it seemed less inclined now to believe in Fidel's economic promises, Cuba was nevertheless profoundly grateful to him for this second liberation. The missile crisis bound the Cubans still closer to their leader. His new policy seemed to be off to a good start— Fidel and his team did not feel cut off from the rank and file and were not haunted by the fears that paralyze the unpopular leaders of European Communist countries.

The relative impunity with which they survived their first political and economic disaster did not, however, cause them to search their souls in an attempt to prevent future mistakes of the same type; they simply replaced their reliance on Soviet aid with the faith that Cuba's rapid economic expansion called for a great leap in sugar production, their "heavy industry." For the rest they continued in their old ways as if nothing untoward had happened. In fact, all that had changed were the slogans. Instead of promising the workers prosperity in the near future, Fidel now declared that a massive increase in sugar production was so noble a task that only the ignorant or malicious could doubt its salutary effects. Clearly, the new Castroist program continued to be based on the old priorities—

The reckoning

accumulation first, solution of social problems next—and was no more realistic than the last. The Russian experience had shown that the shift of manpower from the countryside to the industrial centers is a painful process. The exodus in the opposite direction, from the towns to the cane fields, is no easier, even if it is only periodic and seasonal. Purely administrative rearrangements and a second agrarian reform could not alleviate Cuba's most pressing problems, simply because the new measures were geared exclusively to the needs of the productive machinery and not to the enhancement of the worker's role in that machinery or in society at large.

As was only to be expected, therefore, the results of the new policy proved disappointing: the wheels of the economic machine refused to turn. More than any of his comrades, Che realized that something was amiss with the system itself. In his polemics against the "reformists" in Eastern Europe, he rightly pointed out that a factory in a socialist society cannot be just an improved version of a capitalist factory. He had, in fact, put his finger on a fundamental problem: he had come to suspect that building the material foundations of socialism might not be the chief priority, that socialism could never be built without the prior transformation of the political consciousness of the workers. He was not given time to develop these ideas more fully or to define what social mechanisms are generators of a truly socialist spirit.

His general views nevertheless had such a marked effect that Fidel himself incorporated them into his "heresy," soon after 1965. Moreover, Cubans had come to see—however vaguely—that it was recourse to moral incentives which had enabled China to transform the social attitudes of her entire working population, thus paving the way for a society, much fairer, more dynamic, and much more revolutionary than the Russian. It was against this background that Fidel coined the Guevarist, if not frankly Chinese, slogan: "We must create wealth through a new consciousness, and not a new consciousness through wealth." But, unlike the Chinese, Fidel seems to have tried to produce that consciousness mainly by speeches and appeals to the "vanguard."

This was probably because he felt entitled to ignore the "petty trifles" of daily life, because he had staked everything on a fabulous increase in agricultural production. His program, in fact, grew more ambitious as his evaluation of the agricultural potential of the island became more optimistic. He was determined to make Cuba even more egalitarian than China, through a distributive system in which money would have no importance: its sole basis would be the voluntary and full cooperation of the workers. And once he was set on so remarkable a course, it was not surprising that he should have turned a blind eye to the persistence of poverty and to the organization of labor on a hierarchic and authoritarian scale that made a mockery of the very collectivist values Cubans were being asked to uphold. Between the doctrine, the official promises, and the harsh realities, an abyss had opened up which was glaringly obvious.

This bitter pill was only slightly sweetened by Cuba's solidarity with the Latin American revolutionaries and by hopes in Che's success. But feelings of solidarity are not long-term substitutes for food shortages or for dissatisfaction with a hierarchic and arbitrary political machine. The result was that everything in Cuba seemed to have a purely temporary character, pending the success of the Latin American enterprise.

That is precisely why Fidel found it possible to accommodate himself for a time to the *"problemas y contradicciones"* of Cuban life. But after Che's death, when what was supposed to be temporary was beginning to look permanent, Fidel felt impelled to put some order into his house, and to give a more coherent framework to a policy which, until then, had consisted of coining slogans of the Chinese type while staking everything on developments of the Russian type. It was then that he threw the honor of the Cuban Revolution behind the ten-million-ton *zafra,* that he abandoned all his old Guevarist longings and extolled the absolute virtues of work and discipline.

According to the logic of the Russian precedent, he ought

542

The reckoning

to have gone on to organize a great national competition (on the Stakhanovite model) geared to material incentives, especially since moral incentives had ceased to work in the prevailing social climate. But money had meanwhile depreciated so fast that it would not have served as a real incentive, certainly not enough to warrant the sacrifice of a principle so dear to Che. There was only one cure: military conscription.

Here, something should be added parenthetically: the Cuban defense force in no way resembles the Chinese, which is the only truly politicized military force in the world. The Cuban army has a classically hierarchic structure and hence is basically authoritarian, even though it serves the people and is headed by former *guerrilleros* from the Sierra Maestra. Thus, when he decided to organize Cuban society on the model of his army, Fidel was implicitly admitting that he lacked less drastic means of implementing his policies. Moreover, the army not only introduced its language, methods, and rigid discipline into the economy, but also supplied the additional labor force needed to fulfill the plan. Fidel let it be known that, in case the masses proved recalcitrant, he would have no hesitation in calling up tens of thousands of reservists. We can only hope that these pressures will have eased after July 1970.

Thus the gap between the Castroist program and post-revolutionary reality has given rise to a whole chain of disappointments which in turn have caused more resentment, forcing Fidel to use even more authoritarian methods. In all fairness, however, we must not view these developments in isolation. We must remember that during the same period most underdeveloped countries, though massively aided by the United States and its capitalist allies, nevertheless regressed economically, suffering famines and poverty on a scale that has become quite unthinkable in postrevolutionary Cuba. If this retrospective survey of the Castroist past shows anything at all, it merely demonstrates that the Soviet bloc is no more capable of solving the problems of underdevelopment than are its imperialist rivals. It should also not be forgotten that a country as small

543

and as vulnerable as Cuba had little chance of standing up to its powerful protectors and rejecting their economic recipes and "socialist" dogmas. It was inevitable that Cuba should have repeated many of the "classic" errors of the Soviet Union.

All the same, the repetition of this drama on the Cuban stage is a most astonishing and saddening spectacle, especially because the Cuban Revolution has been so unlike the rest. It was not born of a cruel civil war as Russia's was during the twenties; it was not imported from outside as "socialism" was in the European People's Democracies following the Second World War. Its leaders were not scarred by Stalinist dogmas or mistaken ideas of discipline. They were shining examples of originality, and so popular that all other "socialist" regimes turned green with envy. How then did it happen that a movement so close to the pulse of the masses, so open-minded and disinterested, lost touch with reality on the morrow of its victory over the old order? Why did Castro adopt economic plans that had to be quickly abandoned again or that could only be implemented by methods quite out of keeping with the historical promises of the Revolution?

The Cuban experience demonstrates that the choice of ultra-ambitious economic objectives is not just a relic from the Stalinist past. All revolutionary leaders in underdeveloped countries have a tendency to rush off in pursuit of economic pipedreams because they can think of no better way to solve the vast problems of their heterogeneous society. They lack the material resources to immediately rectify all the injustices accumulated under earlier regimes, and they are almost fatalistically led to believe that accelerated economic expansion is the most revolutionary, the most leftist of all possible policies, the only one capable of liquidating the miserable heritage of the past in record time. It should be remembered that, in 1927, when Stalin first drove his country into forced industrialization and collectivization, people believed that he had come around to the views of the Trotskyist opposition, to the extent that such leading leftist critics as Eugen Preobrazhensky became converts to Stalin's cause. But though this policy can be justified on social as well as doctrinal grounds, it is nevertheless completely mistaken; its results have been far more devastating than anyone would have thought possible at the time.

The reader may remember the strange question President Dorticós asked me one day in Havana: "What is the aim of the Revolution?" The answer is quite simple and, shorn of theoretical embellishment, goes something like this: "The aim of the Revolution is to hand over to the workers in town and country, that is, to the immense majority of the people, effective control of all social institutions, so that they can freely organize their working life and decide on the collective distribution of its fruits." This program is admittedly simple in the extreme but, as Bertolt Brecht has put it, it is also one of the most difficult to achieve. There can be no doubt about that. But it is none the less true that this program cannot be circumvented or postponed *sine die*. No revolution has culminated in socialism which has been content to rely exclusively on the promotion of quick economic growth. On the contrary, those countries which have tried to force the economy by authoritarian methods have had to admit defeat in the long run. Nor can the rewards of such a policy be considered fair recompense for the hardships of military conscription. The logic of "primitive socialist accumulation" is such, moreover, that it has to lean heavily on capitalistic methods (hierarchic organization of production, arbitrary decisions as to the utilization of the social product, etc.) . Prolonged recourse to such methods is bound to introduce tremendous social and political dislocations which are not offset by the attempts of all revolutionary regimes to uplift the underprivileged of yesterday.

Though it may appear to be "leftist," any coercive attempt to create the "material foundations of socialism" does not solve any real problems of postrevolutionary society, and, ultimately, it is bound to pervert socialist values and to lead to new social crystalizations and to new types of oppression. But there is little need to make this point to the Cuban leaders; in earlier

545

chapters we saw how critical they themselves were, during their "heretical" period, of this emphasis on the construction of the material bases. The fact that Cuba has fallen into the same trap in no way proves that these criticisms have lost their force. On the contrary, recent Cuban developments have shown that if the economic battle is waged in the Soviet manner, the workers, having forfeited all rights, also lose their political initiative. As a result, they become incapable of developing a socialist consciousness or of working for the fundamental objectives of the revolution. True, the very fact that Cuban leaders, though fully aware of all these evils, have nevertheless seen fit to embark on a policy of militarization and conscription seems to prove that good will is not enough, and that, under certain circumstances, coercion becomes unavoidable. Fidel Castro himself confessed to me, in sorrow, that he saw no chance of granting the workers the right to self-determination in the near future, let alone of introducing a truly socialist mode of production.

But his arguments would have looked more convincing if one country had not shown the world that, underdevelopment notwithstanding, it is possible to run a society on collectivist and egalitarian principles. It is not by chance that that country— China—has always exerted a secret fascination on Cubans. They keep marveling at eye-witness reports that despite her undeniable poverty, China has nevertheless succeeded in filling her workers and peasants with a truly collectivist attitude. Nor were Cubans the only ones to be moved by these events; throughout the Third World, China is admired for her contented working class, among whom mutual aid is a matter of course, and who are encouraged to use their own initiative in solving even the most complex economic problems. Prince Sihanouk of Cambodia, who was the first to mention these facts to me before my visit to China, also told me that Mao Tse-tung was fortunate to govern a nation that worked so much harder than others. Fidel and his companions were also intrigued when I told them that during my stay in China, no one had complained about absenteeism or about any of the other labor problems of all underdeveloped countries.

546

The reckoning

It would be naïve to think that the exemplary behavior of the Chinese workers is due solely to their indoctrination and intensive education from on high. Edifying sermons alone have never worked such miracles. If the Chinese have changed, they owe it to a social system that enables them to apply Maoist values in their daily lives, to the fact that the Communist Party of China, instead of postponing the implementation of its revolutionary program, has made it the top priority immediately. Ever since 1958, it has systematically relied on the social radicalization of the masses, on their profound politicization, on rank-and-file initiative and decision-making (especially in the communes). In brief, it has set itself the task of unifying society, not by dictatorial conscription for the sake of grandiose economic plans, but by respecting the wish of the masses to work collectively and so to effect a radical change in current social relationships. The Party leaves it to the masses themselves to put an end to old habits and outdated social structures. Moreover, it has gone on to question its own role as an institution, and to challenge its own bureaucratized cadres. This is the precise meaning of the Great Cultural Revolution. To the Chinese themselves it is the prelude to a birth of truly revolutionary, popular institutions, to an ever deeper transformation of social relationships.

The implementation of the Maoist program is not, of course, a completely painless process either, as the tremors of the Cultural Revolution have shown only too clearly.[48] China has not yet come to the end of her road, and there will surely be many more zigzags as she continues along it.[49] But the Chi-

48. In my *China: The Other Communism* (Hill and Wang, New York, 1967), I have discussed at length the dark and bright sides of China's historic experience, including the "voluntarist" illusions common during the Great Leap Forward. Hence there is no further need for me to insist on the fact that even the fundamentally correct decision to trust in the masses is not a complete guarantee against tactical errors, especially not in a country as marked by its singular past and economic backwardness as China.
49. On the objective reasons for these inevitable zigzags the reader might like to hear this conclusion by Rossana Rossanda: "Only one socialist country, namely China, has been able in the course of its revolution—and quite especially during its tumultuous Cultural Revolution—to change

547

nese, at least, will try to lessen their effects by keeping firmly to the spirit and letter of their revolutionary doctrine. They will not be party to the building, in the name of socialism, of a society that is socialist only in name. So great is their originality that those (even of the Left) conditioned by the "growth-rate syndrome," so typical of both capitalist and Soviet economists, are completely bewildered by its objectives. It is a curious fact that, despite the moral and material crisis that is currently gripping East and West alike, many otherwise objective observers have ended up with the conviction that every regime, no matter what its political color, must concern itself first and foremost with the business of economic growth (the targets, of course, being fixed by the power elite). "The Chinese must be mad," they will tell you, "to ignore this fact; they are sacrificing their future on the altar of doctrinal delusions, or else their Cultural Revolution is simply a Machiavellian plot." In reality it is not their future which the Chinese have sacrificed but the notorious dogma of "primitive socialist accumulation"

---

the theoretical terms in the relationship Party/Masses, by calling for the permanent consultation of the masses, and for a permanent reference not only to their objective needs but also to their particular level of consciousness (with the 'poor peasant,' i.e., the most needy, as the axis of the construction of the movement wherever the Red Army and its propagandists appear) : it is these criteria which decide the fitness of the political line and to which the Party must subordinate its plans. However, this insistence on the material condition is itself guaranteed by the charismatic nature of the 'correct thought' of Mao, the leaven of [political] consciousness, the guarantor of the subjective process. This duality sets up an explosive tension which, from time to time, bursts asunder the concrete forms of the political organization or the state administration, but only to create another in its place, no less rigidly centralized, and with its own forms outside the masses. It seems that instead of speaking of a dialectic process we should speak of an unresolved antinomy, kept alive as a practical, empirical system with its own reciprocal corrective features; perhaps this is the only system which, working with immature productive and partly immature social forces, ensures that the Class/Party relations do not congeal into a hierarchical structure, to which it would otherwise tend by virtue of the immensity of the problems to be resolved." See Rossana Rossanda: "De Marx à Marx" in *Il Manifesto*, No. 4, Rome, September 1969. To be reprinted in *Socialist Register*, 1970.

under the supervision of an authoritarian bureaucracy. In spite of their sacrifice the Chinese are, by all accounts, doing much better than most of their "socialist" critics, even in the field of economic growth. Theirs is, moreover, the only socialist country that seems to be moving forward without suffering all those distortions and frustrations that all "sovietized" societies in Eastern Europe seem to be heir to.

Each social experiment is, of course, unique in its way. It would therefore be idle to suggest to the Cubans that they should copy the Maoist model. Cuba's ability to stand on her own feet is infinitely smaller than China's; the island is small and lacking in human resources. Therefore, even if the Cubans did try to follow the Chinese example, they would have to proceed along quite different paths to achieve the same essential aims: fostering the growth of political consciousness before economic growth; trust in the ability of the masses to determine their own destiny; building revolutionary institutions in harmony with the professed principles of the revolution. The last thing they need be called upon to do is to plaster the walls of Havana with such slogans as "Let us create two, three Cultural Revolutions," as some French pro-Maoists saw fit to do in 1968. None of this is really in the cards for Cuba at this stage, but it is true to say that at this hour, on the eve of their next stage, Cubans would do well to pay greater heed to the Chinese precedent.

The choice before Fidel Castro as the great fiesta of July 1970 approaches is not one between different economic plans, or between new productive wagers designed to fill the workers with fresh enthusiasm and to mobilize their energies once again. The innovation all Cubans so fervently desire is the complete reorganization, from top to bottom, of their social system, a reorganization that will give workers a greater say over their lives and will no longer leave them at the mercy of the errors of remote planners, however well-intentioned. In short, the true novelty would be the creation, as Cuba takes her next step, of all those social institutions Cubans so cruelly miss today.

549

Guerrillas in Power

This conclusion is not just a pious wish by a European friend of the Cuban Revolution. In 1967, I heard the same sentiments expressed by several of Cuba's own political leaders. And anyone reading the works of Ernesto Che Guevara will discover a similar concern—in spirit if not in the letter. For what else was his last public speech, in Algiers, and his last message to Tricontinental, if not an appeal to his comrades to guard against the kind of "socialism" that bases its methods of foreign trade and home production increasingly on those of the capitalist countries, and which daily draws further apart from those who believe in the real revolution, in true social justice? Cubans can still make a choice that will save them from this calamity. They still have the means to start on a road that will lead them to a free and equal society. One does not have to be a dreamer to think that this is, in fact, the road they will choose.

Appendixes

Appendices

Appendix A: A chronology

1. From War of Independence to "Mediatized Republic"

1868

October 10. Carlos Manuel de Céspedes gathers a small group of men in his sugar mill, *La Demajagua,* frees his slaves, and forms a rebel column pledged to overthrow the Spanish colonial power. The column is defeated in the battle of Yara, but the insurrection spreads to Bayamo, which falls to the patriots.

October 24. Máximo Gómez, Dominican citizen, former sergeant in the Spanish army, and friend of the Cuban conspirators, leads the machete charge against the royal army at Pinos de Baire. The insurrection spreads to the provinces of Oriente and Camagüey, and partly to Las Villas, but Havana and the western provinces remain under Spanish control.

553

Guerrillas in Power

[First British Trade Union Congress. Publication of Marx's *Capital*.]

1869

April 10. The insurgents hold the first Cuban Constitutional Assembly at Guaimaro, in Camagüey, and proclaim Manuel de Céspedes president of the "Republic in arms."

December. The Assembly deposes General Quesada, commander in chief, suspected of dictatorial ambitions. Disagreements between the representatives of Oriente and Camagüey, which were to mark the entire Ten Year War, begin to make themselves felt.

[Opening of the Suez Canal. Birth of Gandhi (1869–1948).]

1870

The young poet, José Martí Pérez, barely seventeen years old, is sentenced to seven years hard labor for his patriotic activities. He is taken to the Isle of Pines, and later to Spain, where he studies law at Madrid University.

U.S. President Grant refuses to recognize the insurgent republic.

[Birth of Lenin (1870–1924). Franco-German war.]

1871

General Máximo Gómez launches a general offensive in Guantánamo, during which the Maceo brothers, Antonio and José, two mulattos and future generals of the "Mambi" army (a name the insurgents themselves bestowed on their troops) play a distinguished part. In Havana, the Spaniards execute eight hostages, all of them medical students, *November 27*.

[Paris commune. Amadeus I of Savoy succeeds to the Spanish throne.]

1874

Carlos Manuel de Céspedes is surprised by the Spaniards in his refuge of San Lorenzo (Sierra Maestra) and mortally wounded. General Máximo Gómez invades the western provinces and defeats the enemy after a three-day battle at Las Guasimas. Increasing political tension between the civil leaders of the

Appendix A: A Chronology

insurrection. The Assembly elects and dismisses three presidents in a single year. Spain appoints General Martínez Campos *capitán general* of the island, and charges him to find a peaceful solution to the conflict.

[Spanish coup d'état: Alphonse XII proclaimed king. Coup d'état in Mexico: Porfirio Díaz sets himself up as dictator.]

1878

February. General Martínez Campos signs a peace treaty with the insurgents at Zanjon. Cuba is granted a measure of autonomy within the Spanish Empire and representation in the *Cortés*. At Baragua, in Oriente, General Antonio Maceo informs Martínez Campos that he is not in favor of this "agreement for peace without independence for Cuba," and that he will continue to fight.

[Rumania, Serbia and Montenegro become independent.]

1880

February 13. Abolition of slavery in Cuba. Population: 1,631,687 inhabitants, including 528,798 Negroes.[1]

José Martí arrives in New York, after his second deportation to Spain (1879), and on January 24 becomes president of the Cuban Revolutionary Committee. General Calixto García arrives in Cuba to revive the "little war" (*la guerra chiquita*), but fails.

[Mounting agitation in Ireland for Home Rule. War between Peru, Bolivia, and Chile.]

1884

Generals Gómez and Maceo, the two Mambi commanders, organize an expedition, but their 1884 Movement fails.

October 20. José Martí meets the two Mambi commanders in New York.

[Fabian Society founded in London.]

1. In 1953, the population of Cuba was: Whites, 72.8 per cent; Mestizos, 14.5 per cent; Negroes, 12.4 per cent; Asiatics, 0.3 per cent (*Encyclopaedia Britannica*, 1966).

555

Guerrillas in Power

1892

January 5. José Martí launches the Cuban Revolutionary Party, one of the first in Latin America to adopt a popular and democratic program.

March 14. José Martí founds *La Patria,* the official organ of the Cuban Revolutionary Party.

[Encyclical *Rerum novarum.*]

1895

March 25. José Martí and Máximo Gómez publish the Montecristi manifesto and appeal for a new war against the Spanish occupiers. The U.S. government seizes three ships of the La Fernandina expedition, on which the Mambi were setting out for Cuba. Antonio Maceo and Frol Crombet disembark with about twenty men at Duaba in Oriente, but are scattered by the Spaniards.

April 11. José Martí and Máximo Gómez and their men disembark at Playitas.

May 5. Martí, Gómez and Maceo decide their strategy at *La Majorana.*

May 19. José Martí, the "apostle of independence," killed in the Two Rivers battle.

September 16. The insurgent constitutional convention meets in the village of Jimaguayu in Camagüey, and adopts a new constitution.

October 22. The columns of Maceo and Gómez begin the invasion of the Western provinces. (Sixty-three years later, in 1958, Camilo Cienfuegos and Che Guevara would take the same path from the Sierra toward the Western plains).

[Eloy Alfaro becomes president-dictator of Ecuador. Bolivia loses access to the sea. Sun Yat-sen organizes the first insurrection against the Ching dynasty.]

1896

Maceo's column advances to the province of Pinar del Río, Gómez' establishes itself in the province of Havana. General Calixto García dominates the Eastern provinces. The Spaniards content themselves with defending the bigger towns and appoint

556

Appendix A: A Chronology

a new *capitán general,* Valeriano Weyler, a savage reactionary, who sets up concentration camps. Famine in Havana: 52,000 deaths.

December 7. General Antonio Maceo (the "bronze titan") falls in the battle of San Pedro, Havana Province.

[Strike by 30,000 textile workers in Petrograd.]

1897

October 31. Valeriano Weyler is recalled to Spain and replaced by General Ramón Blanco, instructed to sign a peace with the Cubans.

November 25. Spain offers complete autonomy to the island, but the insurgents refuse to compromise and call for national independence. Disorders in Havana fomented by Spanish extremists. President McKinley sends the cruiser *Maine* to the Bay of Havana in order to "protect the lives and property of U.S. citizens."

[Russia occupies Port Arthur. Germany establishes an enclave in the Province of Shantung.]

1898

February 15. A mysterious explosion on board the *Maine* kills 266 American sailors.

April 18. The American Senate and Chamber adopt the Joint Declaration requesting Spain to renounce control of Cuba, and to retire its forces from the island, and authorizing President McKinley to employ force to attain these objectives.

April 25. The United States declares war with Spain.

July 16. After a series of defeats at sea and on land, the Spanish forces in Oriente province capitulate at Santiago. U.S. General Shafter excludes Calixto García, commander of the Cuban army, from the capitulation ceremony.

August 12. Spain signs a "peace protocol" in Washington and agrees to all American demands.

October 1. Spanish-American peace conference opens in Paris.

December 10. Signing of the Treaty of Paris, by which Cuba is granted independence, and Puerto Rico, Guam, and the Philippines are ceded to the United States.

557

Guerrillas in Power

[First Congress of Russian Social Democratic Party in Minsk. Kaiser Wilhelm II announces the building of the German Navy. (Eight years later, the German fleet had become the second greatest naval power in the world.)]

1899

January 1. The last Spanish *capitán general,* A. Jiménez Castellanos, hands over power to General John R. Brode, the first U.S. military governor. The island now has 1,572,197 inhabitants (i.e., 3.6 per cent less than during the previous census). Despite the insistence of General Máximo Gómez, the American military authorities refuse to recognize the Cuban National Assembly.

March 12. General Máximo Gómez, acting against the wishes of the Assembly and the occupying power, retires from public life. Mass demonstrations in Havana and on the whole island fail to persuade him to change his mind.

December 5. President McKinley declares that Cuba is bound to the United States by "ties of singular intimacy and strength."

[Dispute between Brazil and Bolivia about the Acre territory (190,000 km²). America sides with Brazil, which annexes the territory.]

1900

November 5. First meeting of the Constituent Assembly, composed of thirty members under the presidency of General L. Wood, U.S. Military Governor.

[Lenin publishes *Iskra.*]

1901

June. Governor Wood demands that the Constituent Assembly incorporate in the Cuban Constitution an amendment by Senator Orville Platt, previously approved by Congress, granting the United States the right to intervene in Cuba whenever its interests demand it.

June 12. Platt Amendment adopted by a vote of 16 to 11, with 3 abstentions, despite the strong opposition of Juan Gualaberto Gómez, an old friend of José Martí and a delegate of the Cuban Revolutionary Party in Havana. "By accepting this amendment, you are handing the Americans the key to our house."

[The new President of the United States, Theodore Roosevelt,

promises to use "big stick" to guarantee U.S. presence in Latin America.]
1902
May 20. Governor Wood hands over power to the first President of the Cuban Republic, Estrada Palma, and puts an end to the military occupation of the island. But, thanks to the Platt Amendment, the Americans retain the right to "mediate" between Cubans, whence the name of "mediatized Republic."
[The United States establishes the Republic of Panama, and resumes the construction of the canal.]

2. From the "Mediatized Republic" to Fulgencio Batista's coup d'état

1903
May 22. Signing of permanent treaty between the United States and the Republic of Cuba. The United States is granted control of the naval base of Guantánamo Bay, the administration of the Isle of Pines (until 1925) and a number of economic privileges. According to Manuel Sanguily, this treaty gave the United States everything against which the Cuban people had risen up under Spanish rule.
[Second Congress of the Russian Social-Democratic Party in London. Split into Bolsheviks and Mensheviks.]
1904
February 28. Elections are fraudulently tampered with. "This was a farce enacted more shamefully than in the colonial days." (Emilio Terry) Two great parties emerge at the end of the year: the Conservative Republican Party (also called the Moderate Party) and the National Liberal Party. President Estrada Palma belongs to the Conservative Party. Carlos Balinos, one of the first Cuban Marxists and a former member of the Cuban Revolutionary Party founds the Workers' Party (later called the Socialist Workers' Party).
[France and Great Britain form the *Entente Cordiale*. Russia would join it three years later, when it would become known as the *Triple Entente*.]

Guerrillas in Power

1905

June 17. Death of Máximo Gómez, chief of the Mambi army, and the last of the great leaders of the War of Independence.

September 11. Estrada Palma offers himself for reelection. The Liberals prepare for armed insurrection, knowing that the election results will be faked.

[Russo-Japanese war. Workers' revolution in Russia.]

1906

May 20. Liberal coup d'état fails; numerous arrests (including Juan Gualaberto Gómez); first armed skirmishes in the provinces.

September 10. President Estrada Palma suspends the Constitution and calls for U.S. intervention.

September 19. U.S. Secretary of War, William H. Taft, arrives in Havana on board the cruiser *Des Moines.*

September 29. After ten days of fruitless "mediation," William H. Taft deposes Estrada Palma, dissolves the legislature, appoints himself governor and sets up a provisional administration pending new elections. 2,000 Marines disembark in Havana. Judge Charles Magoon of Nebraska, assisted by General Enoch Crowder, governs the island for two years and four months. The population exceeds the two million mark (2,048,980 inhabitants).

[President Roosevelt receives the Nobel Peace Prize. The United States intervenes in the war between Guatemala and El Salvador. Czar Nicholas II dissolves the first Duma.]

1909

January 28. The American governors hand over power to the new President, General José Miguel Gómez, elected on the Liberal ticket in November of the previous year. During the four years of his rule, corruption reaches new heights. President Gómez becomes known as Don Pépe Tiburón ("shark").

[U.S. intervention in Nicaragua.]

1912

May 20. Armed uprising by Negroes against the law forbidding the formation of "movements composed of persons of the same race or color" (the Morua Amendment). The insurgents, led

Appendix A: A Chronology

by Evaristo Estenoz and Pedro Ivonet, hold large areas of Oriente province but do not commit a single outrage against the whites. President Gómez declares martial law in Oriente and orders the army to wipe out the insurgents. Evaristo Estenoz is killed on June 27; Ivonet is murdered in prison. Officially, 3,000 blacks are executed, but General Monteagudo admits in his report to the President: "It is impossible to give the precise number of deaths, because the campaign has degenerated into a *carnicería* (carnage)."

[The Bolsheviks become an independent party. The United States steps up its repression against the Mexican revolution.]

1913–1920

General Mario García Menocal, elected on the Moderate Conservative label, becomes president. In 1917, when his term of office is extended for a further four years, the liberals form a *guerrita* and protest against the fraud. The President of the United States, Woodrow Wilson, offers his support to General Menocal and declares that his administration will not recognize any Cuban government brought in by revolutionary means. The Marines stationed in Guantánamo Bay advance as far as Camagüey to make a show of force and to discourage any revolt on the part of the liberals. In 1914, Cuba declares war on Germany and brings in military conscription. A symbolic Cuban detachment leaves for Europe, and at the end of the war, Cuba is granted German reparations. Spectacular rise in sugar prices up to the record level of 22.6 cents a pound is responsible for "Dances of the Millions" during the years 1919–20, and the stability of the regime of General Mario G. Menocal. Population in 1919: 2,889,004.

[First World War (1914–1918). Bolshevik revolution in Russia (October 1917). Foundation of Third International. The first Latin American Communist Party founded in the Argentine (1918).]

1921

After a sudden drop in sugar prices (from 22.6 to 3.25 cents) Cuba experiences her first economic crisis. The liberal, Alfredo Zayas, becomes president of the republic, and the United States

561

grants him a credit of $50 million, on condition that an American commissioner—General Enoch Crowder—is put in charge of these funds. The Crowder Commission interferes in all aspects of Cuba's political life, inciting a wave of anti-American and anti-imperialist feeling. In Havana, a clandestine Association of Veterans and Patriots is formed for the express purpose of overthrowing the government by force. One of its leaders is the young poet, Rubén Martínez Villena (aged 23).

[Treaty of Riga: end of Russo-Polish war, and of the civil war in the Soviet Union. Kronstadt uprising crushed by the Red Army.]

1923

February. Progressive intellectuals form the Movement for University Reform. Jorge Mañach founds the *Revista de Avance,* an avant-garde literary journal virulently opposed to the regime. Rubén Martínez Villena organizes the Protest of the Thirteen, and on March 23 accuses Zayas publicly of corruption; with a group of friends he prevents the president from speaking at the inaugural meeting of the Academy of Sciences.

October 15. The first National Congress of Students, organized and presided over by Julio Antonio Mella, passes a declaration on the rights and duties of students, but also anti-imperialist resolutions against the policy of isolating Russia, and for the independence of India, the Philippines, Ireland, Egypt, and Morocco.

[Sun Yat-sen signs an agreement with Adolf Yoffé, the representative of the Soviet government. The Communist Party of China enters the Kuomintang. Mussolini comes to power in Italy.]

1924

February 2. Foundation of the Cuban Railwaymen's Union, which immediately proclaims a three weeks' strike. Julio Antonio Mella organizes a general strike of tobacco workers and founds the José Martí University, which is run from trade union offices.

April. In America, Rubén Martínez Villena, Antonio Fernández and Calixto García plan an air raid against military objec-

tives in Havana, to coincide with an uprising led by the Association of Veterans and Patriots. They are arrested by the U.S. authorities and the uprising of April 30 fails (only in Cienfuegos do the insurgents score some brief successes). Alfredo Zayas decides not to offer himself for re-election. General Crowder proposes to set up a provisional administration on the Magoon model; he finally supports General Gerardo Machado, the prototype of the Latin American dictator.
[First Labour Government in Great Britain. First Congress of the new Kuomintang in Canton. Death of Lenin. Marines land in Honduras to "protect the lives and property of United States citizens."]
1925
February 15–18. Foundation of the National Workers' Confederation of Cuba, in Camagüey. *August 16–17:* Foundation of the Communist Party for Cuba in Havana.
November 27. Julio Antonio Mella, arrested for an infringement of the explosives law, goes on a 19-day hunger strike. He is released and expelled from the island.
[American intervention in Panama. Death of Sun Yat-sen.]
1927
March 28. General Machado asks parliament to change the Constitution, so as to extend his presidential mandate by seven years, and later, for a further seven years.
June 21. After three months of continual debating, the chamber adopts the amendment proposed by Machado. A wave of indignation sweeps the country. Students found the *Directorio Revolucionario Estudiantil.* Among its founders: Antonio Guiteras Holmes, a pharmacology student; Rubén Martínez Villena, a member of the Communist Party.
[The Fifteenth Congress of the Communist Party of the Soviet Union expels all left-wing opponents (Trotsky, Zinoviev, Kamenev). Chiang Kai-shek crushes the insurrection in Shanghai.]
1929
January 10. The dictator's henchmen assassinate Mella in Mexico.
May 20. Machado "re-elected" just as America is hit by eco-

nomic crisis. Antonio Guiteras leaves the university to become the representative of Lederle, a pharmaceutical firm. He manufactures the first anti-Machadoist bombs. Machado bans all meetings and public assemblies. [Beginning of forced collectivization in the U.S.S.R. Europe hit by economic crisis.]

1930

April 19. The Supreme Court overrules the presidential decree against public meetings. 50,000 persons demonstrate against the dictatorship in Central Park, Havana.

September 30. Mass demonstration by students: police fire and kill Rafael Trejo, one of the student leaders. The dictator closes the university. The orthodox Right led by ex-president Menocal joins the opposition. Foundation of the clandestine ABC Party. [Getulio Vargas becomes president of Brazil. Trujillo comes to power in the Dominican Republic.]

1931

August. Menocal organizes an armed landing in Río Verde (province of Pinar del Río) but fails. Wave of repression on the island. Antonio Guiteras is arrested, but released in December. The *Directorio Estudiantil* starts a terrorist campaign in Havana. Population in 1931: 3,962,344. [In Great Britain, Ramsay MacDonald forms National Government. The Labour Party loses four fifths of its seats in the General Election.]

1933

August 12. Following a strike of transport workers, which turns into a general strike, the dictator is forced to flee the country. The American mediator, Sumner Welles, backs Manuel de Céspedes as provisional president.

September 4. Sergeants' revolt causes fall of provisional government. A *pentarquía* presided over by Dr. Ramón Grau San Martín takes power.

September 11. Grau San Martín and Antonio Guiteras form revolutionary government. The United States withholds recognition. The Communist Party calls for all power to the Soviets.

September 29. The army fires on the crowd attending the funeral of Julio Antonio Mella.

October 2. The army crushes the uprising of officers barricaded in the Hotel Nacional in Havana.

October–November. Government proclaims 8-hour working day, university autonomy, state control of the electricity company.

December. The Cuban delegate attacks the Platt Amendment and American interference at the Montevideo Conference.

[Hitler becomes Chancellor of Germany. Franklin Delano Roosevelt starts his first presidential term and proclaims goodneighbor policy toward Latin America.]

1934

January 15. Colonel Batista overthrows the Grau-Guiteras government. Colonel Mendieta becomes provisional President. Wave of repression on the island. The United States recognizes the new regime.

May 29. The American government agrees to waive the Platt Amendment. Antonio Guiteras founds the *Jóven Cuba* Party. Death of Rubén Martínez Villena. Blas Roca becomes general secretary of the Cuban Communist Party.

[Beginning of Long March by the Chinese Red Army. Growing fascist menace in France.]

1935

March. Antonio Guiteras organizes a workers' strike in the sugar mills.

May 8. Guiteras and Carlos Aponte are killed at El Morrillo.

September. The Communist Party invites all opposition parties to join a national anti-fascist front.

[The Seventh Congress of the Comintern calls for the formation of popular (anti-fascist) fronts.]

1936

January 10. Miguel Mariano Gómez "voted" president in an election boycotted by the opposition parties.

December 24. The Assembly deposes Miguel Mariano Gómez

and appoints Federico Laredo Bru in his stead, but *de facto* power is in the hands of the minister of defense, General Fulgencio Batista.

[Victory of the Popular Front in France. Franco uprising against the Spanish Republican Government.]

1938

March. General Fulgencio Batista meets Blas Roca.

September 13. The Cuban Communist Party recognized as a legal organization; government authorizes the formation of a Confederation of Cuban Trade Unions.

November 12. The Communist Party asks its members to give Batista an enthusiastic welcome on his return from Washington. Batista restores the autonomy of the university and agrees to call a Constituent Assembly.

[Munich agreements. Dismemberment of Czechoslovakia. Formation of the Berlin-Rome-Tokyo Axis.]

1939

November 11. The opposition defeats the Batista-Communist coalition at the elections. Dr. Grau San Martín voted president of the Constituent Assembly.

[German-Soviet Pact. The Second World War.]

1940

July 1. The Assembly adopts a new constitution to come in force on October 10, the anniversary of the declaration of the War of Independence of 1868.

July 14. Fulgencio Batista "elected" president of Cuba.

[Defeat of France. Pétain sets up a collaborationist regime in Vichy.]

1942

July 20. Cuba declares war on Germany, Japan, and Italy.

July 23. Batista appeals to all parties to form a Government of National Unity.

July 24. The Communist Party joins the Government: Juan Marinello and Carlos Rafael Rodríguez become ministers without portfolio.

[The battle of Stalingrad marks the great turning point of the Second World War.]

Appendix A: A Chronology

1944

October 10. Dr. Ramón Grau San Martín succeeds Batista as president of the Republic. The Communist Party changes its name and becomes the Popular Socialist Party (PSP). It promises to cooperate with the new government in ensuring the social peace and progress of the island. Population in 1943: 4,778,583.

[Allied landing in Normandy. Liberation of Paris. Warsaw uprising crushed by Germans.]

1946

January 24–28. The Third Assembly of the PSP decides to go into opposition. At the University of Havana, Fidel Castro is elected president of the Association of Law Students.

[Churchill's speech in Fulton heralds the beginning of the Cold War.]

1947

August–October. Cayo Confites expedition intended to liberate the Dominican Republic.

September 15. Bloody clashes between the two ex-revolutionary police groups in Havana, throw total discredit on the Grau administration.

October. Fidel Castro joins the Party of the Cuban People (*Ortodoxo*) founded by Senator Eduardo Chibás.

[Civil war in China. Perón, the new dictator of the Argentine, in conflict with Great Britain.]

1948

April. Fidel Castro attends the conference of Latin-American students in Bogotá (Colombia), which coincides with the assassination of Eleicir Gaitán, followed by a vast popular uprising.

June. Prío Socarrás, minister of labor, elected president of the Republic (he took office on October 10).

[Coup d'état by General Odria in Peru. Communist Party seizes power in Czechoslovakia.]

1952

March 10. General Fulgencio Batista seizes power, ten weeks after a general election that swept the *Ortodoxos* into office. The political parties condemn the *golpe* but remain passive.

567

Guerrillas in Power

Fidel Castro lays a charge against the usurper before the Supreme Court, but then decides to take direct action. Several clandestine movements are formed, particularly in university circles.

[Puerto Rico becomes a "free state" associated with the United States. Coup d'état by General Pérez Jiménez in Venezuela. Paz Estenssoro carried into power by Bolivian revolution.]

3. From resistance to revolution

1953

July 26. 120 young people, led by Fidel Castro, attack the Moncada barracks in Santiago de Cuba. The attempt fails. Several of the assailants are tortured or killed by the army (among the victims: Abel Santamaría, Castro's second in command). In September, Fidel Castro, his brother Raúl, Juan Almeida, Jésus Montané and others are tried in Santiago. The Court decides to hear Fidel's case separately and *in camera* on October 16. On that occasion, Fidel delivers his now famous plea: *History Will Absolve Me*. Sentenced to 15 years of prison, he is reunited with many of the Moncada survivors in a special penitentiary on the Isle of Pines.

[Death of Stalin. Beginning of CIA operation to overthrow President Jácobo Arbenz of Guatemala. Workers' revolt in East Berlin.]

1954

Fidel Castro begins to organize the July 26th Movement while still in prison.

November. General Batista "elected" president of the republic.

[An insurrection in Algeria marks the beginning of the seven years' war against the French colonial regime.]

1955

May. Batista declares a general amnesty. Castro and his companions are freed and return in triumph to Havana.

July 8. Fidel Castro leaves for Mexico, the United States, Costa

568

Rica and once again for Mexico to reorganize Cuban exiles and to prepare an armed landing. In Mexico he meets Ernesto Che Guevara, a young physician from the Argentine, who joins the movement.

[Fall of Perón in the Argentine. Four Power Conference (U.S.A., U.S.S.R., France, Britain) in Geneva. Kubitschek elected President of Brazil.]

1956

September. After breaking officially with the *Ortodoxos,* Fidel Castro signs a united action pact with José Antonio Echeverría, leader of the *Directorio Revolutionario,* in Mexico. He announces his impending landing in Cuba and proclaims "This year we shall be free or else we shall be martyrs."

November 25. Granma leaves Tuxpán, Mexico, with 82 armed men aboard.

November 30. Uprising in Santiago directed by Frank País and Pepito Tey (who is killed in action).

December 2. Granma landing.

December 5. The army surprises the expeditionaries at Alegría del Pío.

December 18–25. Some twenty expeditionaries are reunited in the Sierra Maestra, and form the first Cuban guerrilla center.

[Twentieth Congress of the Communist Party of the Soviet Union. Polish and Hungarian October uprising. Anglo-French-Israeli attack on Egypt. Rigoberto López, a student, kills the Nicaraguan dictator, Somoza.]

1957

January 17. 17 *guerrilleros* make a successful attack on the La Plata barracks.

February 17. Fidel Castro interviewed, in the Sierra Maestra, by Herbert Matthews of *The New York Times.*

Early March. Frank País sends the *guerrilleros* 50 men from Santiago.

March 13. Members of the *Directorio* attack the presidential palace in Havana. José Antonio Echeverría killed by the police. Wave of repression on the entire island.

May 28. The *guerrilleros* seize a large quantity of arms in the El Uvero barracks.

June–July. The urban resistance movement (Llano), organizes a series of spectacular attacks in Havana, Santiago, and other towns.

July 30. The police shoot down Frank País in the streets of Santiago.

Early August. A spontaneous strike paralyzes almost all the western provinces of the island. In the Sierra Maestra, Fidel Castro sets up a "second rebel column" with Ernesto Che Guevara in command.

September 5. Sailors' revolt in Cienfuegos: the air force bombards the town.

November. The *guerrilleros* declare El Hombrito, in the Sierra Maestra, a free territory with its own small industries, radio, hospital, etc.

November 30. All the opposition parties, with the exception of the PSP, adopt a pro-American program to be implemented after Batista's defeat (Miami Pact).

December 14. Fidel Castro denounces the Miami Pact as a reactionary trick, and declares that Captain Lester Rodríguez, then on an arms-buying mission in the United States, has no authority to sign it in the name of the July 26th Movement.

December 18. Fangio, the Argentinian racing driver, held prisoner in Havana for 48 hours.

[Duvalier seizes power in Haiti. Mao Tse-tung attends international conference of Communist parties in Moscow. After eliminating the "anti-party group" and deposing Marshal Zhukov, Nikita Khrushchev becomes top man in the U.S.S.R. The Soviet Union launches its first Sputnik.]

1958

January–March. New series of spectacular attacks in the cities: Havana without electricity or water for three days. The international airport of Rancho Boyeros gutted.

March 10. Raúl Castro and a column of 67 open a Second Front (the Frank País Front) in the Sierra de Cristal, Northern Oriente.

570

Appendix A: A Chronology

March 12. Fidel Castro, as commander in chief, and Faustino Pérez as national coordinator of the July 26th Movement, issue a 22-point appeal to the nation, in which they call for a general strike and ask Cubans to withhold their taxes and to avoid the highways after April 1. They announce that, after their victory, Dr. Manuel Urrutia will become provisional president of the republic.

April 9. General strike collapses in Havana; street battles in several towns (especially in Sagua la Grande).

May 5. Meeting of national leadership of July 26th Movement in the Sierra Maestra: Fidel Castro becomes the sole leader of the movement. In Havana, Faustino Pérez is replaced by Marcelo Fernández (Zorilo).

End of May. Great army offensive against the Sierra Maestra.

May 28. After three days of fighting, the army occupies Las Mercedes.

June. The army continues its advance.

June 25. The army occupies Las Vegas, a four-hour march from La Plata, the rebel capital.

June 29. Rebel counteroffensive near San Domingo river. Two army battalions routed.

July 10. After violent battles at El Jigue, the rebels take 250 prisoners and hand them over to the Red Cross (Operation Trojan Horse).

July 29. The columns of Che Guevara and Camilo Cienfuegos recapture Las Vegas. Fidel Castro's column routs the troops of Sánchez Mosquera, during the second battle of Santo Domingo.

August 7. The *guerrilleros* recapture Las Mercedes. The army withdraws from the Sierra Maestra after three months of battles.

August 29. The columns of Camilo Cienfuegos and Ernesto Che Guevara invade the plains of Camagüey and Las Villas.

September. Fidel Castro's column descends into Oriente.

November 3. Batista "re-elected" president, but the poll is so small (98 per cent of the electorate abstains in Santiago; 75 per cent in Havana) that he becomes the chief victim of his own electoral farce.

December 9. In Las Vegas province, Che Guevara signs a pact with the *Directorio Revolucionario* and the PSP. On the national plane, the July 26th Movement is a signatory of the Caracas pact of July 20, embracing the entire Left and Center-Left, whereas the Miami Pact excluded the Communists.

December. Raúl Castro opens the first Congress of Peasants in the liberated Sierra de Cristal.

December 24. Che's column occupies Sancti Spiritus and moves toward Santa Clara.

December 27–30. Batista's air force bombards Santa Clara. Camilo Cienfuegos' and Che Guevara's columns meet outside Santa Clara.

December 31. The garrison of Santa Clara capitulates. Batista flees to the Dominican Republic. General Cantillo tries to establish a "peace government" presided over by Judge Piedra.

[French army revolt in Algeria. General de Gaulle comes to power in France. China launches a campaign for peoples' communes and calls for a great leap forward both economically and socially. Pérez Jiménez overthrown in Venezuela. Frondizi succeeds at the polls in the Argentine. Eighth Congress of Chinese Communist Party. Vice-President Nixon tours Latin America. Llevas Camargo becomes president of Colombia. Ydígoras Fuentes becomes president of Guatemala. The U.S.S.R. sends a memorandum to France, Great Britain and the United States on the subject of Berlin and a peace treaty with the two Germanys.]

1959

January 1. Fidel Castro calls a general strike.

January 2. The rebels occupy Santiago, whence Castro delivers his first address to the nation.

January 3. Che and Camilo advance on Havana.

January 4. Members of the *Directorio* entrench themselves in the presidential palace and the university.

January 5. The Provisional President, Manuel Urrutia enters the presidential palace in Havana. Fidel crosses the island on his way toward the capital.

January 8. Fidel Castro enters Havana in triumph and appeals for the unity of all revolutionaries.

Appendix A: A Chronology

[Twenty-first Congress of Soviet Communist Party. Seven-year plan inaugurated in the U.S.S.R. Conservative government elected in Great Britain. Khrushchev visits the United States.]

4. *From the Revolution to the ten-million-ton* zafra

1959 *Año de la Liberación*

January 23. Fidel Castro goes to Caracas in order to thank the Venezuelan people for their aid during the struggle against the dictatorship.

February 13. Fidel Castro becomes prime minister.

March 10. The Government passes Law No. 135, lowering all rents on the island by 50 per cent.

April 15. Fidel Castro goes to the United States at the invitation of leading newspaper publishers.

April 27. Fidel Castro arrives in Canada.

May 2. At a meeting of twenty-one South American countries in Buenos Aires, Fidel Castro demands thirty thousand million dollars' worth of aid to Latin America over the next ten years.

May 17. Fidel Castro signs the agrarian reform bill in La Plata, the former rebel capital in the Sierra Maestra.

June 14. Ministerial reshuffle. Raúl Roa becomes minister of foreign affairs; Major Pedro Miret minister of agriculture.

July 16. Fidel resigns his post in the government, and publicly denounces President Urrutia.

July 18. The Council of Ministers appoints Dr. Osvaldo Dorticós president of the republic.

July 26. Fidel withdraws his resignation and becomes prime minister.

September 8. Ernesto Che Guevara returns from a three months' trip to Africa and Asia, having signed economic and cultural agreements with Egypt, India, Pakistan, Indonesia, and Japan.

October 29. Major Camilo Cienfuegos' aircraft lost in a storm.

November 18. 3,000 delegates participate in the Tenth National Congress of the Revolutionary Confederation of Labor (CTCR).

November 26. Second ministerial reshuffle following the resignations of Major Faustino Pérez and Manuel Ray. Che Guevara appointed director of the National Bank.
December 14. The Revolutionary Tribunal of Havana sentences
Major Hubert Matos, accused of plotting against the revolution,
to 20 years hard labor.
December 23. By Law No. 677, greater social security is made
available to all workers.
[After his trip to the United States, Nikita Khrushchev attends
the tenth anniversary of the Chinese revolution in Peking but
leaves without signing a common communiqué. Peasant Leagues
in Northeast Brazil led by Juliano. Mao Tse-tung resigns as
president of the Chinese Republic, in order to devote himself
to ideological questions. Liu Shao-ch'i elected president of
China.]
    1960 *Año de la reforma agraria*
February 4. Mikoyan arrives in Havana and signs a commercial
treaty with Cuba.
March 4. Explosion on the French ship *La Coubre* in Havana
causes 70 deaths. The Castroist press blames the CIA.
March 16. Law No. 757 inaugurates the *Junta Central de
Planificación* (Juceplan) with instructions to plan the economic
development of the island.
April 8. In a letter to the Federation of Chilean Students, Presi-
dent Eisenhower accuses Fidel Castro of betraying the ideals of
the Cuban Revolution.
April 19. President Dorticós refutes Eisenhower's arguments and
denounces American pressure against the Cuban Revolution.
April 25. Bank of Foreign Trade established.
May 8. Diplomatic relations between the U.S.S.R. and Cuba
resumed.
July 5. The United States refuses to buy the residue of the 1960
Cuban sugar quota, i.e., 700,000 tons.
July 9. The Soviet government agrees to buy what Cuban sugar
the Americans refuse to take.
July 10. At a mass meeting outside the Presidential Palace,

Appendix A: A Chronology

Ernesto Che Guevara thanks the U.S.S.R. and declares: "Cuba is a glorious island in the center of the Caribbean, defended by the rockets of the greatest power in history."

July 23. First commercial treaty between China and Cuba.

August 6. After unsuccessful mediation attempts by President Frondizi of the Argentine, the government nationalizes 36 sugar mills and refineries, and the Telephone Company. The value of these nationalized estates is thought to be $800 million.

August 15. At a meeting of the Organization of American States in San José, Costa Rica, the United States pushes through a resolution condemning Cuba.

September 2. In reply to the San José resolution, Fidel Castro issues the First Havana Declaration during a mass meeting on Revolution Square.

September 14. Fidel Castro leaves for New York to attend the Fifteenth Assembly of the United Nations.

October 15. By Law No. 890, the Cuban government nationalizes 382 major enterprises and banks.

October 19. The United States declares a partial embargo on trade with Cuba.

[Russians shoot down American U-2 spy plane. Failure of Paris Summit Conference. Semi-public recriminations between the U.S.S.R. and China. The U.S.S.R. recalls all technicians from China and starts what amounts to a total economic blockade. Yon Sosa establishes a guerrilla center in Guatemala. Paz Estenssoro becomes president of Bolivia for the second time. Quadros elected president of Brazil. World Conference of 81 Communist Parties in Moscow. Belgian Congo becomes independent. Secession attempts in Katanga; Prime Minister Lumumba appeals to the United Nations. Lumumba assassinated.]

1961 *Año de la Educacion*

January 1. 100,000 young people leave Havana to start the great literacy campaign in the countryside.

January 3. The United States breaks off diplomatic relations with Cuba.

January 5. A young, black "alphabetizer," Conrado Benítez, is assassinated in the mountains of Escambray, where a strong counterrevolutionary center is being established.

February 23. Ernesto Che Guevara appointed minister of industry; Major Alberto Mora, minister of foreign trade; Máximo Berman, minister of home trade; José Llanusa Gobel, director of the National Institute of Sports and Physical Education.

April 15. 7 dead and 53 wounded during an air raid on Havana and Santiago airports, prior to the landing of the anti-Castroist expeditionary force set up by the CIA.

April 16. During the funeral of the victims, Fidel Castro proclaims the socialist character of the Cuban Revolution.

April 17. Expeditionary force lands on Playa Girón, in the Bay of Pigs; 48 hours later more than 1,200 invaders are taken prisoner.

April 25. The United States declares a total embargo on all trade with Cuba.

May 1. The U.S.S.R. bestows the Lenin Peace Prize on Fidel Castro.

August 5. Financial reforms. The parity of the peso is maintained, but bank accounts are blocked and private persons may no longer withdraw more than 660 pesos per month.

August 10. Che Guevara leads the Cuban delegation to Punta del Este, where the Organization of American States subscribes to the American Alliance for Progress.

August 26. First national conference on production. The minister of economics, Regino Botí, presents the draft of a four-year industrialization plan.

November 11. Venezuela breaks off diplomatic relations with Cuba.

December 2. In a speech on the impending formation of the Unified Party of the Socialist Revolution, Fidel Castro declares: "I am a Marxist-Leninist and I shall remain one until the end of my life."

[Generals' revolt in Algiers. Franco-Algerian Conference in Evian, promising Algerian independence in 1962. Twenty-second Congress of the Communist Party of the U.S.S.R. The new President of the United States, John F. Kennedy, inaugurates the Alliance for Progress in Latin America, and intensifies the anti-guerrilla campaign in Vietnam and Laos. Split in the ruling party of Venezuela. Split in the APRA party of Peru. Luis de la Puente sets up a rebel APRA. Hugo Blanco organizes peasant federations. Vice-President Goulart takes over from President Quadros in Brazil.]

1962 *Año de la Planificación*

January 25. President Dorticós leads the Cuban delegation to a new conference in Punta del Este, which expels Cuba from the Organization of American States by 14 to 6. (Brazil, Argentina, Mexico, Chile, Bolivia, and Ecuador).

February 4: In reply to the resolution of Punta del Este, Fidel Castro issues the Second Havana Declaration.

March 8. Inauguration of ORI (Organizaciones Revolucionarias Integradas).

March 12. Law No. 1015 introduces rationing for most foods and articles of clothing.

March 26. In a radio-television address, Fidel Castro denounces the sectarianism of Aníbal Escalante.

June 22. Law No. 1035 stipulates penalties against speculators and hoarders of food-stuffs.

October 3. President Dorticós attends the Seventeenth Assembly of the United Nations in New York.

October 16. Ahmed Ben Bella, president of Algeria, visits Havana.

October 21–28. Missile crisis.

October 30. The Secretary-General of the United Nations, U Thant, arrives in Havana to discuss the dismantling of Soviet missiles.

November 2. Mikoyan arrives in Havana.

November 20. The President of the United States calls off the quarantine measures against Cuba adopted during the missile crisis.

December 21. The United States agrees to supply Cuba with equipment and pharmaceutical products to the tune of $63 million (collected by private subscription) in exchange for prisoners taken during the Playa Girón invasion.

Guerrillas in Power

[Military coup d'état in the Argentine. Progressive military uprisings in Puerto Cabello and Carupano (Venezuela). The *guerrilleros* take to the mountains. Haya de la Torre wins elections in Peru, but is prevented from taking office by the army. China accuses the Soviet Union of betraying Communism. Armed conflict between India and China.]

1963 *Año de la Organisación*

April 27–June 3. Fidel Castro pays his first visit to the U.S.S.R.

June 4. In a radio-television address, Fidel announces a new economic policy based on the Soviet-Cuban sugar agreement.

June 12. Foundation of the National Sugar Council which becomes a special ministry for the sugar industry.

June 13. Ernesto Che Guevara visits Algeria.

October 4. The Second Agrarian Reform restricts privately-owned estates to 5 *caballerías* (approximately 100 acres).

October 5–7. Hurricane Flora devastates the eastern regions of Cuba.

December 30. Nikolai Podgorny arrives in Havana.

[President J. F. Kennedy assassinated in Dallas, Texas. Communist Party banned in Venezuela; the government candidate, Leoni, wins the presidential elections.]

1964 *Año de la Economia*

January 13–23. Second visit to the U.S.S.R. by Fidel Castro.

January 24. In an address to the nation, Fidel Castro announces the impending arrival of Soviet cane-cutting machines and declares that Cuba will produce ten million tons of sugar in 1970. "Everyone to work!"

March 17. Ernesto Che Guevara leaves for Geneva to attend a United Nations Conference on trade and development in the Third World.

March 26. Trial of Marcos A. Rodríguez. He is sentenced to death for informing on members of the *Directorio Revolucionario* during the anti-Batista struggle.

October 1. President Dorticós leaves for the second conference of non-aligned countries in Cairo.

October 15. President Dorticós leaves for Moscow where Khrushchev's resignation has just been announced.

578

Appendix A: A Chronology

November 5. Ernesto Che Guevara pays his last visit to the Soviet Union.

November 19. Joaquín Ordoqui resigns from the leadership of the Party and the vice-ministry of defense. He and his wife Edith García Buchacha are arrested a few weeks later.

December 9. Ernesto Che Guevara addresses the Nineteenth General Assembly of the United Nations.

[In Peru, Hugo Blanco is arrested and sentenced to 25 years imprisonment. Military coup d'état in Guatemala. Khrushchev replaced by the Brezhnev-Kosygin-Podgorny triumvirate. Coup d'état in Brazil: Marshal Castelo Branco proclaims himself president. The Christian-Democrat, Frei, elected president of Chile. Labour Party wins the British elections. Lyndon Johnson elected President of the United States.]

1965 *Año de la Agricultura*

January 1. Ernesto Che Guevara arrives in Congo-Brazzaville.

January 19. Publication of joint communiqué by Conference of Latin American Communist Parties held in Cuba at the end of 1964 (date not specified). The document subscribes to the Soviet view on the unity of the Communist movement, but does not explicitly condemn China.

January 30–February 5. Ernesto Che Guevara pays his last visit to Peking after his African tour (Ghana, Guinea, Algeria).

February 14. Fidel Castro takes personal charge of INRA and becomes *de facto* minister of agriculture.

February 17. Three-year Soviet-Cuban trade agreement signed. The U.S.S.R. grants Cuba a new credit of $167 million.

February 20. Che Guevara arrives in Algeria for the Second Economic Conference on Afro-Asian Solidarity. He delivers his last public speech and criticizes "socialist" methods of aid and trade.

March 1. Raúl Castro leads a Cuban delegation to Moscow on the occasion of a preparatory meeting, charged to convene a world conference of Communist parties.

March 15. Ernesto Che Guevara returns to Havana after his Afro-Asian tour. Fidel Castro and President Dorticós receive him at the airport.

579

April 20. In a statement to foreign correspondents Fidel Castro declares: "Major Ernesto Che Guevara will be found where he is most useful to the revolution."

May 3. Cuba complains to the Security Council against U.S. intervention in the Dominican Republic.

September 28. Cuba agrees to a mini-airbridge between Veradero and Miami so as to facilitate the departure of Cubans anxious to emigrate.

October 3. Fidel Castro presents the Central Committee of the Communist Party of Cuba to the nation and reads the farewell letter of Ernesto Che Guevara.

October 7. Armando Hart is appointed secretary of the PCC, and hands over the ministry of education to José Llanusa Gobel.

[Soviet Premier visits Hanoi and Peking. American military escalation; start of the daily pounding of North Vietnam. Coup d'état in Jakarta; massacre of 500,000 Indonesian Communists. 42,000 marines land in the Dominican Republic to "protect the lives and property of American citizens" and to prevent the return to power of President Bosch. Savage repression against striking miners in Bolivia; 150 strikers shot. Luis de la Puente, the leader of the Peruvian *guerrilleros,* killed in action. Coup d'état in Algeria. Colonel Boumedienne supplants Ben Bella.]

   1966   *Año de la Solidaridad*

January 2. Fidel Castro criticizes China for its refusal to increase rice deliveries to Cuba.

January 3–15. "Tricontinental" conference in Havana. Foundation of OSPAAAL (Organization for the Solidarity of the People of Africa, Asia and Latin America) with provisional headquarters in Havana.

January 16. Delegates from 27 Latin American countries found the Latin American Solidarity Organization (OLAS).

February 16. Replying to a declaration by the Chinese government Fidel Castro declares: "China has abused the faith of the Cuban people."

August 22–26. The Second Congress of the Cuban Revolu-

Appendix A: A Chronology

tionary Trade Union movement (CTCR) deplores absenteeism and the low output of Cuban workers.

September 28. Fidel Castro denounces "those who have nothing but pesos in their heads" and declares his preference for moral incentives.

November 6. The Cuban government offers to release those sentenced for counterrevolutionary activities, if Latin American countries liberate their imprisoned revolutionaries.

[Coup d'état in Argentina: General Ongania proclaims himself president. Marshal Costa e Silva succeeds Marshal Castelo Branco as president of Brazil. Méndez Montenegro elected president of Guatemala. Balaguer, the U.S. sponsored candidate, elected president of the Dominican Republic. Great proletarian cultural revolution in China. Twenty-third Congress of the Communist Party of the Soviet Union.]

1967 *Año del Vietnam heroico*

January 28. In a speech in San Andrés, Fidel Castro announces Cuba's withdrawal from the international copyright convention.

March 6–9. In a series of editorials attributed to Armando Hart, *Granma* invites Cubans to wage a decisive battle against bureaucracy.

March 13. Fidel Castro attacks the leaders of the Venezuelan Communist Party for their ambiguous attitude toward the guerrilla struggle led by Douglas Bravo (a former member of the Politburo of the Venezuelan Communist Party and commander in chief of the National Liberation Front).

April. Ernesto Che Guevara addresses a message to OSPAAAL and invites Latin American revolutionaries to create two, three, many Vietnams.

June 27. Premier Kosygin pays a brief visit to Cuba after his meeting with President Johnson at Glassboro.

July 26. Fidel Castro declares that, if attacked, Cuba would fight by itself and would never sign a truce.

August 4–11. First OLAS conference. In his closing speech, Fidel Castro repeats his attacks on the Venezuelan Communist Party

581

and condemns Soviet aid to reactionary governments in Latin America.

October 8. Death of Ernesto Che Guevara in Bolivia.

October 15–18. National mourning in Cuba.

November 6. Major Machado, minister of health, represents Cuba at the celebrations of the fiftieth anniversary of the Russian Revolution. The absence of Fidel Castro and Dorticós in Moscow marks a resurgence of Cuban-Soviet disagreements.

[Six-day war in the Middle East; Israel occupies Jerusalem, Sinai, Western Jordan and the Golan heights. The Communist party of Venezuela expels Douglas Bravo. The Chilean Senate vetoes President Frei's visit to the United States. Régis Debray sentenced to thirty years of prison in Bolivia. Caldera elected President of Venezuela.]

1968 *Año del Guerrillero heróico*

January 2. Fidel Castro introduces petrol rationing, and declares that the dignity of the Revolution prevents Cuba from begging for additional Soviet supplies.

January 4–11. International Cultural Congress in Havana. During the closing speech Fidel Castro attacks "pseudo-revolutionaries" who, in times of crisis, instead of heading the struggle take to the extreme rear.

January 28. The Central Committee of the Cuban Communist Party decides to hand over Aníbal Escalante and 8 other members of the former PSP accused of microfactional activities to the revolutionary tribunal. They and 32 non-Party members are given sentences ranging from 3 to 15 years.

March 13. Fidel Castro launches a Great Revolutionary Offensive which culminates in the nationalization of all trade and services. General mobilization of manpower for agriculture and quite particularly for sugar production.

August 17. The minister of labor, Jorge Risquet, announces the introduction of labor cards recording acts of indiscipline, etc.

August 2. Fidel Castro approves of Soviet intervention in Czechoslovakia.

Appendix A: A Chronology

November 21. Cuban–East German communiqué on the necessity of fighting "against all forms of revisionism and opportunism."

[Tet offensive of the NLF in South Vietnam, followed by the cessation of the U.S. bombardment of North Vietnam and Paris talks. May revolt in France. "Political spring" in Czechoslovakia followed by Soviet pressure and military intervention. Coup d'état by General Velasco Alvarado in Peru. Massacre of Mexican students at Tlalolco.]

1969 *Año del Esfuerzo decisivo*

January 2. Fidel Castro introduces sugar rationing.

June 10. The Cuban delegate to the World Conference of Communist parties in Moscow, Carlos Rafael Rodríguez, declares his country's "indefectible solidarity with the U.S.S.R."

July 9. Fidel Castro approves the revolutionary measures of the military junta in Peru.

July. Visit of Soviet naval squadron to Havana. Soviet sailors cut sugar cane.

September 24. Armando Hart praises Soviet achievements under Stalin and declares that Cuba must emulate them.

November 12. Marshal Grechko, Soviet minister of defense, visits Havana.

December. Arrival of U.S. volunteer brigade (*Venceremos*) to help in the ten-million-ton *zafra.* Arrival of Vietnamese brigade for the same purpose.

[Resignation of General de Gaulle. Georges Pompidou elected president of France. Coup d'état by General Ovanda in Bolivia. The Brazilian urban resistance movement achieves the release of seventeen political prisoners in exchange for the United States Ambassador. Ninth Congress of the Communist Party of China.]

1970 *Año de los diez millones*

January 18. The second millionth ton of sugar produced on schedule.

February. Arrival of North Korean and Bulgarian volunteer brigades.

February 10. Fidel Castro declares that, despite bad weather conditions at the beginning of the year, the sugar target will be reached on the appointed date, July 15.
[Douglas Bravo, leader of the Venezuelan guerrilla movement, criticizes Cuba's support of the U.S.S.R.]

Appendix B: Brief economic survey of Cuba

(SOURCES: *"Panorama económico latino-americano,"* Havana, No. 295 and No. 294, 1968; Year Book of P.A.L., 1967; *Cuba,* special edition on the Tenth Anniversary of the Cuban Revolution; Reports of the Cuban delegation at the fourteenth session of the F.A.O., 1967, Rome; Weekly summary of *Granma;* Annual statistics of the United Nations, 1969).

Population: 7,937,200 inhabitants (as estimated on June 30, 1967).

8,033,000 inhabitants (as estimated on June 30, 1968).

Area: 110,921 square kilometers.

Density of population: 72.4 inhabitants to the square kilometer (estimated on June 30, 1968).

Population growth rate: 2.2 per cent per annum.

Working population: 2,508,000 (including persons aged over 14 years as estimated on June 30, 1964. The percentage of the working population to the whole population was 33.7 per cent, and distribution by professions was as follows:

Guerrillas in Power

		per cent
Agriculture	838,000 or	33.4
Industry and mines	375,700 or	15
Building	119,000 or	4.7
Transport	89,700 or	3.6
Commerce	252,900 or	10.1
Services and others	832,700 or	33.2

Principal towns: Havana, 1,008,500 inhabitants (as estimated on June 30, 1967). Greater Havana, i.e., the capital plus the satellite towns of Guanabacoa, Cojimar, San Miguel del Padrón and Marinao: 1,700,300 inhabitants; Santiago de Cuba: 259,000; Camagüey: 178,000; Santa Clara: 137,700; Guantánamo: 135,100; Holguín: 100,500; Cienfuegos: 91,800.
Percentage of urban population: 53.4 per cent of total population (as estimated on June 30, 1967).
National income: In millions of pesos, at 1965 rate:

Year	Amount
1962	3,509.5
1963	3,544.2
1964	3,856.6
1965	3,888.2
1966	3,727.4

TABLE 1

Cuban imports and exports from 1958 to 1965, in millions of dollars (fixed rate)

	1958	1959–63	1964	1965	1966a
Exports	733,519	2,945,481	713,825	686,000	593,000
Imports	777,094	3,520,063	1,008,471	865,000	926,000
Balance	− 43,575	− 574,582	− 294,646	−179,000	−333,000

a) UN data.

586

Appendix B: Brief Economic Survey of Cuba

TABLE 2

Geographic distribution of Cuban exports (in percentage by groups of countries)

GROUPS OF COUNTRIES	1959	1960	1961	1962	1963	1964a
Socialist countries	2.2	24.2	74.7	82.0	67.4	59.0
Other countries	97.8	75.6	25.3	18.0	32.6	41.0

a) Percentage based on the first six months of the year.

TABLE 3

Composition of main Cuban exports (in percentages represented by the three principal products)

PRODUCTS	1959	1960	1961	1962	1963	1964	1965
Sugar and sugar products	76.9	79.4	85.0	82.9	87.3	87.8	86.2
Non ferrous metals	2.5	1.1	1.3	7.2	6.5	5.2	3.6
Tobacco	8.5	10.2	6.4	4.8	4.0	4.0	4.75

TABLE 4

Some data on Cuban trade with the Socialist countriesa in millions of dollars (fixed rate)

Country	1958	percentage	1959–63	1964	percentage
U.S.S.R.					
Exports	14,172	74.6	801,789	274,937	65.1
Imports	——	——	1,215,165	408,579	59.7
Balance	+14,172		− 413,376	−133,642	
CHINA					
Exports	3,622		285,451	81,402	19.3
Imports	18	19.2	279,400	106,318	15.5
Balance	+ 3,604	0.9	+ 6,051	− 24,916	
CZECHOSLOVAKIA					
Exports	16		93,281	14,790	3.5
Imports	1,952	——	125,835	65,838	9.6
Balance	− 1,936	97.9	− 32,554	− 51,048	

587

Guerrillas in Power

TABLE 4 *(Continued)*

Country	1958	percentage	1959–63	1964	percentage
EAST GERMANY					
Exports	——	——	72,820	16,147	3.8
Imports	——	——	90,328		5.6
Balance			— 17,508	38,358	
POLAND					
Exports	——	——	75,024	7,996	1.9
Imports	——	——	73,853	20,148	2.9
Balance		+	1,171	— 12,152	
BULGARIA					
Exports	——	——	27,542	14,934	3.5
Imports	——	——	24,025	11,561	1.7
Balance		+	3,517	+ 3,373	
HUNGARY					
Exports	——	——	23,671	696	0.2
Imports			33,946	14,993	2.1
Balance			— 10,275	— 14,297	

a) The total volume of trade with Albania, Korea, Mongolia, Rumania, Vietnam and Yugoslavia in 1964 was $11,572 million (exports) and $18,456 million (imports) giving a deficit of $6,884 million.

TABLE 5

Data on commerce between Cuba and the main socialist countries in 1965, expressed as percentages of Cuba's total imports and exports

Country	Exports	Imports
U.S.S.R.	47	40.2
CHINA	14.6	10.7
CZECHOSLOVAKIA	6.6	6.3
GERMAN DEMOCRATIC REPUBLIC	4.1	3.7

Appendix B: Brief Economic Survey of Cuba

CUBAN INDUSTRIAL AND AGRICULTURAL PRODUCTION

	Industrial Production	Agricultural Production[a]
	1959 = 100	1952–57 = 100
1960	113	130
1961	120	105
1962	122	92
1963	129	100
1964	138	120
1965	150	136

a) SOURCE: P.A.L., Havana, 1968.

	Industrial Production[a]	Agricultural Production
	1963 = 100	1963 = 100
1964	107	108
1965	116	129
1966		109
1967		133

a) SOURCE: figures published by U.N.; industrial indices for 1966 and 1967 not published.

	Food Production[a] 1952–57 = 100		Food Production[b] 1963 = 100
1960	135	1962	114
1961	105	1964	108
1962	91	1965	132
1963	101	1966	110
1964	120	1967	135

a) SOURCE: P.A.L., Havana, 1968.
b) SOURCE: figures published by U.N., 1969.

589

Guerrillas in Power

Data on Industrial Production[a]

Products	Year	Volume
Steel	1967	120,000 metric tons
Raw Sugar	1967	6,100,000 metric tons
Leather Footwear	1966	12.6 million pairs
Cotton	1966	108.4 million square meters
Paper and Cardboard	1966	91,884 metric tons
Cigarettes	1966	18,455 million
Cigars	1966	657 million

a) Precise data on the production of textiles, glass, metal articles, beer, wood, detergents and fertilizers are not included in this table, taken from P.A.L., Havana, 1968.

Cement Production and Imports
(in metric tons)

Year	Production	Imports
1958	735,602	4,235
1959	672,670	4,433
1960	813,273	621
1961	870,860	11,195
1962	778,930	111,613
1963	811,621	16,621
1964	805,600	33,424
1965	801,111	51,010
1966	750,400	144,568
1967	835,100	277,700
Plans for 1968–71		
1968	1,113,800	
1969	1,851,900	
1970	2,108,800	
1971	2,395,300	

Source: *Bohemia,* January 17, 1969.

Appendix B: Brief Economic Survey of Cuba

Chief Agricultural Products in 1966 (in metric tons) [a]

Tobacco	51,261
Coffee	33,405
Potatoes	104,040
Tomatoes	132,911
Malanga	69,272

a) SOURCE: P.A.L., Havana, 1968.

Other Important Crops: maize, rice, fiber, cocoa, citrus fruits (citrus has become a major crop during the last two years).

Electricity: production in 1967: 3,099 million KWH; consumption per inhabitant: 950 KWH (in 1965).

Principal mining products[a]:

Nickel	34,900 metric tons (1967)
Petroleum	113,600 metric tons (1967)
Chromium (Cr_2O_3 content)	18,200 metric tons (1965)
Manganese (Mn content)	33,000 metric tons (1965)

Other mining products: iron, copper, sulphur, cobalt and salt.

a) SOURCE: P.A.L., Havana, 1968.

Livestock: Cattle (1967 census): 7,146,768 head (roughly 55 per cent belonging to the State sector). Milk production: 1,190 million litres in 1966; 1,195 million in 1967 (370 millions from the State sector). A great effort is being made to improve the cattle, the poor quality of which is shown on the following table.

Comparative yield of 100 head of cattle in different countries 1961

COUNTRY	MEAT (TONS)	MILK (TONS)
U.S.A.	7.6	59
France	7.3	122
Denmark	6.6	154
West Germany	7.3	154
Italy	5.9	97
Belgium	7.4	143
Austria	6.5	122
Argentine	4.9	102
New Zealand	3.9	84
Australia	4.6	36
Cuba (1964–1965)	2.7	11

SOURCE: *Juceplan,* mentioned in the report of the Cuban delegation to the XIV F.A.O. Conference, Rome, 1967.

591

Guerrillas in Power

Fish: the total weight of fish, crustaceans and mollusks caught in 1967, was 62,881.3 tons, exceeding the 1965 figure by 56.3 per cent.

Ports: The leading Cuban ports are: Havana, Santiago de Cuba, Nuevitas, Matanzas, Cienfuegos and Mariel. In addition there are some twenty other serviceable ports of lesser importance.

Merchant Marine: Comprises 47 ships, with a gross registered tonnage of 333,000 tons.

Civil Aviation: The national company (La Cubana de Aviación) provides a national and international service. Three international companies make use of the international airport of José Marti de Rancho Boyeros, 13 miles from the capital. These are: Aeroflot (U.S.S.R.), C.S.A. (Czechoslovakia) and Iberia (Spain).

Railway Network: The total network covers 18,115 km., of which 30 per cent are passenger lines, and the remaining 70 per cent serve the sugar industry.

Roads: Cuba's road system covers 20,134.3 km., of which 34 per cent were paved in 1967. The central motorway (*Carretera central*) covers 1,145 km.

Appendix C: Cuban tractor imports before and after the revolution

YEAR	NUMBER OF UNITS	1952 = 100
1952	2,247	100
1953	1,409	62.7
1954	1,150	51.2
1955	1,280	57.0
1956	1,413	62.9
1957	2,484	110.5
1958	2,408	107.2

Average 1952–58	1,770	75.2
1960	3,081	137.1
1961	5,614	249.9
1962	4,291	191.0
1963	3,443	152.2
1964	3,880	172.3
1965	6,574	292.6
1966	3,839	170.9
Average 1960–66	4,388	195.7

SOURCE: *Juceplan*, mentioned in *La Economia Cubana*, report to the O.L.A.S. conference.[1]

1. According to the report of the Cuban delegation to the 14th session of the FAO in Rome, Cuba imported 5,696 tractors in 1967, and was due to import 6,988 tractors in 1968.

Data on Cuban heavy equipment imports, 1960–1967	
Trucks of various types	29,372
Buses (from socialist countries)	3,557
British buses (Leyland)	928
Jeeps	7,314
Bulldozers	1,614
Excavators and cranes	873

SOURCE: *Bohemia*, No. 3, January 17, 1969.

Appendix D: National education

Special schools, opened in 1961

	1961–62	1968–69	Increase
Number of schools	20	110	90
Teachers	148	1,118	970
Pupils	843	7,947	7,104

Technical and Professional Education

Industrial Colleges	1958–59	1968–69	Increase
Number of Schools	20	38	18
Teachers	818	2,180	1,362
Pupils	6,259	29,975	23,716

Agricultural Colleges			
Number of Schools	——	37	37
Teachers	——	2,335	2,335
Pupils	——	36,812	36,812

Fishery Colleges			
Number of Schools	——	2	2
Teachers	——	175	175
Pupils	——	3,115	3,115

Universities

Number of Universities	3	6	3
Teachers	1,053	4,449	3,396
Pupils	25,599	40,147	14,548

Number of scholarships at all levels in October 1968: 244,718
Number of half-boarders at all levels: 160,818
SOURCE: *Cuba,* Special edition published on the occasion of the tenth anniversary of the revolution, January 1969.

Appendix E: Public health

	1958	1968
Number of Hospitals	44	221
Polyclinics	—	260
Blood Banks	1	15
Hospital Beds	21,780	40,402
Social Assistance Beds	3,965	7,258
Number of physicians	6,300	7,000
Budget of Ministry of Public Health	22 million pesos	263 million pesos
Medical Education		
Medical Schools	1	3
Stomatology Faculties	1	2
Research Institutes	1	9
University Hospital Centers	4	32
Hospital Schools	—	7
Nursing Colleges	6	13
Auxiliary Nursing Colleges	—	58

Some advances in preventive medicine

Poliomyelitis	Epidemics every four or five years; average: 300 cases per year.	Thanks to mass vaccinations no cases for the past three years.
Malaria	Several thousand cases every year; 3,519 in 1962.	Only seven cases in 1967; none in 1968.
Deaths from gastro-enteritis	2,784	1,346

SOURCE: *Cuba,* January 1969.

597

Appendix F: The Cuban state executive

President of the Republic: Osvaldo Dorticós Torrado.
Prime Minister: Fidel Castro Ruz.

Vice - Premier and Minister of the Revolutionary Army: Raúl Castro Ruz.

Ministers:
Foreign Affairs: Raúl Roa García.
Interior: Sergio Del Valle Jiménez.
Education: José Llanusa Gobel.
Foreign Trade: Marcelo Fernández Font.
Internal Trade: Manuel Luzardo García.
Communications: Jesús Montané Oropesa.
Transport: Faure Chomón Mediavilla.

598

Appendix F: The Cuban State Executive

Labor: Jorge Risquet Valdés.
Justice: Alfredo Yabur Maluf.
Public Health: Eliodoro Martínez Junco.
Heavy Industry: Joel Domenech Benítez.
Light Industry: Manuel E. Escalona Chavez.
Metallurgy and Mining: Arthuro Guzmán Pascual.
Food: José A. Naranjo.
Sugar Industries: Francisco Pardón.
President of the National Bank: Orlando Pérez Rodríguez.
Economic, Technical and Scientific Coordination: Carlos
    Rafael Rodríguez.
Government Secretariat-General: Celia Sánchez Manduley.

Index

Index

Guerrillas in Power

Index

China, 291, 310, 335, 342, 428, 499–
500, 503; Castroism and, 52, 303,
307, 371, 372, 396n., 541; and
Cuban Revolution, 44, 232, 301;
Cuban trade with, 27, 222, 423;
Cultural Revolution, 305, 308,
363, 397, 441, 547, 548; Fidel and,
304–305, 355, 372, 386; and
Korean war, 294n.; and labor
movement, 366; and missile crisis,
276–277; politicization of military,
543; socialism in, 546; and Soviet
Union, 198–199, 200, 202, 259, 266,
268, 270, 275, 280, 281, 293, 298n.,
302, 303, 372n., 515, 529; and Stalinism, 519–520
Choi Yong-kun, 515
Chomón, Faure, 146, 169, 190, 246n.,
285, 286n., 458n.
Chou En-lai, 302, 303
Churchill, Winston, 102n.
Cienfuegos, 317, 356, 421, 446; naval
uprising at, 165n.; soviets near,
76n.
Cienfuegos, Camilo, 42, 164n., 167,
168, 174n., 183, 239, 376
Cienfuegos, Osmani, 247n., 298, 304
cigars, 440; rationing of, 430n.
citrus fruits, 283, 348, 353, 382, 439
Civil Defense Organization, 457n.
civil servants, Fidel and, 460, 461
civil war, 68; in Colombia, 122; and
Cuban revolution, 158, 165n., 213,
544
class consciousness: Fidel on, 453;
and Soviet policy, 528
class struggle, 80, 107, 367
clothing, shortages of, 429
coal mining, 49
Coca-Cola, 24, 212
Coello, Carlos, 389n.
coexistence, doctrine of, 51–52, 159,
201, 244, 521; Castroism and, 209,
266–267, 307, 334, 371, 381, 385,
511; and Czech invasion, 509;
Khrushchev and, 155, 194, 196–
197, 199, 200, 207; and Latin
American Communists, 391; and

missile crisis, 258, 268–269, 279,
280; Stalin and, 100; Vietnam
and, 293, 497
coffee production, 211, 283, 346,
347, 348, 349, 351, 439, 447, 477;
forced, 516n.
Cold War, 4, 13, 97, 108, 123, 129,
177, 205, 269, 295, 527; and Czech
invasion, 508–509; and world
revolution, 528
collaborationism, 106
collectivization, forced, 517, 518,
532, 544
Colombia, 107, 122, 344, 365, 379,
390, 403
colonialism, viii, 87, 227, 393, 427–
428
Colorado Group, 128n.
Columbia Barracks, speech by Fidel
at, 169–170
Columbus, Christopher, 4, 209
Comintern, 60, 80, 82, 98, 150, 191,
538; Castro and, 280; critics of,
156; dissolution of, 101, 106, 107;
expulsion of Polish Communists,
385
commerce, ministry of, 180n.
Committees for the Defense of the
Revolution, 447, 454, 457, 511n.
communications, 324; ministry of,
180n., 311
Communism, 58; Cuban attitudes
toward, 11n., 38; Dorticos Torrado on, 357–359, 360–361; Che
Guevara and, 45; Khrushchev on,
264, 265; socialist transition to,
358–359, 362, 363; U.S. attitudes
toward, 4–5, 12–13, 18, 257. See
also Communist parties
Communist Manifesto, 238
Communist parties, 244, 293, 294n.;
Castroism and, ix, 370–371, 399,
402, 479; Chinese, 547; conferences of, 204, 207, 208n., 266, 301–
302, 514; Czech, 505, 506, 507,
527n.; Italian, 477, 523; Latin
American, 100, 101, 123, 159, 245,
246, 267, 295, 303–304, 340, 371,

605

Index

Czechoslovakia, 44*n.*, 48, 194, 216, 268*n.*, 318, 338, 470; experts from, 215, 223, 229–230, 282, 505; growth rate in, 319*n.;* rank-and-file activity in, 331; Soviet invasion, 490, 503–509, 510, 511, 525, 526–527, 530–531; Stalinist period, 530*n.*

Daily Worker (London) , 323
Daniel, Jean, 261
death sentence, 110. *See also* executions
Debray, Régis, 76*n.*, 159, 374–379, 381, 390*n.*, 491
debureaucratization, 457, 460–462, 463
decentralization, problems of, 464–465*n.*
de Gaulle, Charles, 95*n.*, 252, 498
de la Torre, Cándido, 144*n.*
del Cerro, Angelo, 147*n.*
del Valle, Sergio, 247*n.*, 284*n.*, 458*n.*
democracy: parliamentary, 4, 368–369; problems of in Cuba, 451–452, 454, 459, 482; rank-and-file, 179, 451; rhetoric of, 177, 178.
See also democratization
Democratic Action Party (AD) , 373
"democratic centralism," 531–532
Democratic Republican Party, 89
Democratic Socialist Party of Colombia, 107
democratization, 466–467, 527*n.*
depression, economic, 67
Desnoes, Edmundo, 427*n.*
de-Stalinization, 141*n.*, 195, 197, 198, 264–265, 520
Deutscher, Isaac, 383, 525
dialectical materialism, 437*n.*
Díaz, Jesús, 396*n.*
Díaz, José, 94
Díaz, Julio, 164*n.*
Díaz, Porfirio, 111*n.*
Díaz Balart, Mirta, 135*n.*
Díaz Balart, Rafael, 135
Díaz Lanz, Pedro Luis, 171, 182
Díaz Ordaz, Gustavo, 501, 502, 503

Diefenbaker, John, 253
Dimitrov, Georgi, 82
Directorio Estudiantil Universitario, 37*n.*, 68–70, 77, 80, 124, 169, 246
Directorio Revolucionario, 57, 129, 137–138, 145, 169, 170, 175*n.*, 285*n.*
Dobrynin, Anatol, 250, 262
Doctor Zhivago, 237
Dominican Republic, 118, 168, 185
Dorticós Torrado, Dr. Osvaldo, 41, 165*n.*, 183, 217*n.*, 246*n.*, 302, 356, 392, 427*n.*, 458*n.*, 471; on aim of revolution, 545; on Che Guevara, 393*n.*
Draper, Theodore, 16, 48*n.*
drought, 409
Dubček, Alexander, 504, 505
Dubois, Jules, 132*n.*, 136, 142*n.*
Duclos, Jacques, 106–107
Dulles, John Foster, 41, 252*n.*
Dumont, René, 22*n.*, 34*n.*–35*n.*, 424, 516*n.*
Duras, Marguerite, 341
Dutschke, Rudi, 65

East Germany, 268, 269, 506*n.*, 512–513
Echeverría, José Antonio, 129, 137–138, 145, 146, 247
economic affairs, ministry of, 217*n.*
economic blockade, U.S., *see* trade embargo
economic development, 112, 425; Soviet, 193–194
economic growth, 112*n.*, 216, 217, 226; and building of socialism, 517, 545–546; priority given to, 528–529, 548; Soviet, 319
economic planning, 35, 48, 215–217, 223, 327–332, 357, 361–363, 408, 535; peasants and, 350–352; problems of Cuba, 464–465*n.*, 539, 544, 549; Soviet, 264, 318–319
economic system, Castroist, 464–466
economics: ministry of, 180*n.;* Polish school of, 318, 328

607

Index

Index

611

Index

McNamara, Robert, 251–252, 307n.
maize, 347
Makarenko, Anton, 38
Makarenko Pedagogical Institute, 313
Mañach, Jorge, 70, 90, 111
Mandel, Ernest, 327n.
Manicheanism, 10, 12, 181
Manzanillo, 142, 150, 337
Mao Tse-tung, 198–199, 200, 203, 294, 362, 372n., 376, 378, 425, 496, 515; Fidel on, 305, 481; Sihanouk on, 546
Maoism, 44, 159, 199, 294, 301, 303, 332, 372; Dorticós and, 302; program in China, 547–548; and Stalinism, 520n.
Marcellin, Raymond, 498
Marinello, Juan, 85n., 90, 104, 105, 146
market economy, Che Guevara on, 325, 332, 359
marriages, rumored ban on, 468, 484, 485
Martí y Pérez, José, 38, 62, 63, 68n., 70, 111, 118, 120, 124, 128, 364, 366; Fidel and, 161, 170–171, 178, 271
Martínez, Fernando, 396n.
Martínez Sánchez, Augusto, 180, 246n.
Martínez Tamayo, José María, 389n.
Martínez Villena, Rubén, 62, 66, 67, 71, 125
Marx, Karl, 125, 328, 356, 359, 360, 367; Fidel and, 123, 479; Che Guevara and, 393
Marxism, 69; and Cuban revolution, 10, 38, 47, 90, 158, 245, 309, 358, 360; Fidel on, 177, 241, 403, 480, 488, 525
Marxism-Leninism, 47, 53, 156, 198, 235–236, 272, 303, 369, 437; Fidel and, 158, 178, 275; in Latin America, 378n., 379, 492
Masetti, Jorge Ricardo, 389n.

Masferrer, Rolando, 114, 118, 121n., 128n.
Matanzas, 165n., 314n., 421
Matar, José, 468
material incentives, 524, 541, 543
Matos, Hubert, 168, 171, 172, 183–184, 472n., 488
Matta, 398
Matthews, Herbert, 143, 488
Mauny, Eric de, 19n., 22
Mayakovsky, Vladimir, 69, 209, 210, 214, 238
meat: black market, 433; importation of, 315; prices, 429n.; rationing, 225
Medical Federation of Cuba, 81
Mella, Julio Antonio, 65–67, 77n., 79n., 110, 463n.
Mendieta, Carlos, 68, 77
Menéndez, Jesús, 108n.
Menéndez, Marcelino, 468n.
Merle, Robert, 91n.–92n.
Mexico, 9, 27, 41–42, 87, 110, 123, 188, 245; Cuban Communists in, 141, 285n.; Fidel in, 136–137, 138, 162, 389, 536n.; in missile crisis, 279; student revolt in, 501–503; U.S. and, 244, 267n.
Meyer, Charles A., 521n.
Meyer, Karl E., 17n.
Miami, Cubans in, 112, 113, 126, 144, 149, 151n., 176n., 224, 475
"microfactionalism," 468–469, 472, 473, 485
Middle East, 307n., 343, 400n.
Mikoyan, Anastas, 188, 189, 238, 275–278
Miliband, Ralph, 398, 400n.
militarism: Fidel and, 160, 448–449, 494–495, 528; Soviet, 526, 531n.
military training, 32, 39
Military Units to Aid Production (UMAP), 395
Militia, 454, 457, 474
milk: consumption, projected, 218; delivery, 220; production, 315, 347, 477; rationing, 225–226n., 347. See also condensed milk

Index

Mills, C. Wright, 8–11, 21*n*., 37, 46, 176–177, 246, 452, 477, 530*n*.
Minas del Frío, 313
mining, 49, 50*n*. *See also* nickel
"mini-Stalinism," 248, 271, 394, 453, 457, 468, 473
Miret, Pedro, 180*n*.
Miró Cardona, José, 17, 181, 183
missile crisis, 159, 227*n*., 231, 249–281, 292, 293, 309, 323, 371, 402, 540
Mitin, M. B., 38, 46, 47
Miyar, Chomi, 356
Moa, 353; arrests at, 178; nickel refinery at, 50*n*., 211, 337
Molotov, V. M., 264
Moncada Fortress, attack on, 3, 132, 133–135, 136, 137*n*., 158, 160, 161, 316, 336, 390, 492; martyrs of, 309; PSP and, 138–139; veterans of, 311, 474*n*.
money: Cuban attitudes toward, 431, 438; Fidel on, 342–345, 355, 358, 432, 542
Monje, Mario, 392*n*.
Monroe Doctrine, 188
Montané, Jesús (Chucho), 133, 134, 311, 312, 314, 316, 339
Montecristi Manifesto, 118*n*.
Montés, César, 493*n*.
Monthly Review, 298, 390*n*., 476
Mora, Alberto, 221, 327
Morales, Calixto, 164*n*.
Moscow trials, 470–471
Movement of the Revolutionary Left (MIR), 373
Movimiento Socialista Revolucionario (MSR), 116, 117, 118, 121
Mujal, Eusebio, 126*n*.
Mujalism, 126, 330
Munich agreement, 277
Muñoz, Dr., 134
Mussolini, Benito, 71

National Assembly of the People of Cuba, 29*n*.
National Association of Small Farmers (ANAP), 30, 31, 454, 457
National Bank of Cuba, 34*n*., 42
National Council of Culture, 306, 312, 341
national defense, ministry of, 472. *See also* Militia
National Institute for Agrarian Reform (INRA), 9, 22*n*., 23*n*., 29, 30, 31, 33, 34, 43
National Institute of the Tourist Industry (INIT), 23, 33
National Labor Confederation of Cuba, 63
National Labor Front (Frente Obrero Nacional), 151
National Liberation Front (Vietnam), 292, 293*n*., 496
National Revolutionary Movement (MNR), 137*n*.
National Union of University Teachers (SNESUP), French, 498*n*.
nationalism, 43, 530
nationalization, 45, 58, 181–182, 447; and Coca-Cola, 24; compensation for, 432–433*n*.; in Mexico, 501; in Peru, 523; of private enterprises, 442; problems of, 214–215, 224–225; of sugar refineries, 26; of U.S. estates, 6, 206; of utilities, 23
Nazism, 434
Nemchinov, Professor, 318
neocolonialism, viii, 87
neutralism, 8, 26, 293*n*. *See also* nonaligned countries
New Statesman, 12, 48*n*., 303*n*.
New York Times, The, 143, 165*n*., 206*n*., 257, 296*n*., 521
Newsweek, 19*n*.
Nicaragua, 119, 120*n*.
Nicaro, 353; nickel refinery at, 50*n*., 337–338, 339
nickel, 26, 49–50, 52, 211, 225, 227, 228, 337–338, 425, 456; prices, 535
nightclubs, 17. *See also* cabarets
Niquero, 142

Index

of, 314, 450, 454; exploitation of, 30, 368, 427; Fidel and, 142*n*., 144–145, 516*n*.; and food production, 226; and government reforms, 23, 29–31, 336, 350–352, 443, 455; in guerrilla campaign, 163–164; and land reform, 48, 181; Latin American, 391*n*.; and literacy brigades, 37; and revolution, 367

Peña, Lázaro, 97, 106, 141, 247*n*.

Peña Vilaboa, José, 67*n*.

Pentagon, 201, 292, 385; and missile crisis, 254

People's Democracies, 51, 155, 190, 197, 198, 267, 293, 298*n*., 318, 323, 516, 526*n*.; "socialism" imported to, 544

Peredo, Inti, 493*n*.

Pérez, Faustino, 40*n*., 137, 142, 152–153, 162, 164, 174*n*., 175*n*., 180, 184, 284*n*., 344, 345

Pérez, José Miguel, 66*n*.

Pérez Damera, General, 121

Pérez Jiménez, Marcos, 4, 373*n*.–374*n*.

Perón, Juan, 119; followers, 122

Perrot, Roy, 19*n*., 22

Peru, 388*n*., 391*n*., 522, 523, 524, 536*n*.

peso, Cuban, exchange rate, 21*n*., 417, 430

Pham Van Dong, 515

Piedra (Cuban magistrate), 168

Pignon, Edouard, 398, 441

Pinar del Río province, 28, 30–31, 35, 36, 167, 415–416

Plank, John, 521

Platt Amendment, 60–61, 76, 77

Playa Girón, *see* Bay of Pigs

PM (film), 241*n*., 245

Podgorny, Nikolai, 265

Poland, 3, 197, 220, 223, 268*n*., 318, 323, 328, 384, 385, 506*n*.; uprising in, 530*n*.

Policarpio Group, 128*n*.

police: "action groups" and, 115–117; under Batista, 73*n*., 110, 145–146, 285*n*.; Castroist, 457, 473, 474; "expert squad," 68, 70, 72; Mexican, 142, 144*n*., 501; Venezuelan, 374*n*.

Politburo, 269

Ponce, José, 133*n*.

Popular Socialist Party, *see* Partido Socialista Popular

Populism, 367

porros, *see* Patriotic League

port facilities, *see* harbor installations

positional warfare, transition to, 166 ff.

postal communications, 223*n*.

Power Elite, The, 9

Pravda, 29, 35, 36, 191, 258*n*., 259*n*., 266*n*., 284*n*., 296, 372, 391, 392, 425, 439*n*., 511, 515; (Slovak) 504*n*.

Preobrazhensky, Eugen, 328, 544

prices, in revolutionary countries, 405, 429*n*. *See also* sugar

"primitive socialist accumulation," 519, 537, 545, 548

Prío Socarrás, Carlos, 69, 115, 125, 126, 127–128, 137, 138; and guerrillas, 144

priorities, economic, 465*n*.

prisoners, 166, 469, 475; treatment of, 374*n*., 474; under Batista, 81, 146

private property, Cuban policy and, 5, 14, 350, 351

private trade, 436–438, 440–441, 442–443, 447, 457, 460. *See also* black market

Proctor & Gamble, 212, 220

Production, National Convention on, 217, 220, 225

profit motive, Che Guevara on, 326, 332

profiteers, 30, 441, 442–443, 460

proletariat, Cuban, 62, 75, 80, 126*n*., 158, 159, 179; dictatorship of, 525–526*n*., 528, 531; revolutionary transformation, 360, 367, 370

Index

Revolutionary Defense Committees, *see* Committees for the Defense of the Revolution

Revolutionary Executive Tribunal, 128n., 469–470

Revolutionary Reconstruction Group, 73

Reyes, Eliseo, 389n.

rice: deliveries by Chinese, 304–305, 386; prices, 429n.; production, 346, 347, 535; rationing, 225n.

Richard-Continental, 421, 422n.

Risquet, Jorge, 345, 517n.

Roa, Raúl, 6n., 56, 69, 78n., 79n., 111n.

Roca, Blas, 58, 67, 79–93 *passim*, 98, 104, 105, 139, 140n., 233, 243, 246n., 332, 394, 458n., 514; and Escalante, 248, 469n.; and PSP self-criticism, 149

Rodríguez, Armando, 164n.

Rodríguez, Carlos Rafael, 57, 76n., 90, 92, 93, 104, 141, 151, 153, 234, 246n., 284, 418, 458n., 469; Che Guevara and, 327; sent to Moscow, 514, 515; and Venezuelan Communists, 536n.

Rodríguez, Fructoso, 285n.

Rodríguez, Lester, 176n.

Rodríguez, Luis Orlando, 180n.

Rodríguez, Marcos, 138n., 285n., 286n., 472n.

Rodríguez, Marquitos, 285n.

Rodríguez, René, 164

Rodríguez Saens, Luis M., 468n.

Roosevelt, Franklin D., 13, 27, 28, 71, 83–84, 87, 88, 91–92, 96, 99, 101, 102n.

Rosario Guevara, Maria, 333n.

Rosi, Francesco, 391n., 476

Rossanda, Rossana, 311, 547n.–548n.

Rostov, market practices in, 434–436

Ruá Rodríguez, Manuel, 314

Ruiz, Señor, 353–354

Rumania, 293, 477, 506n.

Rusk, Dean, 307n.

Russell, Bertrand, 398, 502

Russell, Sam, 323

Sabbatini, Mario, 157n.

sabotage, 31, 47, 148, 165n., 447, 448, 517

Salabarria, Mario, 116, 117, 118, 121

Salagrida (Cuban politician), 95n.

Salon de Mai exhibition, 309, 394, 473

Salvador, David, 151,153,173n.–174n.

Sánchez, Osvaldo, 141, 153

Sánchez, Universo, 164n.

Sánchez Arango, Aureliano, 138n., 144

Sánchez Díaz, Antonio, 389n.

Sánchez Manduley, Celia, 56, 142, 174n., 178, 345, 473, 477, 483, 486

Sánchez White, Calixto, 144n.

Sancti Spiritus, 167, 180n.

Sandino, César Augusto, 120

Sandri, R., 523n.

Santa Clara: Communist congress at, 85; in rebel campaign, 167

Santa Lucía, soviet at, 76

Santamaría, Abel, 133, 134

Santamaría, Haydée, 134, 161, 162, 163n., 174n., 176n., 247n., 316

Santiago, 138, 142, 143, 150, 160, 163, 164n., 165, 182, 316; Carnival at, 336–337; cement factory at, 212

Santo Domingo, 117, 119, 121, 303n.

Sartre, Jean-Paul, 7, 239, 240n., 398, 453, 502

Satiukov, Pavel, 266n.

Schlesinger, Arthur, Jr., 14–15, 19, 249–250

Schools for Revolutionary Education, 53, 242, 247

Second Havana Declaration, 29n., 280, 379

Second World War, 28n., 61, 95n., 98, 100 ff., 111, 123, 197, 245, 282, 298n., 434, 450, 520

Seers, Dudley, 226n.

Seguridad, 457

self-criticism, 79, 149, 202, 219, 226, 272; cultural, 240; by Fidel, 533n.

Selnich, Andrés, 388n.

619

Index